FUBAR

AMERICAN HISTORY Z

FUBAR

AMERICAN HISTORY Z

EDITOR IN CHIEF:
JEFF McCOMSEY

ART DIRECTOR:
STEVE BECKER

STORY EDITOR:
JEFF McCLELLAND

DISTRIBUTION MANAGER
PETER SIMETI

FRONT COVER BY:
LEONARDO PIETRO

BACK COVER BY:
GRAEY ERB

FUBAR VOL 3 2012 FIRST EDITION
FIRST PRINTING.

PRINTED IN THE U.S.A.

Special thanks
to the large army of Small-Press Commandos
that went above and beyond the call of duty
to make this book a reality.

SMALL-PRESS
COMMANDOS
Fortuna audaces iuvat

FUBAR

AMERICAN HISTORY Z

AT THE WORLD'S END

STORY BY:
MAGNUS ASPLI

ART BY:
PABLO PEPPINO

LETTERS BY:
JEFF McCOMSEY

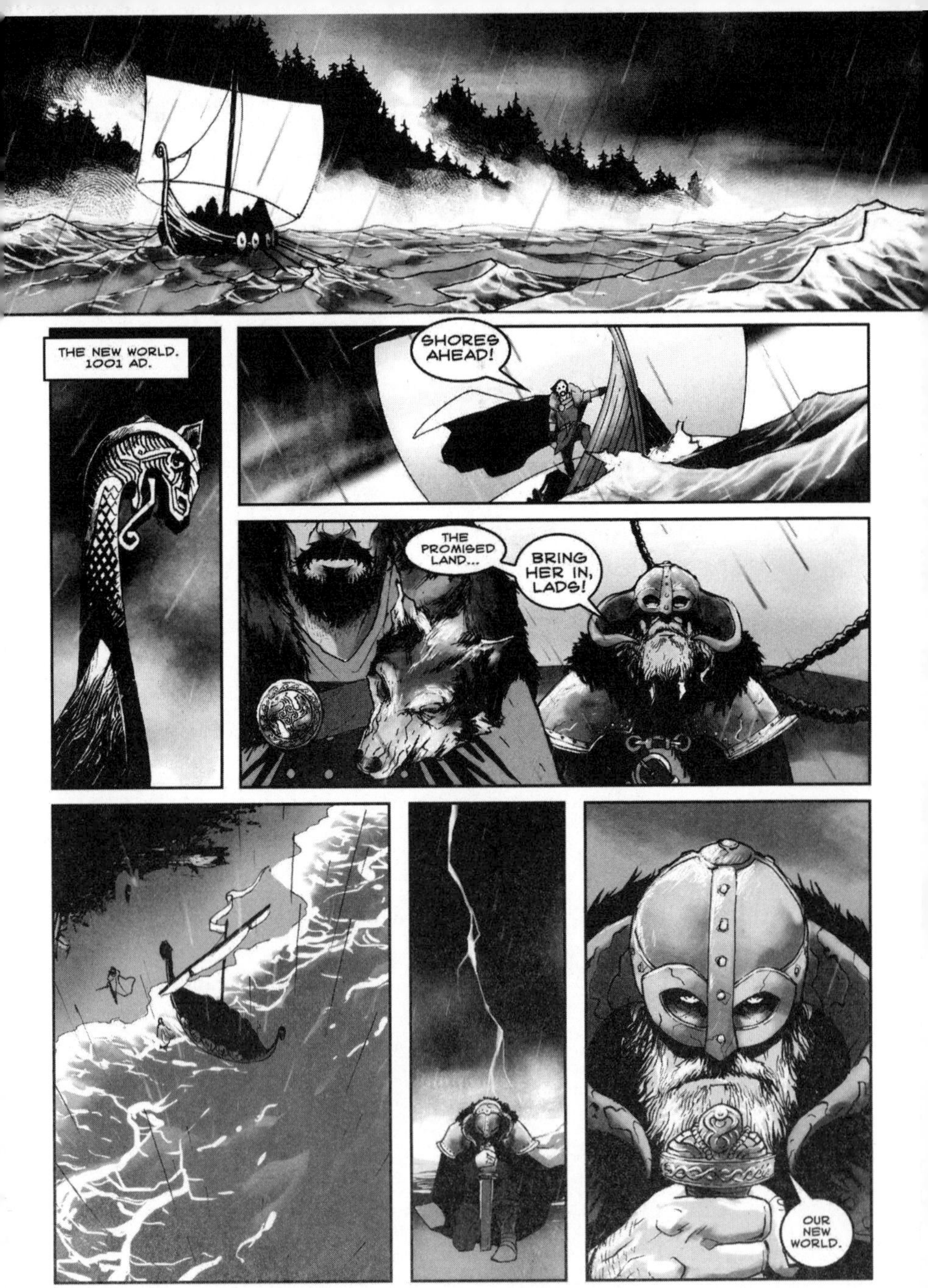
THE NEW WORLD. 1001 AD.
SHORES AHEAD!
THE PROMISED LAND...
BRING HER IN, LADS!
OUR NEW WORLD.

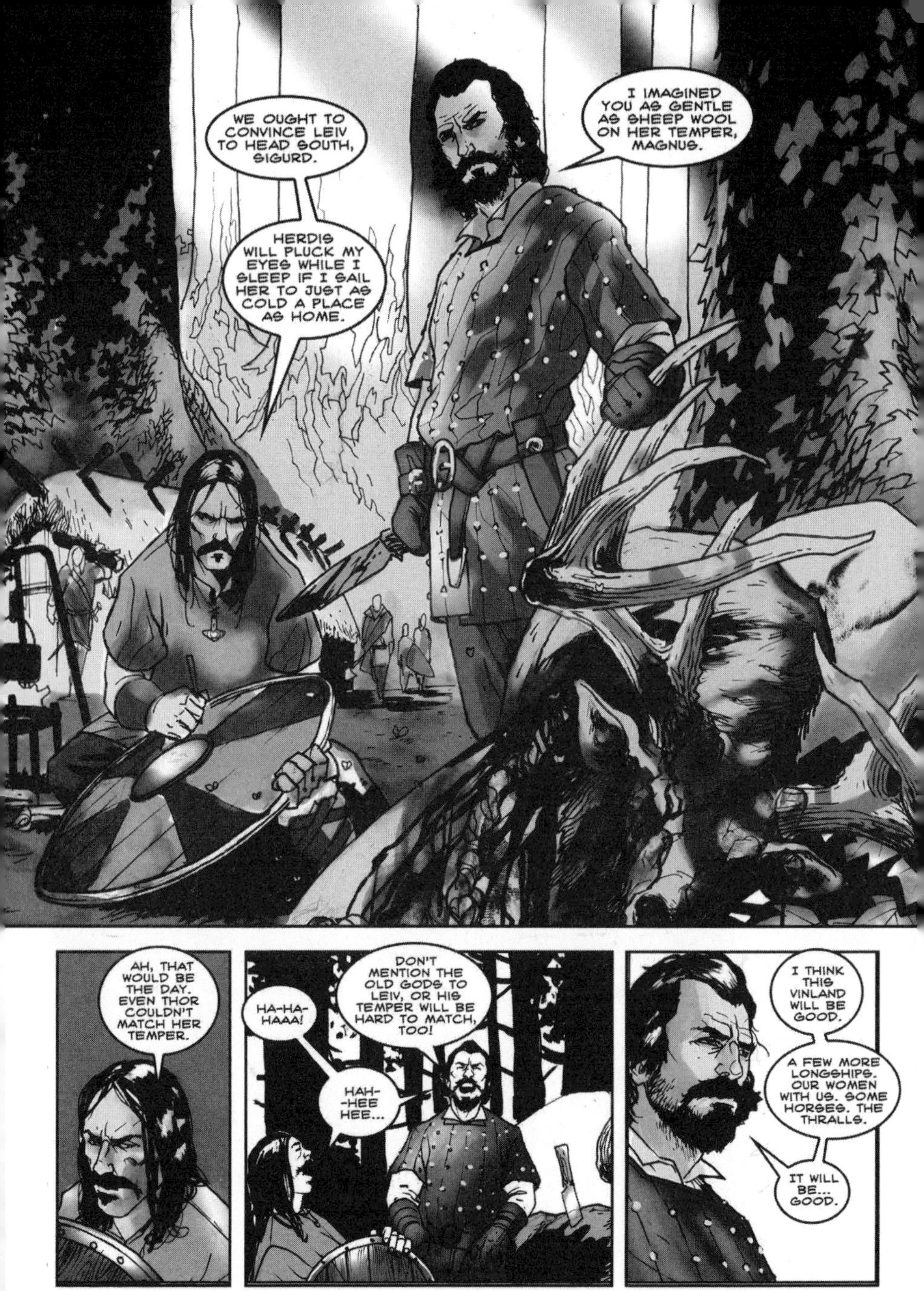
WE OUGHT TO CONVINCE LEIV TO HEAD SOUTH, SIGURD.
I IMAGINED YOU AS GENTLE AS SHEEP WOOL ON HER TEMPER, MAGNUS.
HERDIS WILL PLUCK MY EYES WHILE I SLEEP IF I SAIL HER TO JUST AS COLD A PLACE AS HOME.
AH, THAT WOULD BE THE DAY. EVEN THOR COULDN'T MATCH HER TEMPER.
DON'T MENTION THE OLD GODS TO LEIV, OR HIS TEMPER WILL BE HARD TO MATCH, TOO!
HA-HA-HAAA!
HAH--HEE HEE...
I THINK THIS VINLAND WILL BE GOOD.
A FEW MORE LONGSHIPS. OUR WOMEN WITH US. SOME HORSES. THE THRALLS.
IT WILL BE... GOOD.

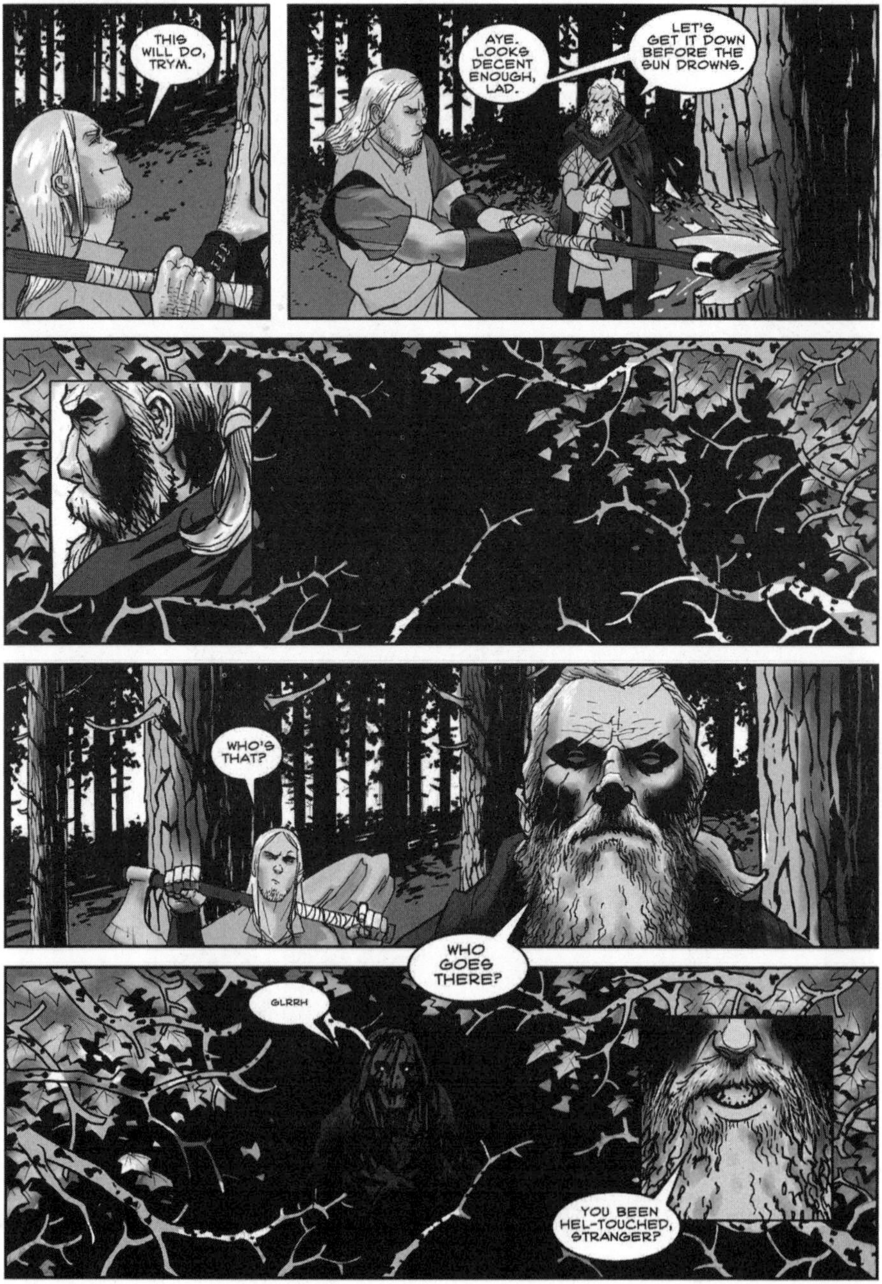
THIS WILL DO, TRYM.
AYE. LOOKS DECENT ENOUGH, LAD.
LET'S GET IT DOWN BEFORE THE SUN DROWNS.
WHO'S THAT?
WHO GOES THERE?
GLRRH
YOU BEEN HEL-TOUCHED, STRANGER?

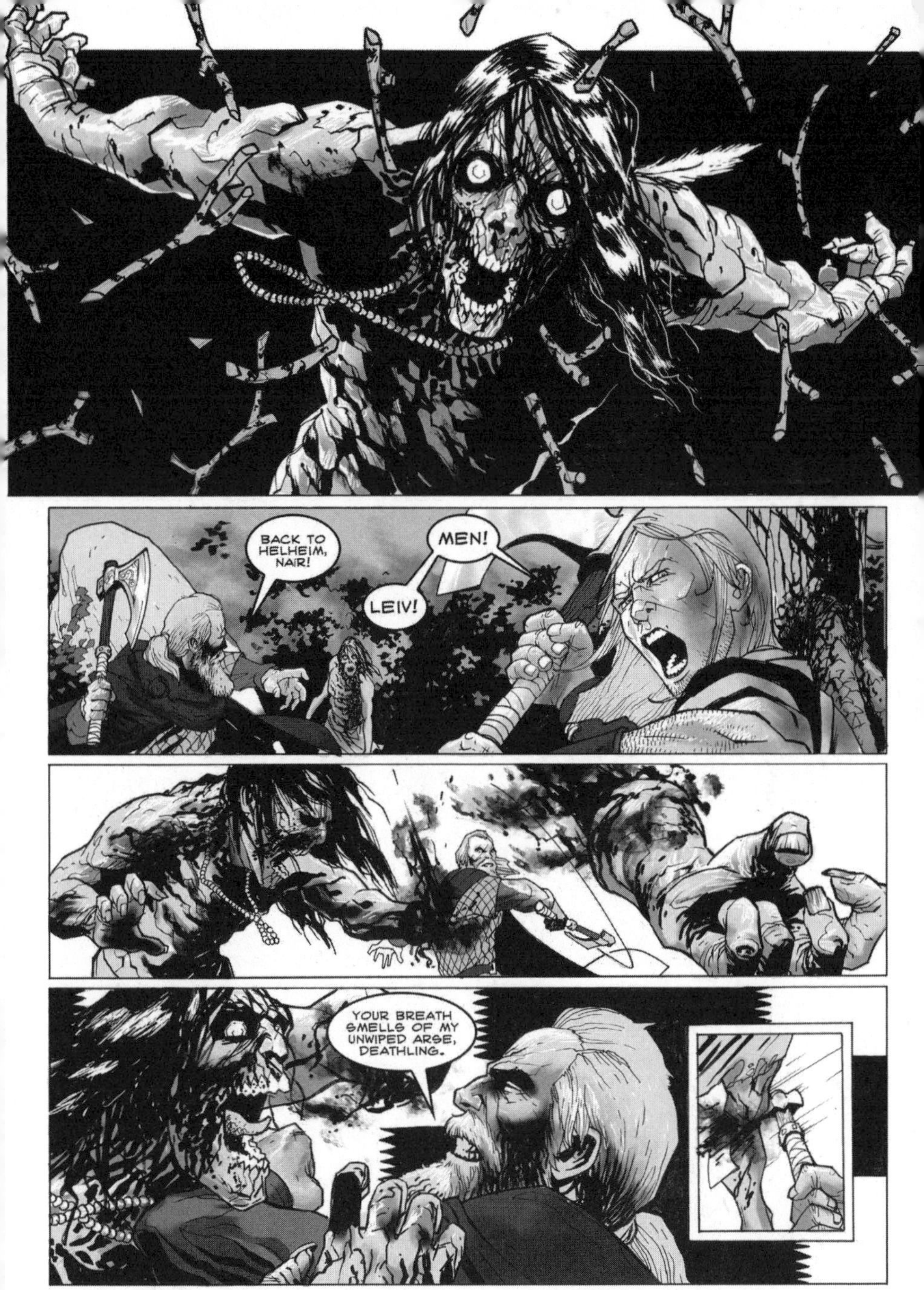
BACK TO HELHEIM, NAIR!
MEN!
LEIV!
YOUR BREATH SMELLS OF MY UNWIPED ARSE, DEATHLING.

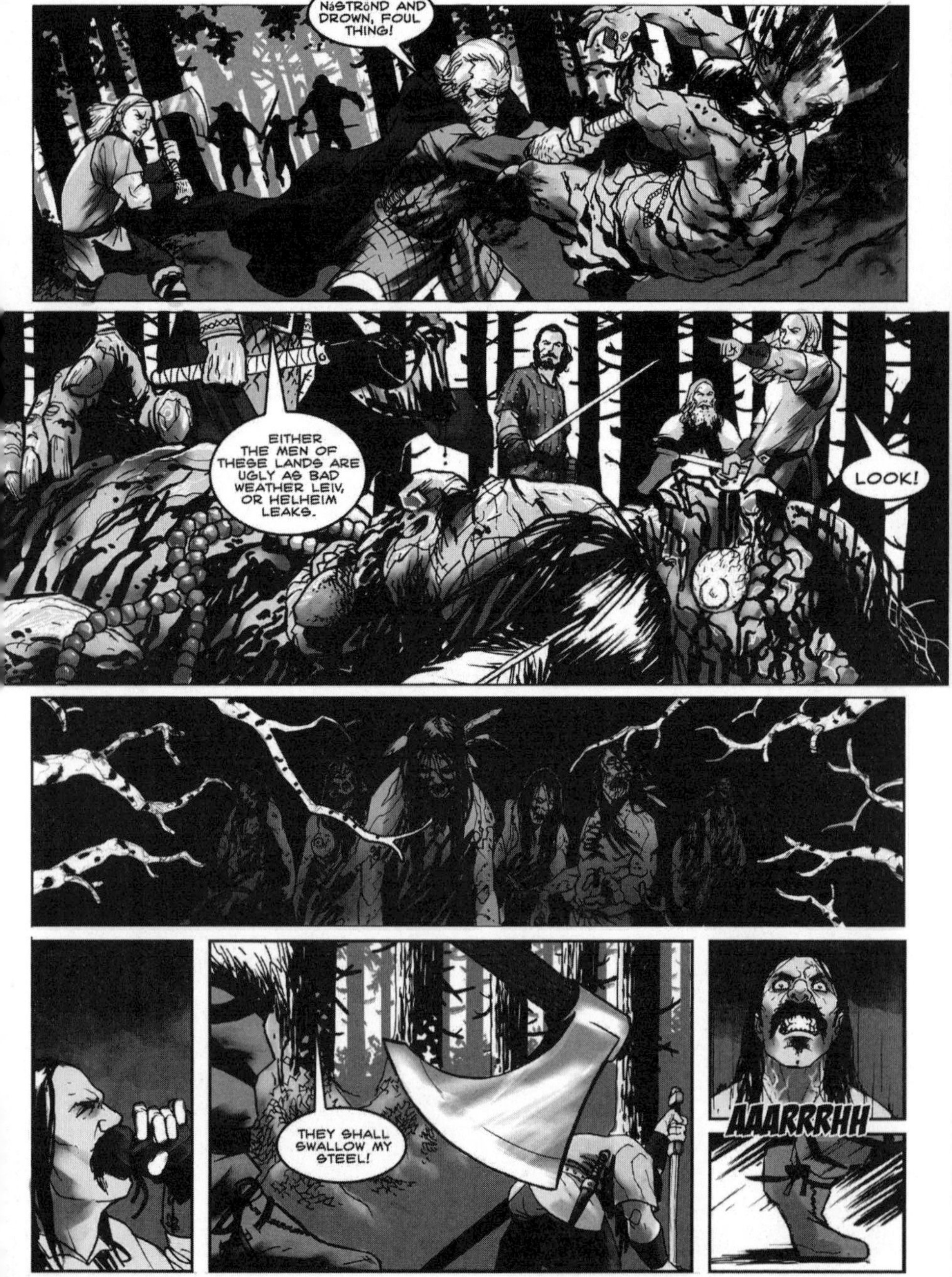
TO NáSTRöND AND DROWN, FOUL THING!
EITHER THE MEN OF THESE LANDS ARE UGLY AS BAD WEATHER LEIV, OR HELHEIM LEAKS.
LOOK!
THEY SHALL SWALLOW MY STEEL!
AAARRRHH

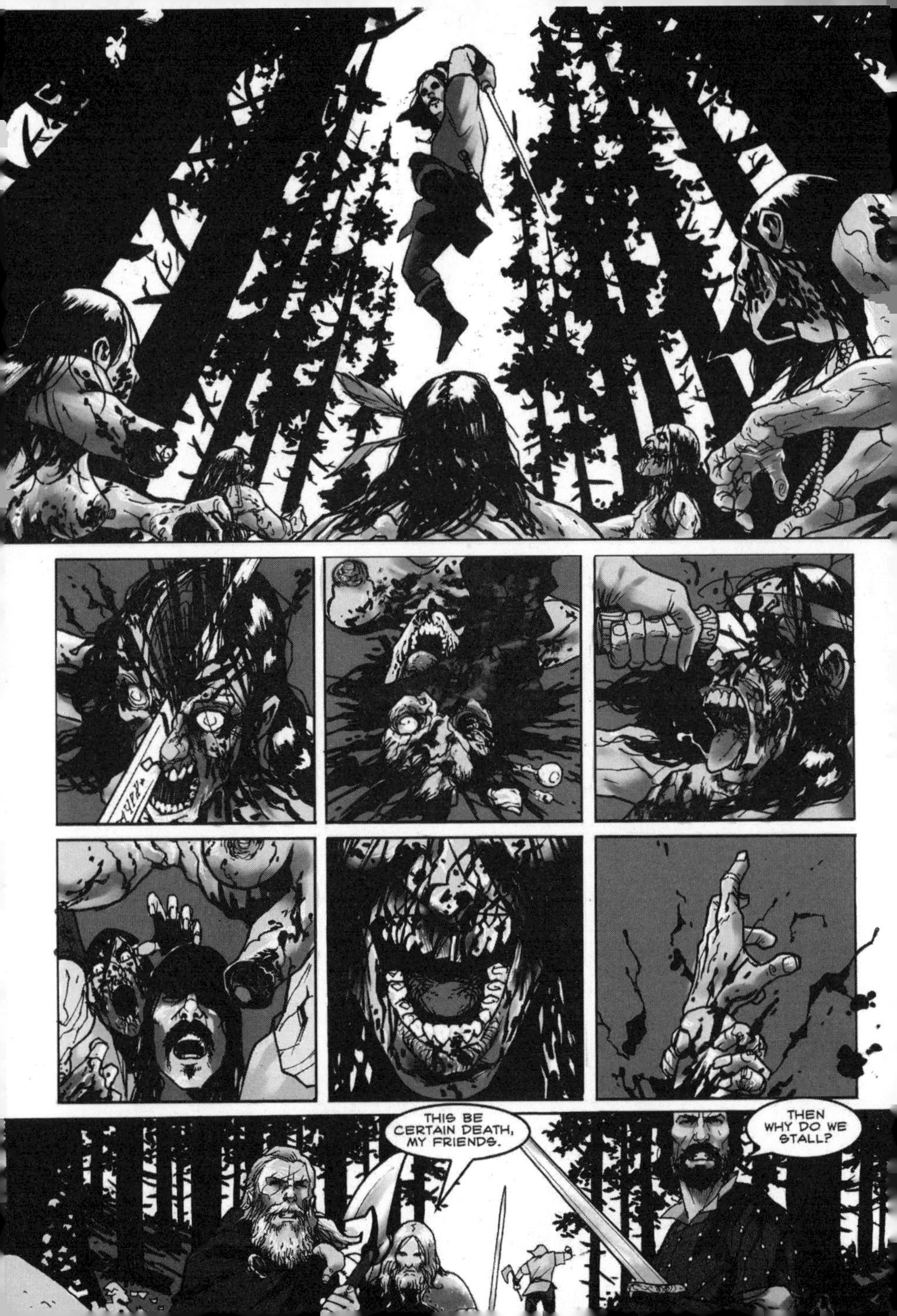

THIS BE CERTAIN DEATH, MY FRIENDS.
THEN WHY DO WE STALL?

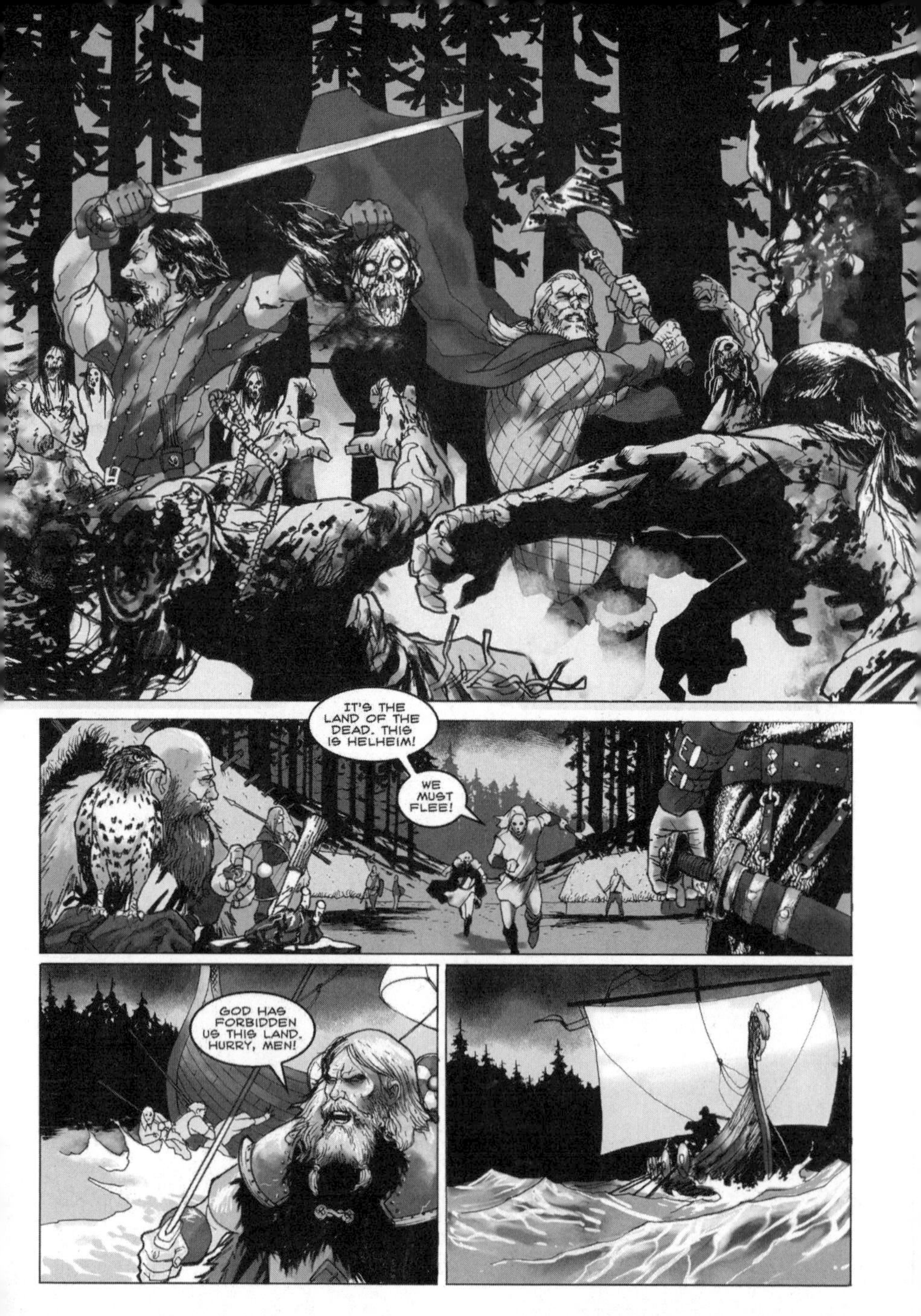
IT'S THE LAND OF THE DEAD. THIS IS HELHEIM!
WE MUST FLEE!
GOD HAS FORBIDDEN US THIS LAND. HURRY, MEN!

OUR RISEN BROTHERS AND SISTERS COWED THE INTRUDERS!

OUR LANDS ARE SAFE. THE CLAN SPIRIT IS ETERNALLY GRATEFUL, NONOS. YOU HAVE SAVED US.

NOW, LAY TO REST OUR BRETHREN BEFORE THEY FIND OUR VILLAGE.

LAY TO REST? I...

THE BEGINNING OF THE END

AT THE WORLD'S END

STORY BY: MAGNUS ASPLI   ART BY: PABLO PEPPINO   LETTERS BY: JEFF McCOMSEY

THE FIRST THANKSGIVING

STORY BY:
ERIC ESQUIVEL

ART AND LETTERS BY:
ANDER SARABIA

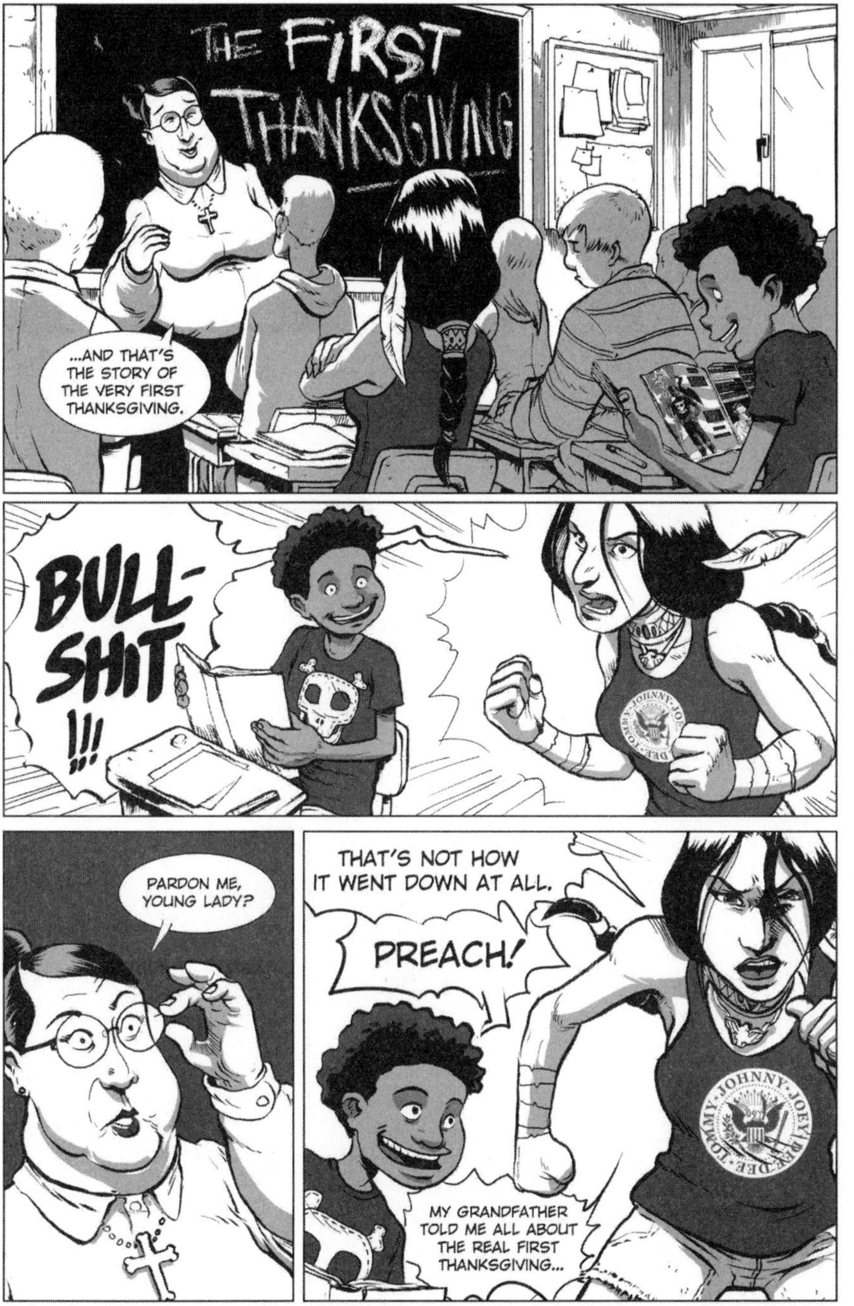
THE FIRST THANKSGIVING
...AND THAT'S THE STORY OF THE VERY FIRST THANKSGIVING.
BULL-SHIT!!!
JOHNNY JOEY DEE-DEE TOMMY
PARDON ME, YOUNG LADY?
THAT'S NOT HOW IT WENT DOWN AT ALL.
PREACH!
JOHNNY JOEY DEE-DEE TOMMY
MY GRANDFATHER TOLD ME ALL ABOUT THE REAL FIRST THANKSGIVING...

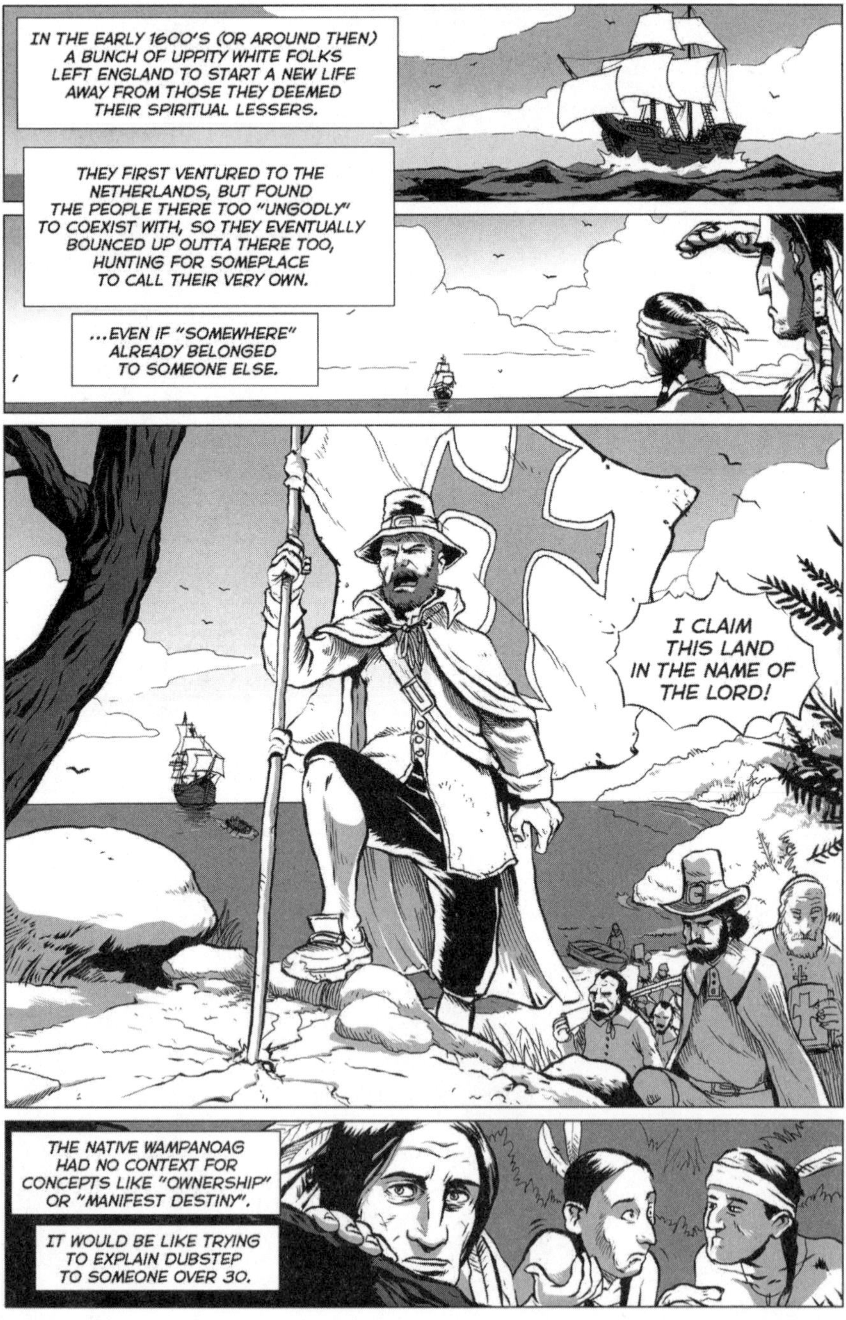

IN THE EARLY 1600'S (OR AROUND THEN) A BUNCH OF UPPITY WHITE FOLKS LEFT ENGLAND TO START A NEW LIFE AWAY FROM THOSE THEY DEEMED THEIR SPIRITUAL LESSERS.
THEY FIRST VENTURED TO THE NETHERLANDS, BUT FOUND THE PEOPLE THERE TOO "UNGODLY" TO COEXIST WITH, SO THEY EVENTUALLY BOUNCED UP OUTTA THERE TOO, HUNTING FOR SOMEPLACE TO CALL THEIR VERY OWN.
...EVEN IF "SOMEWHERE" ALREADY BELONGED TO SOMEONE ELSE.
I CLAIM THIS LAND IN THE NAME OF THE LORD!
THE NATIVE WAMPANOAG HAD NO CONTEXT FOR CONCEPTS LIKE "OWNERSHIP" OR "MANIFEST DESTINY".
IT WOULD BE LIKE TRYING TO EXPLAIN DUBSTEP TO SOMEONE OVER 30.

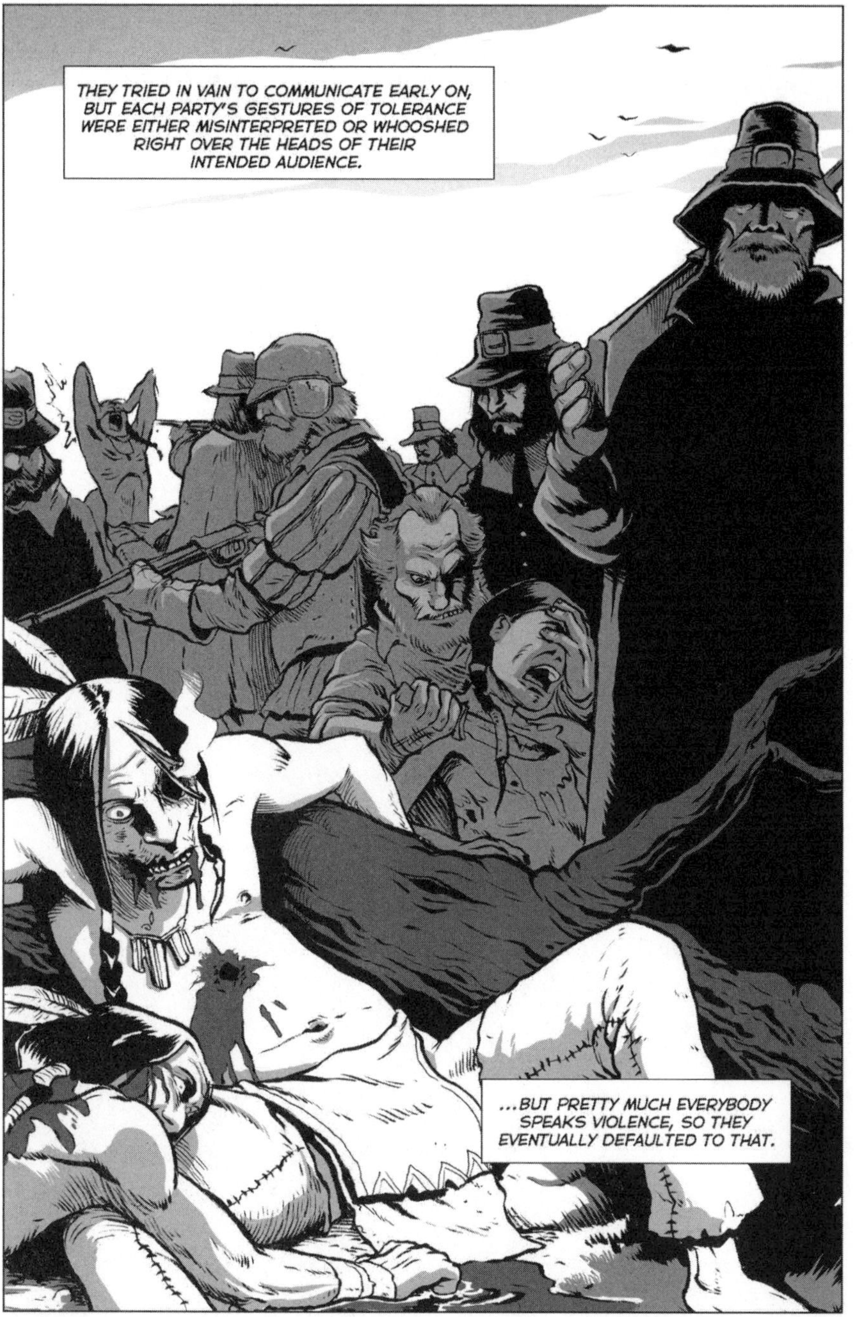
THEY TRIED IN VAIN TO COMMUNICATE EARLY ON, BUT EACH PARTY'S GESTURES OF TOLERANCE WERE EITHER MISINTERPRETED OR WHOOSHED RIGHT OVER THE HEADS OF THEIR INTENDED AUDIENCE.
...BUT PRETTY MUCH EVERYBODY SPEAKS VIOLENCE, SO THEY EVENTUALLY DEFAULTED TO THAT.

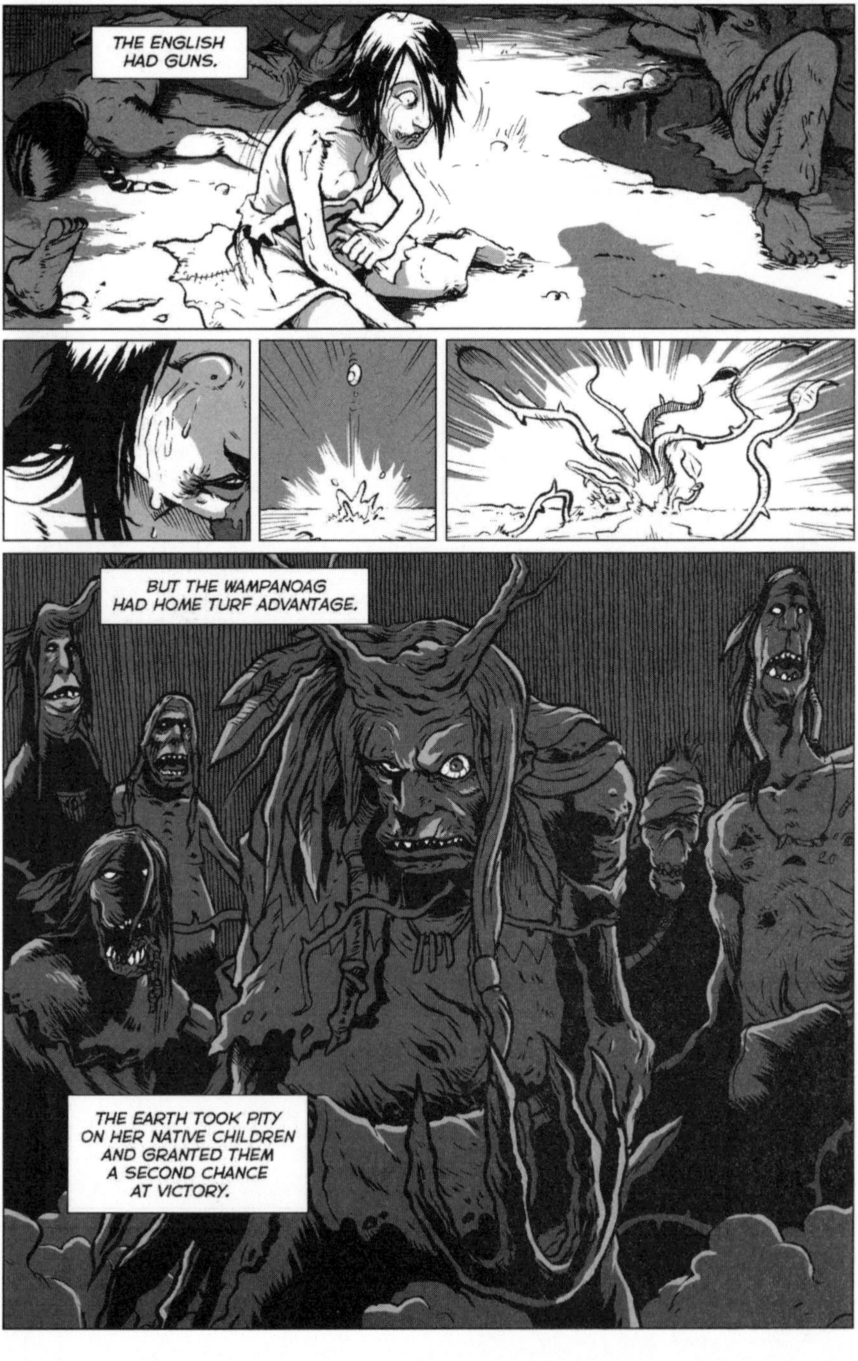
THE ENGLISH HAD GUNS.
BUT THE WAMPANOAG HAD HOME TURF ADVANTAGE.
THE EARTH TOOK PITY ON HER NATIVE CHILDREN AND GRANTED THEM A SECOND CHANCE AT VICTORY.

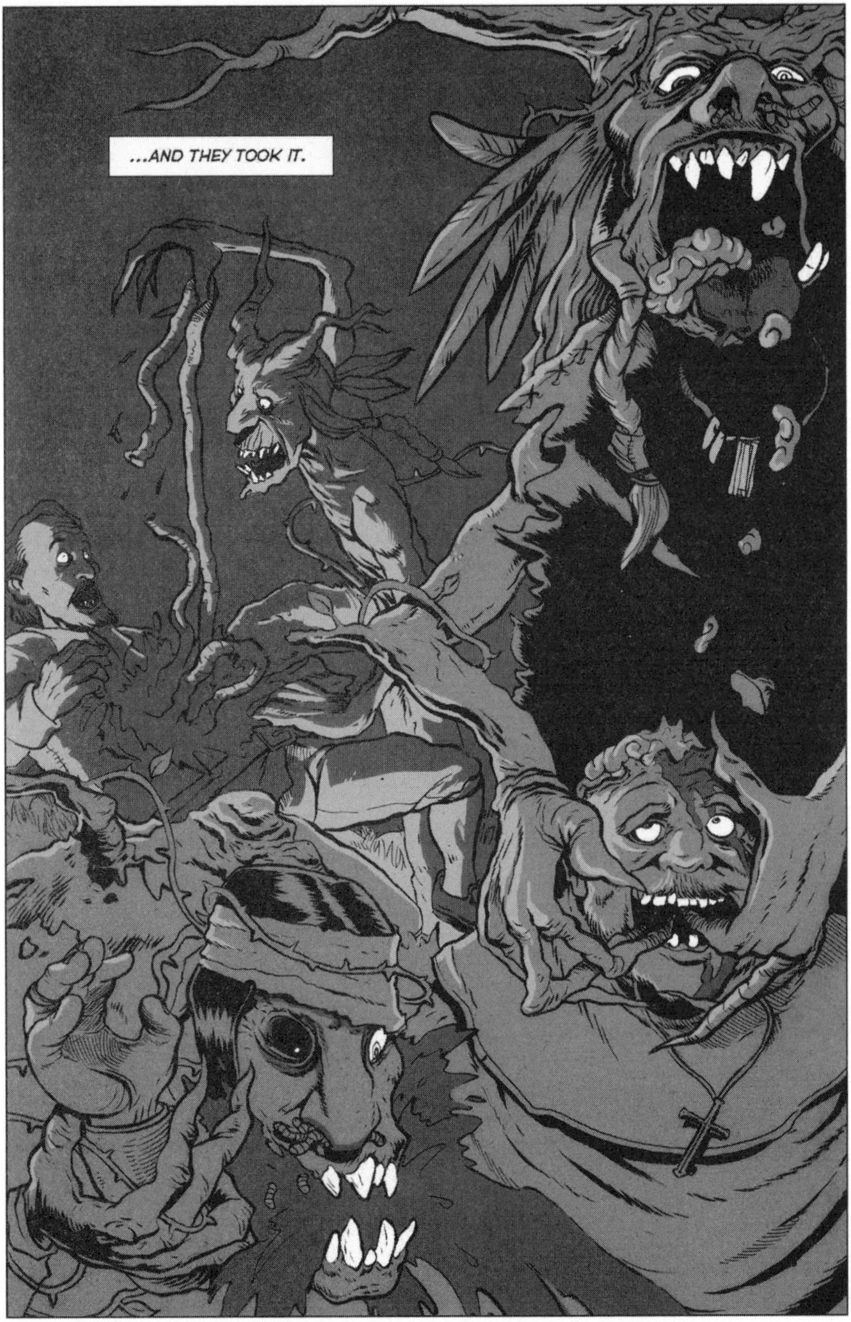
...AND THEY TOOK IT.

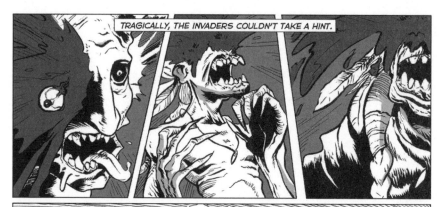

TRAGICALLY, THE INVADERS COULDN'T TAKE A HINT.

THEY SENT REINFORCEMENTS ARMED WITH PROFANE WEAPONRY AND A RIGHTEOUS INDIGNATION THAT JUSTIFIED A LEVEL OF VIOLENCE HERETOFORE UNSEEN.

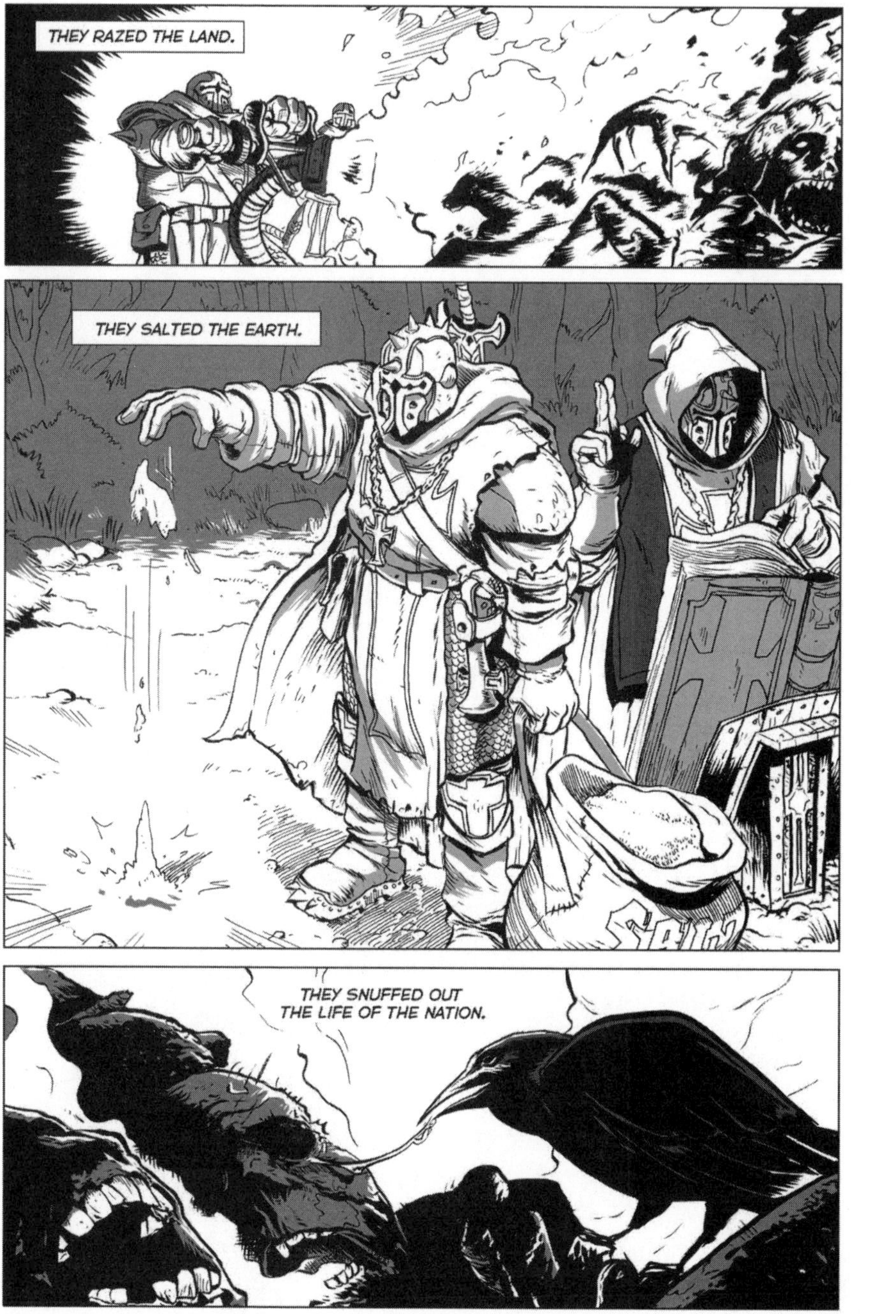
THEY RAZED THE LAND.
THEY SALTED THE EARTH.
THEY SNUFFED OUT THE LIFE OF THE NATION.

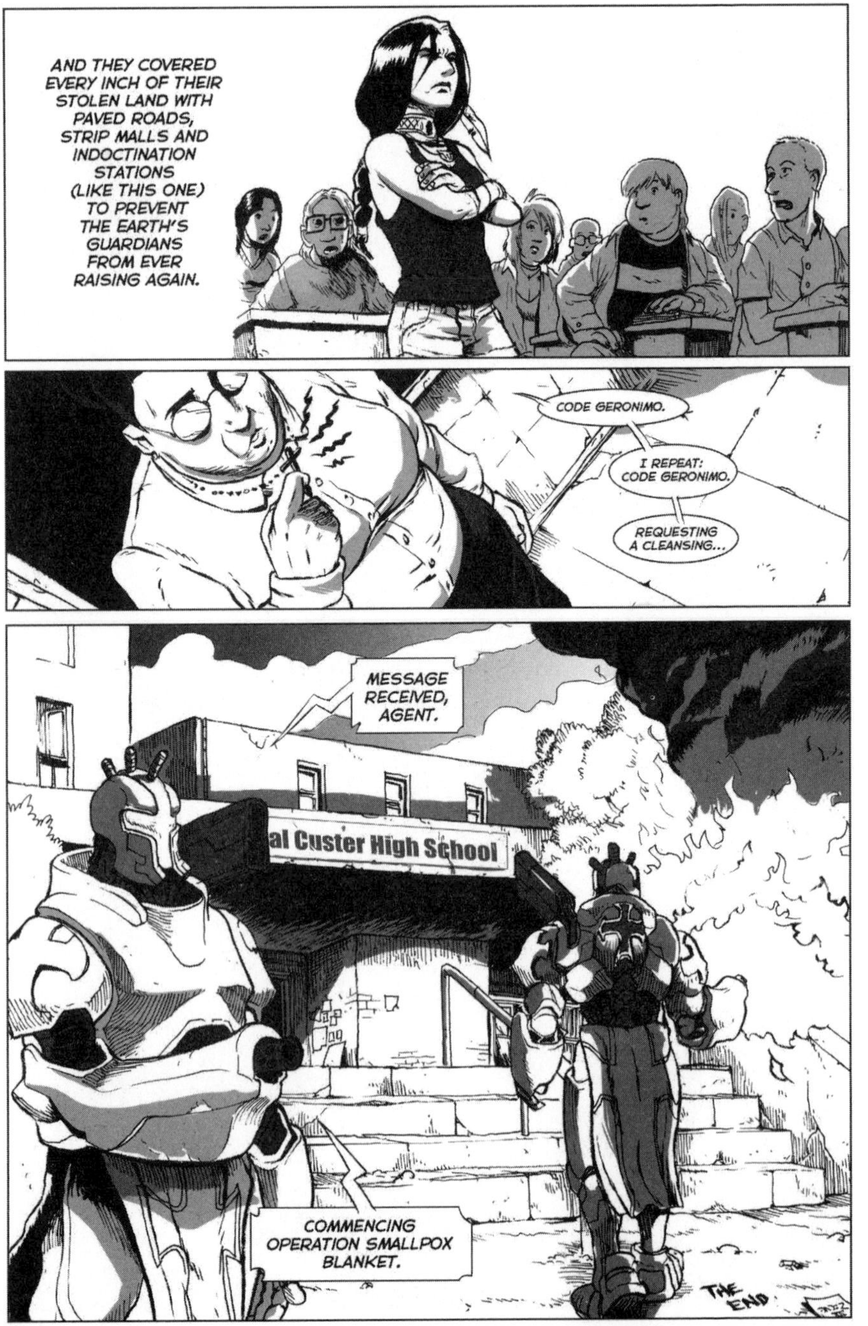
AND THEY COVERED EVERY INCH OF THEIR STOLEN LAND WITH PAVED ROADS, STRIP MALLS AND INDOCTINATION STATIONS (LIKE THIS ONE) TO PREVENT THE EARTH'S GUARDIANS FROM EVER RAISING AGAIN.
CODE GERONIMO.
I REPEAT: CODE GERONIMO.
REQUESTING A CLEANSING...
MESSAGE RECEIVED, AGENT.
al Custer High School
COMMENCING OPERATION SMALLPOX BLANKET.
THE END

TRUTH OR VIRGINIA DARE

STORY BY:
JENNIE WOOD

ART AND LETTERS BY:
GLEN OSTRANDER

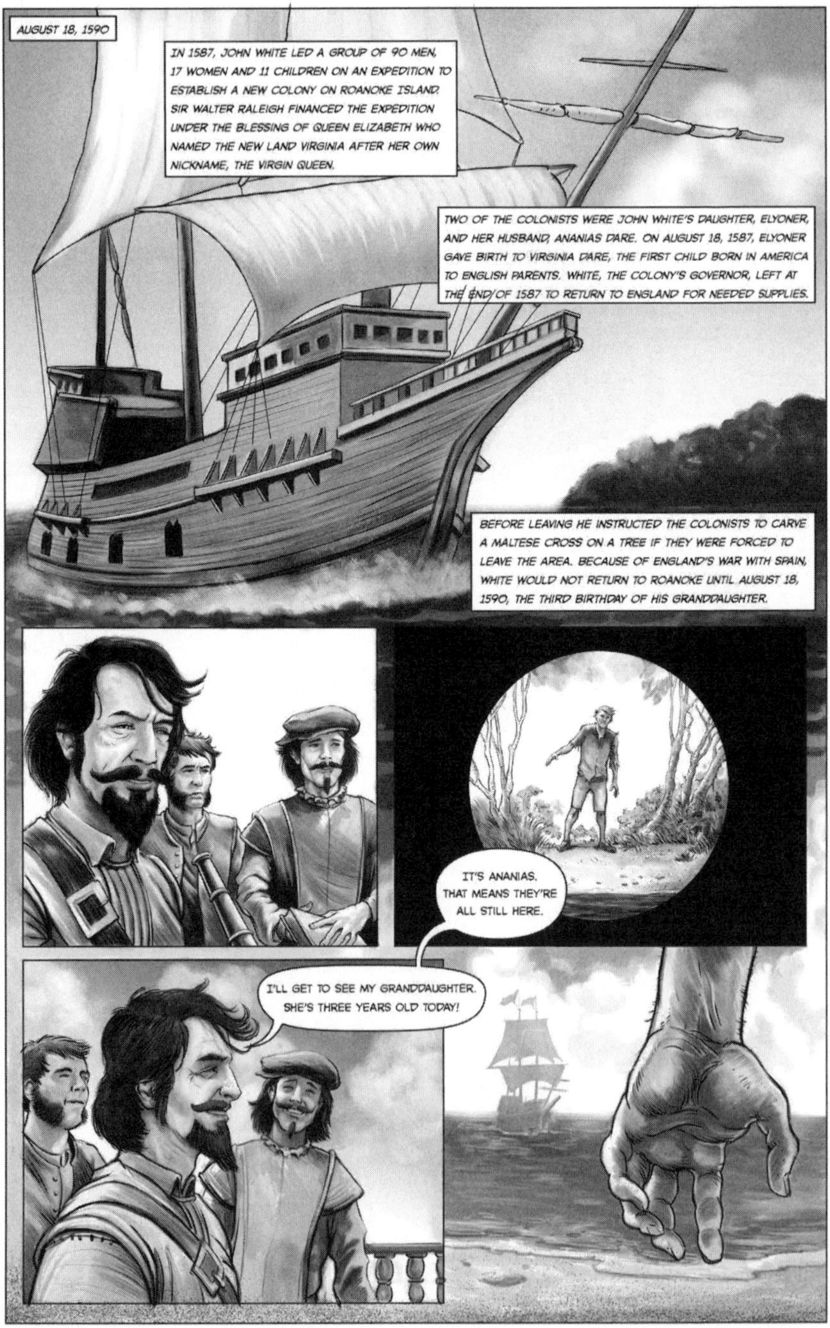
AUGUST 18, 1590
IN 1587, JOHN WHITE LED A GROUP OF 90 MEN, 17 WOMEN AND 11 CHILDREN ON AN EXPEDITION TO ESTABLISH A NEW COLONY ON ROANOKE ISLAND. SIR WALTER RALEIGH FINANCED THE EXPEDITION UNDER THE BLESSING OF QUEEN ELIZABETH WHO NAMED THE NEW LAND VIRGINIA AFTER HER OWN NICKNAME, THE VIRGIN QUEEN.
TWO OF THE COLONISTS WERE JOHN WHITE'S DAUGHTER, ELYONER, AND HER HUSBAND, ANANIAS DARE. ON AUGUST 18, 1587, ELYONER GAVE BIRTH TO VIRGINIA DARE, THE FIRST CHILD BORN IN AMERICA TO ENGLISH PARENTS. WHITE, THE COLONY'S GOVERNOR, LEFT AT THE END OF 1587 TO RETURN TO ENGLAND FOR NEEDED SUPPLIES.
BEFORE LEAVING HE INSTRUCTED THE COLONISTS TO CARVE A MALTESE CROSS ON A TREE IF THEY WERE FORCED TO LEAVE THE AREA. BECAUSE OF ENGLAND'S WAR WITH SPAIN, WHITE WOULD NOT RETURN TO ROANOKE UNTIL AUGUST 18, 1590, THE THIRD BIRTHDAY OF HIS GRANDDAUGHTER.
IT'S ANANIAS. THAT MEANS THEY'RE ALL STILL HERE.
I'LL GET TO SEE MY GRANDDAUGHTER. SHE'S THREE YEARS OLD TODAY!

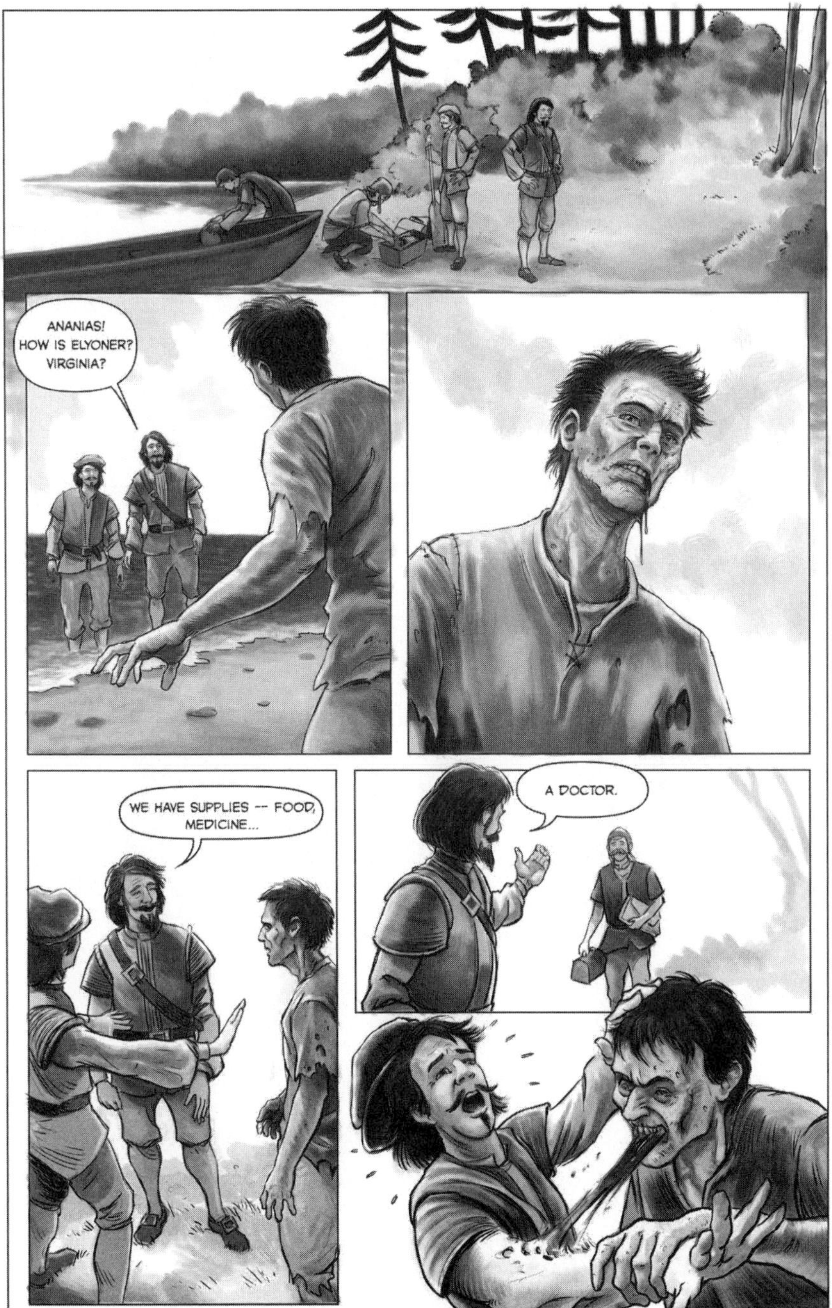
ANANIAS! HOW IS ELYONER? VIRGINIA?
WE HAVE SUPPLIES -- FOOD, MEDICINE...
A DOCTOR.

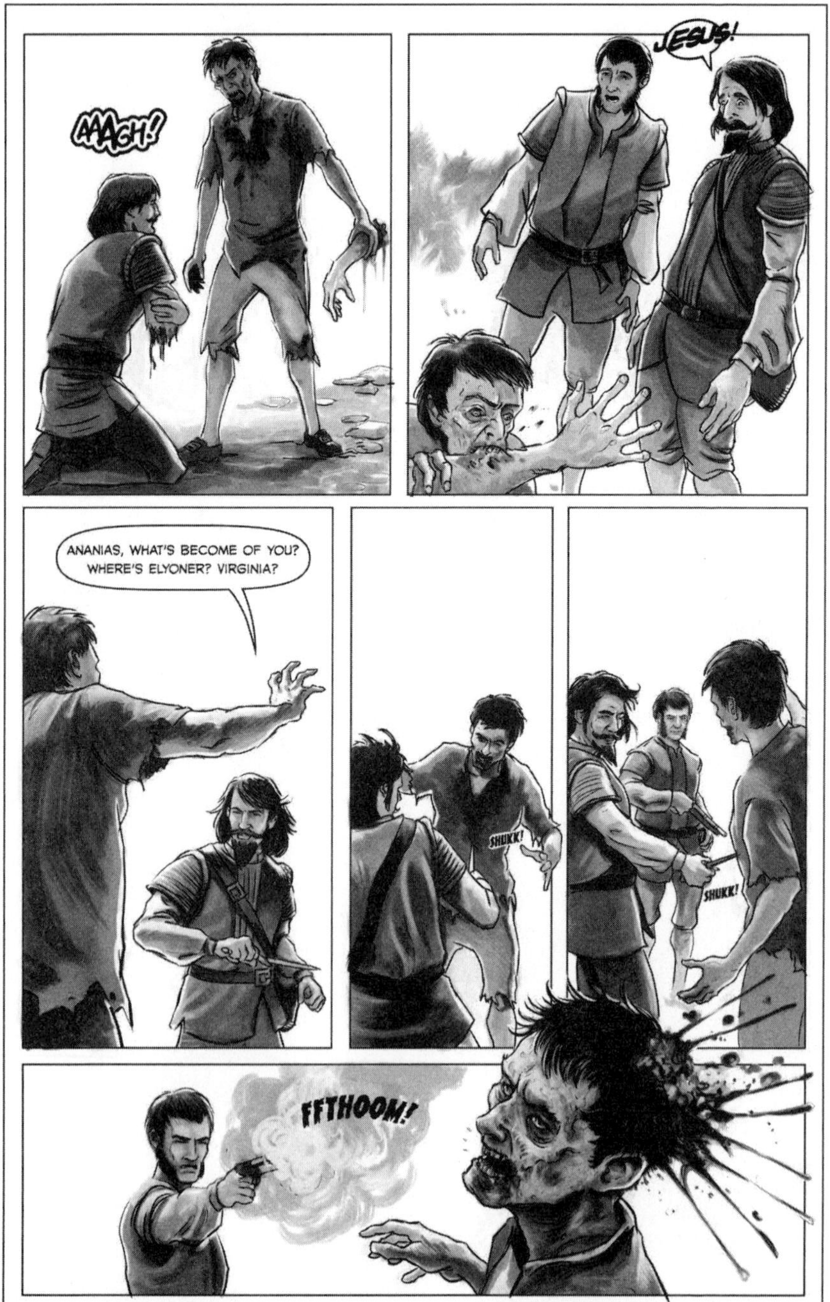
AAACH!
JESUS!
ANANIAS, WHAT'S BECOME OF YOU? WHERE'S ELYONER? VIRGINIA?
SHUKK!
SHUKK!
FFTHOOM!

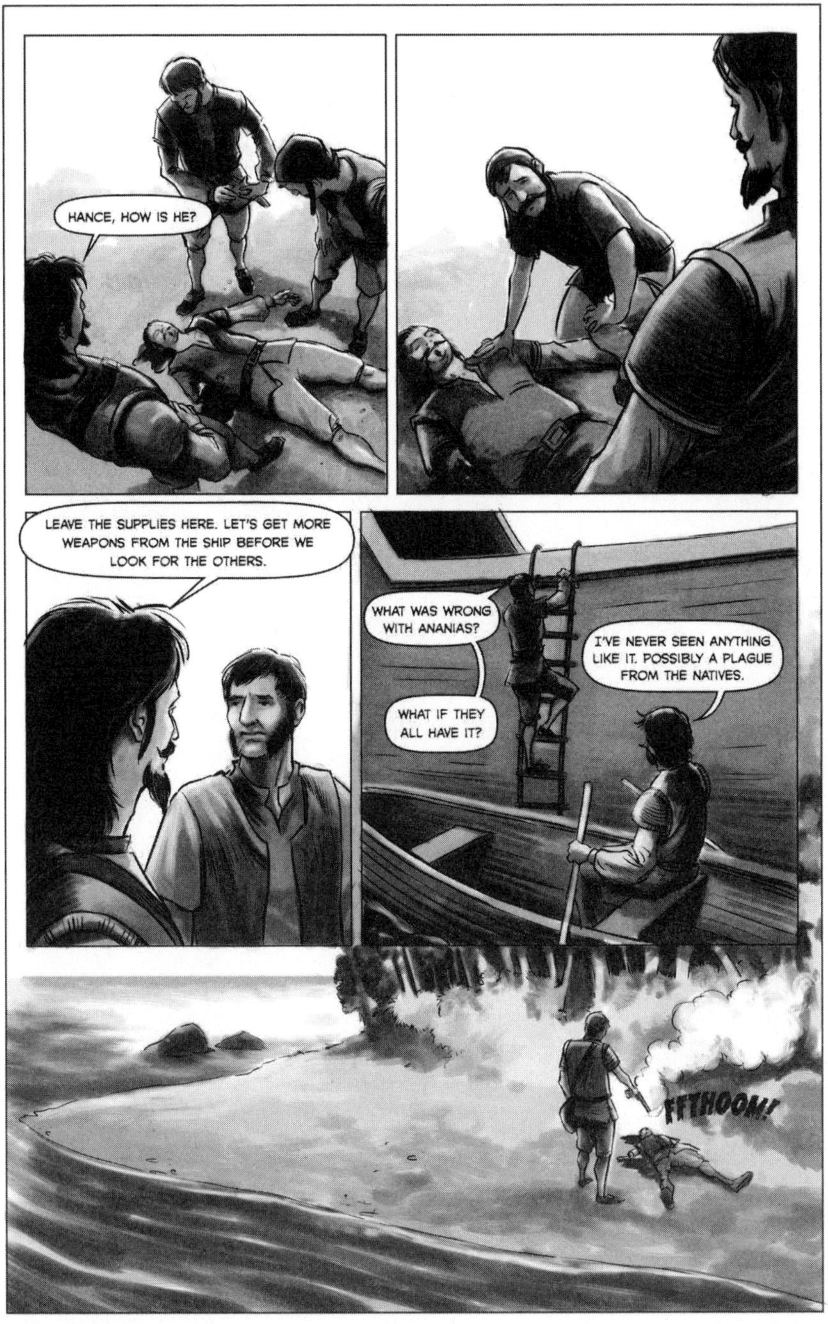
HANCE, HOW IS HE?
LEAVE THE SUPPLIES HERE. LET'S GET MORE WEAPONS FROM THE SHIP BEFORE WE LOOK FOR THE OTHERS.
WHAT WAS WRONG WITH ANANIAS?
I'VE NEVER SEEN ANYTHING LIKE IT. POSSIBLY A PLAGUE FROM THE NATIVES.
WHAT IF THEY ALL HAVE IT?
FFTHOOM!

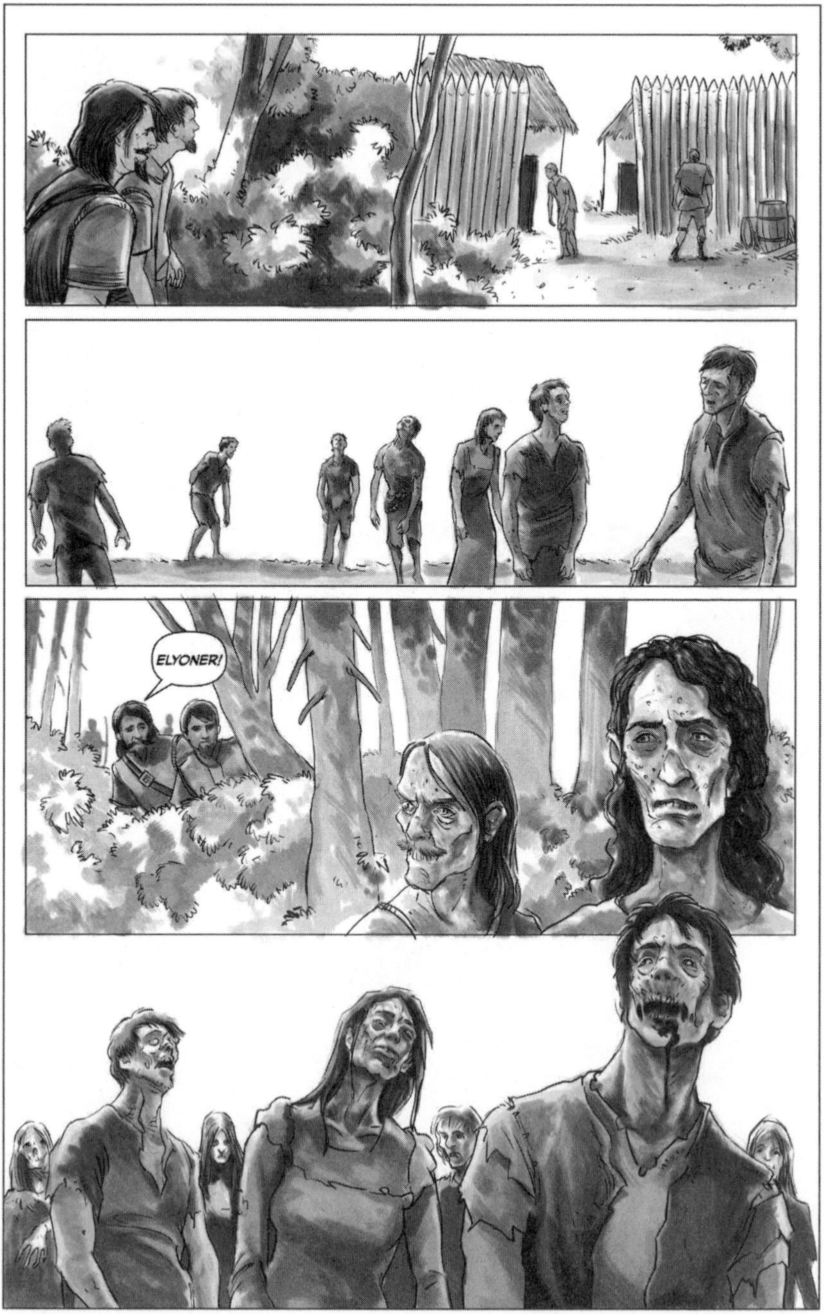
ELYONER!

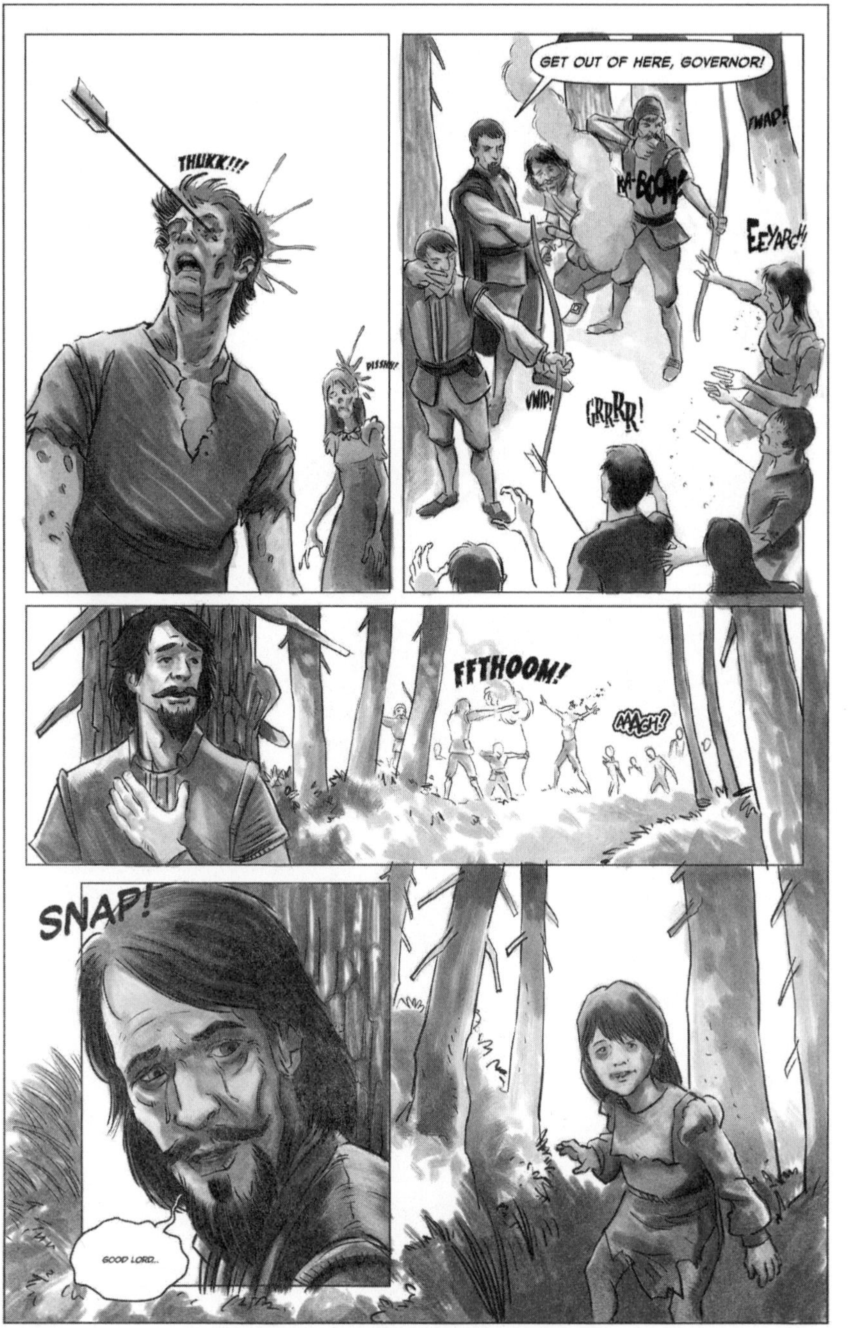
THUKK!!!
PISSHH!
GET OUT OF HERE, GOVERNOR!
FWAP!
KA-BOOM!
EEYARGH!
VWIP!
GRRRR!
FFTHOOM!
AAAGH!
SNAP!
GOOD LORD..

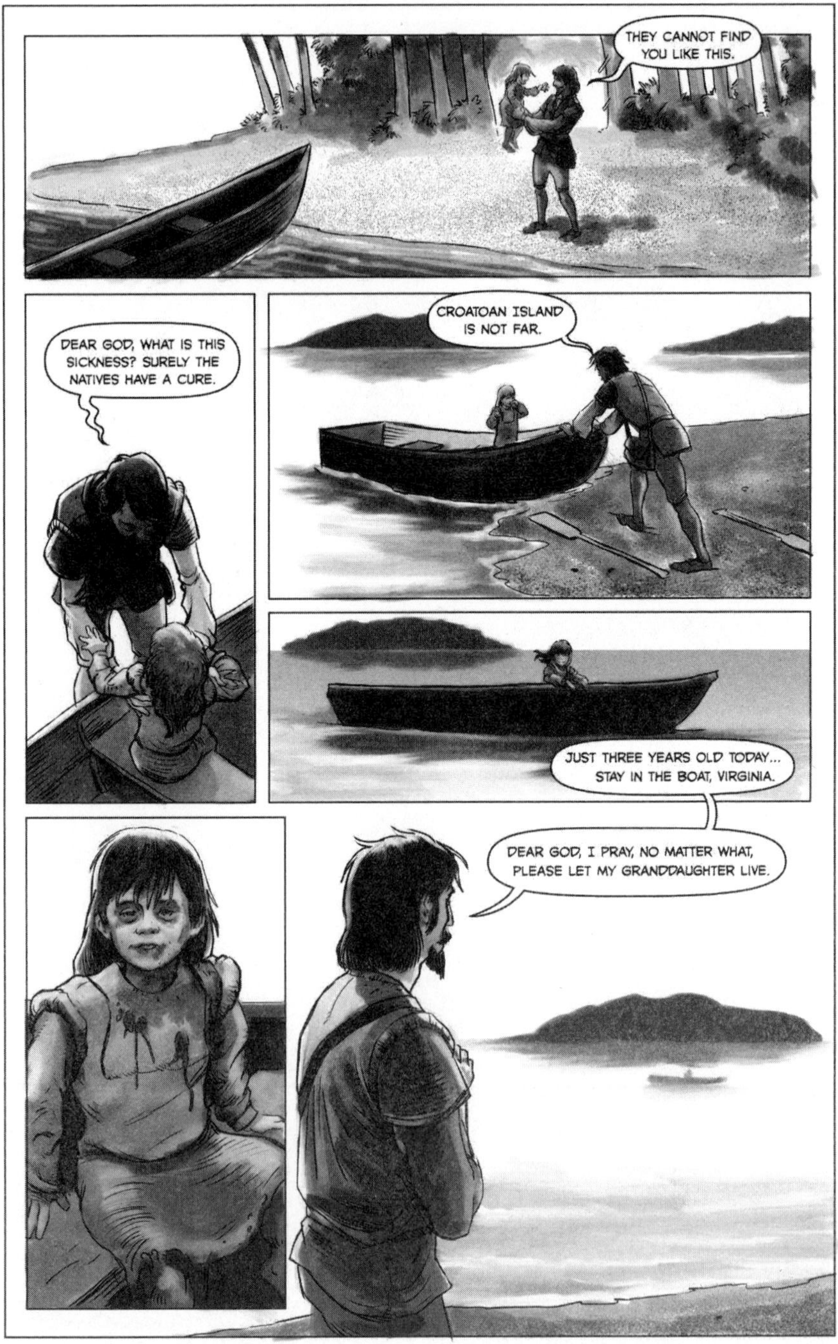
THEY CANNOT FIND YOU LIKE THIS.
DEAR GOD, WHAT IS THIS SICKNESS? SURELY THE NATIVES HAVE A CURE.
CROATOAN ISLAND IS NOT FAR.
JUST THREE YEARS OLD TODAY... STAY IN THE BOAT, VIRGINIA.
DEAR GOD, I PRAY, NO MATTER WHAT, PLEASE LET MY GRANDDAUGHTER LIVE.

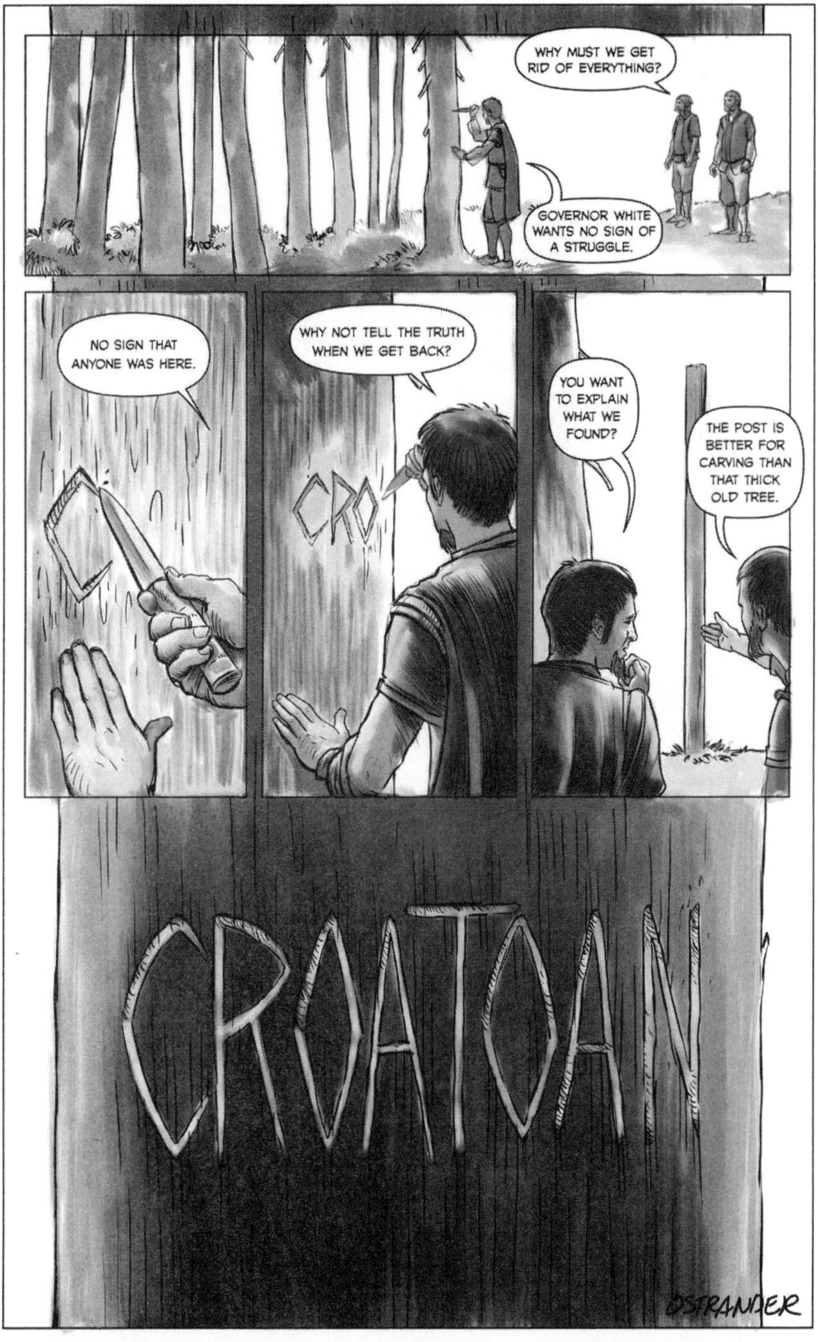
WHY MUST WE GET RID OF EVERYTHING?
GOVERNOR WHITE WANTS NO SIGN OF A STRUGGLE.
NO SIGN THAT ANYONE WAS HERE.
WHY NOT TELL THE TRUTH WHEN WE GET BACK?
CRO
YOU WANT TO EXPLAIN WHAT WE FOUND?
THE POST IS BETTER FOR CARVING THAN THAT THICK OLD TREE.
CROATOAN
OSTRANDER

THE DESIRED EFFECT

STORY AND LETTERS BY:
RACHEL DEERING

ART BY:
ANDRES ESPARZA

GREYSCALES BY:
JEFF McCOMSEY

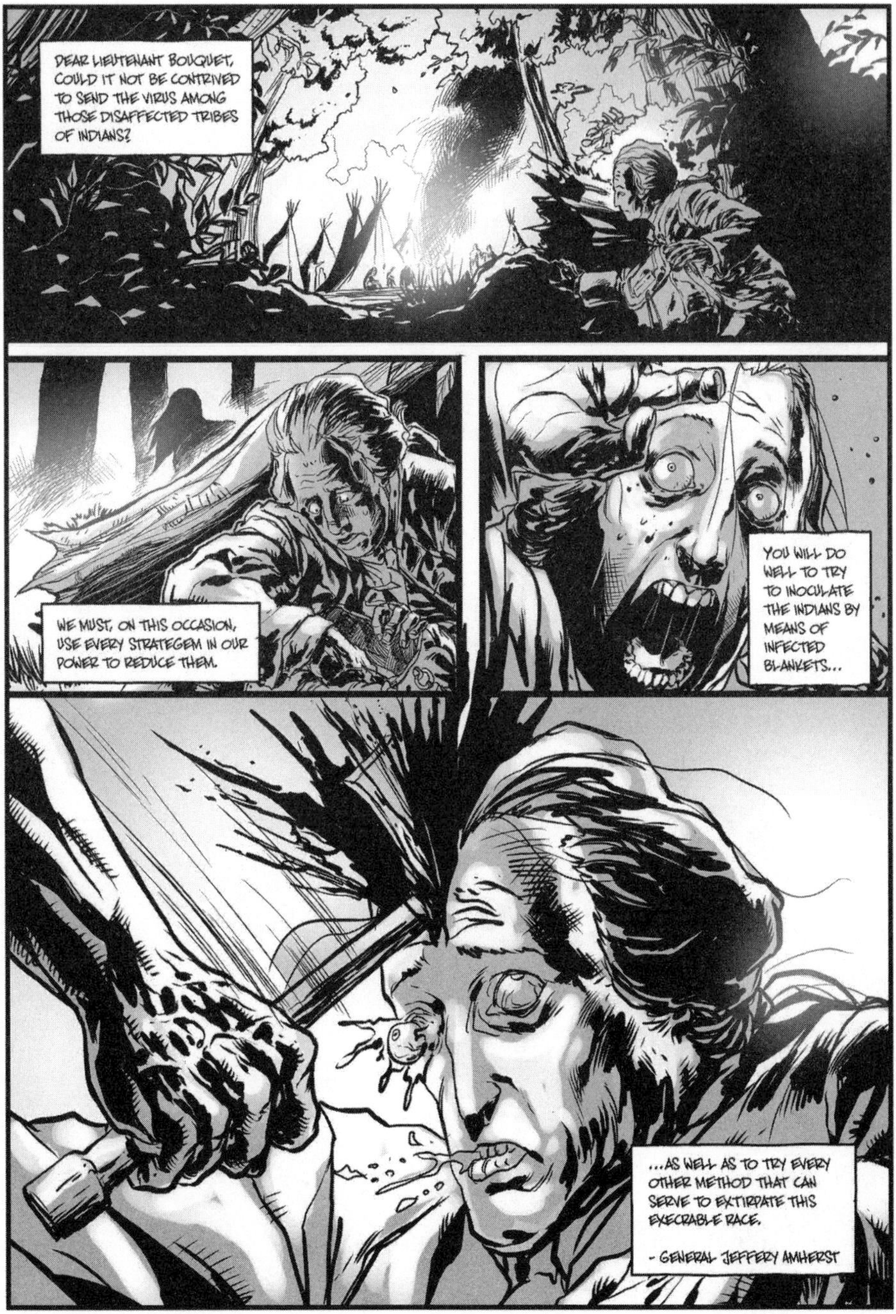
DEAR LIEUTENANT BOUQUET, COULD IT NOT BE CONTRIVED TO SEND THE VIRUS AMONG THOSE DISAFFECTED TRIBES OF INDIANS?
WE MUST, ON THIS OCCASION, USE EVERY STRATEGEM IN OUR POWER TO REDUCE THEM.
YOU WILL DO WELL TO TRY TO INOCULATE THE INDIANS BY MEANS OF INFECTED BLANKETS...
...AS WELL AS TO TRY EVERY OTHER METHOD THAT CAN SERVE TO EXTIRPATE THIS EXECRABLE RACE.
- GENERAL JEFFERY AMHERST

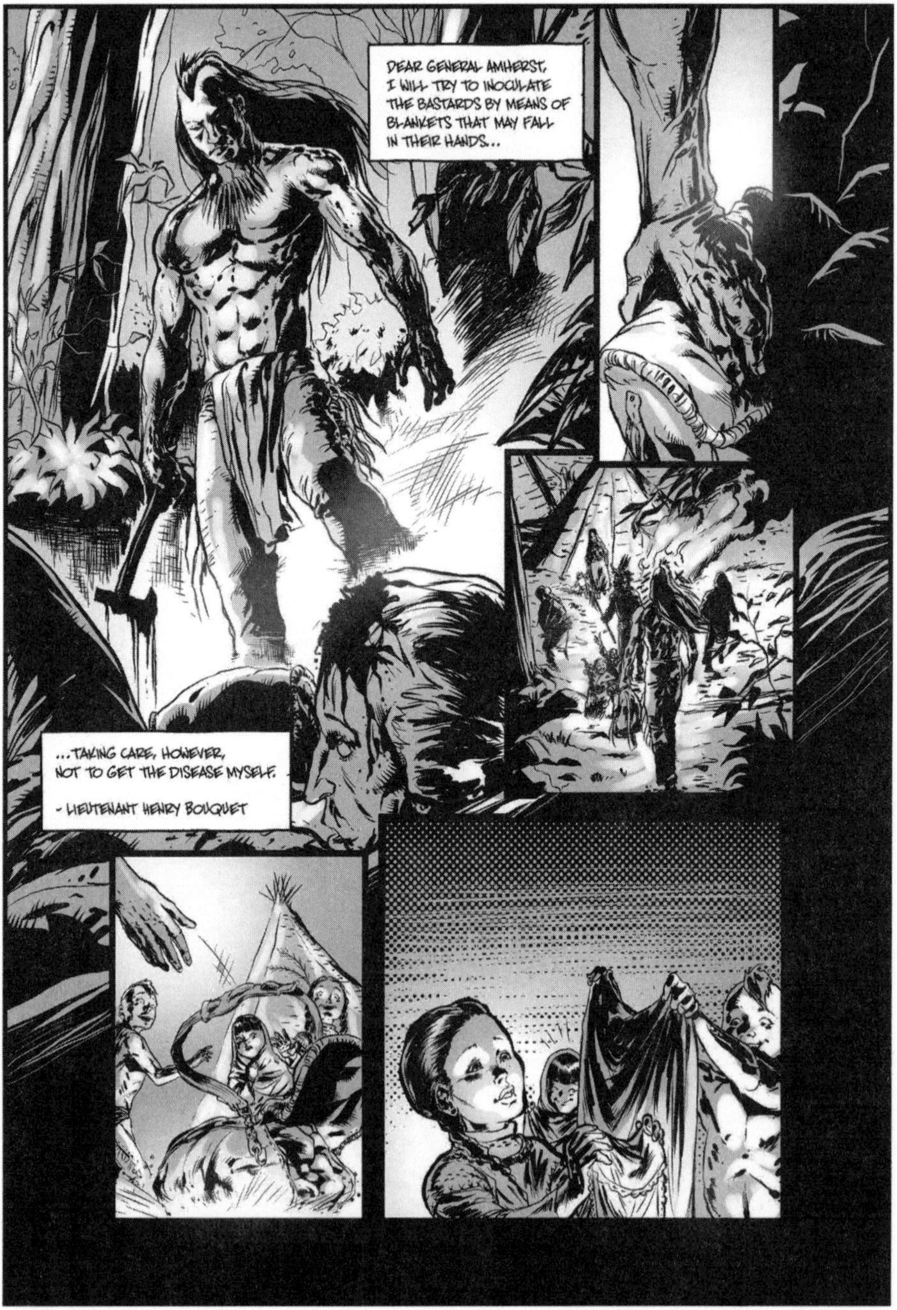
DEAR GENERAL AMHERST, I WILL TRY TO INOCULATE THE BASTARDS BY MEANS OF BLANKETS THAT MAY FALL IN THEIR HANDS...
...TAKING CARE, HOWEVER, NOT TO GET THE DISEASE MYSELF.
- LIEUTENANT HENRY BOUQUET

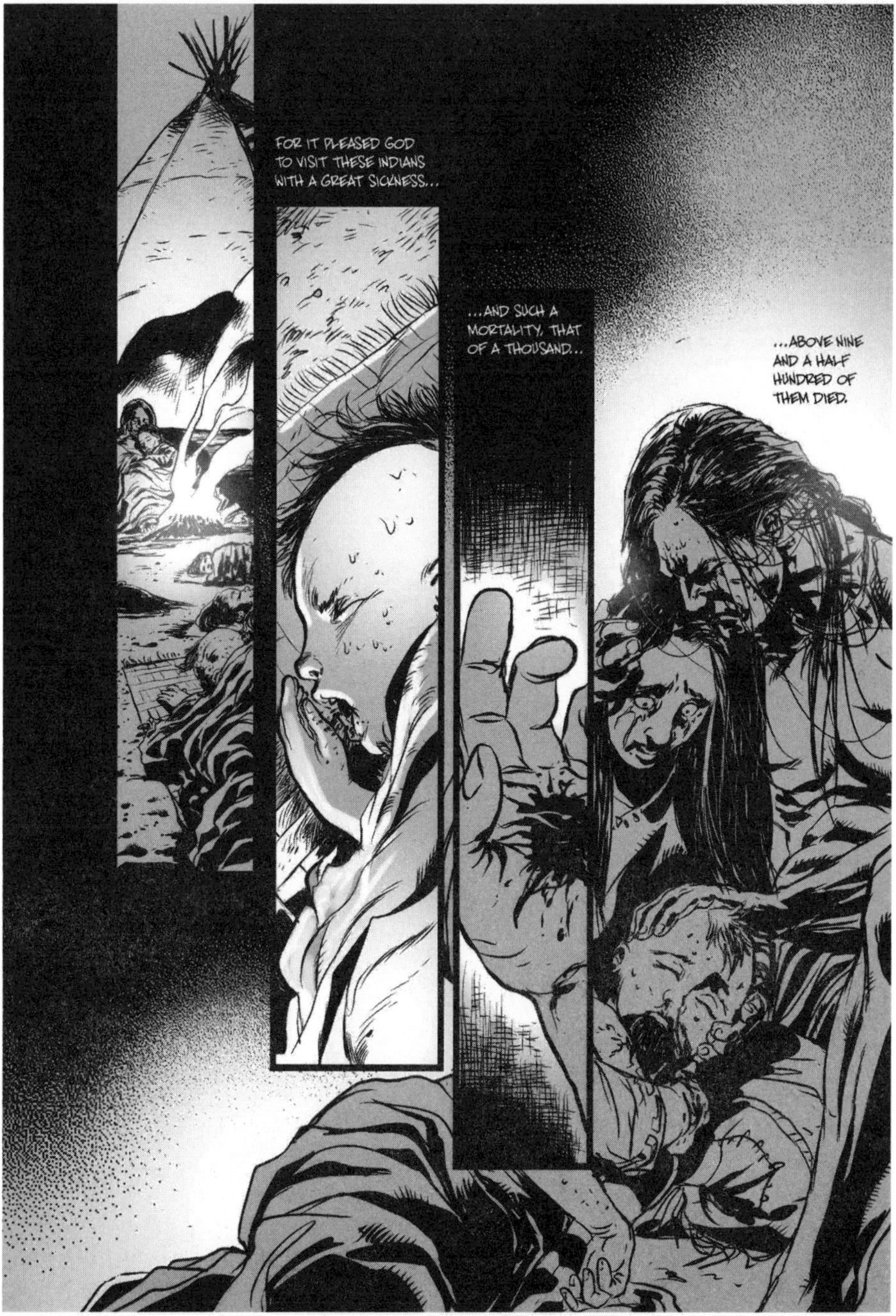
FOR IT PLEASED GOD TO VISIT THESE INDIANS WITH A GREAT SICKNESS...
...AND SUCH A MORTALITY, THAT OF A THOUSAND...
...ABOVE NINE AND A HALF HUNDRED OF THEM DIED.

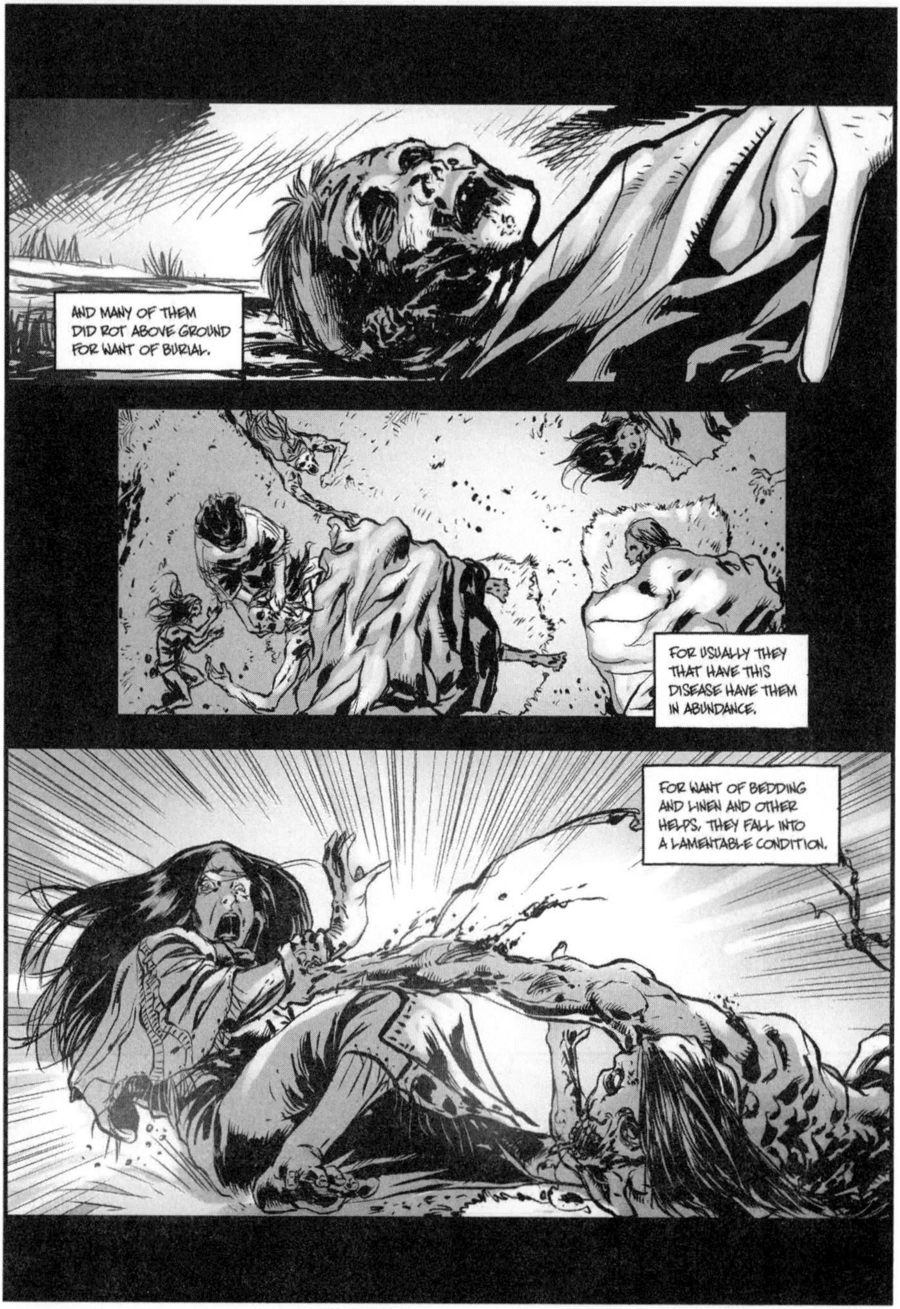
AND MANY OF THEM DID ROT ABOVE GROUND FOR WANT OF BURIAL.
FOR USUALLY THEY THAT HAVE THIS DISEASE HAVE THEM IN ABUNDANCE.
FOR WANT OF BEDDING AND LINEN AND OTHER HELPS, THEY FALL INTO A LAMENTABLE CONDITION.

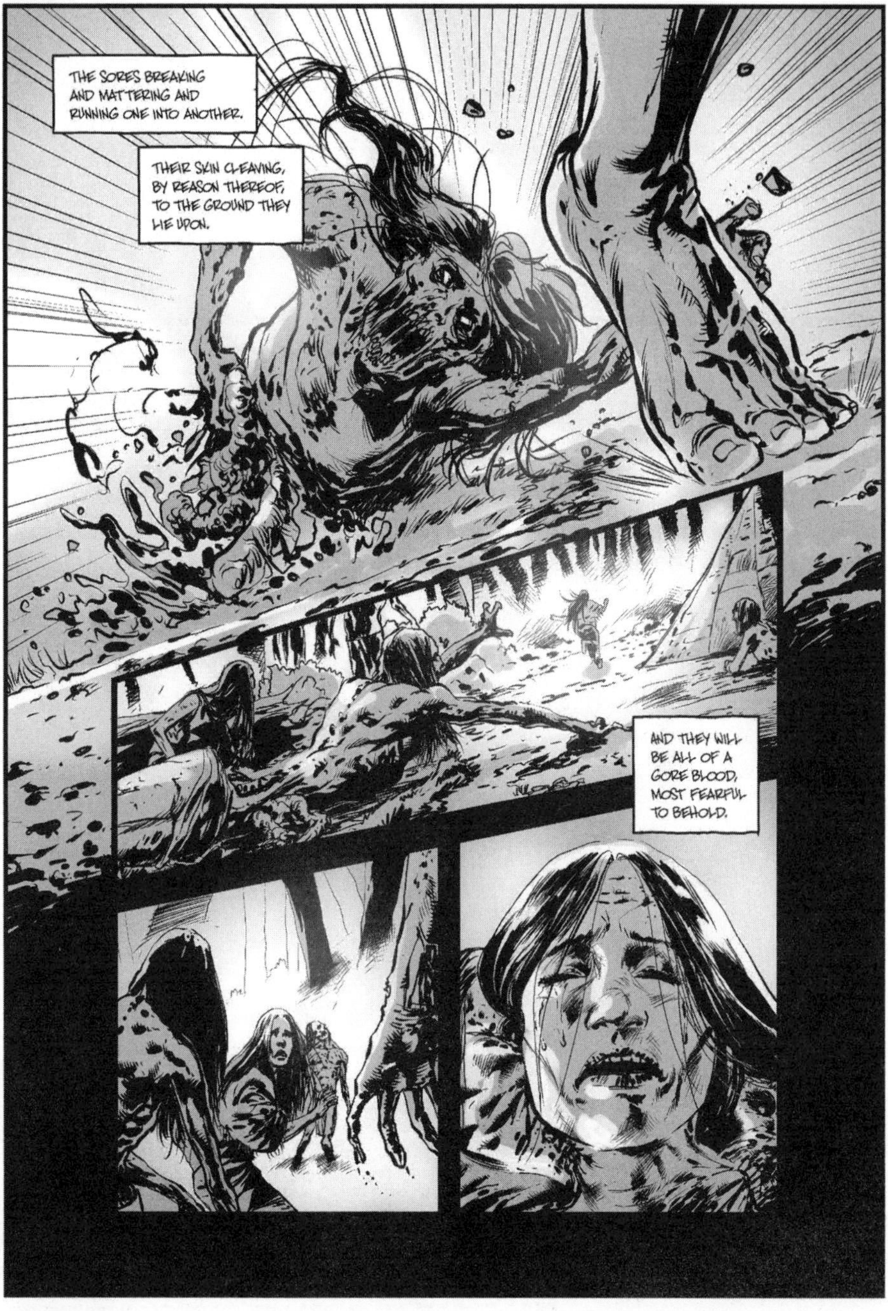
THE SORES BREAKING AND MATTERING AND RUNNING ONE INTO ANOTHER.
THEIR SKIN CLEAVING, BY REASON THEREOF, TO THE GROUND THEY LIE UPON.
AND THEY WILL BE ALL OF A GORE BLOOD, MOST FEARFUL TO BEHOLD.

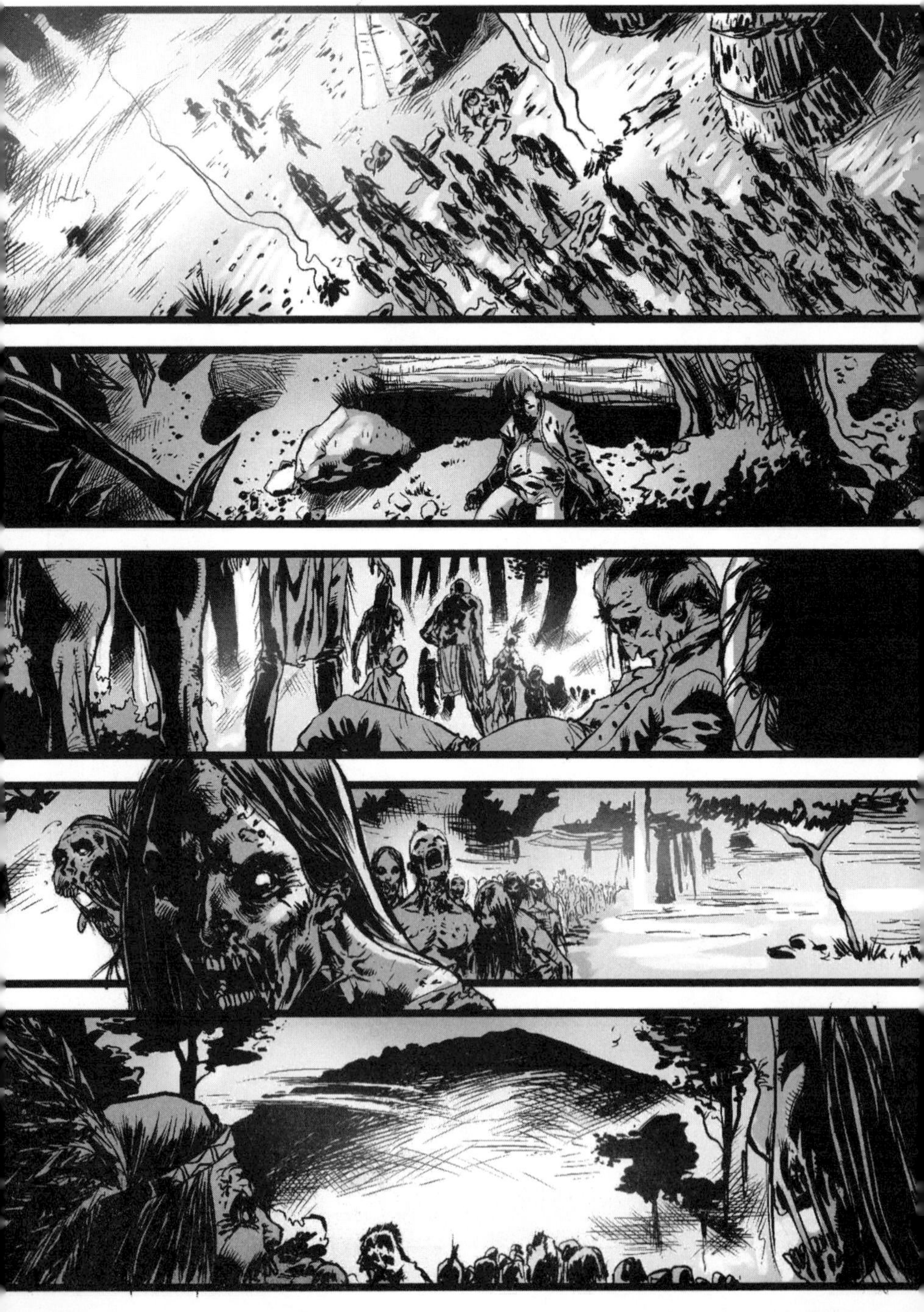

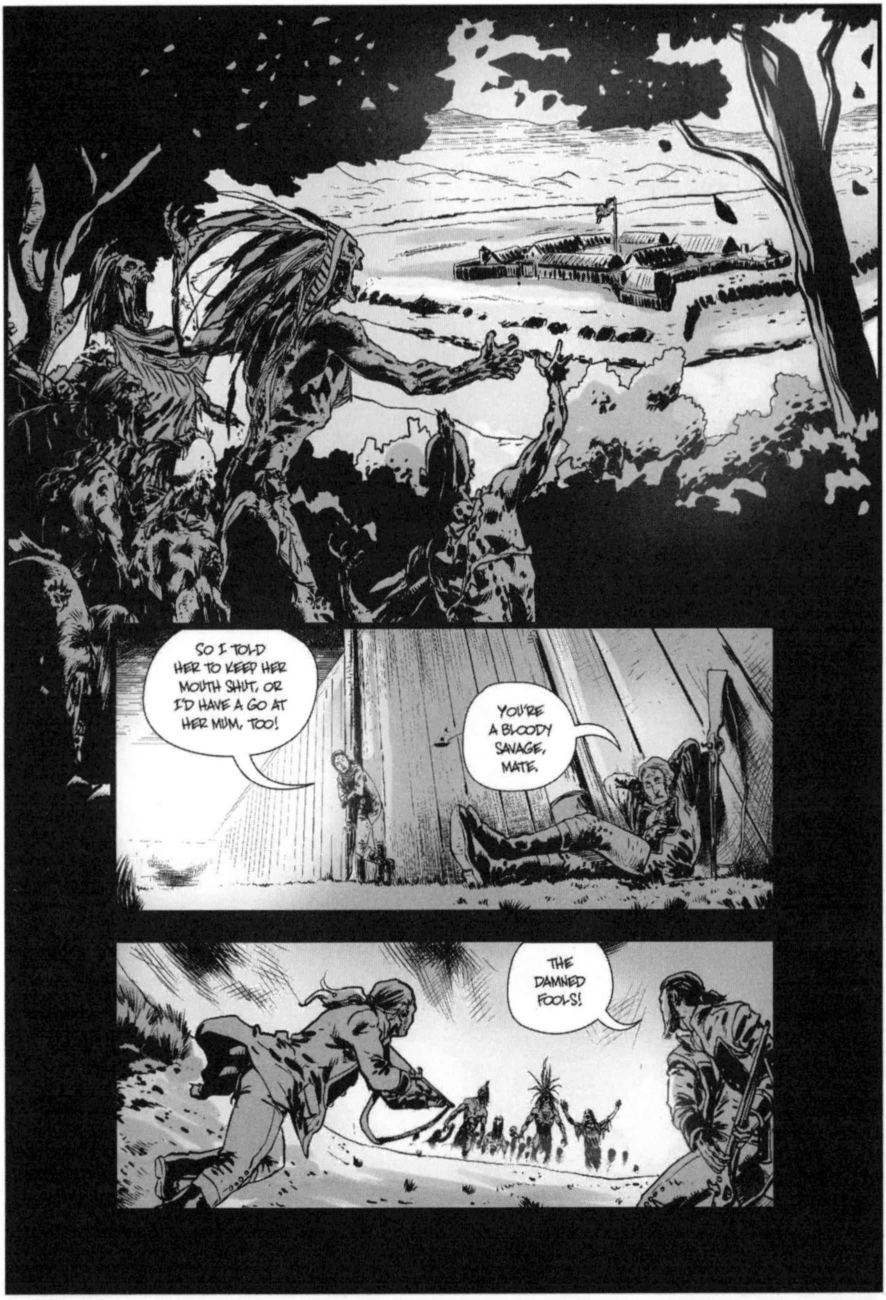
SO I TOLD HER TO KEEP HER MOUTH SHUT, OR I'D HAVE A GO AT HER MUM, TOO!
YOU'RE A BLOODY SAVAGE, MATE.
THE DAMNED FOOLS!

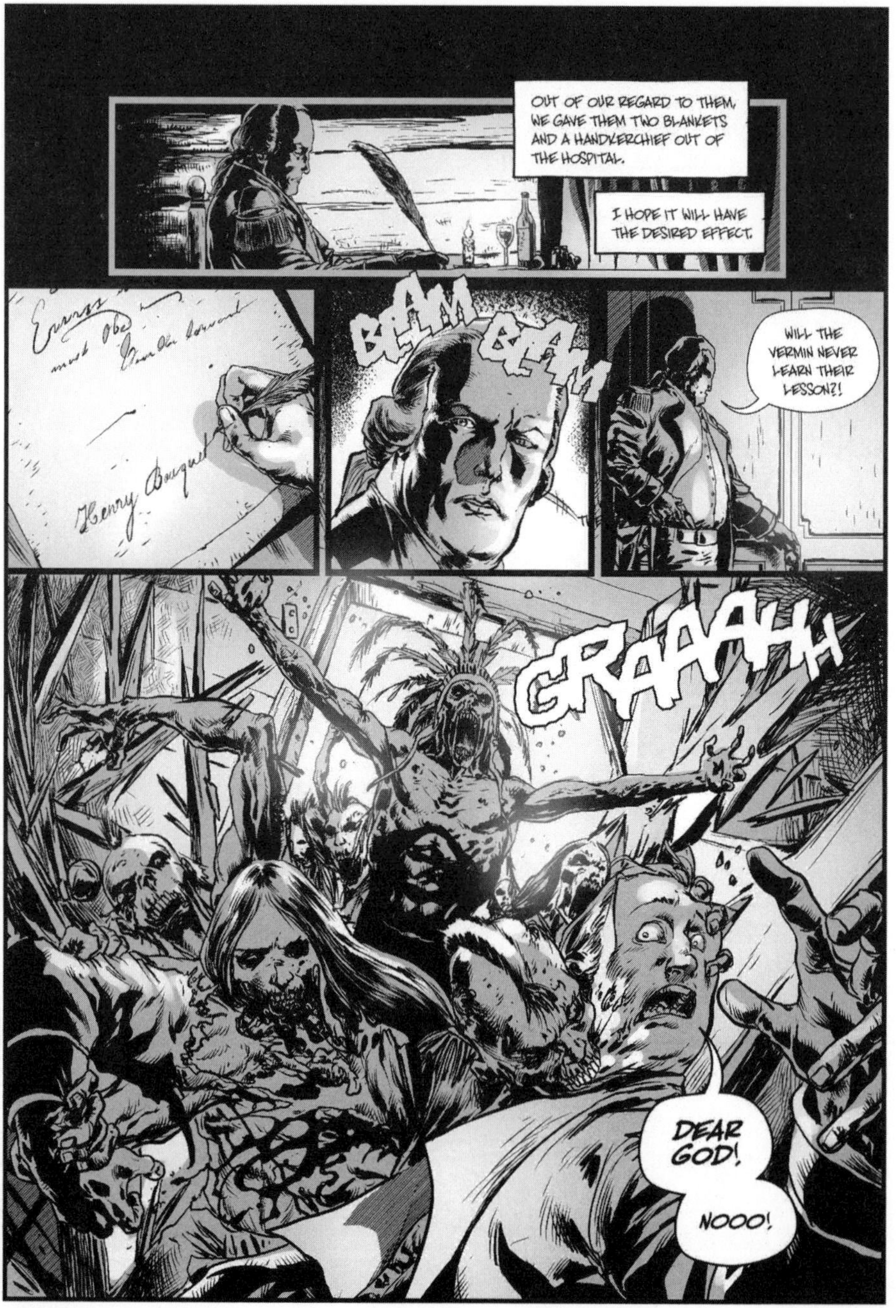
OUT OF OUR REGARD TO THEM, WE GAVE THEM TWO BLANKETS AND A HANDKERCHIEF OUT OF THE HOSPITAL.
I HOPE IT WILL HAVE THE DESIRED EFFECT.
Henry Bouquet
BLAM BLAM
WILL THE VERMIN NEVER LEARN THEIR LESSON?!
GRAAAHH
DEAR GOD!
NOOO!

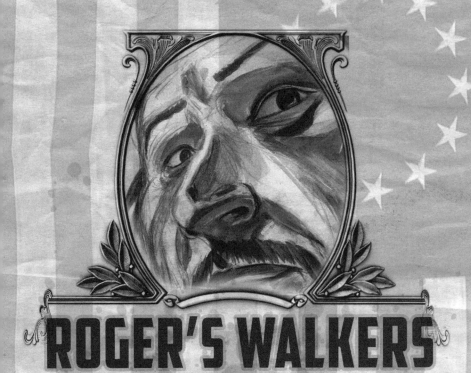

ROGER'S WALKERS

STORY BY:
SHAWN WILLIAMS

ART AND LETTERS BY:
DOUGLAS DRAPER

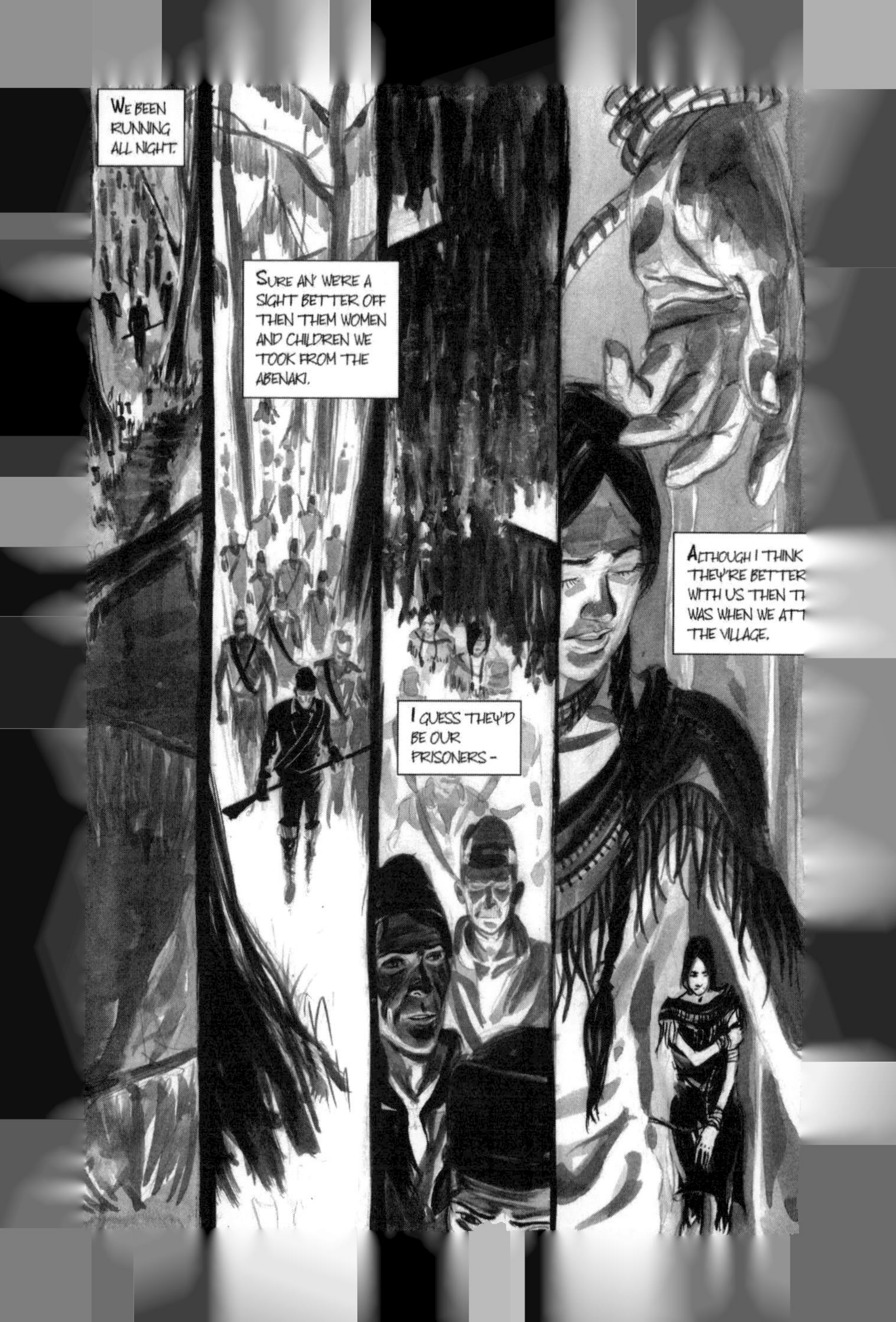
WE BEEN RUNNING ALL NIGHT.
SURE AN' WE'RE A SIGHT BETTER OFF THEN THEM WOMEN AND CHILDREN WE TOOK FROM THE ABENAKI.
I GUESS THEY'D BE OUR PRISONERS -
ALTHOUGH I THINK THEY'RE BETTER WITH US THEN TH WAS WHEN WE ATT THE VILLAGE.

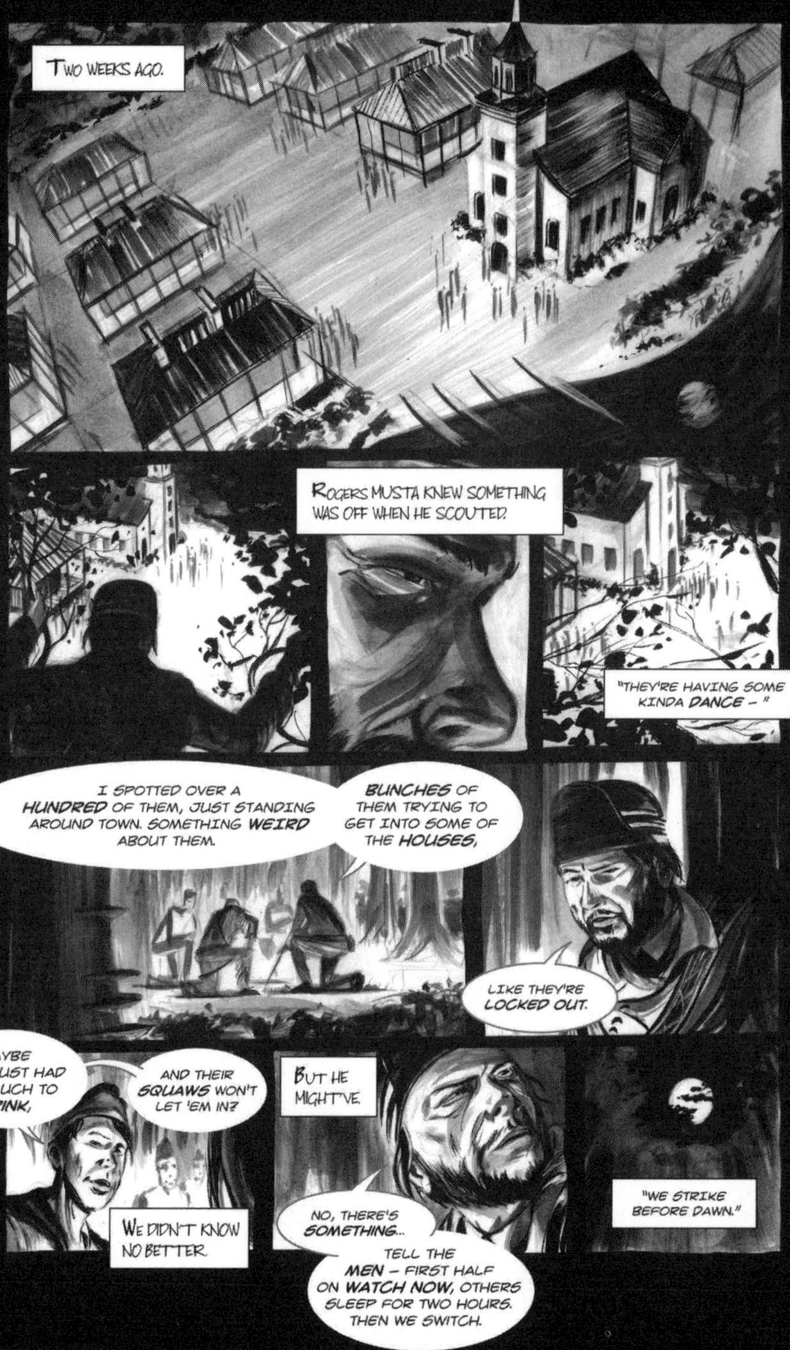
TWO WEEKS AGO.
ROGERS MUSTA KNEW SOMETHING WAS OFF WHEN HE SCOUTED.
"THEY'RE HAVING SOME KINDA DANCE –"
I SPOTTED OVER A HUNDRED OF THEM, JUST STANDING AROUND TOWN. SOMETHING WEIRD ABOUT THEM.
BUNCHES OF THEM TRYING TO GET INTO SOME OF THE HOUSES,
LIKE THEY'RE LOCKED OUT.
MAYBE THEY JUST HAD TOO MUCH TO DRINK,
AND THEIR SQUAWS WON'T LET 'EM IN?
WE DIDN'T KNOW NO BETTER.
BUT HE MIGHT'VE.
NO, THERE'S SOMETHING...
TELL THE MEN – FIRST HALF ON WATCH NOW, OTHERS SLEEP FOR TWO HOURS. THEN WE SWITCH.
"WE STRIKE BEFORE DAWN."

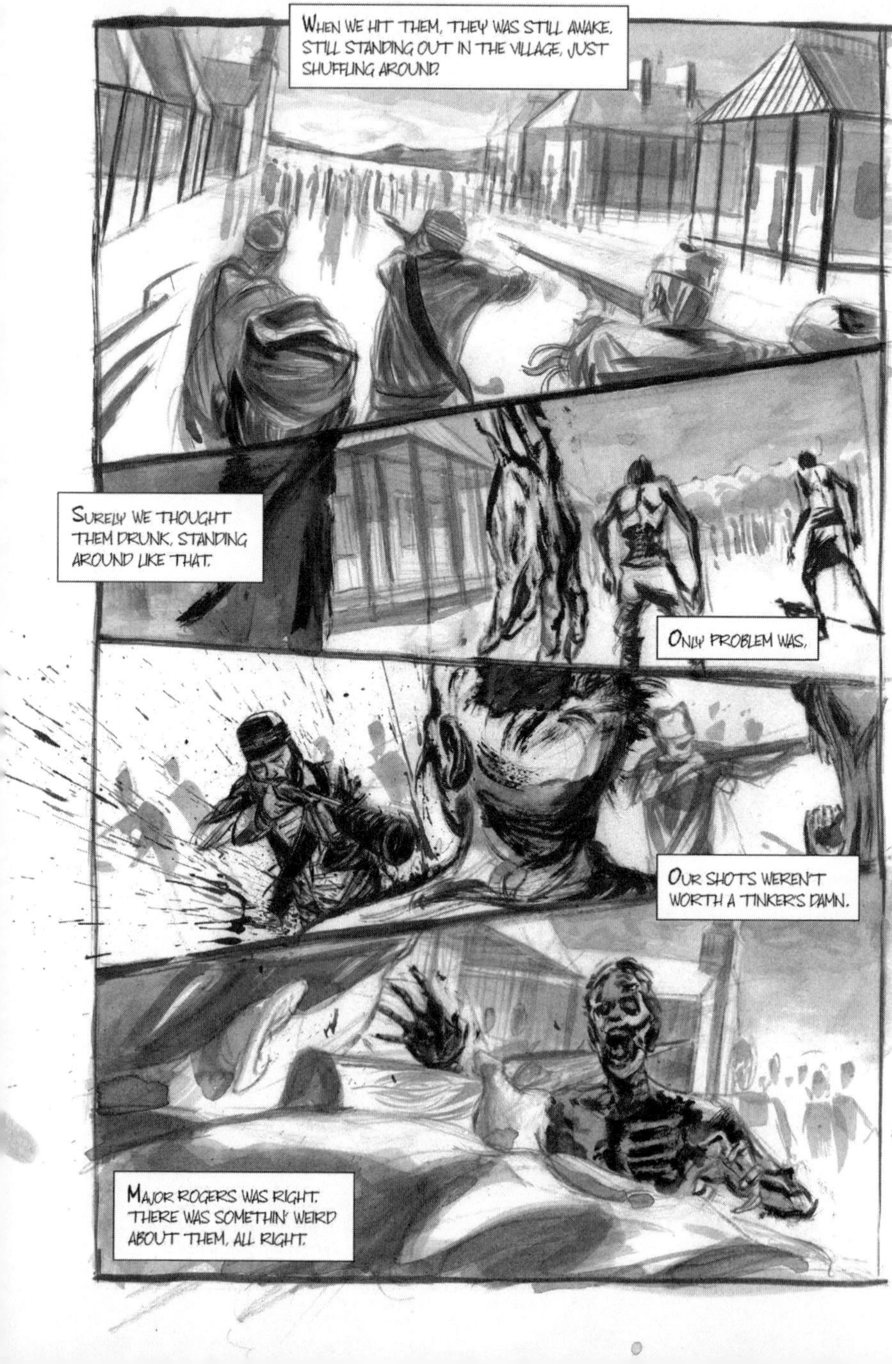
WHEN WE HIT THEM, THEY WAS STILL AWAKE, STILL STANDING OUT IN THE VILLAGE, JUST SHUFFLING AROUND.
SURELY WE THOUGHT THEM DRUNK, STANDING AROUND LIKE THAT.
ONLY PROBLEM WAS,
OUR SHOTS WEREN'T WORTH A TINKER'S DAMN.
MAJOR ROGERS WAS RIGHT. THERE WAS SOMETHIN' WEIRD ABOUT THEM, ALL RIGHT.

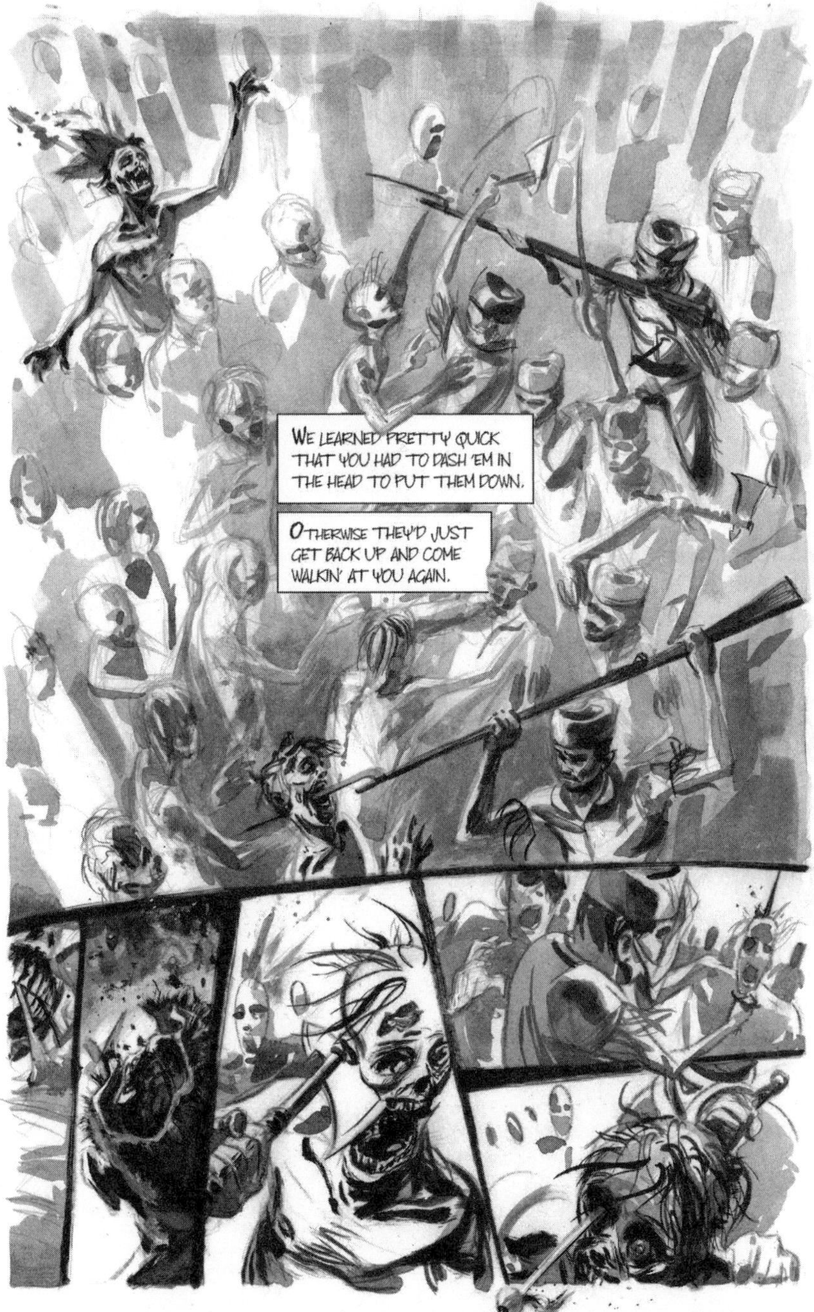
WE LEARNED PRETTY QUICK THAT YOU HAD TO DASH 'EM IN THE HEAD TO PUT THEM DOWN.
OTHERWISE THEY'D JUST GET BACK UP AND COME WALKIN' AT YOU AGAIN.

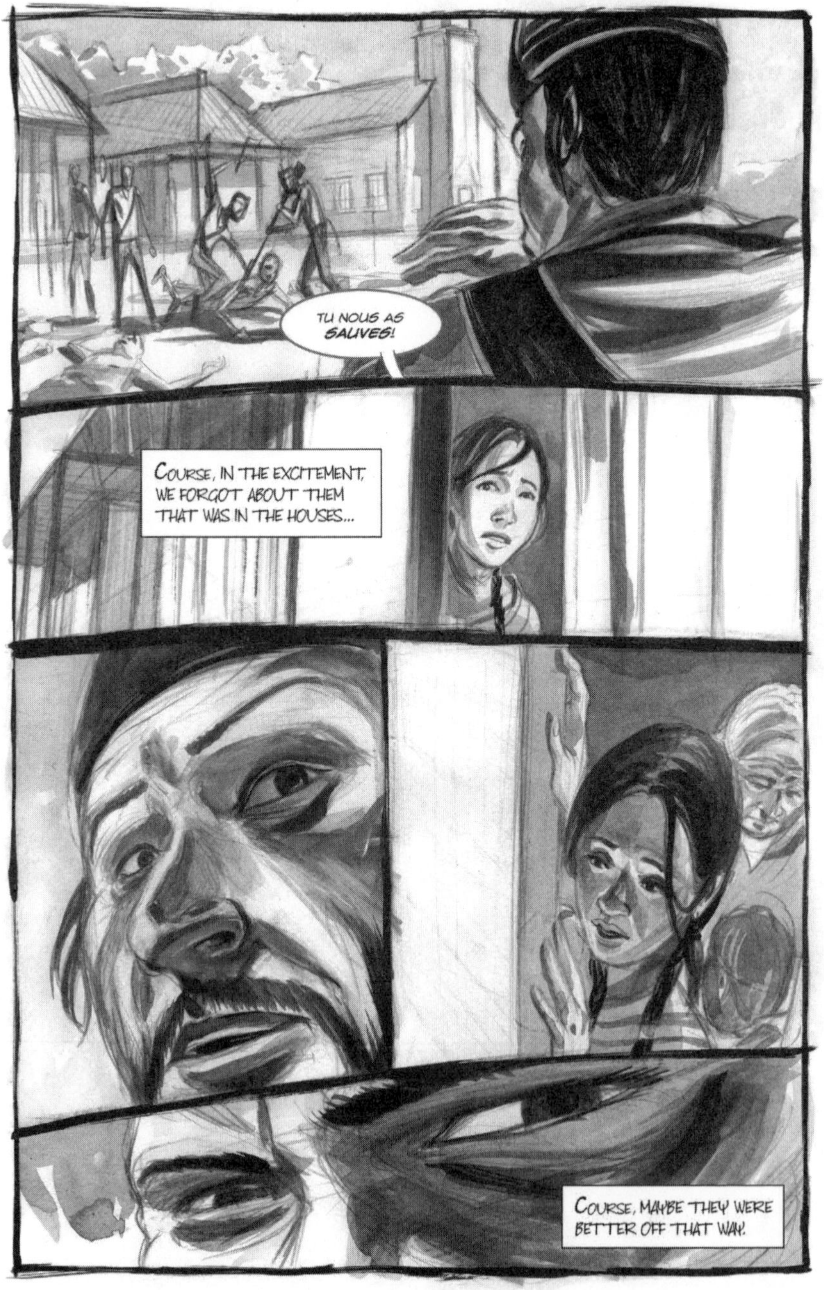
TU NOUS AS SAUVES!
COURSE, IN THE EXCITEMENT, WE FORGOT ABOUT THEM THAT WAS IN THE HOUSES...
COURSE, MAYBE THEY WERE BETTER OFF THAT WAY.

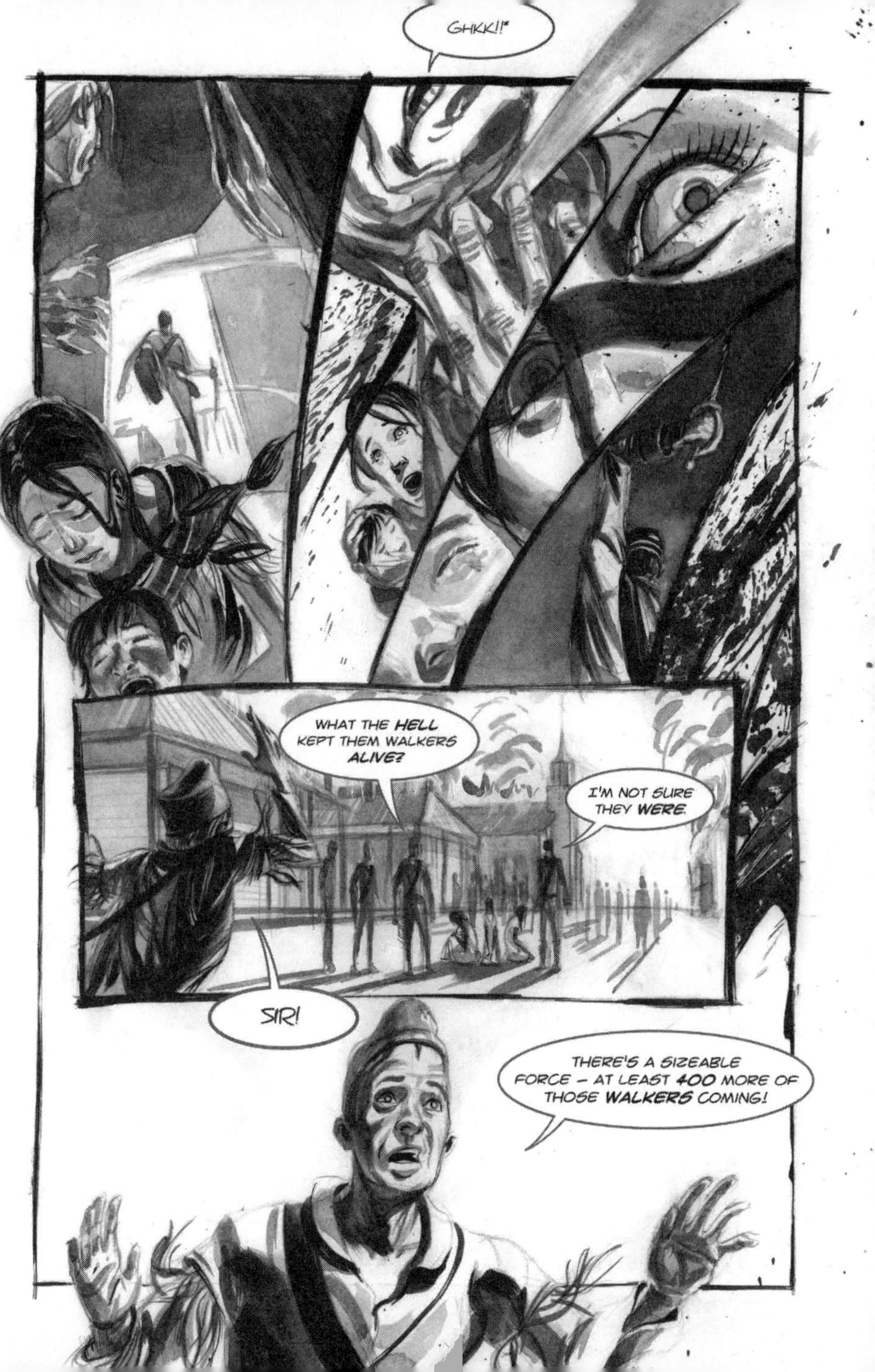
GHKK!!*
WHAT THE HELL KEPT THEM WALKERS ALIVE?
I'M NOT SURE THEY WERE.
SIR!
THERE'S A SIZEABLE FORCE – AT LEAST 400 MORE OF THOSE WALKERS COMING!

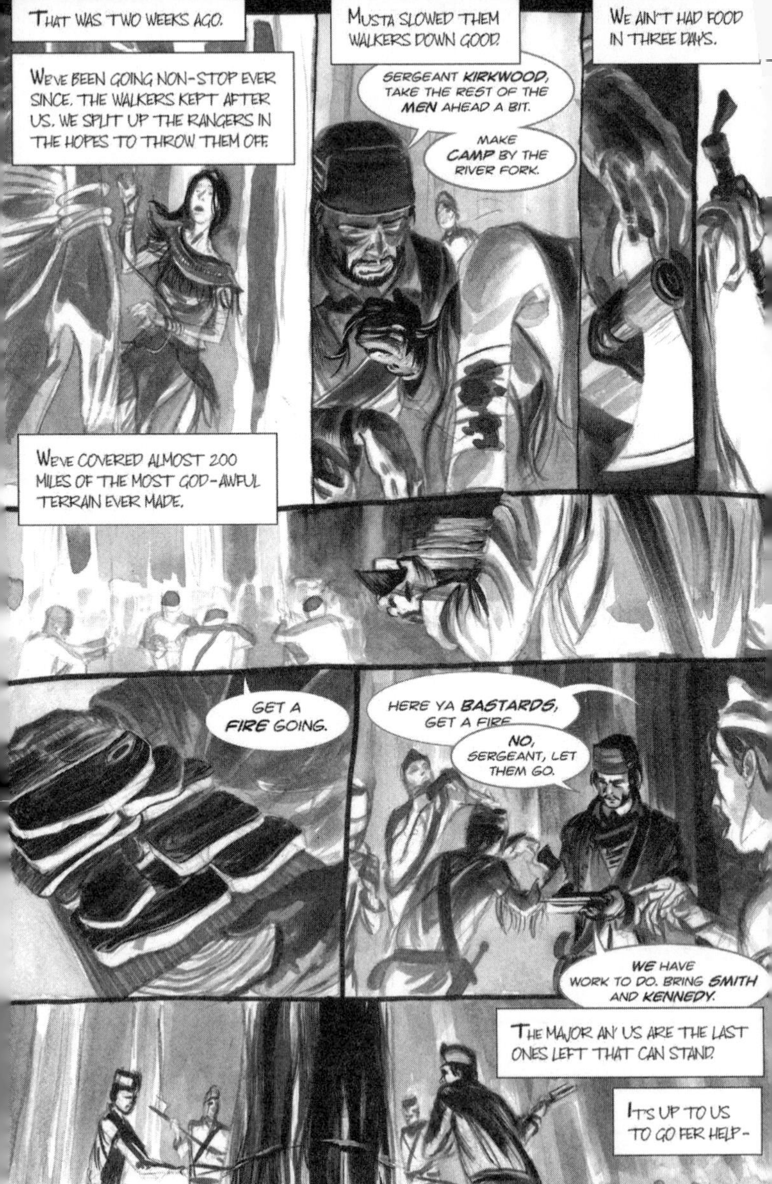

THAT WAS TWO WEEKS AGO.
WE'VE BEEN GOING NON-STOP EVER SINCE. THE WALKERS KEPT AFTER US. WE SPLIT UP THE RANGERS IN THE HOPES TO THROW THEM OFF.
MUSTA SLOWED THEM WALKERS DOWN GOOD.
SERGEANT KIRKWOOD, TAKE THE REST OF THE MEN AHEAD A BIT.
MAKE CAMP BY THE RIVER FORK.
WE AIN'T HAD FOOD IN THREE DAYS.
WE'VE COVERED ALMOST 200 MILES OF THE MOST GOD-AWFUL TERRAIN EVER MADE.
GET A FIRE GOING.
HERE YA BASTARDS, GET A FIRE
NO, SERGEANT, LET THEM GO.
WE HAVE WORK TO DO. BRING SMITH AND KENNEDY.
THE MAJOR AN' US ARE THE LAST ONES LEFT THAT CAN STAND.
IT'S UP TO US TO GO FER HELP-
DOWN THE RIVER TO NUMBER FOUR.

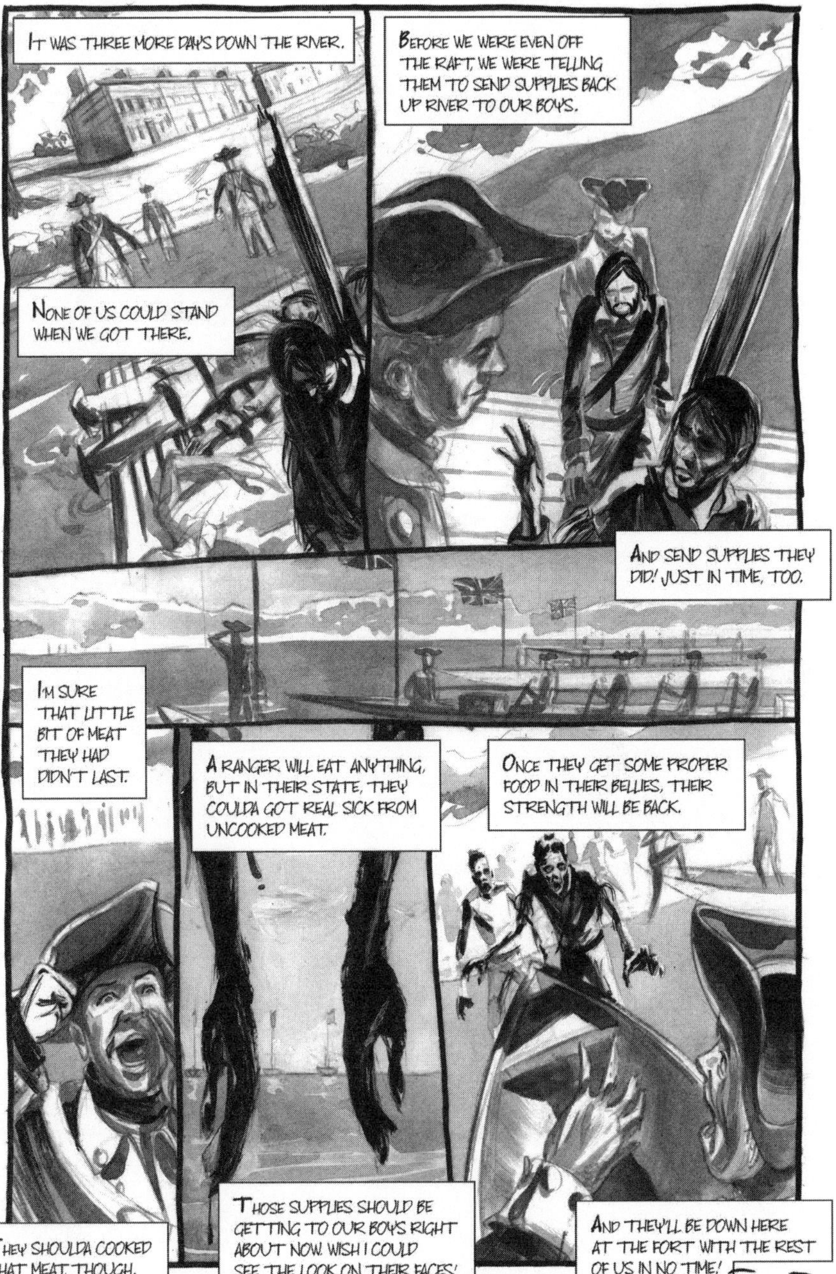
It was three more days down the river.
None of us could stand when we got there.
Before we were even off the raft, we were telling them to send supplies back up river to our boys.
And send supplies they did! Just in time, too.
I'm sure that little bit of meat they had didn't last.
A ranger will eat anything, but in their state, they coulda got real sick from uncooked meat.
Once they get some proper food in their bellies, their strength will be back.
They shoulda cooked that meat, though.
Those supplies should be getting to our boys right about now. Wish I could see the look on their faces!
And they'll be down here at the fort with the rest of us in no time!
The End

PAUL REVERE'S LAST RIDE

STORY AND LETTERS BY:
JEFF McCOMSEY

ART BY:
JIM McMUNN

. EXCERPTS FROM THE POEM
"THE MIDNIGHT RIDE OF PAUL REVERE"
BY HENRY WADSWORTH LONGFELLOW

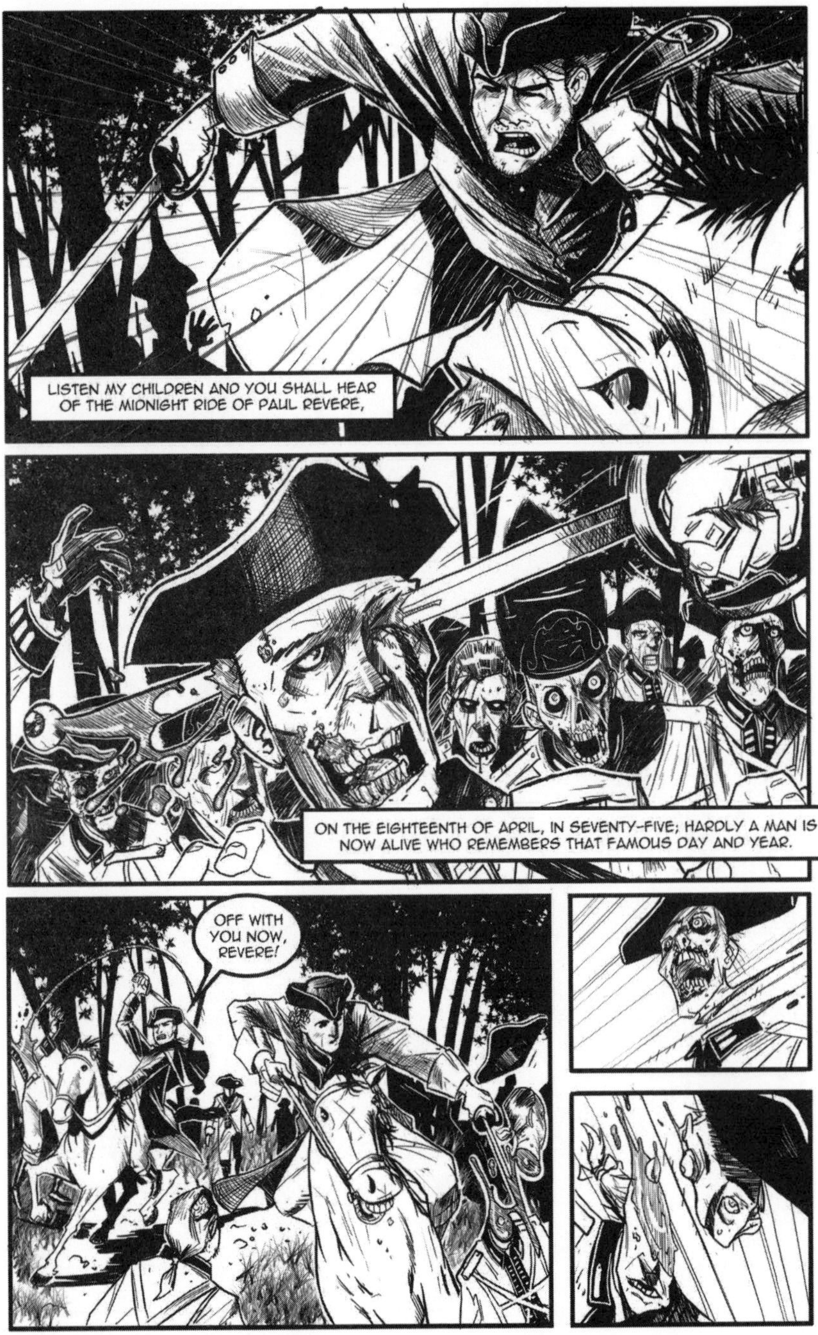
LISTEN MY CHILDREN AND YOU SHALL HEAR OF THE MIDNIGHT RIDE OF PAUL REVERE,
ON THE EIGHTEENTH OF APRIL, IN SEVENTY-FIVE; HARDLY A MAN IS NOW ALIVE WHO REMEMBERS THAT FAMOUS DAY AND YEAR.
OFF WITH YOU NOW, REVERE!

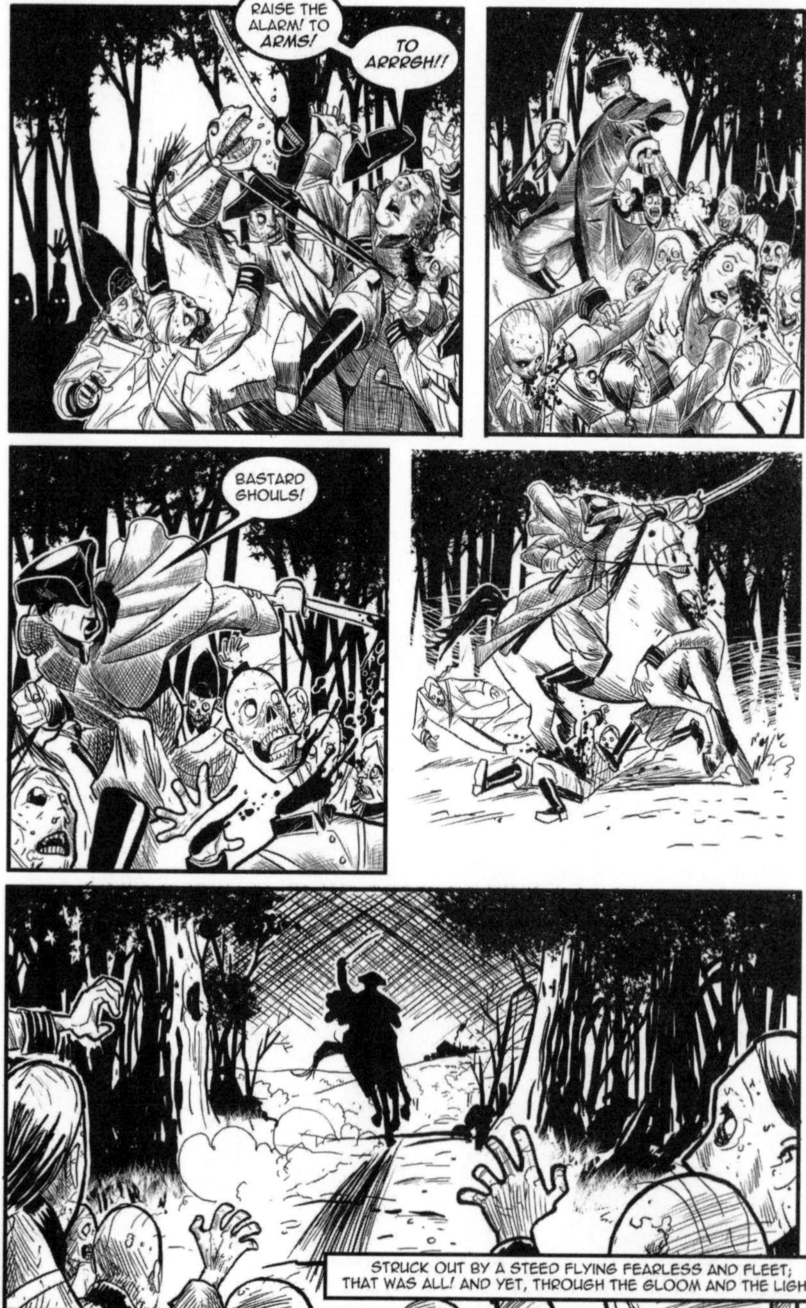
RAISE THE ALARM! TO ARMS!
TO ARRRGH!!
BASTARD GHOULS!
STRUCK OUT BY A STEED FLYING FEARLESS AND FLEET;
THAT WAS ALL! AND YET, THROUGH THE GLOOM AND THE LIGHT,

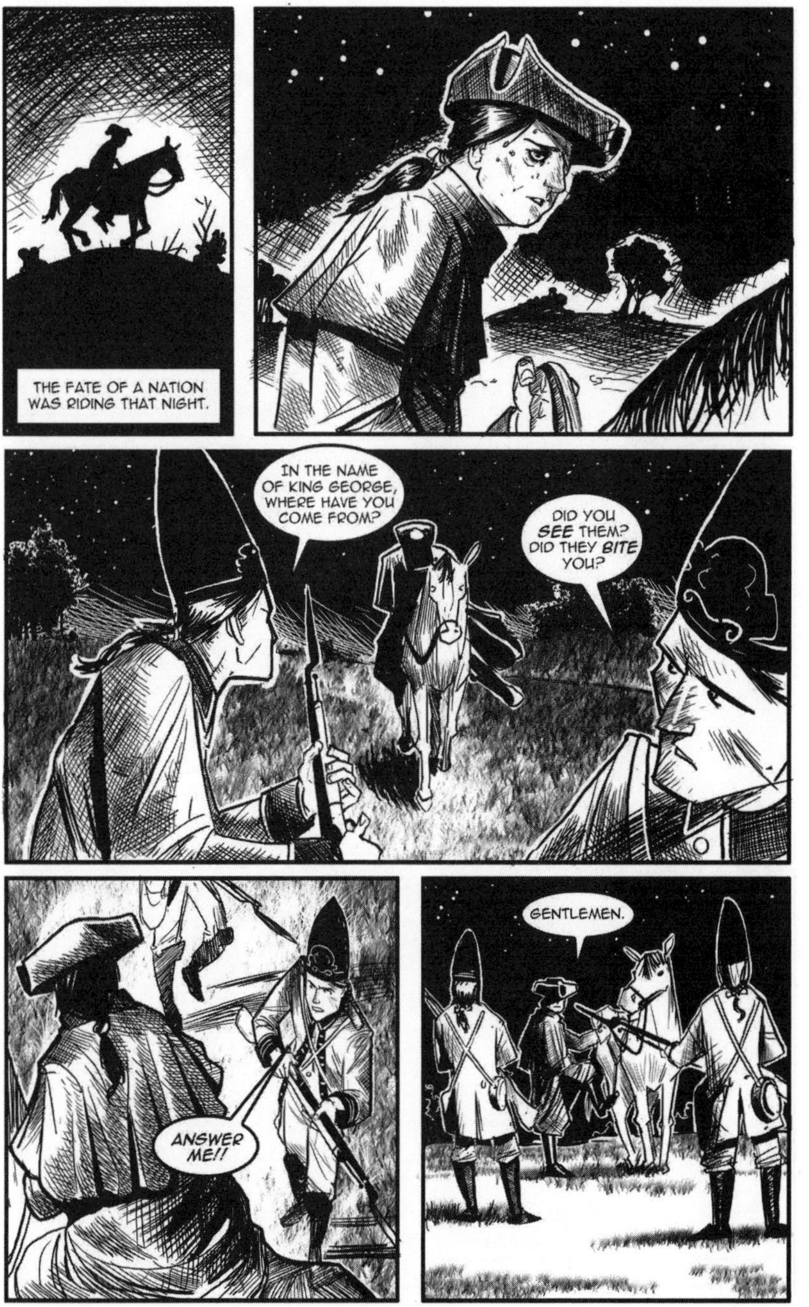
THE FATE OF A NATION WAS RIDING THAT NIGHT.
IN THE NAME OF KING GEORGE, WHERE HAVE YOU COME FROM?
DID YOU *SEE* THEM? DID THEY *BITE* YOU?
ANSWER ME!!
GENTLEMEN.

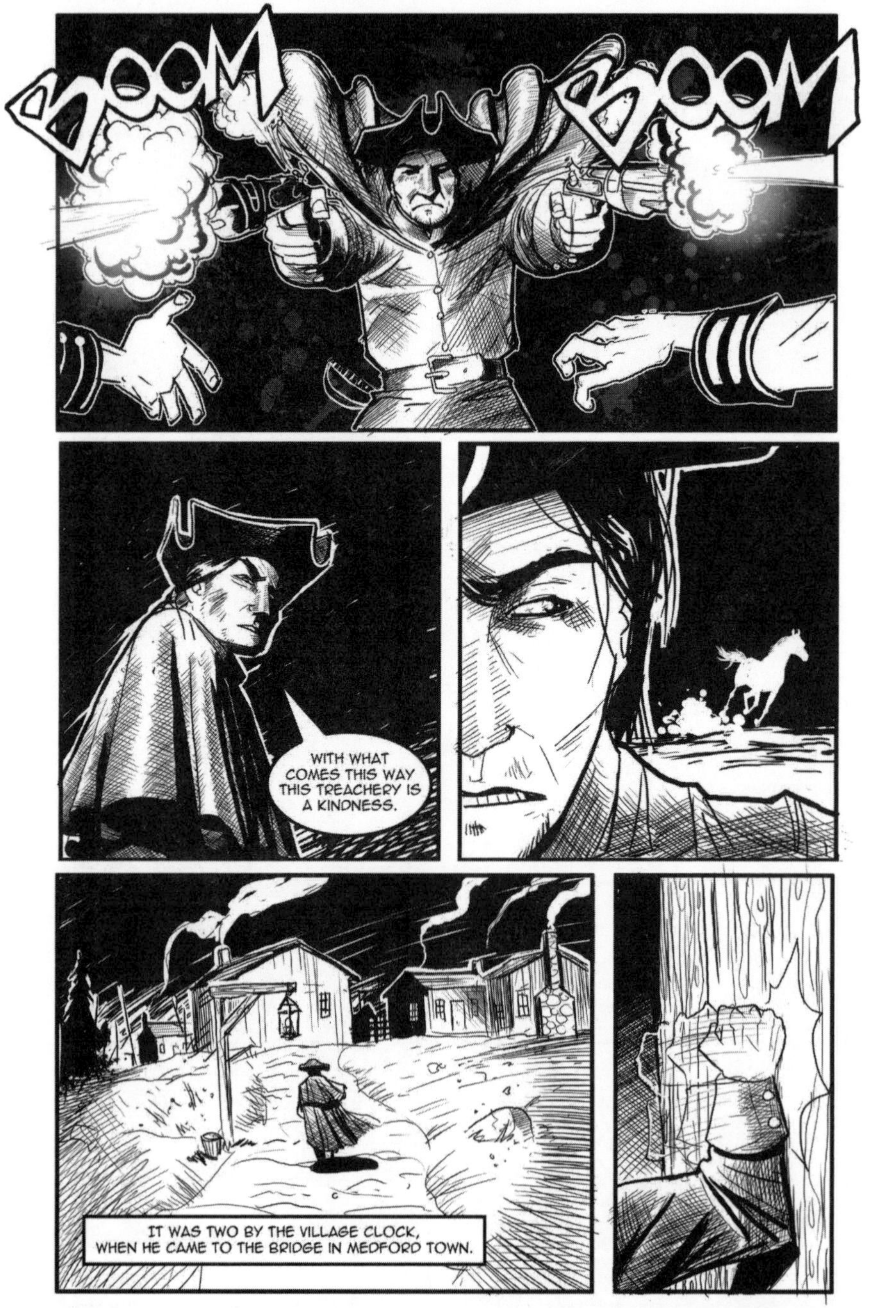
BOOM
BOOM
WITH WHAT COMES THIS WAY THIS TREACHERY IS A KINDNESS.
IT WAS TWO BY THE VILLAGE CLOCK, WHEN HE CAME TO THE BRIDGE IN MEDFORD TOWN.

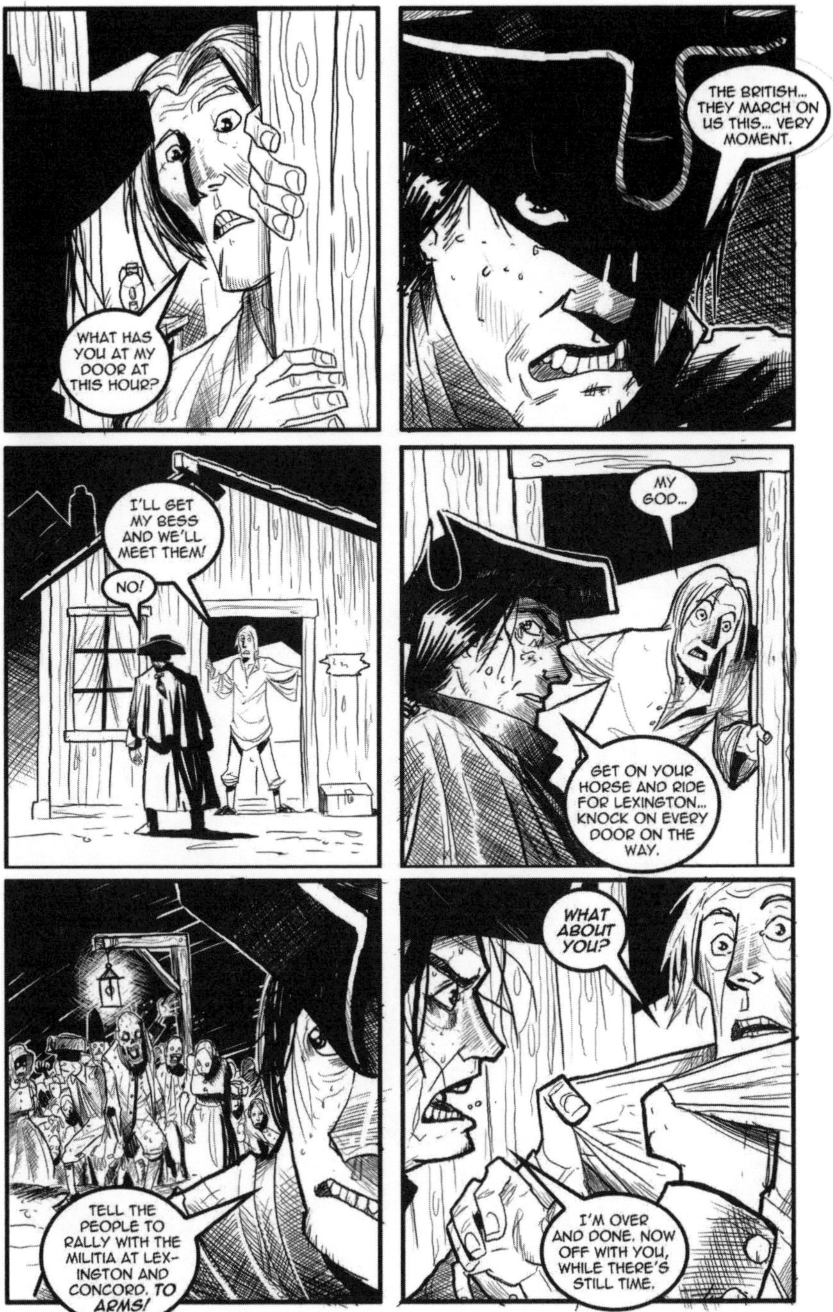
WHAT HAS YOU AT MY DOOR AT THIS HOUR?
THE BRITISH... THEY MARCH ON US THIS... VERY MOMENT.
I'LL GET MY BESS AND WE'LL MEET THEM!
NO!
MY GOD...
GET ON YOUR HORSE AND RIDE FOR LEXINGTON... KNOCK ON EVERY DOOR ON THE WAY.
TELL THE PEOPLE TO RALLY WITH THE MILITIA AT LEX-INGTON AND CONCORD. *TO ARMS!*
WHAT ABOUT YOU?
I'M OVER AND DONE. NOW OFF WITH YOU, WHILE THERE'S STILL TIME.

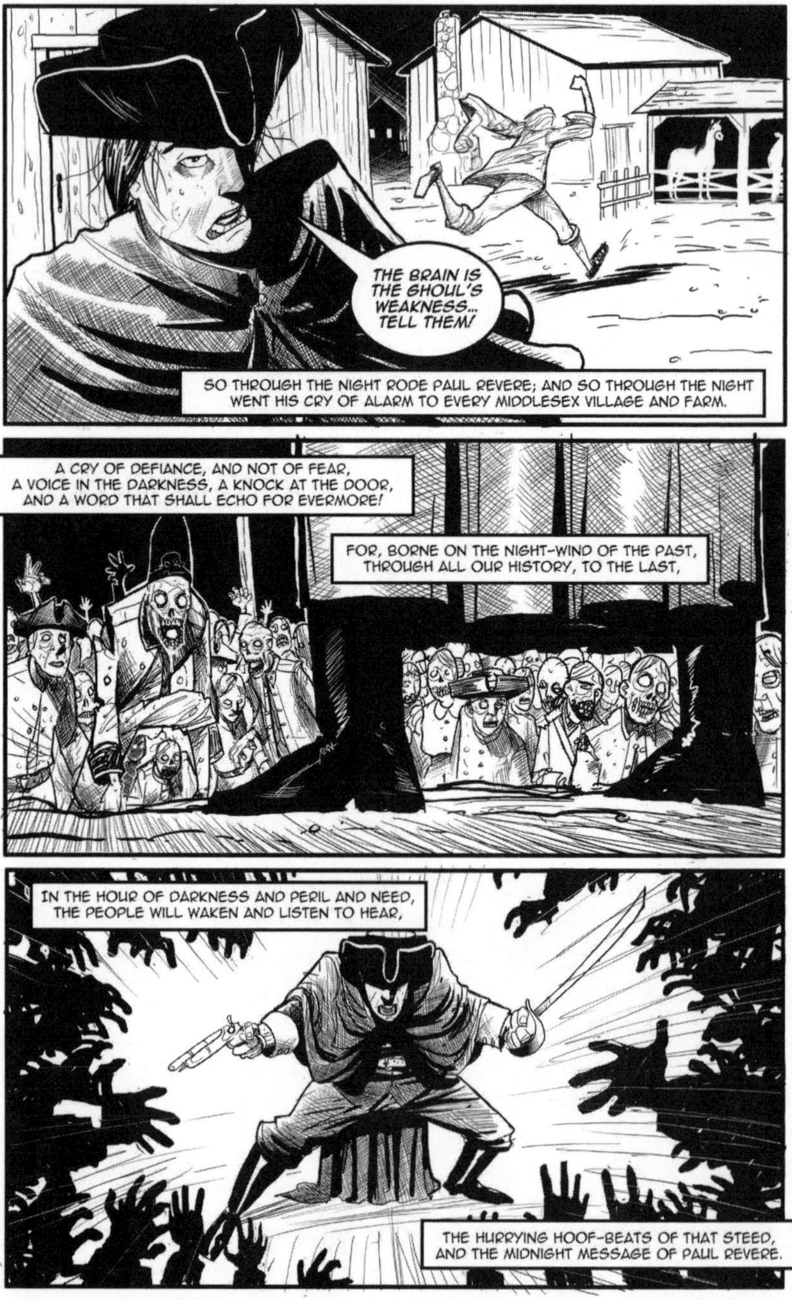
THE BRAIN IS THE GHOUL'S WEAKNESS... TELL THEM!
SO THROUGH THE NIGHT RODE PAUL REVERE; AND SO THROUGH THE NIGHT WENT HIS CRY OF ALARM TO EVERY MIDDLESEX VILLAGE AND FARM.
A CRY OF DEFIANCE, AND NOT OF FEAR, A VOICE IN THE DARKNESS, A KNOCK AT THE DOOR, AND A WORD THAT SHALL ECHO FOR EVERMORE!
FOR, BORNE ON THE NIGHT-WIND OF THE PAST, THROUGH ALL OUR HISTORY, TO THE LAST,
IN THE HOUR OF DARKNESS AND PERIL AND NEED, THE PEOPLE WILL WAKEN AND LISTEN TO HEAR,
THE HURRYING HOOF-BEATS OF THAT STEED, AND THE MIDNIGHT MESSAGE OF PAUL REVERE.

GIVE ME MEAT

STORY BY
GLENN MØANE
PENCILS BY:
DREW ZUCKER
INKS BY:
PHILIP SEVY
LETTERS BY:
TED WOODS
GREYSCALES BY:
JEFF MCCOMSEY

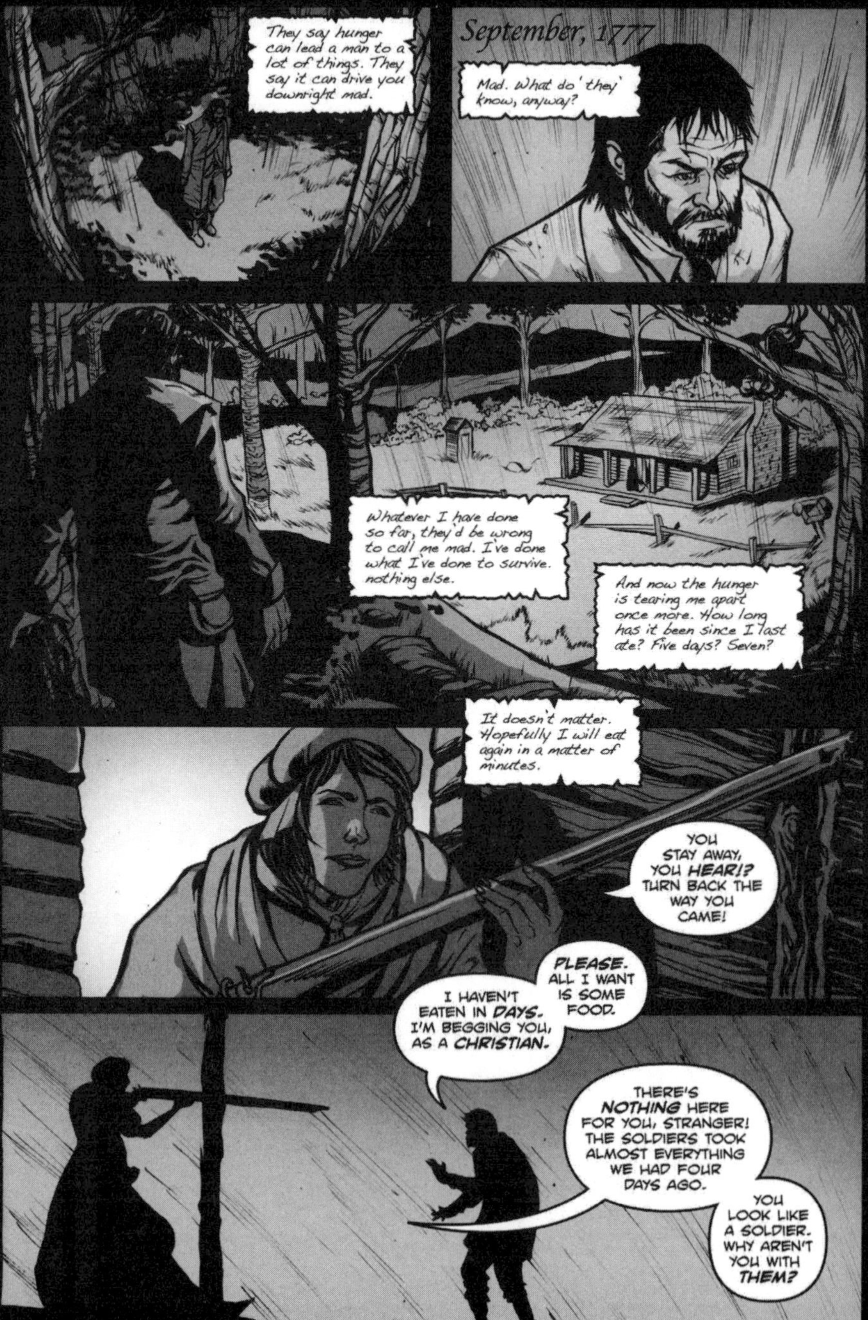

They say hunger can lead a man to a lot of things. They say it can drive you downright mad.
September, 1777
Mad. What do 'they' know, anyway?
Whatever I have done so far, they'd be wrong to call me mad. I've done what I've done to survive. nothing else.
And now the hunger is tearing me apart once more. How long has it been since I last ate? Five days? Seven?
It doesn't matter. Hopefully I will eat again in a matter of minutes.
YOU STAY AWAY, YOU HEAR!? TURN BACK THE WAY YOU CAME!
PLEASE. ALL I WANT IS SOME FOOD.
I HAVEN'T EATEN IN DAYS. I'M BEGGING YOU, AS A CHRISTIAN.
THERE'S NOTHING HERE FOR YOU, STRANGER! THE SOLDIERS TOOK ALMOST EVERYTHING WE HAD FOUR DAYS AGO.
YOU LOOK LIKE A SOLDIER. WHY AREN'T YOU WITH THEM?

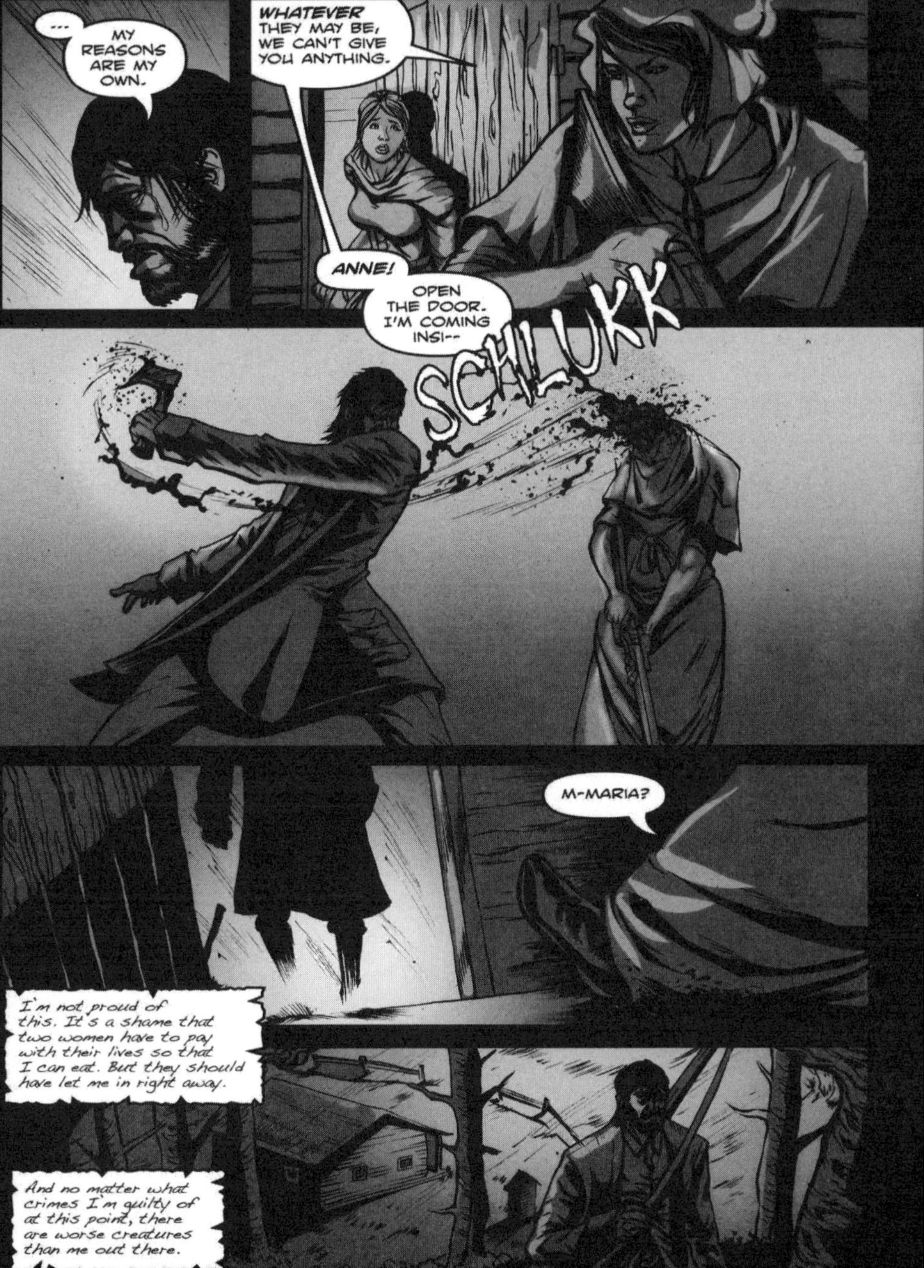
... MY REASONS ARE MY OWN.
WHATEVER THEY MAY BE, WE CAN'T GIVE YOU ANYTHING.
ANNE!
OPEN THE DOOR. I'M COMING INSI--
SCHLUKK
M-MARIA?
I'm not proud of this. It's a shame that two women have to pay with their lives so that I can eat. But they should have let me in right away.
And no matter what crimes I'm guilty of at this point, there are worse creatures than me out there.

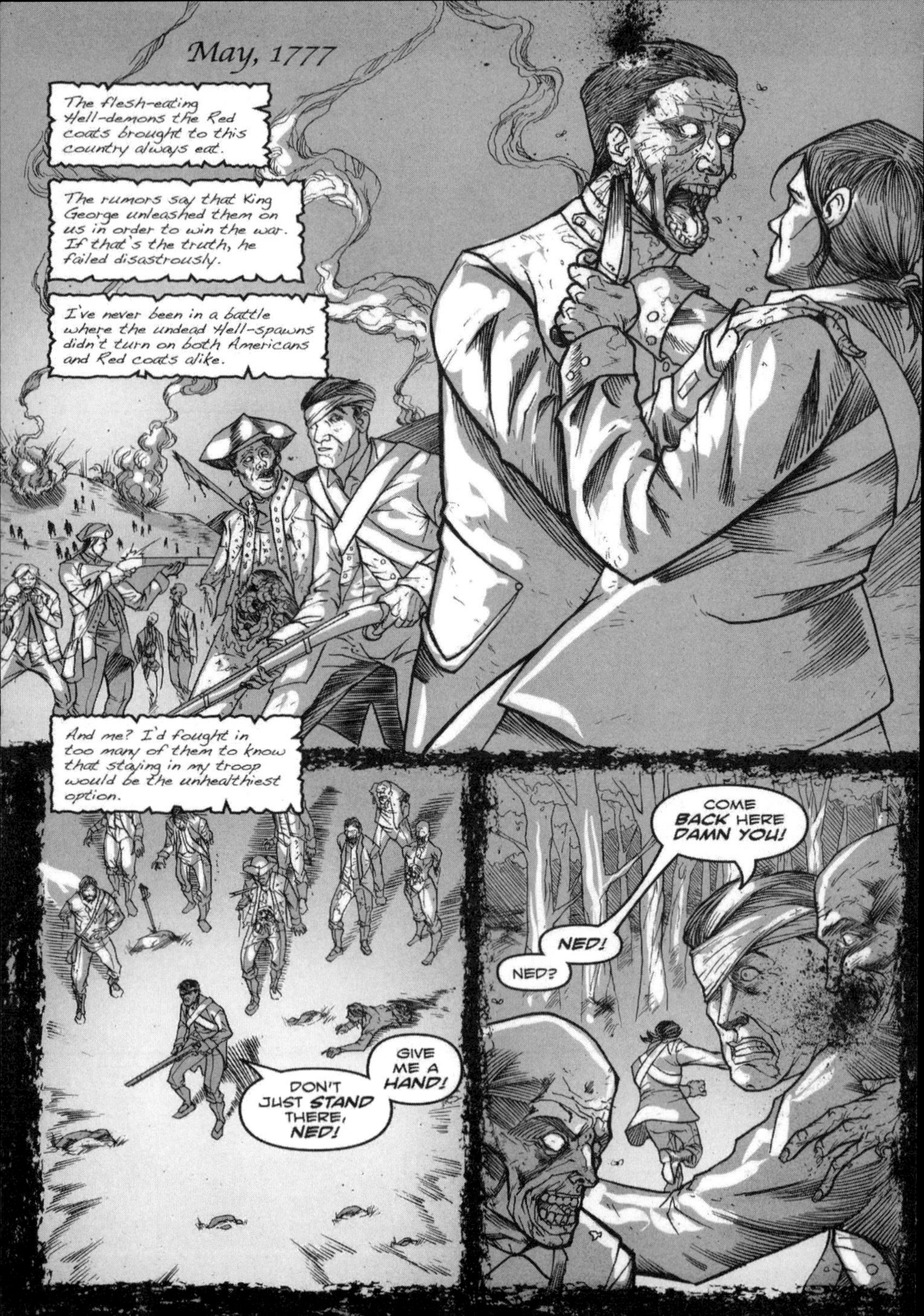
May, 1777
The flesh-eating Hell-demons the Red coats brought to this country always eat.
The rumors say that King George unleashed them on us in order to win the war. If that's the truth, he failed disastrously.
I've never been in a battle where the undead Hell-spawns didn't turn on both Americans and Red coats alike.
And me? I'd fought in too many of them to know that staying in my troop would be the unhealthiest option.
GIVE ME A HAND!
DON'T JUST STAND THERE, NED!
COME BACK HERE DAMN YOU!
NED!
NED?

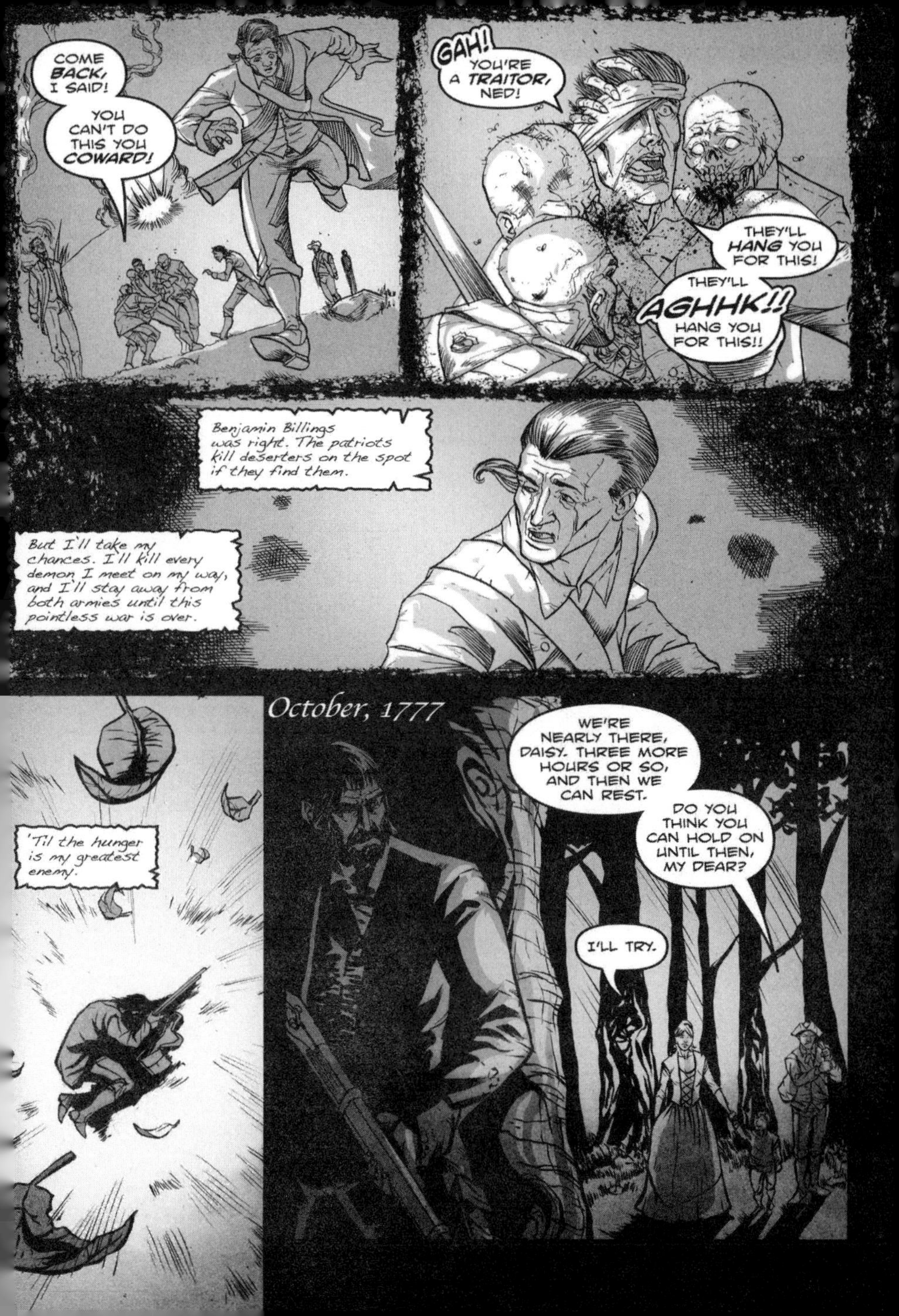

COME BACK, I SAID!
YOU CAN'T DO THIS YOU COWARD!
GAH! YOU'RE A TRAITOR, NED!
THEY'LL HANG YOU FOR THIS!
THEY'LL AGHHK!! HANG YOU FOR THIS!!
Benjamin Billings was right. The patriots kill deserters on the spot if they find them.
But I'll take my chances. I'll kill every demon I meet on my way, and I'll stay away from both armies until this pointless war is over.
'Til the hunger is my greatest enemy.
October, 1777
WE'RE NEARLY THERE, DAISY. THREE MORE HOURS OR SO, AND THEN WE CAN REST.
DO YOU THINK YOU CAN HOLD ON UNTIL THEN, MY DEAR?
I'LL TRY.

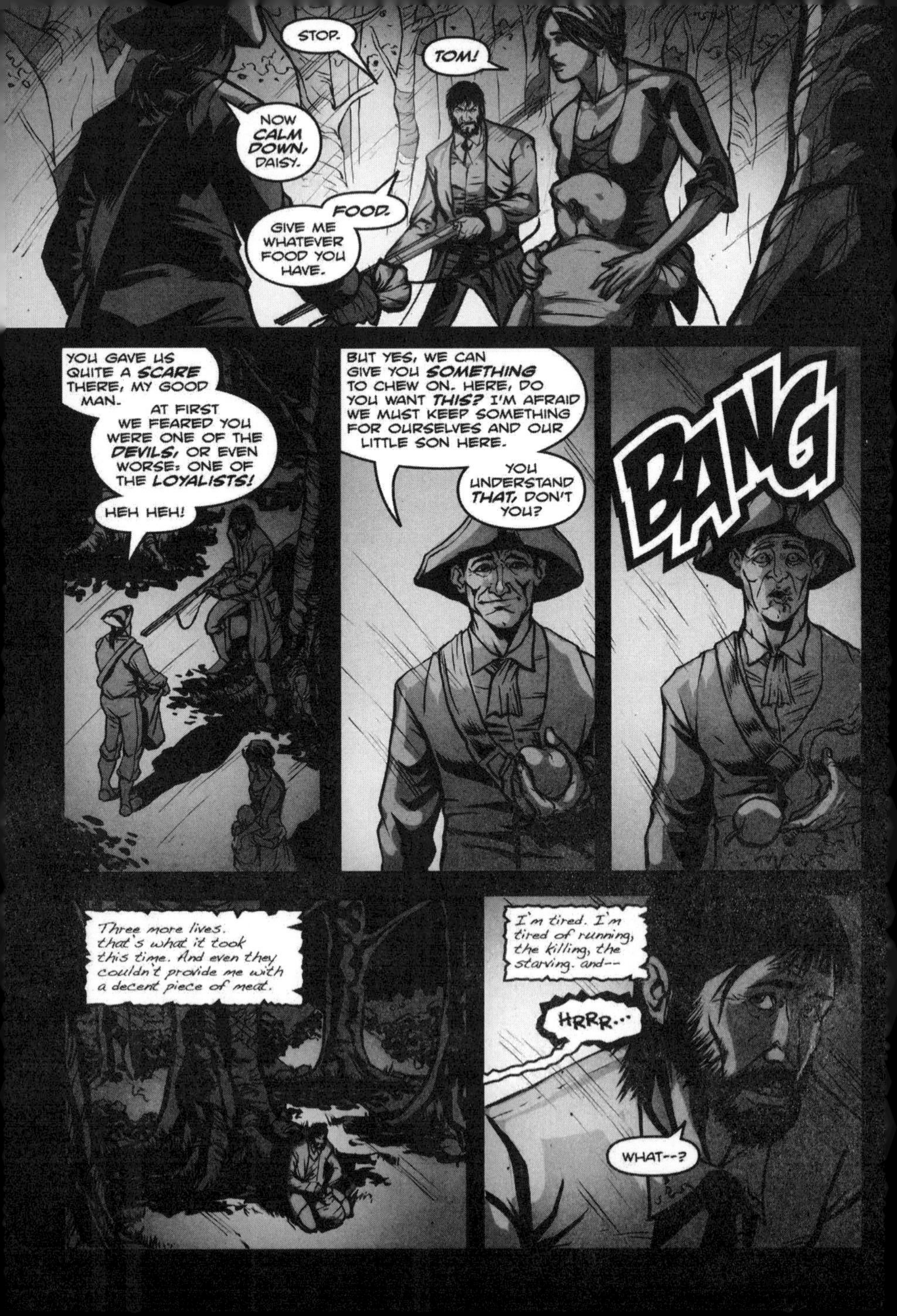

STOP.
TOM!
NOW CALM DOWN, DAISY.
FOOD. GIVE ME WHATEVER FOOD YOU HAVE.
YOU GAVE US QUITE A SCARE THERE, MY GOOD MAN.
AT FIRST WE FEARED YOU WERE ONE OF THE DEVILS, OR EVEN WORSE: ONE OF THE LOYALISTS!
HEH HEH!
BUT YES, WE CAN GIVE YOU SOMETHING TO CHEW ON. HERE, DO YOU WANT THIS? I'M AFRAID WE MUST KEEP SOMETHING FOR OURSELVES AND OUR LITTLE SON HERE.
YOU UNDERSTAND THAT, DON'T YOU?
BANG
Three more lives. that's what it took this time. And even they couldn't provide me with a decent piece of meat.
I'm tired. I'm tired of running, the killing, the starving. and--
HRRR...
WHAT--?

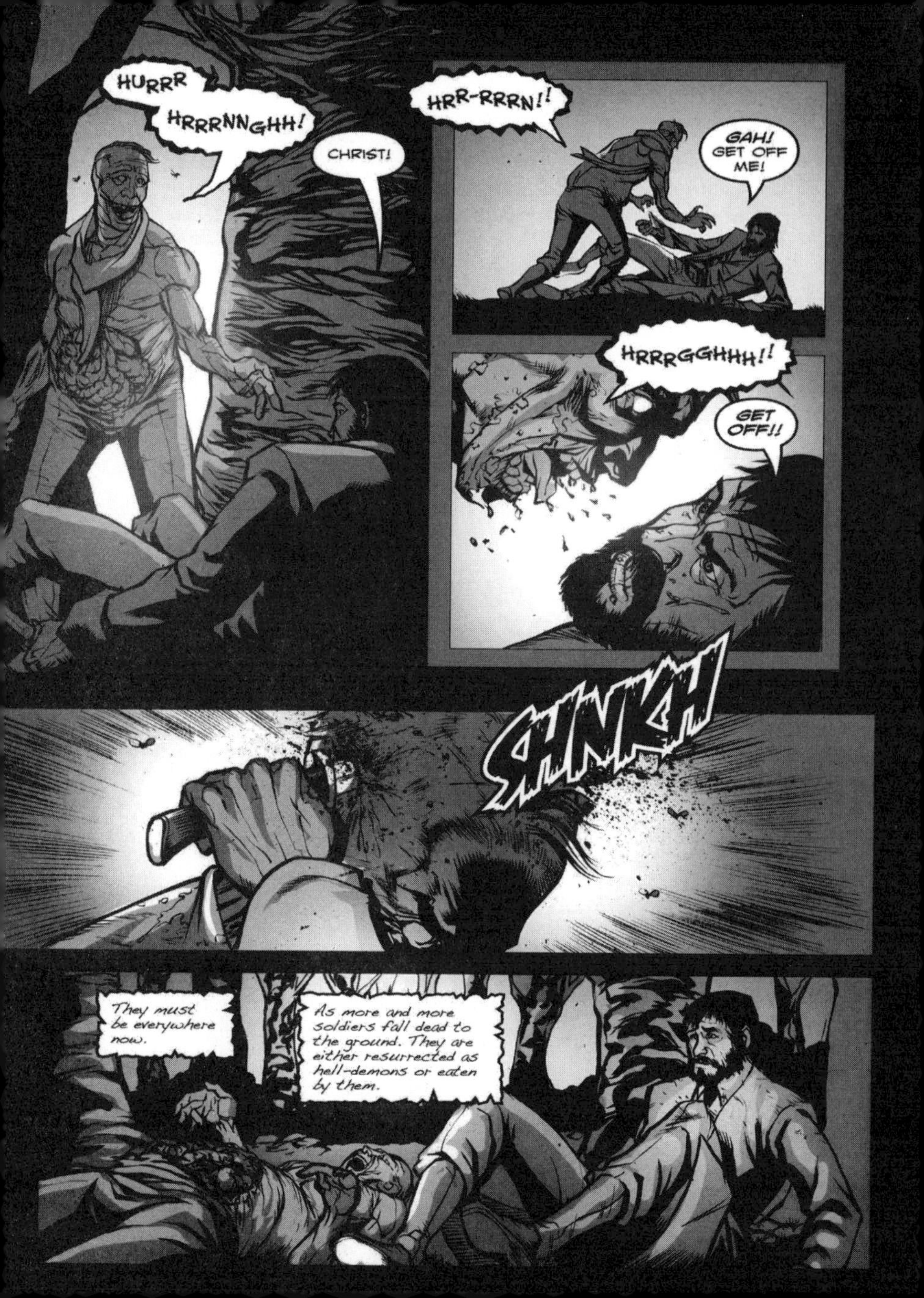
HURRR
HRRRNNGHH!
CHRIST!
HRR-RRRN!!
GAH! GET OFF ME!
HRRRGGHHH!!
GET OFF!!
SHNKH
They must be everywhere now.
As more and more soldiers fall dead to the ground. They are either resurrected as hell-demons or eaten by them.

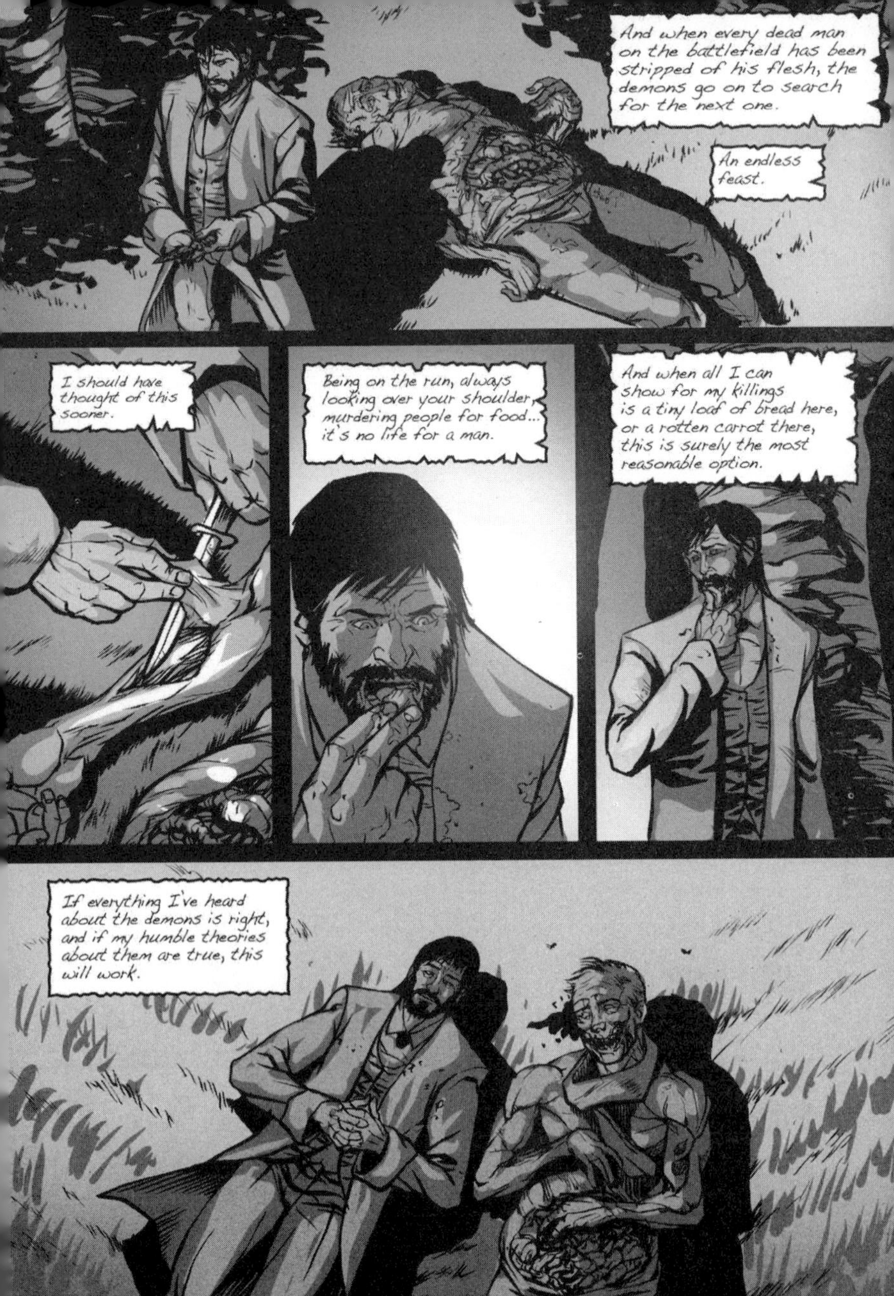
And when every dead man on the battlefield has been stripped of his flesh, the demons go on to search for the next one.
An endless feast.
I should have thought of this sooner.
Being on the run, always looking over your shoulder, murdering people for food... it's no life for a man.
And when all I can show for my killings is a tiny loaf of bread here, or a rotten carrot there, this is surely the most reasonable option.
If everything I've heard about the demons is right, and if my humble theories about them are true, this will work.

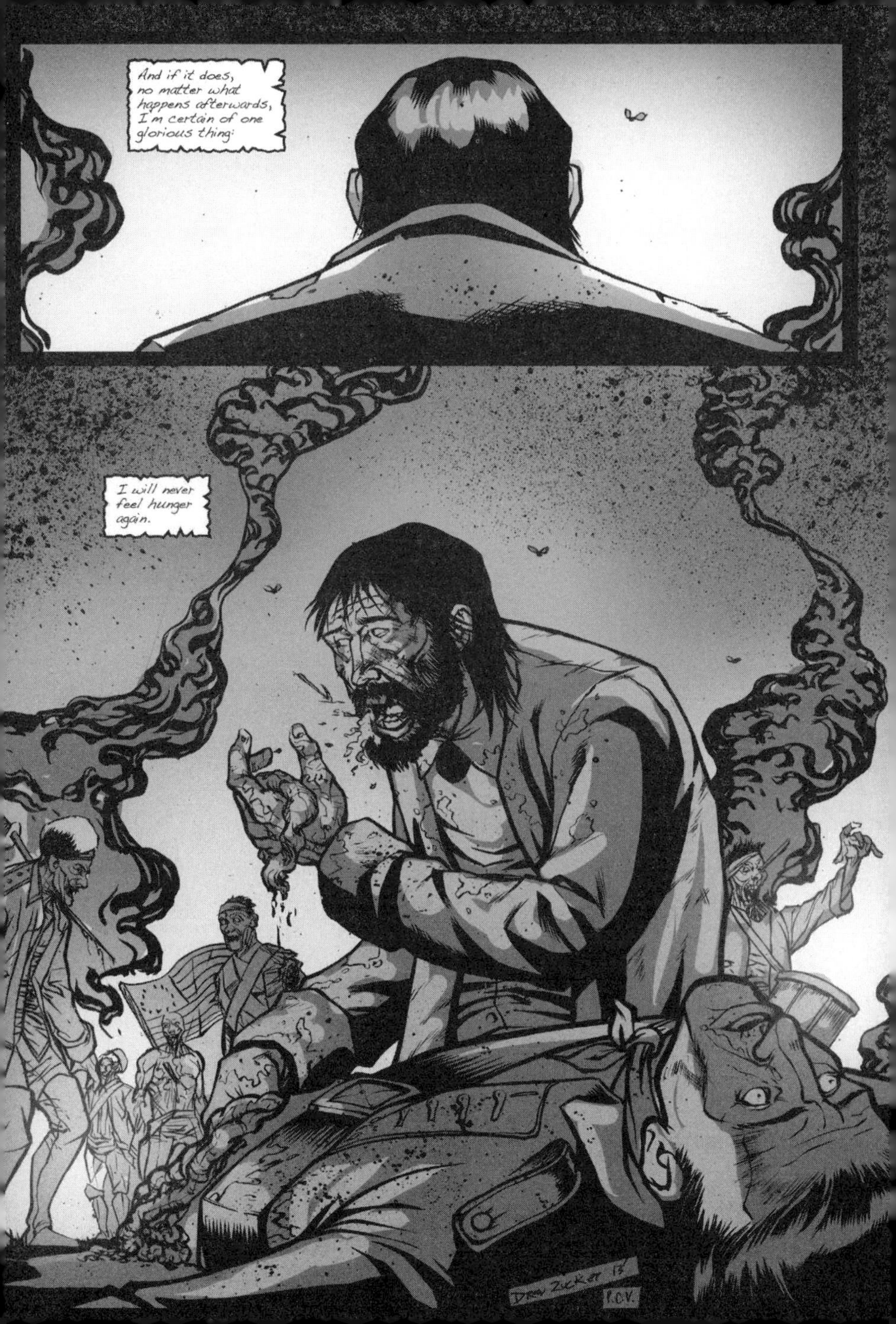
And if it does, no matter what happens afterwards, I'm certain of one glorious thing:
I will never feel hunger again.
Drew Zucker 13
P.C.V.

VALLEY FORGE

STORY AND LETTERS BY:
SHAWN ALDRIDGE

ART BY:
CHRIS PETERSON

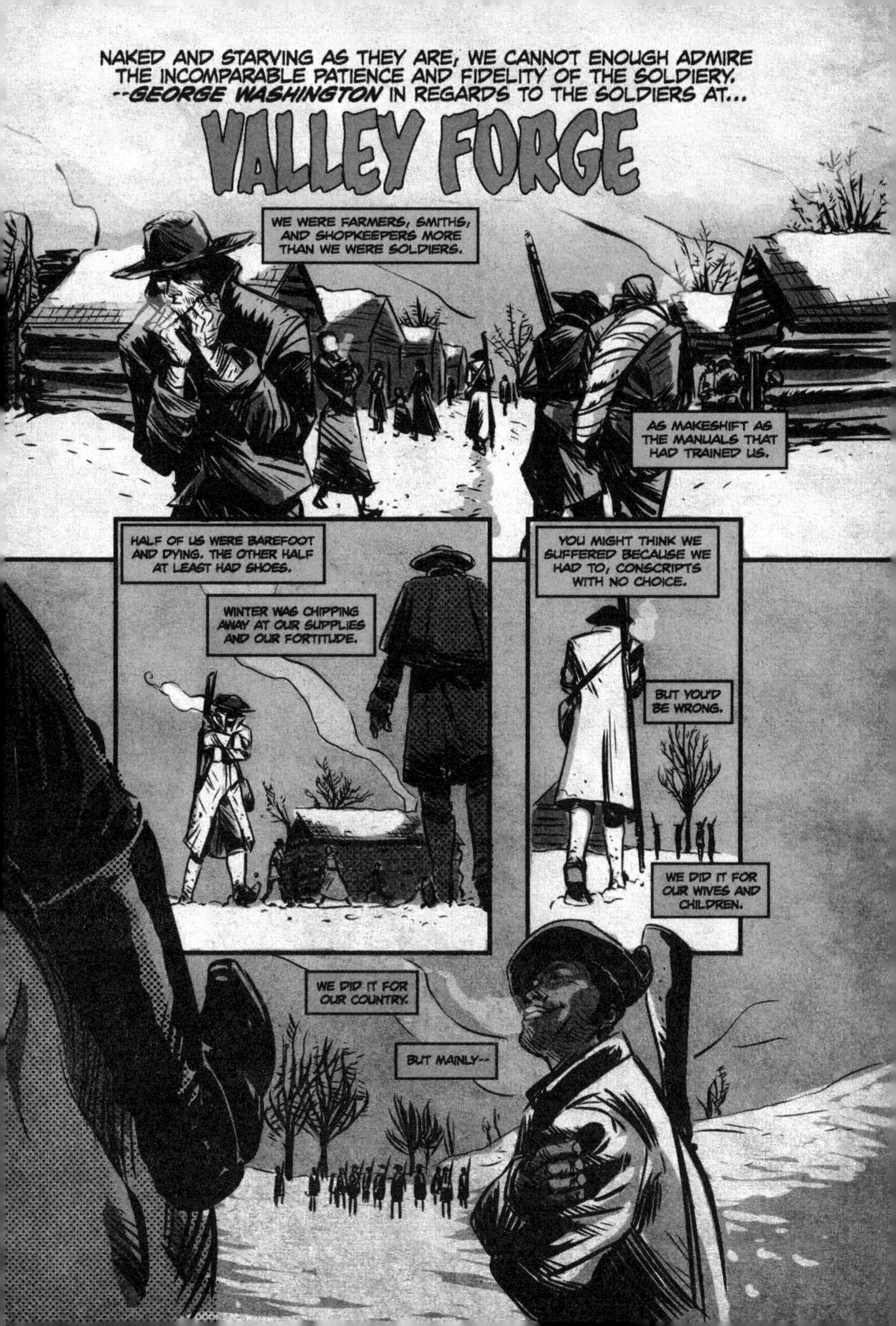
NAKED AND STARVING AS THEY ARE, WE CANNOT ENOUGH ADMIRE THE INCOMPARABLE PATIENCE AND FIDELITY OF THE SOLDIERY.
--GEORGE WASHINGTON IN REGARDS TO THE SOLDIERS AT...
VALLEY FORGE
WE WERE FARMERS, SMITHS, AND SHOPKEEPERS MORE THAN WE WERE SOLDIERS.
AS MAKESHIFT AS THE MANUALS THAT HAD TRAINED US.
HALF OF US WERE BAREFOOT AND DYING. THE OTHER HALF AT LEAST HAD SHOES.
WINTER WAS CHIPPING AWAY AT OUR SUPPLIES AND OUR FORTITUDE.
YOU MIGHT THINK WE SUFFERED BECAUSE WE HAD TO, CONSCRIPTS WITH NO CHOICE.
BUT YOU'D BE WRONG.
WE DID IT FOR OUR WIVES AND CHILDREN.
WE DID IT FOR OUR COUNTRY.
BUT MAINLY--

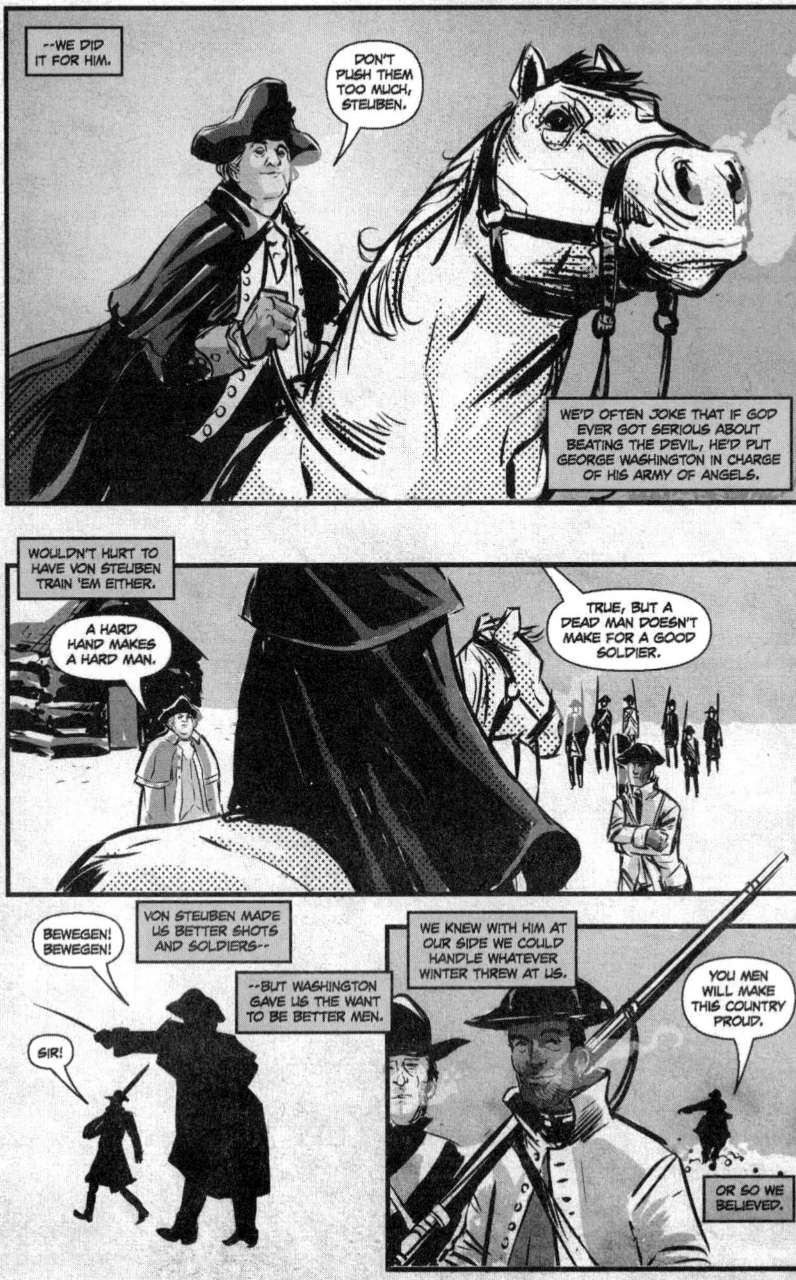
--WE DID IT FOR HIM.
DON'T PUSH THEM TOO MUCH, STEUBEN.
WE'D OFTEN JOKE THAT IF GOD EVER GOT SERIOUS ABOUT BEATING THE DEVIL, HE'D PUT GEORGE WASHINGTON IN CHARGE OF HIS ARMY OF ANGELS.
WOULDN'T HURT TO HAVE VON STEUBEN TRAIN 'EM EITHER.
A HARD HAND MAKES A HARD MAN.
TRUE, BUT A DEAD MAN DOESN'T MAKE FOR A GOOD SOLDIER.
BEWEGEN! BEWEGEN!
VON STEUBEN MADE US BETTER SHOTS AND SOLDIERS--
SIR!
--BUT WASHINGTON GAVE US THE WANT TO BE BETTER MEN.
WE KNEW WITH HIM AT OUR SIDE WE COULD HANDLE WHATEVER WINTER THREW AT US.
YOU MEN WILL MAKE THIS COUNTRY PROUD.
OR SO WE BELIEVED.

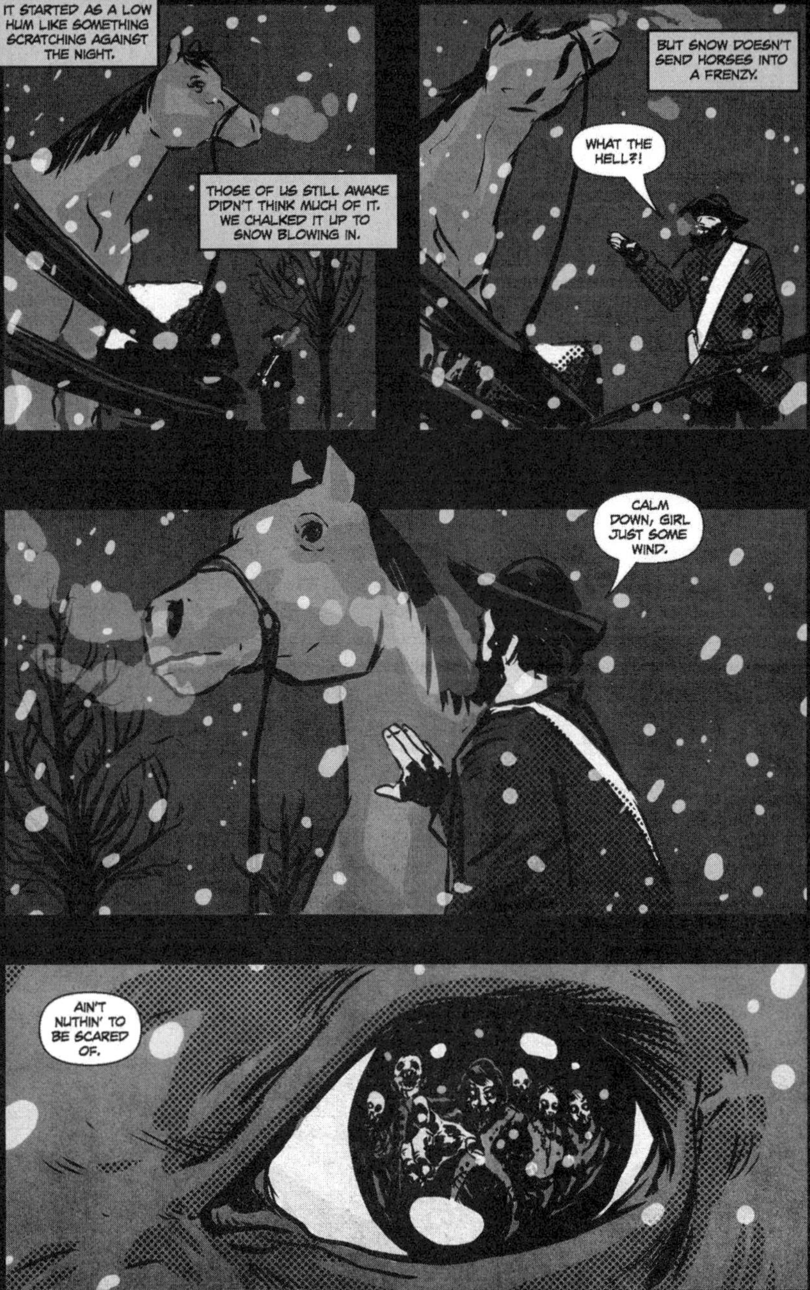
IT STARTED AS A LOW HUM LIKE SOMETHING SCRATCHING AGAINST THE NIGHT.
THOSE OF US STILL AWAKE DIDN'T THINK MUCH OF IT. WE CHALKED IT UP TO SNOW BLOWING IN.
BUT SNOW DOESN'T SEND HORSES INTO A FRENZY.
WHAT THE HELL?!
CALM DOWN, GIRL JUST SOME WIND.
AIN'T NUTHIN' TO BE SCARED OF.

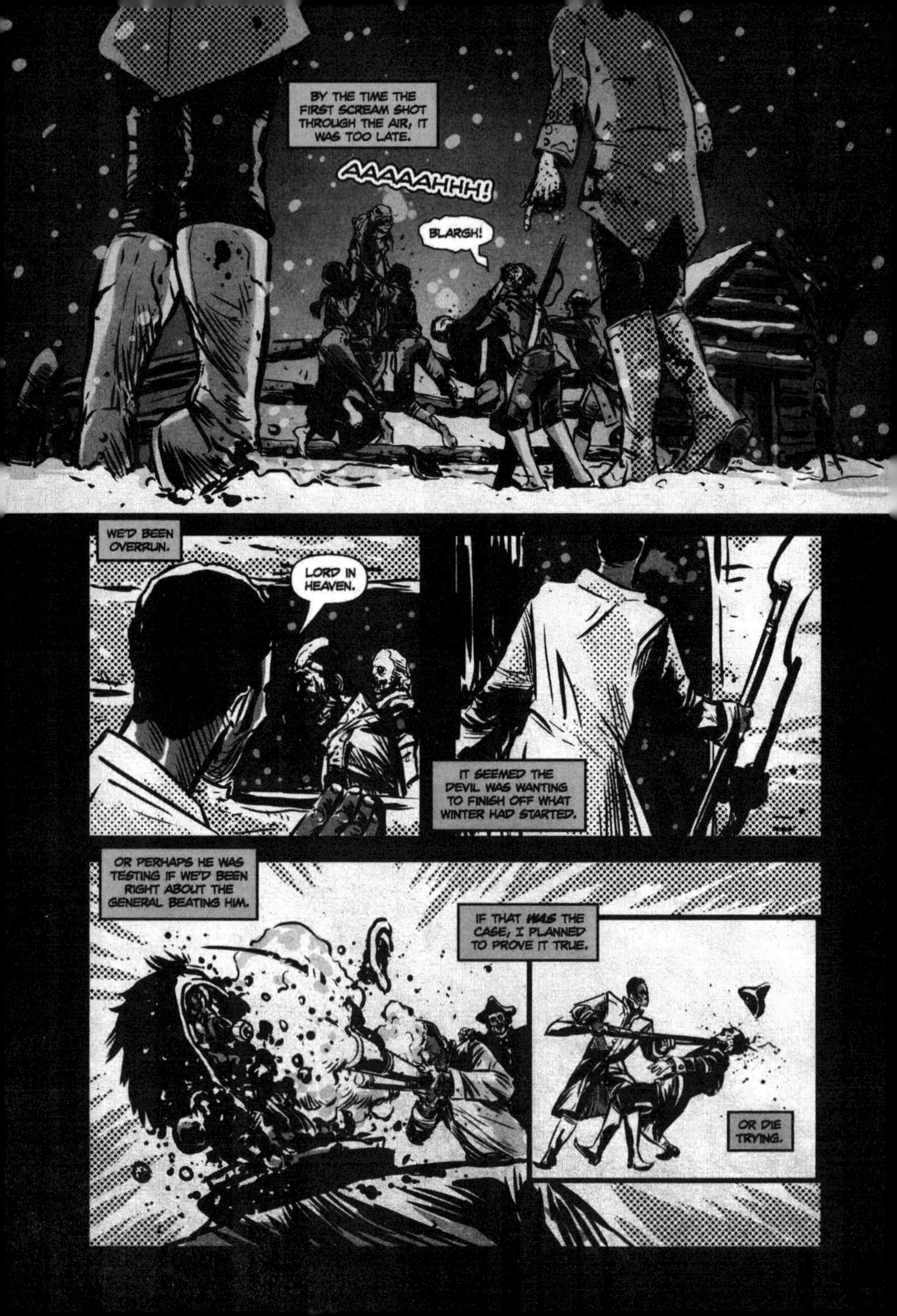
BY THE TIME THE FIRST SCREAM SHOT THROUGH THE AIR, IT WAS TOO LATE.
AAAAAHHH!
BLARGH!
WE'D BEEN OVERRUN.
LORD IN HEAVEN.
IT SEEMED THE DEVIL WAS WANTING TO FINISH OFF WHAT WINTER HAD STARTED.
OR PERHAPS HE WAS TESTING IF WE'D BEEN RIGHT ABOUT THE GENERAL BEATING HIM.
IF THAT WAS THE CASE, I PLANNED TO PROVE IT TRUE.
OR DIE TRYING.

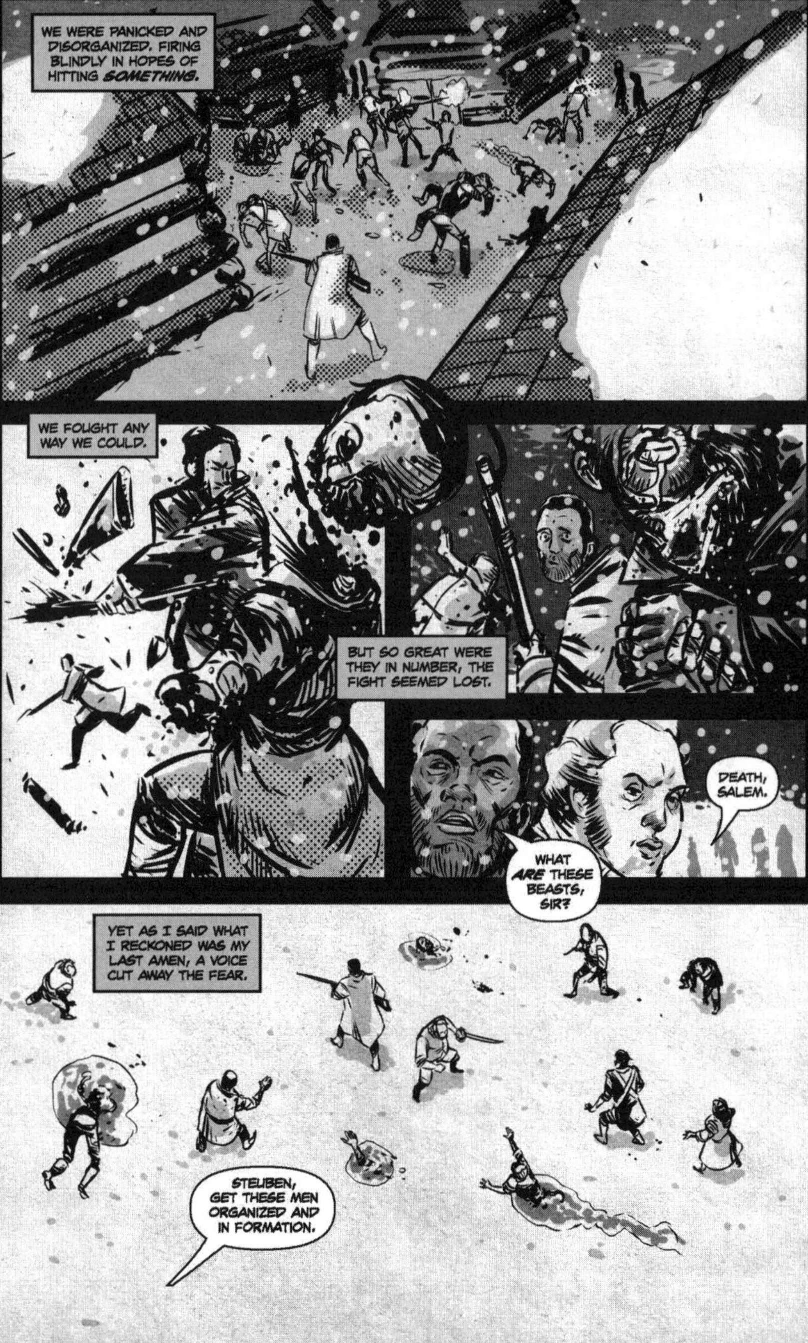

WE WERE PANICKED AND DISORGANIZED. FIRING BLINDLY IN HOPES OF HITTING *SOMETHING.*
WE FOUGHT ANY WAY WE COULD.
BUT SO GREAT WERE THEY IN NUMBER, THE FIGHT SEEMED LOST.
WHAT *ARE* THESE BEASTS, SIR?
DEATH, SALEM.
YET AS I SAID WHAT I RECKONED WAS MY LAST AMEN, A VOICE CUT AWAY THE FEAR.
STEUBEN, GET THESE MEN ORGANIZED AND IN FORMATION.

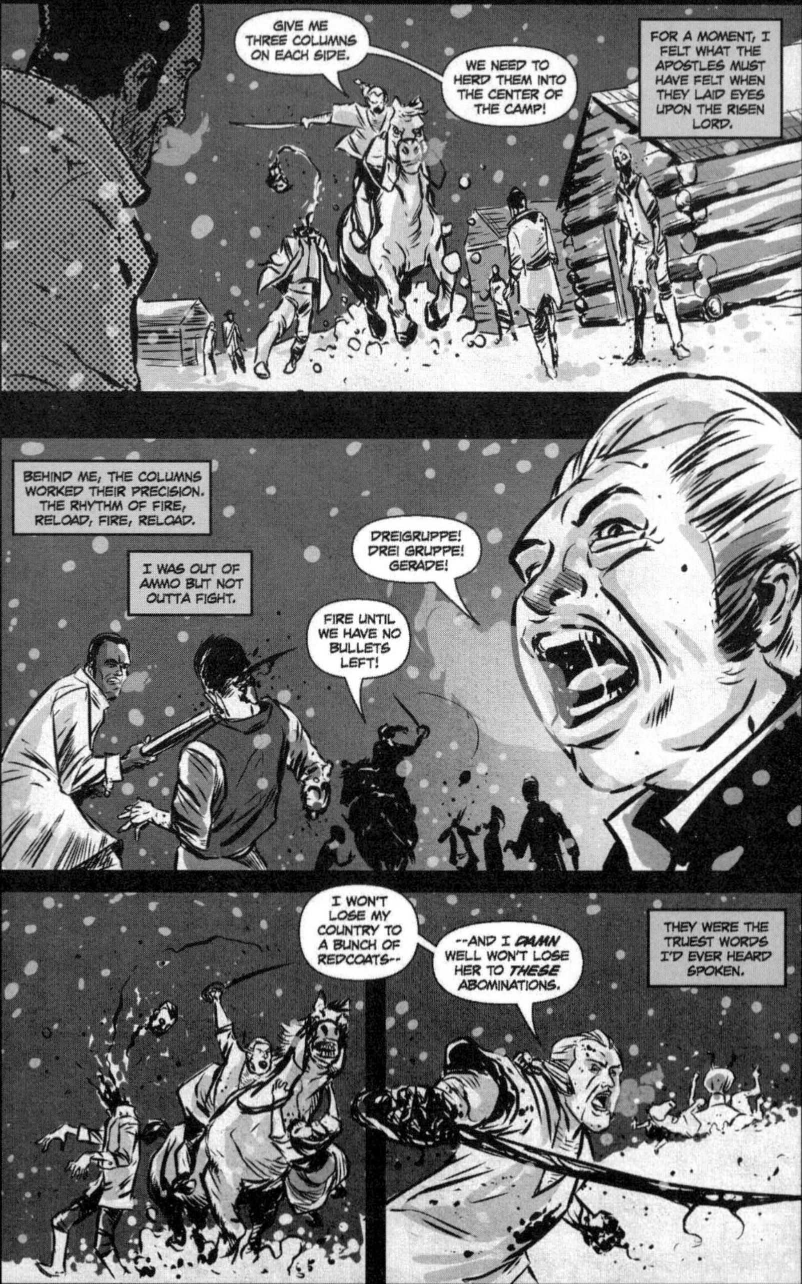
GIVE ME THREE COLUMNS ON EACH SIDE.
WE NEED TO HERD THEM INTO THE CENTER OF THE CAMP!
FOR A MOMENT, I FELT WHAT THE APOSTLES MUST HAVE FELT WHEN THEY LAID EYES UPON THE RISEN LORD.
BEHIND ME, THE COLUMNS WORKED THEIR PRECISION. THE RHYTHM OF FIRE, RELOAD, FIRE, RELOAD.
I WAS OUT OF AMMO BUT NOT OUTTA FIGHT.
DREIGRUPPE! DREI GRUPPE! GERADE!
FIRE UNTIL WE HAVE NO BULLETS LEFT!
I WON'T LOSE MY COUNTRY TO A BUNCH OF REDCOATS--
--AND I *DAMN* WELL WON'T LOSE HER TO *THESE* ABOMINATIONS.
THEY WERE THE TRUEST WORDS I'D EVER HEARD SPOKEN.

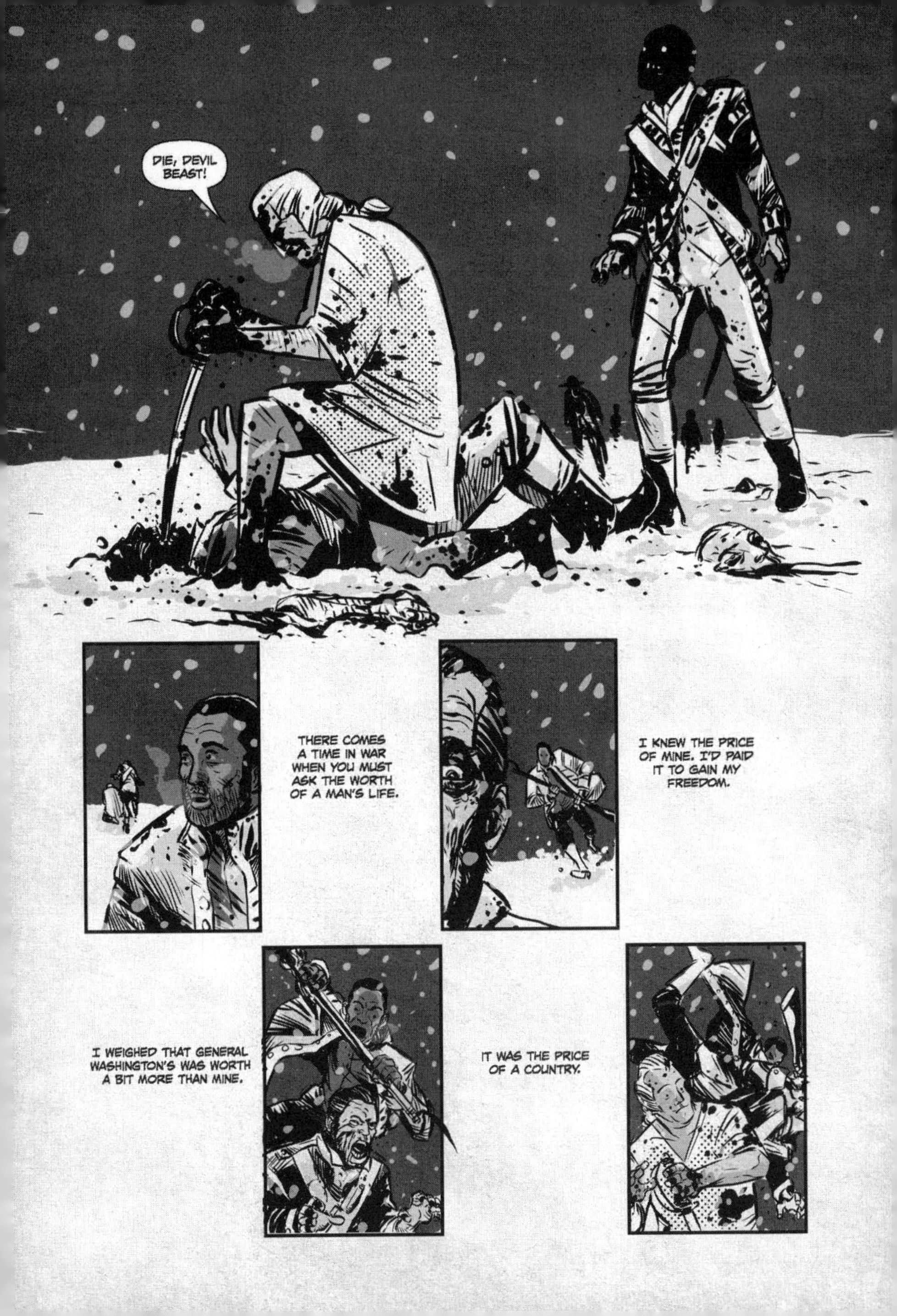
DIE, DEVIL BEAST!
THERE COMES A TIME IN WAR WHEN YOU MUST ASK THE WORTH OF A MAN'S LIFE.
I KNEW THE PRICE OF MINE. I'D PAID IT TO GAIN MY FREEDOM.
I WEIGHED THAT GENERAL WASHINGTON'S WAS WORTH A BIT MORE THAN MINE.
IT WAS THE PRICE OF A COUNTRY.

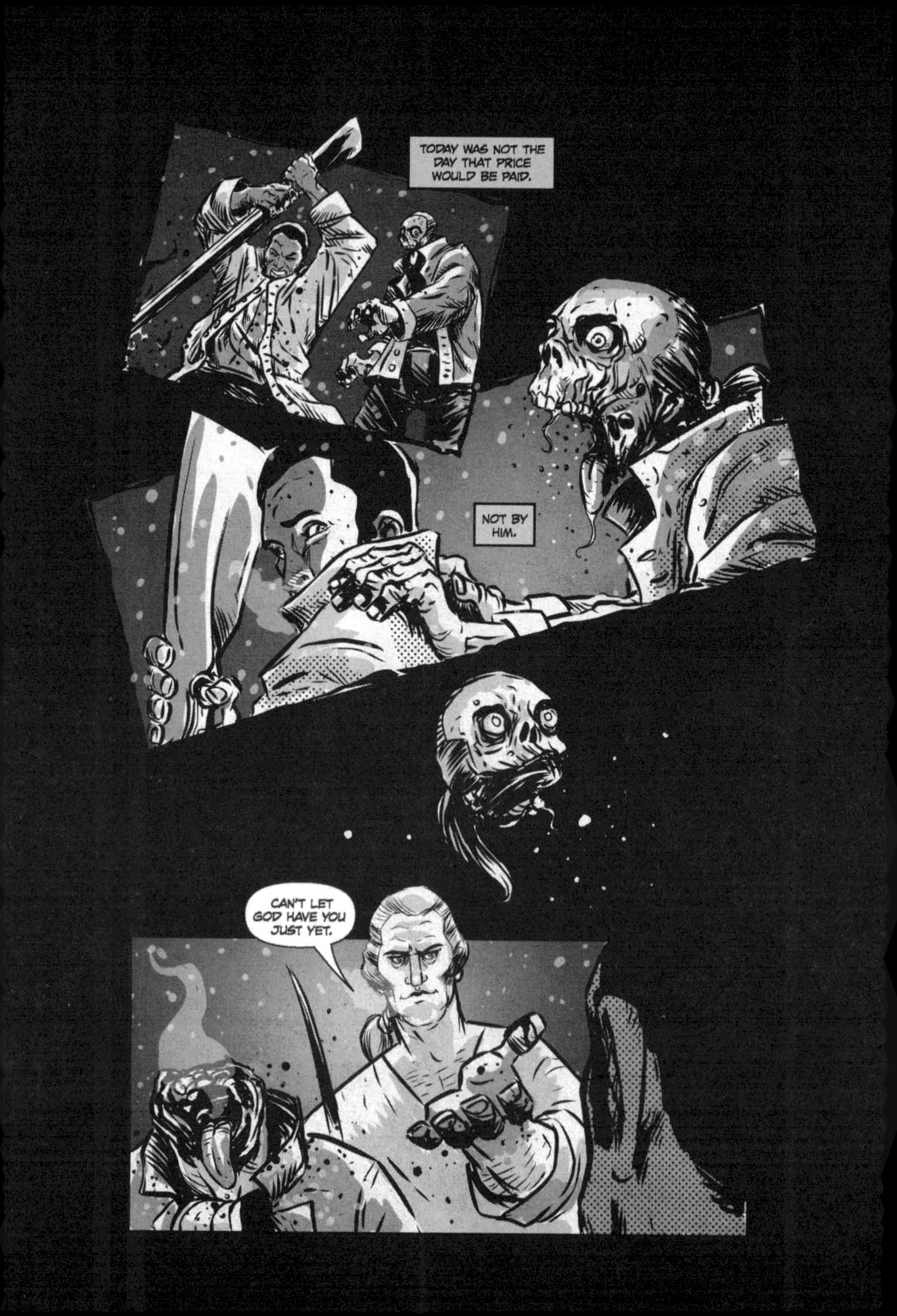
TODAY WAS NOT THE DAY THAT PRICE WOULD BE PAID.
NOT BY HIM.
CAN'T LET GOD HAVE YOU JUST YET.

JUST DESERTS

STORY BY:
ANDREW FOLEY

ART BY:
PEEBO MONDIA

LETTERS BY:
JEFF McCOMSEY

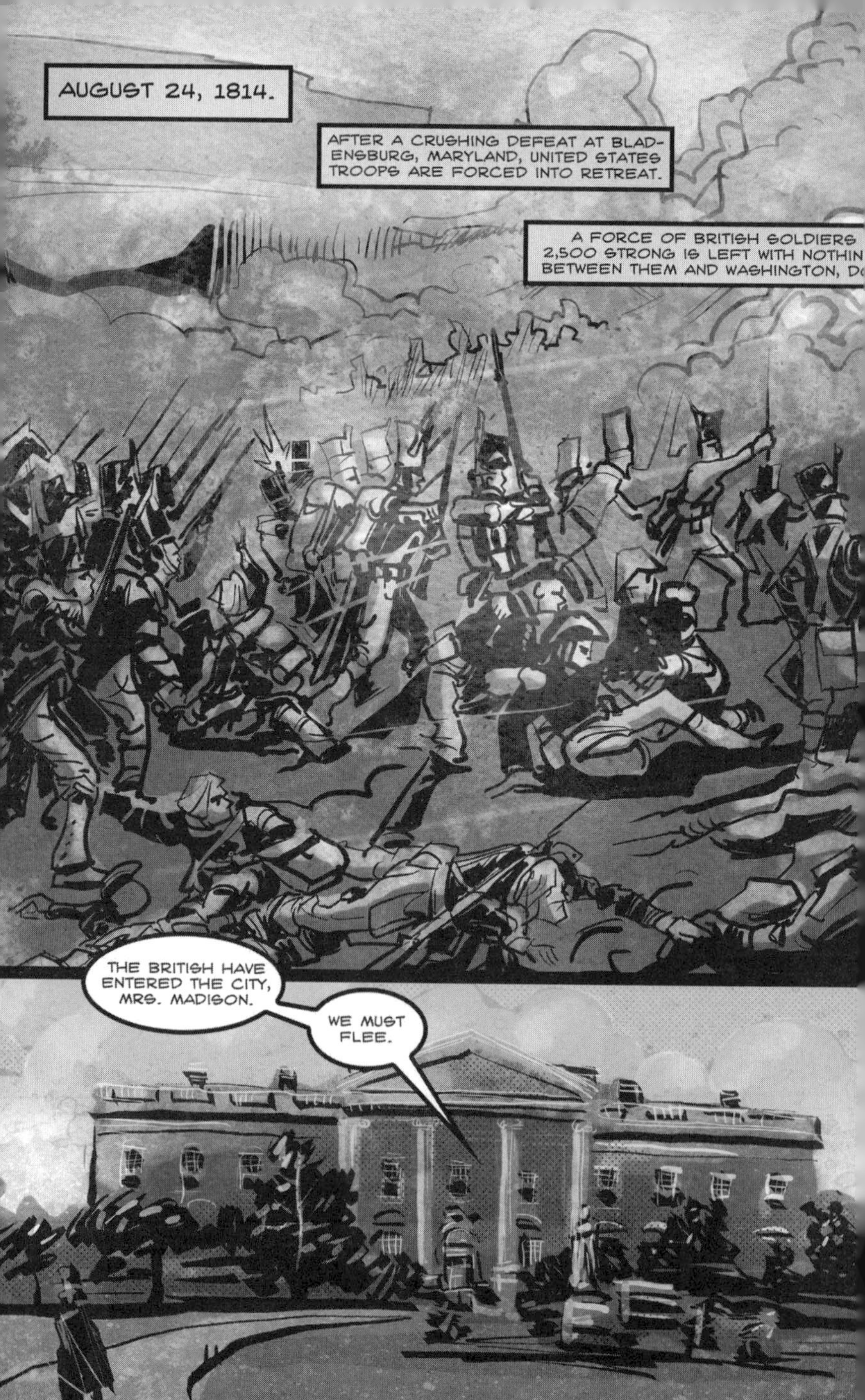
AUGUST 24, 1814.
AFTER A CRUSHING DEFEAT AT BLADENSBURG, MARYLAND, UNITED STATES TROOPS ARE FORCED INTO RETREAT.
A FORCE OF BRITISH SOLDIERS 2,500 STRONG IS LEFT WITH NOTHIN BETWEEN THEM AND WASHINGTON, D
THE BRITISH HAVE ENTERED THE CITY, MRS. MADISON.
WE MUST FLEE.

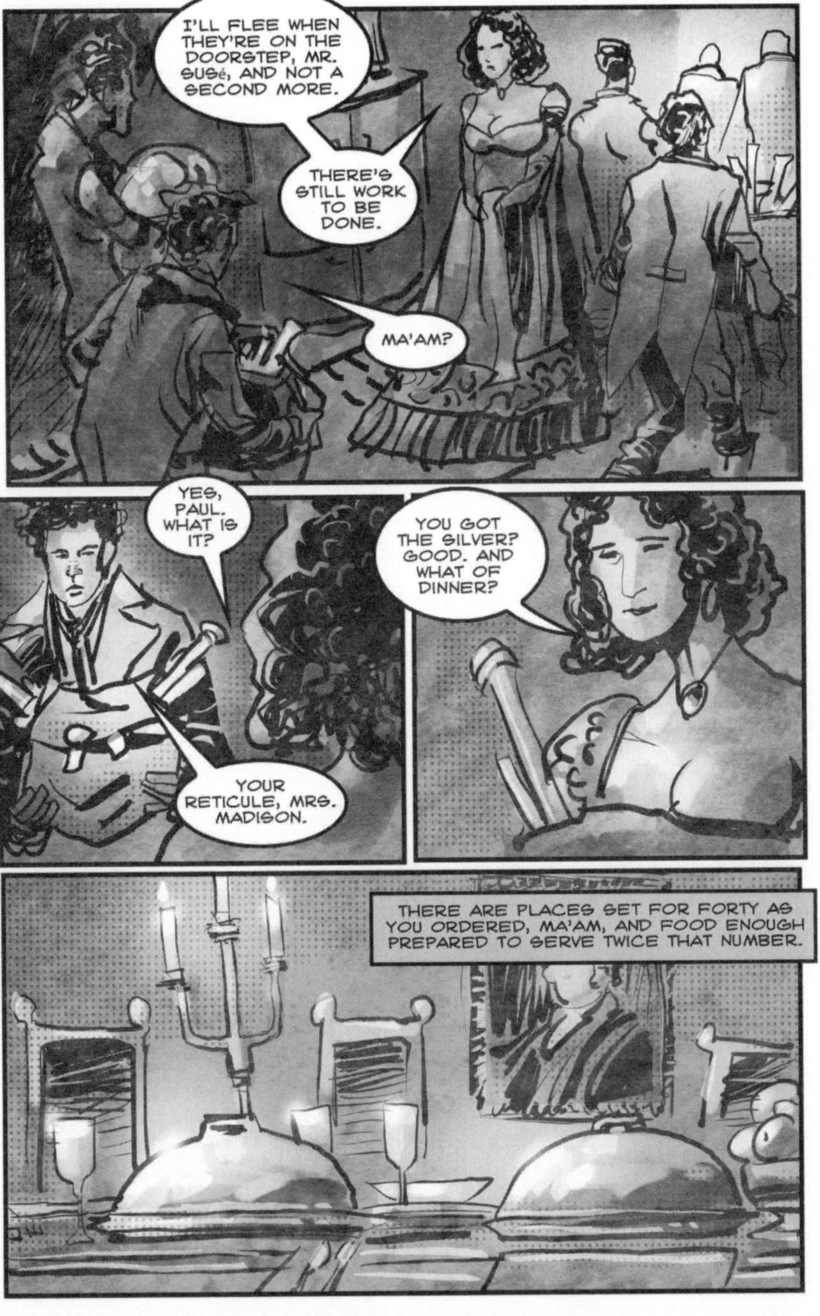
I'LL FLEE WHEN THEY'RE ON THE DOORSTEP, MR. SUSé, AND NOT A SECOND MORE.
THERE'S STILL WORK TO BE DONE.
MA'AM?
YES, PAUL. WHAT IS IT?
YOUR RETICULE, MRS. MADISON.
YOU GOT THE SILVER? GOOD. AND WHAT OF DINNER?
THERE ARE PLACES SET FOR FORTY AS YOU ORDERED, MA'AM, AND FOOD ENOUGH PREPARED TO SERVE TWICE THAT NUMBER.

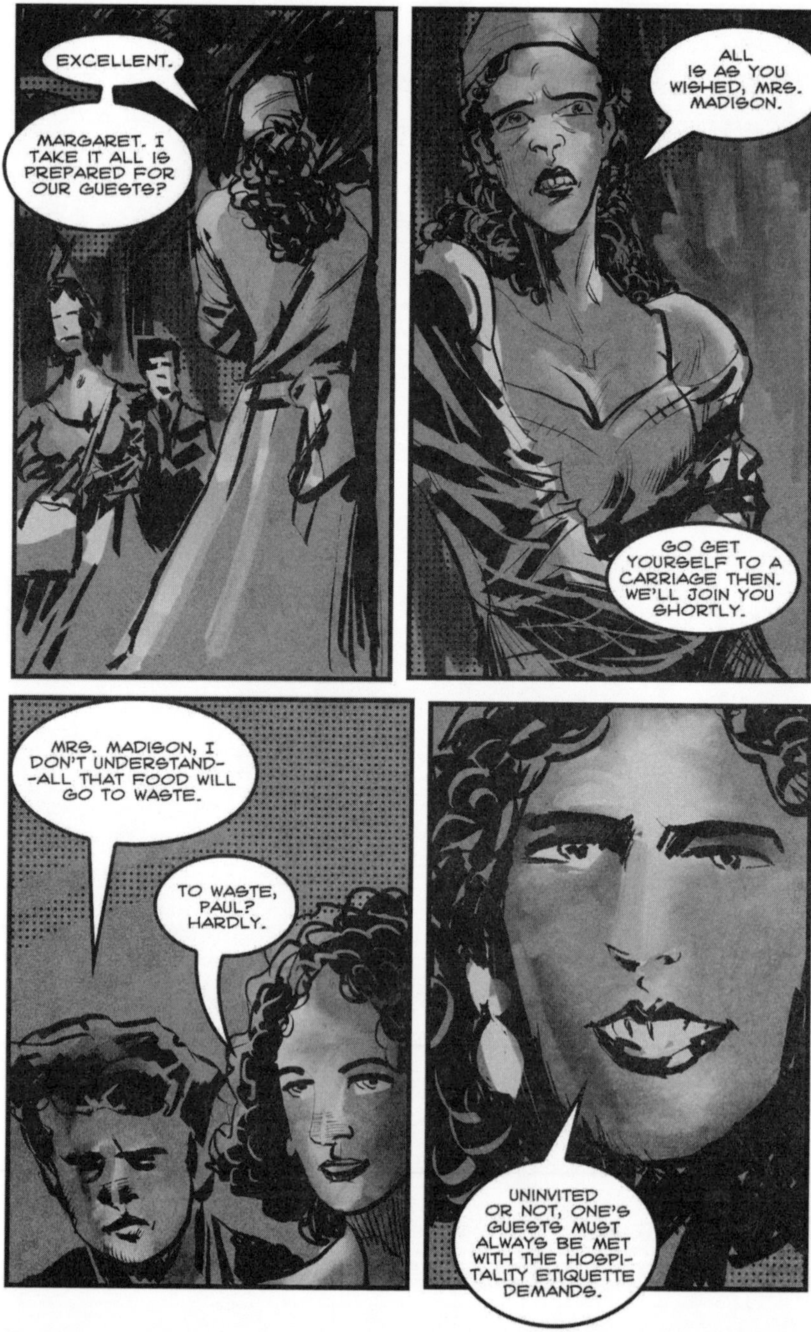
EXCELLENT.
MARGARET. I TAKE IT ALL IS PREPARED FOR OUR GUESTS?
ALL IS AS YOU WISHED, MRS. MADISON.
GO GET YOURSELF TO A CARRIAGE THEN. WE'LL JOIN YOU SHORTLY.
MRS. MADISON, I DON'T UNDERSTAND--ALL THAT FOOD WILL GO TO WASTE.
TO WASTE, PAUL? HARDLY.
UNINVITED OR NOT, ONE'S GUESTS MUST ALWAYS BE MET WITH THE HOSPITALITY ETIQUETTE DEMANDS.

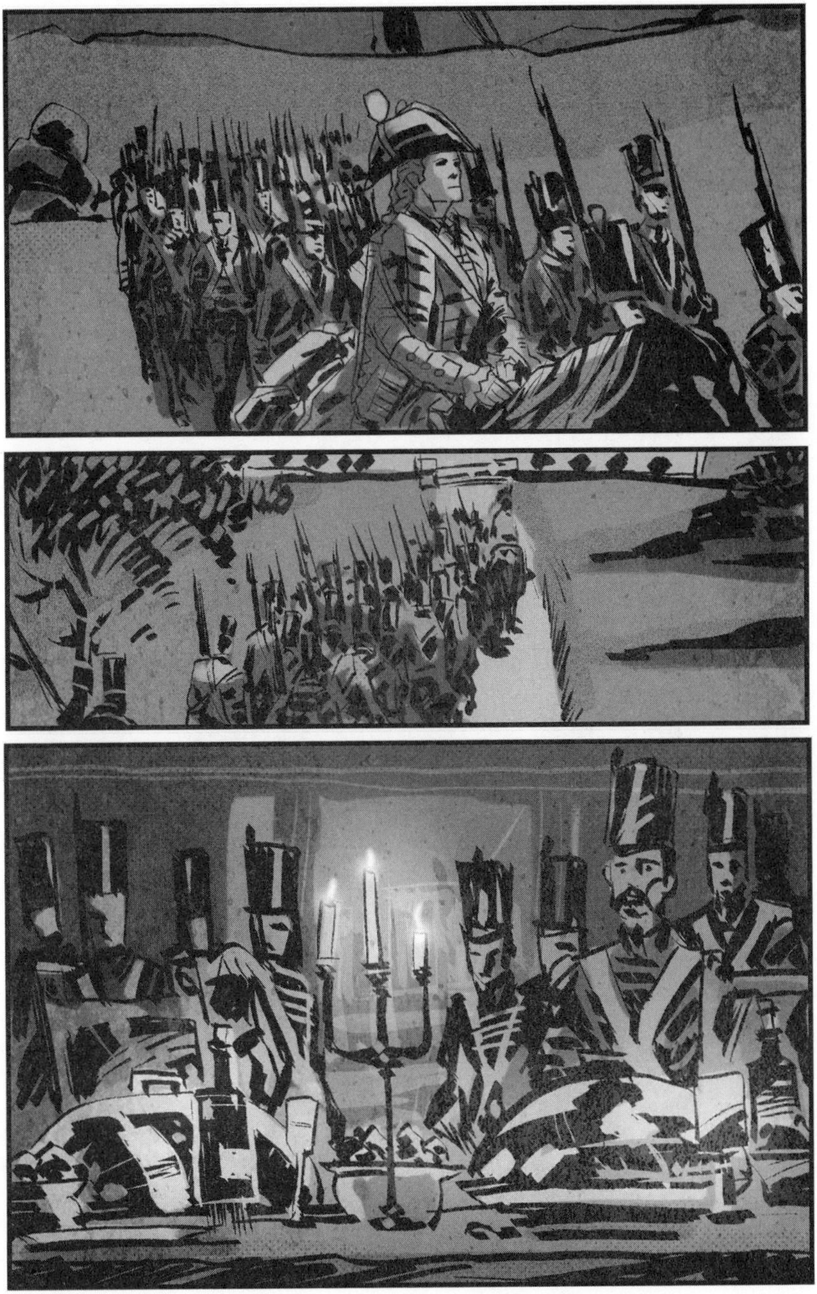

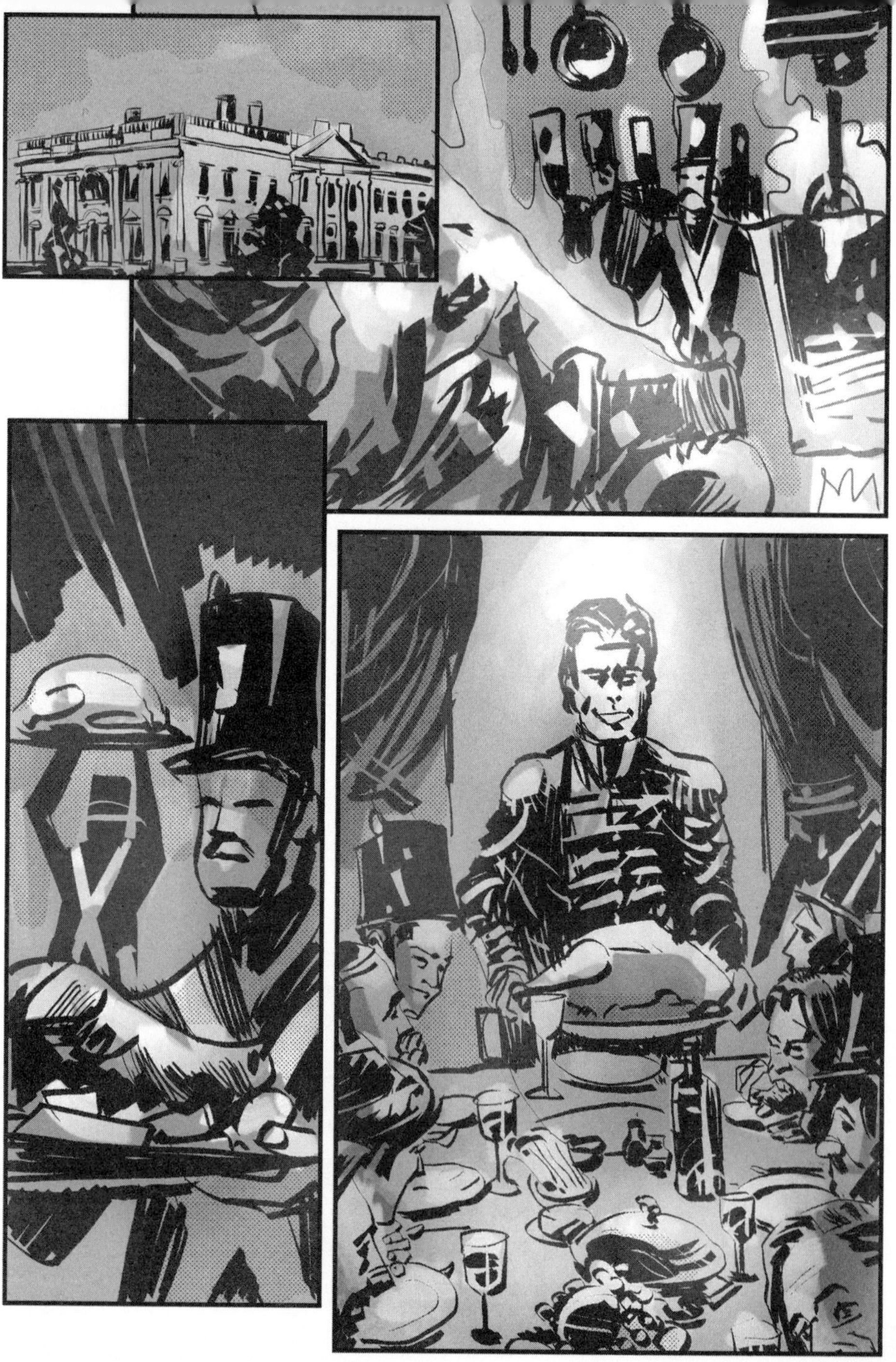

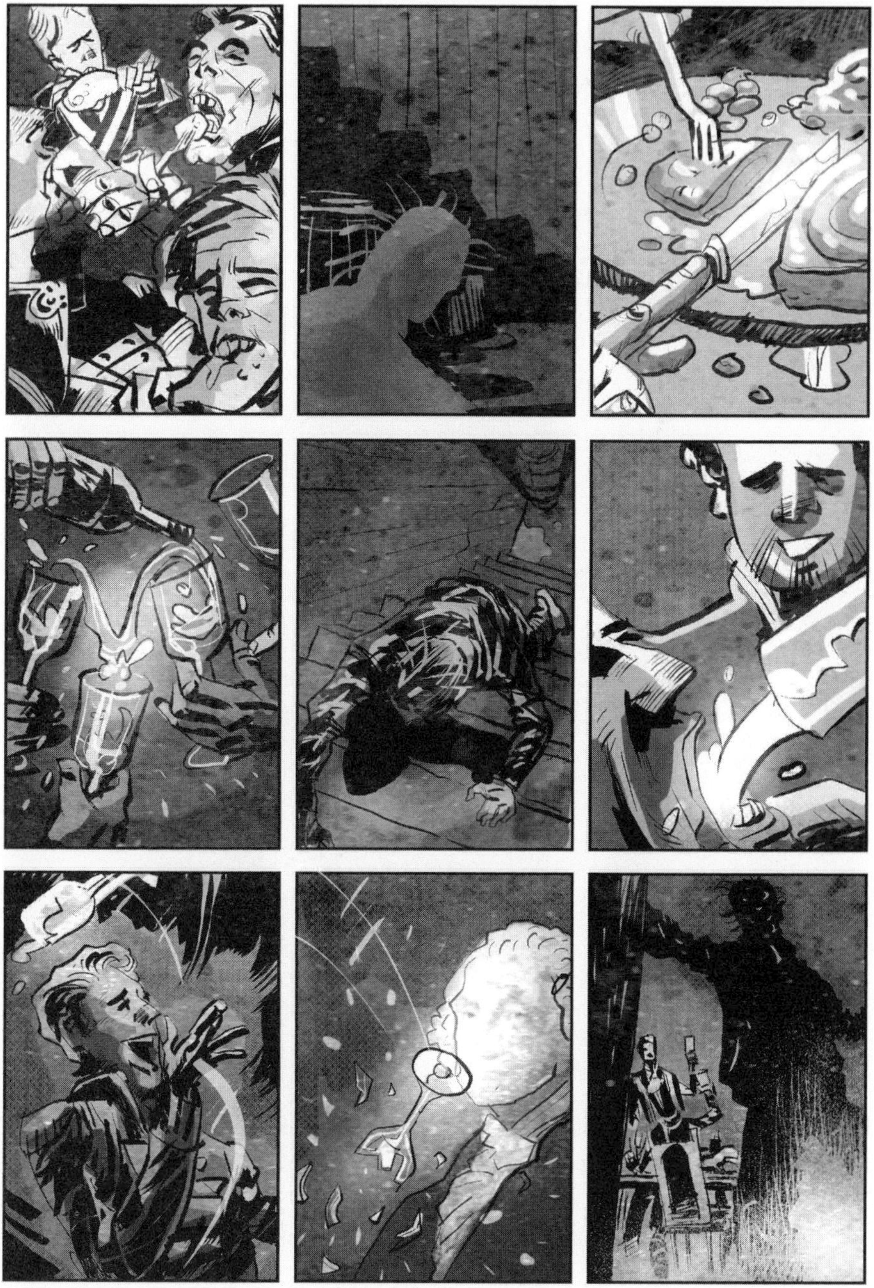

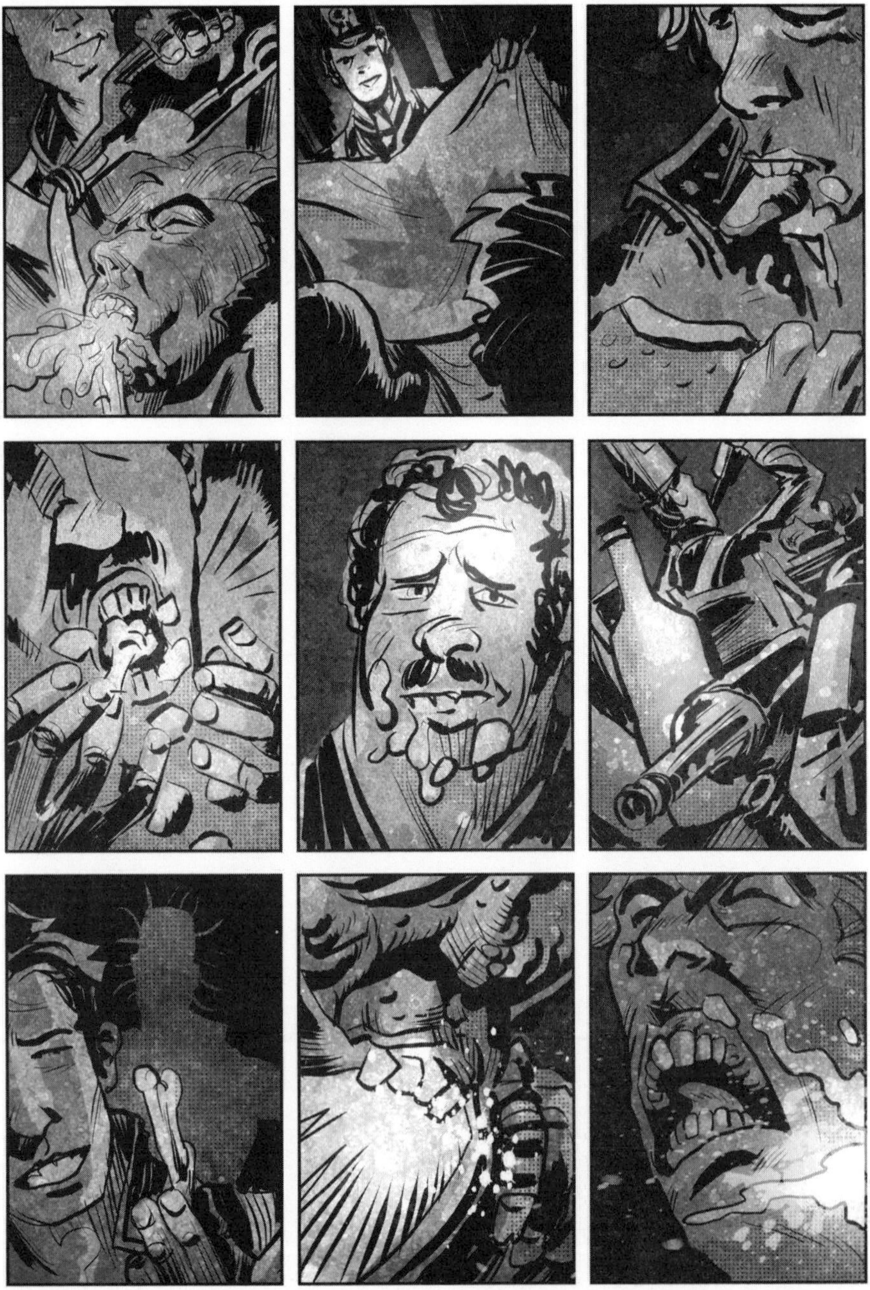

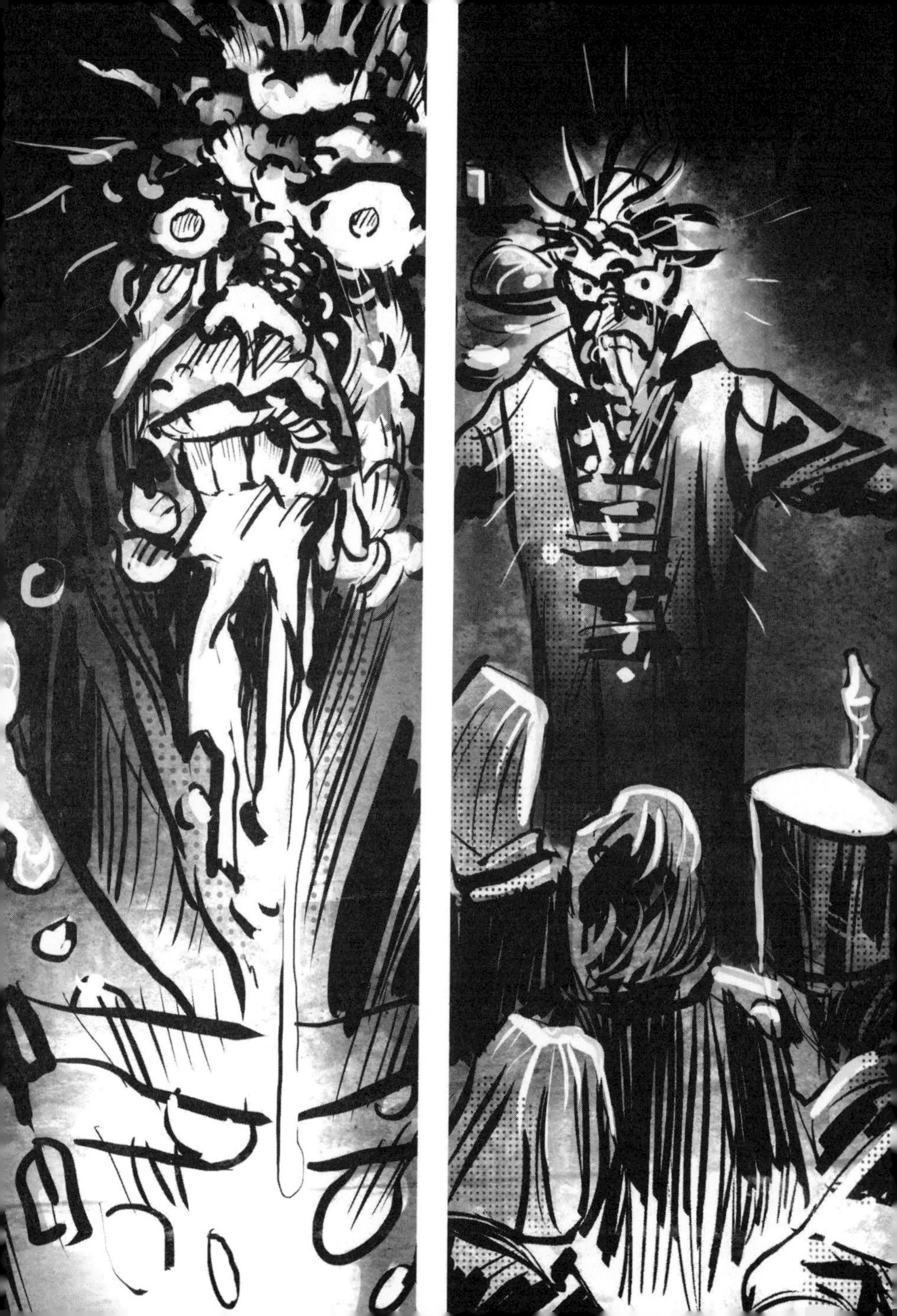

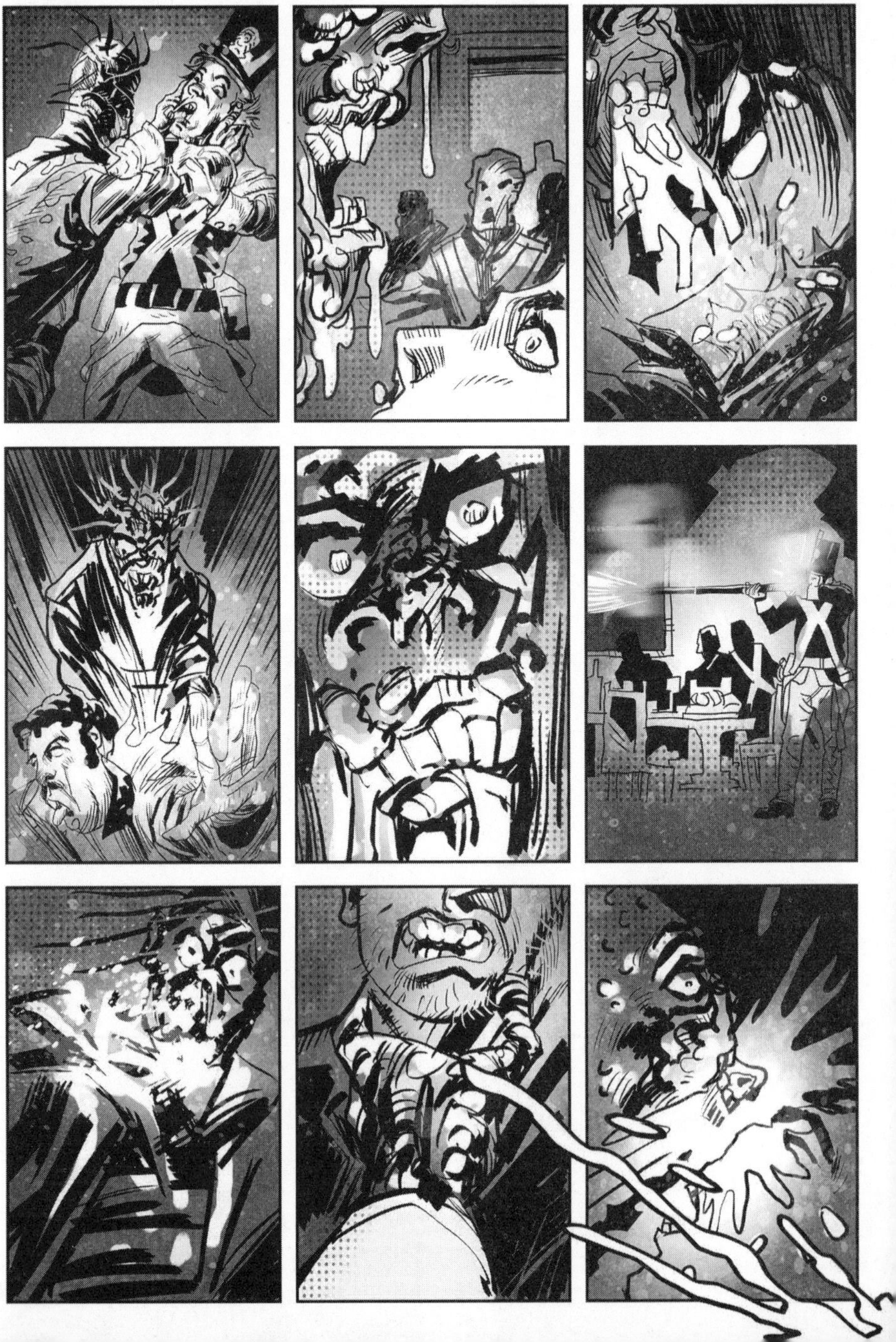

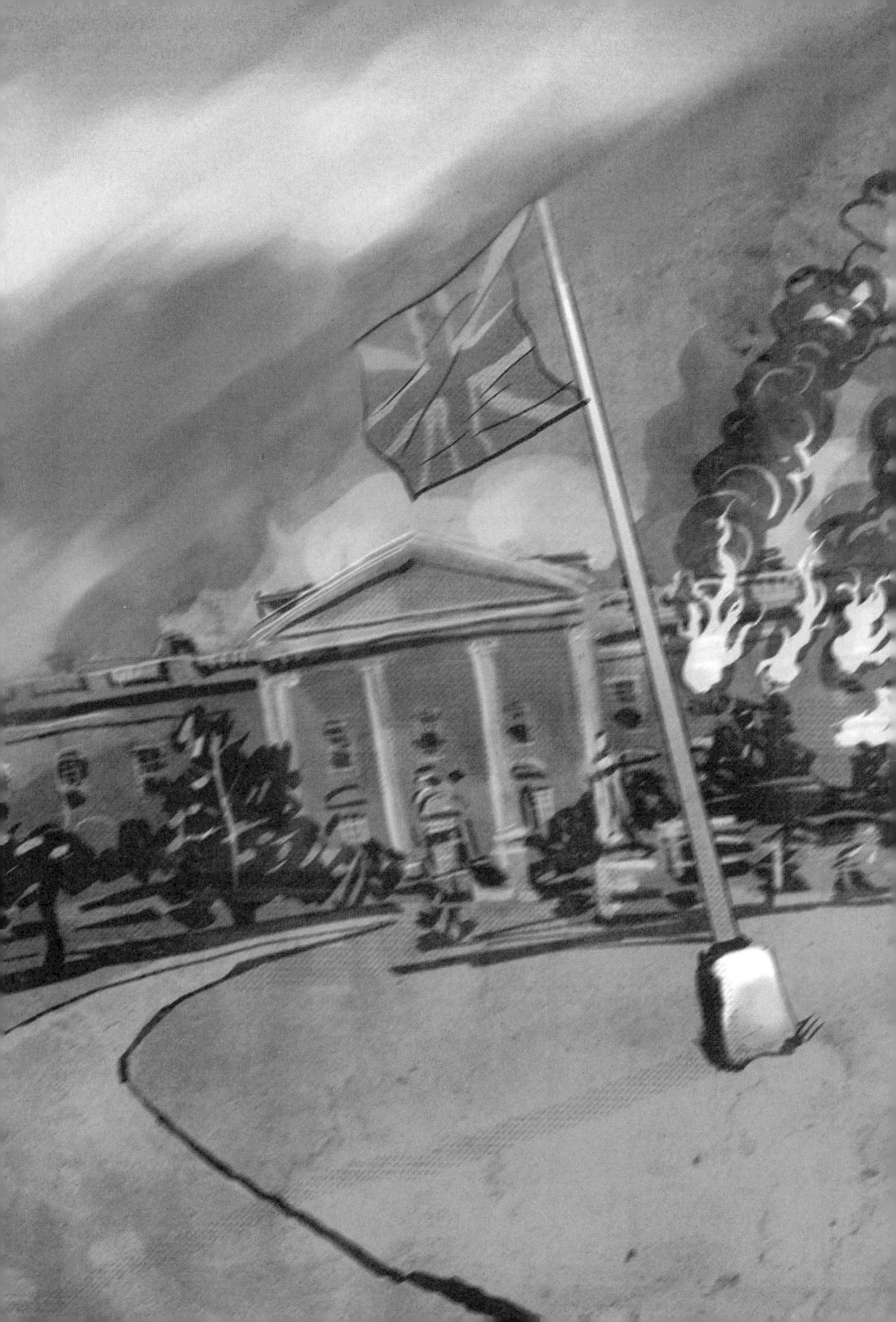

REMEMBER THE ALAMO

STORY AND LETTERS BY:
JEFF McCLELLAND
PENCILS BY:
STEVE BECKER
INKS BY:
JEFF McCOMSEY
GREYSCALES BY:
BARRY SACHS

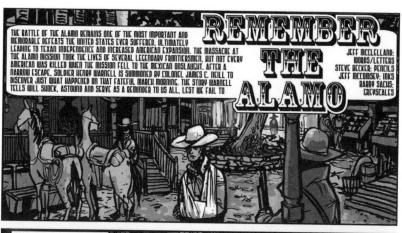

REMEMBER THE ALAMO

THE BATTLE OF THE ALAMO REMAINS ONE OF THE MOST IMPORTANT AND MEMORABLE DEFEATS THE UNITED STATES EVER SUFFERED, ULTIMATELY LEADING TO TEXAN INDEPENDENCE AND INCREASED AMERICAN EXPANSION. THE MASSACRE AT THE ALAMO MISSION TOOK THE LIVES OF SEVERAL LEGENDARY FRONTIERSMEN, BUT NOT EVERY AMERICAN WAS KILLED WHEN THE MISSION FELL TO THE MEXICAN ONSLAUGHT. AFTER A NARROW ESCAPE, SOLDIER HENRY WARNELL IS SUMMONED BY COLONEL JAMES C. NEILL TO DISCOVER JUST WHAT HAPPENED ON THAT FATEFUL MARCH MORNING. THE STORY WARNELL TELLS WILL SHOCK, ASTOUND AND SERVE AS A REMINDER TO US ALL, LEST WE FAIL TO

JEFF MCCLELLAND: WORDS/LETTERS
STEVE BECKER: PENCILS
JEFF MCCONKEY: INKS
BARRY SACHS: CREYSCALES

APRIL, 1836. GONZALES, TEXAS.

C'MON IN.

HAVE A SEAT, MR. WARNELL.

YES, SIR.

AH, DON'T NEED NONE OF THAT FORMAL BULLSHIT. JUST SIT DOWN AND LET'S TALK.

I TAKE IT YOU KNOW WHY YOU WERE CALLED, MR. WARNELL.

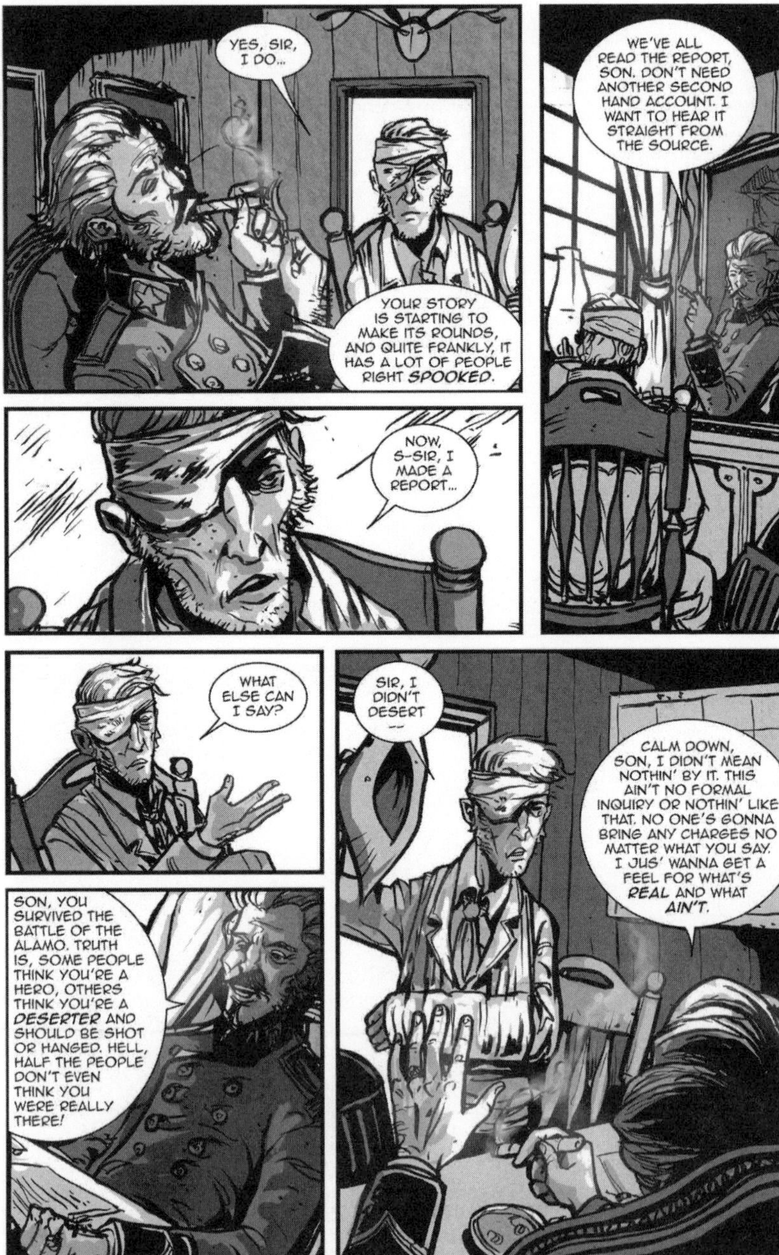
YES, SIR, I DO...
YOUR STORY IS STARTING TO MAKE ITS ROUNDS, AND QUITE FRANKLY, IT HAS A LOT OF PEOPLE RIGHT SPOOKED.
WE'VE ALL READ THE REPORT, SON. DON'T NEED ANOTHER SECOND HAND ACCOUNT. I WANT TO HEAR IT STRAIGHT FROM THE SOURCE.
NOW, S-SIR, I MADE A REPORT...
WHAT ELSE CAN I SAY?
SON, YOU SURVIVED THE BATTLE OF THE ALAMO. TRUTH IS, SOME PEOPLE THINK YOU'RE A HERO, OTHERS THINK YOU'RE A DESERTER AND SHOULD BE SHOT OR HANGED. HELL, HALF THE PEOPLE DON'T EVEN THINK YOU WERE REALLY THERE!
SIR, I DIDN'T DESERT —
CALM DOWN, SON, I DIDN'T MEAN NOTHIN' BY IT. THIS AIN'T NO FORMAL INQUIRY OR NOTHIN' LIKE THAT. NO ONE'S GONNA BRING ANY CHARGES NO MATTER WHAT YOU SAY. I JUS' WANNA GET A FEEL FOR WHAT'S REAL AND WHAT AIN'T.

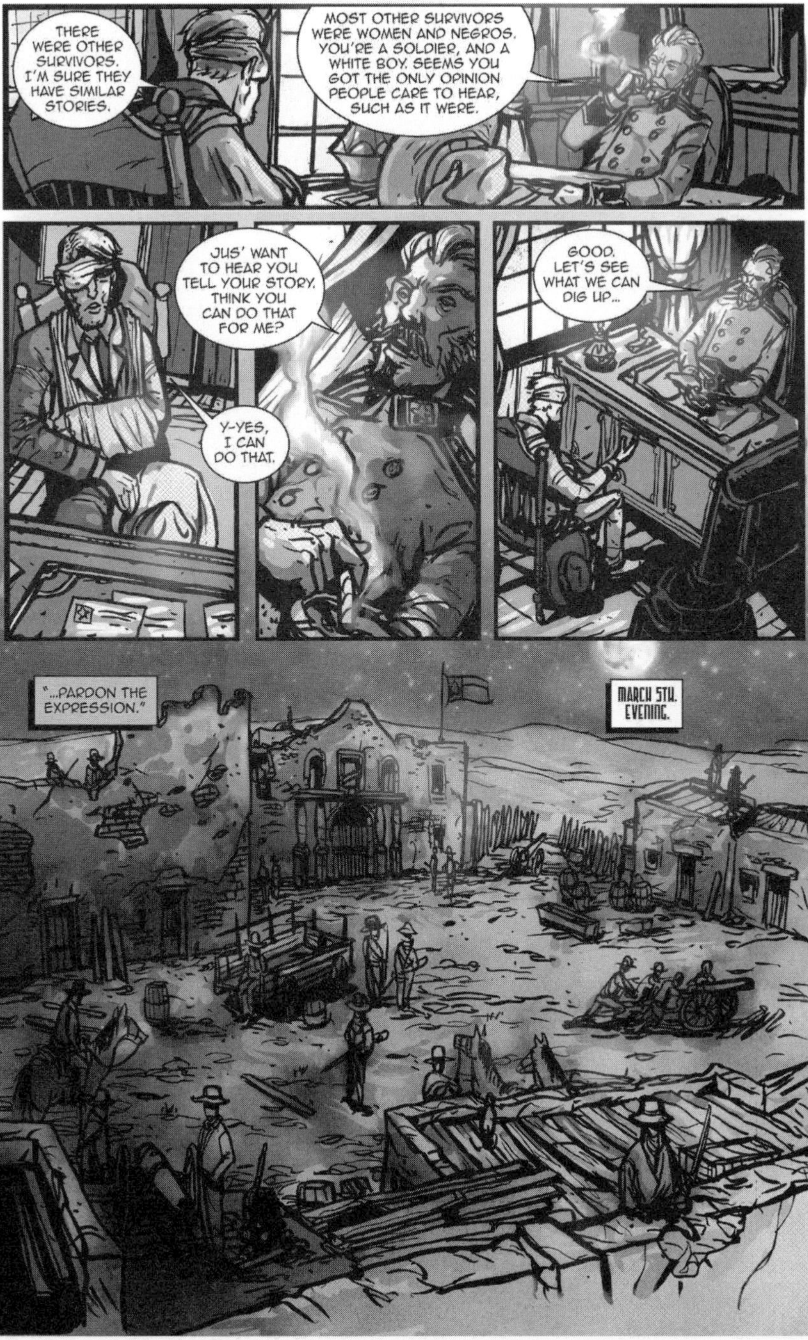
THERE WERE OTHER SURVIVORS. I'M SURE THEY HAVE SIMILAR STORIES.
MOST OTHER SURVIVORS WERE WOMEN AND NEGROS. YOU'RE A SOLDIER, AND A WHITE BOY. SEEMS YOU GOT THE ONLY OPINION PEOPLE CARE TO HEAR, SUCH AS IT WERE.
JUS' WANT TO HEAR YOU TELL YOUR STORY. THINK YOU CAN DO THAT FOR ME?
Y-YES, I CAN DO THAT.
GOOD. LET'S SEE WHAT WE CAN DIG UP...
"...PARDON THE EXPRESSION."
MARCH 5TH. EVENING.

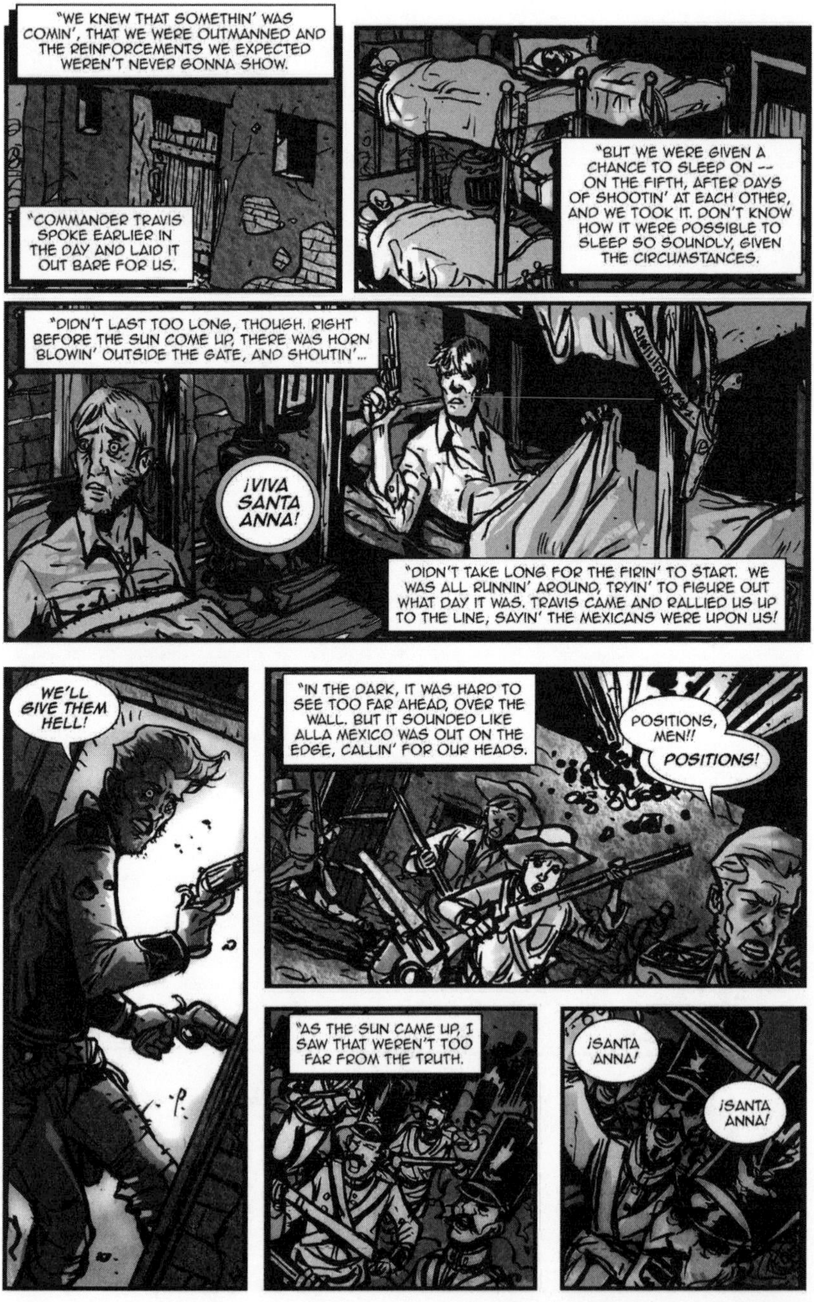
"WE KNEW THAT SOMETHIN' WAS COMIN', THAT WE WERE OUTMANNED AND THE REINFORCEMENTS WE EXPECTED WEREN'T NEVER GONNA SHOW.
"COMMANDER TRAVIS SPOKE EARLIER IN THE DAY AND LAID IT OUT BARE FOR US.
"BUT WE WERE GIVEN A CHANCE TO SLEEP ON -- ON THE FIFTH, AFTER DAYS OF SHOOTIN' AT EACH OTHER, AND WE TOOK IT. DON'T KNOW HOW IT WERE POSSIBLE TO SLEEP SO SOUNDLY, GIVEN THE CIRCUMSTANCES.
"DIDN'T LAST TOO LONG, THOUGH. RIGHT BEFORE THE SUN COME UP, THERE WAS HORN BLOWIN' OUTSIDE THE GATE, AND SHOUTIN'...
¡VIVA SANTA ANNA!
"DIDN'T TAKE LONG FOR THE FIRIN' TO START. WE WAS ALL RUNNIN' AROUND, TRYIN' TO FIGURE OUT WHAT DAY IT WAS. TRAVIS CAME AND RALLIED US UP TO THE LINE, SAYIN' THE MEXICANS WERE UPON US!
WE'LL GIVE THEM HELL!
"IN THE DARK, IT WAS HARD TO SEE TOO FAR AHEAD, OVER THE WALL. BUT IT SOUNDED LIKE ALLA MEXICO WAS OUT ON THE EDGE, CALLIN' FOR OUR HEADS.
POSITIONS, MEN!! POSITIONS!
"AS THE SUN CAME UP, I SAW THAT WEREN'T TOO FAR FROM THE TRUTH.
¡SANTA ANNA!
¡SANTA ANNA!

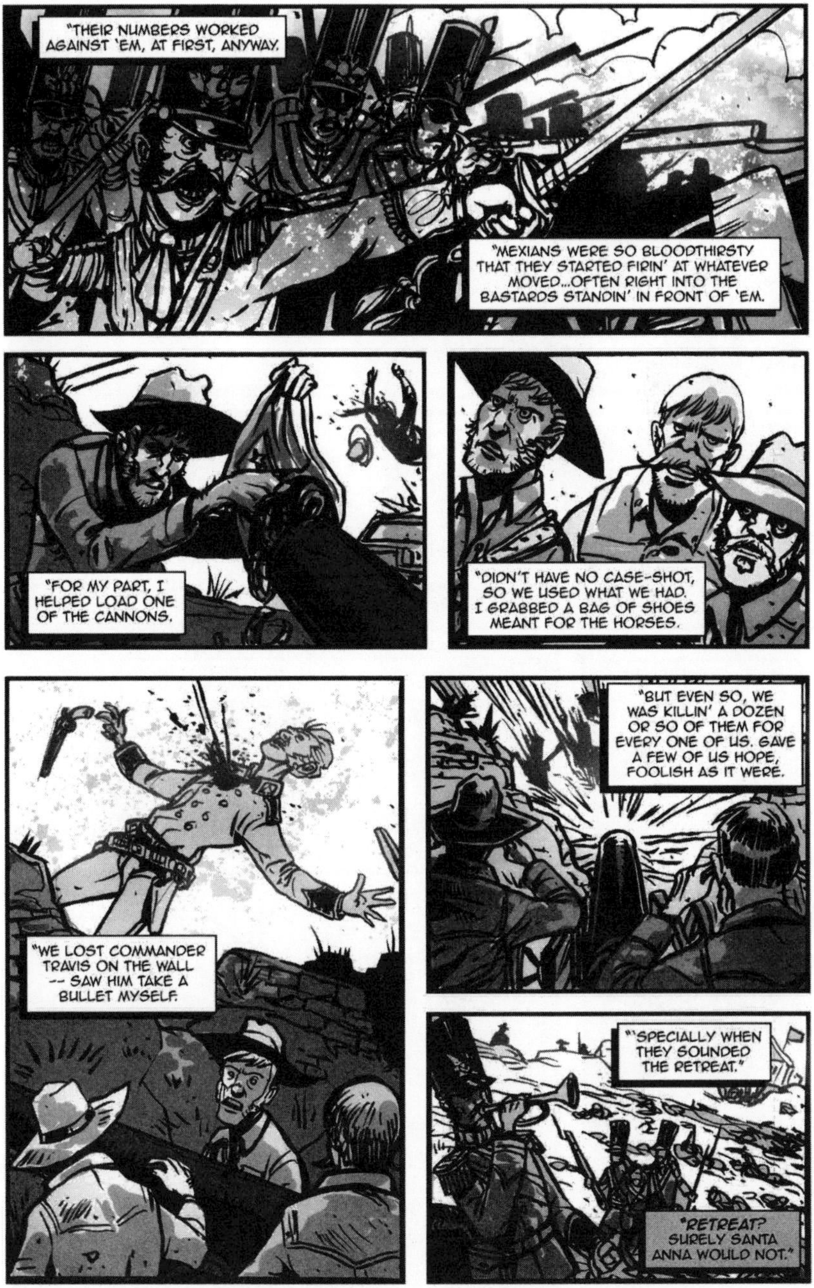
"THEIR NUMBERS WORKED AGAINST 'EM, AT FIRST, ANYWAY.
"MEXIANS WERE SO BLOODTHIRSTY THAT THEY STARTED FIRIN' AT WHATEVER MOVED...OFTEN RIGHT INTO THE BASTARDS STANDIN' IN FRONT OF 'EM.
"FOR MY PART, I HELPED LOAD ONE OF THE CANNONS.
"DIDN'T HAVE NO CASE-SHOT, SO WE USED WHAT WE HAD. I GRABBED A BAG OF SHOES MEANT FOR THE HORSES.
"WE LOST COMMANDER TRAVIS ON THE WALL -- SAW HIM TAKE A BULLET MYSELF.
"BUT EVEN SO, WE WAS KILLIN' A DOZEN OR SO OF THEM FOR EVERY ONE OF US. GAVE A FEW OF US HOPE, FOOLISH AS IT WERE.
"'SPECIALLY WHEN THEY SOUNDED THE RETREAT."
"RETREAT? SURELY SANTA ANNA WOULD NOT."

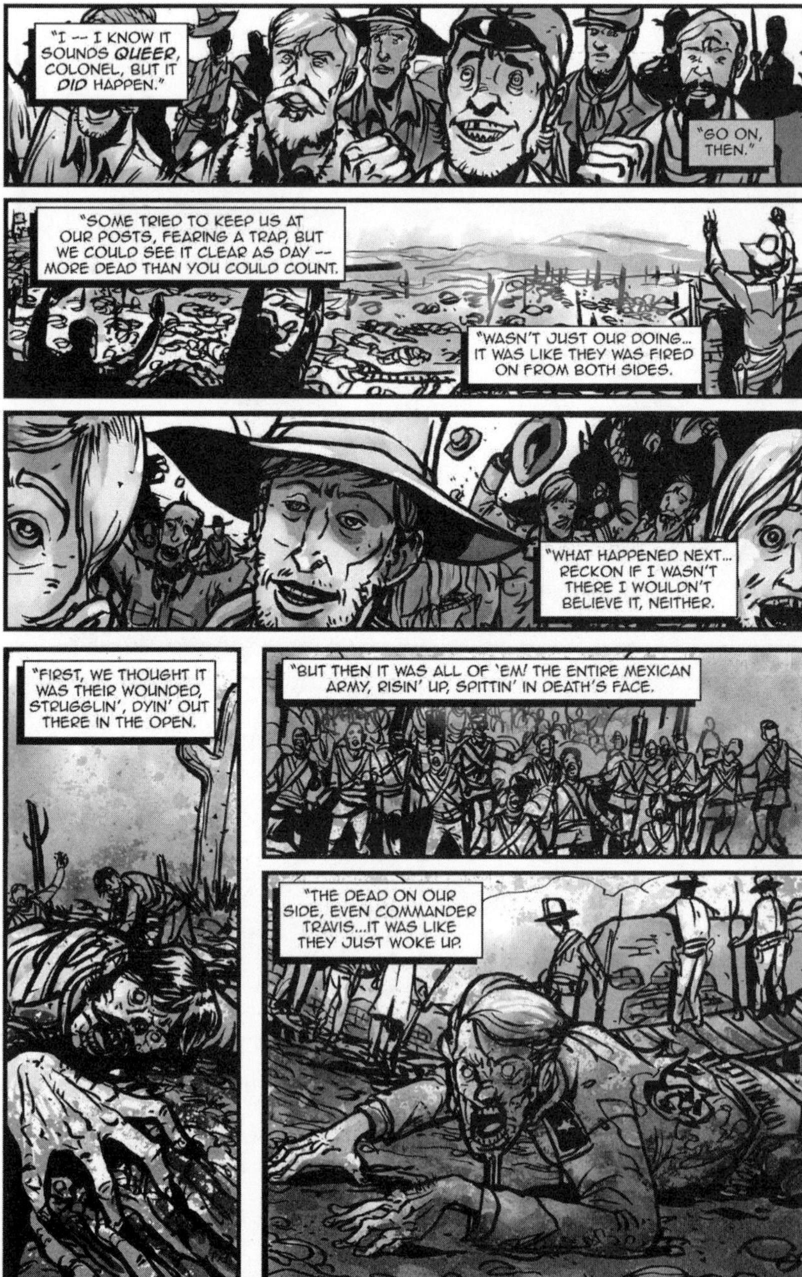
"I -- I KNOW IT SOUNDS QUEER, COLONEL, BUT IT DID HAPPEN."
"GO ON, THEN."
"SOME TRIED TO KEEP US AT OUR POSTS, FEARING A TRAP, BUT WE COULD SEE IT CLEAR AS DAY -- MORE DEAD THAN YOU COULD COUNT.
"WASN'T JUST OUR DOING... IT WAS LIKE THEY WAS FIRED ON FROM BOTH SIDES.
"WHAT HAPPENED NEXT... RECKON IF I WASN'T THERE I WOULDN'T BELIEVE IT, NEITHER.
"FIRST, WE THOUGHT IT WAS THEIR WOUNDED, STRUGGLIN', DYIN' OUT THERE IN THE OPEN.
"BUT THEN IT WAS ALL OF 'EM! THE ENTIRE MEXICAN ARMY, RISIN' UP, SPITTIN' IN DEATH'S FACE.
"THE DEAD ON OUR SIDE, EVEN COMMANDER TRAVIS...IT WAS LIKE THEY JUST WOKE UP.

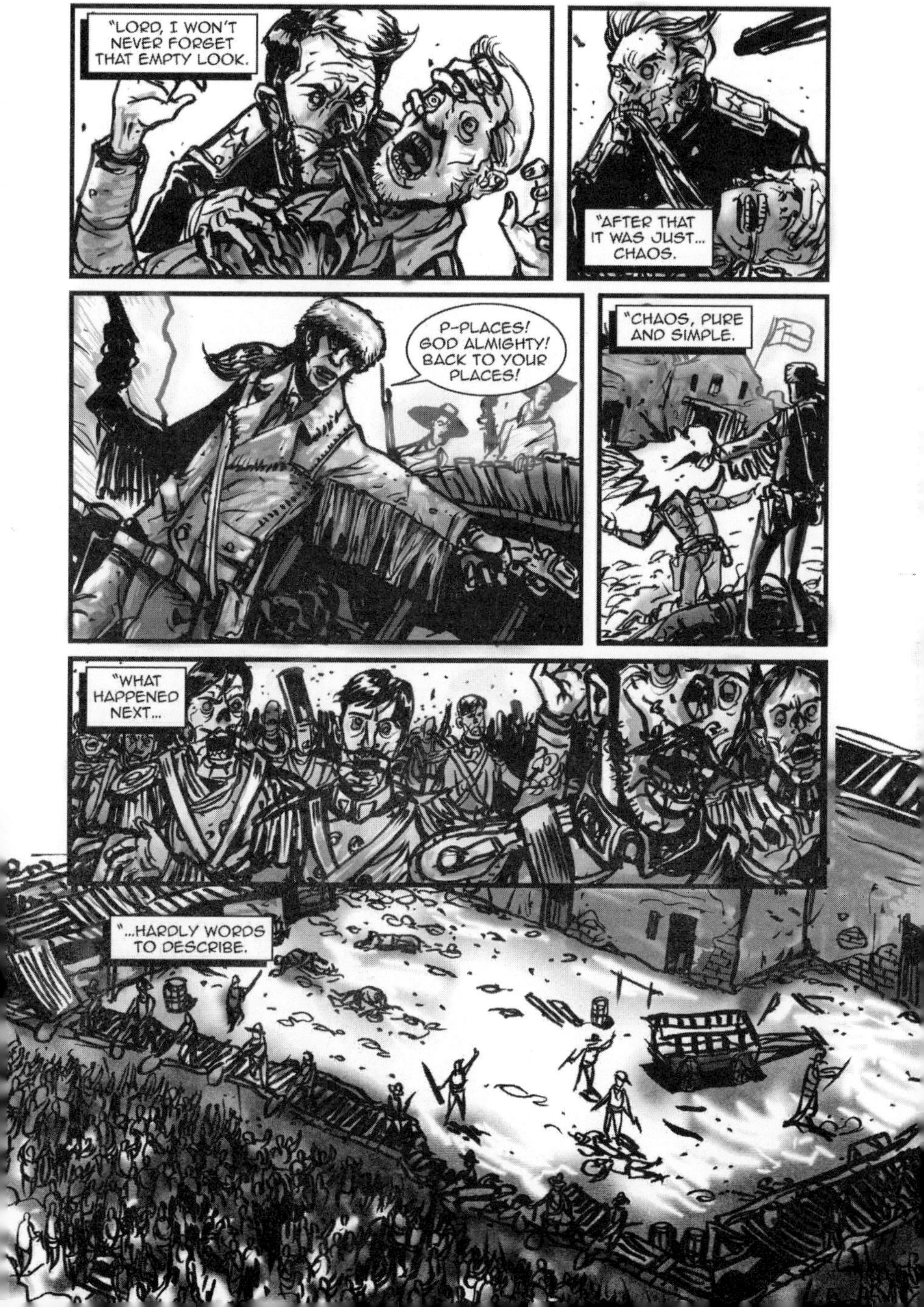
"LORD, I WON'T NEVER FORGET THAT EMPTY LOOK.
"AFTER THAT IT WAS JUST... CHAOS.
P-PLACES! GOD ALMIGHTY! BACK TO YOUR PLACES!
"CHAOS, PURE AND SIMPLE.
"WHAT HAPPENED NEXT...
"...HARDLY WORDS TO DESCRIBE.

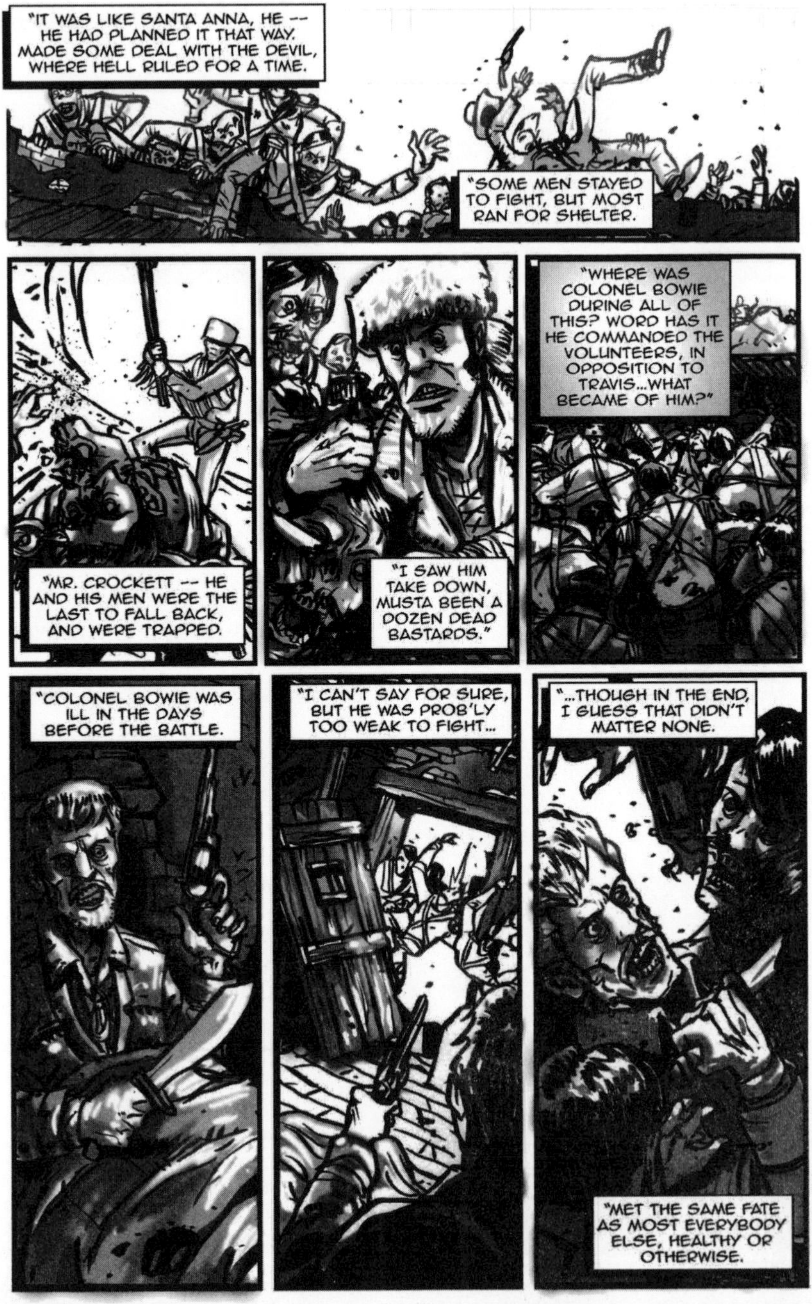
"IT WAS LIKE SANTA ANNA, HE -- HE HAD PLANNED IT THAT WAY. MADE SOME DEAL WITH THE DEVIL, WHERE HELL RULED FOR A TIME.
"SOME MEN STAYED TO FIGHT, BUT MOST RAN FOR SHELTER.
"MR. CROCKETT -- HE AND HIS MEN WERE THE LAST TO FALL BACK, AND WERE TRAPPED.
"I SAW HIM TAKE DOWN, MUSTA BEEN A DOZEN DEAD BASTARDS."
"WHERE WAS COLONEL BOWIE DURING ALL OF THIS? WORD HAS IT HE COMMANDED THE VOLUNTEERS, IN OPPOSITION TO TRAVIS...WHAT BECAME OF HIM?"
"COLONEL BOWIE WAS ILL IN THE DAYS BEFORE THE BATTLE.
"I CAN'T SAY FOR SURE, BUT HE WAS PROB'LY TOO WEAK TO FIGHT...
"...THOUGH IN THE END, I GUESS THAT DIDN'T MATTER NONE.
"MET THE SAME FATE AS MOST EVERYBODY ELSE, HEALTHY OR OTHERWISE.

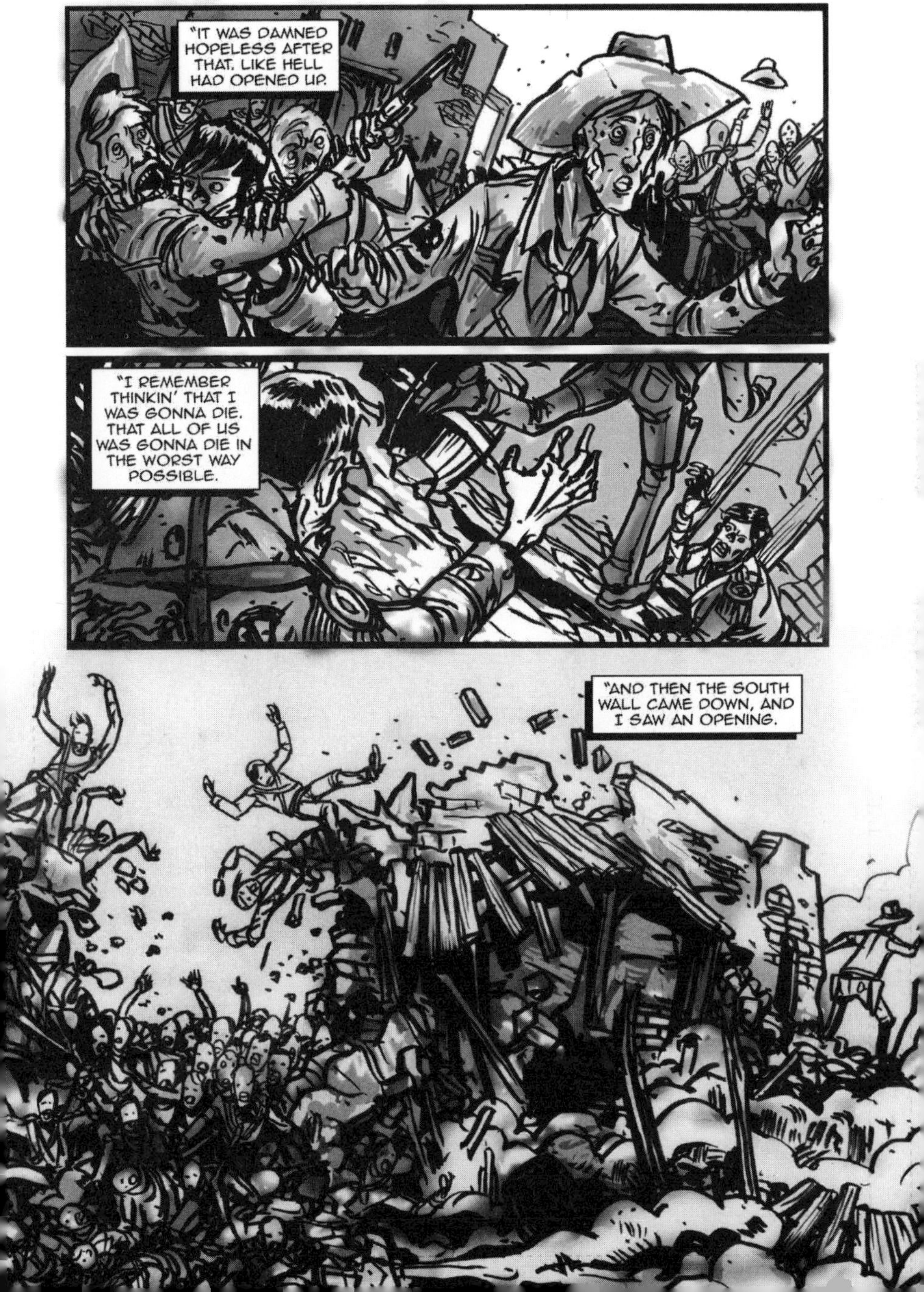
"IT WAS DAMNED HOPELESS AFTER THAT. LIKE HELL HAD OPENED UP.
"I REMEMBER THINKIN' THAT I WAS GONNA DIE. THAT ALL OF US WAS GONNA DIE IN THE WORST WAY POSSIBLE.
"AND THEN THE SOUTH WALL CAME DOWN, AND I SAW AN OPENING.

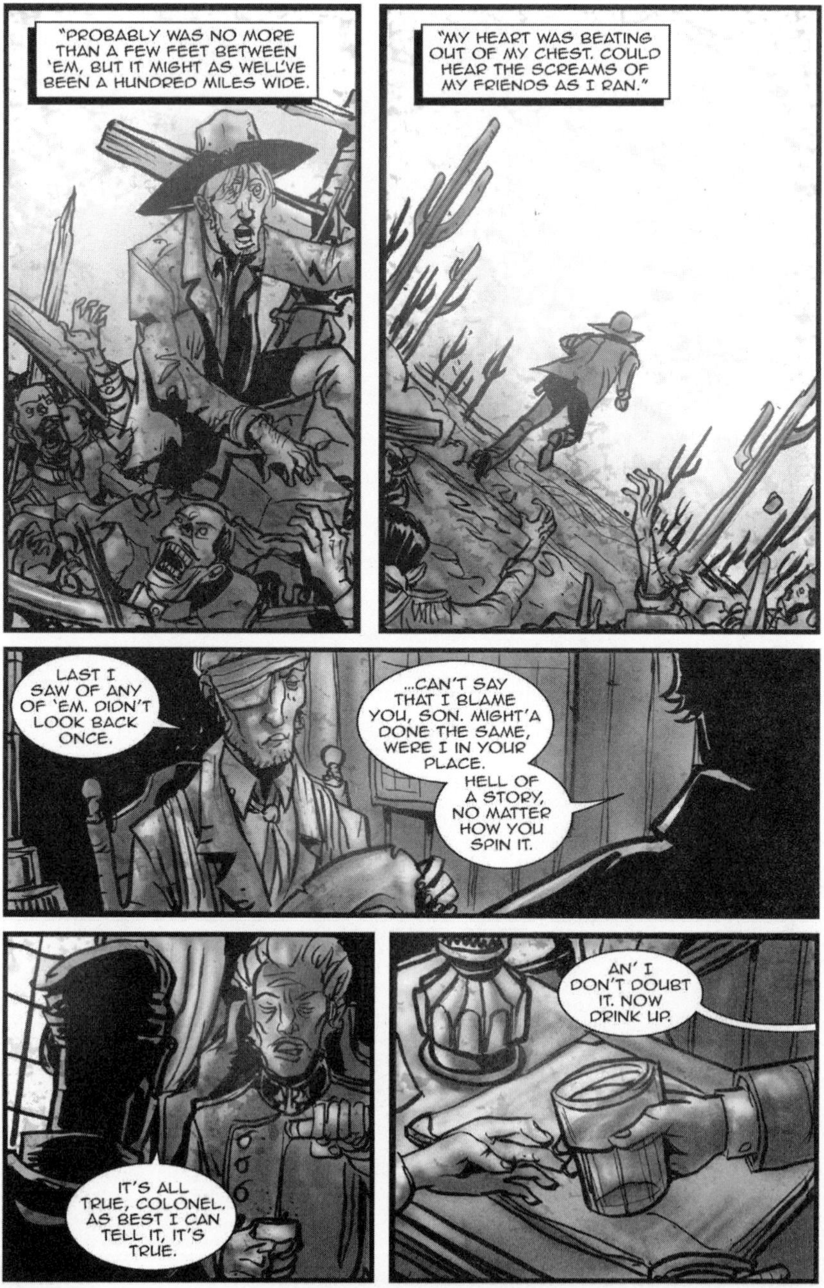
"PROBABLY WAS NO MORE THAN A FEW FEET BETWEEN 'EM, BUT IT MIGHT AS WELL'VE BEEN A HUNDRED MILES WIDE.
"MY HEART WAS BEATING OUT OF MY CHEST. COULD HEAR THE SCREAMS OF MY FRIENDS AS I RAN."
LAST I SAW OF ANY OF 'EM. DIDN'T LOOK BACK ONCE.
...CAN'T SAY THAT I BLAME YOU, SON. MIGHT'A DONE THE SAME, WERE I IN YOUR PLACE.
HELL OF A STORY, NO MATTER HOW YOU SPIN IT.
IT'S ALL TRUE, COLONEL. AS BEST I CAN TELL IT, IT'S TRUE.
AN' I DON'T DOUBT IT. NOW DRINK UP.

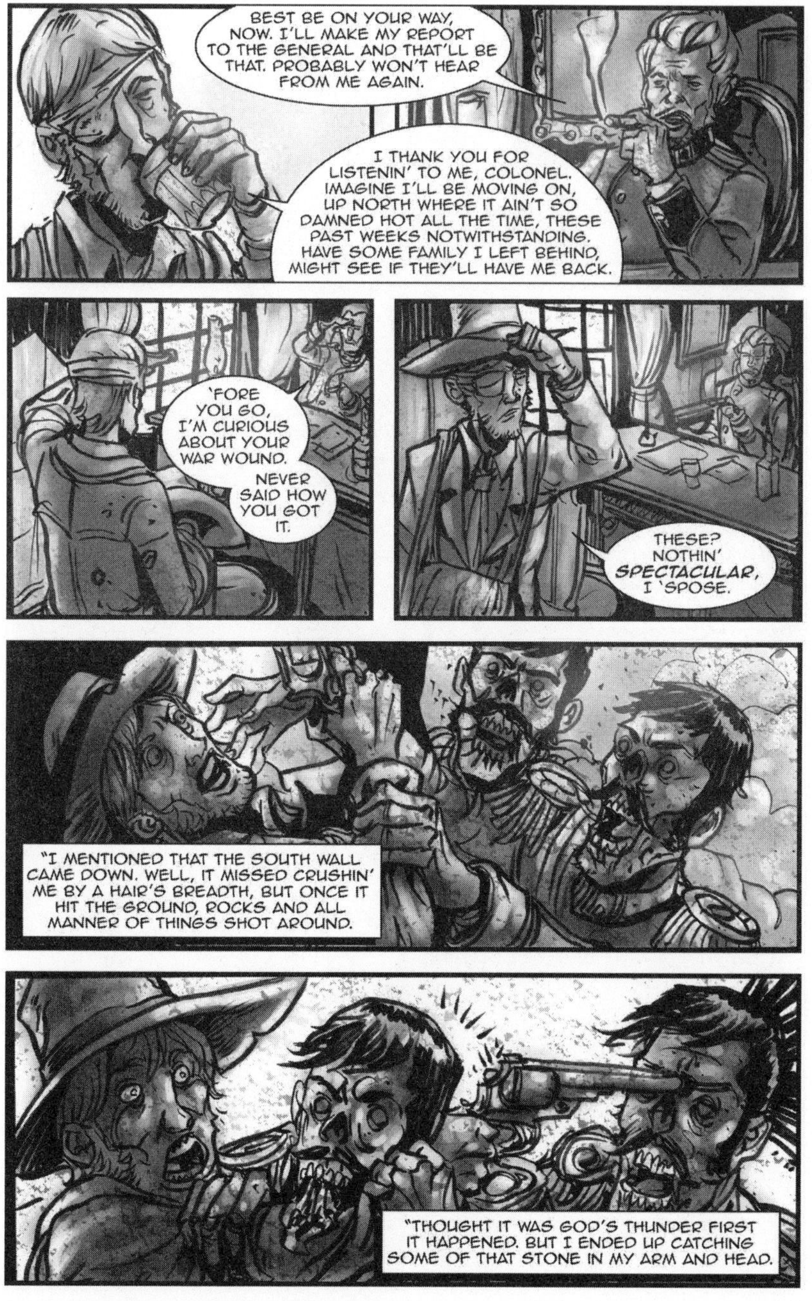
BEST BE ON YOUR WAY, NOW. I'LL MAKE MY REPORT TO THE GENERAL AND THAT'LL BE THAT. PROBABLY WON'T HEAR FROM ME AGAIN.
I THANK YOU FOR LISTENIN' TO ME, COLONEL. IMAGINE I'LL BE MOVING ON, UP NORTH WHERE IT AIN'T SO DAMNED HOT ALL THE TIME, THESE PAST WEEKS NOTWITHSTANDING. HAVE SOME FAMILY I LEFT BEHIND, MIGHT SEE IF THEY'LL HAVE ME BACK.
'FORE YOU GO, I'M CURIOUS ABOUT YOUR WAR WOUND.
NEVER SAID HOW YOU GOT IT.
THESE? NOTHIN' *SPECTACULAR*, I 'SPOSE.
"I MENTIONED THAT THE SOUTH WALL CAME DOWN. WELL, IT MISSED CRUSHIN' ME BY A HAIR'S BREADTH, BUT ONCE IT HIT THE GROUND, ROCKS AND ALL MANNER OF THINGS SHOT AROUND.
"THOUGHT IT WAS GOD'S THUNDER FIRST IT HAPPENED. BUT I ENDED UP CATCHING SOME OF THAT STONE IN MY ARM AND HEAD.

"HAD TO DIG IT OUT, MOST BY HAND.

"LOOKS WORSE THAN IT IS, THOUGH...

"...TRUTH BE TOLD."

Gen. Houston,

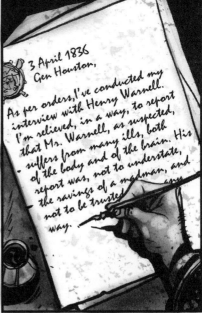

3 April 1836
Gen Houston,

As per orders, I've conducted my interview with Henry Warnell. I'm relieved, in a way, to report that Mr. Warnell, as suspected, suffers from many ills, both of the body and of the brain. His report was, not to understate, the ravings of a madman, and not to be trusted any way.

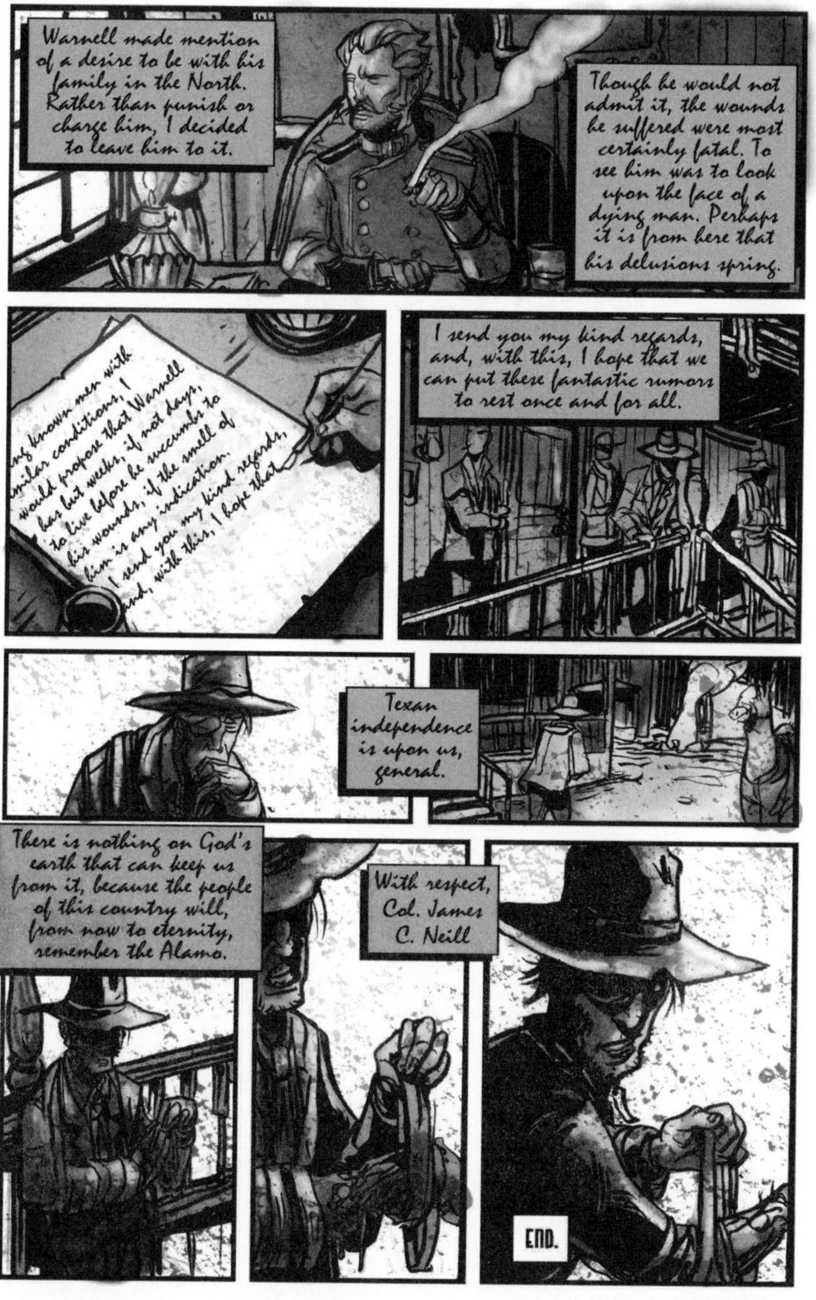
Warnell made mention of a desire to be with his family in the North. Rather than punish or charge him, I decided to leave him to it.
Though he would not admit it, the wounds he suffered were most certainly fatal. To see him was to look upon the face of a dying man. Perhaps it is from here that his delusions spring.
ng known men with milar conditions, I would propose that Warnell has but weeks, if not days, to live before he succumbs to his wounds, if the smell of him is any indication. I send you my kind regards, and, with this, I hope that
I send you my kind regards, and, with this, I hope that we can put these fantastic rumors to rest once and for all.
Texan independence is upon us, general.
There is nothing on God's earth that can keep us from it, because the people of this country will, from now to eternity, remember the Alamo.
With respect, Col. James C. Neill
END.

LEAVING THE DEAD BEHIND

STORY AND ART BY: RAFER ROBERTS

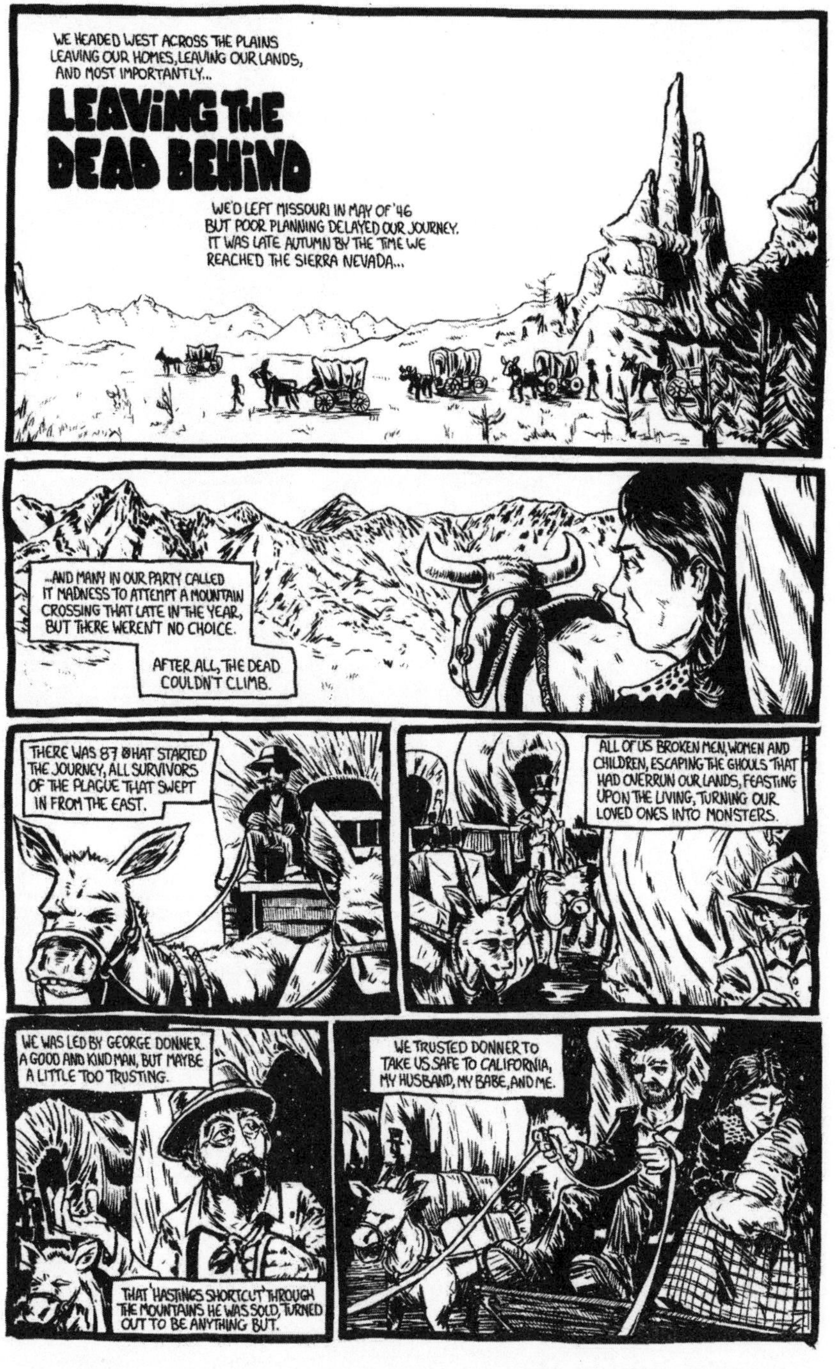
WE HEADED WEST ACROSS THE PLAINS LEAVING OUR HOMES, LEAVING OUR LANDS, AND MOST IMPORTANTLY...
LEAVING THE DEAD BEHIND
WE'D LEFT MISSOURI IN MAY OF '46 BUT POOR PLANNING DELAYED OUR JOURNEY. IT WAS LATE AUTUMN BY THE TIME WE REACHED THE SIERRA NEVADA...
...AND MANY IN OUR PARTY CALLED IT MADNESS TO ATTEMPT A MOUNTAIN CROSSING THAT LATE IN THE YEAR, BUT THERE WEREN'T NO CHOICE.
AFTER ALL, THE DEAD COULDN'T CLIMB.
THERE WAS 87 THAT STARTED THE JOURNEY, ALL SURVIVORS OF THE PLAGUE THAT SWEPT IN FROM THE EAST.
ALL OF US BROKEN MEN, WOMEN AND CHILDREN, ESCAPING THE GHOULS THAT HAD OVERRUN OUR LANDS, FEASTING UPON THE LIVING, TURNING OUR LOVED ONES INTO MONSTERS.
WE WAS LED BY GEORGE DONNER. A GOOD AND KIND MAN, BUT MAYBE A LITTLE TOO TRUSTING.
THAT 'HASTINGS SHORTCUT' THROUGH THE MOUNTAINS HE WAS SOLD, TURNED OUT TO BE ANYTHING BUT.
WE TRUSTED DONNER TO TAKE US SAFE TO CALIFORNIA, MY HUSBAND, MY BABE, AND ME.

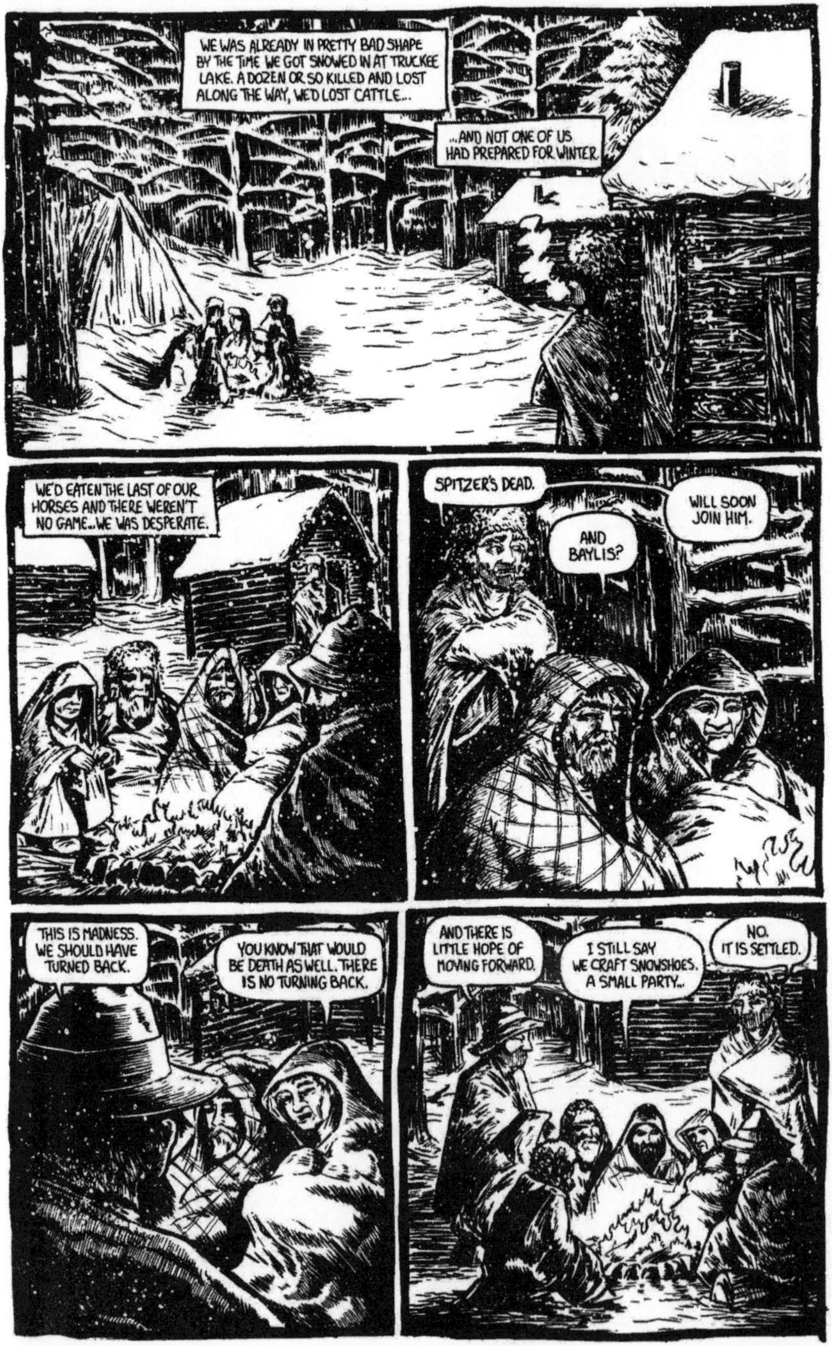
WE WAS ALREADY IN PRETTY BAD SHAPE BY THE TIME WE GOT SNOWED IN AT TRUCKEE LAKE. A DOZEN OR SO KILLED AND LOST ALONG THE WAY, WE'D LOST CATTLE...
...AND NOT ONE OF US HAD PREPARED FOR WINTER.
WE'D EATEN THE LAST OF OUR HORSES AND THERE WEREN'T NO GAME...WE WAS DESPERATE.
SPITZER'S DEAD.
AND BAYLIS?
WILL SOON JOIN HIM.
THIS IS MADNESS. WE SHOULD HAVE TURNED BACK.
YOU KNOW THAT WOULD BE DEATH AS WELL. THERE IS NO TURNING BACK.
AND THERE IS LITTLE HOPE OF MOVING FORWARD.
I STILL SAY WE CRAFT SNOWSHOES. A SMALL PARTY...
NO. IT IS SETTLED.

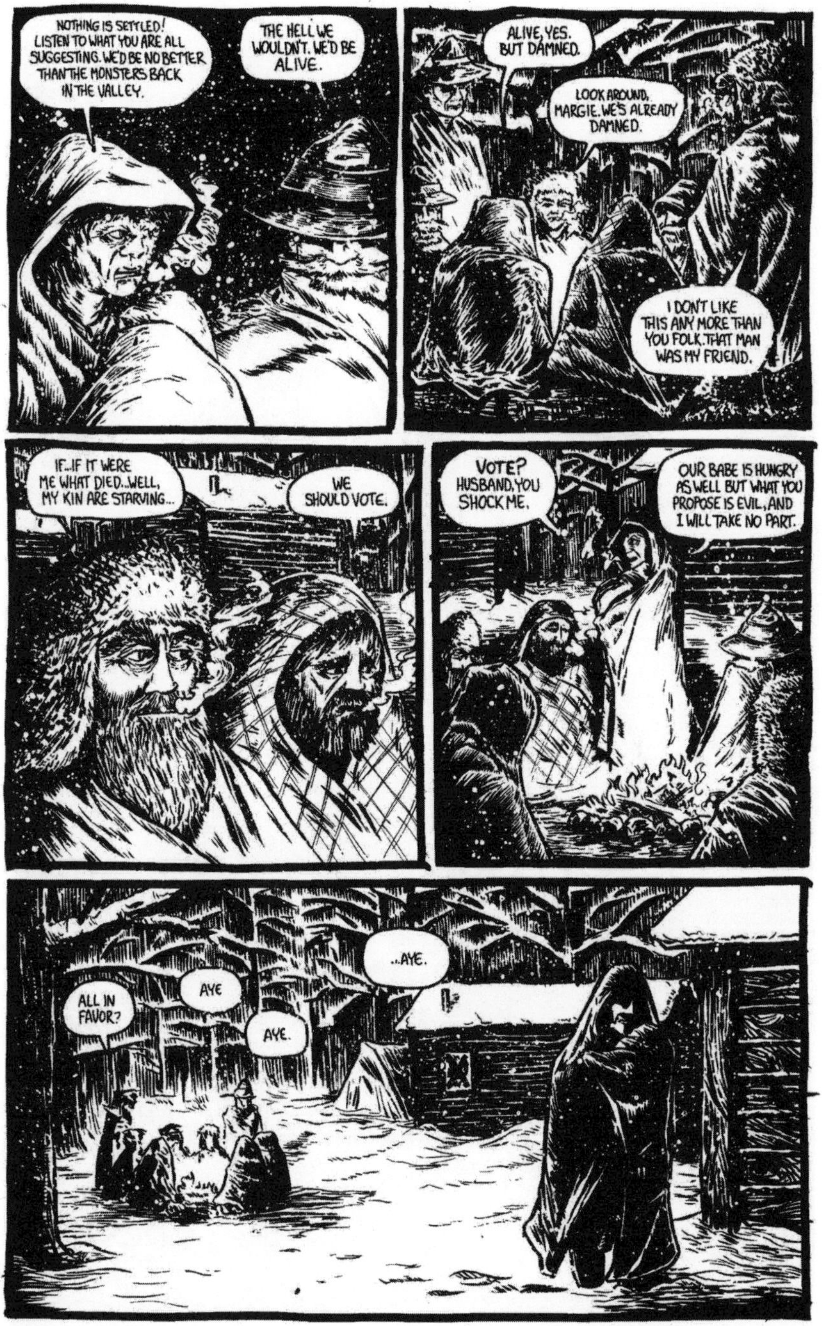
NOTHING IS SETTLED! LISTEN TO WHAT YOU ARE ALL SUGGESTING. WE'D BE NO BETTER THAN THE MONSTERS BACK IN THE VALLEY.
THE HELL WE WOULDN'T. WE'D BE ALIVE.
ALIVE, YES. BUT DAMNED.
LOOK AROUND, MARGIE. WE'S ALREADY DAMNED.
I DON'T LIKE THIS ANY MORE THAN YOU FOLK. THAT MAN WAS MY FRIEND.
IF...IF IT WERE ME WHAT DIED...WELL, MY KIN ARE STARVING...
WE SHOULD VOTE.
VOTE? HUSBAND, YOU SHOCK ME.
OUR BABE IS HUNGRY AS WELL BUT WHAT YOU PROPOSE IS EVIL, AND I WILL TAKE NO PART.
ALL IN FAVOR?
AYE
AYE.
...AYE.

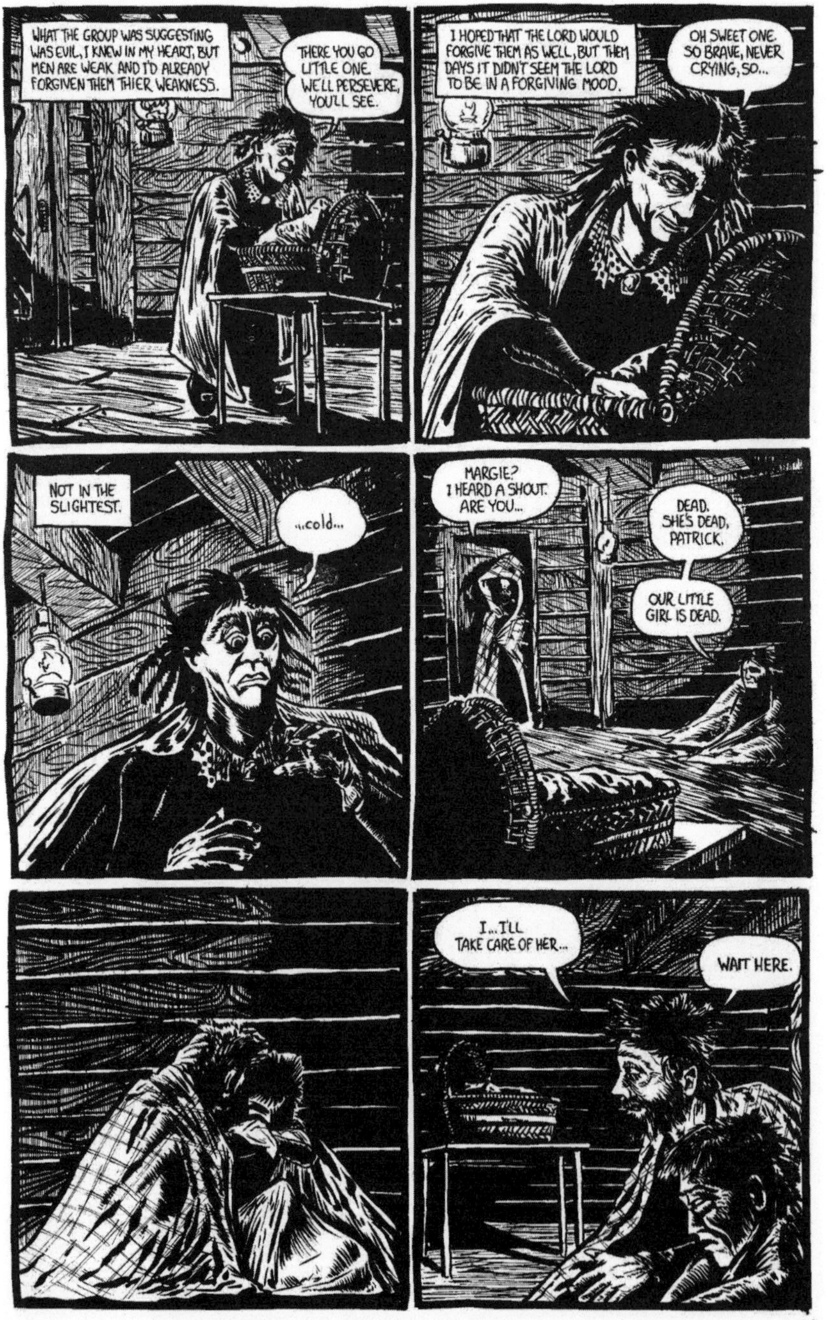
WHAT THE GROUP WAS SUGGESTING WAS EVIL, I KNEW IN MY HEART, BUT MEN ARE WEAK AND I'D ALREADY FORGIVEN THEM THIER WEAKNESS.
THERE YOU GO LITTLE ONE. WE'LL PERSEVERE, YOU'LL SEE.
I HOPED THAT THE LORD WOULD FORGIVE THEM AS WELL, BUT THEM DAYS IT DIDN'T SEEM THE LORD TO BE IN A FORGIVING MOOD.
OH SWEET ONE. SO BRAVE, NEVER CRYING, SO...
NOT IN THE SLIGHTEST.
...cold...
MARGIE? I HEARD A SHOUT. ARE YOU...
DEAD. SHE'S DEAD, PATRICK.
OUR LITTLE GIRL IS DEAD.
I...I'LL TAKE CARE OF HER...
WAIT HERE.

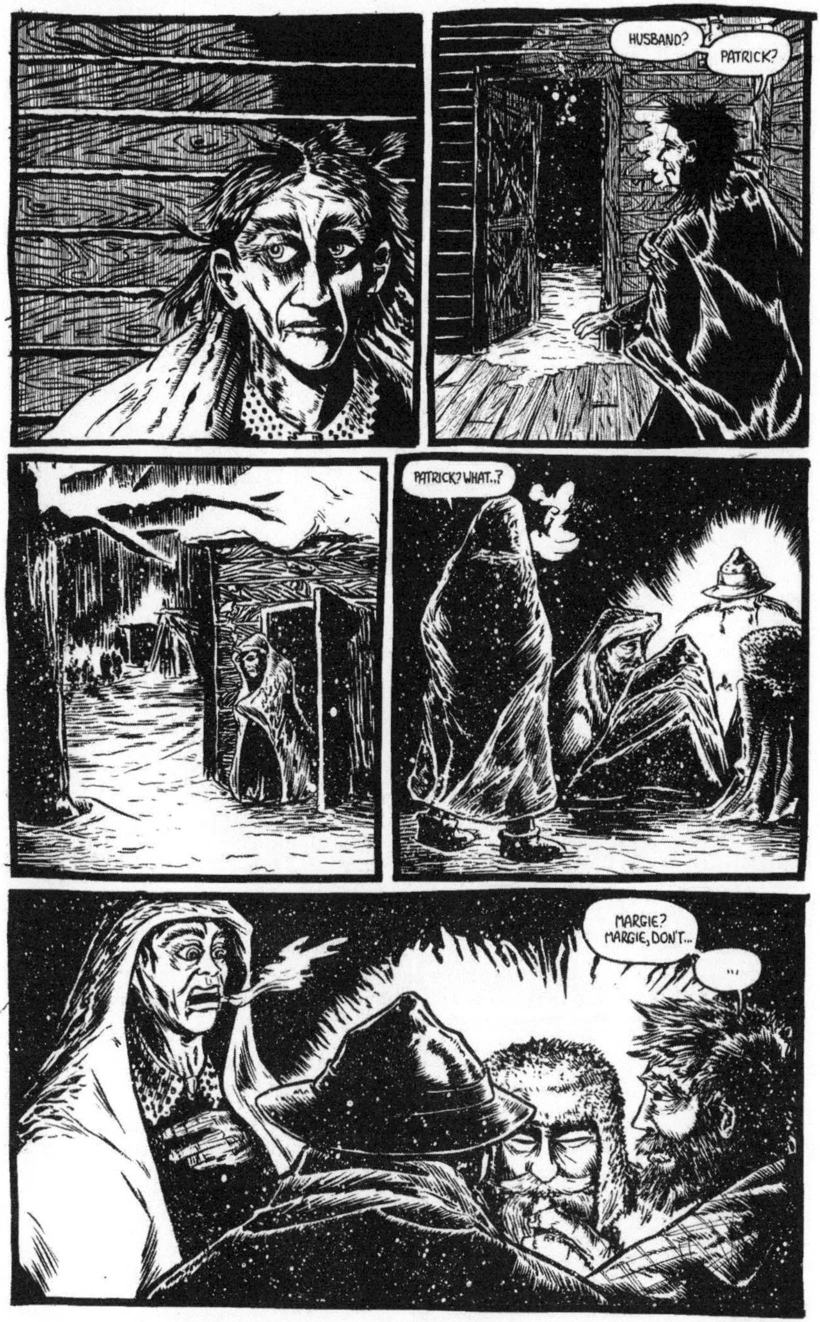
HUSBAND?
PATRICK?
PATRICK? WHAT..?
MARGIE? MARGIE, DON'T...
...

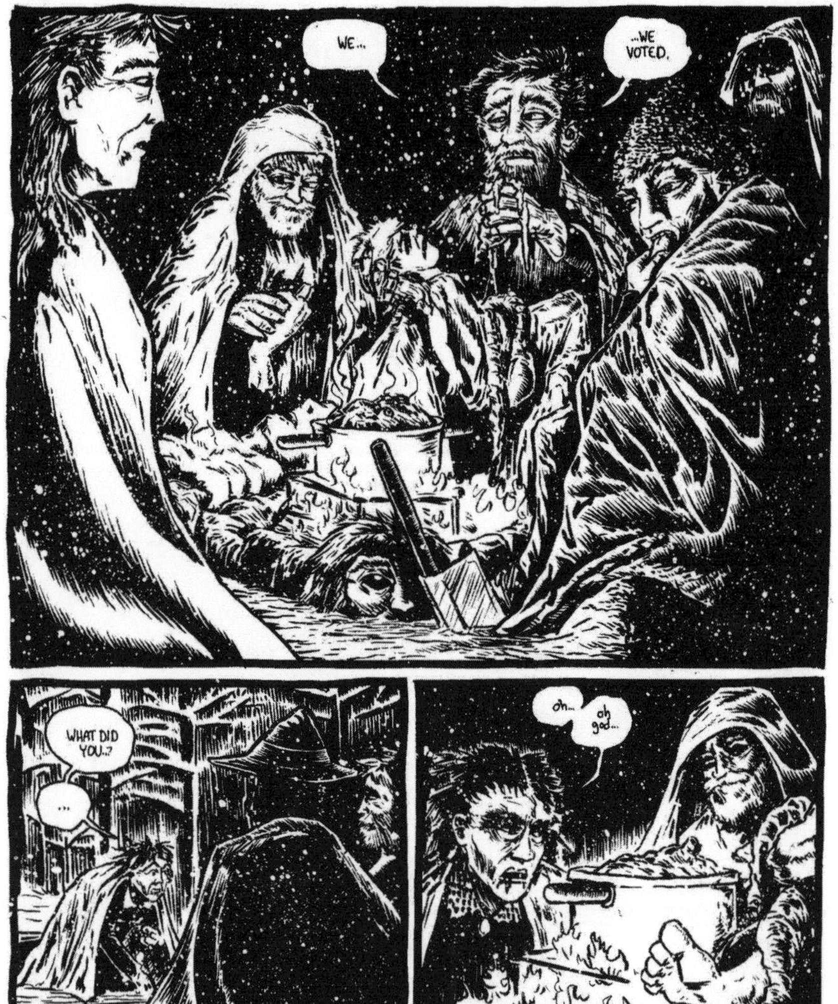
WE...
...WE VOTED.
WHAT DID YOU..?
...
oh... oh god...

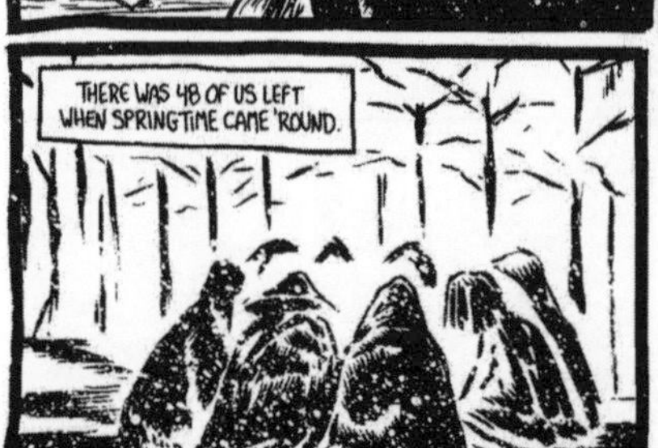
THERE WAS 48 OF US LEFT WHEN SPRINGTIME CAME 'ROUND.

SOME CONTINUED WEST TO CALIFORNIA, SOME STAYED IN THE MOUNTAINS ALL FULL OF SHAME.

I WENT BACK EAST, BACK TO THE LAND OF THE DEAD, THE HOME OF THE FLESH EATING DAMNED...

...BACK TO WHERE I NOW BELONGED.

HARRIET

STORY BY:
TYLER JAMES

ART BY:
STEVE WILLHITE

GREYSCALES AND LETTERS BY:
JEFF McCOMSEY

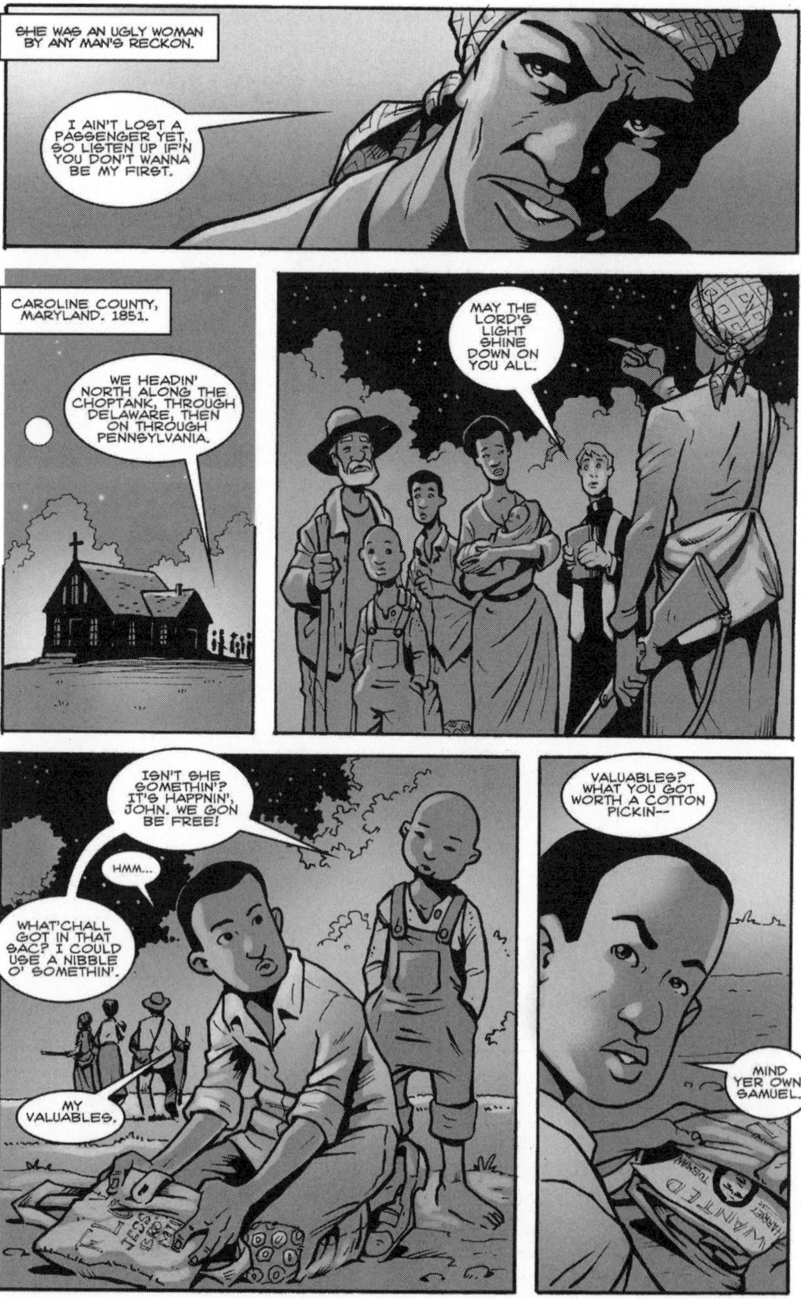
SHE WAS AN UGLY WOMAN BY ANY MAN'S RECKON.
I AIN'T LOST A PASSENGER YET, SO LISTEN UP IF'N YOU DON'T WANNA BE MY FIRST.
CAROLINE COUNTY, MARYLAND. 1851.
WE HEADIN' NORTH ALONG THE CHOPTANK, THROUGH DELAWARE, THEN ON THROUGH PENNSYLVANIA.
MAY THE LORD'S LIGHT SHINE DOWN ON YOU ALL.
ISN'T SHE SOMETHIN'? IT'S HAPPNIN', JOHN. WE GON BE FREE!
HMM...
WHAT'CHALL GOT IN THAT SAC? I COULD USE A NIBBLE O' SOMETHIN'.
MY VALUABLES.
VALUABLES? WHAT YOU GOT WORTH A COTTON PICKIN--
MIND YER OWN, SAMUEL.
WANTED

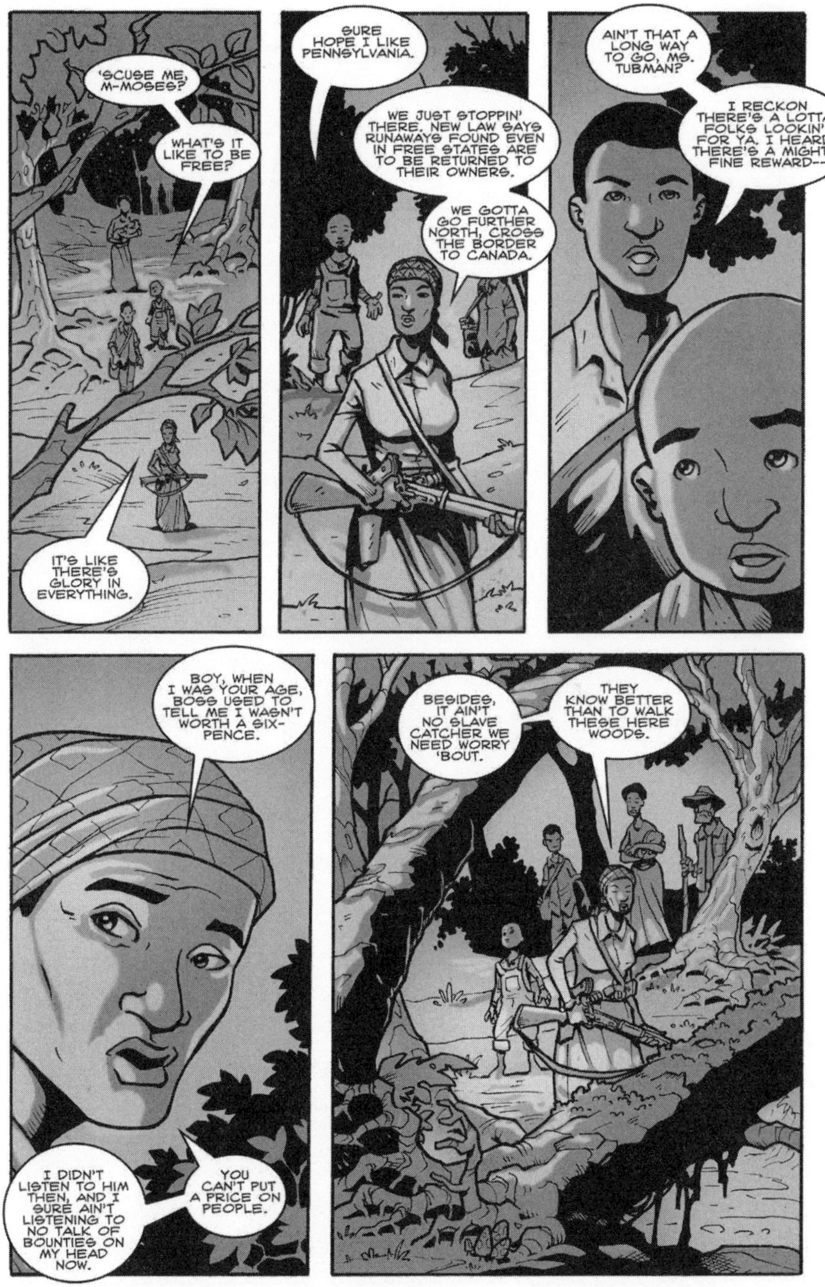
'SCUSE ME, M-MOSES?
WHAT'S IT LIKE TO BE FREE?
IT'S LIKE THERE'S GLORY IN EVERYTHING.
SURE HOPE I LIKE PENNSYLVANIA.
WE JUST STOPPIN' THERE. NEW LAW SAYS RUNAWAYS FOUND EVEN IN FREE STATES ARE TO BE RETURNED TO THEIR OWNERS.
WE GOTTA GO FURTHER NORTH, CROSS THE BORDER TO CANADA.
AIN'T THAT A LONG WAY TO GO, MS. TUBMAN?
I RECKON THERE'S A LOTTA FOLKS LOOKIN' FOR YA. I HEARD THERE'S A MIGHTY FINE REWARD--
BOY, WHEN I WAS YOUR AGE, BOSS USED TO TELL ME I WASN'T WORTH A SIX-PENCE.
YOU CAN'T PUT A PRICE ON PEOPLE.
I DIDN'T LISTEN TO HIM THEN, AND I SURE AIN'T LISTENING TO NO TALK OF BOUNTIES ON MY HEAD NOW.
BESIDES, IT AIN'T NO SLAVE CATCHER WE NEED WORRY 'BOUT.
THEY KNOW BETTER THAN TO WALK THESE HERE WOODS.

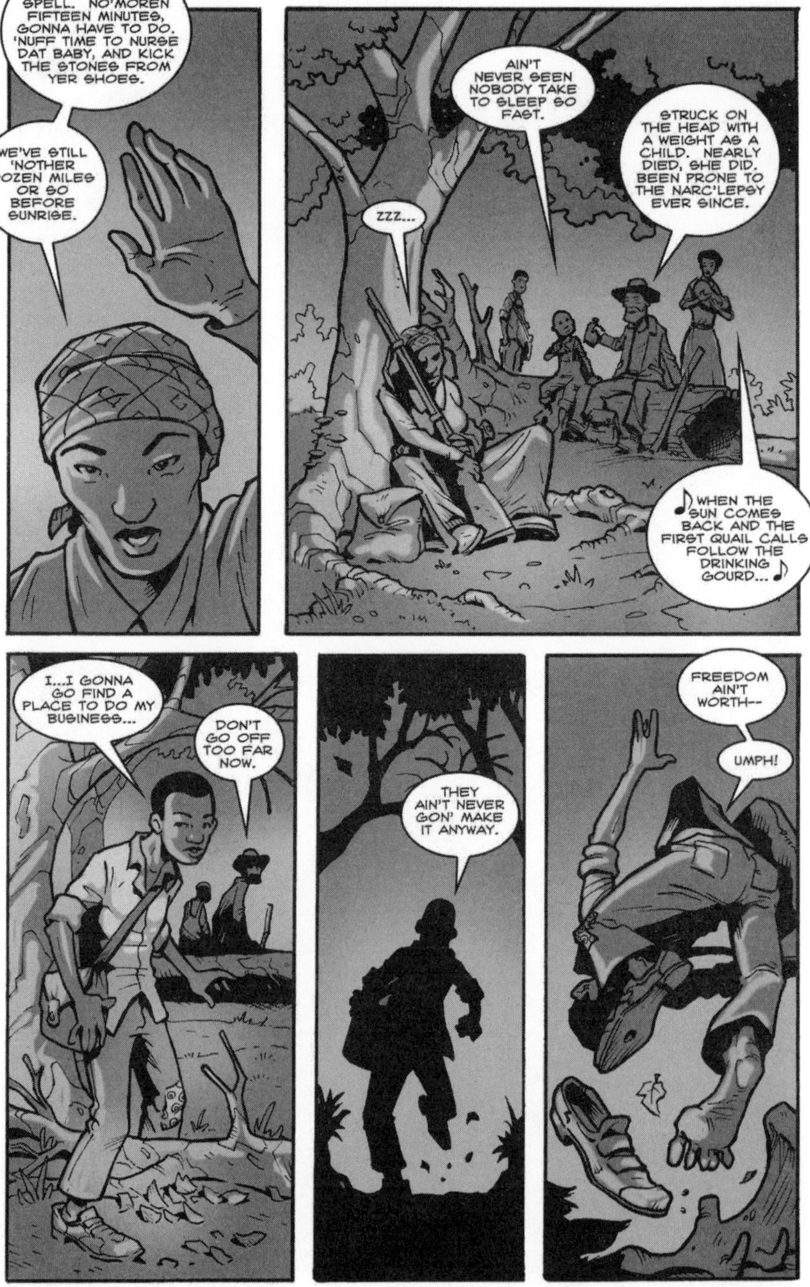
WE'LL REST HERE A SPELL. NO'MOREN FIFTEEN MINUTES, GONNA HAVE TO DO. 'NUFF TIME TO NURSE DAT BABY, AND KICK THE STONES FROM YER SHOES.
WE'VE STILL 'NOTHER DOZEN MILES OR SO BEFORE SUNRISE.
AIN'T NEVER SEEN NOBODY TAKE TO SLEEP SO FAST.
STRUCK ON THE HEAD WITH A WEIGHT AS A CHILD. NEARLY DIED, SHE DID. BEEN PRONE TO THE NARC'LEPSY EVER SINCE.
ZZZ...
♪WHEN THE SUN COMES BACK AND THE FIRST QUAIL CALLS FOLLOW THE DRINKING GOURD...♪
I...I GONNA GO FIND A PLACE TO DO MY BUSINESS...
DON'T GO OFF TOO FAR NOW.
THEY AIN'T NEVER GON' MAKE IT ANYWAY.
FREEDOM AIN'T WORTH--
UMPH!

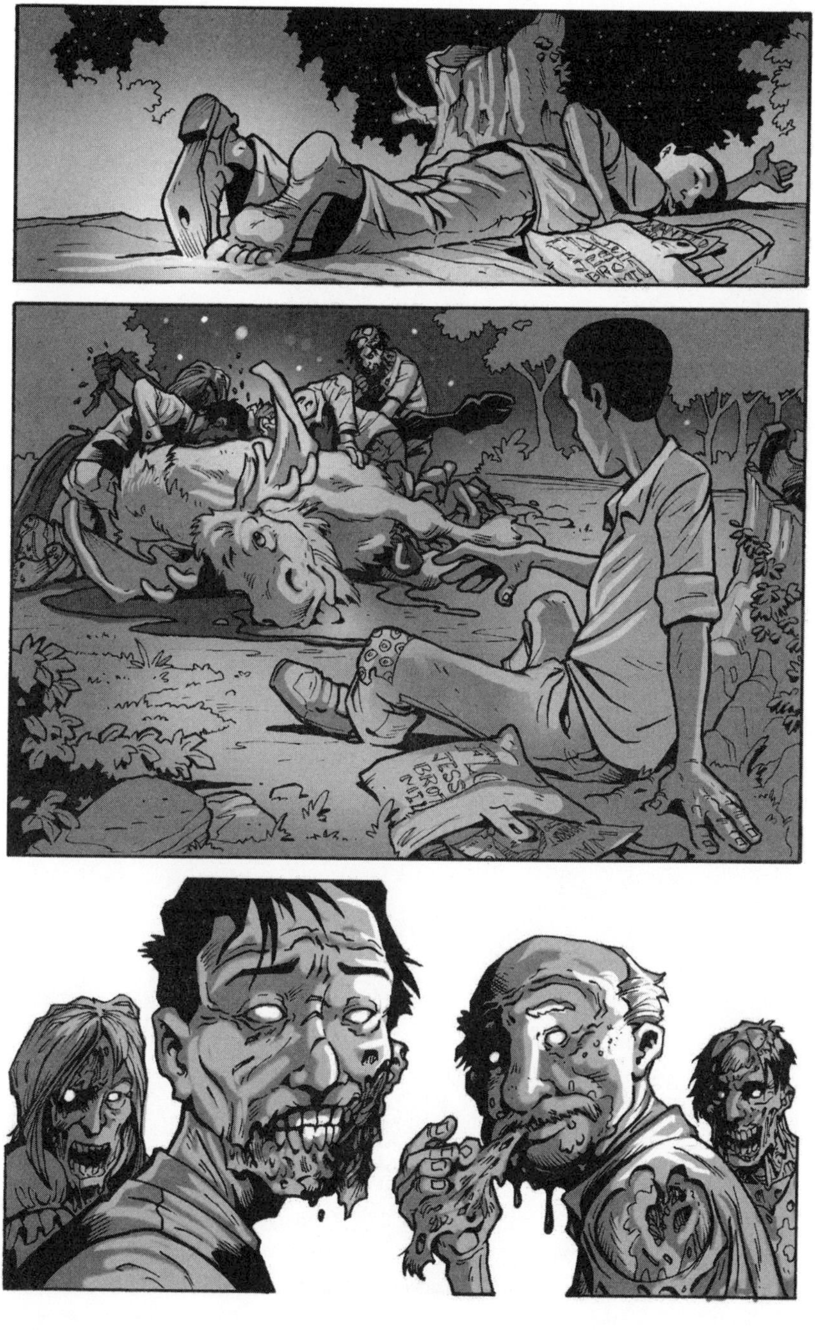

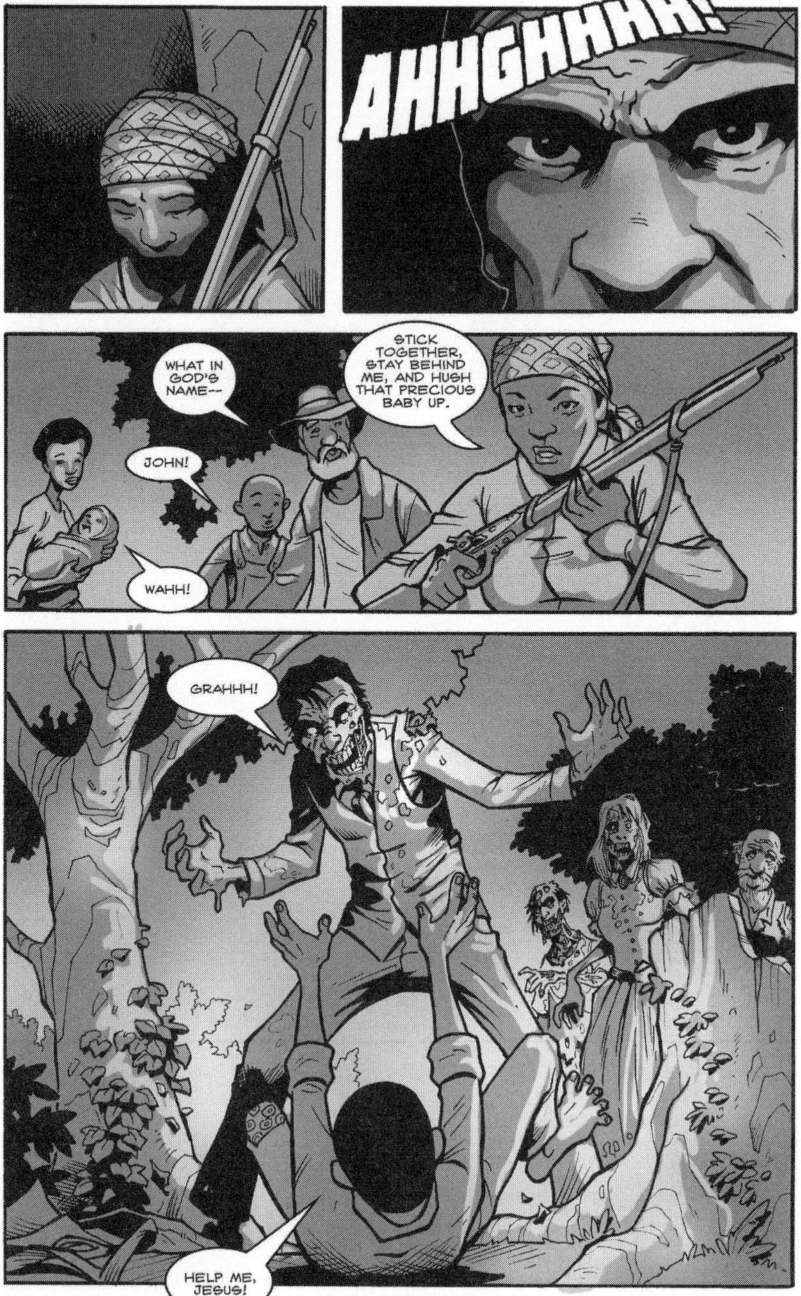
AHHGHHHH!
WHAT IN GOD'S NAME--
STICK TOGETHER, STAY BEHIND ME, AND HUSH THAT PRECIOUS BABY UP.
JOHN!
WAHH!
GRAHHH!
HELP ME, JESUS!

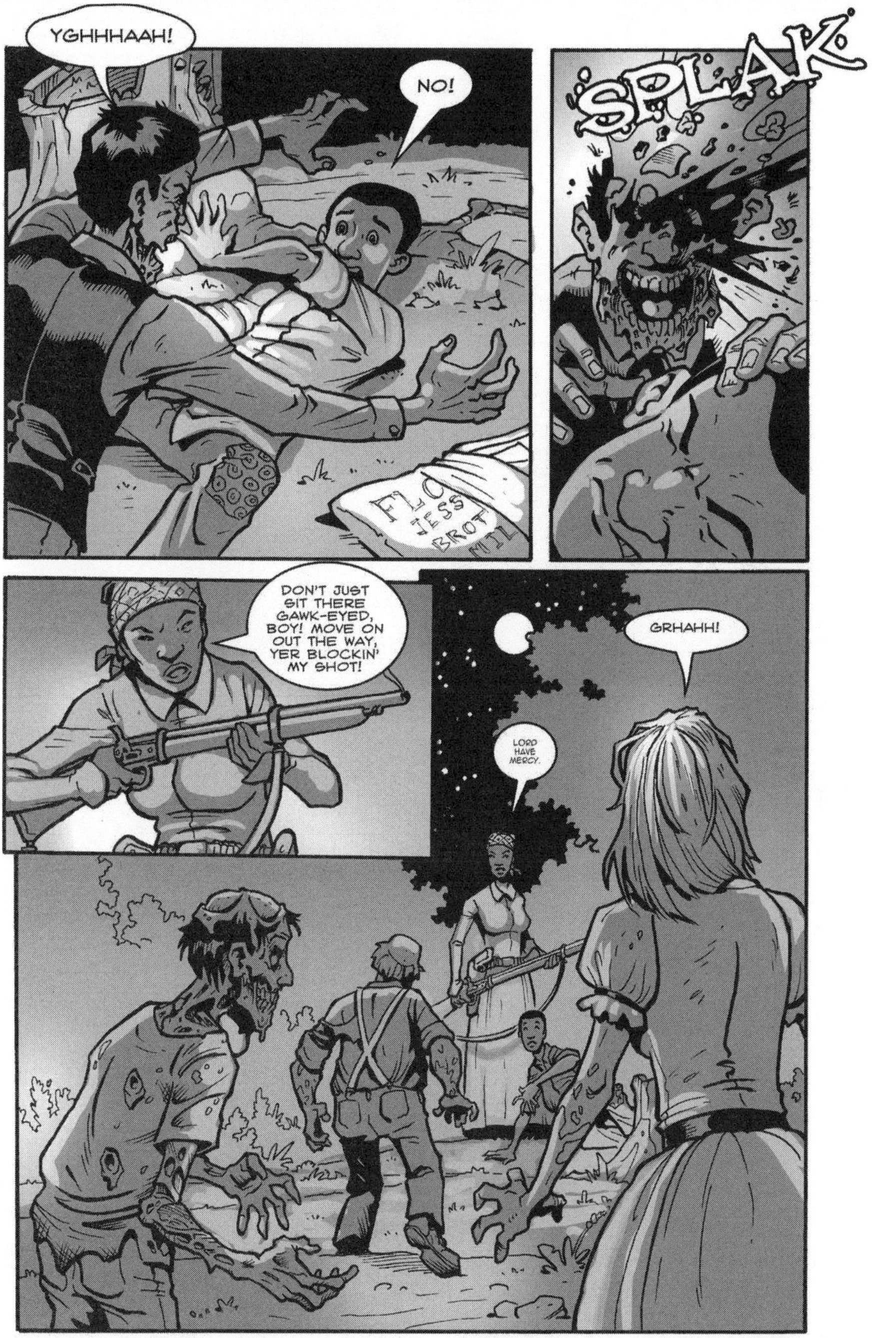
YGHHHAAH!
NO!
SPLAK
DON'T JUST SIT THERE GAWK-EYED, BOY! MOVE ON OUT THE WAY, YER BLOCKIN' MY SHOT!
GRHAHH!
LORD HAVE MERCY.

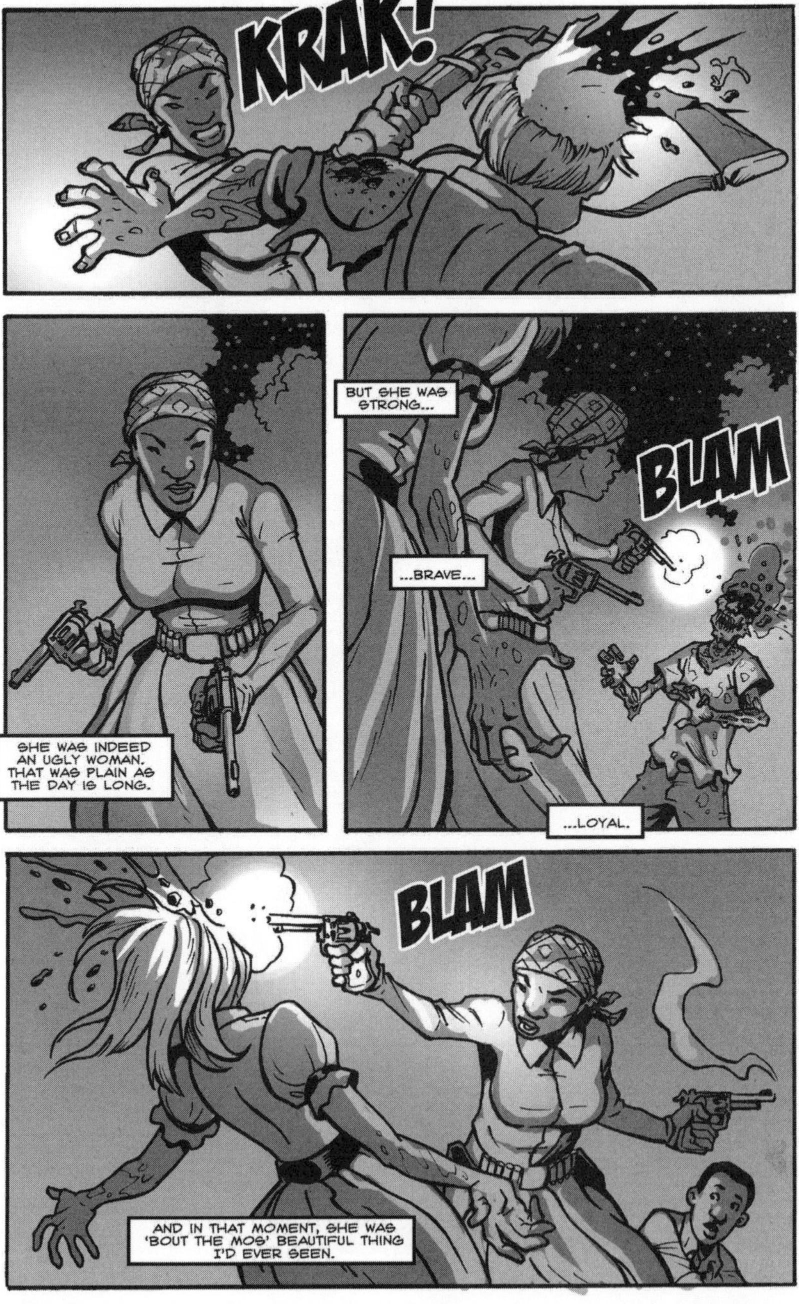
KRAK!
SHE WAS INDEED AN UGLY WOMAN. THAT WAS PLAIN AS THE DAY IS LONG.
BUT SHE WAS STRONG...
...BRAVE...
BLAM
...LOYAL.
BLAM
AND IN THAT MOMENT, SHE WAS 'BOUT THE MOS' BEAUTIFUL THING I'D EVER SEEN.

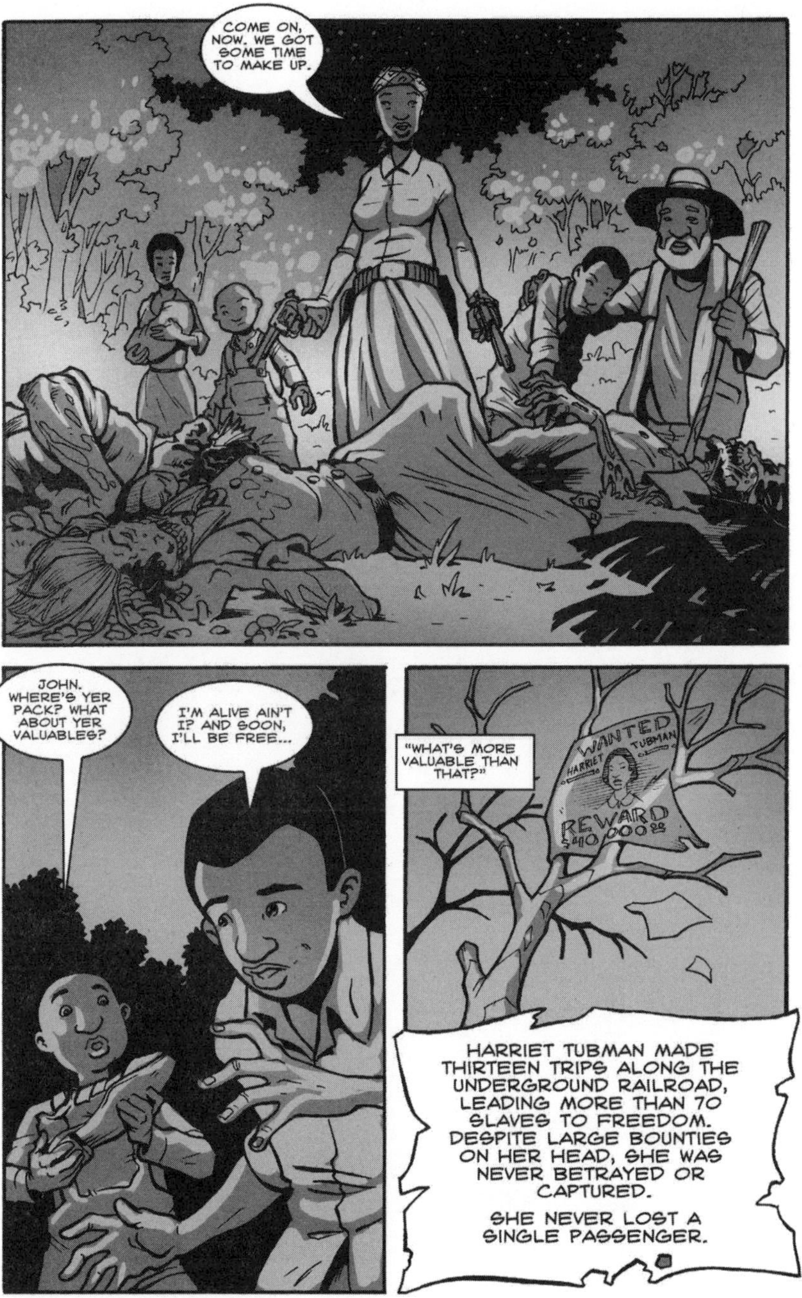
COME ON, NOW. WE GOT SOME TIME TO MAKE UP.
JOHN. WHERE'S YER PACK? WHAT ABOUT YER VALUABLES?
I'M ALIVE AIN'T I? AND SOON, I'LL BE FREE...
"WHAT'S MORE VALUABLE THAN THAT?"
WANTED
HARRIET TUBMAN
REWARD
HARRIET TUBMAN MADE THIRTEEN TRIPS ALONG THE UNDERGROUND RAILROAD, LEADING MORE THAN 70 SLAVES TO FREEDOM. DESPITE LARGE BOUNTIES ON HER HEAD, SHE WAS NEVER BETRAYED OR CAPTURED.
SHE NEVER LOST A SINGLE PASSENGER.

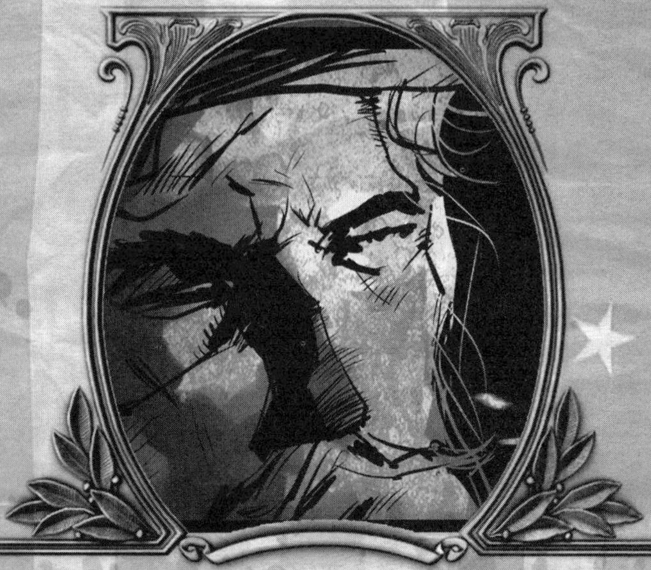

UNSPOKEN FAITH

STORY AND ART BY: PEEBO MONDIA

IN LOVING MEMORY OF LYDIA JURILLA SMITH
1942–2012

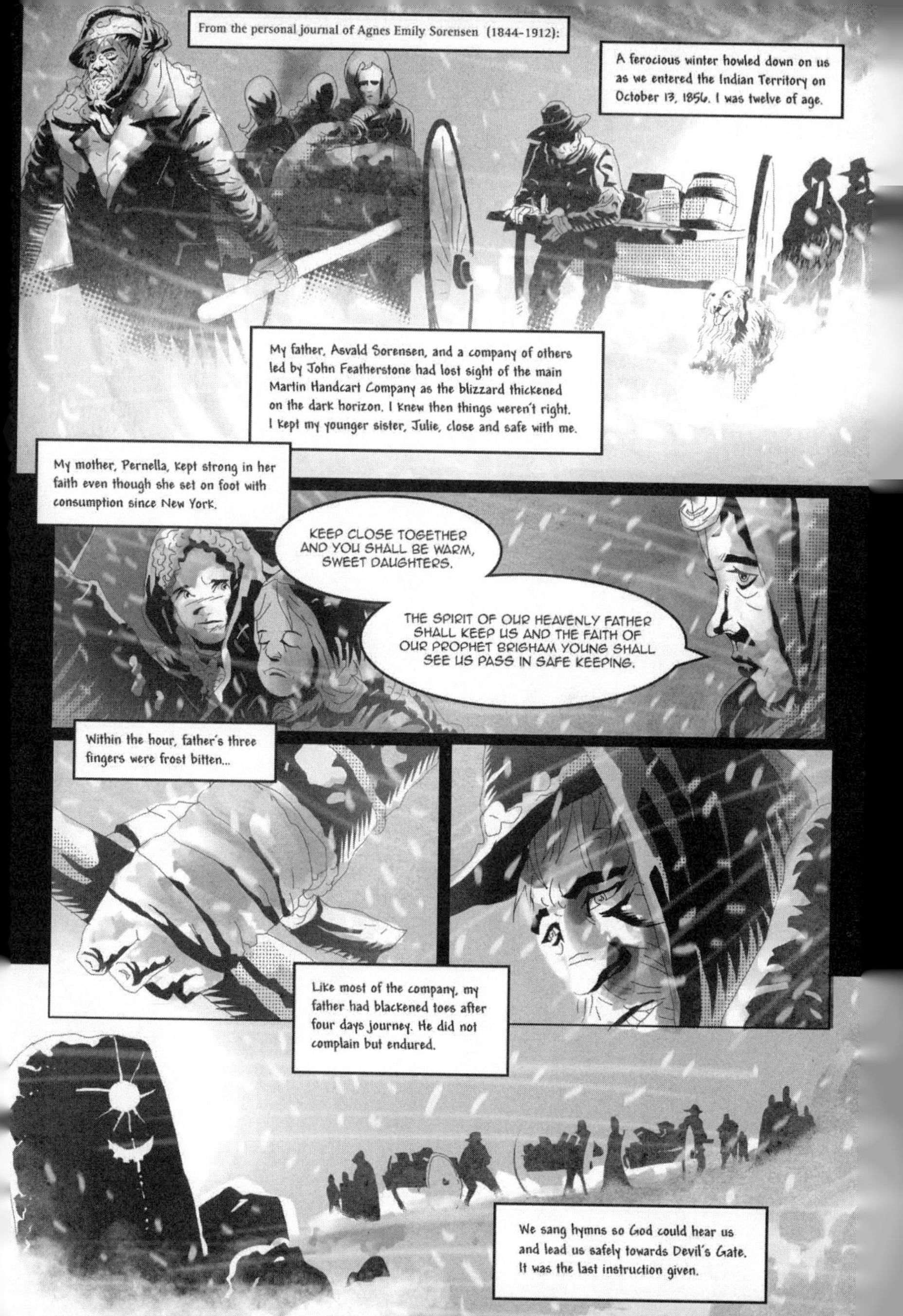
From the personal journal of Agnes Emily Sorensen (1844-1912):
A ferocious winter howled down on us as we entered the Indian Territory on October 13, 1856. I was twelve of age.
My father, Asvald Sorensen, and a company of others led by John Featherstone had lost sight of the main Martin Handcart Company as the blizzard thickened on the dark horizon. I knew then things weren't right. I kept my younger sister, Julie, close and safe with me.
My mother, Pernella, kept strong in her faith even though she set on foot with consumption since New York.
KEEP CLOSE TOGETHER AND YOU SHALL BE WARM, SWEET DAUGHTERS.
THE SPIRIT OF OUR HEAVENLY FATHER SHALL KEEP US AND THE FAITH OF OUR PROPHET BRIGHAM YOUNG SHALL SEE US PASS IN SAFE KEEPING.
Within the hour, father's three fingers were frost bitten...
Like most of the company, my father had blackened toes after four days journey. He did not complain but endured.
We sang hymns so God could hear us and lead us safely towards Devil's Gate. It was the last instruction given.

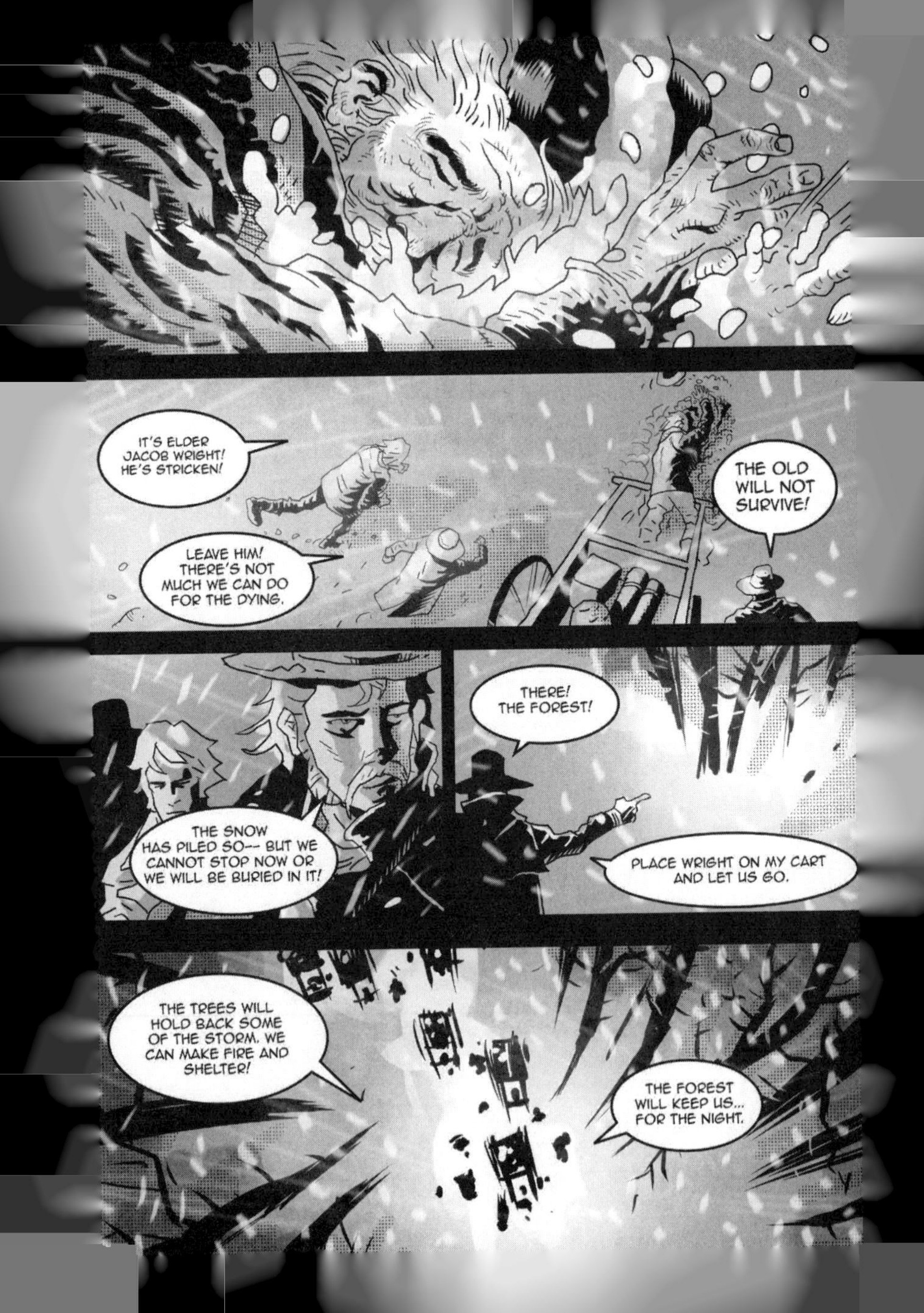
IT'S ELDER JACOB WRIGHT! HE'S STRICKEN!
THE OLD WILL NOT SURVIVE!
LEAVE HIM! THERE'S NOT MUCH WE CAN DO FOR THE DYING.
THERE! THE FOREST!
THE SNOW HAS PILED SO-- BUT WE CANNOT STOP NOW OR WE WILL BE BURIED IN IT!
PLACE WRIGHT ON MY CART AND LET US GO.
THE TREES WILL HOLD BACK SOME OF THE STORM. WE CAN MAKE FIRE AND SHELTER!
THE FOREST WILL KEEP US... FOR THE NIGHT.

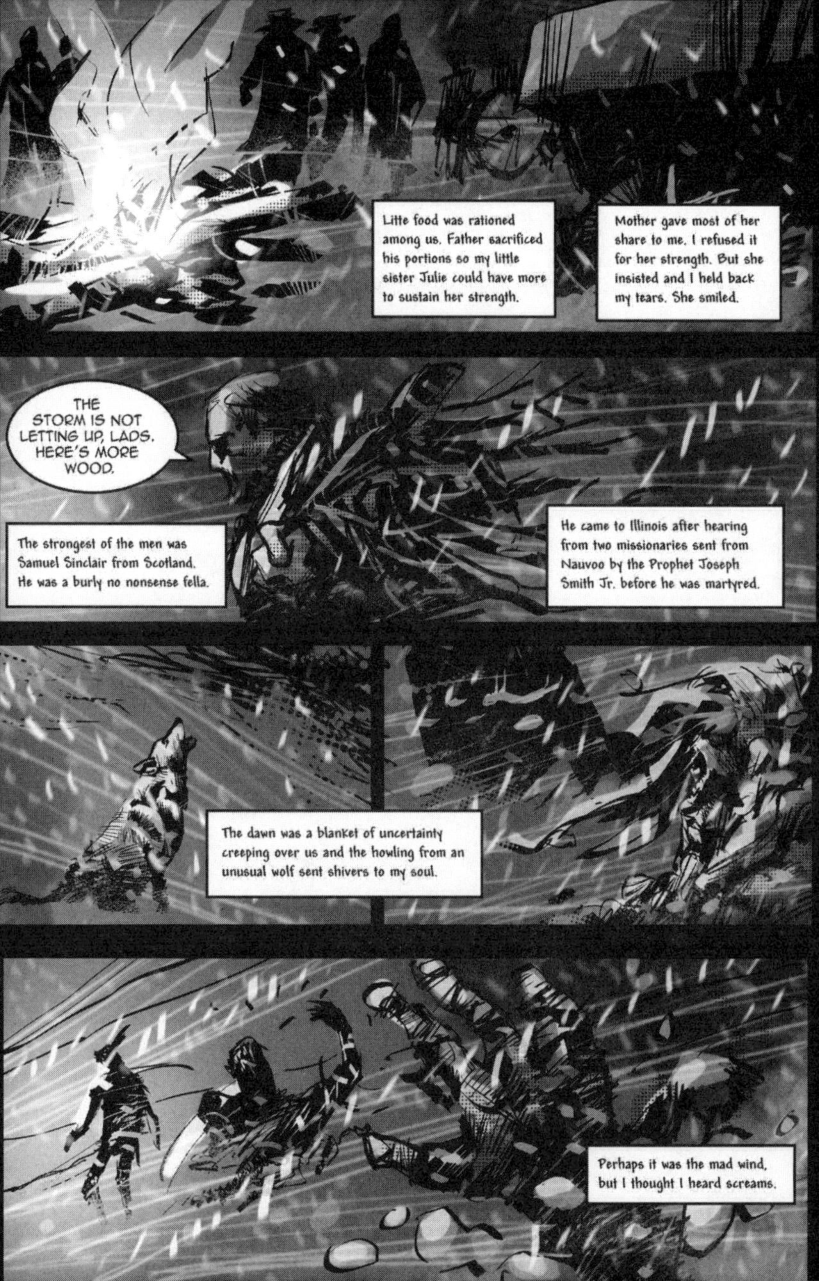

Litte food was rationed among us. Father sacrificed his portions so my little sister Julie could have more to sustain her strength.
Mother gave most of her share to me. I refused it for her strength. But she insisted and I held back my tears. She smiled.
THE STORM IS NOT LETTING UP, LADS. HERE'S MORE WOOD.
The strongest of the men was Samuel Sinclair from Scotland. He was a burly no nonsense fella.
He came to Illinois after hearing from two missionaries sent from Nauvoo by the Prophet Joseph Smith Jr. before he was martyred.
The dawn was a blanket of uncertainty creeping over us and the howling from an unusual wolf sent shivers to my soul.
Perhaps it was the mad wind, but I thought I heard screams.

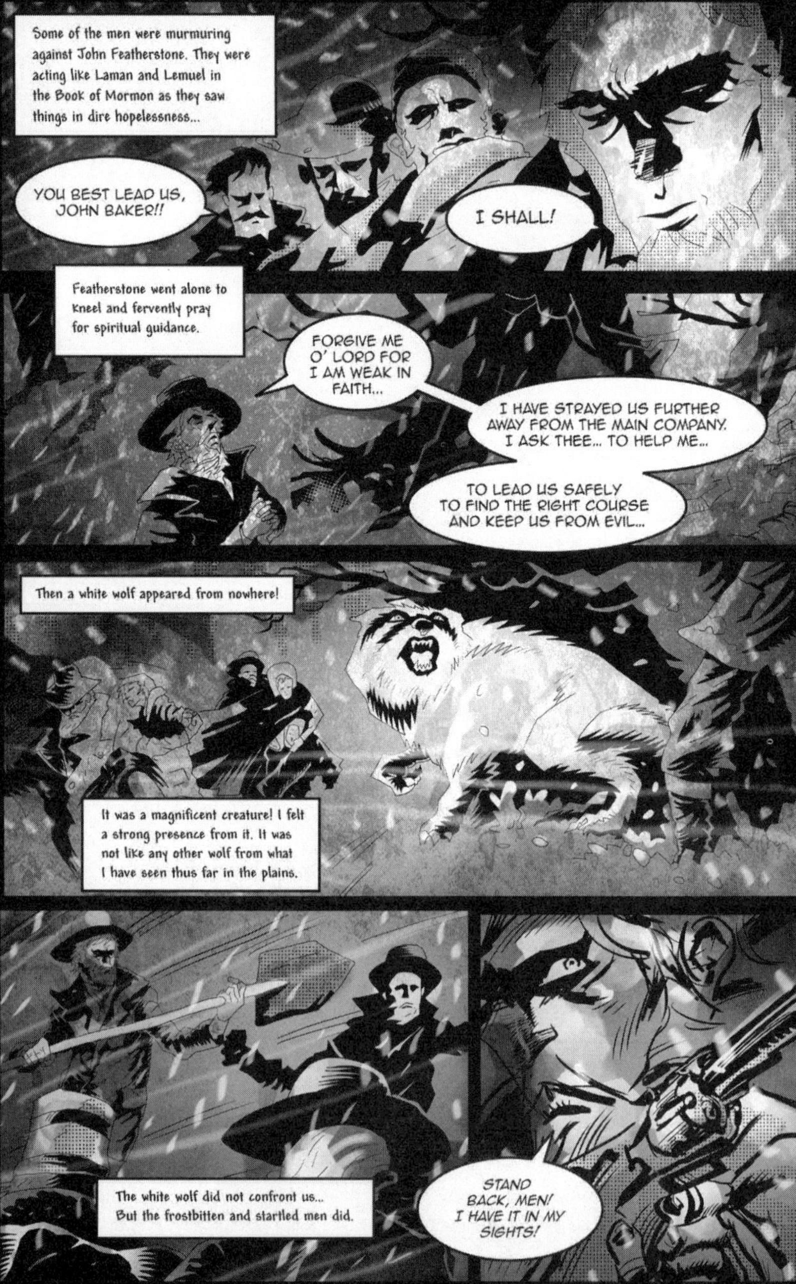
Some of the men were murmuring against John Featherstone. They were acting like Laman and Lemuel in the Book of Mormon as they saw things in dire hopelessness...
YOU BEST LEAD US, JOHN BAKER!!
I SHALL!
Featherstone went alone to kneel and fervently pray for spiritual guidance.
FORGIVE ME O' LORD FOR I AM WEAK IN FAITH...
I HAVE STRAYED US FURTHER AWAY FROM THE MAIN COMPANY. I ASK THEE... TO HELP ME...
TO LEAD US SAFELY TO FIND THE RIGHT COURSE AND KEEP US FROM EVIL...
Then a white wolf appeared from nowhere!
It was a magnificent creature! I felt a strong presence from it. It was not like any other wolf from what I have seen thus far in the plains.
The white wolf did not confront us... But the frostbitten and startled men did.
STAND BACK, MEN! I HAVE IT IN MY SIGHTS!

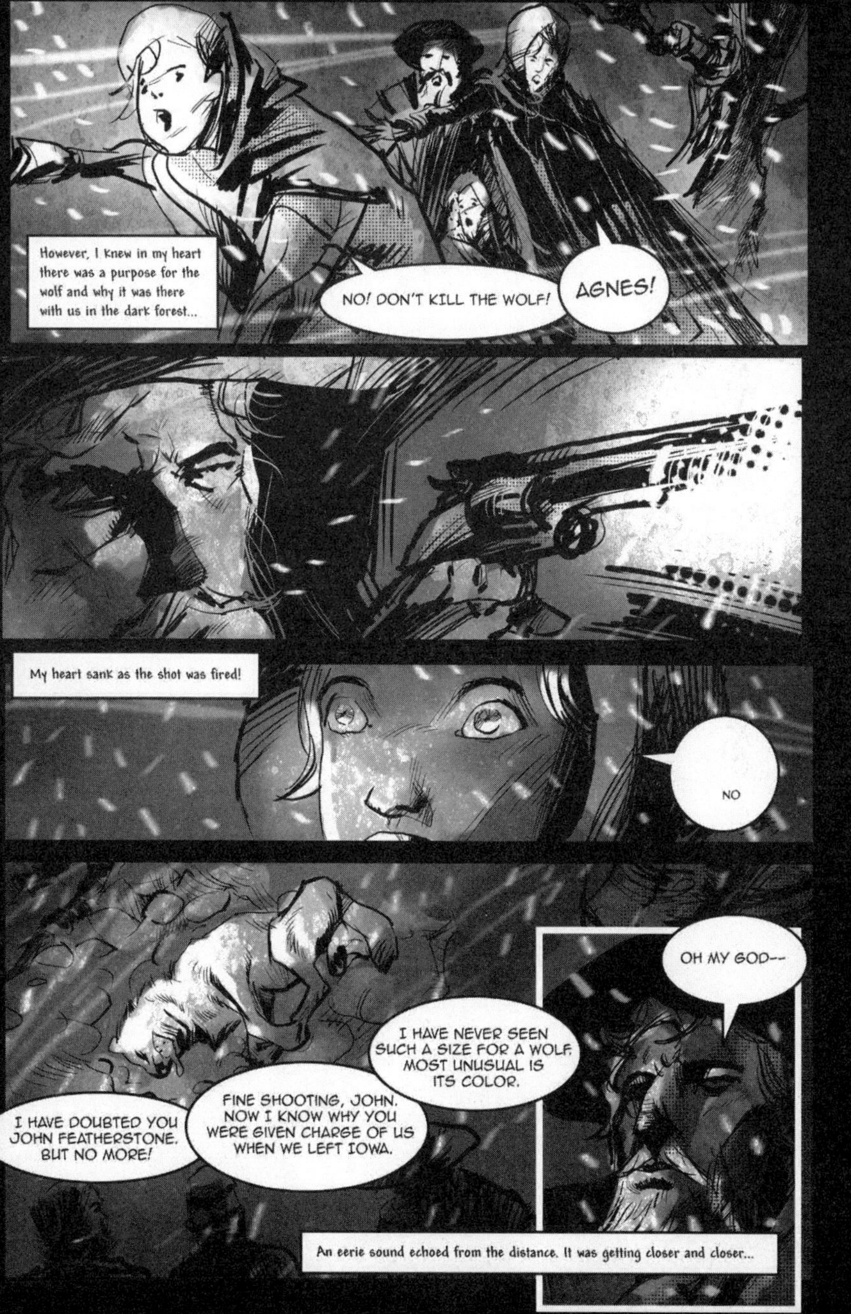
However, I knew in my heart there was a purpose for the wolf and why it was there with us in the dark forest...
NO! DON'T KILL THE WOLF!
AGNES!
My heart sank as the shot was fired!
NO
OH MY GOD--
I HAVE NEVER SEEN SUCH A SIZE FOR A WOLF. MOST UNUSUAL IS ITS COLOR.
FINE SHOOTING, JOHN. NOW I KNOW WHY YOU WERE GIVEN CHARGE OF US WHEN WE LEFT IOWA.
I HAVE DOUBTED YOU JOHN FEATHERSTONE. BUT NO MORE!
An eerie sound echoed from the distance. It was getting closer and closer...

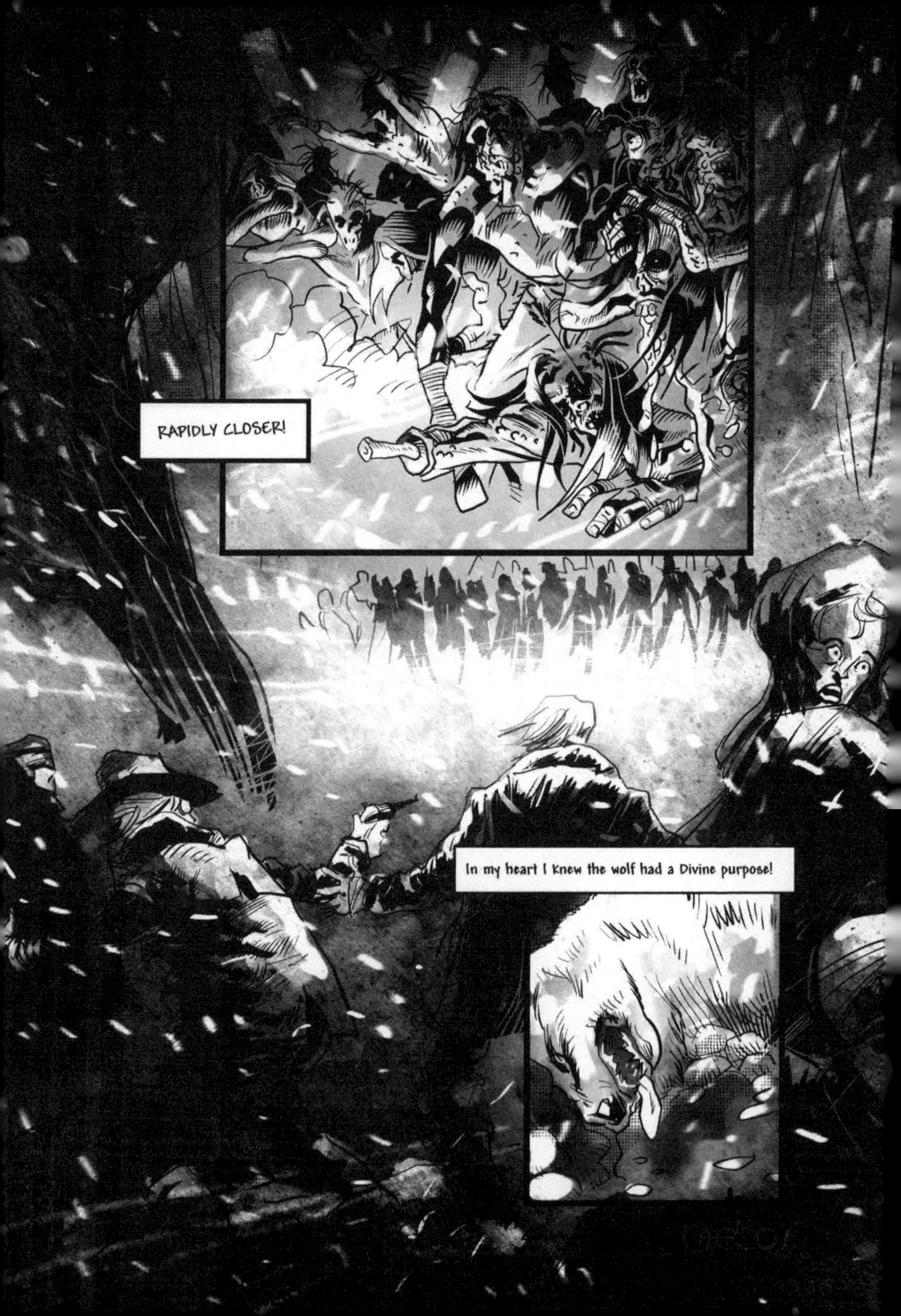
RAPIDLY CLOSER!
In my heart I knew the wolf had a Divine purpose!

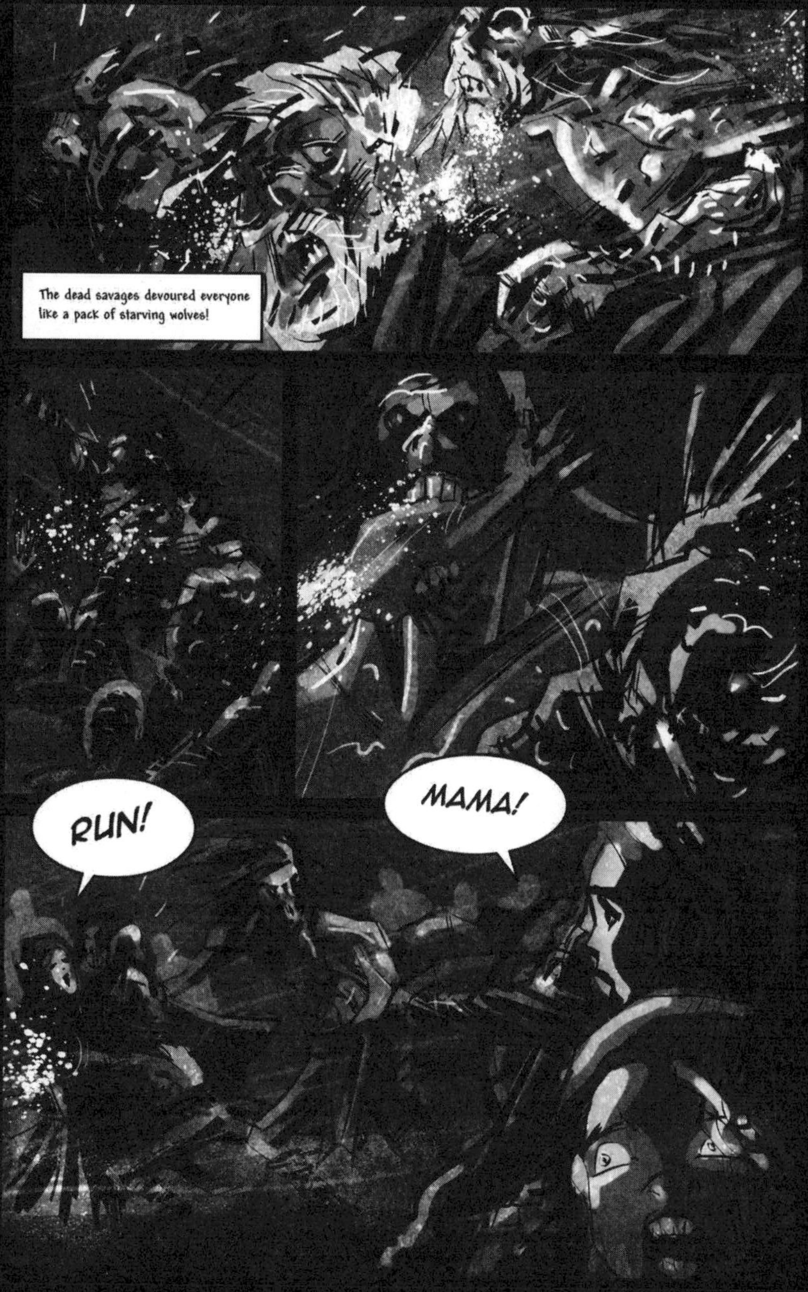
The dead savages devoured everyone like a pack of starving wolves!
RUN!
MAMA!

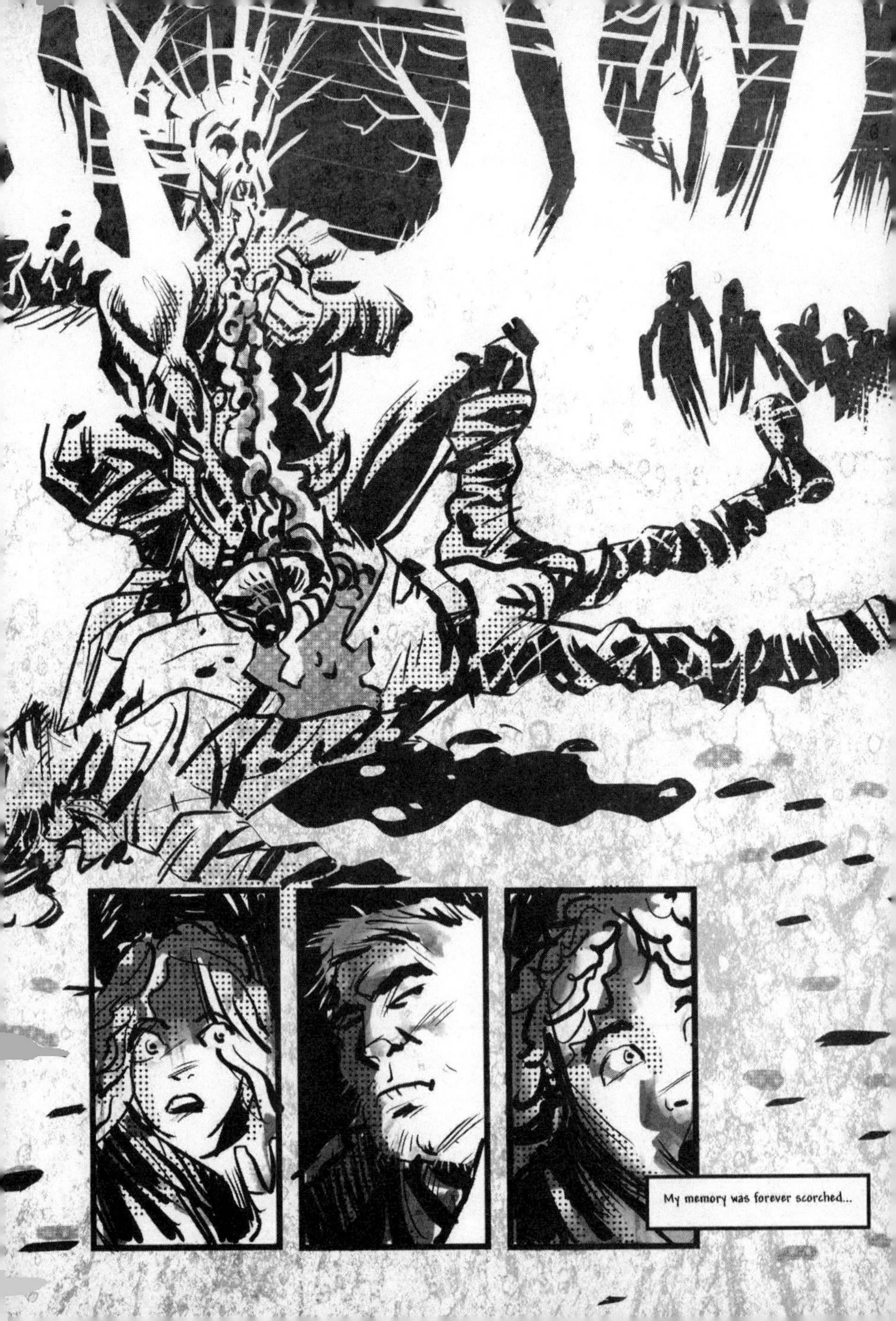
My memory was forever scorched...

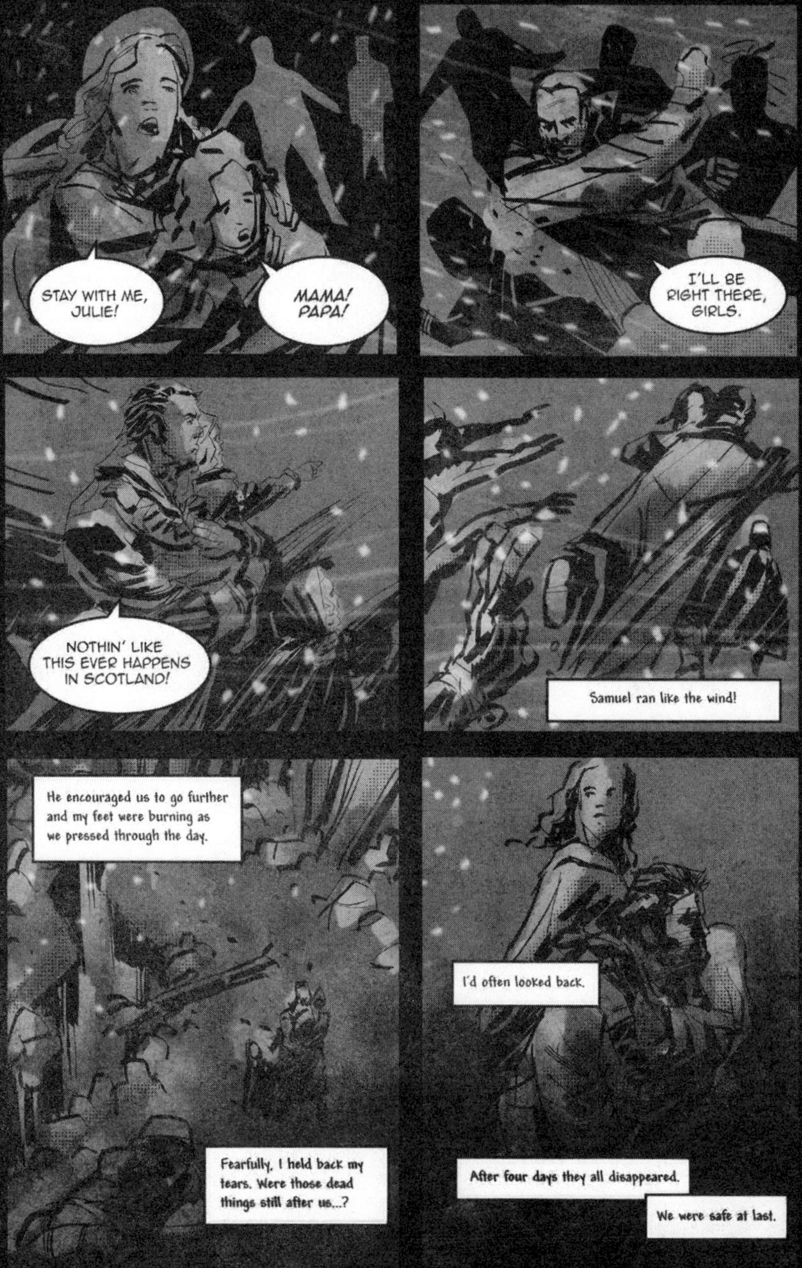
STAY WITH ME, JULIE!
MAMA! PAPA!
I'LL BE RIGHT THERE, GIRLS.
NOTHIN' LIKE THIS EVER HAPPENS IN SCOTLAND!
Samuel ran like the wind!
He encouraged us to go further and my feet were burning as we pressed through the day.
Fearfully, I held back my tears. Were those dead things still after us...?
I'd often looked back.
After four days they all disappeared.
We were safe at last.

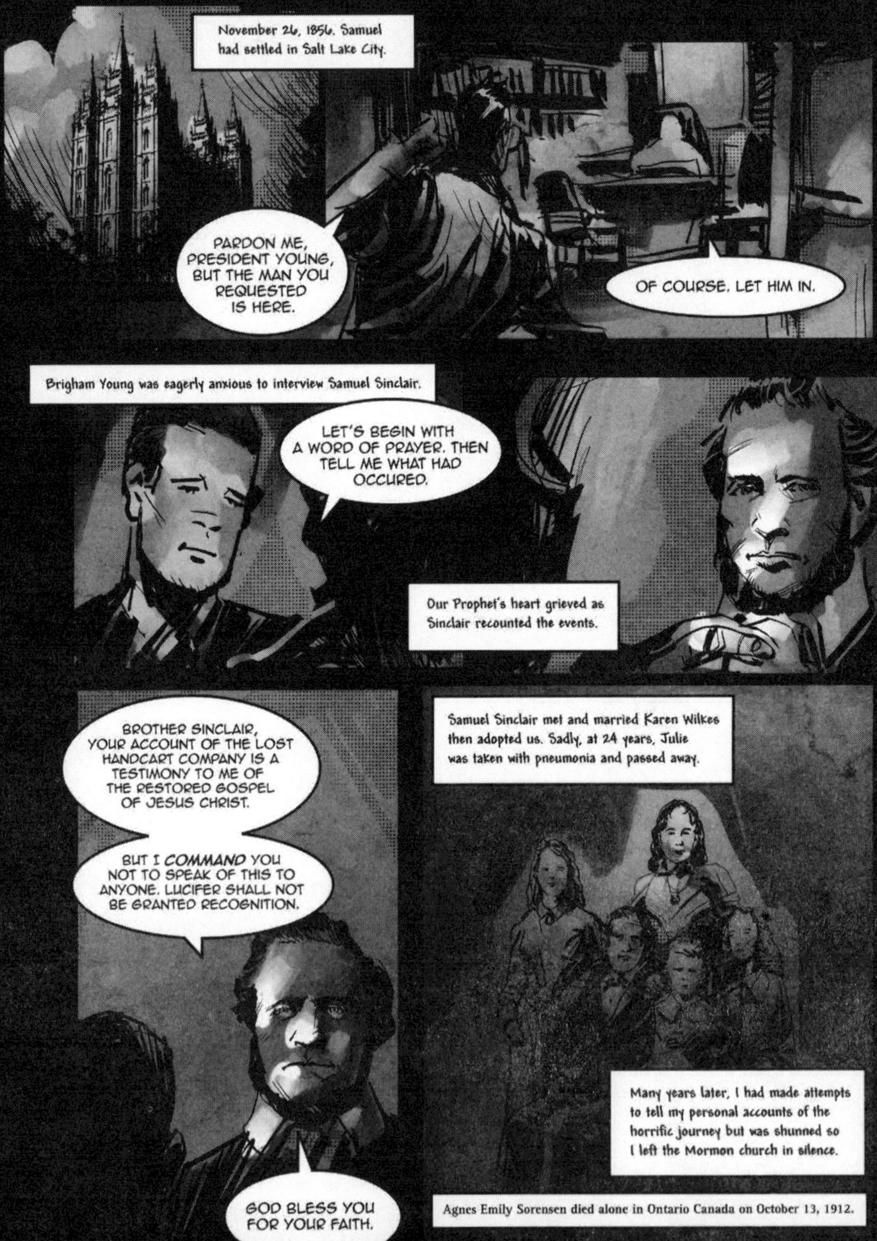
November 26, 1856. Samuel had settled in Salt Lake City.
PARDON ME, PRESIDENT YOUNG, BUT THE MAN YOU REQUESTED IS HERE.
OF COURSE. LET HIM IN.
Brigham Young was eagerly anxious to interview Samuel Sinclair.
LET'S BEGIN WITH A WORD OF PRAYER. THEN TELL ME WHAT HAD OCCURED.
Our Prophet's heart grieved as Sinclair recounted the events.
BROTHER SINCLAIR, YOUR ACCOUNT OF THE LOST HANDCART COMPANY IS A TESTIMONY TO ME OF THE RESTORED GOSPEL OF JESUS CHRIST.
BUT I COMMAND YOU NOT TO SPEAK OF THIS TO ANYONE. LUCIFER SHALL NOT BE GRANTED RECOGNITION.
GOD BLESS YOU FOR YOUR FAITH.
Samuel Sinclair met and married Karen Wilkes then adopted us. Sadly, at 24 years, Julie was taken with pneumonia and passed away.
Many years later, I had made attempts to tell my personal accounts of the horrific journey but was shunned so I left the Mormon church in silence.
Agnes Emily Sorensen died alone in Ontario Canada on October 13, 1912.

In loving memory of Lydia Jurilla Smith 1942-2012

THE END

THAT DEN OF DEVILS

STORY BY:
MIKE PERKINS

ART AND LETTERS BY:
WILL PERKINS

GREYSCALES BY:
JEFF McCOMSEY

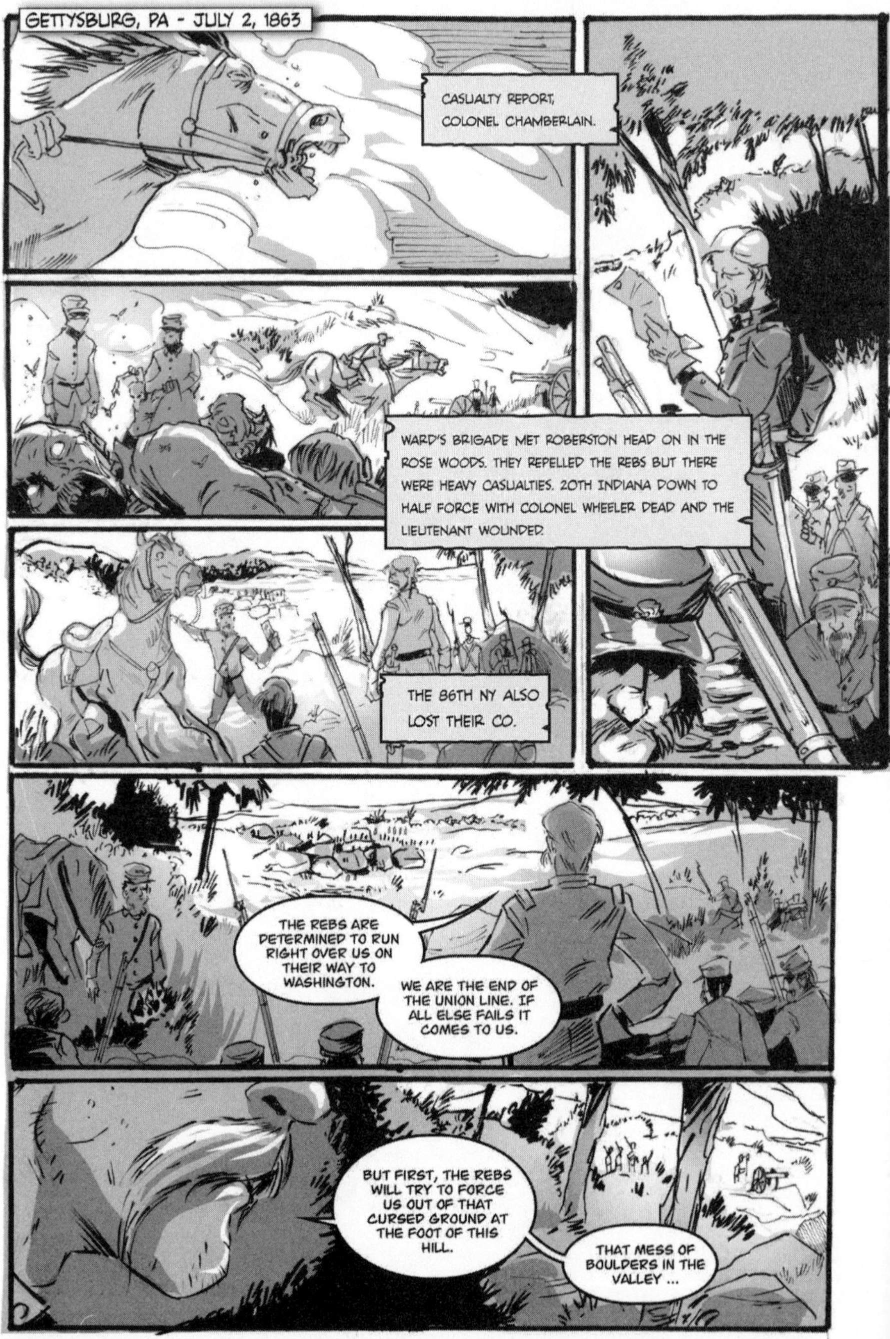
GETTYSBURG, PA - JULY 2, 1863
CASUALTY REPORT, COLONEL CHAMBERLAIN.
WARD'S BRIGADE MET ROBERSTON HEAD ON IN THE ROSE WOODS. THEY REPELLED THE REBS BUT THERE WERE HEAVY CASUALTIES. 20TH INDIANA DOWN TO HALF FORCE WITH COLONEL WHEELER DEAD AND THE LIEUTENANT WOUNDED.
THE 86TH NY ALSO LOST THEIR CO.
THE REBS ARE DETERMINED TO RUN RIGHT OVER US ON THEIR WAY TO WASHINGTON.
WE ARE THE END OF THE UNION LINE. IF ALL ELSE FAILS IT COMES TO US.
BUT FIRST, THE REBS WILL TRY TO FORCE US OUT OF THAT CURSED GROUND AT THE FOOT OF THIS HILL.
THAT MESS OF BOULDERS IN THE VALLEY ...

THAT DEN OF DEVILS

WORDS BY MIKE D. PERKINS   GREYSCALES BY JEFF McCOMSEY   ART AND LETTERS BY WILL PERKINS

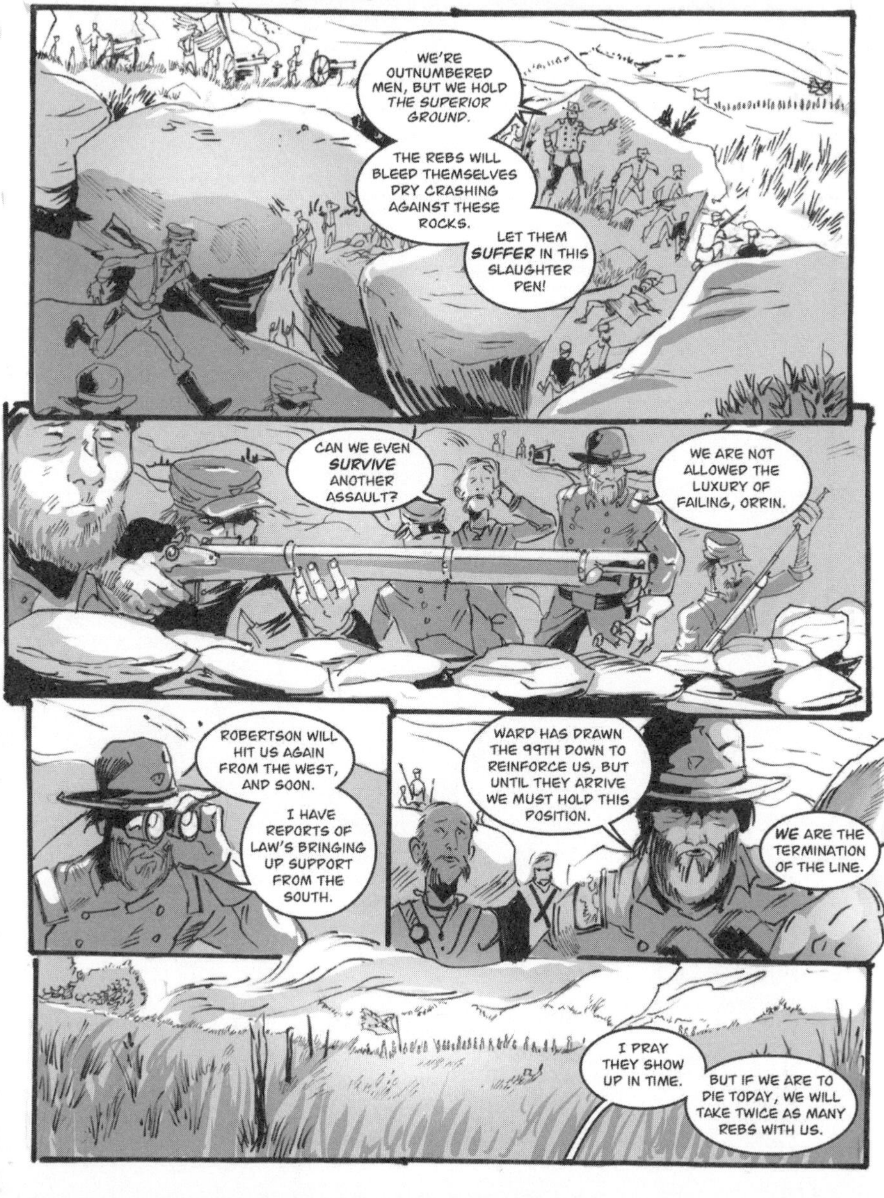

WE'RE OUTNUMBERED MEN, BUT WE HOLD THE SUPERIOR GROUND.
THE REBS WILL BLEED THEMSELVES DRY CRASHING AGAINST THESE ROCKS.
LET THEM SUFFER IN THIS SLAUGHTER PEN!
CAN WE EVEN SURVIVE ANOTHER ASSAULT?
WE ARE NOT ALLOWED THE LUXURY OF FAILING, ORRIN.
ROBERTSON WILL HIT US AGAIN FROM THE WEST, AND SOON.
I HAVE REPORTS OF LAW'S BRINGING UP SUPPORT FROM THE SOUTH.
WARD HAS DRAWN THE 99TH DOWN TO REINFORCE US, BUT UNTIL THEY ARRIVE WE MUST HOLD THIS POSITION.
WE ARE THE TERMINATION OF THE LINE.
I PRAY THEY SHOW UP IN TIME.
BUT IF WE ARE TO DIE TODAY, WE WILL TAKE TWICE AS MANY REBS WITH US.

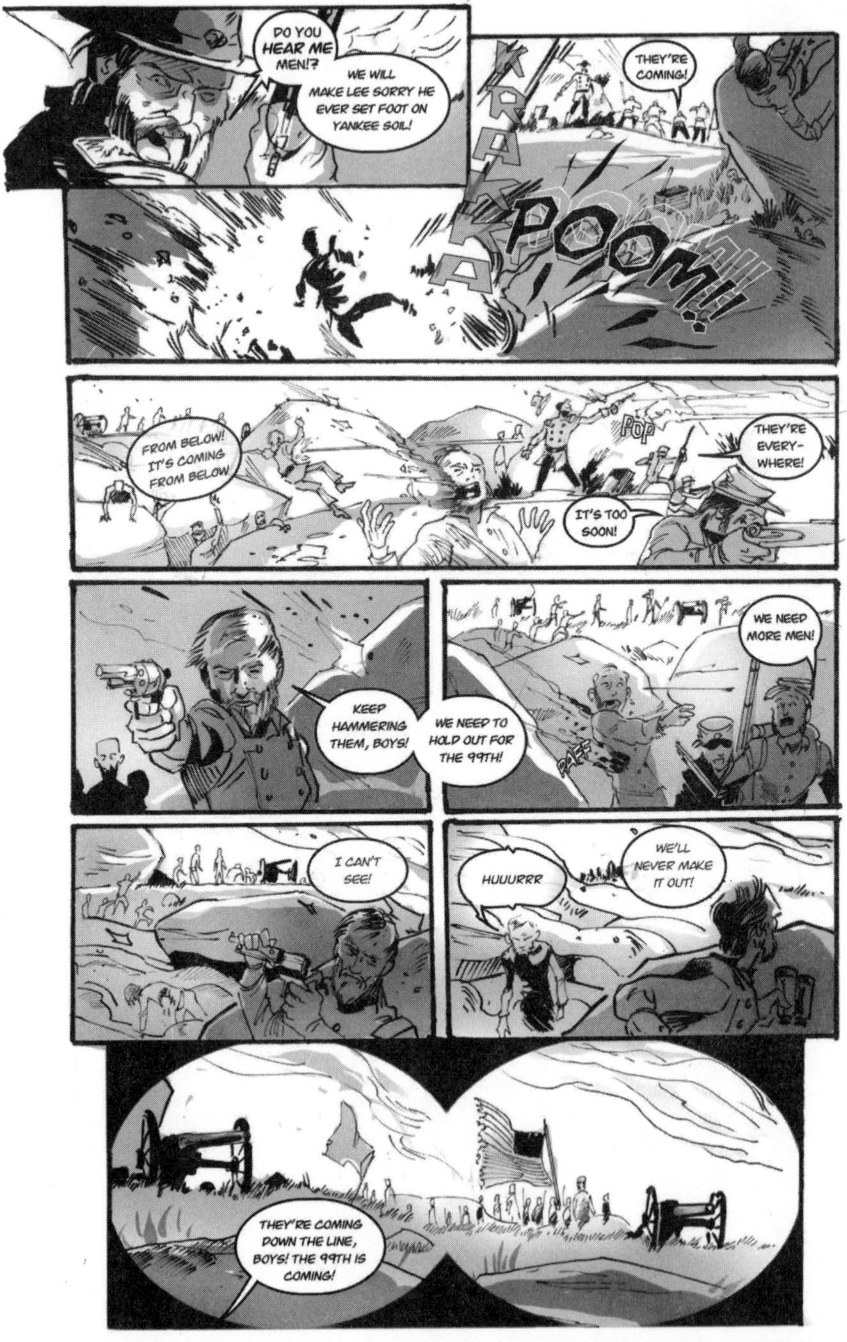
DO YOU HEAR ME MEN!?
WE WILL MAKE LEE SORRY HE EVER SET FOOT ON YANKEE SOIL!
THEY'RE COMING!
KRAKA
POOM!!!
FROM BELOW! IT'S COMING FROM BELOW
POP
THEY'RE EVERY-WHERE!
IT'S TOO SOON!
KEEP HAMMERING THEM, BOYS!
WE NEED TO HOLD OUT FOR THE 99TH!
WE NEED MORE MEN!
PAFF
I CAN'T SEE!
HUUURRR
WE'LL NEVER MAKE IT OUT!
THEY'RE COMING DOWN THE LINE, BOYS! THE 99TH IS COMING!

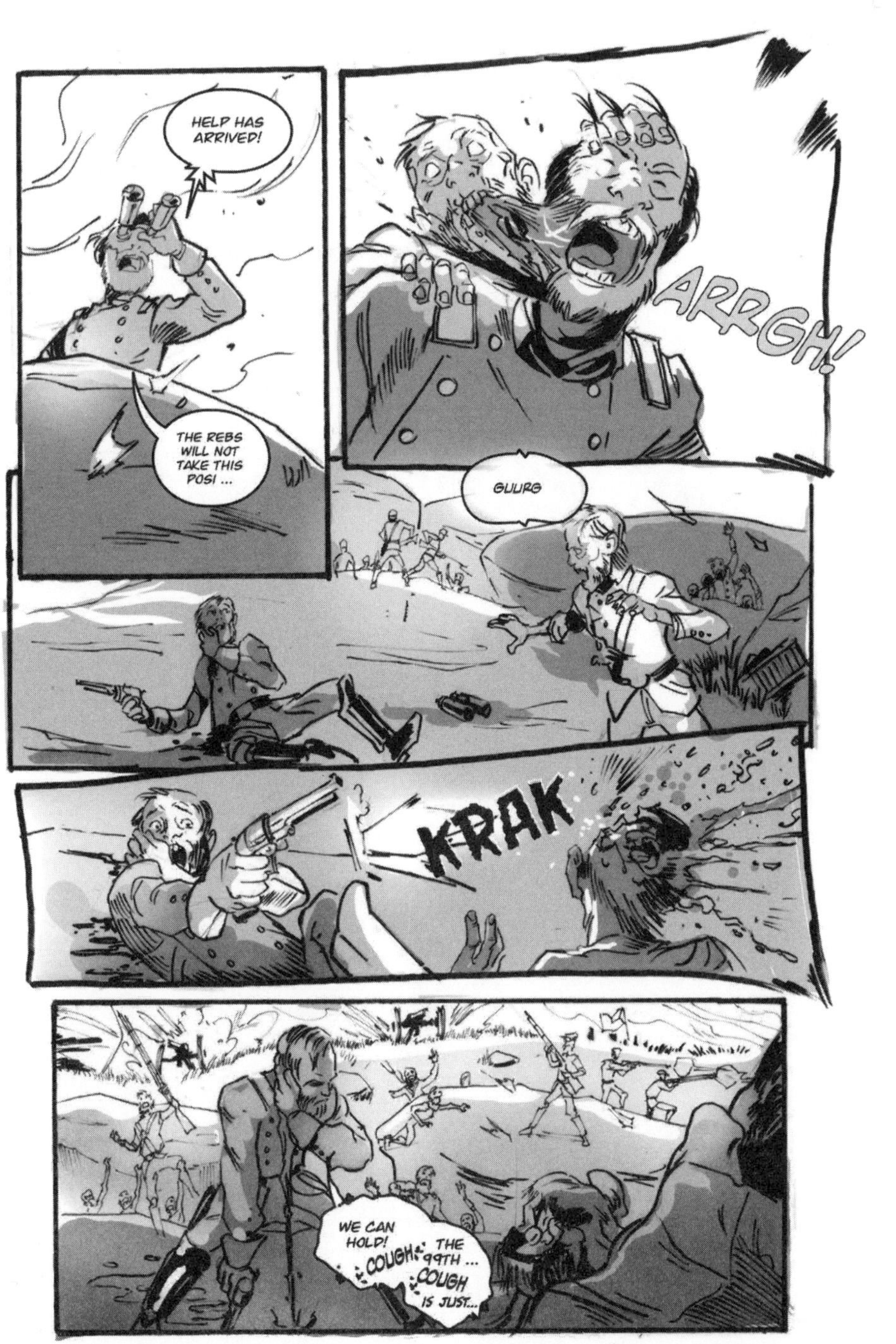
HELP HAS ARRIVED!
THE REBS WILL NOT TAKE THIS POSI ...
ARRGH!
GUURG
KRAK
WE CAN HOLD! COUGH THE 99TH ... COUGH IS JUST...

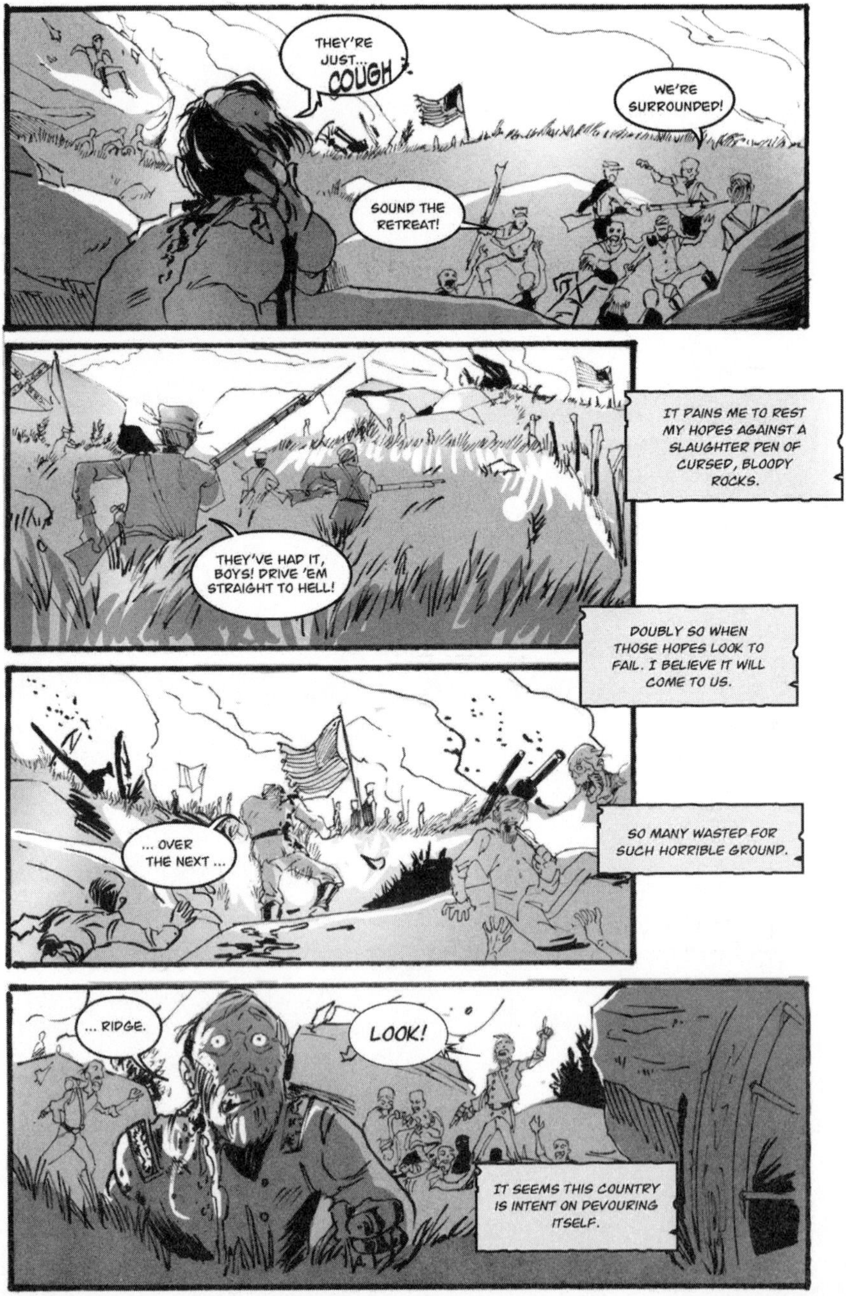
THEY'RE JUST... COUGH
WE'RE SURROUNDED!
SOUND THE RETREAT!
IT PAINS ME TO REST MY HOPES AGAINST A SLAUGHTER PEN OF CURSED, BLOODY ROCKS.
THEY'VE HAD IT, BOYS! DRIVE 'EM STRAIGHT TO HELL!
DOUBLY SO WHEN THOSE HOPES LOOK TO FAIL. I BELIEVE IT WILL COME TO US.
... OVER THE NEXT ...
SO MANY WASTED FOR SUCH HORRIBLE GROUND.
... RIDGE.
LOOK!
IT SEEMS THIS COUNTRY IS INTENT ON DEVOURING ITSELF.

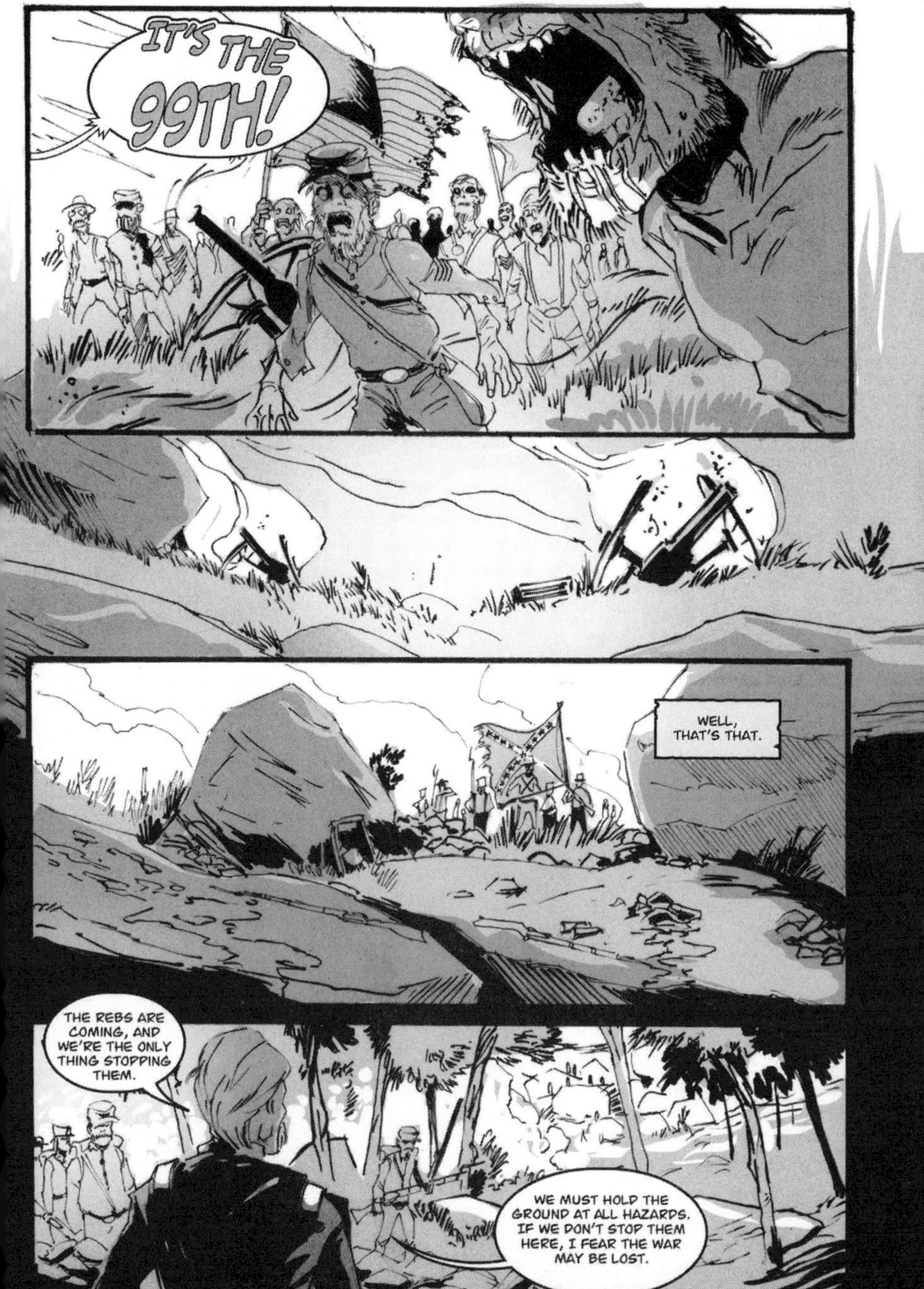
IT'S THE 99TH!
WELL, THAT'S THAT.
THE REBS ARE COMING, AND WE'RE THE ONLY THING STOPPING THEM.
WE MUST HOLD THE GROUND AT ALL HAZARDS. IF WE DON'T STOP THEM HERE, I FEAR THE WAR MAY BE LOST.

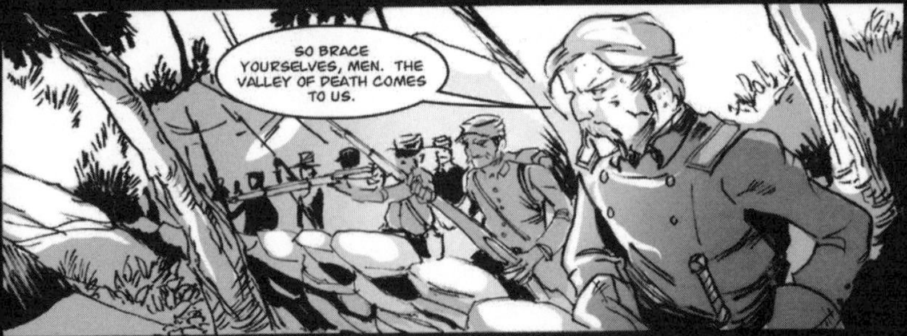
SO BRACE YOURSELVES, MEN. THE VALLEY OF DEATH COMES TO US.

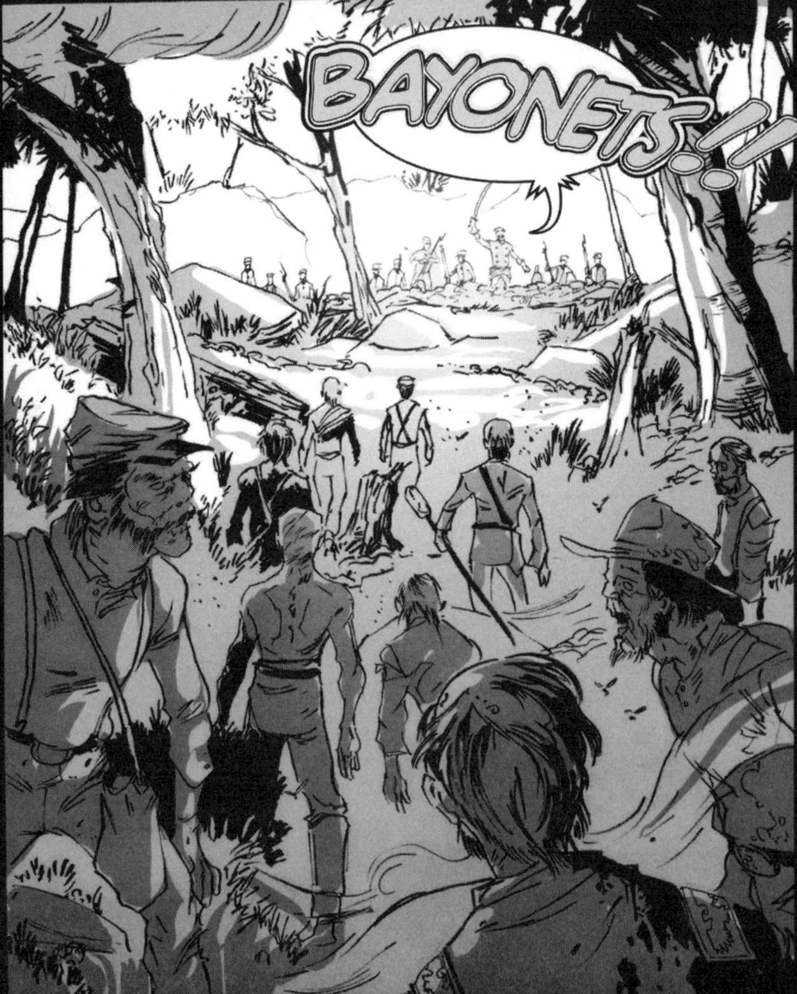
BAYONETS..!!!

ASHES & SMOKE

STORY BY:
MIKE IMBODEN

ART BY:
JOHN SHINE

September 1st

Dearest Mother-

We have won another battle behind the leadership of General Sherman. Lovejoy's Station is ours and General Hood is on the run, his supply lines cut off. Not only was he routed, he destroyed supply depots and an entire train of ammunition during his retreat. Ammunition he could have used against us! If the entire Confederate leadership is anythin like this man, I am happy to say this war may be over soon.

Your Loving Son,
Benjamin

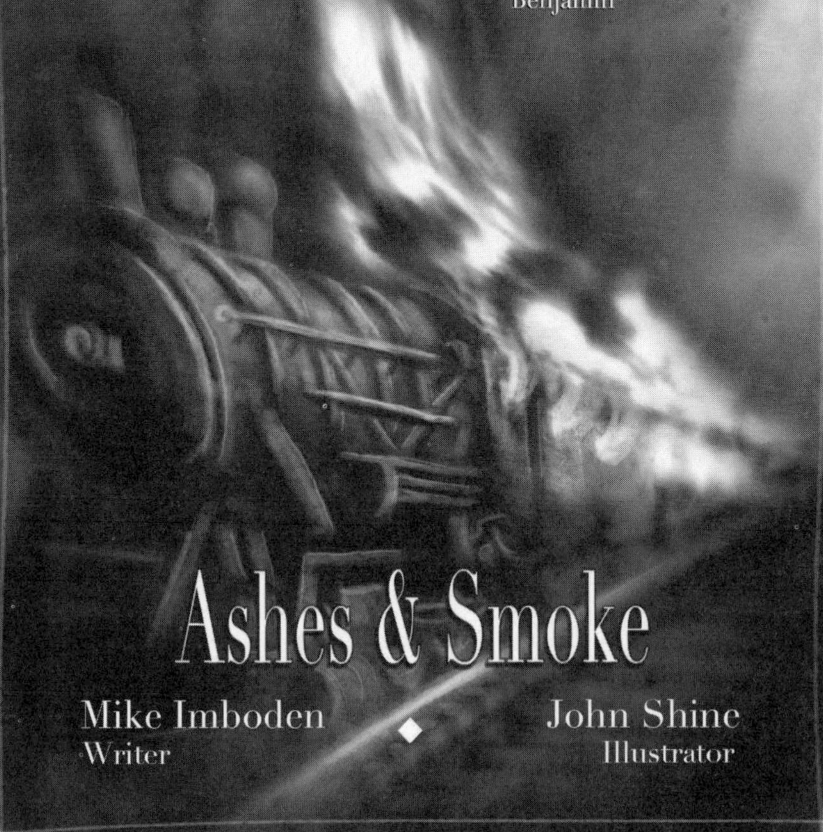

Ashes & Smoke

Mike Imboden
Writer

John Shine
Illustrator

September 2nd

Dearest Mother-

Atlanta is a fine city, considerin its location. Its leaders, however, are as yellow as the corn in the fields. Three men, one who I believe was the Mayor, surrendered the city to General Sherman today. In turn they wanted protection, but would not say from what. General Sherman looked a little upset and I think it's because he felt this Mayor, Calhoun, was tryin to say that WE was the ones he wanted protection from! Can you believe that? President Lincoln himself wants this city under our control, why on earth would we do it harm?

Please tell Carol that I am fine. I hope she is mindin you and doin chores. Remind her to keep an eye on DUSTY. He is a good dog, but he loves chasin rabbits!

Your Loving Son,
Benjamin

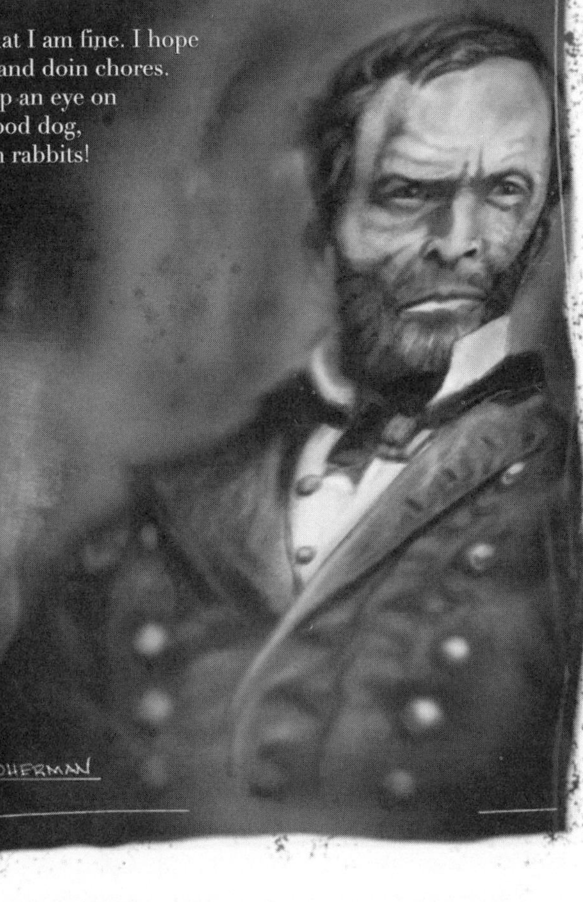

GENERAL SHERMAN

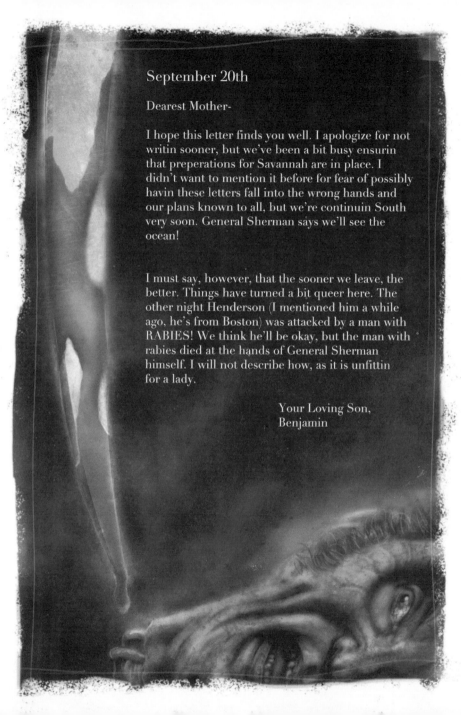

September 20th

Dearest Mother-

I hope this letter finds you well. I apologize for not writin sooner, but we've been a bit busy ensurin that preperations for Savannah are in place. I didn't want to mention it before for fear of possibly havin these letters fall into the wrong hands and our plans known to all, but we're continuin South very soon. General Sherman says we'll see the ocean!

I must say, however, that the sooner we leave, the better. Things have turned a bit queer here. The other night Henderson (I mentioned him a while ago, he's from Boston) was attacked by a man with RABIES! We think he'll be okay, but the man with rabies died at the hands of General Sherman himself. I will not describe how, as it is unfittin for a lady.

Your Loving Son,
Benjamin

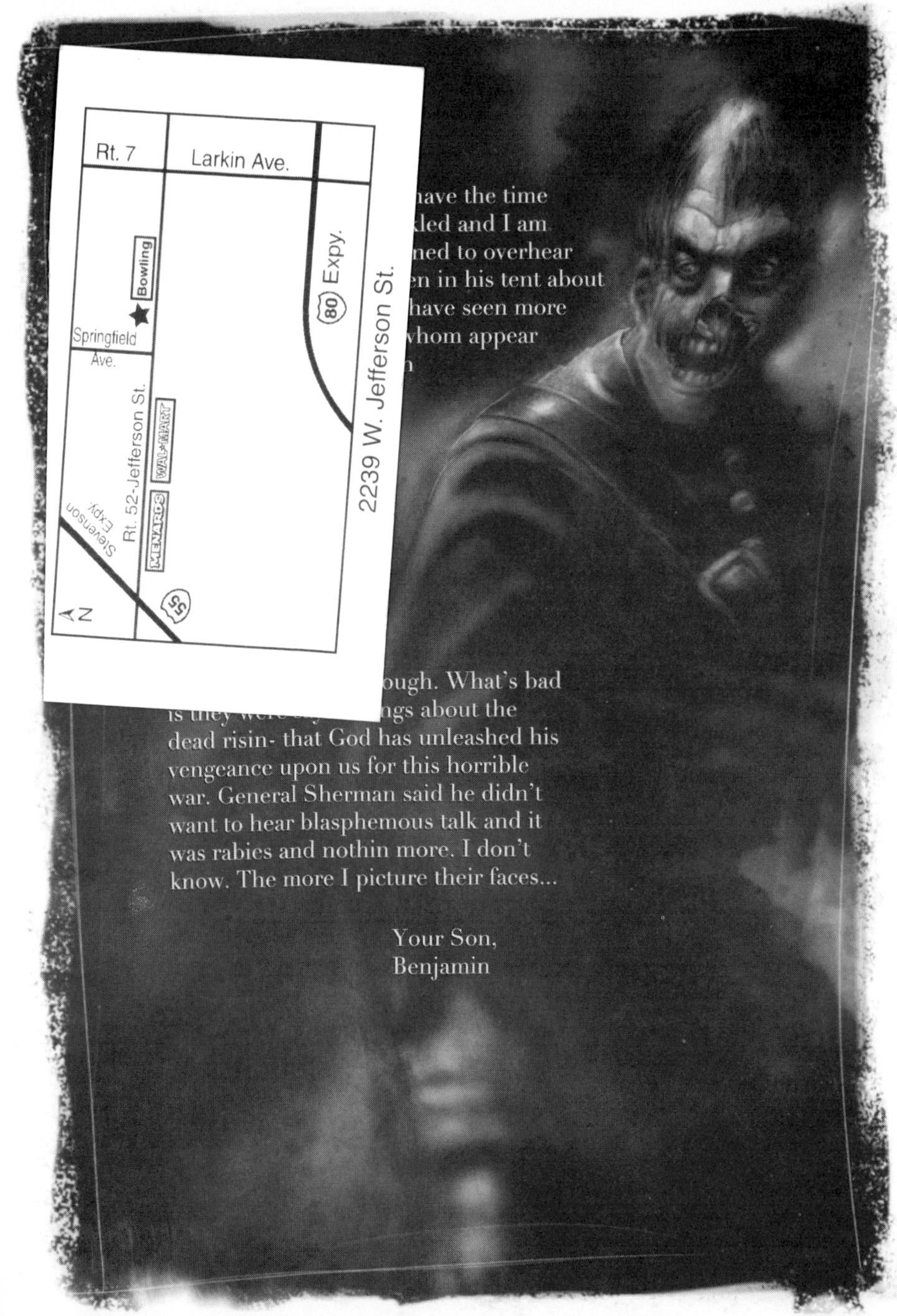
Rt. 7
Larkin Ave.
Bowling
Springfield Ave.
80 Expy.
2239 W. Jefferson St.
Rt. 52-Jefferson St.
WAL*MART
MENARDS
Stevenson Expy.
55
N

have the time
kled and I am
ned to overhear
en in his tent about
have seen more
whom appear
n

ough. What's bad
is they were ngs about the
dead risin- that God has unleashed his
vengeance upon us for this horrible
war. General Sherman said he didn't
want to hear blasphemous talk and it
was rabies and nothin more. I don't
know. The more I picture their faces...

Your Son,
Benjamin

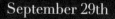

September 29th

Dearest Mother-

Things are bad. A woman was killed tonight by one of her neighbors. I was on patrol and heard the scream. When I turned into the alley I saw the man standin over her with a knife in his hands. She was clutchin her stomach and even with only the light of the moon I could see blood everywhere. The man kept babblin about the DEAD and how he thought she was one'a them.

General Sherman himself took the man into custody but not before tellin us to keep our mouths shut about what the man was sayin. He sounded pretty mad, too. I thought things were gettin better as we'd gone a day without any of the ~~dead~~ rabies-infected men comin around.

Your Son,
Benjamin

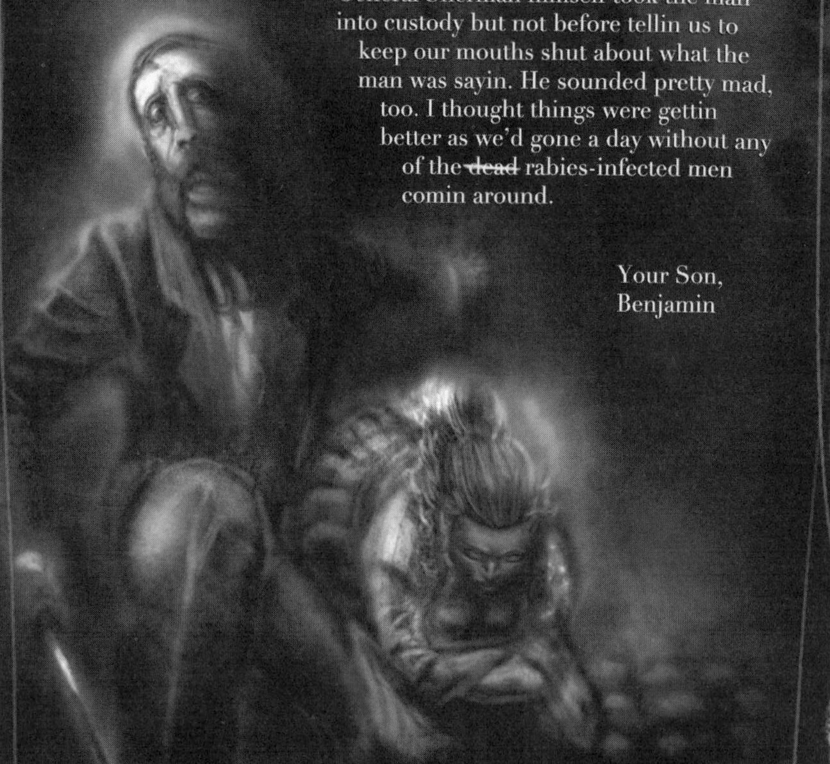

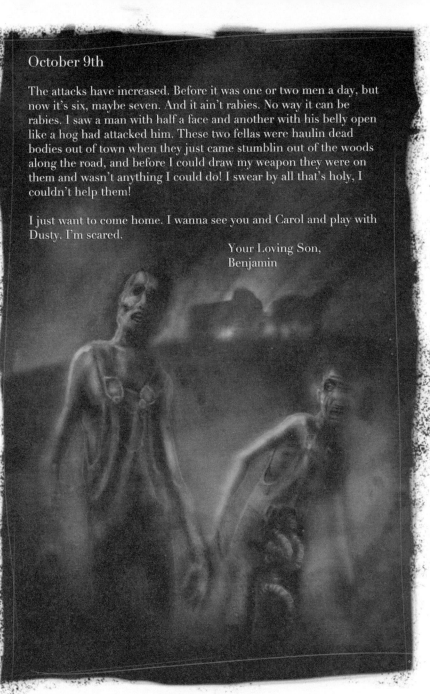

October 9th

The attacks have increased. Before it was one or two men a day, but now it's six, maybe seven. And it ain't rabies. No way it can be rabies. I saw a man with half a face and another with his belly open like a hog had attacked him. These two fellas were haulin dead bodies out of town when they just came stumblin out of the woods along the road, and before I could draw my weapon they were on them and wasn't anything I could do! I swear by all that's holy, I couldn't help them!

I just want to come home. I wanna see you and Carol and play with Dusty. I'm scared.

Your Loving Son,
Benjamin

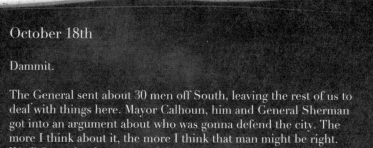

October 18th

Dammit.

The General sent about 30 men off South, leaving the rest of us to deal with things here. Mayor Calhoun, him and General Sherman got into an argument about who was gonna defend the city. The more I think about it, the more I think that man might be right. We DO need to be protected, but who can protect you from the wrath of GOD?!? I wish I was leavin with the rest of the men and... hell, I just might anyway.

Your Son,
Benjamin

October 25th

Dear Father Tim-

I'm writin you because I don't know what to believe anymore.
My faith... my faith is gone. My faith in God and all that is good
is gone. Evil is real and Evil WALKS, Father Tim. THE DEAD
WALK! It ain't rabies like General Sherman said. It ain't nothin
but God's angry hand pullin the dead outta the ground and
movin them around like puppets. What did we do to Him?!?

Tell my mother I love her. I don't know if I'll get outta here
alive.

Sincerely,
Benjamin Cooper

November 7th

Mother-

We've boarded ourselves in a house.
General Sherman has told Mr. Calhoun to
take as many of his people as he can and get
out of the city. Our supplies are limited and
fadin fast and we're all pretty sure we ain't
gonna be able to hold the city much longer.
Every day there are more. Every day we kill
them and every night more return. Men I have
seen die by my own hand among them!

RABIES! We thought it was rabies! Last night a man spoke of this
very thing happenin at Antietam and Gettysburg - how did we not
learn about this until now? Is this why we pushed so hard South?
To find a way out? If only that Confederate bastard hadn't destroyed
those supplies as he ran, we might have had a chance.

Your Son,
Benjamin

November 14th

Atlanta is lost. Our ammunition is gone. We have one last option.

Burn it. Burn it all. Burn it to the ground and pray the flames can do what our bullets could not.

General Sherman said that we are to leave nothin but
  ashes and smoke.

All my love to you and Carol.

Benjamin

THE LION OF LITTLE ROUND TOP

STORY BY
KEVIN JOHNSON
PENCILS BY:
KURT BELCHER
INKS BY:
JASON M. ADAMS
GREYSCALES BY:
SHAWN ALDRIDGE

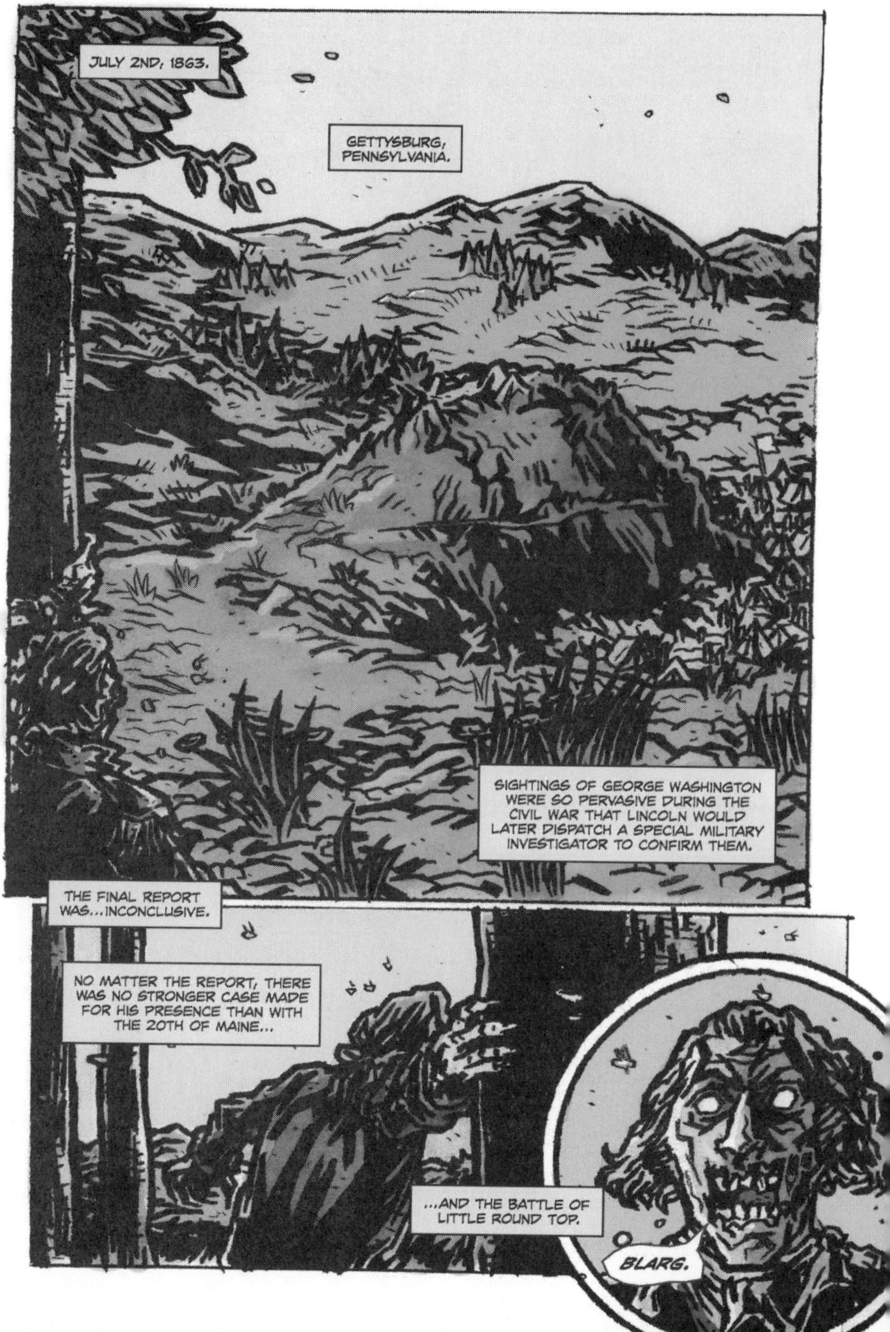
JULY 2ND, 1863.
GETTYSBURG, PENNSYLVANIA.
SIGHTINGS OF GEORGE WASHINGTON WERE SO PERVASIVE DURING THE CIVIL WAR THAT LINCOLN WOULD LATER DISPATCH A SPECIAL MILITARY INVESTIGATOR TO CONFIRM THEM.
THE FINAL REPORT WAS... INCONCLUSIVE.
NO MATTER THE REPORT, THERE WAS NO STRONGER CASE MADE FOR HIS PRESENCE THAN WITH THE 20TH OF MAINE...
...AND THE BATTLE OF LITTLE ROUND TOP.
BLARG.

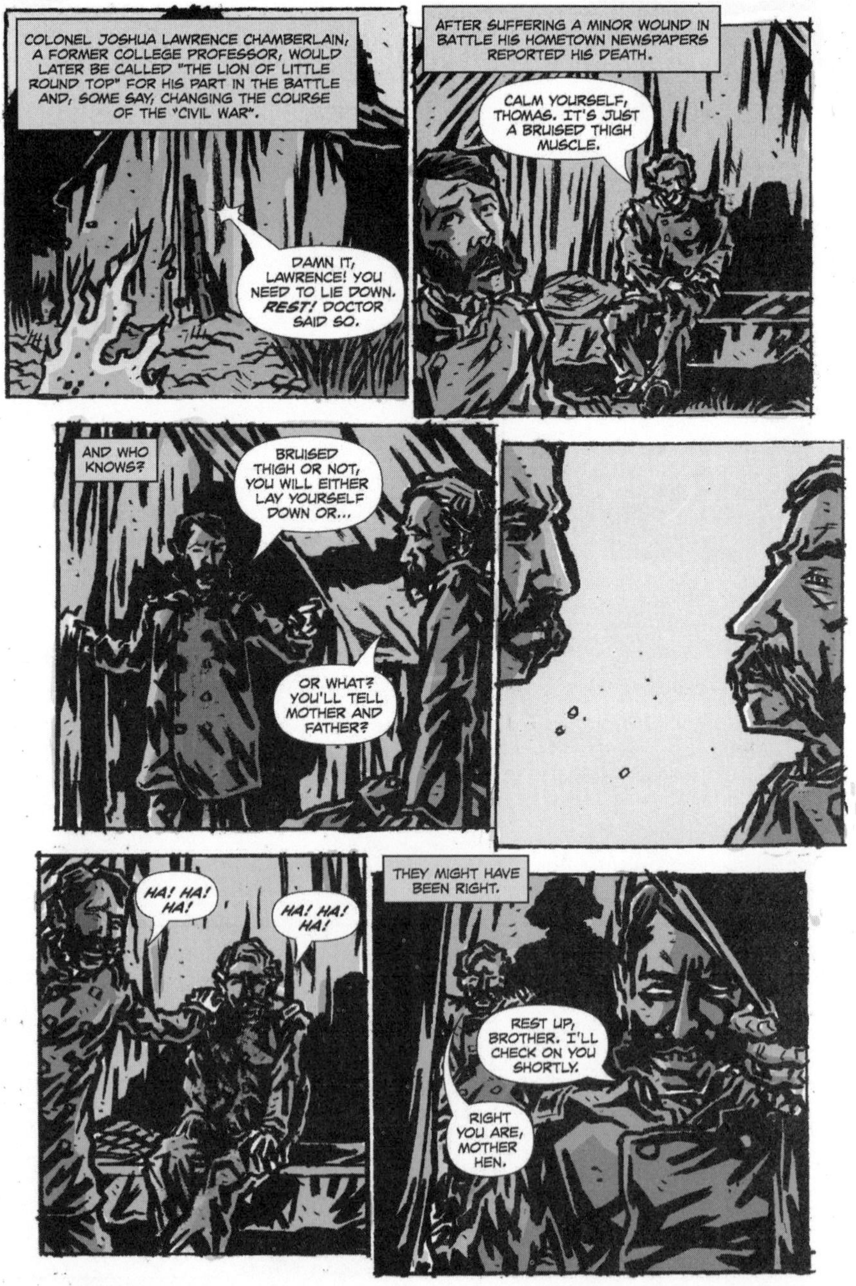

COLONEL JOSHUA LAWRENCE CHAMBERLAIN, A FORMER COLLEGE PROFESSOR, WOULD LATER BE CALLED "THE LION OF LITTLE ROUND TOP" FOR HIS PART IN THE BATTLE AND, SOME SAY, CHANGING THE COURSE OF THE "CIVIL WAR".
DAMN IT, LAWRENCE! YOU NEED TO LIE DOWN. *REST!* DOCTOR SAID SO.
AFTER SUFFERING A MINOR WOUND IN BATTLE HIS HOMETOWN NEWSPAPERS REPORTED HIS DEATH.
CALM YOURSELF, THOMAS. IT'S JUST A BRUISED THIGH MUSCLE.
AND WHO KNOWS?
BRUISED THIGH OR NOT, YOU WILL EITHER LAY YOURSELF DOWN OR...
OR WHAT? YOU'LL TELL MOTHER AND FATHER?
HA! HA! HA!
HA! HA! HA!
THEY MIGHT HAVE BEEN RIGHT.
REST UP, BROTHER. I'LL CHECK ON YOU SHORTLY.
RIGHT YOU ARE, MOTHER HEN.

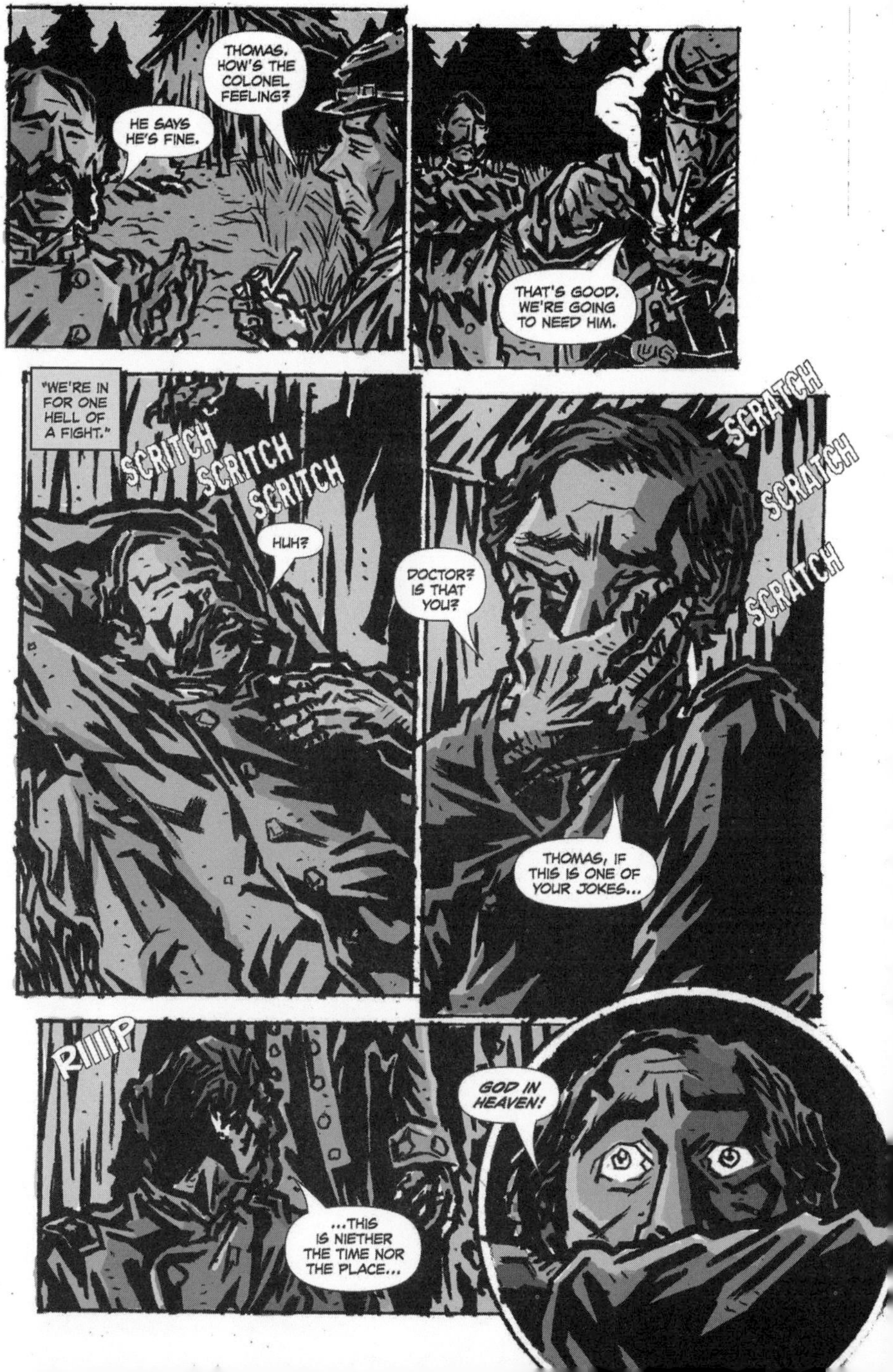
THOMAS. HOW'S THE COLONEL FEELING?
HE SAYS HE'S FINE.
THAT'S GOOD. WE'RE GOING TO NEED HIM.
"WE'RE IN FOR ONE HELL OF A FIGHT."
SCRITCH
SCRITCH
SCRITCH
HUH?
SCRATCH
SCRATCH
SCRATCH
DOCTOR? IS THAT YOU?
THOMAS, IF THIS IS ONE OF YOUR JOKES...
RIIIP
...THIS IS NIETHER THE TIME NOR THE PLACE...
GOD IN HEAVEN!

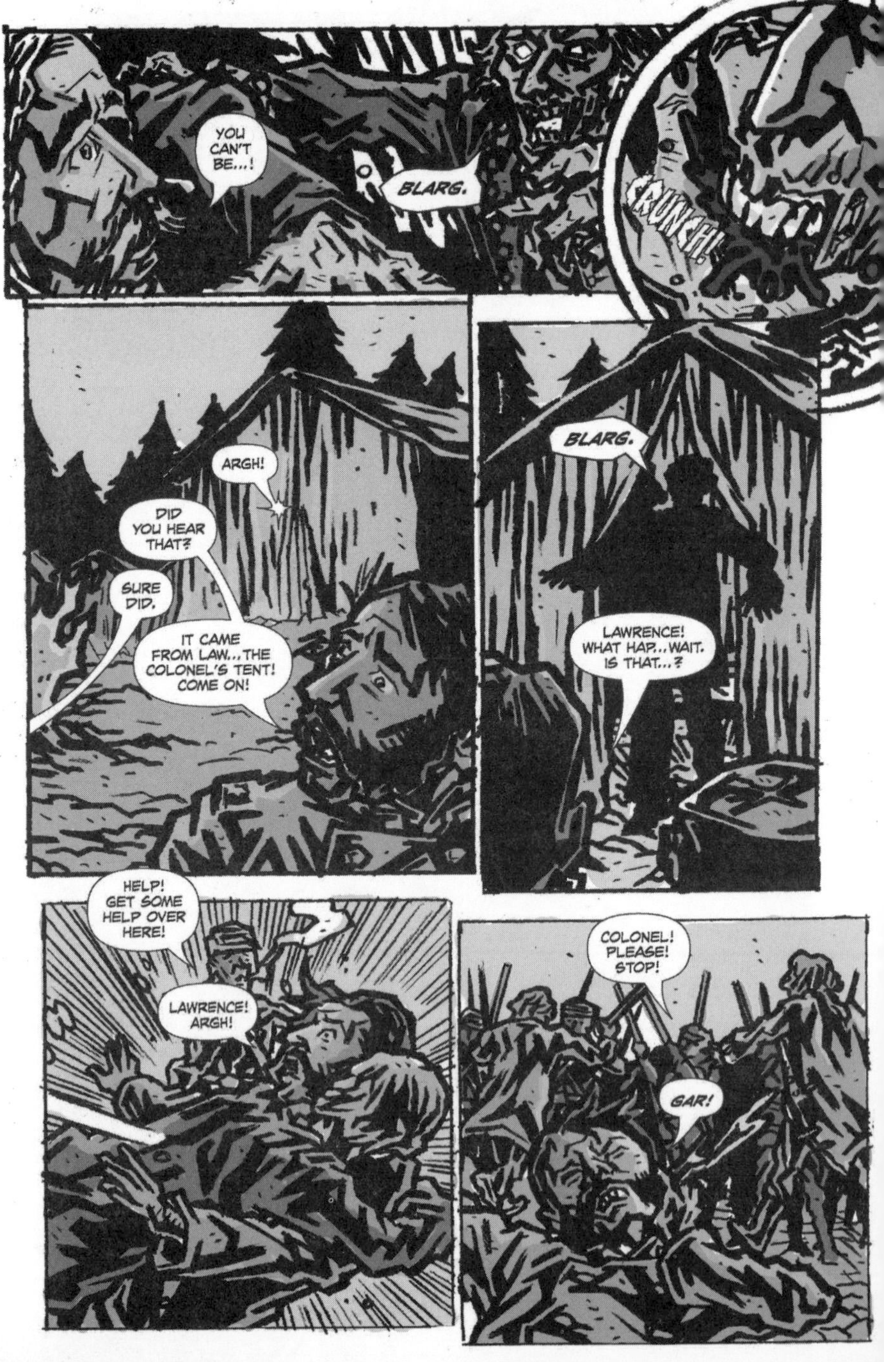
YOU CAN'T BE...!
BLARG.
CRUNCH!
ARGH!
DID YOU HEAR THAT?
SURE DID.
IT CAME FROM LAW...THE COLONEL'S TENT! COME ON!
BLARG.
LAWRENCE! WHAT HAP...WAIT. IS THAT...?
HELP! GET SOME HELP OVER HERE!
LAWRENCE! ARGH!
COLONEL! PLEASE! STOP!
GAR!

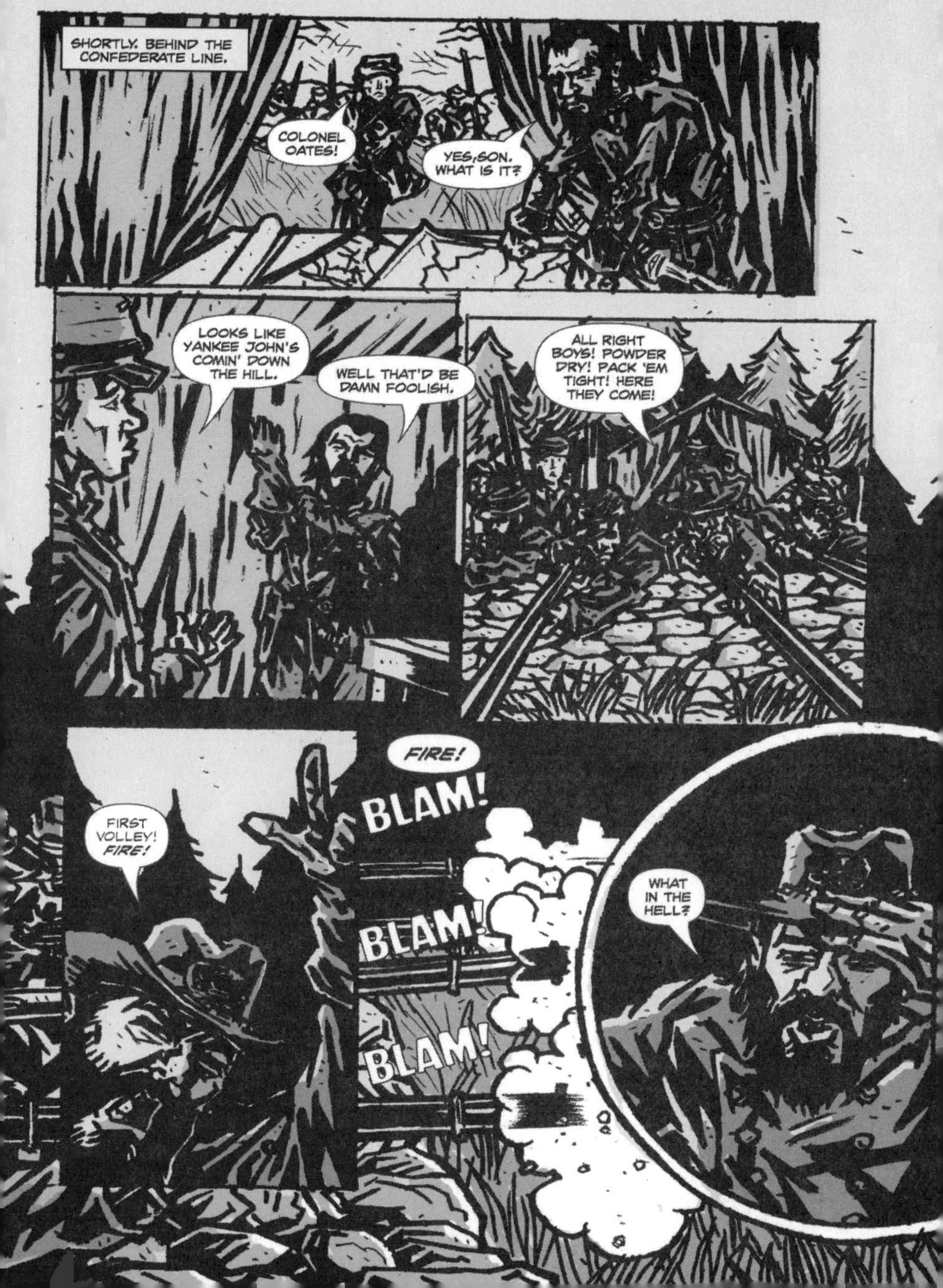

SHORTLY. BEHIND THE CONFEDERATE LINE.
COLONEL OATES!
YES, SON. WHAT IS IT?
LOOKS LIKE YANKEE JOHN'S COMIN' DOWN THE HILL.
WELL THAT'D BE DAMN FOOLISH.
ALL RIGHT BOYS! POWDER DRY! PACK 'EM TIGHT! HERE THEY COME!
FIRST VOLLEY! FIRE!
FIRE!
BLAM!
BLAM!
BLAM!
WHAT IN THE HELL?

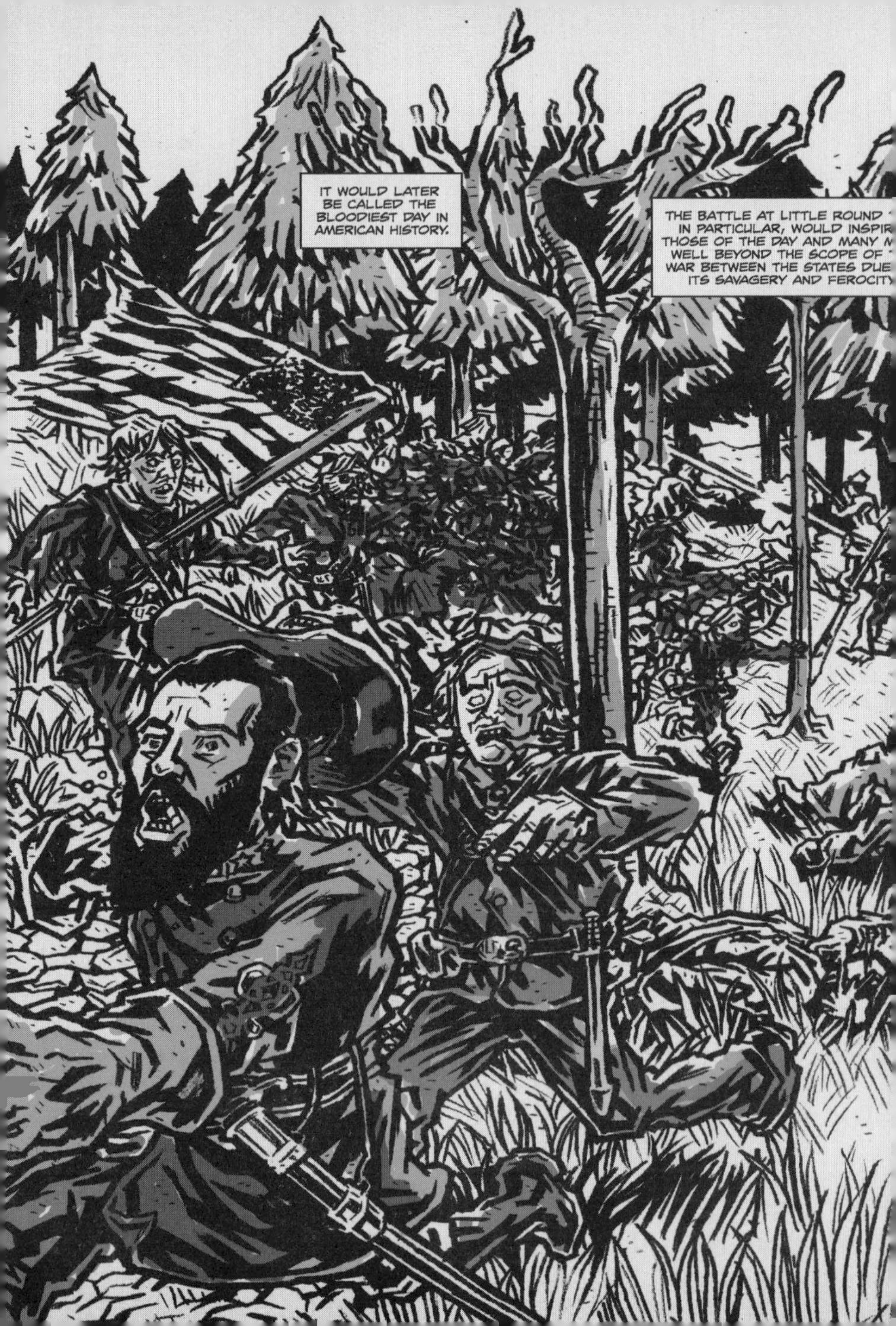
IT WOULD LATER BE CALLED THE BLOODIEST DAY IN AMERICAN HISTORY.
THE BATTLE AT LITTLE ROUND IN PARTICULAR, WOULD INSPIR THOSE OF THE DAY AND MANY M WELL BEYOND THE SCOPE OF WAR BETWEEN THE STATES DUE ITS SAVAGERY AND FEROCITY

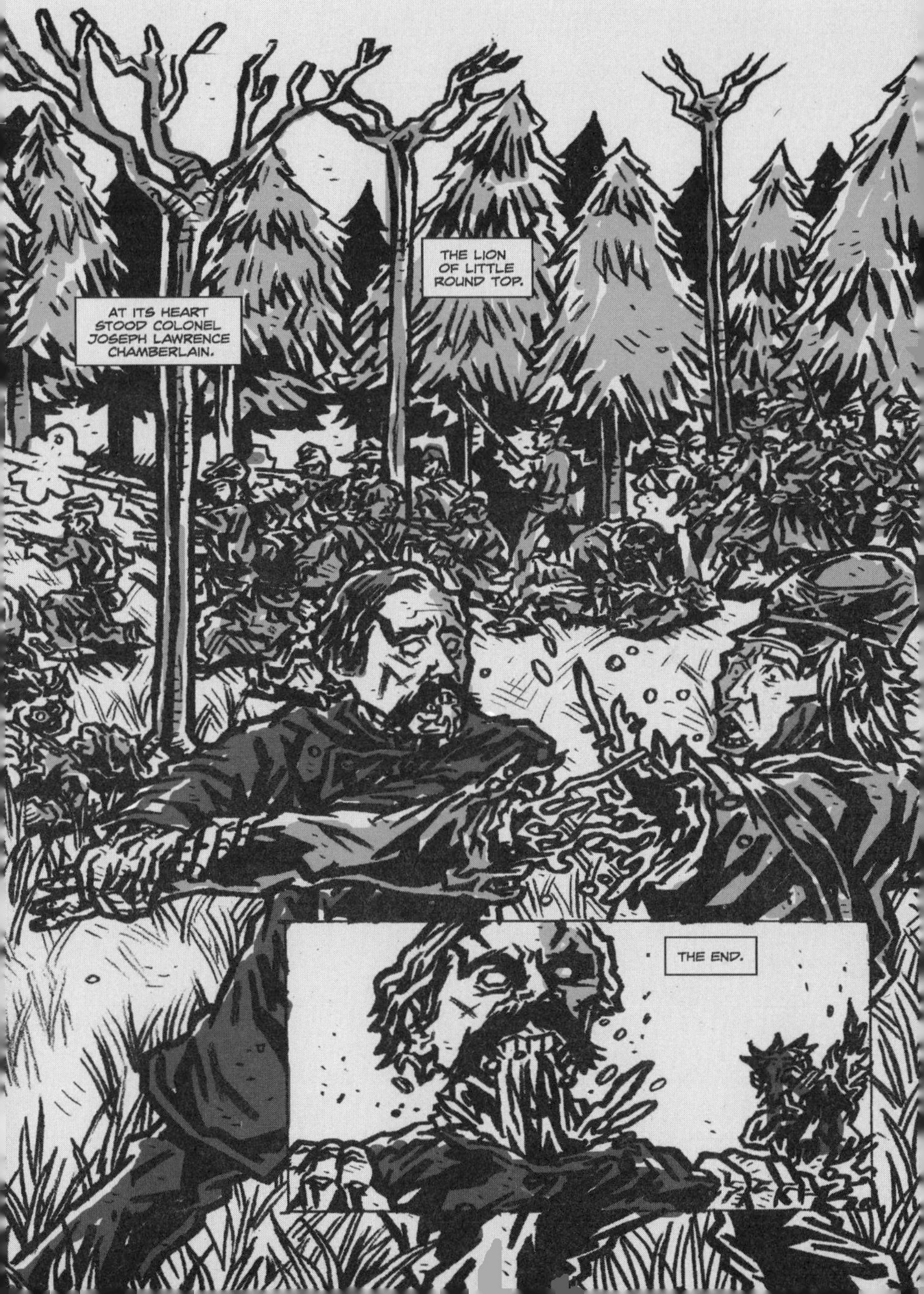
AT ITS HEART STOOD COLONEL JOSEPH LAWRENCE CHAMBERLAIN.
THE LION OF LITTLE ROUND TOP.
THE END.

THE LEGEND OF MOSE THE FIREBOY

STORY BY:
MARK BERTOLINI

ART AND LETTERS BY:
ERIC SPOHN

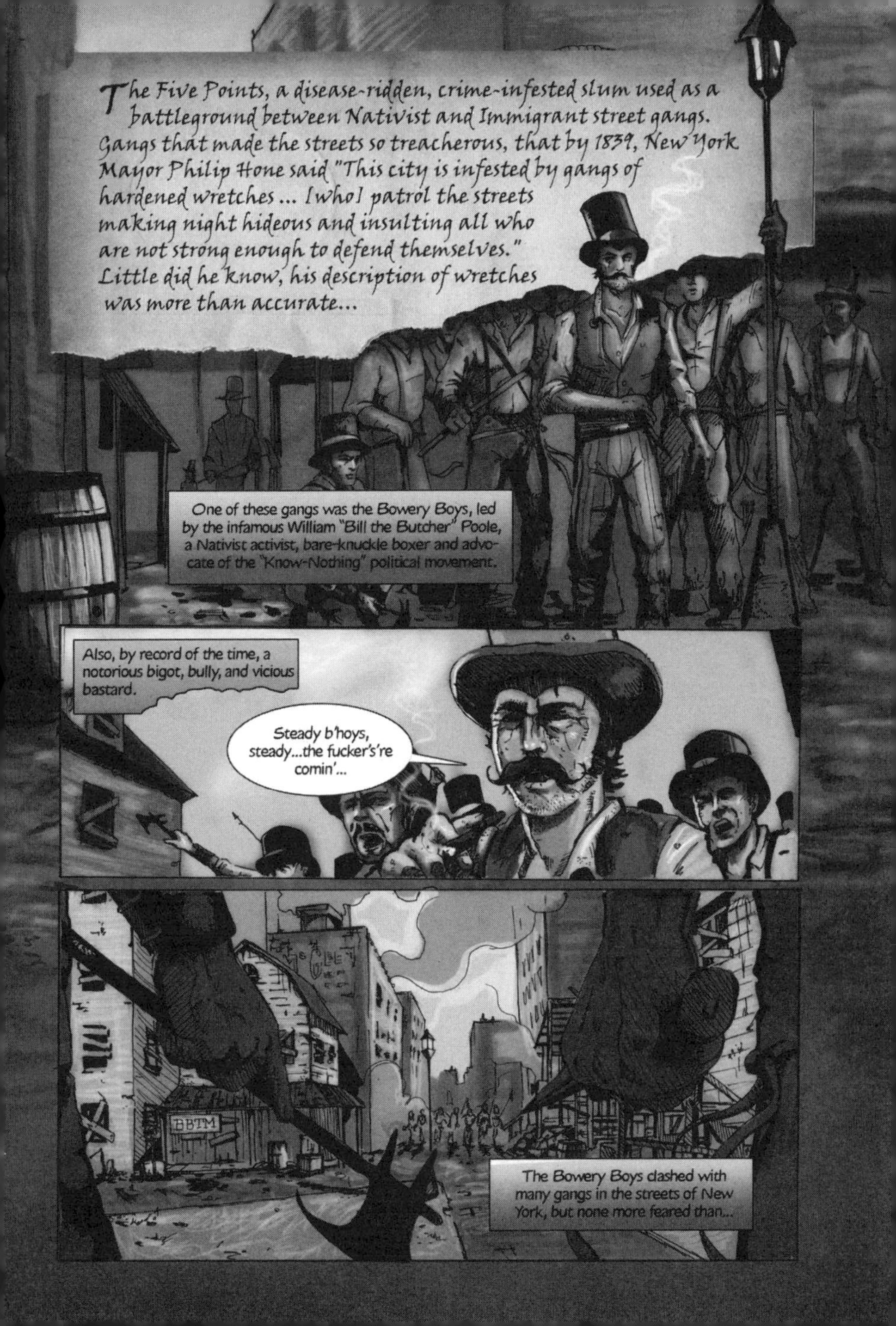
The Five Points, a disease-ridden, crime-infested slum used as a battleground between Nativist and Immigrant street gangs. Gangs that made the streets so treacherous, that by 1839, New York Mayor Philip Hone said "This city is infested by gangs of hardened wretches ... [who] patrol the streets making night hideous and insulting all who are not strong enough to defend themselves." Little did he know, his description of wretches was more than accurate...
One of these gangs was the Bowery Boys, led by the infamous William "Bill the Butcher" Poole, a Nativist activist, bare-knuckle boxer and advocate of the "Know-Nothing" political movement.
Also, by record of the time, a notorious bigot, bully, and vicious bastard.
Steady b'hoys, steady...the fucker's're comin'...
BBTM
The Bowery Boys clashed with many gangs in the streets of New York, but none more feared than...

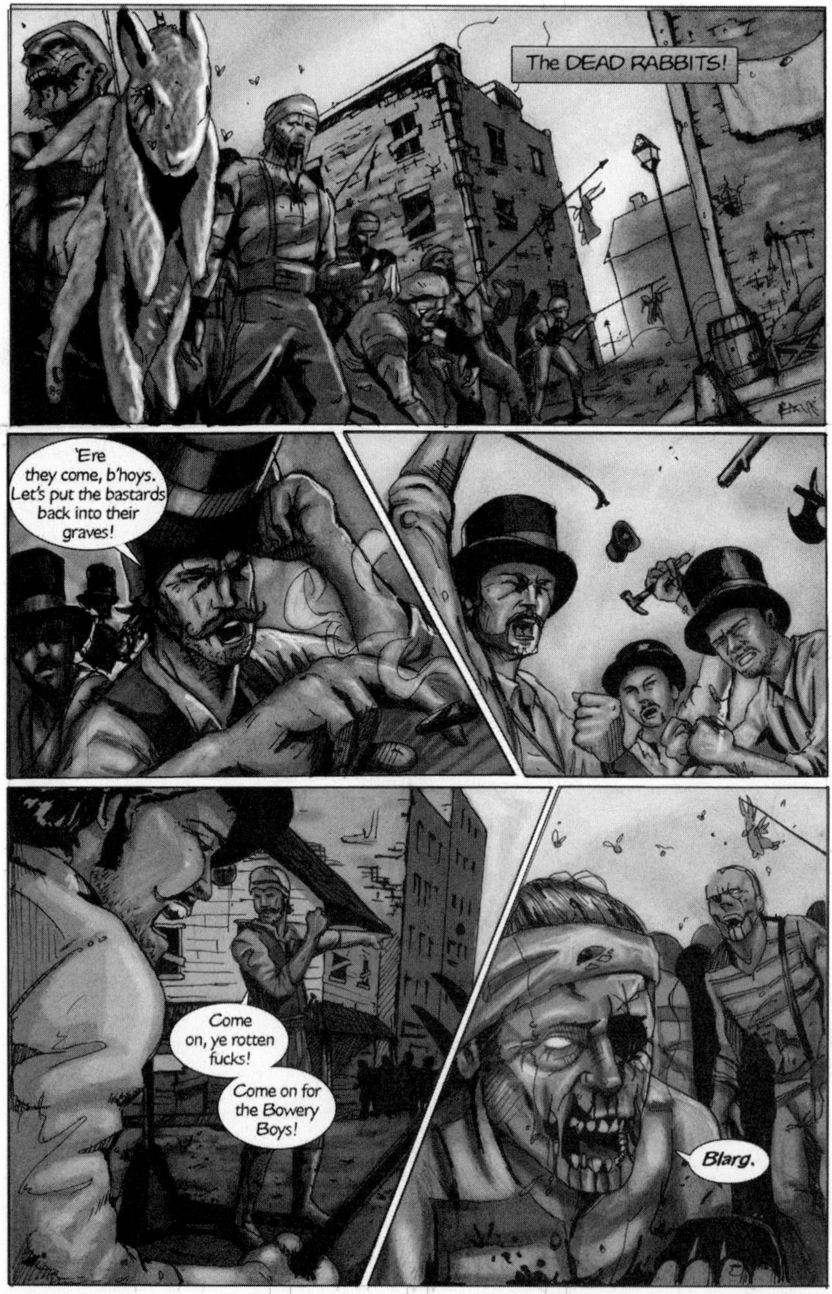

The DEAD RABBITS!
'Ere they come, b'hoys. Let's put the bastards back into their graves!
Come on, ye rotten fucks!
Come on for the Bowery Boys!
Blarg.

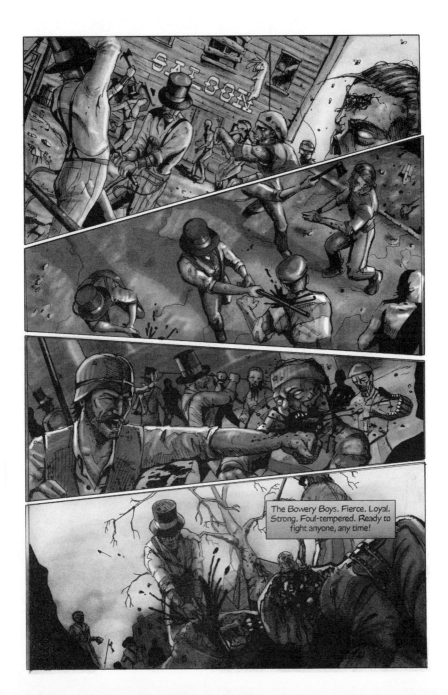

The Bowery Boys. Fierce. Loyal. Strong. Foul-tempered. Ready to fight anyone, any time!

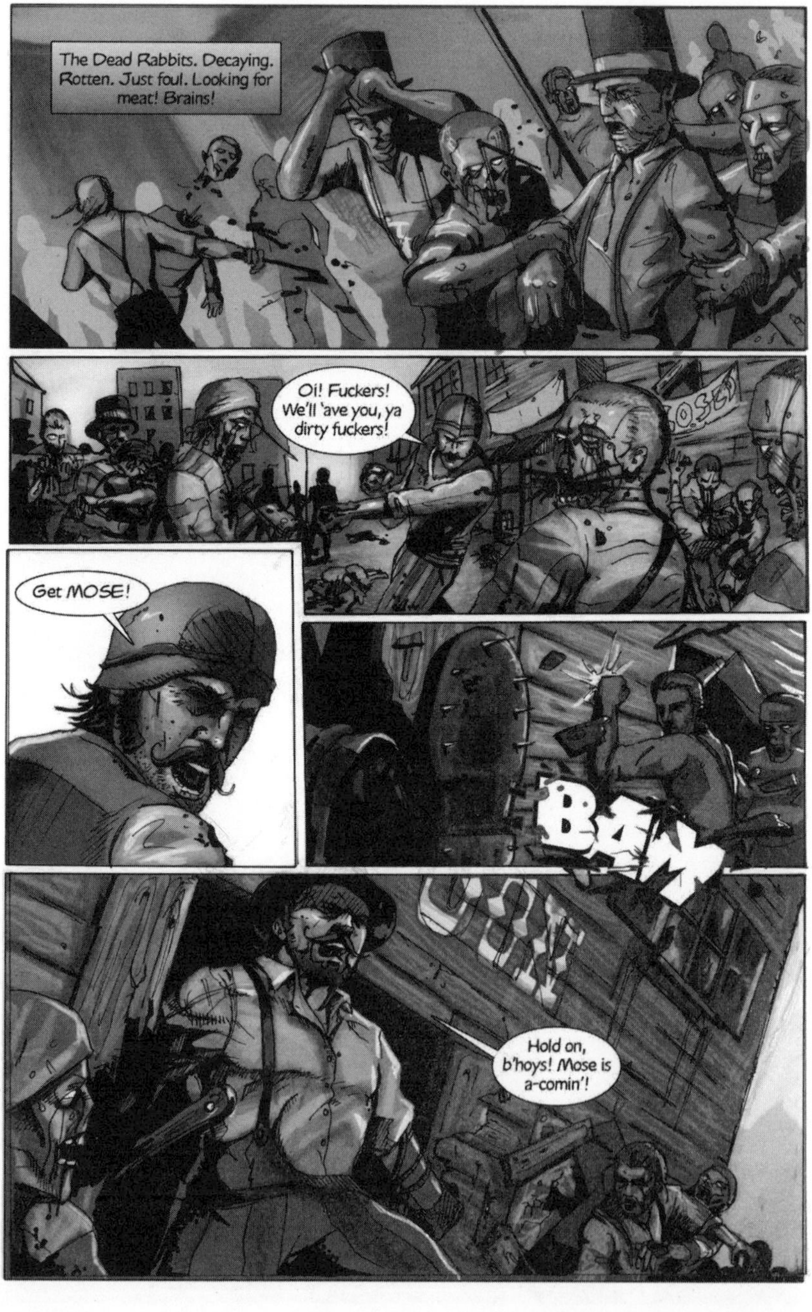
The Dead Rabbits. Decaying. Rotten. Just foul. Looking for meat! Brains!
Oi! Fuckers! We'll 'ave you, ya dirty fuckers!
Get MOSE!
BAM
Hold on, b'hoys! Mose is a-comin'!

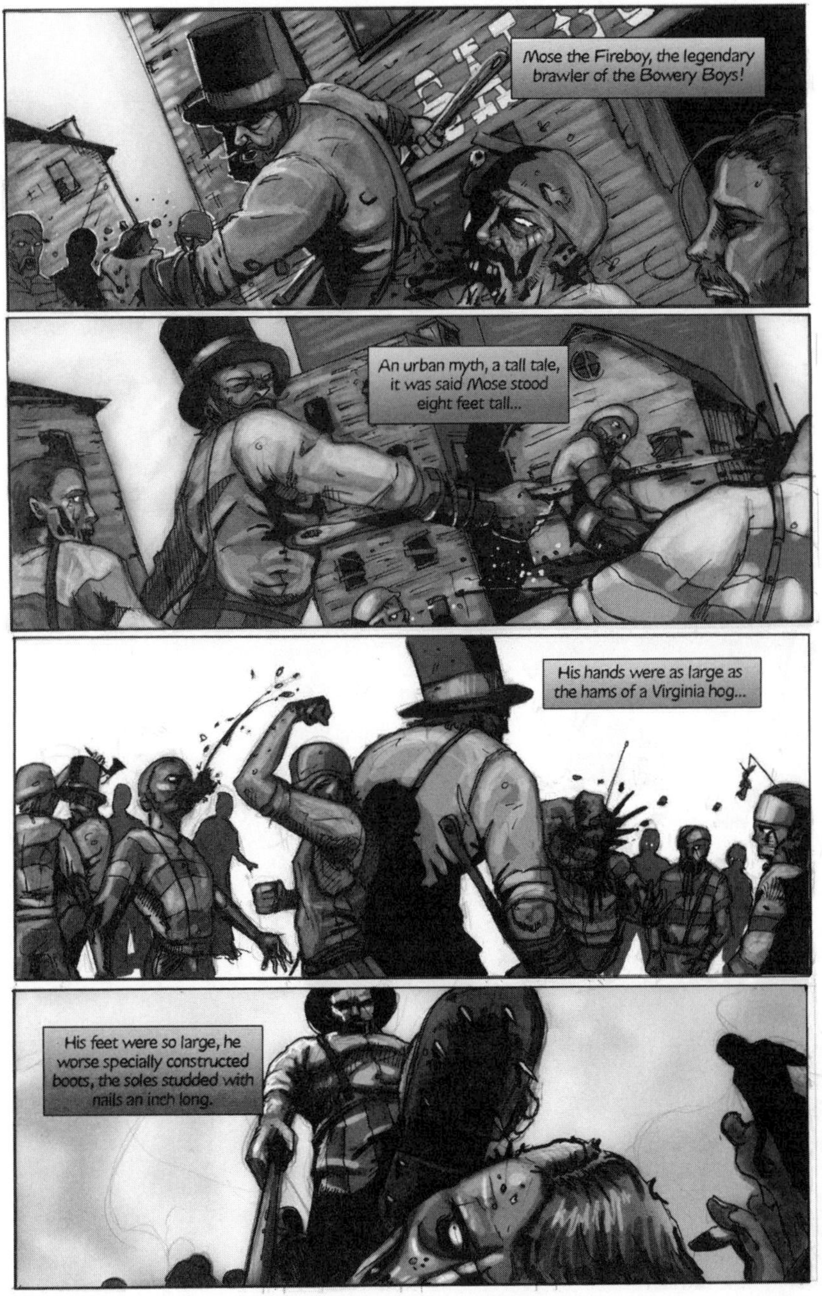
Mose the Fireboy, the legendary brawler of the Bowery Boys!
An urban myth, a tall tale, it was said Mose stood eight feet tall...
His hands were as large as the hams of a Virginia hog...
His feet were so large, he worse specially constructed boots, the soles studded with nails an inch long.

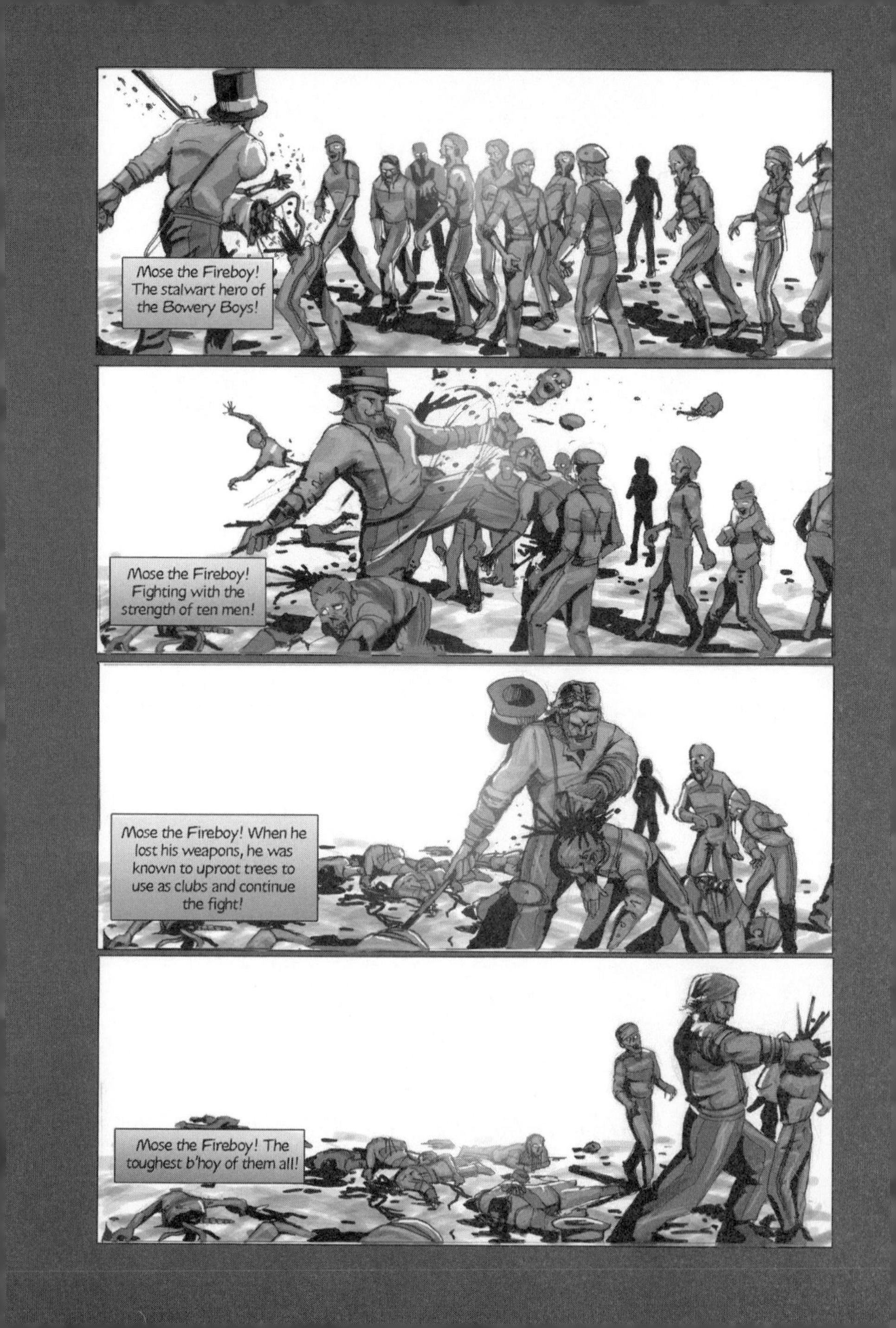
Mose the Fireboy! The stalwart hero of the Bowery Boys!
Mose the Fireboy! Fighting with the strength of ten men!
Mose the Fireboy! When he lost his weapons, he was known to uproot trees to use as clubs and continue the fight!
Mose the Fireboy! The toughest b'hoy of them all!

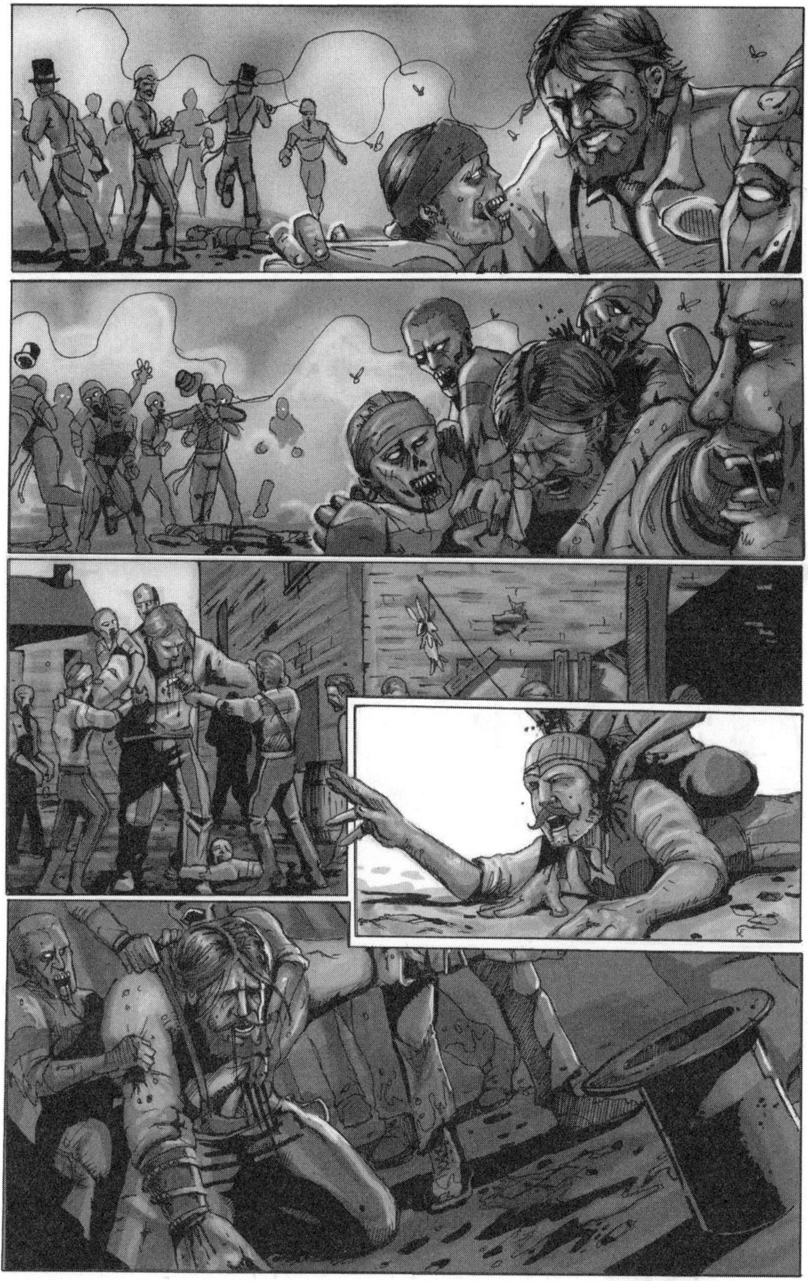

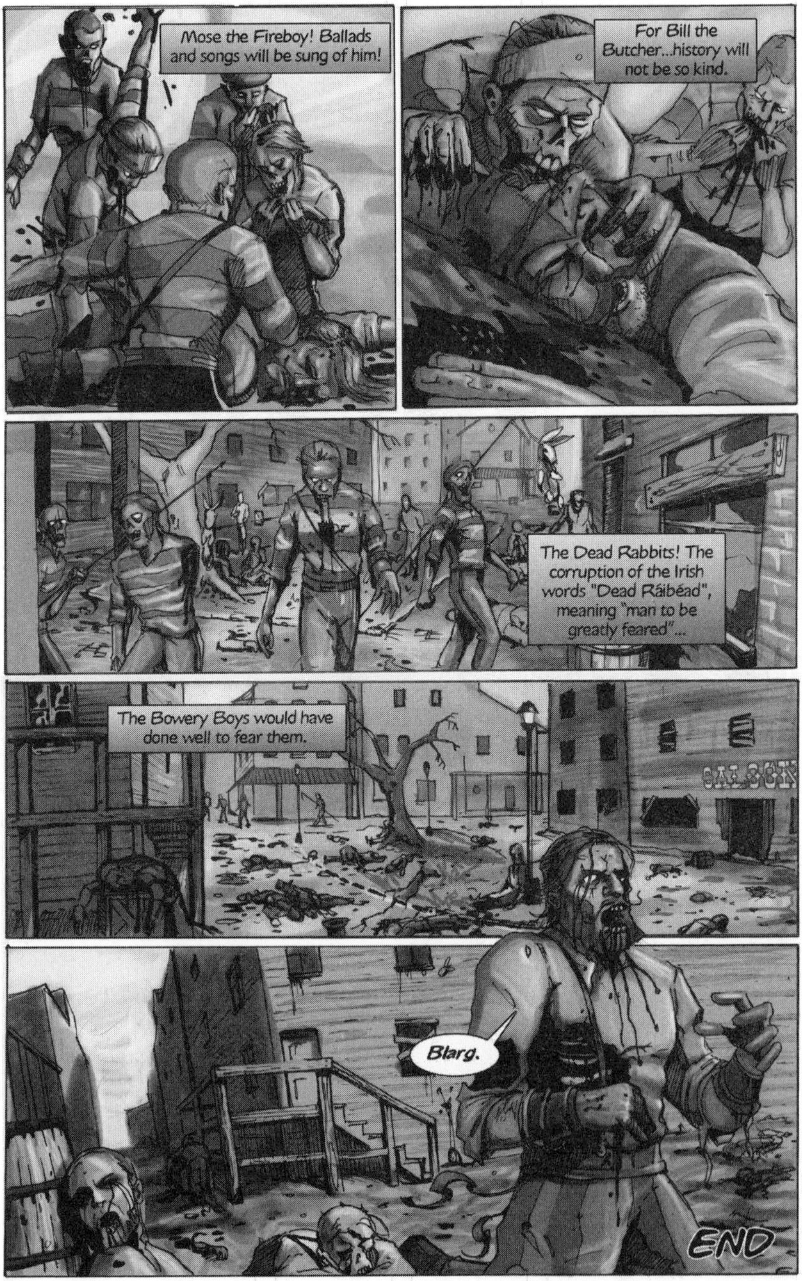

Mose the Fireboy! Ballads and songs will be sung of him!
For Bill the Butcher...history will not be so kind.
The Dead Rabbits! The corruption of the Irish words "Dead Ráibéad", meaning "man to be greatly feared"...
The Bowery Boys would have done well to fear them.
Blarg.
END

BEHIND THE OK CORRAL

STORY AND LETTERS BY:
JEFF McCOMSEY

ART BY:
ROB CROONENBORGHS

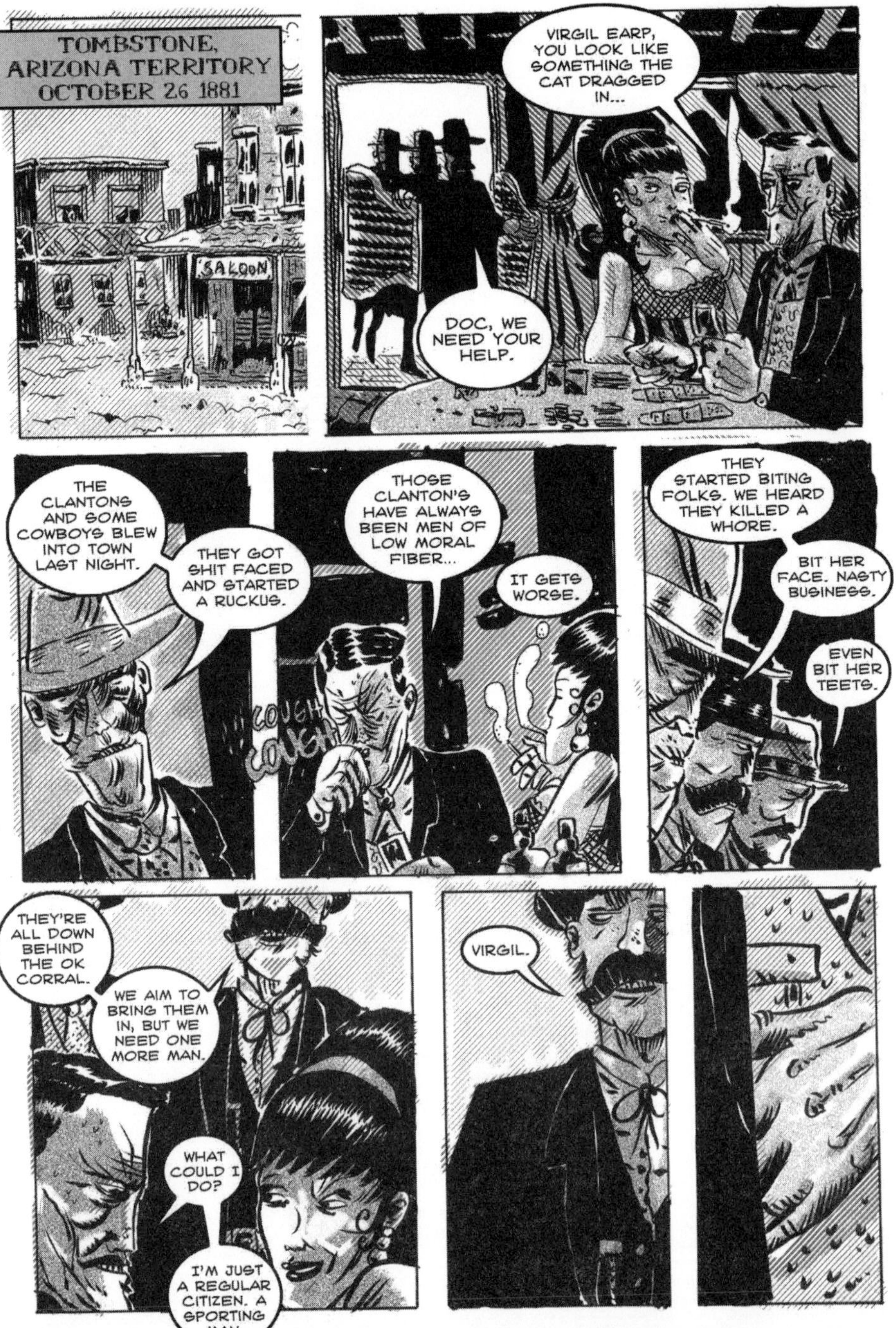
TOMBSTONE, ARIZONA TERRITORY OCTOBER 26 1881
SALOON
VIRGIL EARP, YOU LOOK LIKE SOMETHING THE CAT DRAGGED IN...
DOC, WE NEED YOUR HELP.
THE CLANTONS AND SOME COWBOYS BLEW INTO TOWN LAST NIGHT.
THEY GOT SHIT FACED AND STARTED A RUCKUS.
THOSE CLANTON'S HAVE ALWAYS BEEN MEN OF LOW MORAL FIBER...
COUGH COUGH
IT GETS WORSE.
THEY STARTED BITING FOLKS. WE HEARD THEY KILLED A WHORE.
BIT HER FACE. NASTY BUSINESS.
EVEN BIT HER TEETS.
THEY'RE ALL DOWN BEHIND THE OK CORRAL.
WE AIM TO BRING THEM IN, BUT WE NEED ONE MORE MAN.
WHAT COULD I DO?
I'M JUST A REGULAR CITIZEN. A SPORTING MAN.
VIRGIL.

AND TO THINK DADDY SAID I'D NEVER AMOUNT TO MUCH.

OUGH COUGH OUGH COUGH COUGH COUGH COU

NOW DOC, WE'RE HERE TO DISARM AND ARREST THESE BOYS.

I CONFESS I DON'T HAVE MUCH EXPERIENCE AR-RESTING PEOPLE.

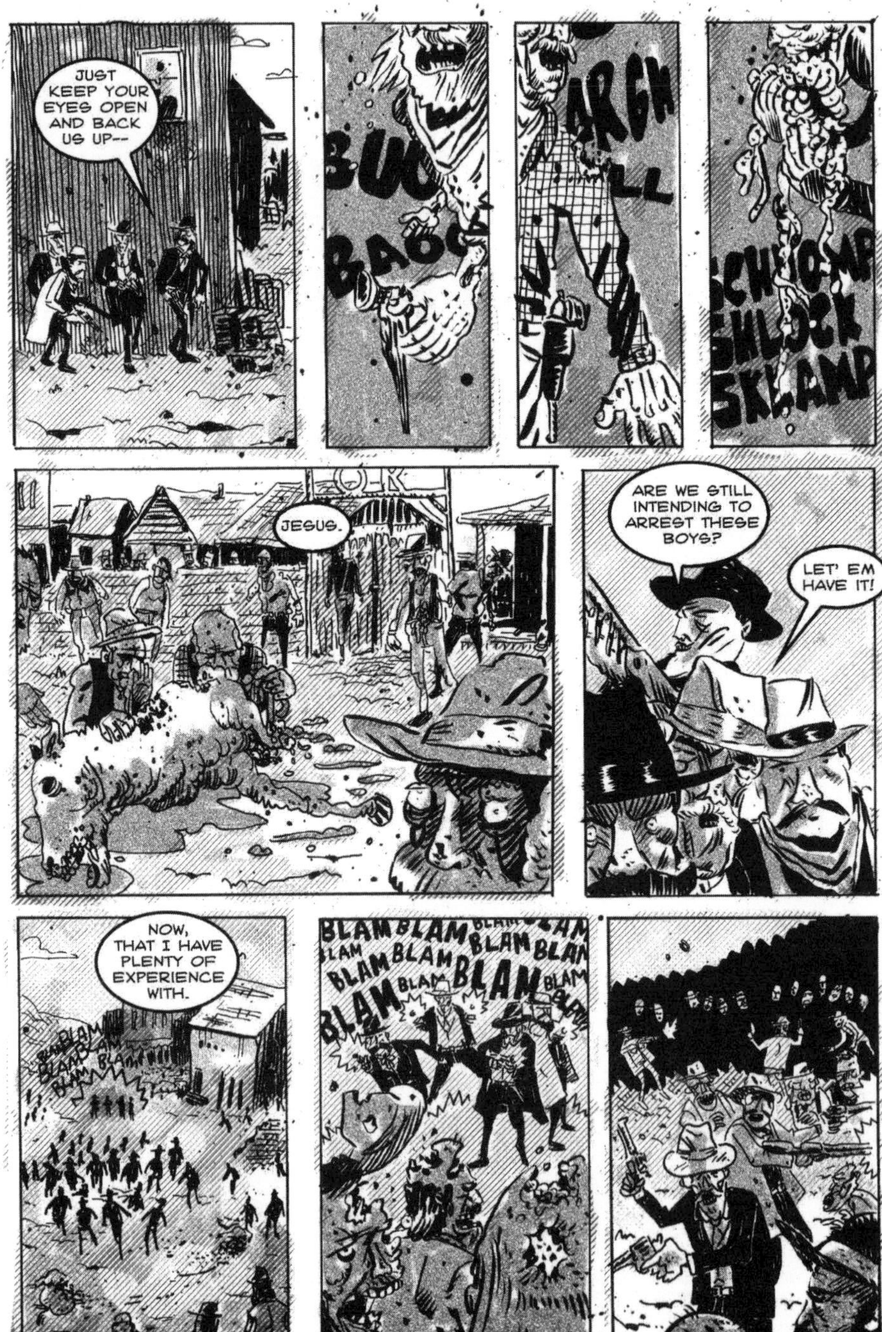
JUST KEEP YOUR EYES OPEN AND BACK US UP--
ARGH
SHLOCK
SKLAMP
JESUS.
ARE WE STILL INTENDING TO ARREST THESE BOYS?
LET' EM HAVE IT!
NOW, THAT I HAVE PLENTY OF EXPERIENCE WITH.
BLAM BLAM BLAM
BLAM BLAM BLAM BLAM BLAM BLAM BLAM BLAM BLAM

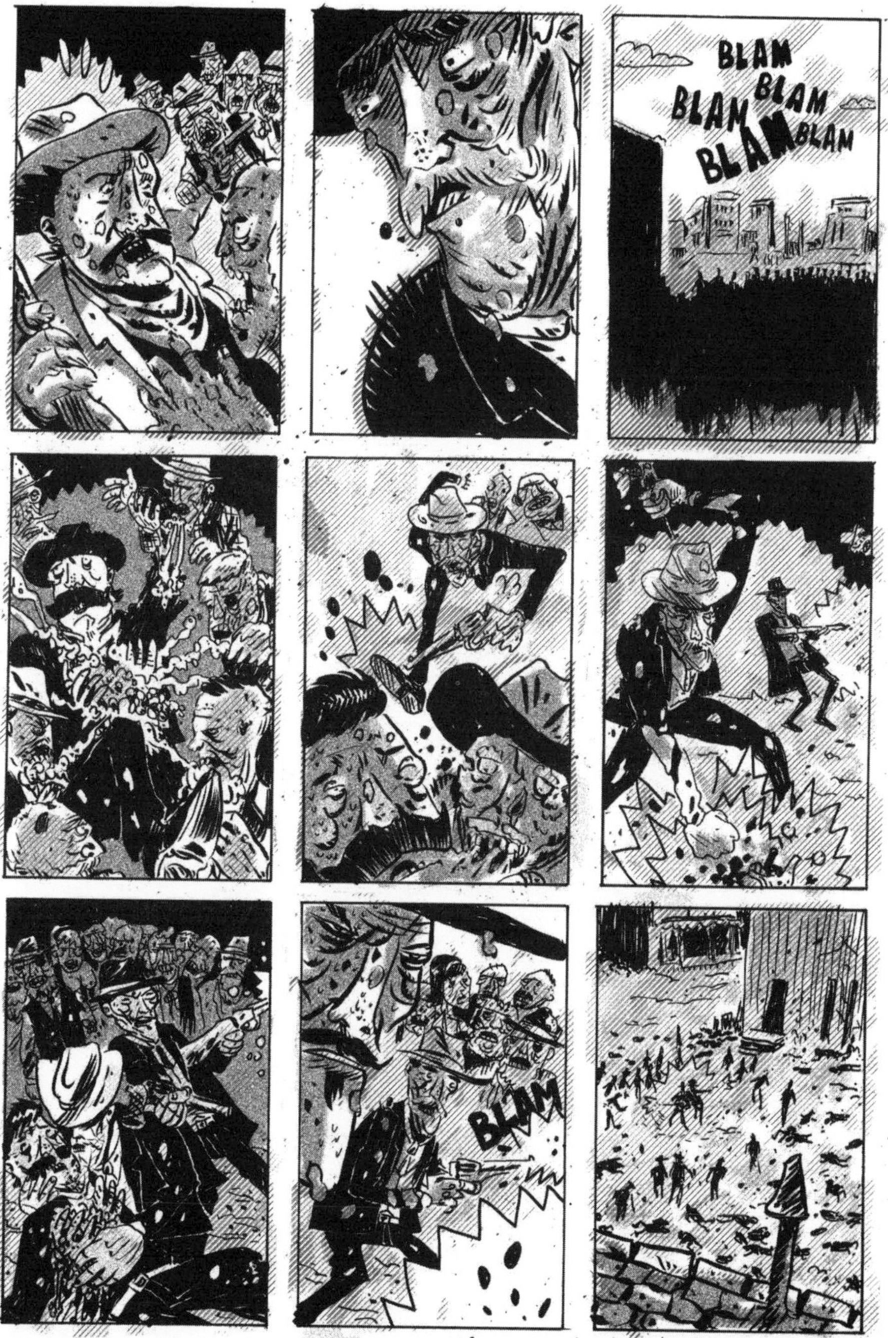
BLAM
BLAM
BLAM
BLAM
BLAM
BLAM

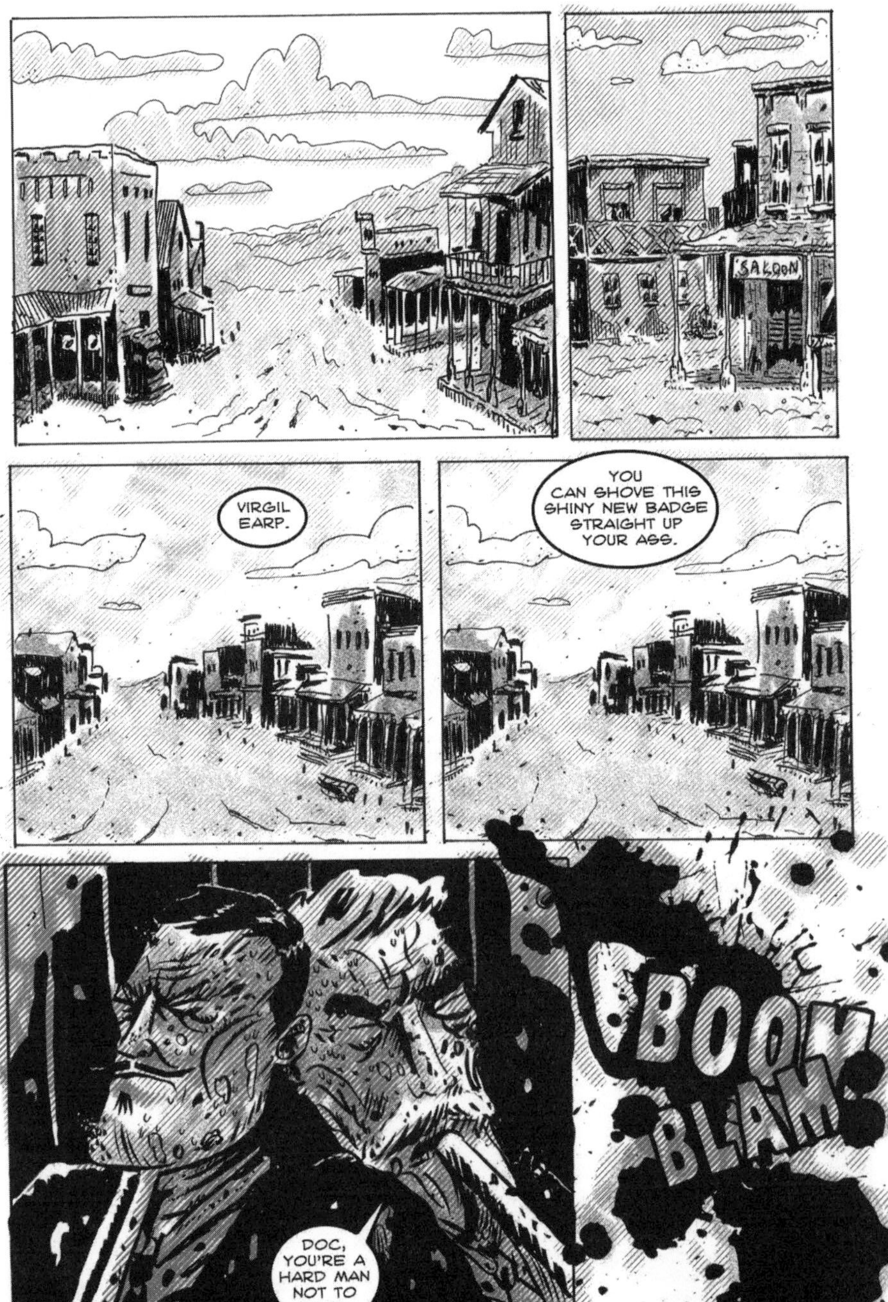
SALOON
VIRGIL EARP.
YOU CAN SHOVE THIS SHINY NEW BADGE STRAIGHT UP YOUR ASS.
BOOM
BLAM
DOC, YOU'RE A HARD MAN NOT TO LIKE.

ZOMBIE BILL'S WILD WEST SHOW

STORY BY:
PARKER LINDSTROM
DAMIAN EBY

ART AND LETTERS BY:
JACOB WARRENFELTZ

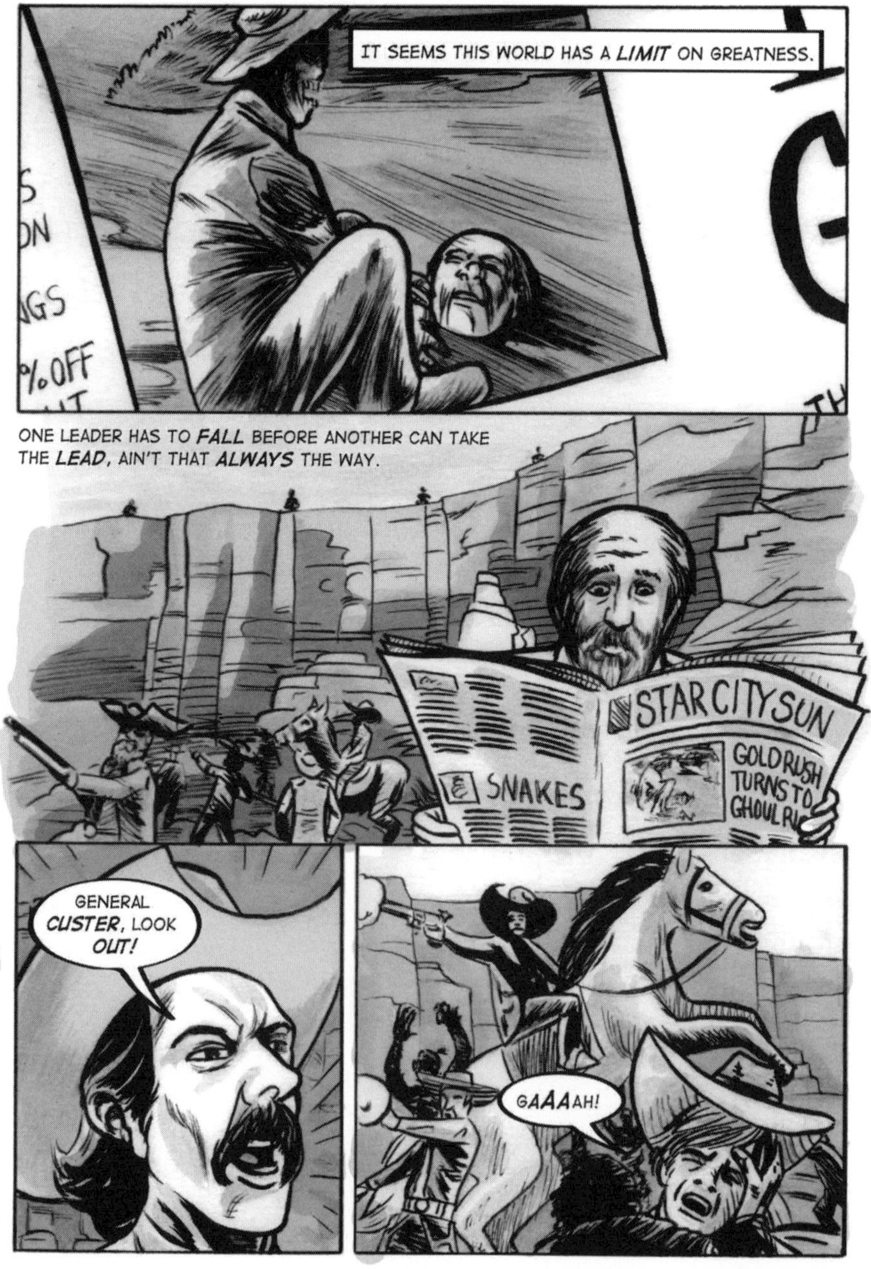
IT SEEMS THIS WORLD HAS A *LIMIT* ON GREATNESS.
ONE LEADER HAS TO *FALL* BEFORE ANOTHER CAN TAKE THE *LEAD*, AIN'T THAT *ALWAYS* THE WAY.
STAR CITY SUN
SNAKES
GOLD RUSH TURNS TO GHOUL RU
GENERAL *CUSTER*, LOOK *OUT!*
GAAAAH!

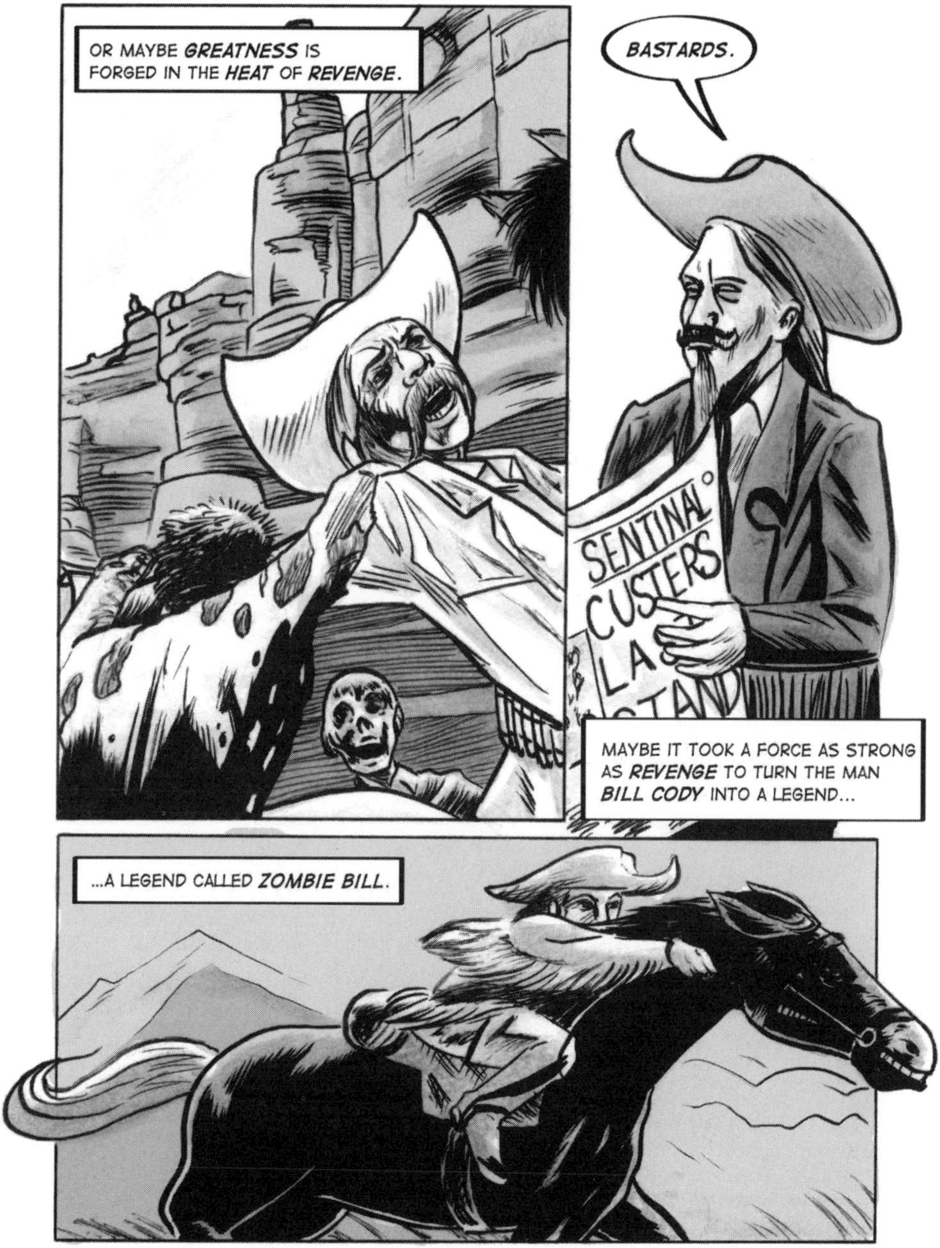
OR MAYBE GREATNESS IS FORGED IN THE HEAT OF REVENGE.
BASTARDS.
SENTINAL CUSTERS LAST STAND
MAYBE IT TOOK A FORCE AS STRONG AS REVENGE TO TURN THE MAN BILL CODY INTO A LEGEND...
...A LEGEND CALLED ZOMBIE BILL.

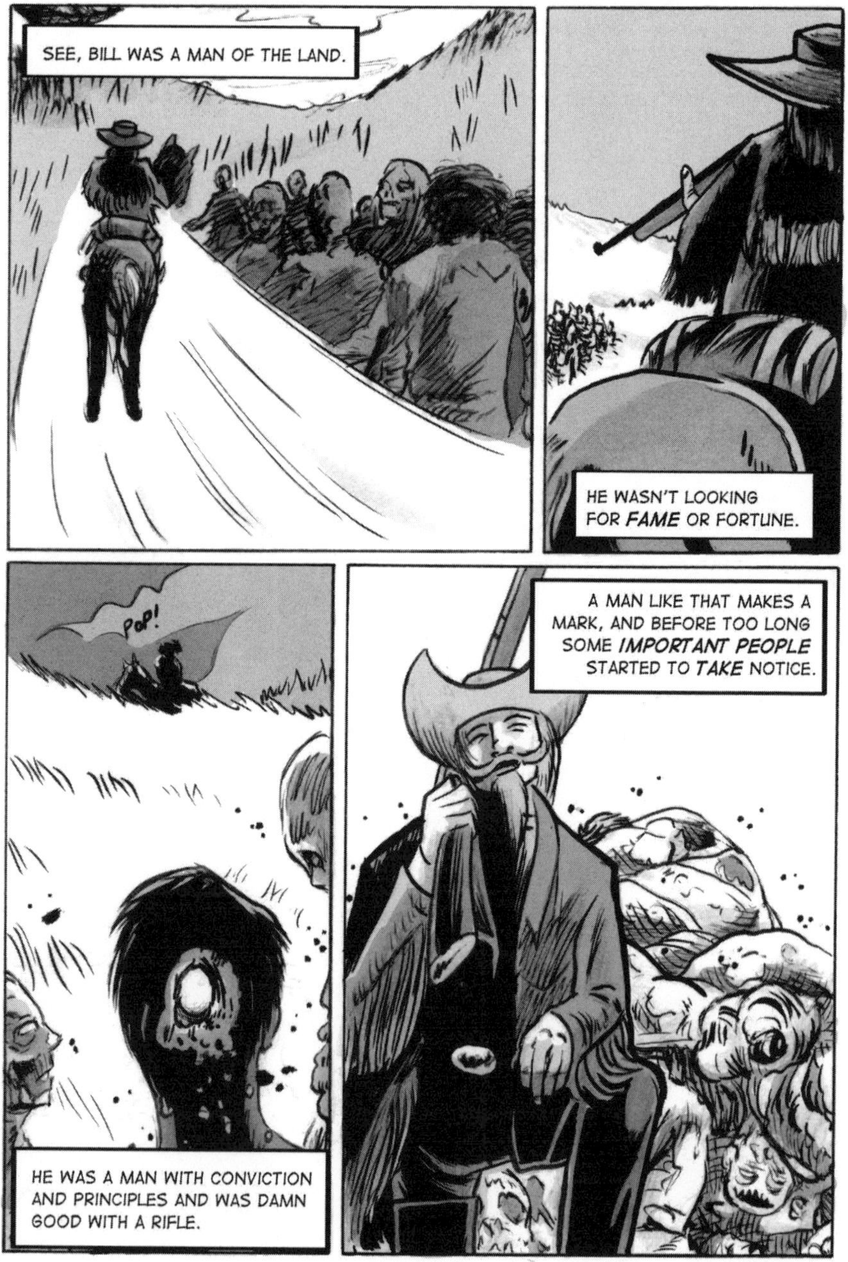
SEE, BILL WAS A MAN OF THE LAND.
HE WASN'T LOOKING FOR *FAME* OR FORTUNE.
POP!
HE WAS A MAN WITH CONVICTION AND PRINCIPLES AND WAS DAMN GOOD WITH A RIFLE.
A MAN LIKE THAT MAKES A MARK, AND BEFORE TOO LONG SOME *IMPORTANT PEOPLE* STARTED TO *TAKE* NOTICE.

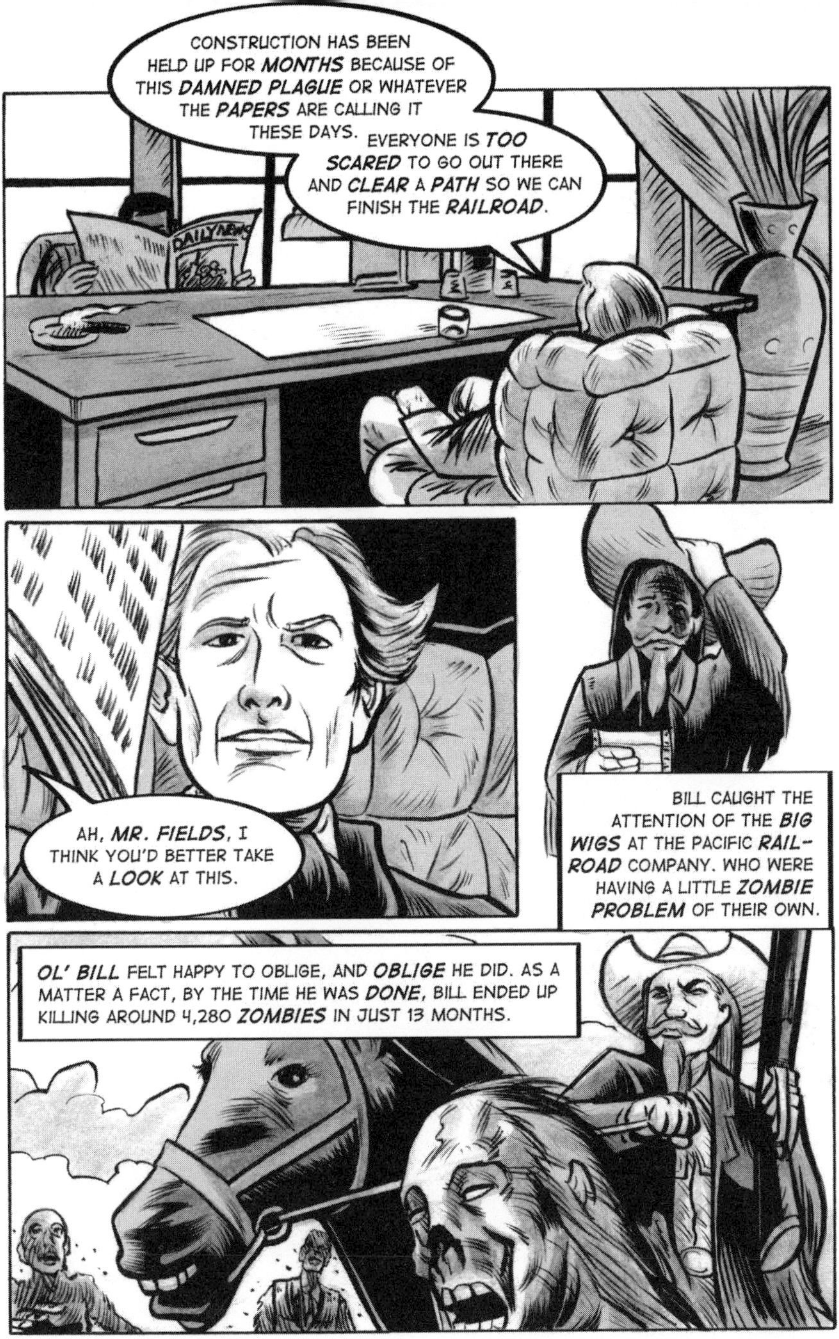
CONSTRUCTION HAS BEEN HELD UP FOR MONTHS BECAUSE OF THIS DAMNED PLAGUE OR WHATEVER THE PAPERS ARE CALLING IT THESE DAYS.
EVERYONE IS TOO SCARED TO GO OUT THERE AND CLEAR A PATH SO WE CAN FINISH THE RAILROAD.
DAILY NEWS
AH, MR. FIELDS, I THINK YOU'D BETTER TAKE A LOOK AT THIS.
BILL CAUGHT THE ATTENTION OF THE BIG WIGS AT THE PACIFIC RAIL-ROAD COMPANY. WHO WERE HAVING A LITTLE ZOMBIE PROBLEM OF THEIR OWN.
OL' BILL FELT HAPPY TO OBLIGE, AND OBLIGE HE DID. AS A MATTER A FACT, BY THE TIME HE WAS DONE, BILL ENDED UP KILLING AROUND 4,280 ZOMBIES IN JUST 13 MONTHS.

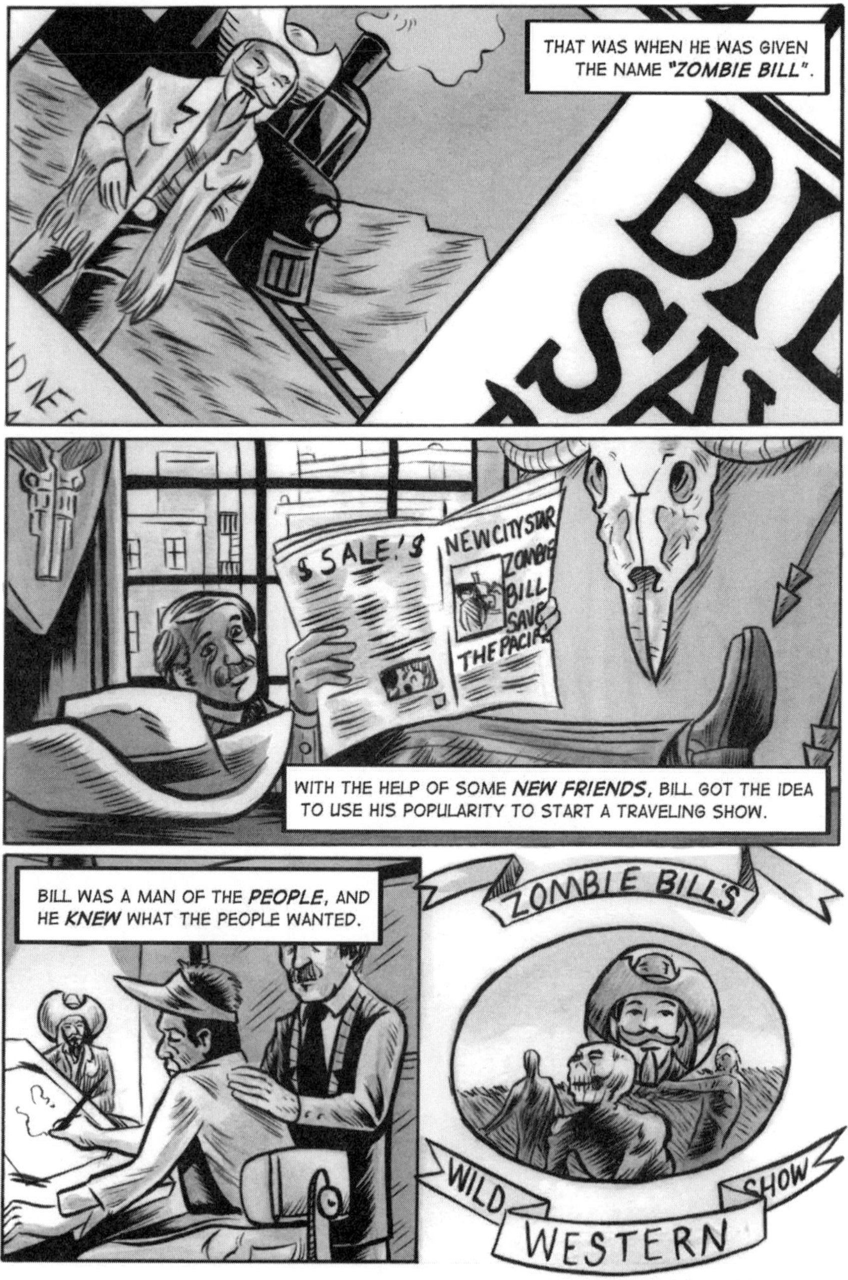
THAT WAS WHEN HE WAS GIVEN THE NAME *"ZOMBIE BILL"*.
NEW CITY STAR
WITH THE HELP OF SOME *NEW FRIENDS*, BILL GOT THE IDEA TO USE HIS POPULARITY TO START A TRAVELING SHOW.
BILL WAS A MAN OF THE *PEOPLE*, AND HE *KNEW* WHAT THE PEOPLE WANTED.
ZOMBIE BILL'S
WILD WESTERN SHOW
SO HE GOT THE *MOST TALENTED* PEOPLE HE KNEW TO *HELP*.

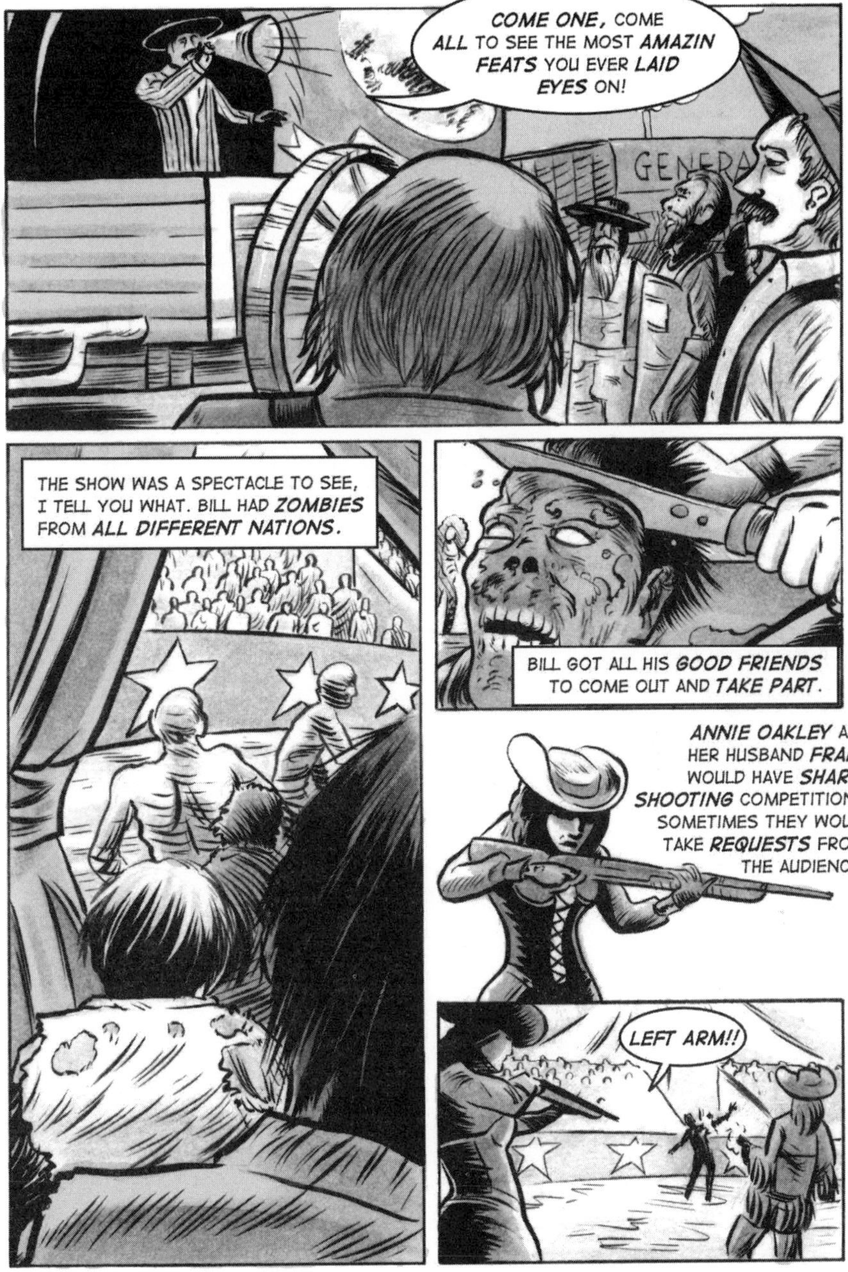
COME ONE, COME ALL TO SEE THE MOST AMAZIN FEATS YOU EVER LAID EYES ON!
THE SHOW WAS A SPECTACLE TO SEE, I TELL YOU WHAT. BILL HAD ZOMBIES FROM ALL DIFFERENT NATIONS.
BILL GOT ALL HIS GOOD FRIENDS TO COME OUT AND TAKE PART.
ANNIE OAKLEY AND HER HUSBAND FRANK WOULD HAVE SHARP-SHOOTING COMPETITIONS. SOMETIMES THEY WOULD TAKE REQUESTS FROM THE AUDIENCE.
LEFT ARM!!

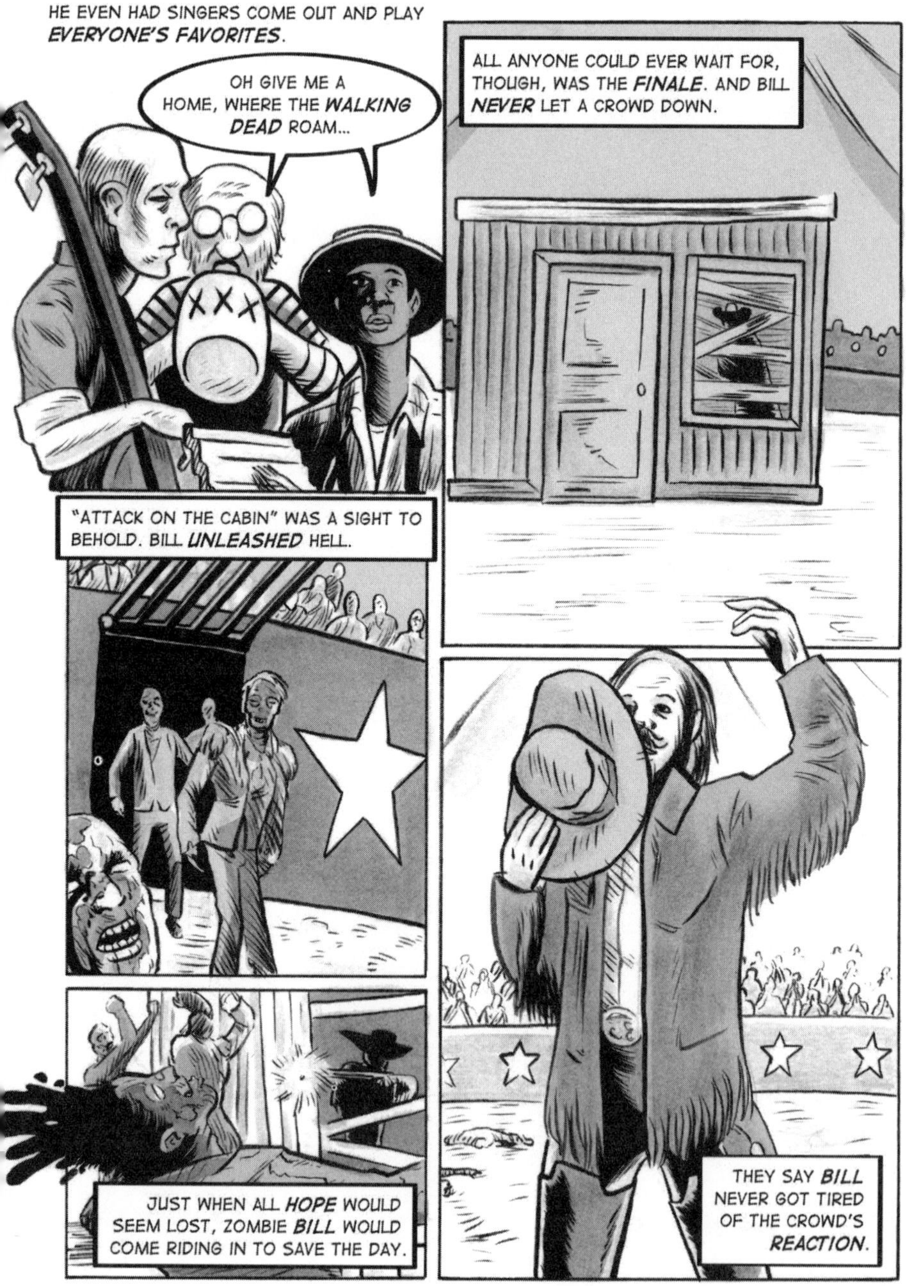
HE EVEN HAD SINGERS COME OUT AND PLAY EVERYONE'S FAVORITES.
OH GIVE ME A HOME, WHERE THE WALKING DEAD ROAM...
ALL ANYONE COULD EVER WAIT FOR, THOUGH, WAS THE FINALE. AND BILL NEVER LET A CROWD DOWN.
"ATTACK ON THE CABIN" WAS A SIGHT TO BEHOLD. BILL UNLEASHED HELL.
JUST WHEN ALL HOPE WOULD SEEM LOST, ZOMBIE BILL WOULD COME RIDING IN TO SAVE THE DAY.
THEY SAY BILL NEVER GOT TIRED OF THE CROWD'S REACTION.

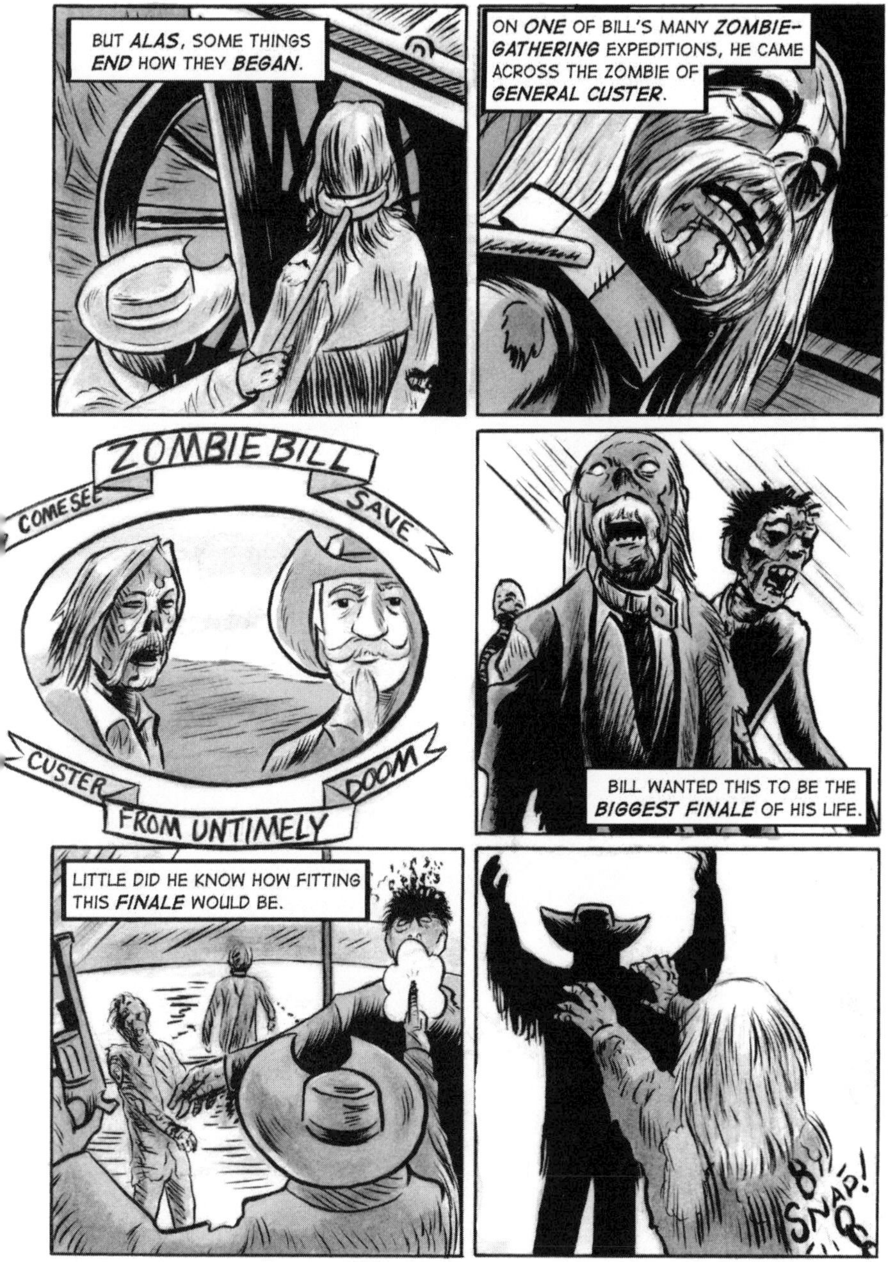
BUT ALAS, SOME THINGS END HOW THEY BEGAN.
ON ONE OF BILL'S MANY ZOMBIE-GATHERING EXPEDITIONS, HE CAME ACROSS THE ZOMBIE OF GENERAL CUSTER.
ZOMBIE BILL
COME SEE
SAVE
CUSTER
FROM UNTIMELY
DOOM
BILL WANTED THIS TO BE THE BIGGEST FINALE OF HIS LIFE.
LITTLE DID HE KNOW HOW FITTING THIS FINALE WOULD BE.
SNAP!

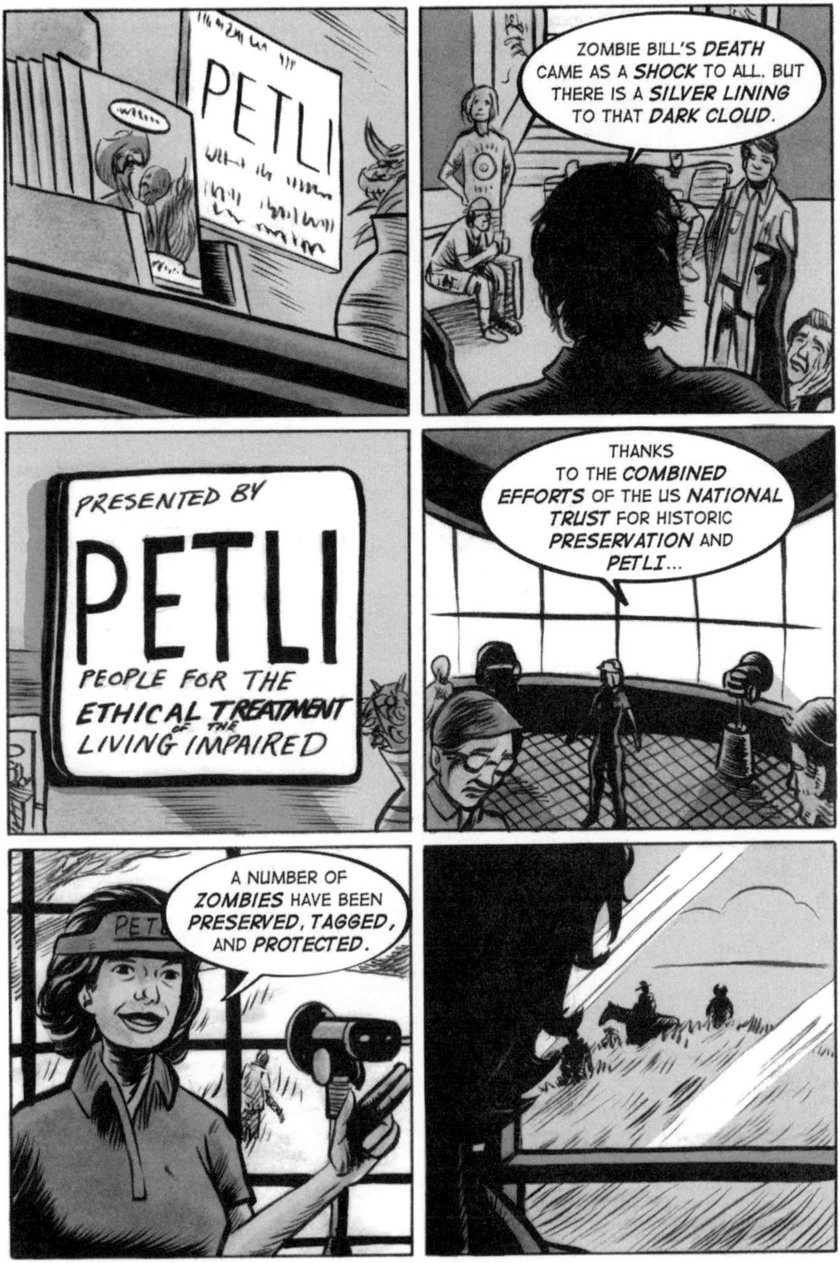
PETLI
ZOMBIE BILL'S DEATH CAME AS A SHOCK TO ALL. BUT THERE IS A SILVER LINING TO THAT DARK CLOUD.
PRESENTED BY
PETLI
PEOPLE FOR THE ETHICAL TREATMENT OF THE LIVING IMPAIRED
THANKS TO THE COMBINED EFFORTS OF THE US NATIONAL TRUST FOR HISTORIC PRESERVATION AND PETLI...
A NUMBER OF ZOMBIES HAVE BEEN PRESERVED, TAGGED, AND PROTECTED.

LIGHTS OUT

STORY AND ART BY:
STEVE BECKER

LETTERS BY:
JEFF McCOMSEY

LIGHTS OUT

STORY AND ART BY: STEVE BECKER

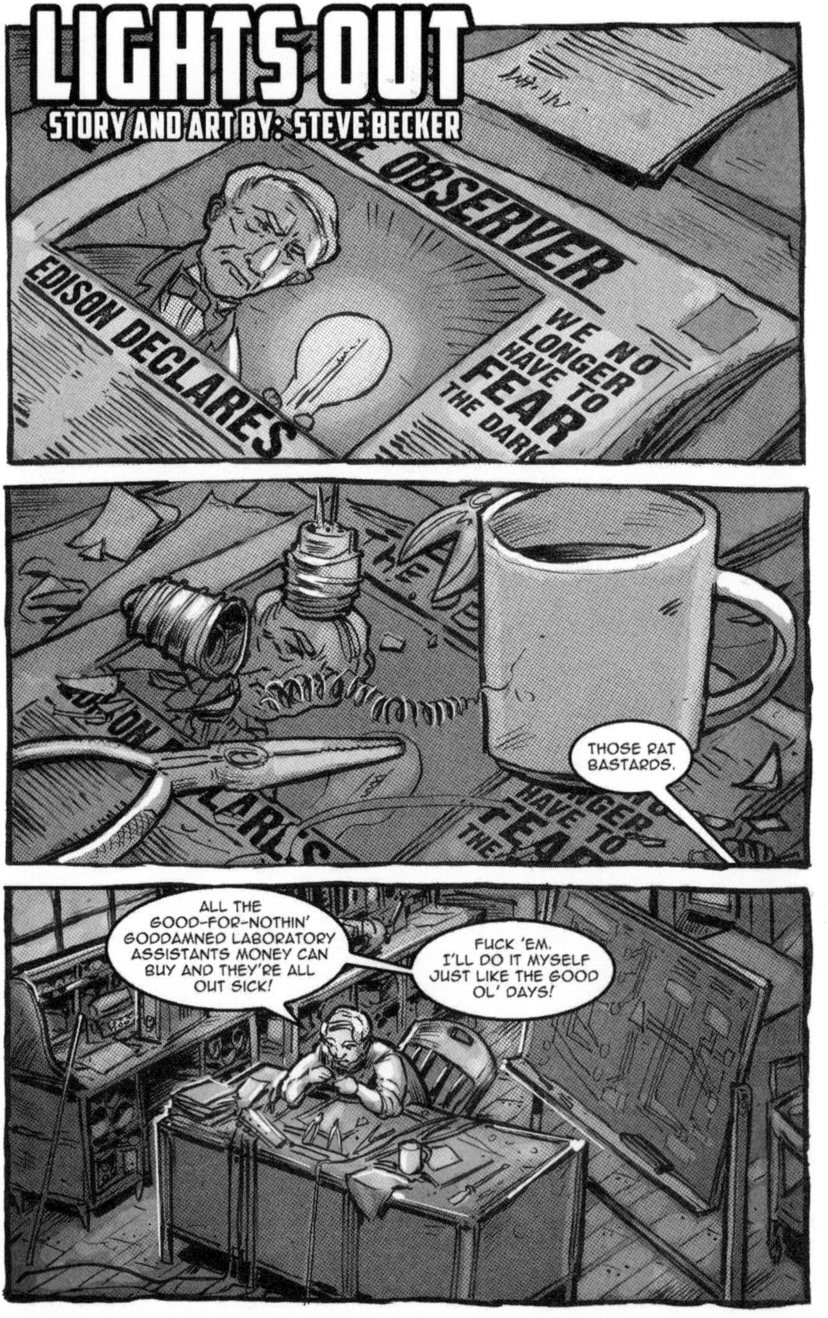

THE OBSERVER
EDISON DECLARES
WE NO LONGER HAVE TO FEAR THE DARK
THOSE RAT BASTARDS.
ALL THE GOOD-FOR-NOTHIN' GODDAMNED LABORATORY ASSISTANTS MONEY CAN BUY AND THEY'RE ALL OUT SICK!
FUCK 'EM. I'LL DO IT MYSELF JUST LIKE THE GOOD OL' DAYS!

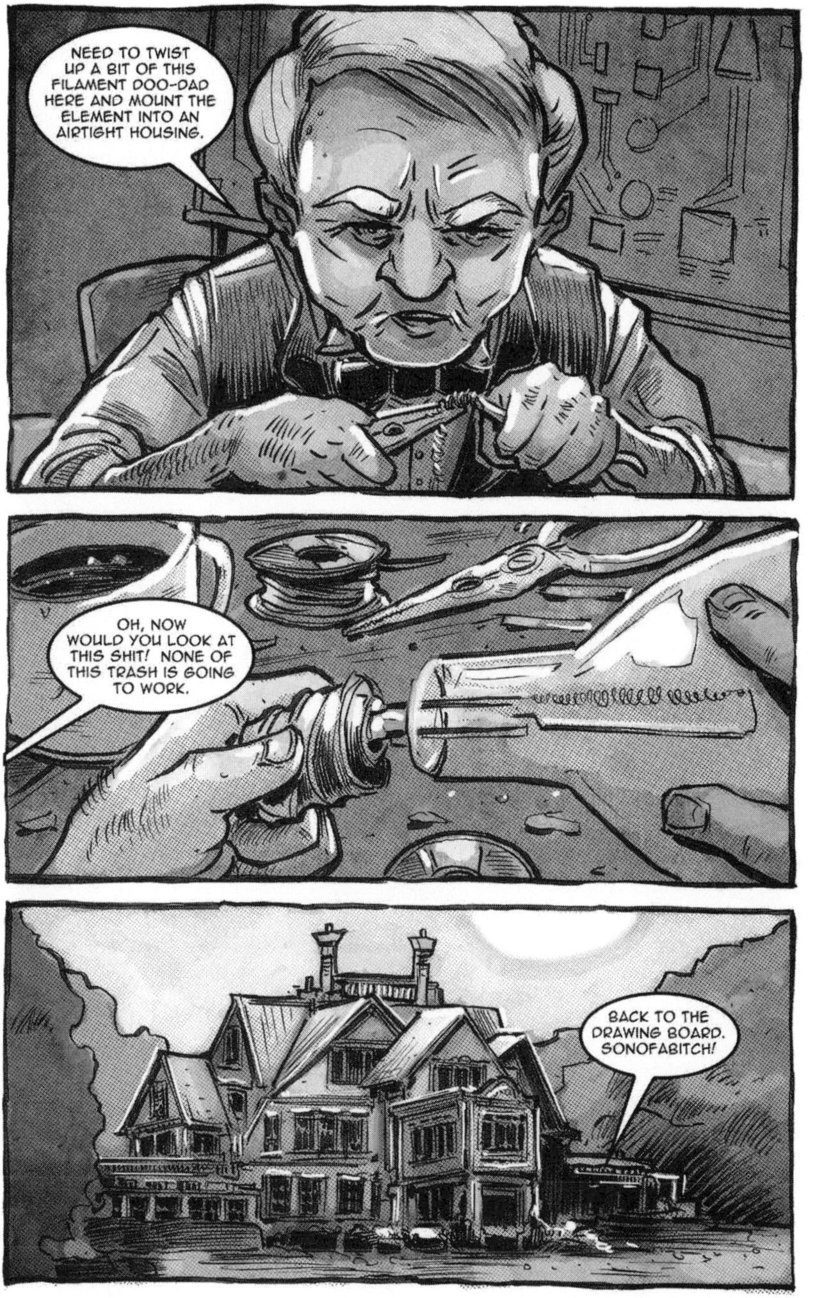
NEED TO TWIST UP A BIT OF THIS FILAMENT DOO-DAD HERE AND MOUNT THE ELEMENT INTO AN AIRTIGHT HOUSING.
OH, NOW WOULD YOU LOOK AT THIS SHIT! NONE OF THIS TRASH IS GOING TO WORK.
BACK TO THE DRAWING BOARD. SONOFABITCH!

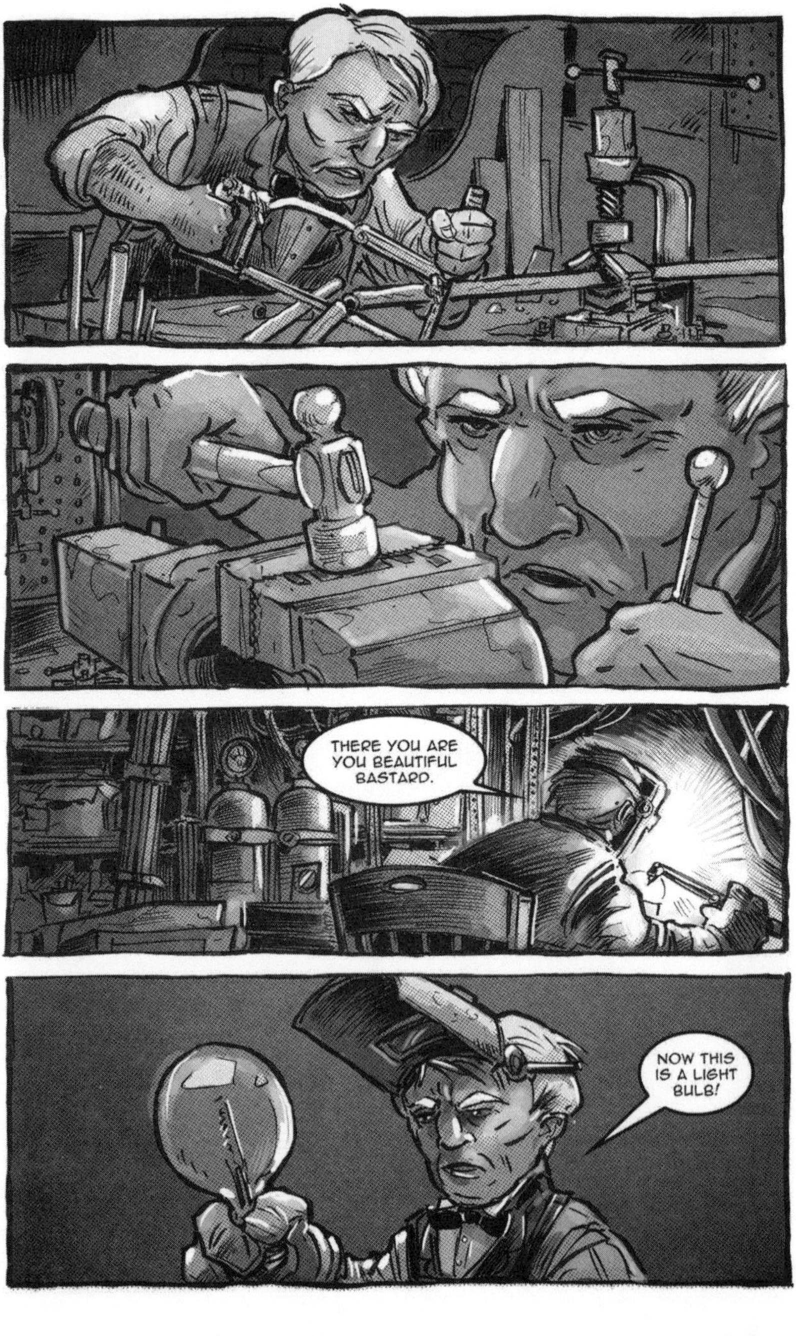
THERE YOU ARE YOU BEAUTIFUL BASTARD.
NOW THIS IS A LIGHT BULB!

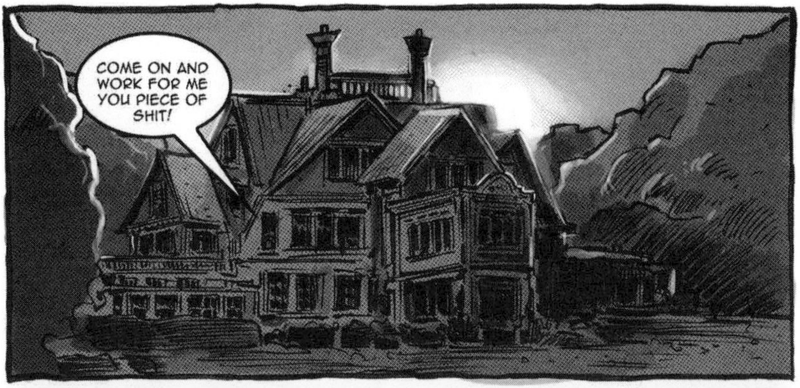
COME ON AND WORK FOR ME YOU PIECE OF SHIT!

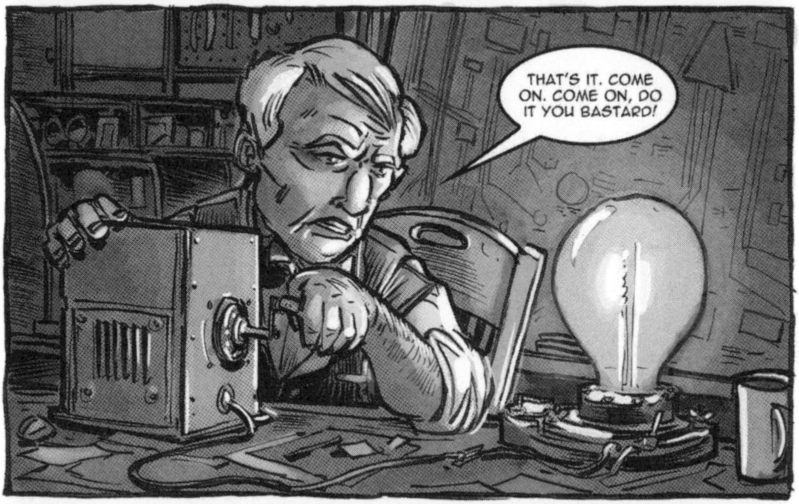
THAT'S IT. COME ON. COME ON, DO IT YOU BASTARD!

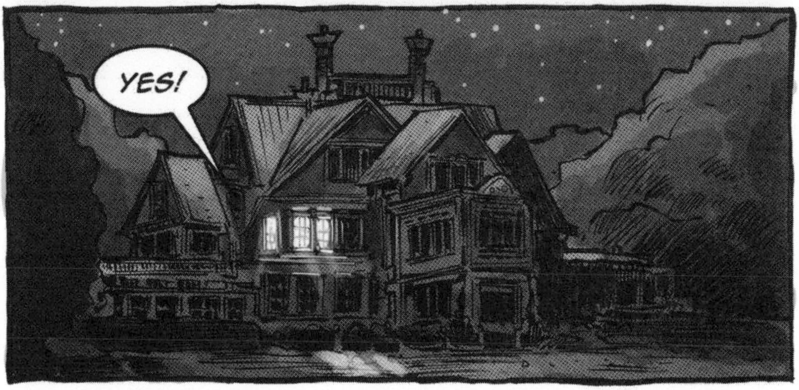
YES!

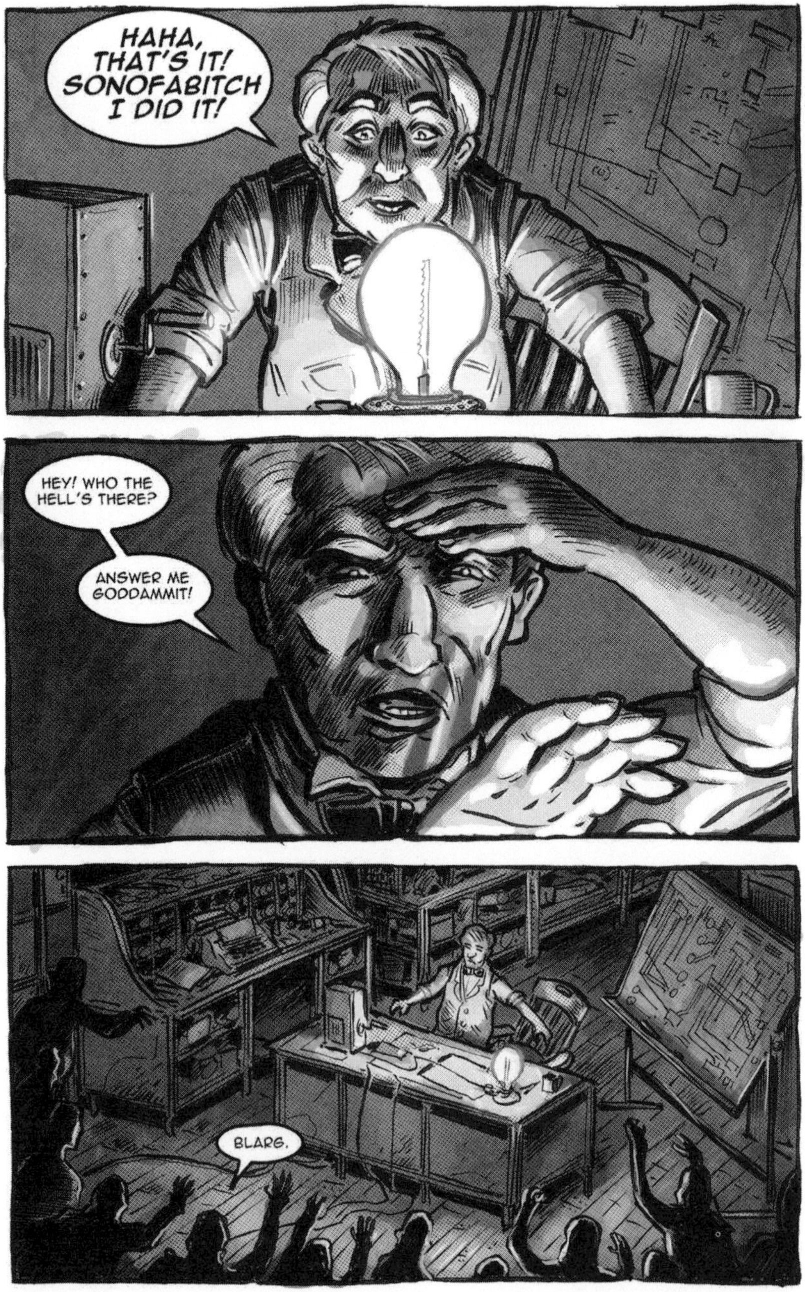
HAHA, THAT'S IT! SONOFABITCH I DID IT!
HEY! WHO THE HELL'S THERE?
ANSWER ME GODDAMMIT!
BLARG.

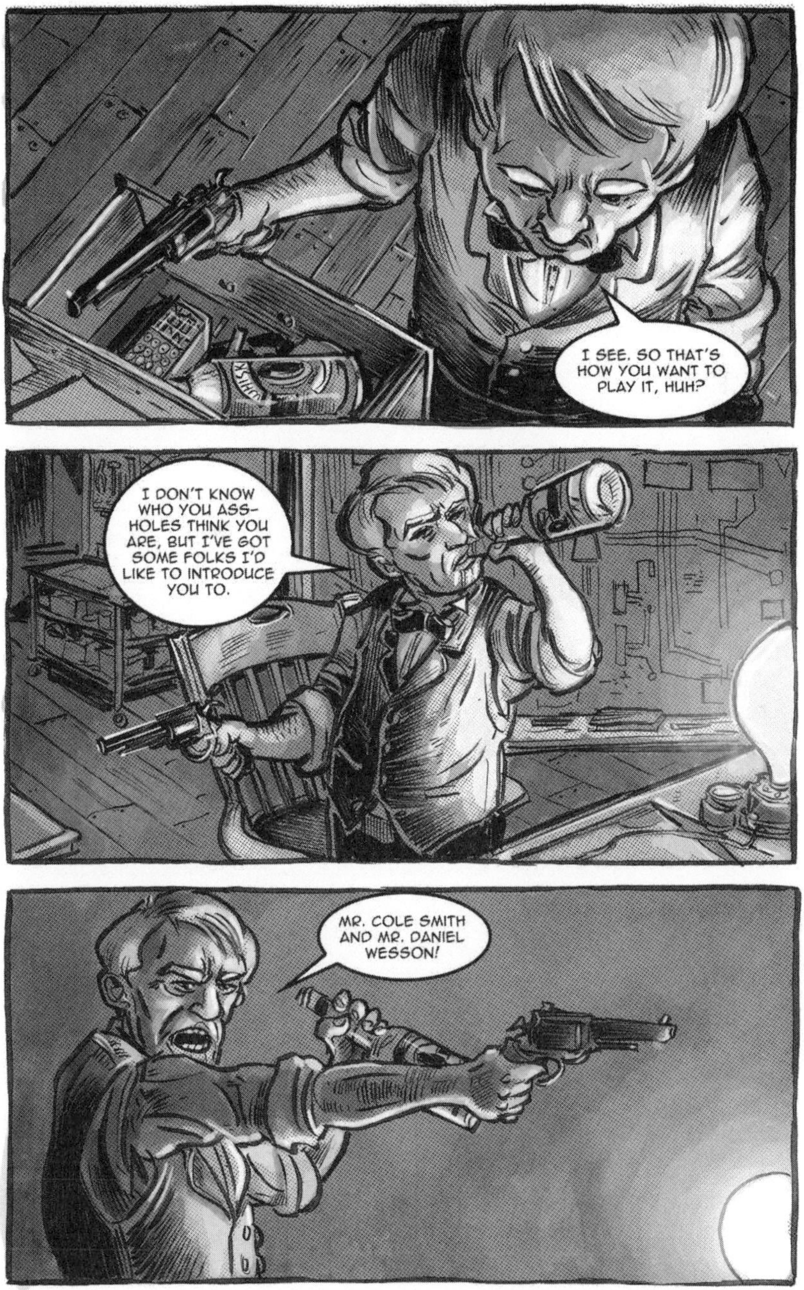
I SEE. SO THAT'S HOW YOU WANT TO PLAY IT, HUH?
I DON'T KNOW WHO YOU ASS-HOLES THINK YOU ARE, BUT I'VE GOT SOME FOLKS I'D LIKE TO INTRODUCE YOU TO.
MR. COLE SMITH AND MR. DANIEL WESSON!

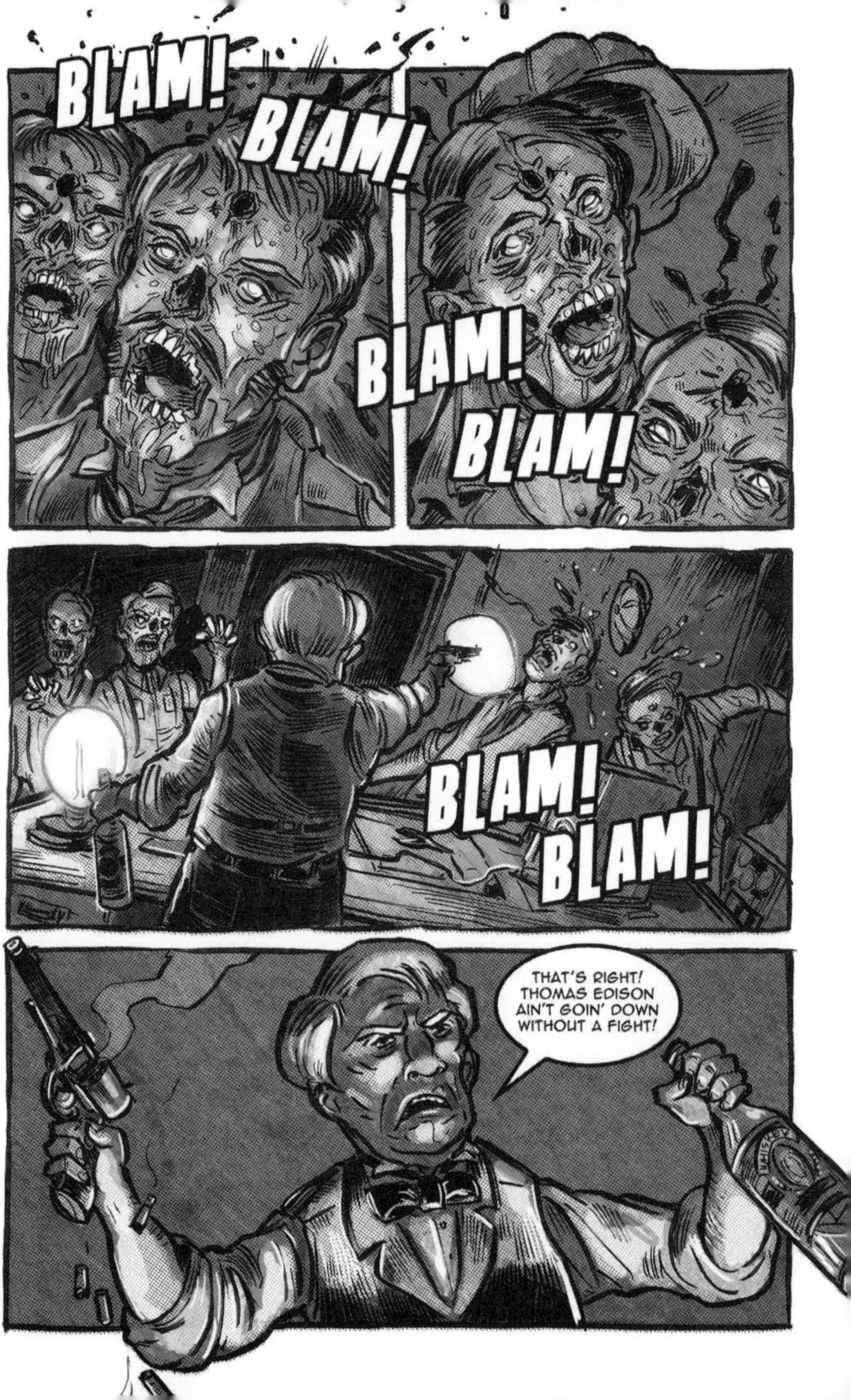
BLAM!
BLAM!
BLAM!
BLAM!
BLAM!
BLAM!
THAT'S RIGHT! THOMAS EDISON AIN'T GOIN' DOWN WITHOUT A FIGHT!
WHISKEY

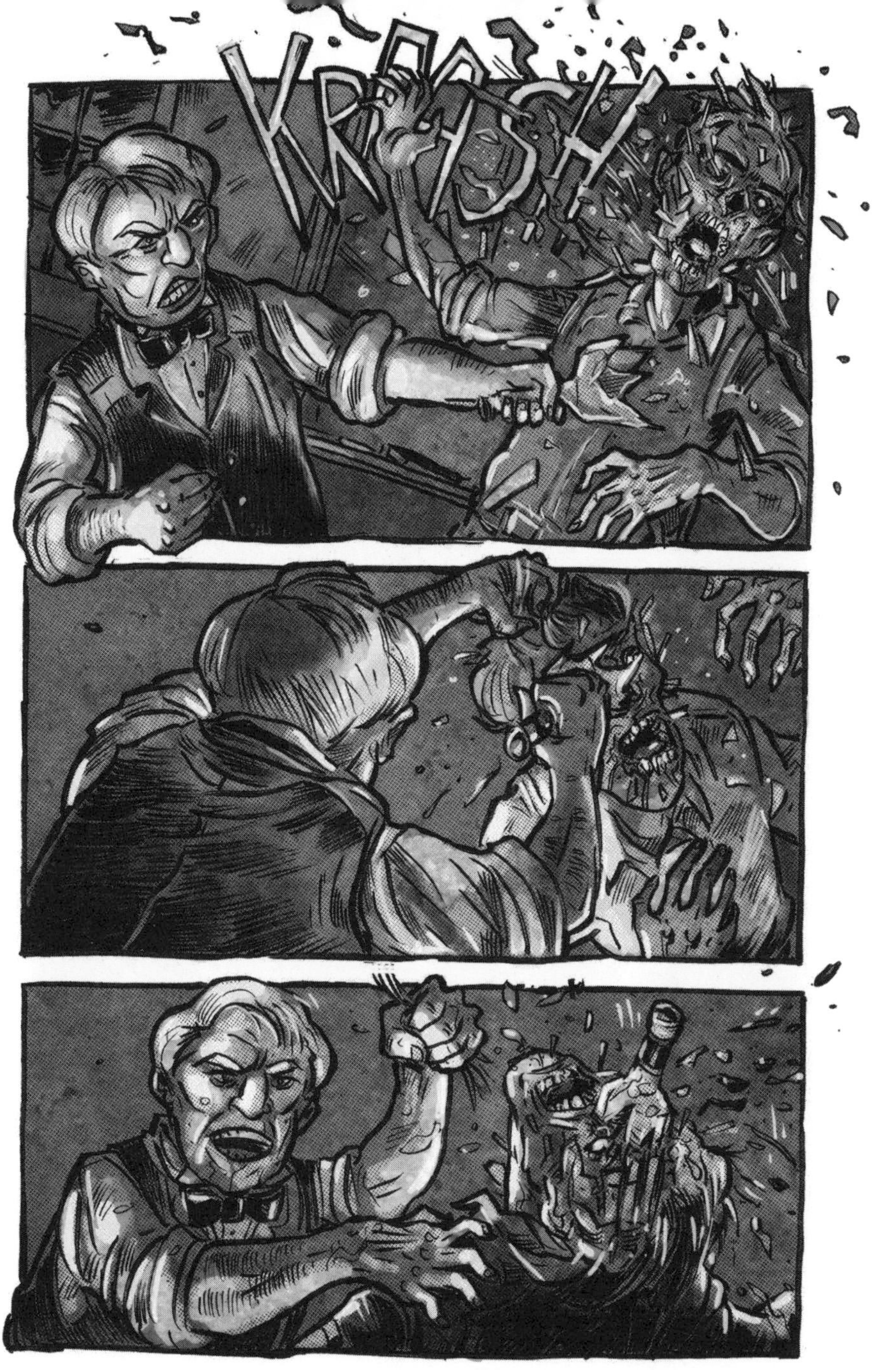
KRAASH

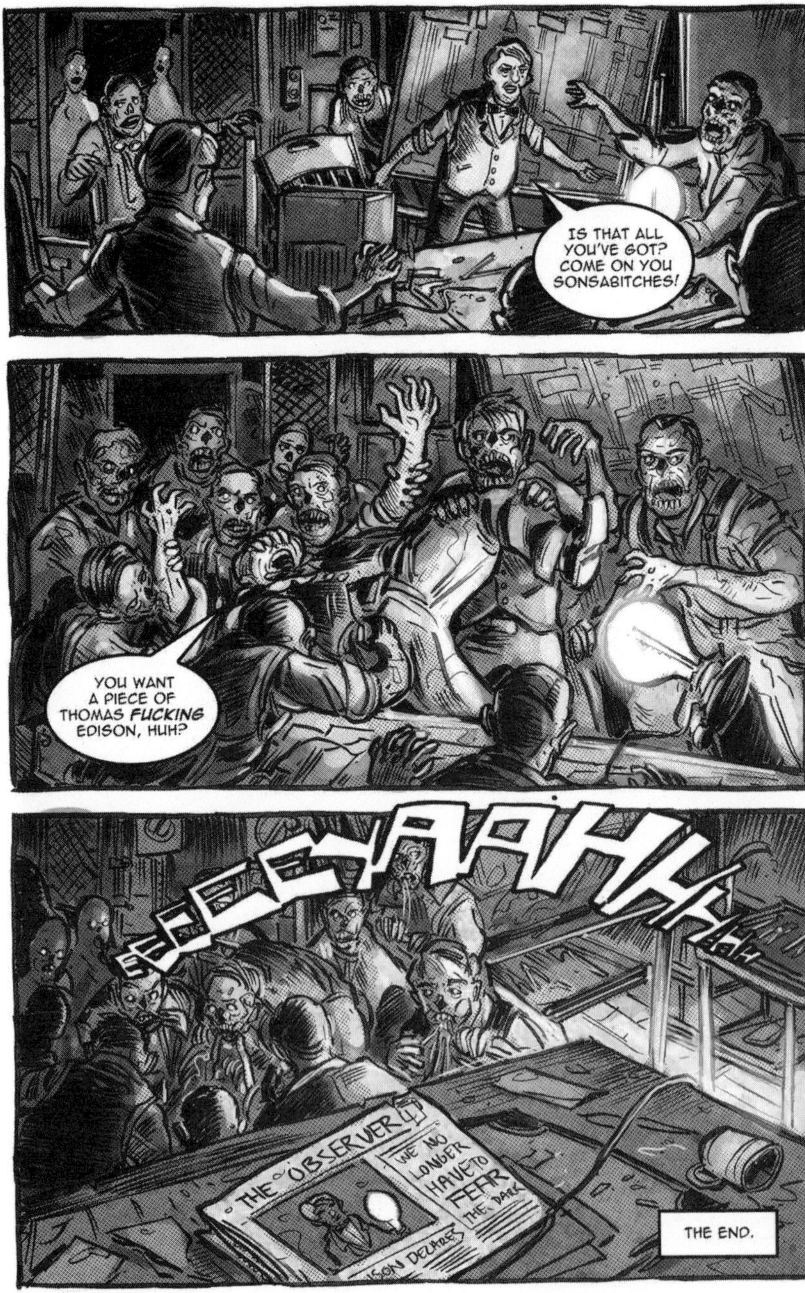
IS THAT ALL YOU'VE GOT? COME ON YOU SONSABITCHES!
YOU WANT A PIECE OF THOMAS *FUCKING* EDISON, HUH?
EEEEEEYAAHHHHHH
THE OBSERVER
WE NO LONGER HAVE TO FEAR THE DARK
THE END.

THE UNTOLD TALE OF JIM BRIDGER

STORY BY:
DAN NOKES

ART BY:
DAVID STOLL

LETTERS BY:
JEFF McCOMSEY

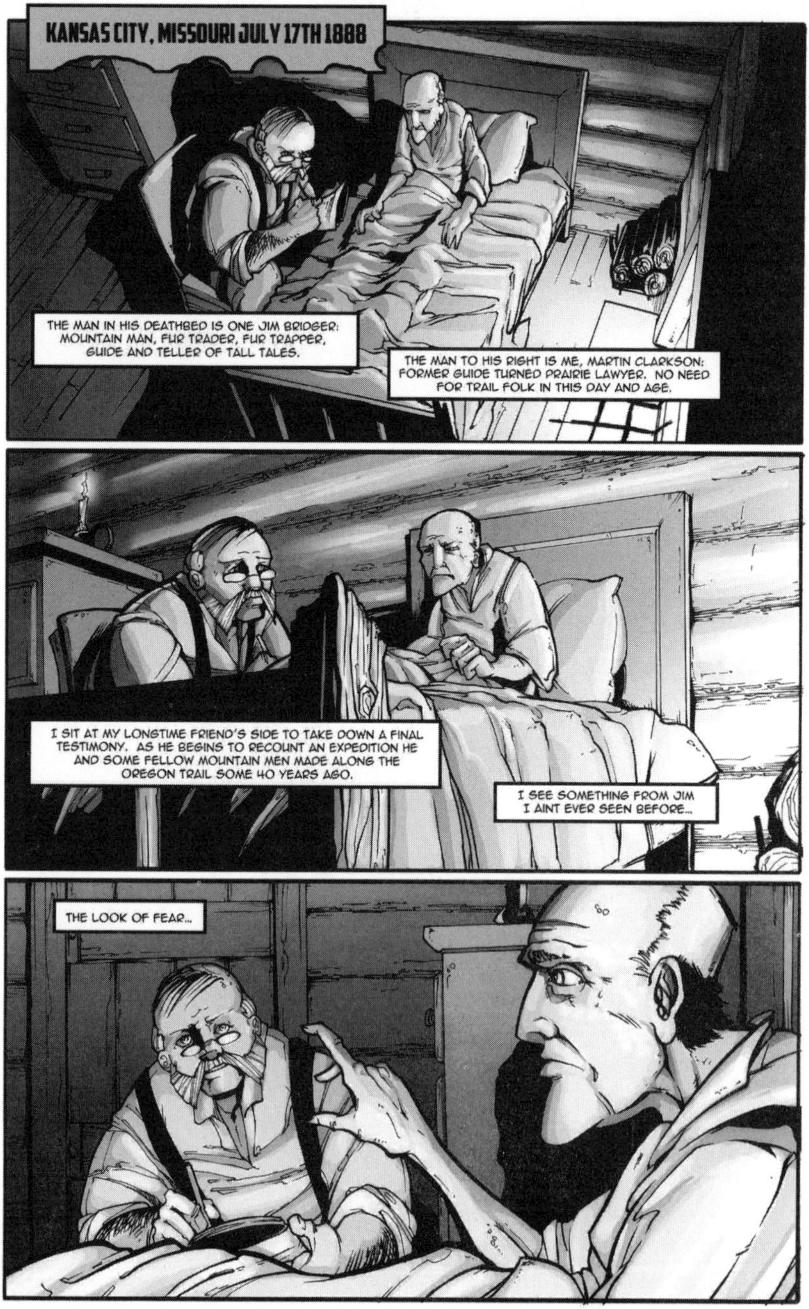
KANSAS CITY, MISSOURI JULY 17TH 1888
THE MAN IN HIS DEATHBED IS ONE JIM BRIDGER: MOUNTAIN MAN, FUR TRADER, FUR TRAPPER, GUIDE AND TELLER OF TALL TALES.
THE MAN TO HIS RIGHT IS ME, MARTIN CLARKSON: FORMER GUIDE TURNED PRAIRIE LAWYER. NO NEED FOR TRAIL FOLK IN THIS DAY AND AGE.
I SIT AT MY LONGTIME FRIEND'S SIDE TO TAKE DOWN A FINAL TESTIMONY. AS HE BEGINS TO RECOUNT AN EXPEDITION HE AND SOME FELLOW MOUNTAIN MEN MADE ALONG THE OREGON TRAIL SOME 40 YEARS AGO.
I SEE SOMETHING FROM JIM I AINT EVER SEEN BEFORE...
THE LOOK OF FEAR...

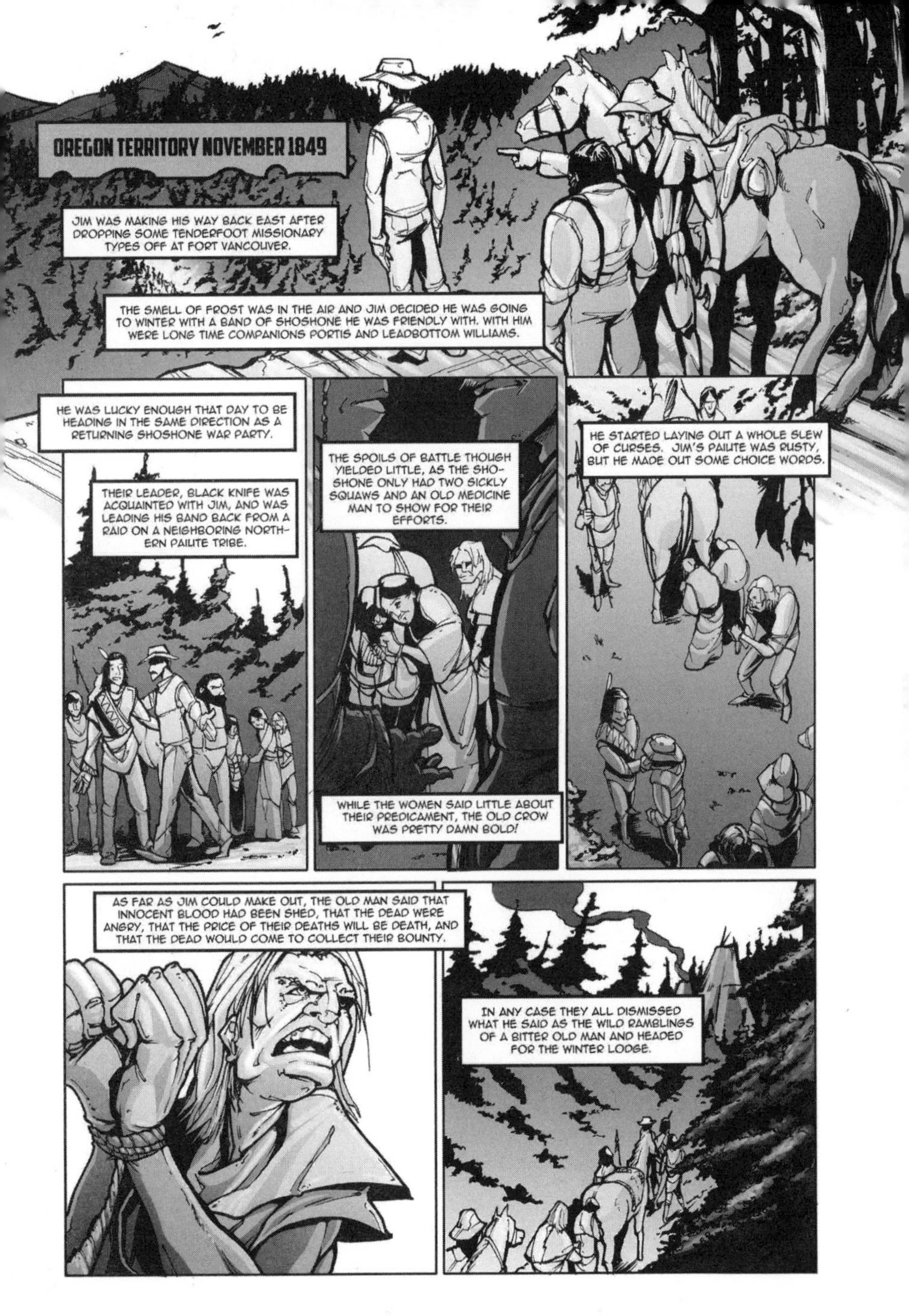
OREGON TERRITORY NOVEMBER 1849
JIM WAS MAKING HIS WAY BACK EAST AFTER DROPPING SOME TENDERFOOT MISSIONARY TYPES OFF AT FORT VANCOUVER.
THE SMELL OF FROST WAS IN THE AIR AND JIM DECIDED HE WAS GOING TO WINTER WITH A BAND OF SHOSHONE HE WAS FRIENDLY WITH. WITH HIM WERE LONG TIME COMPANIONS PORTIS AND LEADBOTTOM WILLIAMS.
HE WAS LUCKY ENOUGH THAT DAY TO BE HEADING IN THE SAME DIRECTION AS A RETURNING SHOSHONE WAR PARTY.
THEIR LEADER, BLACK KNIFE WAS ACQUAINTED WITH JIM, AND WAS LEADING HIS BAND BACK FROM A RAID ON A NEIGHBORING NORTHERN PAILUTE TRIBE.
THE SPOILS OF BATTLE THOUGH YIELDED LITTLE, AS THE SHOSHONE ONLY HAD TWO SICKLY SQUAWS AND AN OLD MEDICINE MAN TO SHOW FOR THEIR EFFORTS.
WHILE THE WOMEN SAID LITTLE ABOUT THEIR PREDICAMENT, THE OLD CROW WAS PRETTY DAMN BOLD!
HE STARTED LAYING OUT A WHOLE SLEW OF CURSES. JIM'S PAILUTE WAS RUSTY, BUT HE MADE OUT SOME CHOICE WORDS.
AS FAR AS JIM COULD MAKE OUT, THE OLD MAN SAID THAT INNOCENT BLOOD HAD BEEN SHED, THAT THE DEAD WERE ANGRY, THAT THE PRICE OF THEIR DEATHS WILL BE DEATH, AND THAT THE DEAD WOULD COME TO COLLECT THEIR BOUNTY.
IN ANY CASE THEY ALL DISMISSED WHAT HE SAID AS THE WILD RAMBLINGS OF A BITTER OLD MAN AND HEADED FOR THE WINTER LODGE.

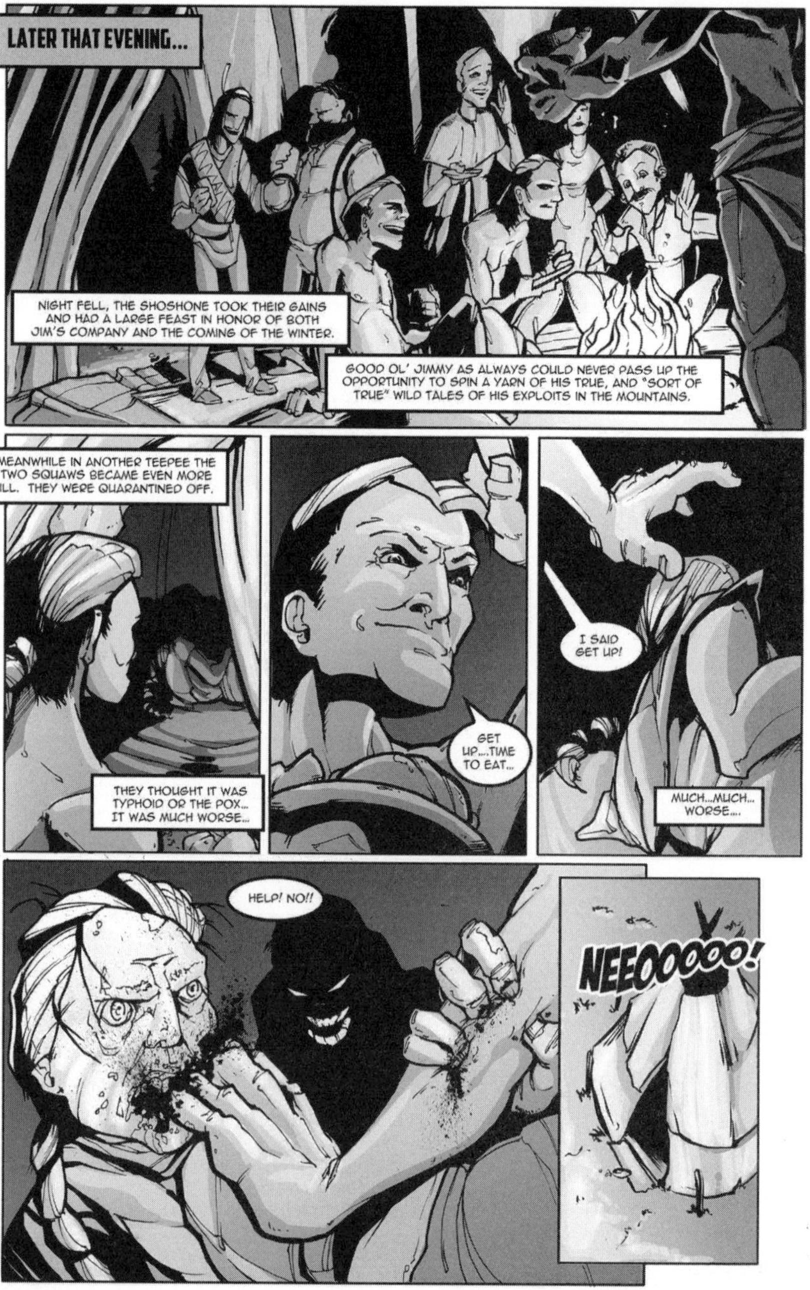
LATER THAT EVENING...
NIGHT FELL, THE SHOSHONE TOOK THEIR GAINS AND HAD A LARGE FEAST IN HONOR OF BOTH JIM'S COMPANY AND THE COMING OF THE WINTER.
GOOD OL' JIMMY AS ALWAYS COULD NEVER PASS UP THE OPPORTUNITY TO SPIN A YARN OF HIS TRUE, AND "SORT OF TRUE" WILD TALES OF HIS EXPLOITS IN THE MOUNTAINS.
MEANWHILE IN ANOTHER TEEPEE THE TWO SQUAWS BECAME EVEN MORE ILL. THEY WERE QUARANTINED OFF.
THEY THOUGHT IT WAS TYPHOID OR THE POX... IT WAS MUCH WORSE...
GET UP....TIME TO EAT...
I SAID GET UP!
MUCH...MUCH... WORSE....
HELP! NO!!
NEEOOOOO!

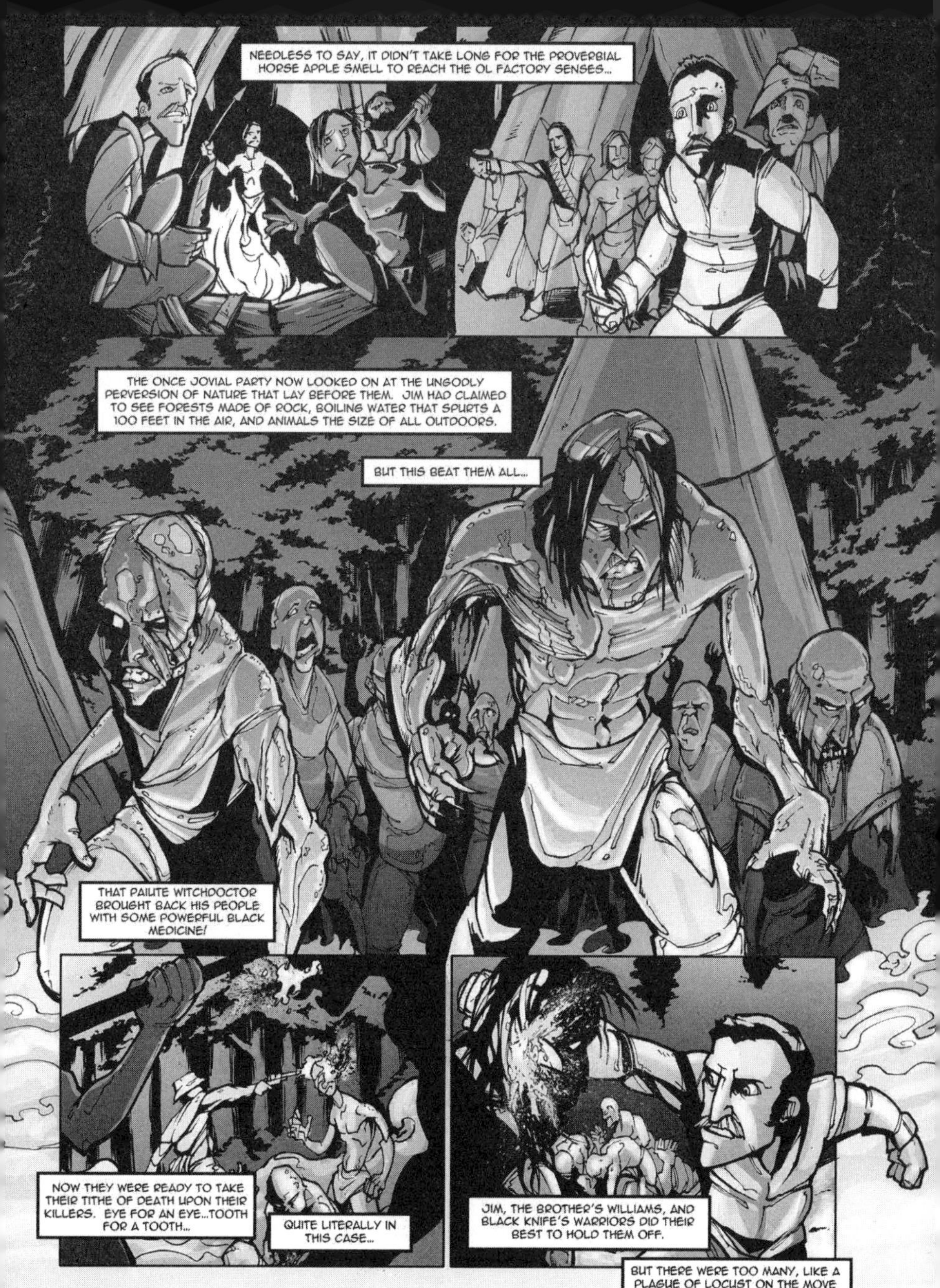
NEEDLESS TO SAY, IT DIDN'T TAKE LONG FOR THE PROVERBIAL HORSE APPLE SMELL TO REACH THE OL FACTORY SENSES...
THE ONCE JOVIAL PARTY NOW LOOKED ON AT THE UNGODLY PERVERSION OF NATURE THAT LAY BEFORE THEM. JIM HAD CLAIMED TO SEE FORESTS MADE OF ROCK, BOILING WATER THAT SPURTS A 100 FEET IN THE AIR, AND ANIMALS THE SIZE OF ALL OUTDOORS.
BUT THIS BEAT THEM ALL...
THAT PAIUTE WITCHDOCTOR BROUGHT BACK HIS PEOPLE WITH SOME POWERFUL BLACK MEDICINE!
NOW THEY WERE READY TO TAKE THEIR TITHE OF DEATH UPON THEIR KILLERS. EYE FOR AN EYE...TOOTH FOR A TOOTH...
QUITE LITERALLY IN THIS CASE...
JIM, THE BROTHER'S WILLIAMS, AND BLACK KNIFE'S WARRIORS DID THEIR BEST TO HOLD THEM OFF.
BUT THERE WERE TOO MANY, LIKE A PLAGUE OF LOCUST ON THE MOVE THROUGH A SUMMER CORNFIELD.

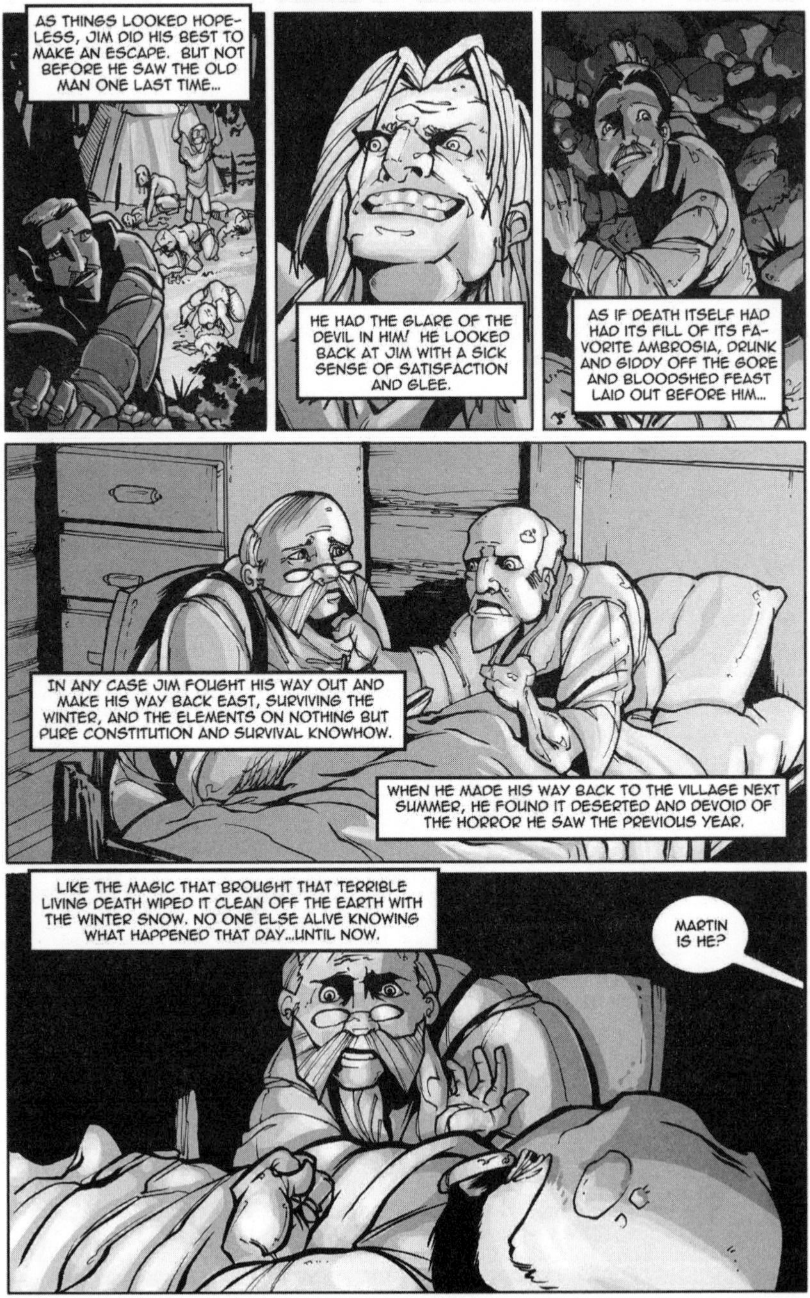
AS THINGS LOOKED HOPELESS, JIM DID HIS BEST TO MAKE AN ESCAPE. BUT NOT BEFORE HE SAW THE OLD MAN ONE LAST TIME...
HE HAD THE GLARE OF THE DEVIL IN HIM! HE LOOKED BACK AT JIM WITH A SICK SENSE OF SATISFACTION AND GLEE.
AS IF DEATH ITSELF HAD HAD ITS FILL OF ITS FAVORITE AMBROSIA, DRUNK AND GIDDY OFF THE GORE AND BLOODSHED FEAST LAID OUT BEFORE HIM...
IN ANY CASE JIM FOUGHT HIS WAY OUT AND MAKE HIS WAY BACK EAST, SURVIVING THE WINTER, AND THE ELEMENTS ON NOTHING BUT PURE CONSTITUTION AND SURVIVAL KNOWHOW.
WHEN HE MADE HIS WAY BACK TO THE VILLAGE NEXT SUMMER, HE FOUND IT DESERTED AND DEVOID OF THE HORROR HE SAW THE PREVIOUS YEAR.
LIKE THE MAGIC THAT BROUGHT THAT TERRIBLE LIVING DEATH WIPED IT CLEAN OFF THE EARTH WITH THE WINTER SNOW. NO ONE ELSE ALIVE KNOWING WHAT HAPPENED THAT DAY...UNTIL NOW.
MARTIN IS HE?

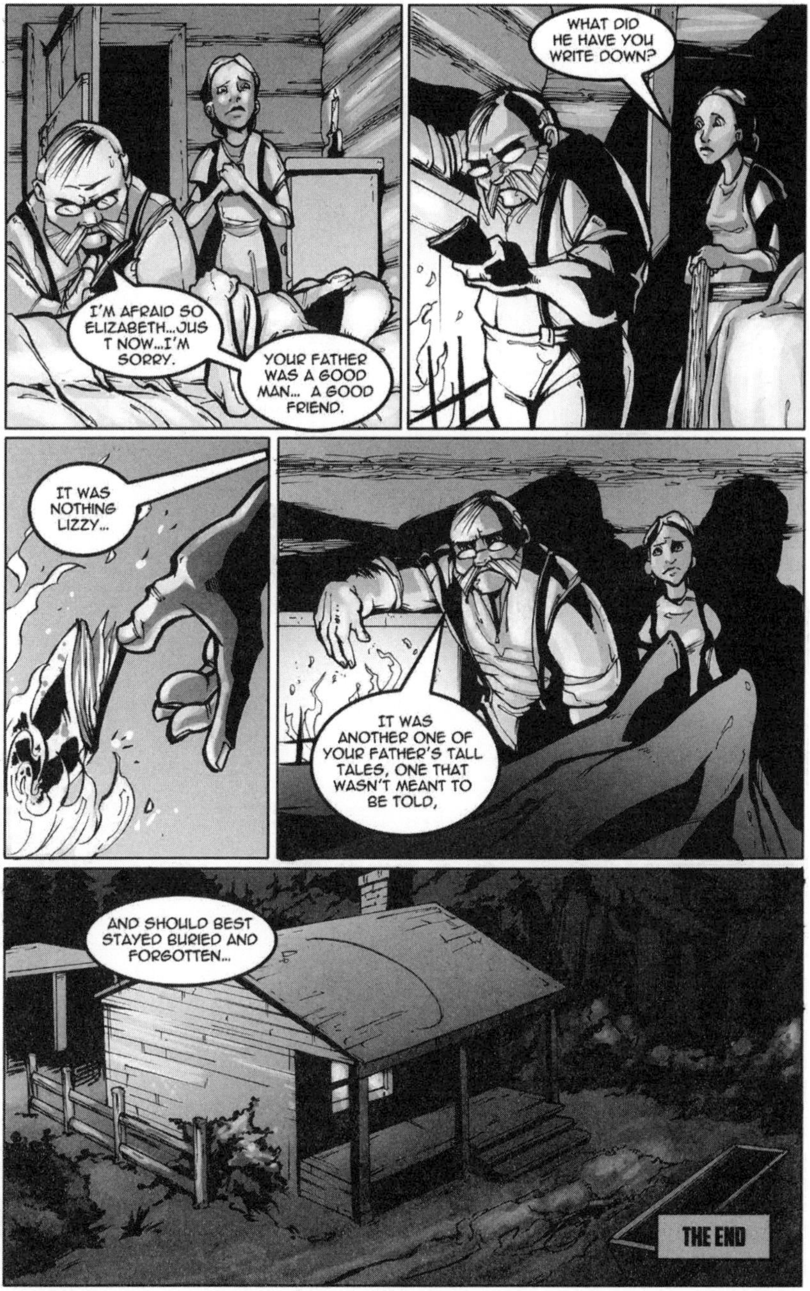
I'M AFRAID SO ELIZABETH...JUS T NOW...I'M SORRY.
YOUR FATHER WAS A GOOD MAN... A GOOD FRIEND.
WHAT DID HE HAVE YOU WRITE DOWN?
IT WAS NOTHING LIZZY...
IT WAS ANOTHER ONE OF YOUR FATHER'S TALL TALES, ONE THAT WASN'T MEANT TO BE TOLD,
AND SHOULD BEST STAYED BURIED AND FORGOTTEN...
THE END

THE GREATER GOOD

STORY BY:
BRANDON BARROWS

ART BY:
ALEX DIOTTO

LETTERS BY:
JEFF McCLELLAND

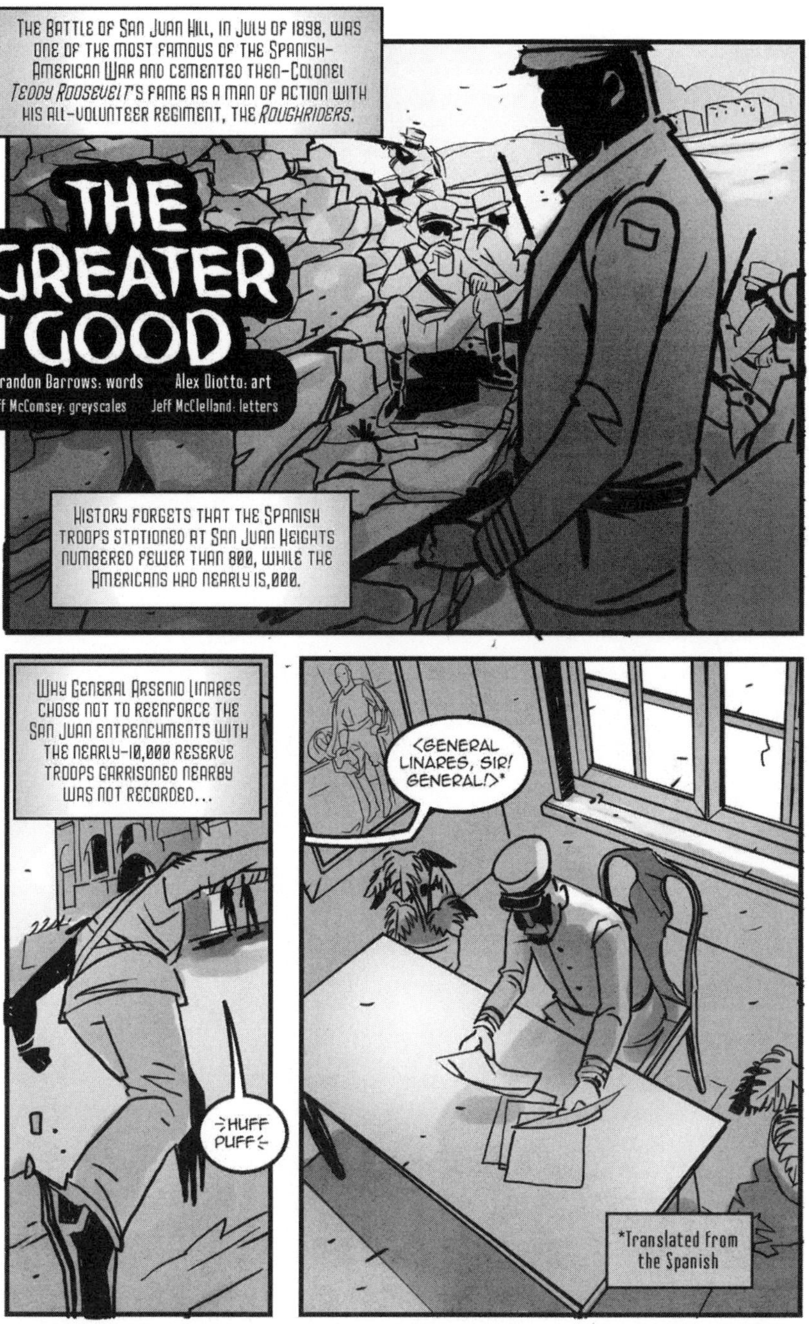
The Battle of San Juan Hill, in July of 1898, was one of the most famous of the Spanish-American War and cemented then-Colonel Teddy Roosevelt's fame as a man of action with his all-volunteer regiment, the Roughriders.
THE GREATER GOOD
Brandon Barrows: words
Alex Diotto: art
Jeff McComsey: greyscales
Jeff McClelland: letters
History forgets that the Spanish troops stationed at San Juan Heights numbered fewer than 800, while the Americans had nearly 15,000.
Why General Arsenio Linares chose not to reenforce the San Juan entrenchments with the nearly-10,000 reserve troops garrisoned nearby was not recorded...
HUFF PUFF
<GENERAL LINARES, SIR! GENERAL!>*
*Translated from the Spanish

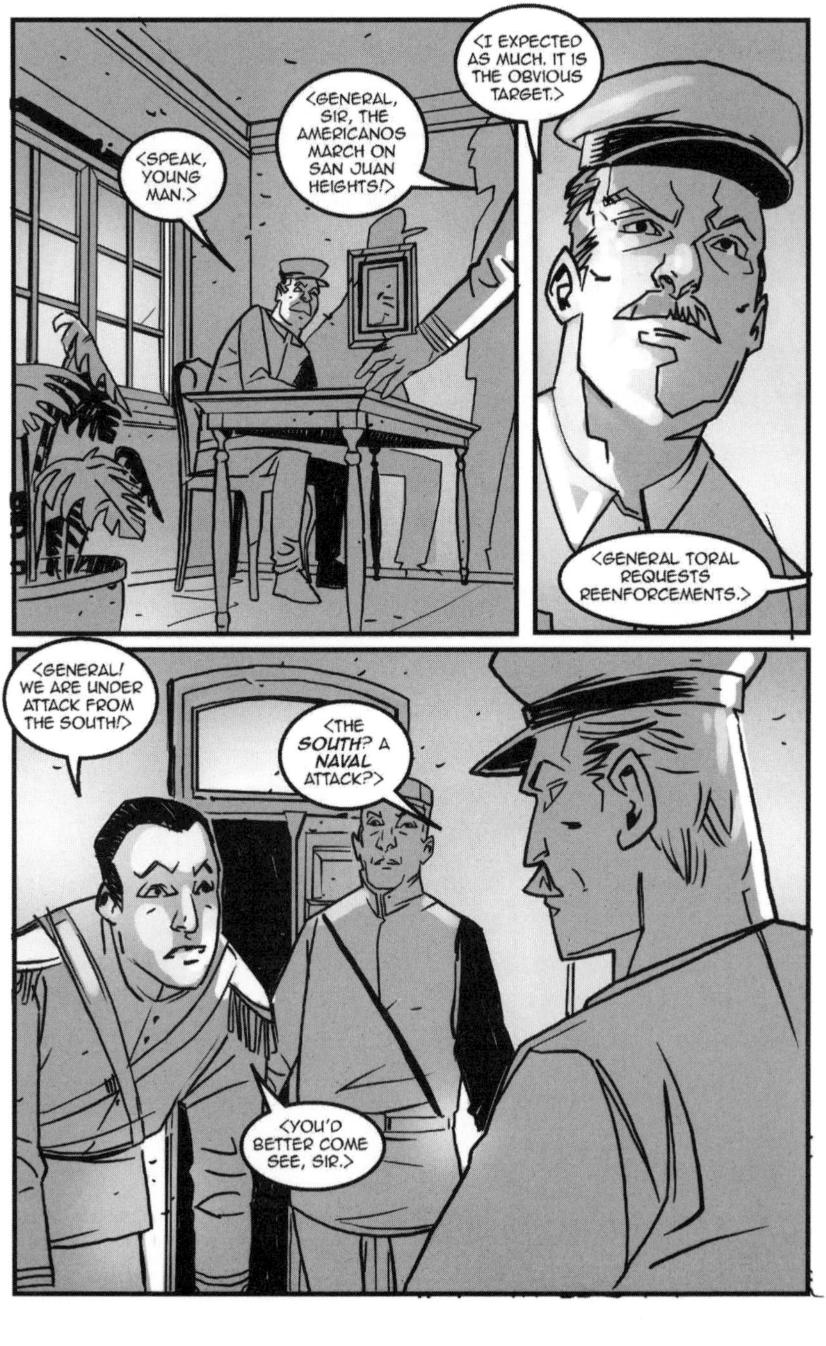
<SPEAK, YOUNG MAN.>
<GENERAL, SIR, THE AMERICANOS MARCH ON SAN JUAN HEIGHTS!>
<I EXPECTED AS MUCH. IT IS THE OBVIOUS TARGET.>
<GENERAL TORAL REQUESTS REENFORCEMENTS.>
<GENERAL! WE ARE UNDER ATTACK FROM THE SOUTH!>
<THE SOUTH? A NAVAL ATTACK?>
<YOU'D BETTER COME SEE, SIR.>

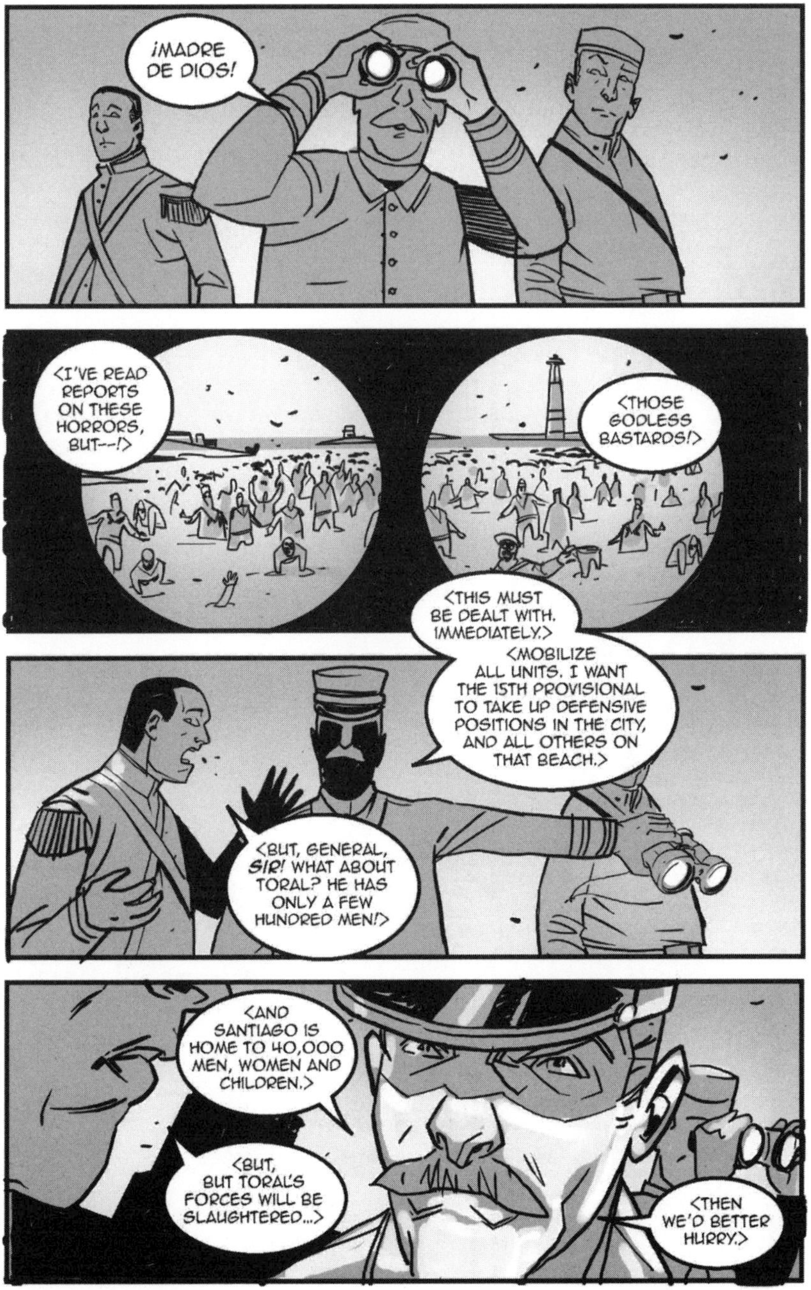
¡MADRE DE DIOS!
<I'VE READ REPORTS ON THESE HORRORS, BUT--!>
<THOSE GODLESS BASTARDS!>
<THIS MUST BE DEALT WITH. IMMEDIATELY.>
<MOBILIZE ALL UNITS. I WANT THE 15TH PROVISIONAL TO TAKE UP DEFENSIVE POSITIONS IN THE CITY, AND ALL OTHERS ON THAT BEACH.>
<BUT, GENERAL, SIR! WHAT ABOUT TORAL? HE HAS ONLY A FEW HUNDRED MEN!>
<AND SANTIAGO IS HOME TO 40,000 MEN, WOMEN AND CHILDREN.>
<BUT, BUT TORAL'S FORCES WILL BE SLAUGHTERED...>
<THEN WE'D BETTER HURRY.>

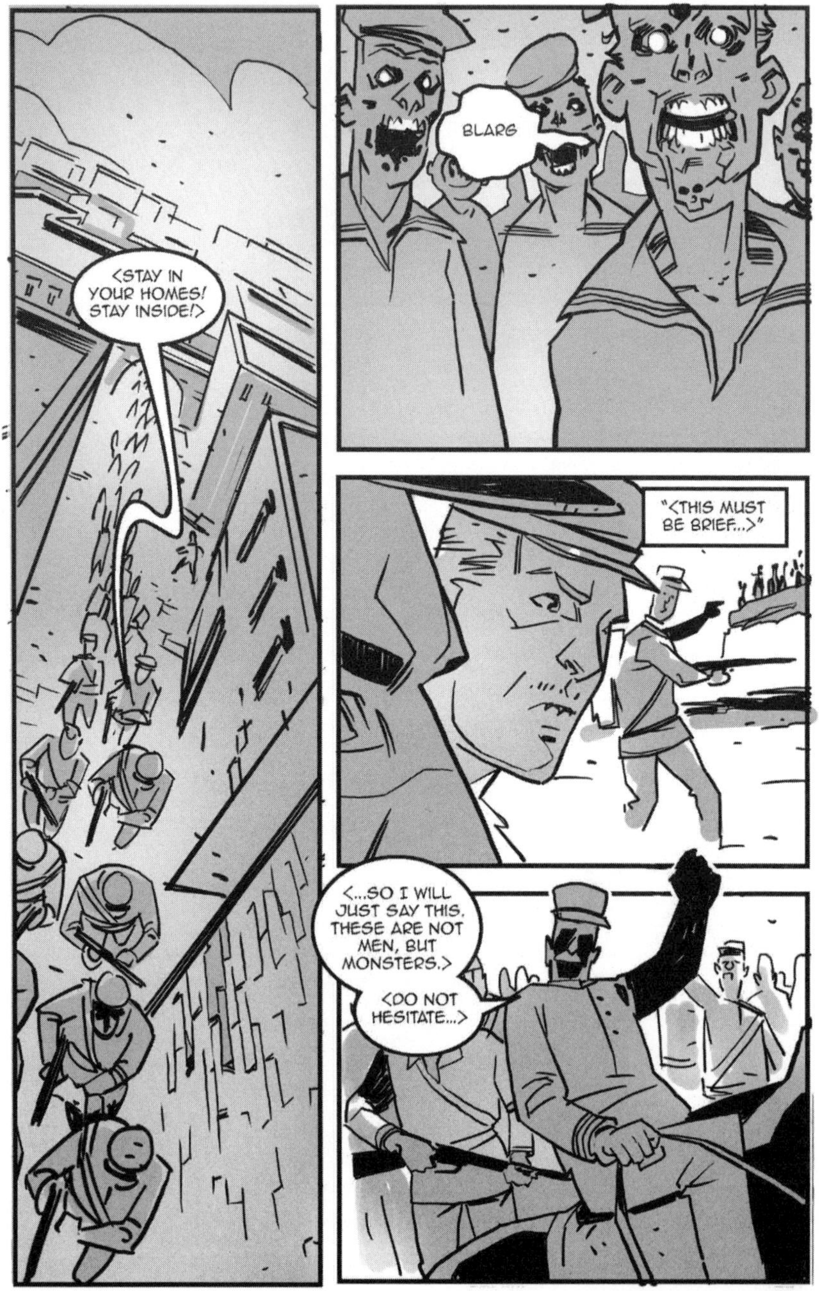
<STAY IN YOUR HOMES! STAY INSIDE!>
BLARG
"<THIS MUST BE BRIEF...>"
<...SO I WILL JUST SAY THIS. THESE ARE NOT MEN, BUT MONSTERS.>
<DO NOT HESITATE...>

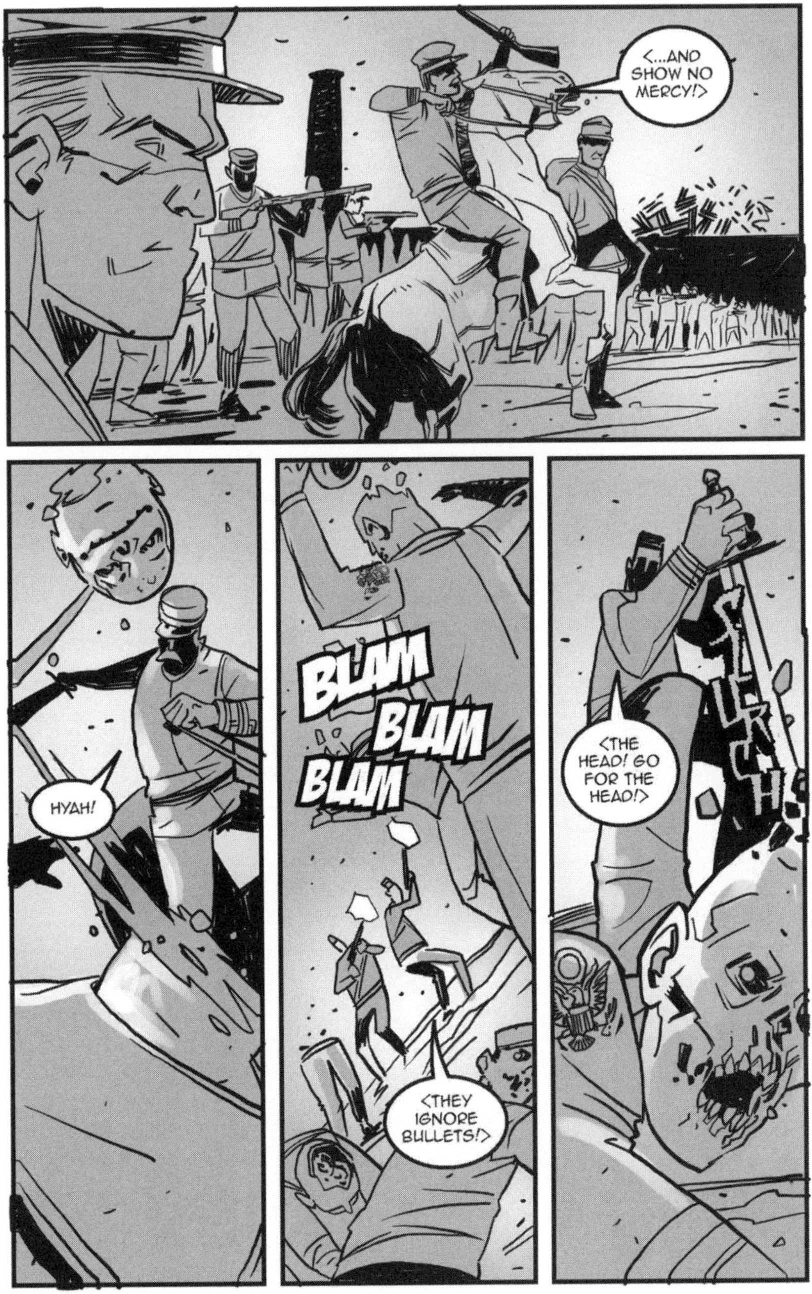

<...AND SHOW NO MERCY!>
HYAH!
BLAM
BLAM
BLAM
<THEY IGNORE BULLETS!>
<THE HEAD! GO FOR THE HEAD!>

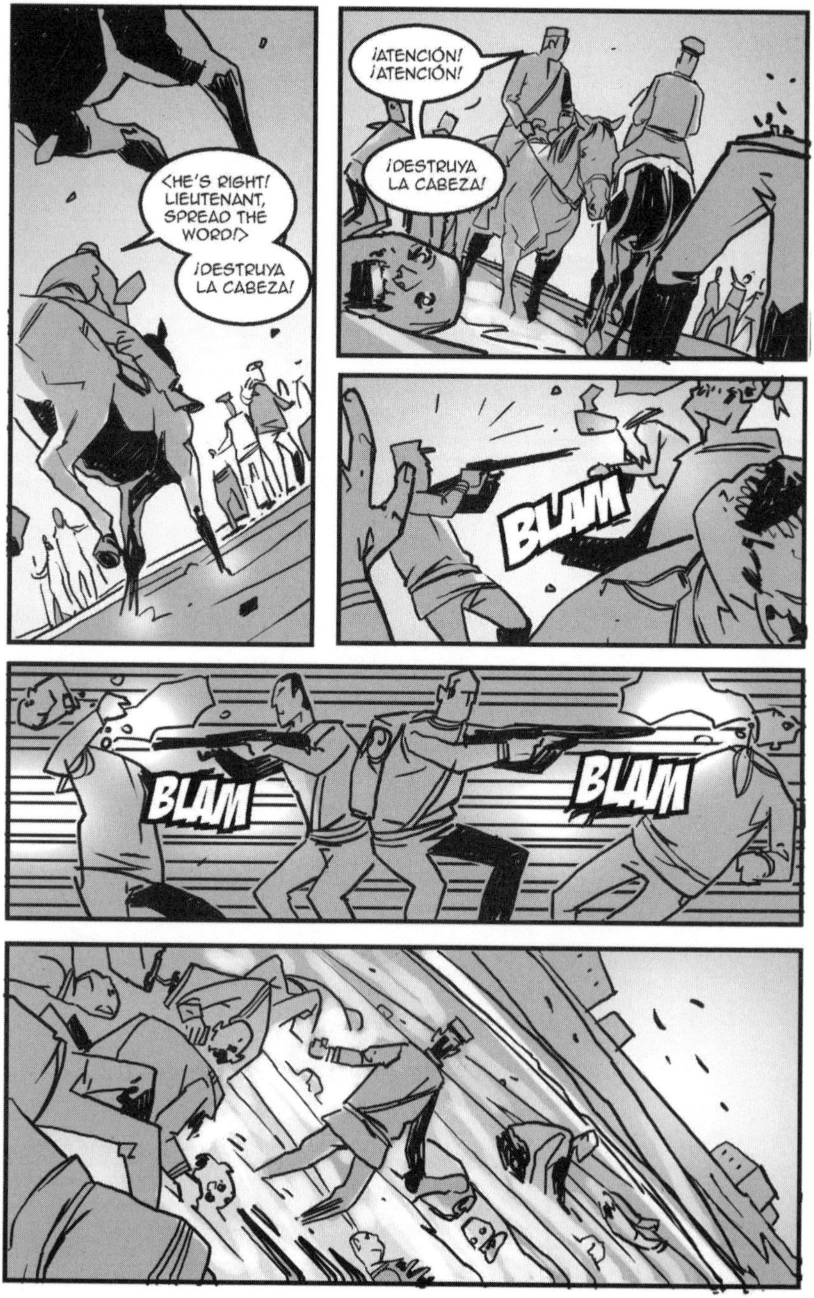
<HE'S RIGHT! LIEUTENANT, SPREAD THE WORD!>
¡DESTRUYA LA CABEZA!
¡ATENCIÓN! ¡ATENCIÓN!
¡DESTRUYA LA CABEZA!
BLAM
BLAM
BLAM

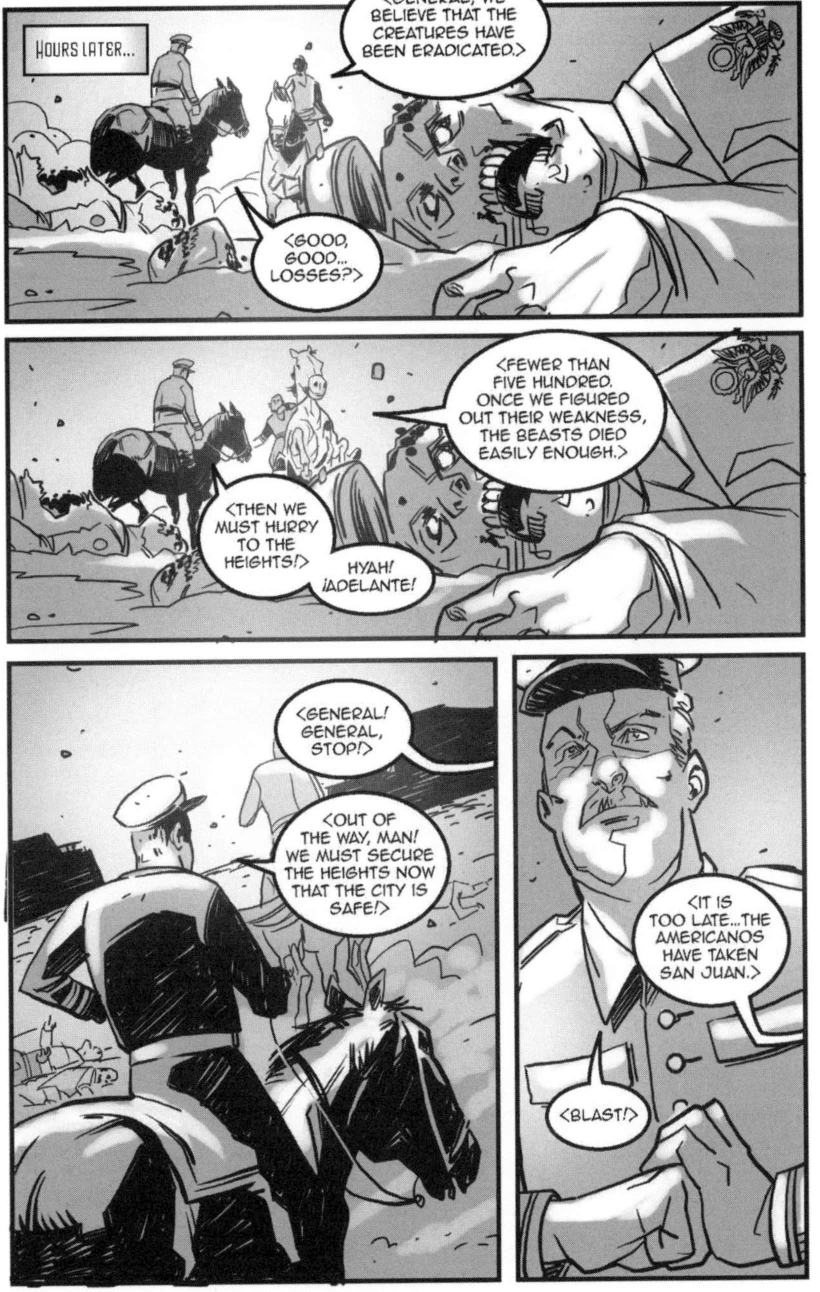
HOURS LATER...
<GENERAL, WE BELIEVE THAT THE CREATURES HAVE BEEN ERADICATED.>
<GOOD, GOOD... LOSSES?>
<FEWER THAN FIVE HUNDRED. ONCE WE FIGURED OUT THEIR WEAKNESS, THE BEASTS DIED EASILY ENOUGH.>
<THEN WE MUST HURRY TO THE HEIGHTS!>
HYAH! ¡ADELANTE!
<GENERAL! GENERAL, STOP!>
<OUT OF THE WAY, MAN! WE MUST SECURE THE HEIGHTS NOW THAT THE CITY IS SAFE!>
<IT IS TOO LATE...THE AMERICANOS HAVE TAKEN SAN JUAN.>
<BLAST!>

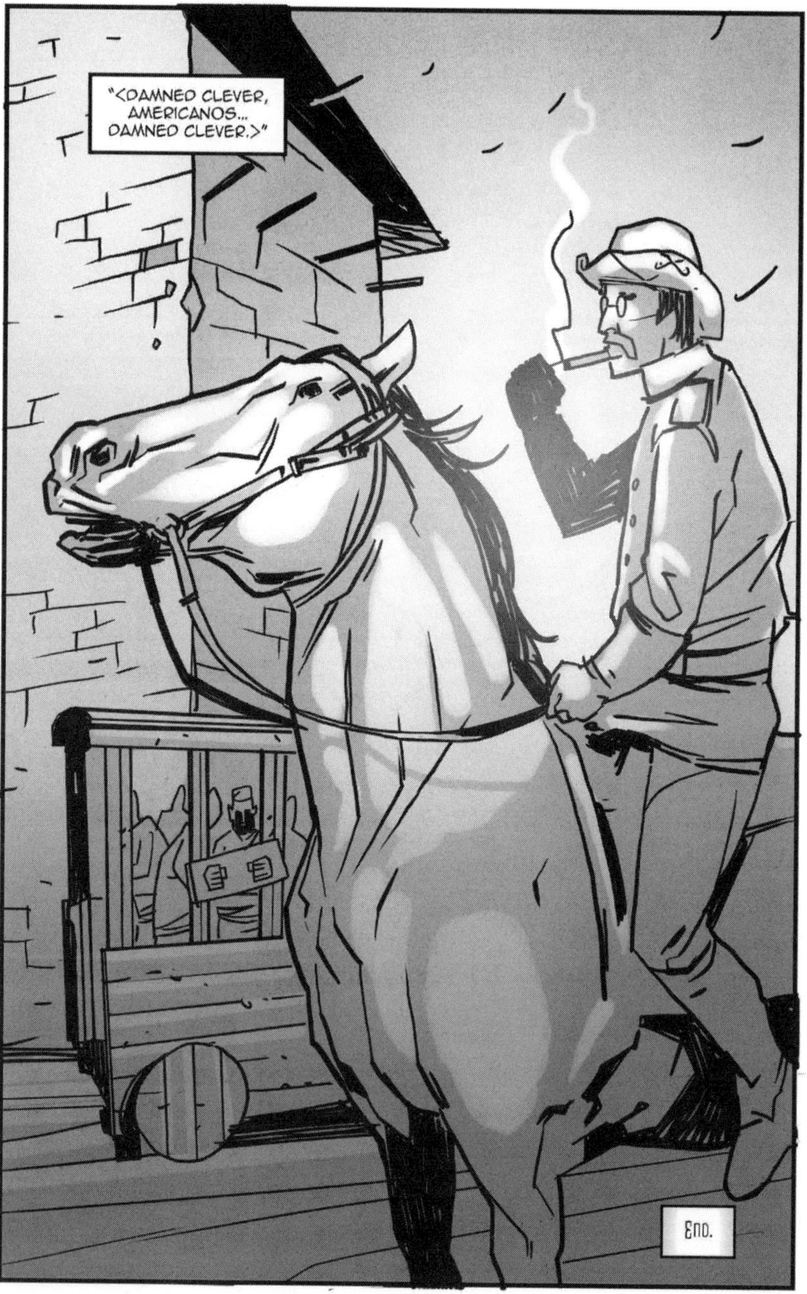
"<DAMNED CLEVER, AMERICANOS... DAMNED CLEVER.>"
END.

HUDDLED MASSES

STORY BY:
BENJAMIN TRUMAN

ART BY:
DOMINIC VIVONA
JEFF McCOMSEY

LETTERS BY:
SHAWN ALDRIDGE

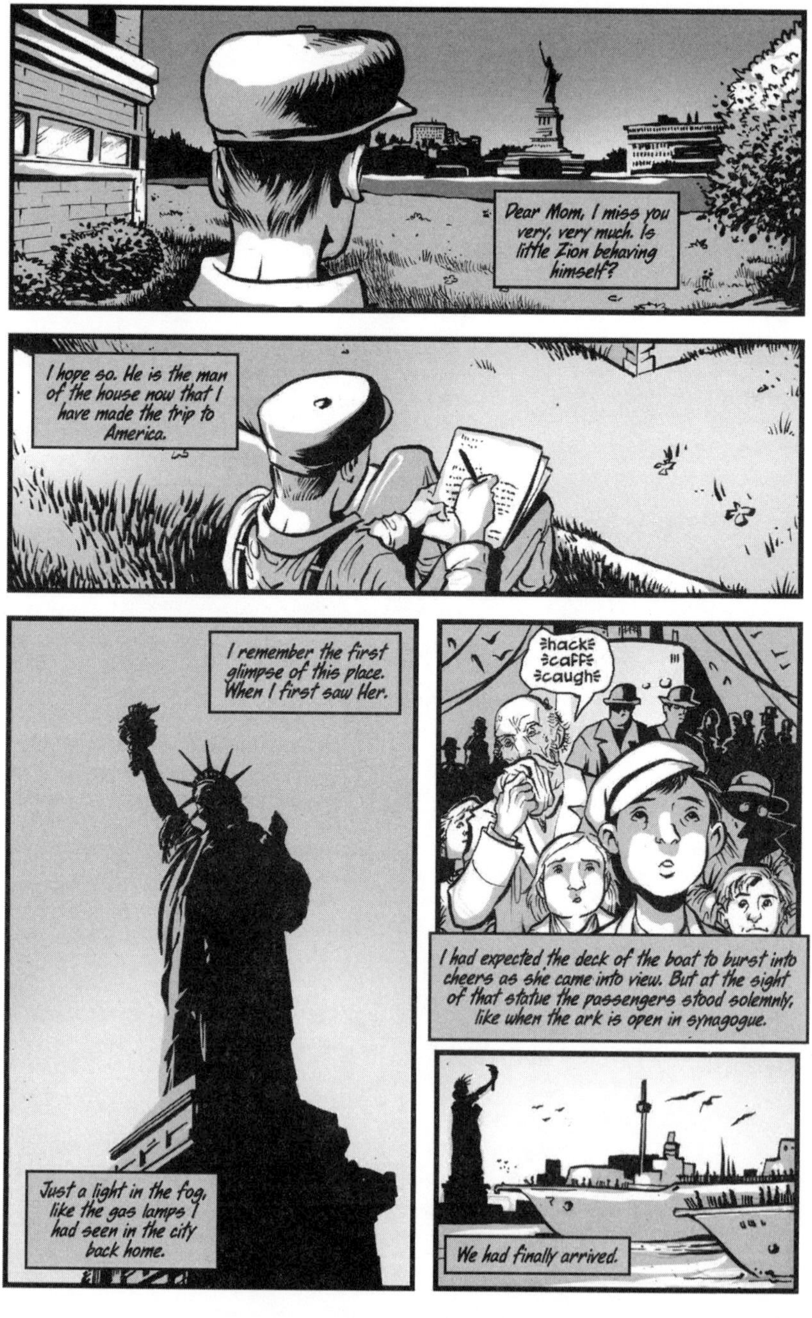

Dear Mom, I miss you very, very much. Is little Zion behaving himself?
I hope so. He is the man of the house now that I have made the trip to America.
I remember the first glimpse of this place. When I first saw Her.
Just a light in the fog, like the gas lamps I had seen in the city back home.
hack caff caugh
I had expected the deck of the boat to burst into cheers as she came into view. But at the sight of that statue the passengers stood solemnly, like when the ark is open in synagogue.
We had finally arrived.

It was like... coming home after a long journey, and warming by the fire.

Except that here, there was no family waiting for me...

...only strangers.

But no matter how differently each of us talked or looked, we were all the same.

Travelers, looking for a home

ǂhackǂ ǂcaffǂ ǂcaughǂ

IS... IS THIS FOR THE FERRY TO THE MAINLAND?

HERE? NO, BOY. THIS IS *PURGATORY.* THAT MARK ON YOUR JACKET MEANS YOU'RE TO BE *QUARANTINED.*

WHAT? BUT I THOUGHT THIS WAS A *FREE* LAND...

HMMPH! EVEN *HERE* WE'RE *OUTSIDERS.* THEY'VE DECIDED I'M NOT FIT FOR THEIR COUNTRY WITH MY *CONDITION.*

I'M TO AWAIT THE *NEXT BOAT* THAT CAN TAKE ME *BACK* TO THE COUNTRY I FLED!

WHO ARE YOU? WHY--?

MY NAME'S GREGORI. AND I'VE TRAVELLED SO FAR... COME TOO CLOSE. NO...I'LL BE OFF THIS ISLAND AND ON THE MAINLAND BEFORE THE--

ǂhackǂ ǂcaffǂ ǂcaughuurkǂ

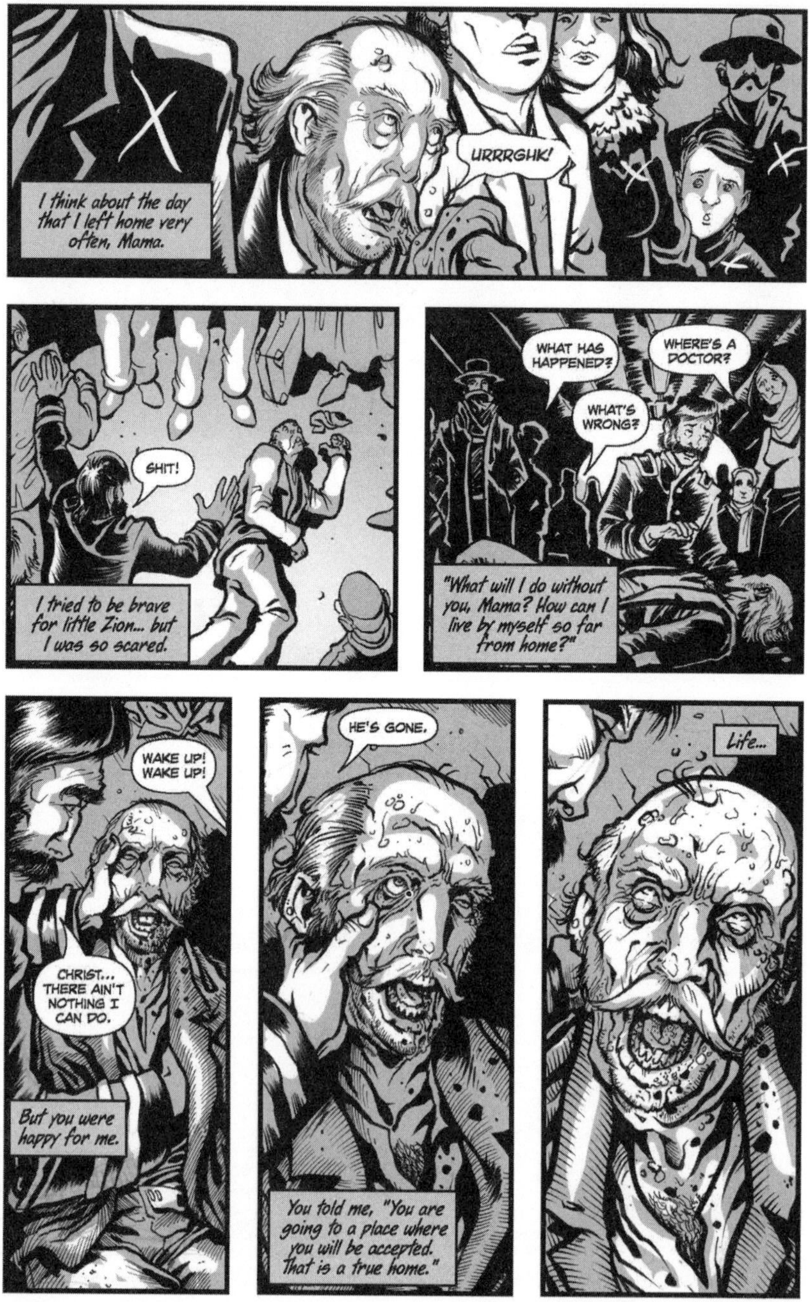
I think about the day that I left home very often, Mama.
URRRGHK!
SHIT!
I tried to be brave for little Zion... but I was so scared.
WHAT HAS HAPPENED?
WHERE'S A DOCTOR?
WHAT'S WRONG?
"What will I do without you, Mama? How can I live by myself so far from home?"
WAKE UP! WAKE UP!
CHRIST... THERE AIN'T NOTHING I CAN DO.
But you were happy for me.
HE'S GONE.
You told me, "You are going to a place where you will be accepted. That is a true home."
Life...

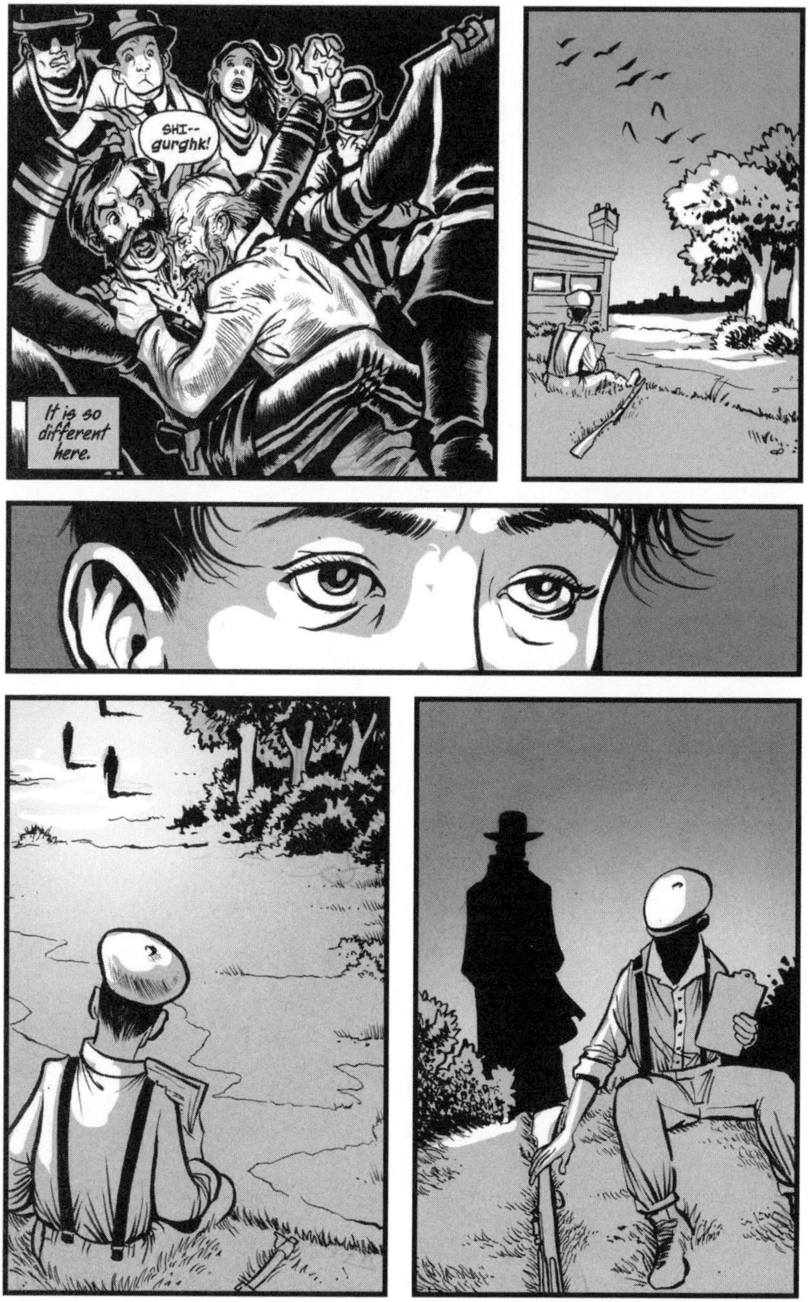
SHI--
gurghk!
It is so different here.

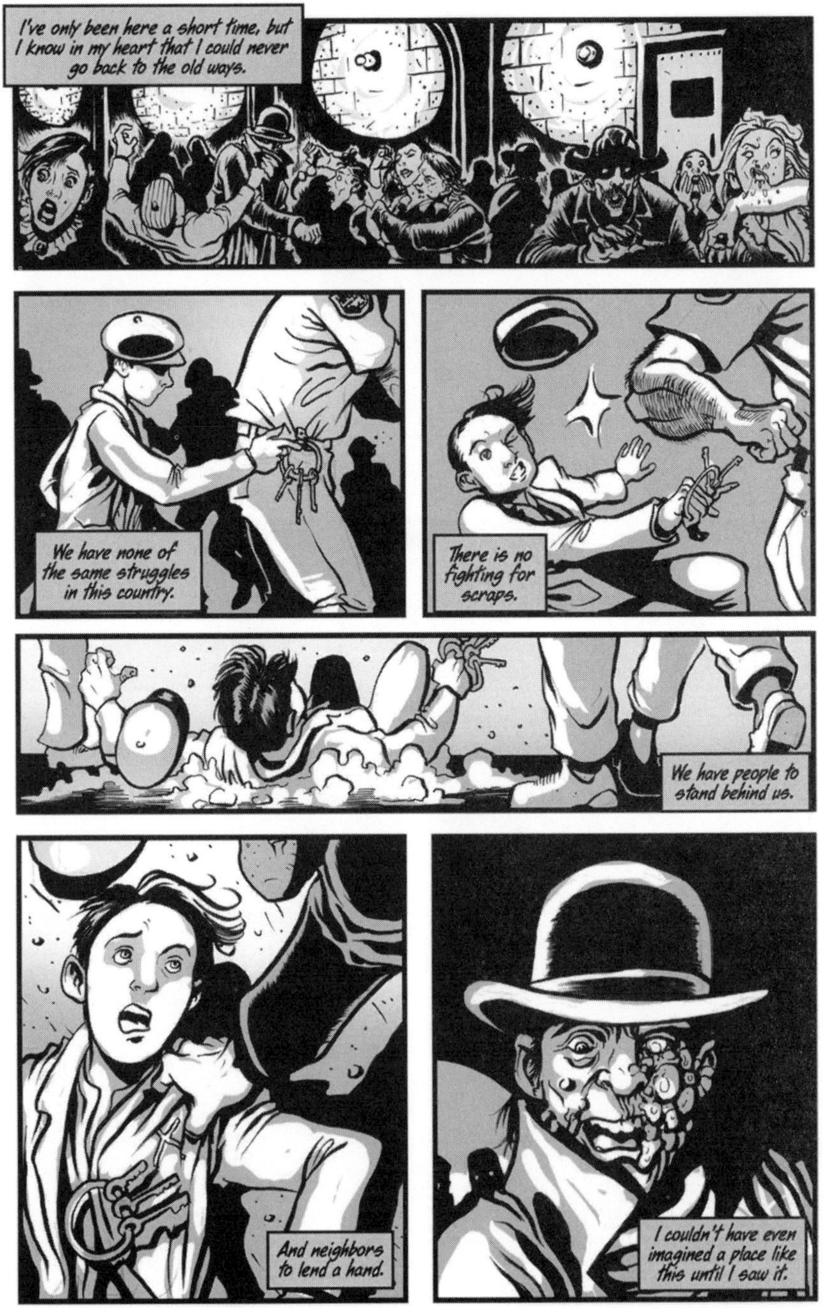
I've only been here a short time, but I know in my heart that I could never go back to the old ways.
We have none of the same struggles in this country.
There is no fighting for scraps.
We have people to stand behind us.
And neighbors to lend a hand.
I couldn't have even imagined a place like this until I saw it.

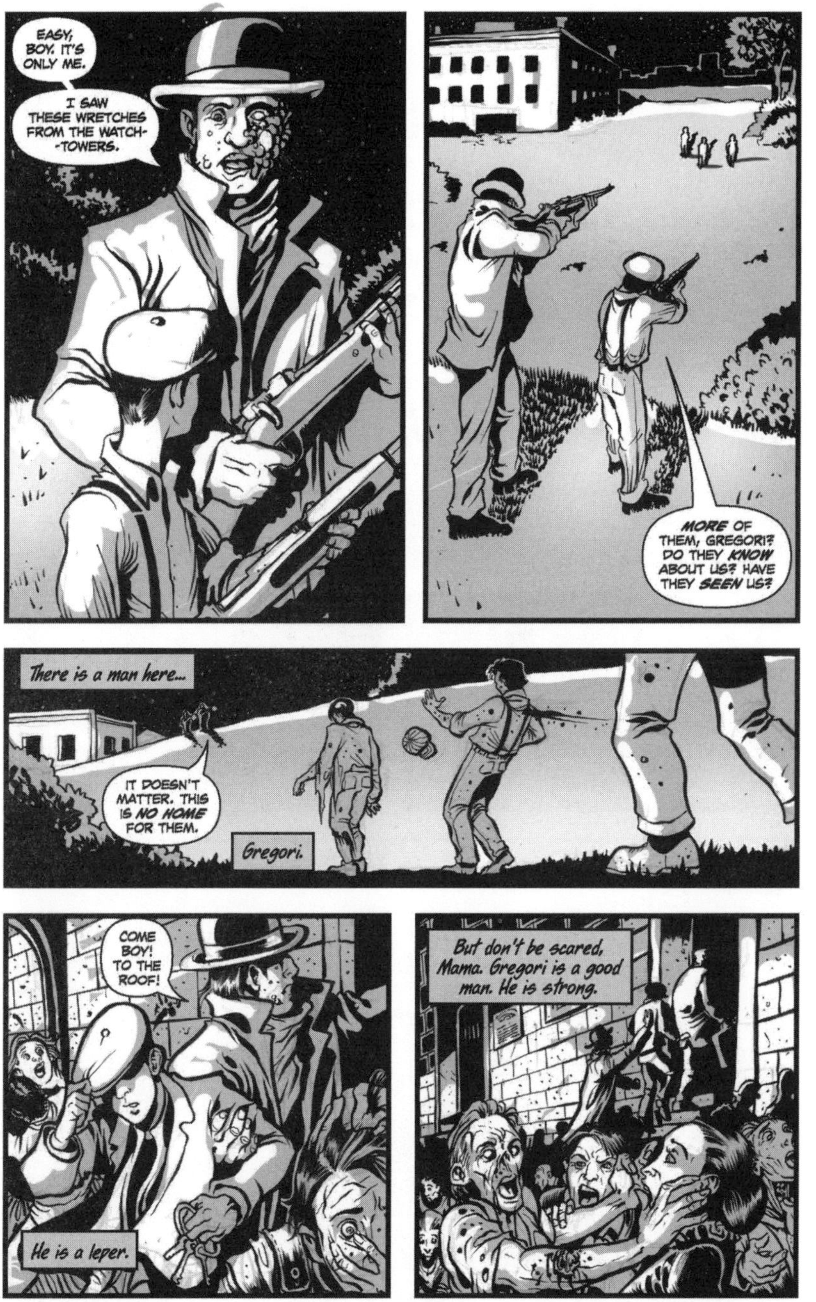
EASY, BOY. IT'S ONLY ME.
I SAW THESE WRETCHES FROM THE WATCH-TOWERS.
MORE OF THEM, GREGORI? DO THEY KNOW ABOUT US? HAVE THEY SEEN US?
There is a man here...
IT DOESN'T MATTER. THIS IS NO HOME FOR THEM.
Gregori.
COME BOY! TO THE ROOF!
He is a leper.
But don't be scared, Mama. Gregori is a good man. He is strong.

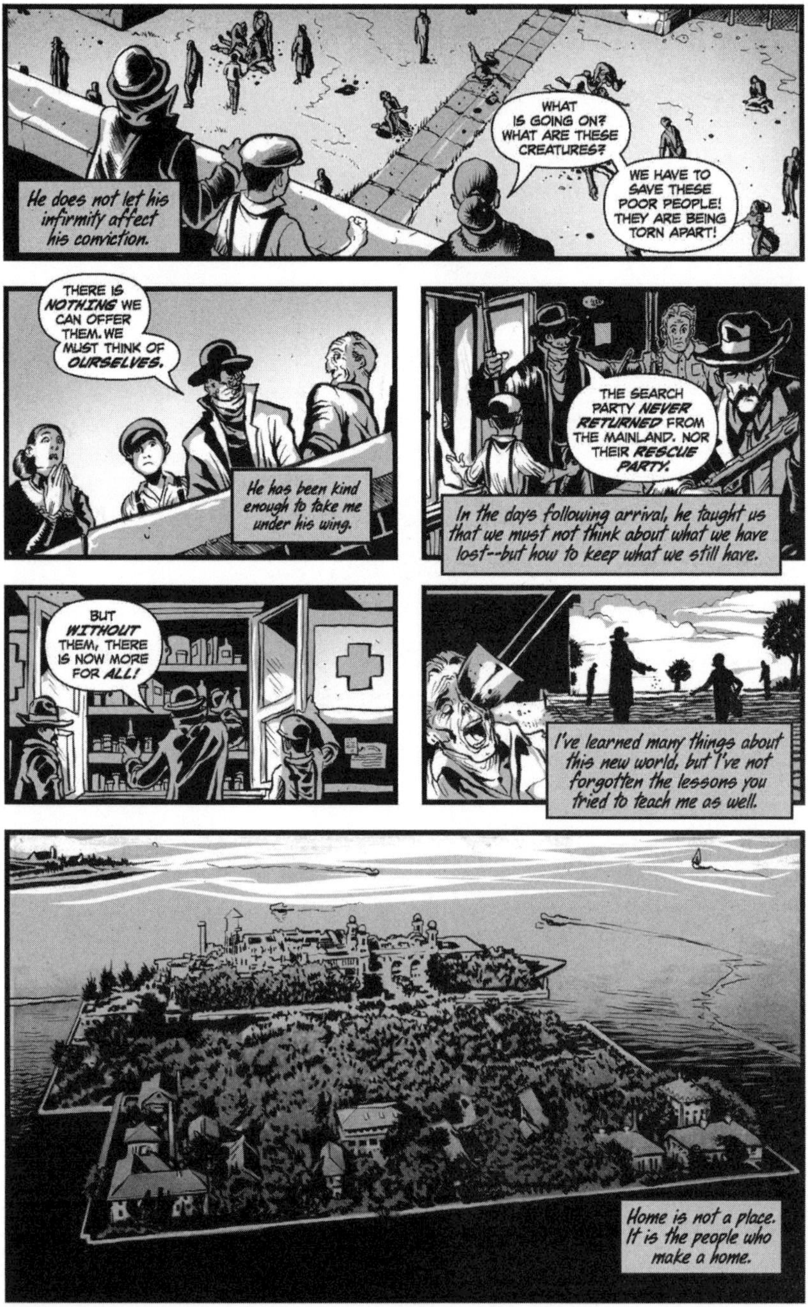

He does not let his infirmity affect his conviction.
WHAT IS GOING ON? WHAT ARE THESE CREATURES?
WE HAVE TO SAVE THESE POOR PEOPLE! THEY ARE BEING TORN APART!
THERE IS NOTHING WE CAN OFFER THEM. WE MUST THINK OF OURSELVES.
He has been kind enough to take me under his wing.
THE SEARCH PARTY NEVER RETURNED FROM THE MAINLAND. NOR THEIR RESCUE PARTY.
In the days following arrival, he taught us that we must not think about what we have lost--but how to keep what we still have.
BUT WITHOUT THEM, THERE IS NOW MORE FOR ALL!
I've learned many things about this new world, but I've not forgotten the lessons you tried to teach me as well.
Home is not a place. It is the people who make a home.

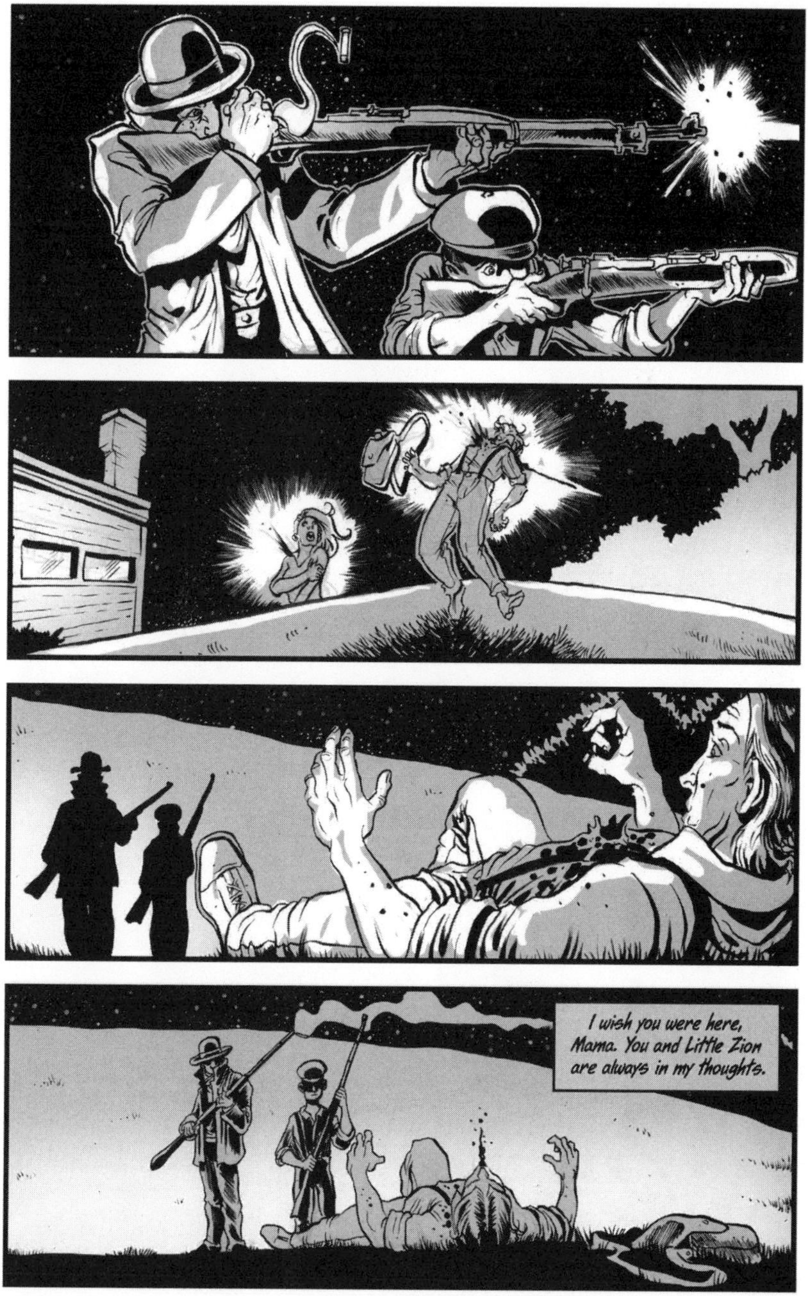
I wish you were here, Mama. You and Little Zion are always in my thoughts.

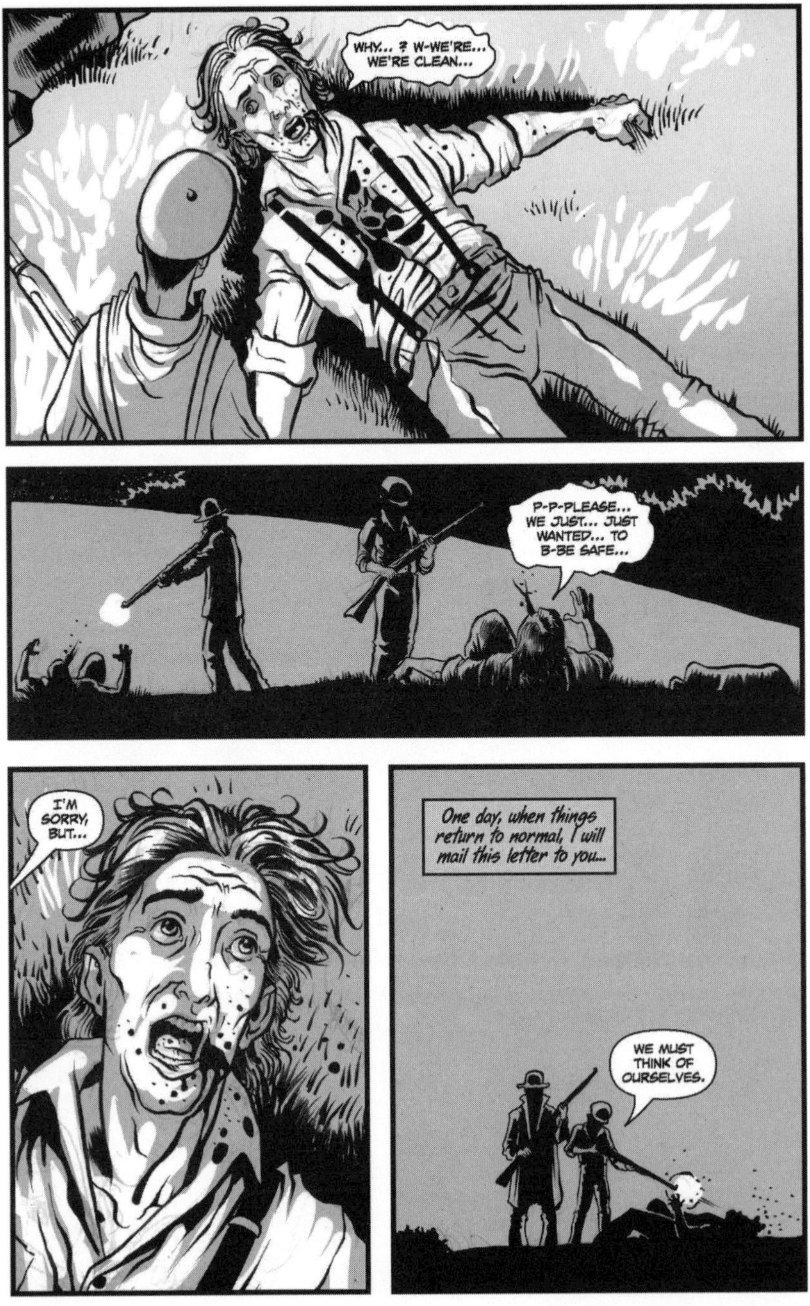
WHY... ? W-WE'RE... WE'RE CLEAN...
P-P-PLEASE... WE JUST... JUST WANTED... TO B-BE SAFE...
I'M SORRY, BUT...
One day, when things return to normal, I will mail this letter to you...
WE MUST THINK OF OURSELVES.

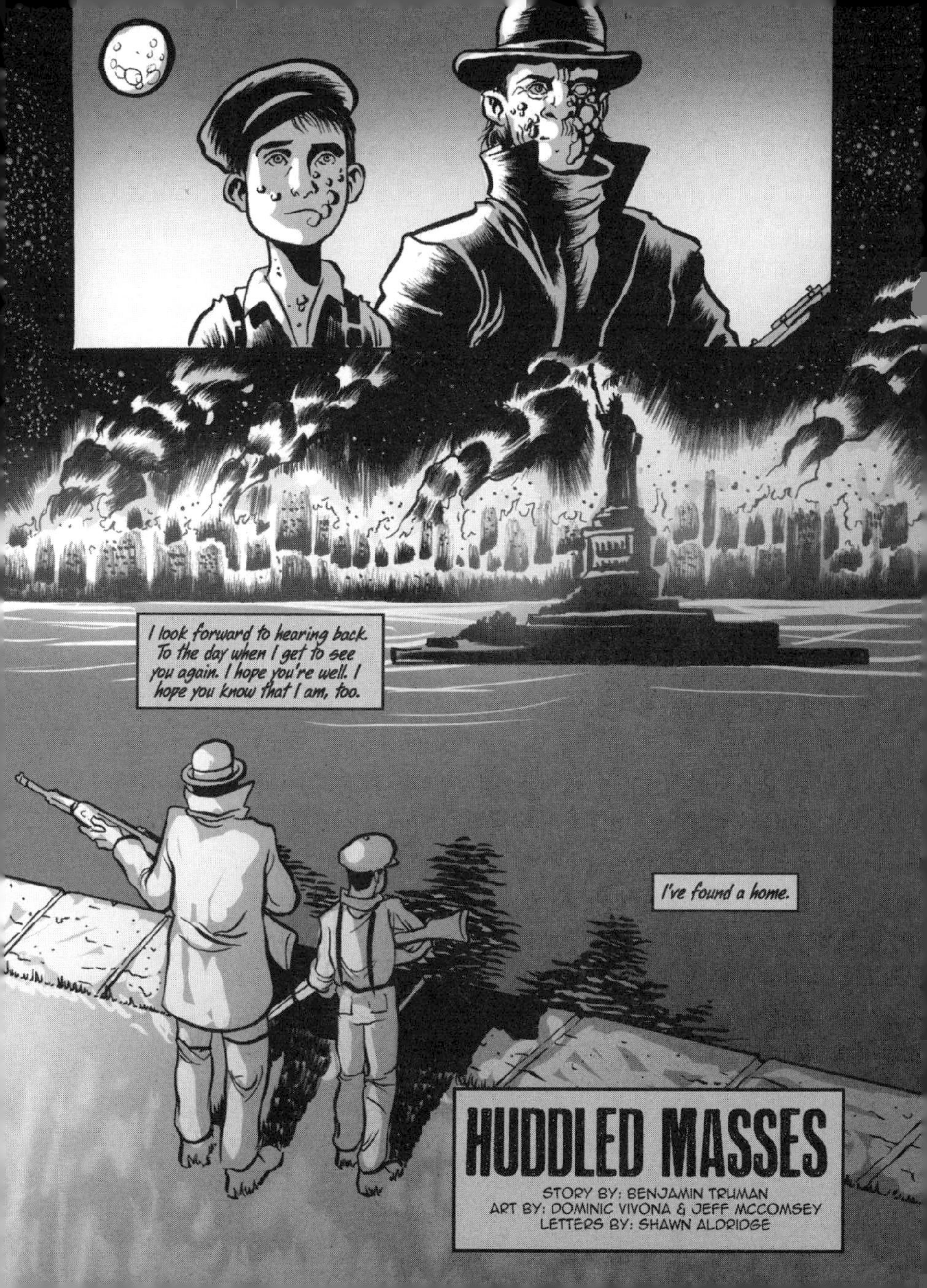
I look forward to hearing back. To the day when I get to see you again. I hope you're well. I hope you know that I am, too.
I've found a home.
HUDDLED MASSES
STORY BY: BENJAMIN TRUMAN
ART BY: DOMINIC VIVONA & JEFF MCCOMSEY
LETTERS BY: SHAWN ALDRIDGE

SO FAR FROM GOD

STORY BY:
CHUCK DIXON

ART BY:
JASON COPLAND

LETTERS BY:
JEFF McCOMSEY

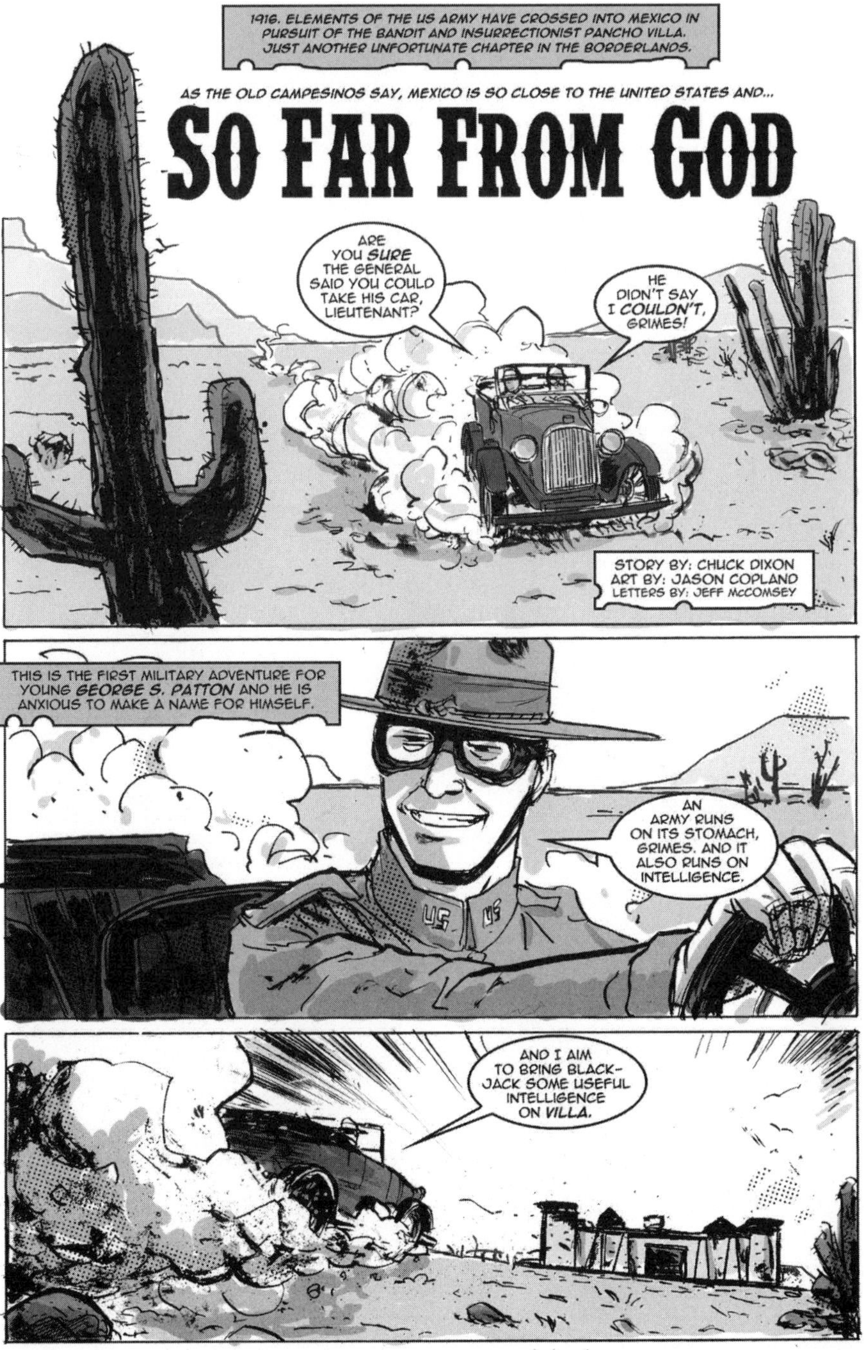
1916. ELEMENTS OF THE US ARMY HAVE CROSSED INTO MEXICO IN PURSUIT OF THE BANDIT AND INSURRECTIONIST PANCHO VILLA. JUST ANOTHER UNFORTUNATE CHAPTER IN THE BORDERLANDS.
AS THE OLD CAMPESINOS SAY, MEXICO IS SO CLOSE TO THE UNITED STATES AND...
SO FAR FROM GOD
ARE YOU SURE THE GENERAL SAID YOU COULD TAKE HIS CAR, LIEUTENANT?
HE DIDN'T SAY I COULDN'T, GRIMES!
STORY BY: CHUCK DIXON
ART BY: JASON COPLAND
LETTERS BY: JEFF McCOMSEY
THIS IS THE FIRST MILITARY ADVENTURE FOR YOUNG GEORGE S. PATTON AND HE IS ANXIOUS TO MAKE A NAME FOR HIMSELF.
AN ARMY RUNS ON ITS STOMACH, GRIMES. AND IT ALSO RUNS ON INTELLIGENCE.
AND I AIM TO BRING BLACK-JACK SOME USEFUL INTELLIGENCE ON VILLA.

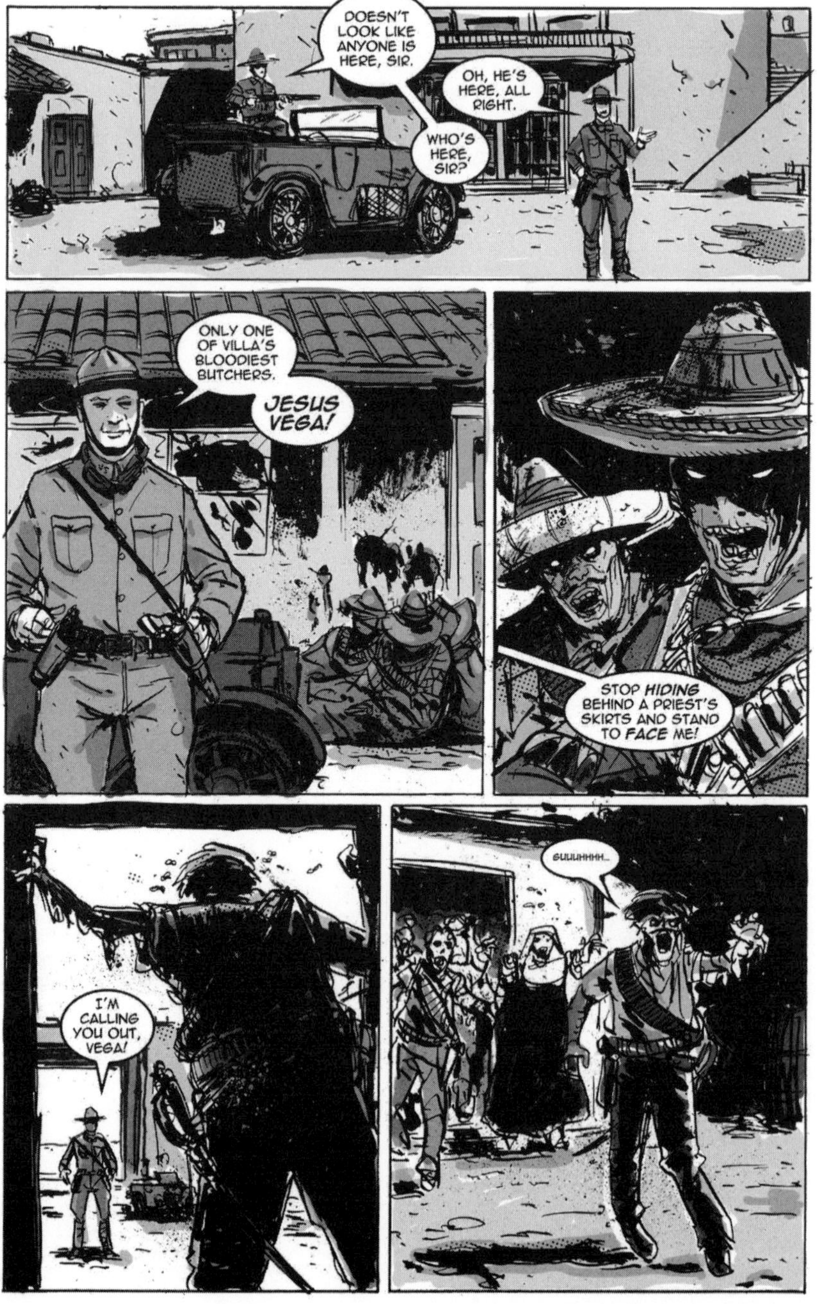
DOESN'T LOOK LIKE ANYONE IS HERE, SIR.
OH, HE'S HERE, ALL RIGHT.
WHO'S HERE, SIR?
ONLY ONE OF VILLA'S BLOODIEST BUTCHERS.
JESUS VEGA!
STOP HIDING BEHIND A PRIEST'S SKIRTS AND STAND TO FACE ME!
I'M CALLING YOU OUT, VEGA!
GUUUHHHH...

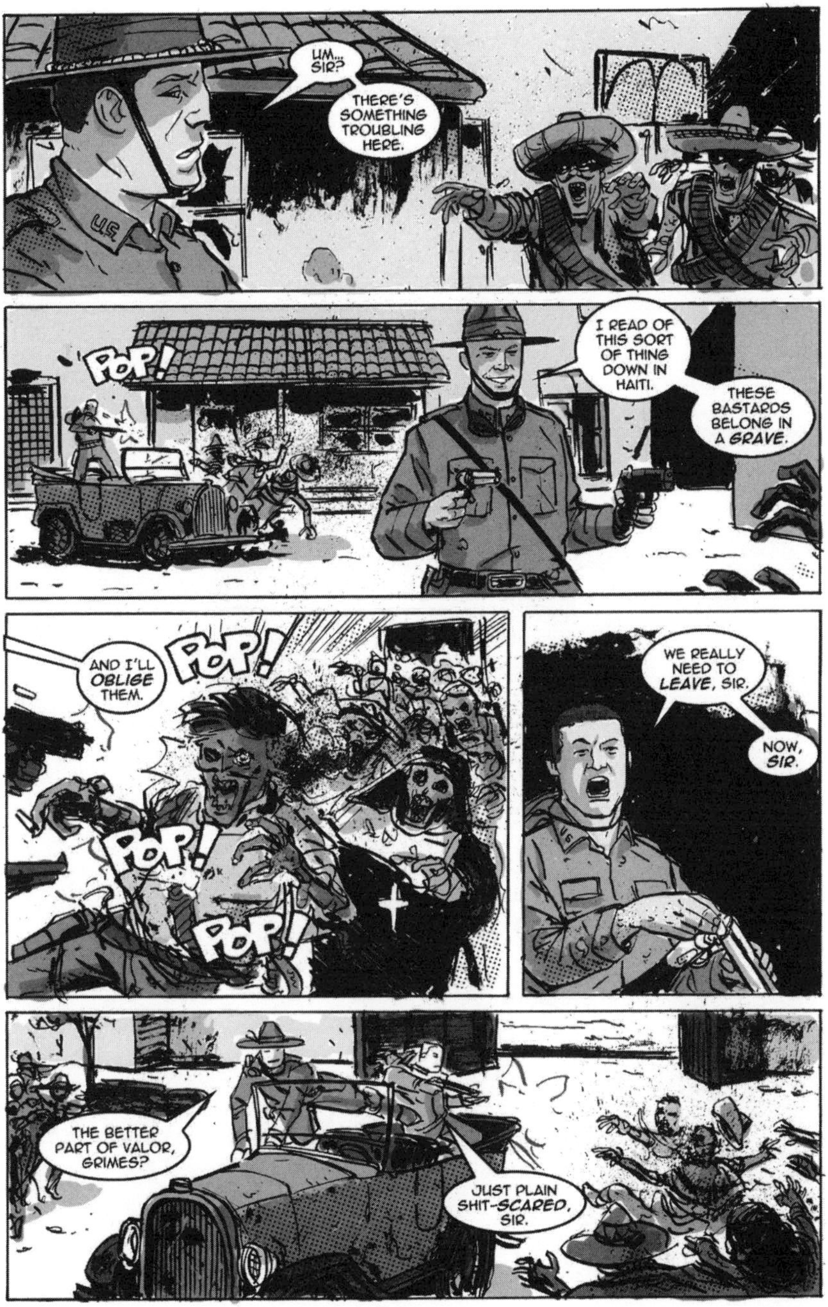

UM... SIR?
THERE'S SOMETHING TROUBLING HERE.
POP!
I READ OF THIS SORT OF THING DOWN IN HAITI.
THESE BASTARDS BELONG IN A GRAVE.
AND I'LL OBLIGE THEM.
POP!
POP!
POP!
WE REALLY NEED TO LEAVE, SIR.
NOW, SIR.
THE BETTER PART OF VALOR, GRIMES?
JUST PLAIN SHIT-SCARED, SIR.

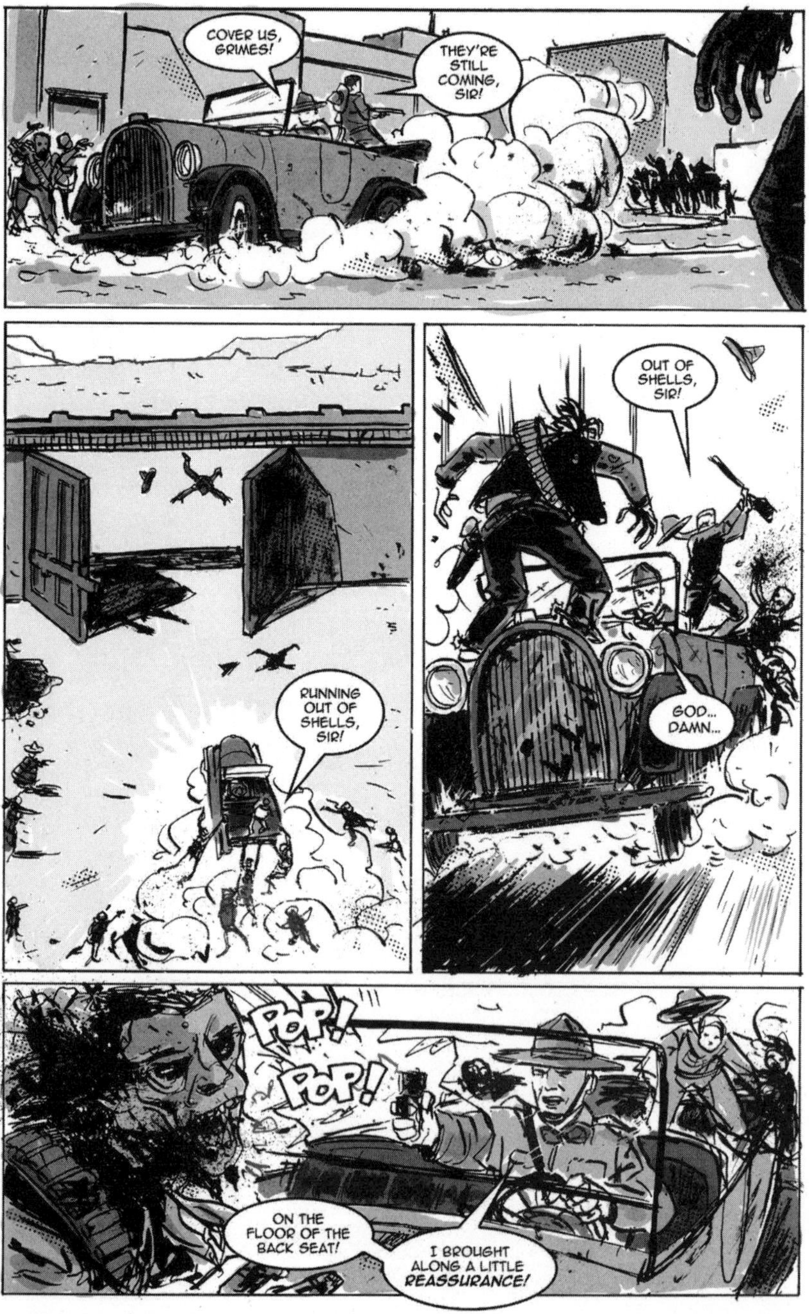
COVER US, GRIMES!
THEY'RE STILL COMING, SIR!
RUNNING OUT OF SHELLS, SIR!
OUT OF SHELLS, SIR!
GOD... DAMN...
POP!
POP!
ON THE FLOOR OF THE BACK SEAT!
I BROUGHT ALONG A LITTLE REASSURANCE!

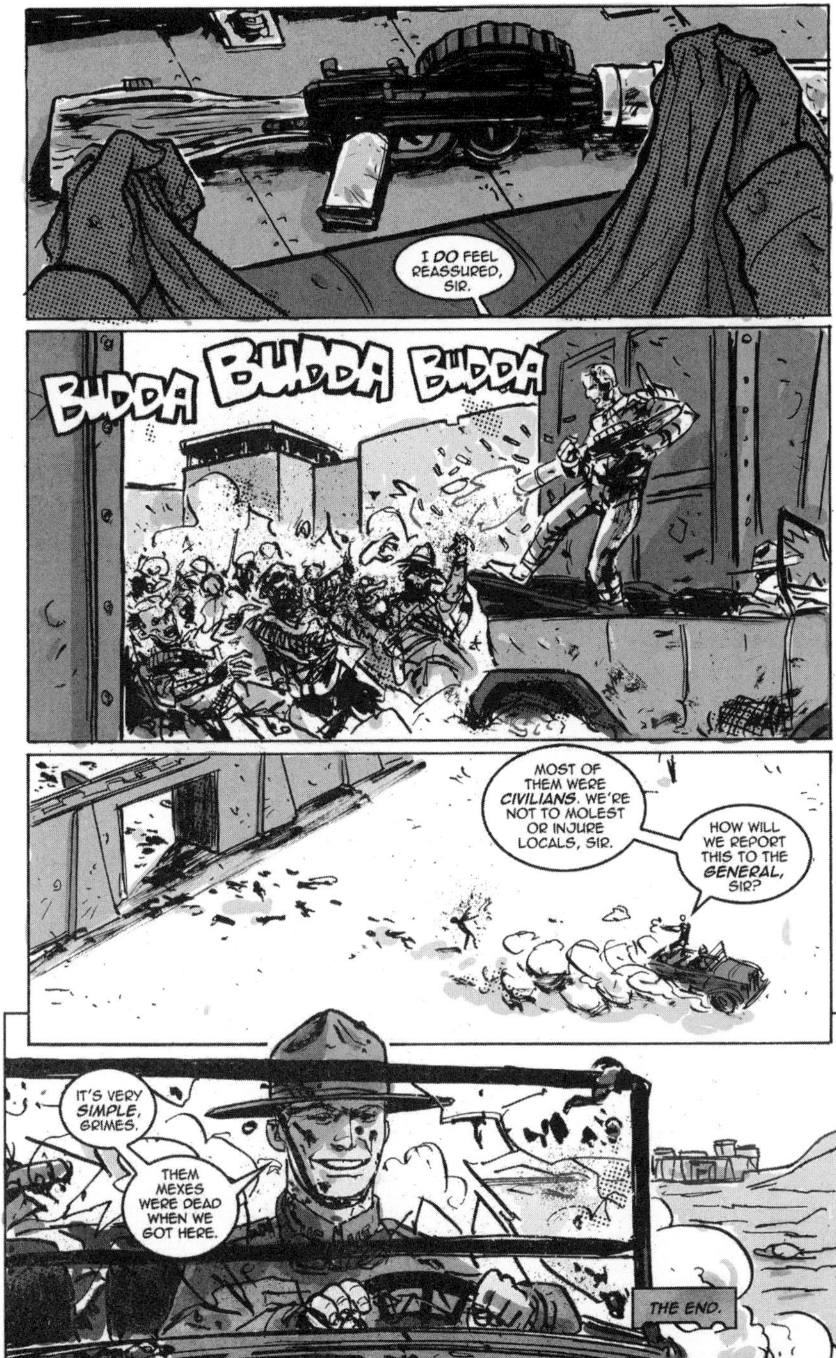
I DO FEEL REASSURED, SIR.
BUDDA BUDDA BUDDA
MOST OF THEM WERE CIVILIANS. WE'RE NOT TO MOLEST OR INJURE LOCALS, SIR.
HOW WILL WE REPORT THIS TO THE GENERAL, SIR?
IT'S VERY SIMPLE, GRIMES.
THEM MEXES WERE DEAD WHEN WE GOT HERE.
THE END.

NO MAN'S LAND

STORY AND LETTERS BY:
STEPHEN LINDSAY

ART BY:
JOHN BROGLIA

GRAYSCALES BY:
DANIEL THOLLIN

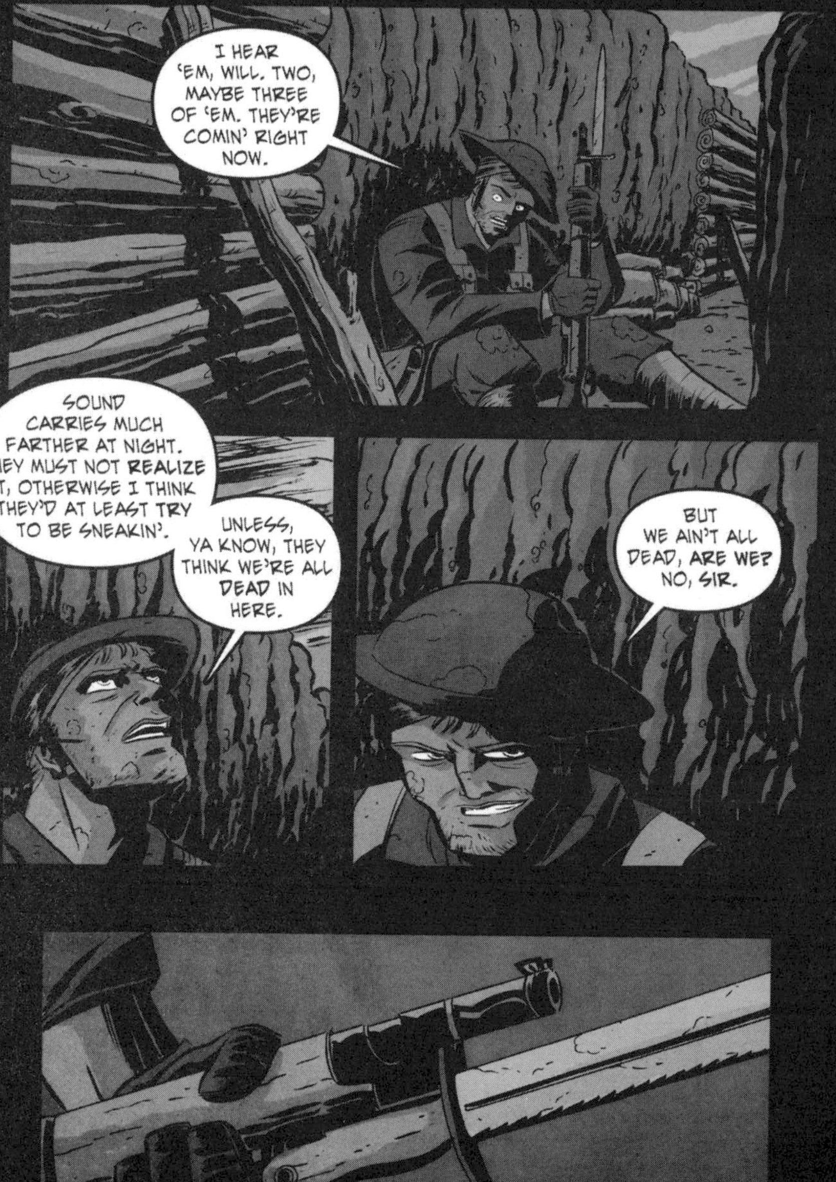
I HEAR 'EM, WILL. TWO, MAYBE THREE OF 'EM. THEY'RE COMIN' RIGHT NOW.
SOUND CARRIES MUCH FARTHER AT NIGHT. THEY MUST NOT REALIZE IT, OTHERWISE I THINK THEY'D AT LEAST TRY TO BE SNEAKIN'.
UNLESS, YA KNOW, THEY THINK WE'RE ALL DEAD IN HERE.
BUT WE AIN'T ALL DEAD, ARE WE? NO, SIR.

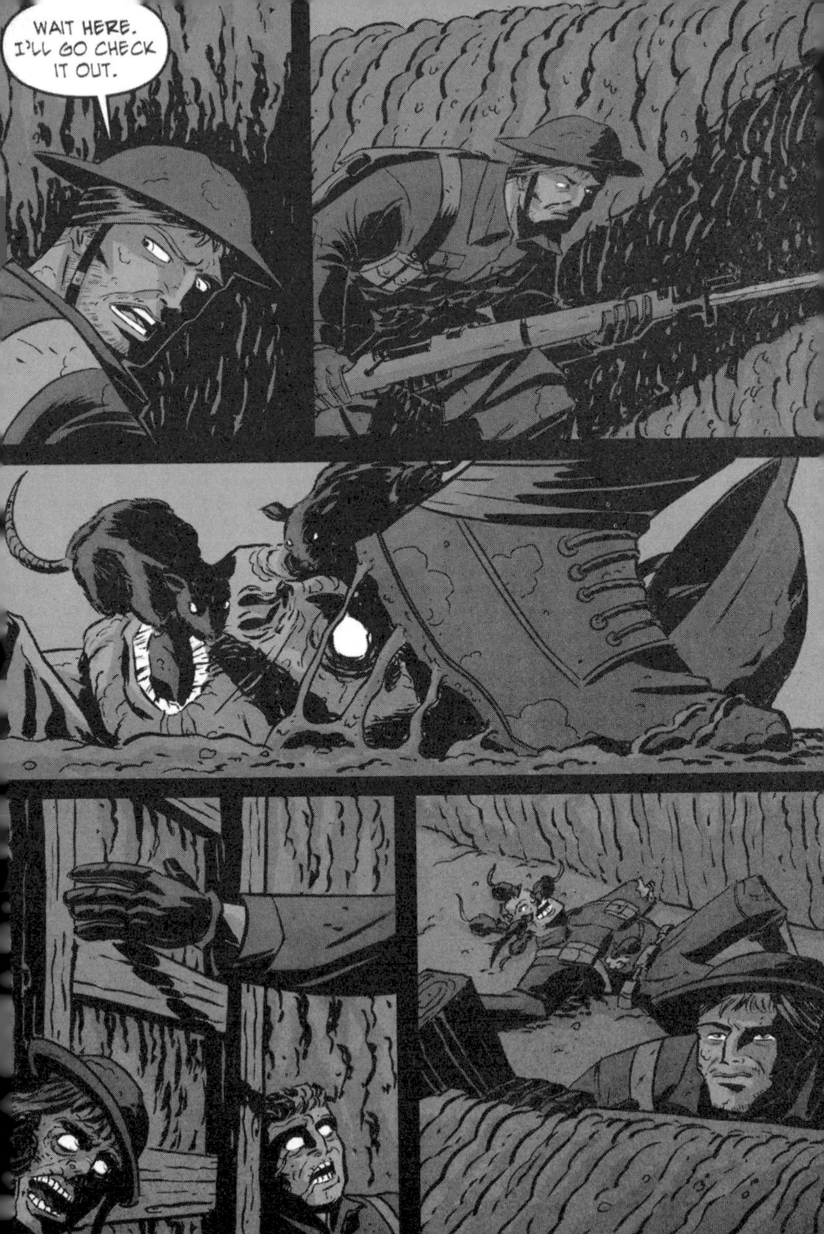
WAIT HERE. I'LL GO CHECK IT OUT.

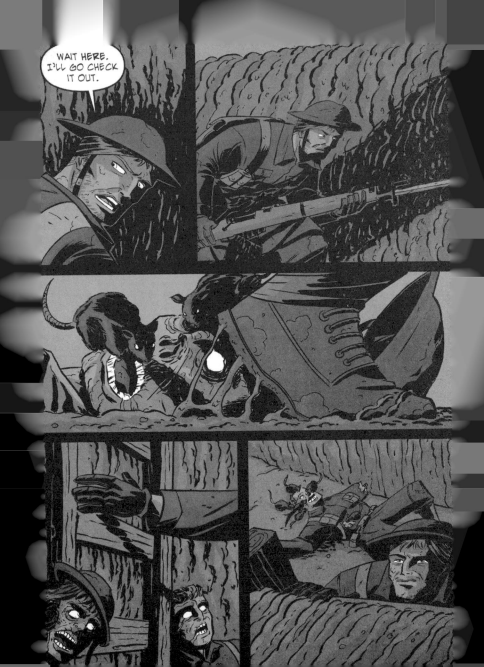

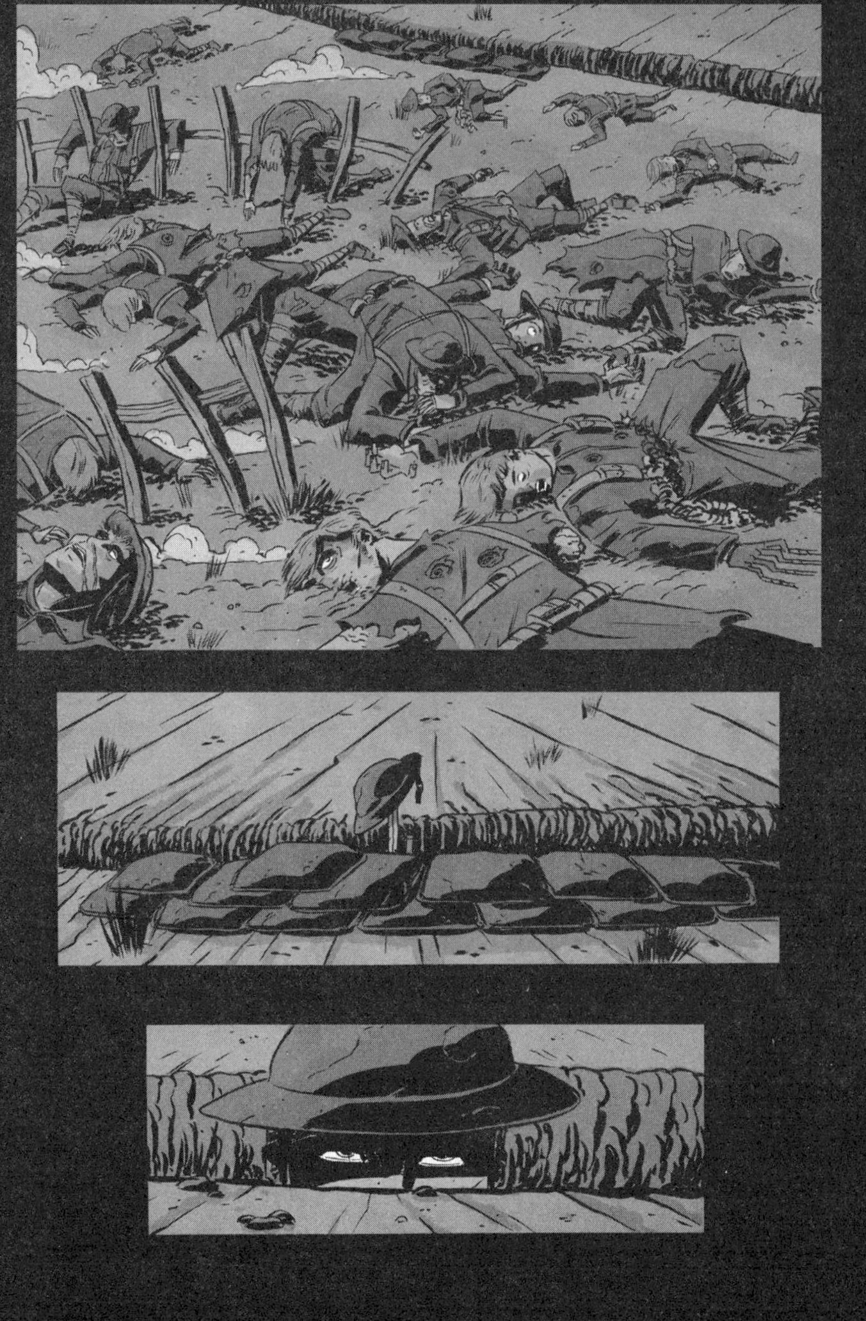

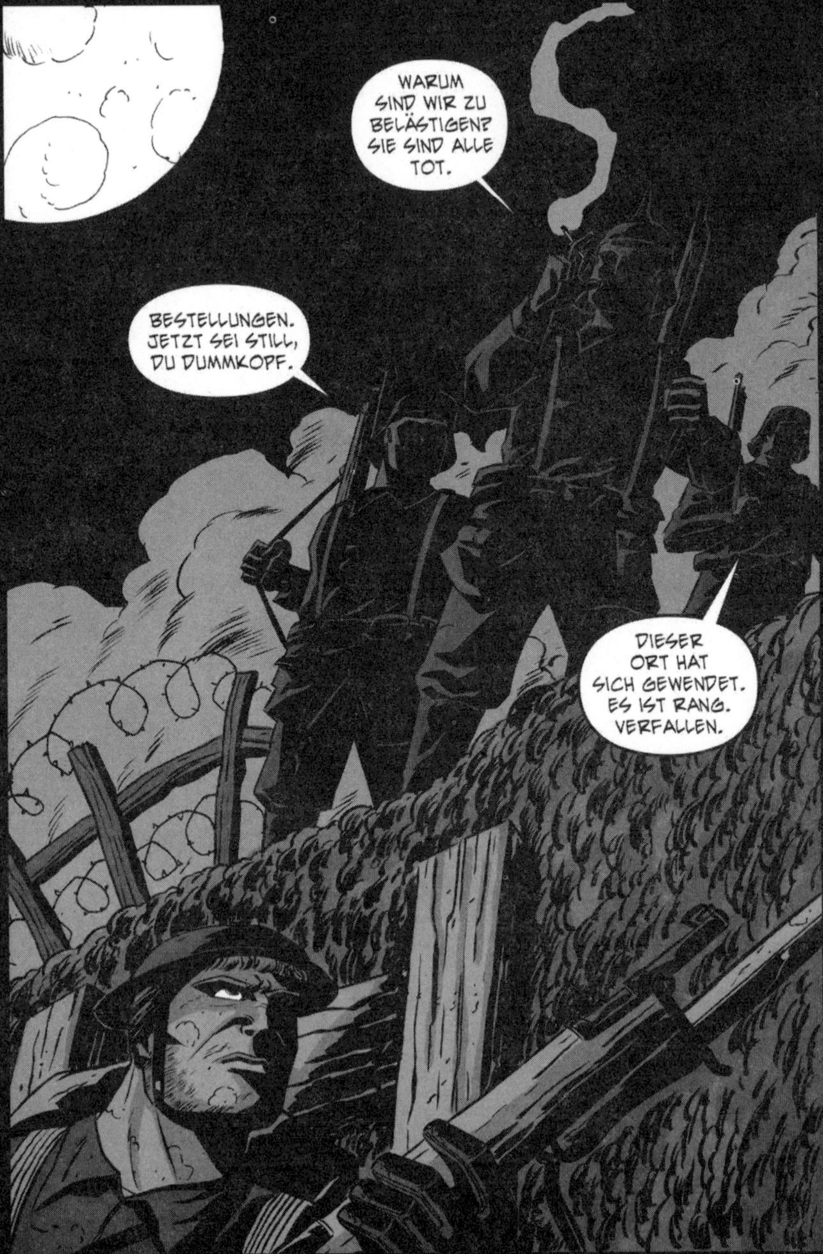
WARUM SIND WIR ZU BELÄSTIGEN? SIE SIND ALLE TOT.
BESTELLUNGEN. JETZT SEI STILL, DU DUMMKOPF.
DIESER ORT HAT SICH GEWENDET. ES IST RANG. VERFALLEN.

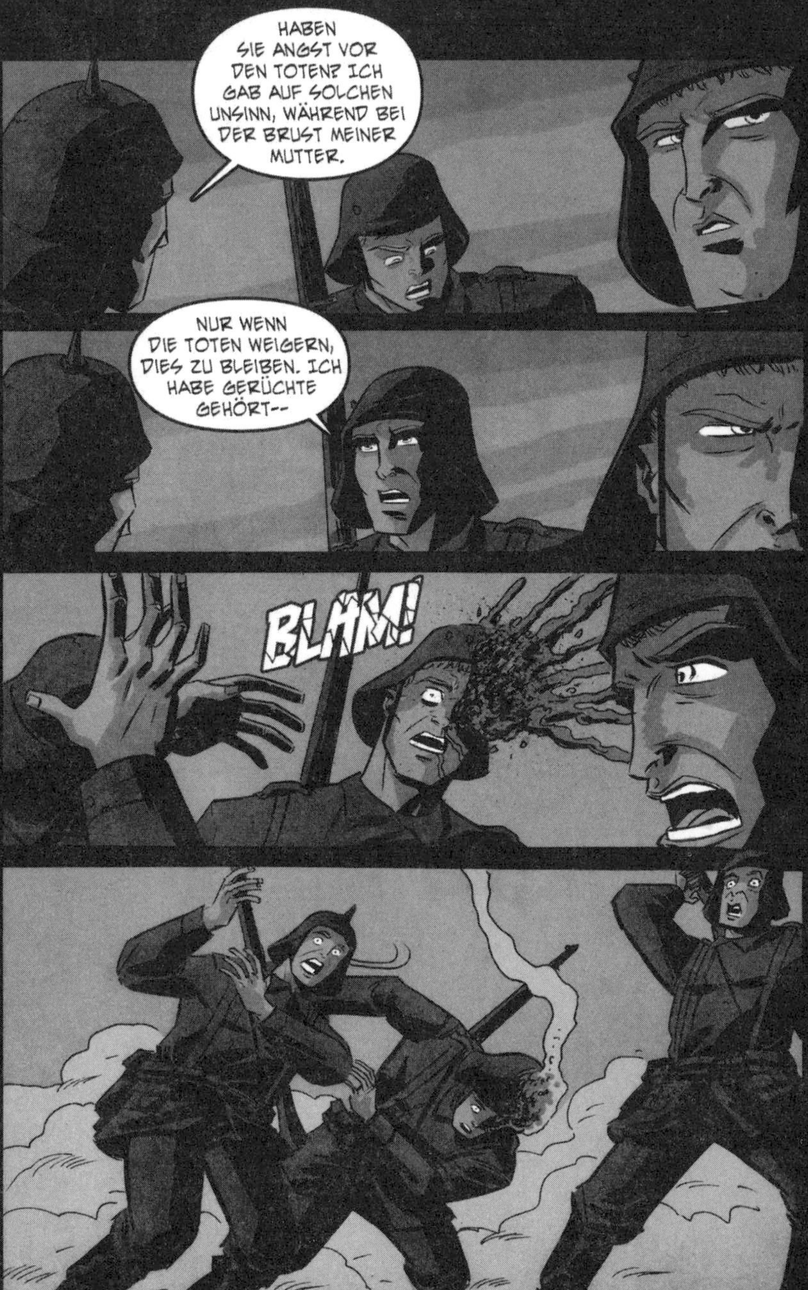
HABEN SIE ANGST VOR DEN TOTEN? ICH GAB AUF SOLCHEN UNSINN, WÄHREND BEI DER BRUST MEINER MUTTER.
NUR WENN DIE TOTEN WEIGERN, DIES ZU BLEIBEN. ICH HABE GERÜCHTE GEHÖRT--
BLAM!

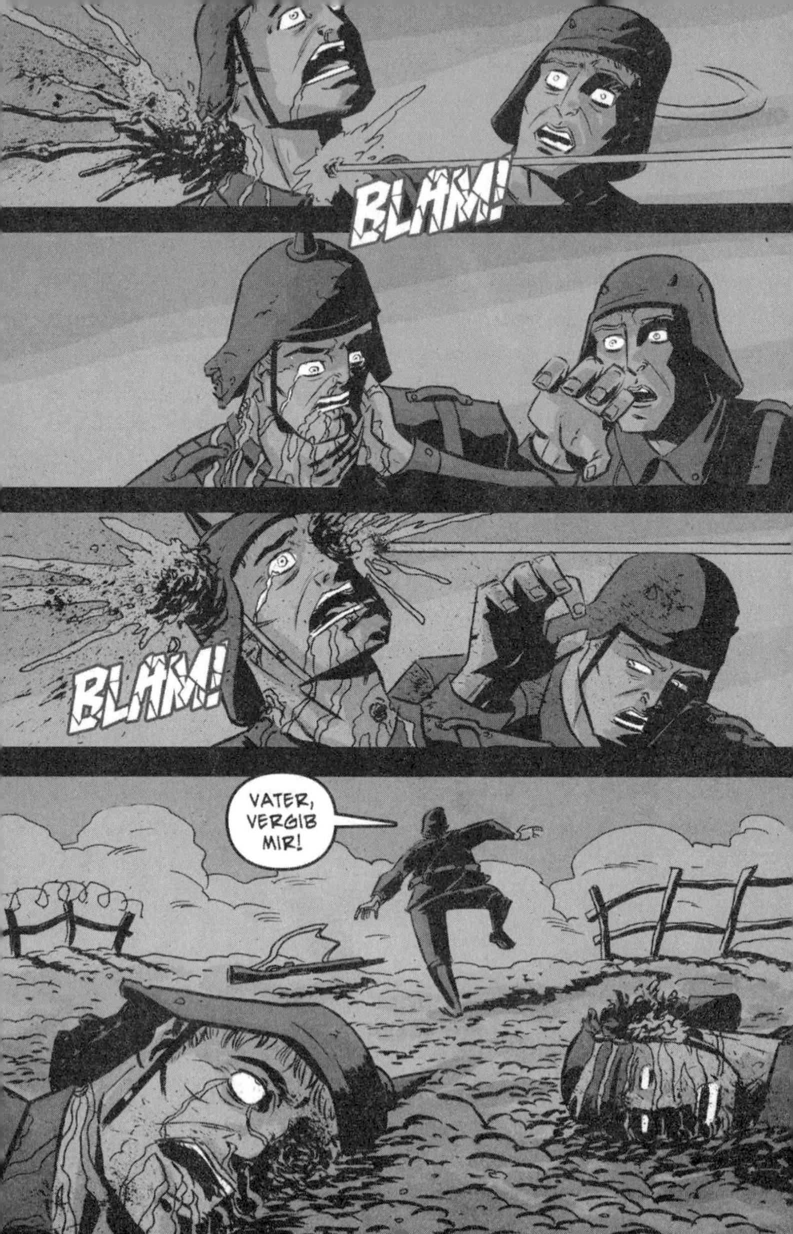
BLAM!
BLAM!
VATER, VERGIB MIR!

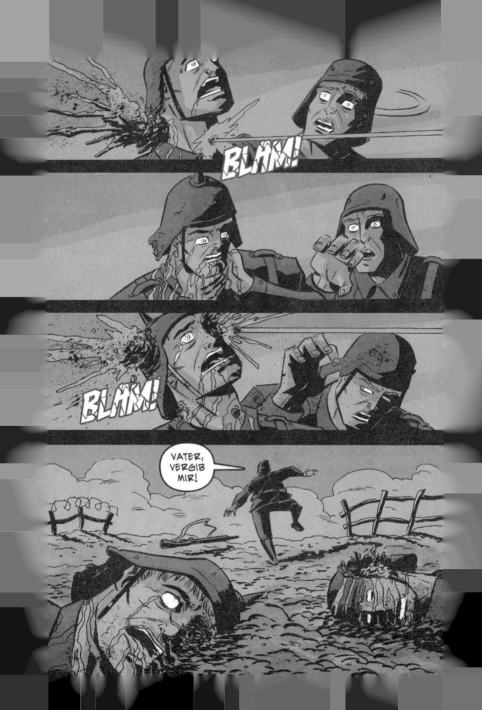

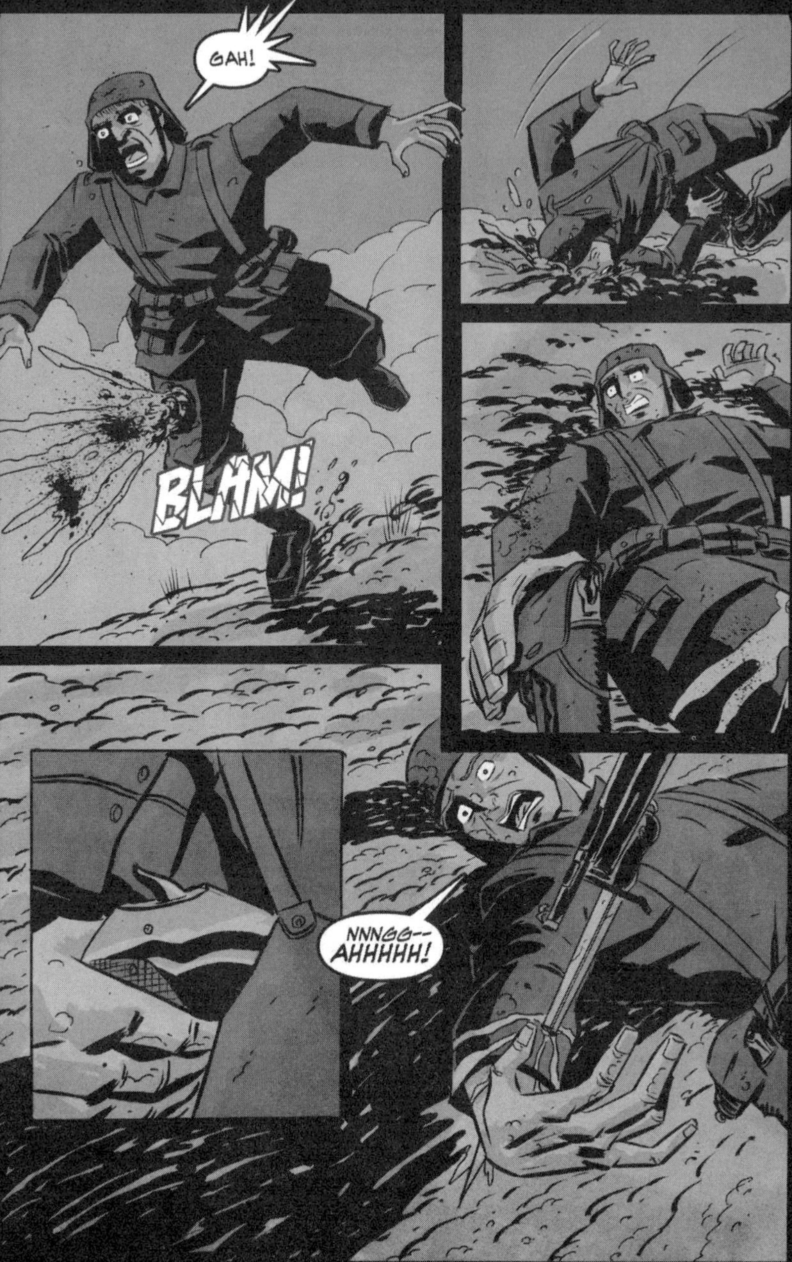
GAH!
BLAM!
NNNGG--AHHHHH!

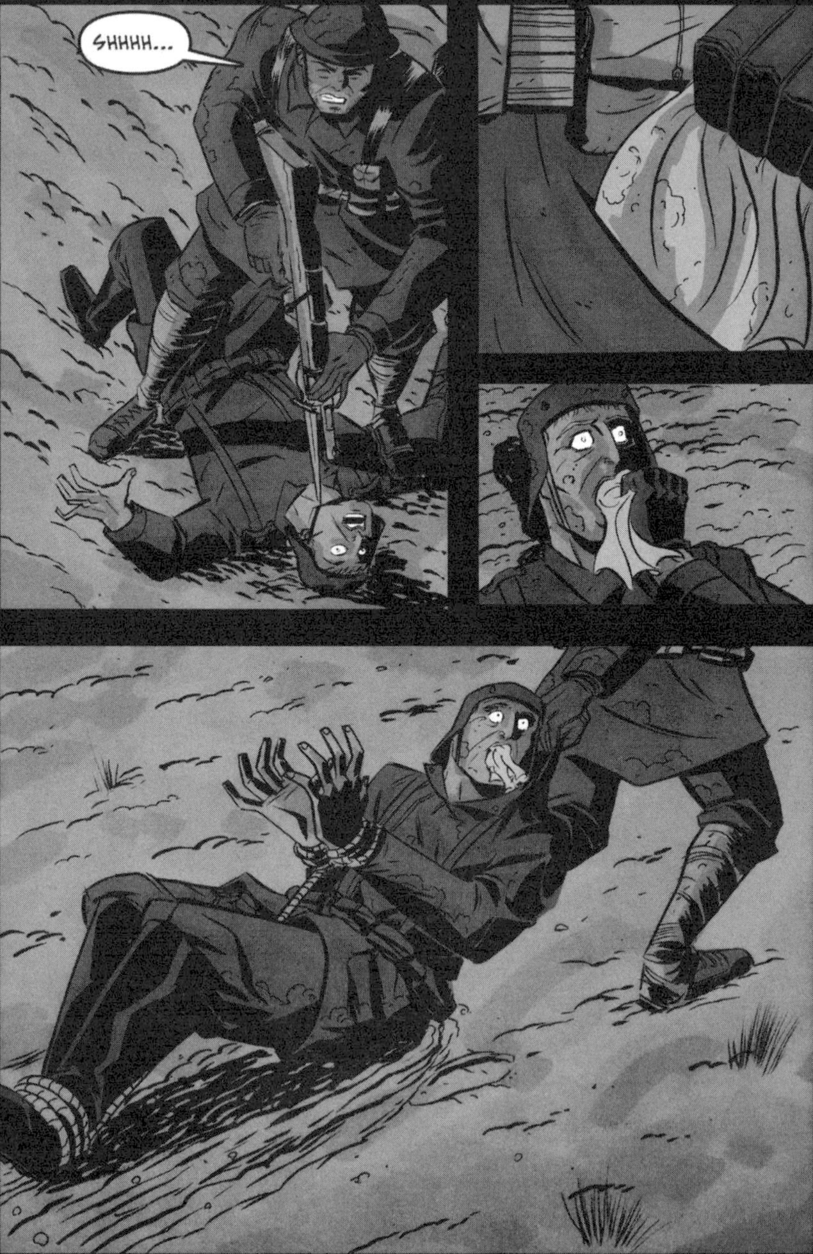
SHHHH...

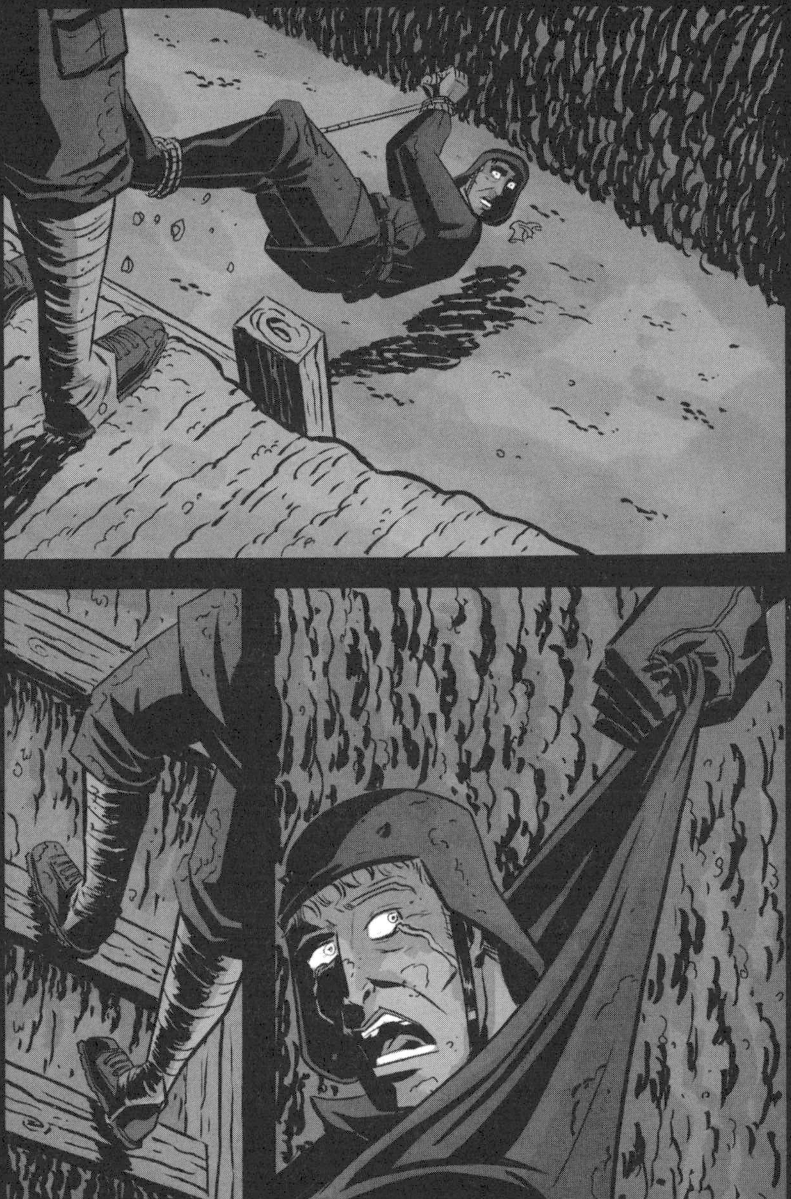

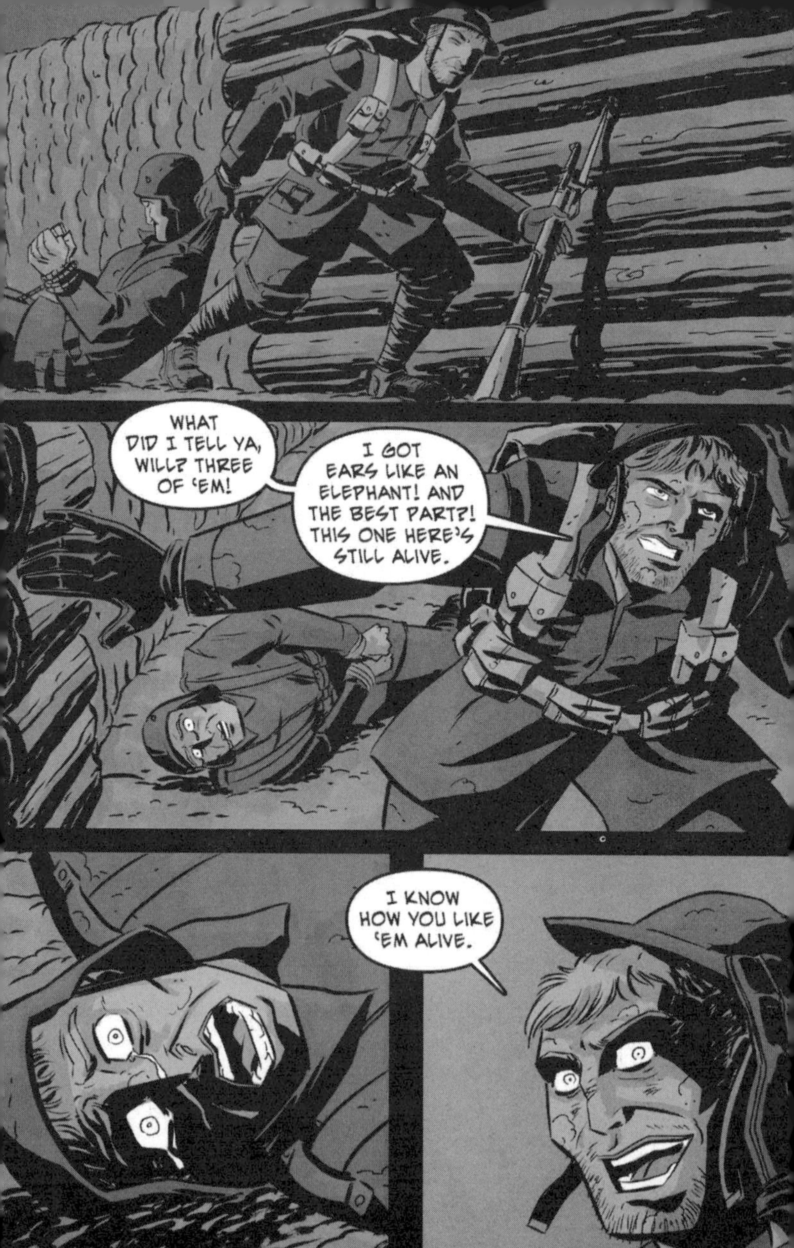
WHAT DID I TELL YA, WILL? THREE OF 'EM!
I GOT EARS LIKE AN ELEPHANT! AND THE BEST PART?! THIS ONE HERE'S STILL ALIVE.
I KNOW HOW YOU LIKE 'EM ALIVE.

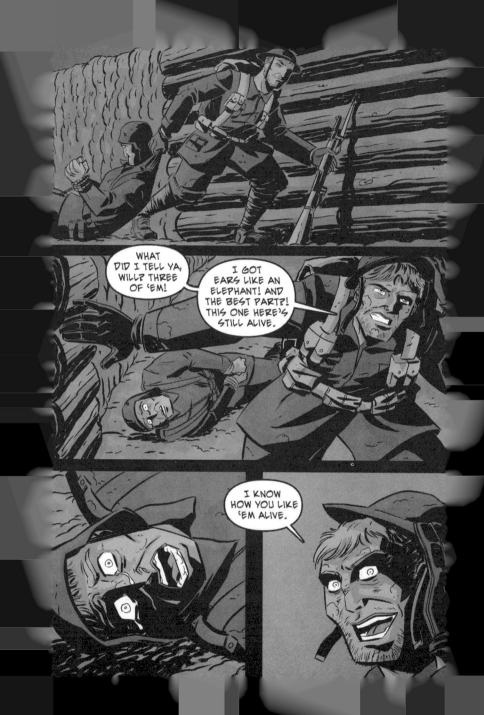

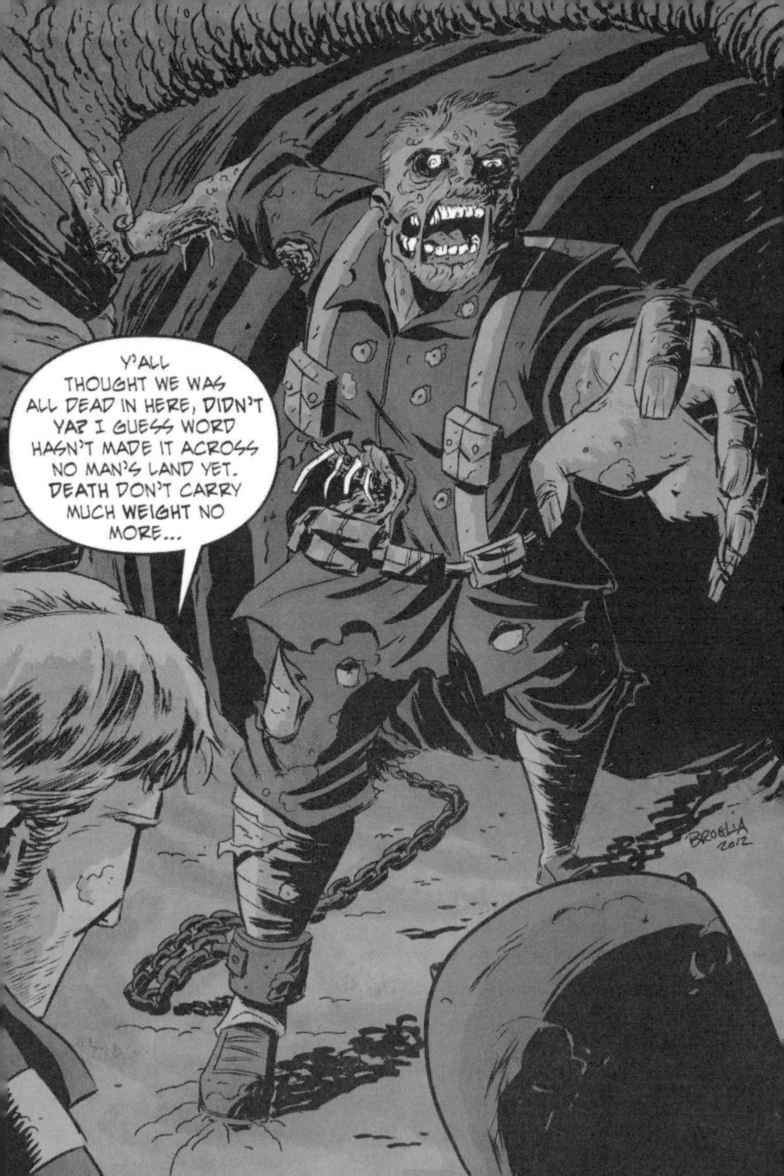
Y'ALL THOUGHT WE WAS ALL DEAD IN HERE, DIDN'T YA? I GUESS WORD HASN'T MADE IT ACROSS NO MAN'S LAND YET. DEATH DON'T CARRY MUCH WEIGHT NO MORE...
BROGLIA 2012
FIN.

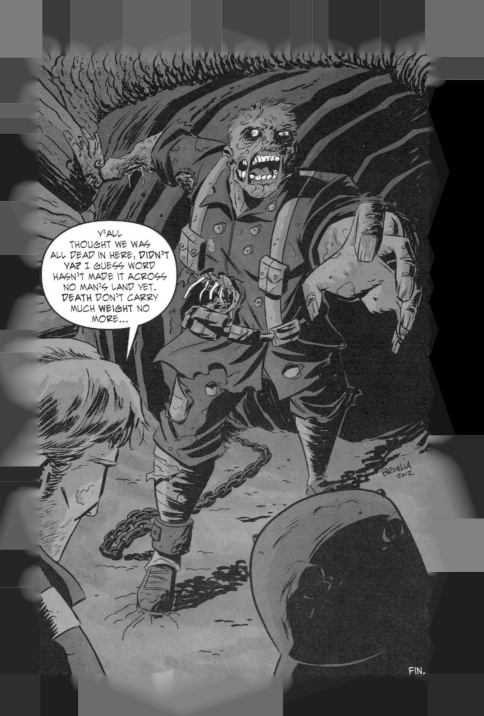

SIXTEEN TONS

STORY BY:
PHIL McCLOREY

ART BY:
GILES CRAWFORD

LETTERS BY:
MICK SCHUBERT

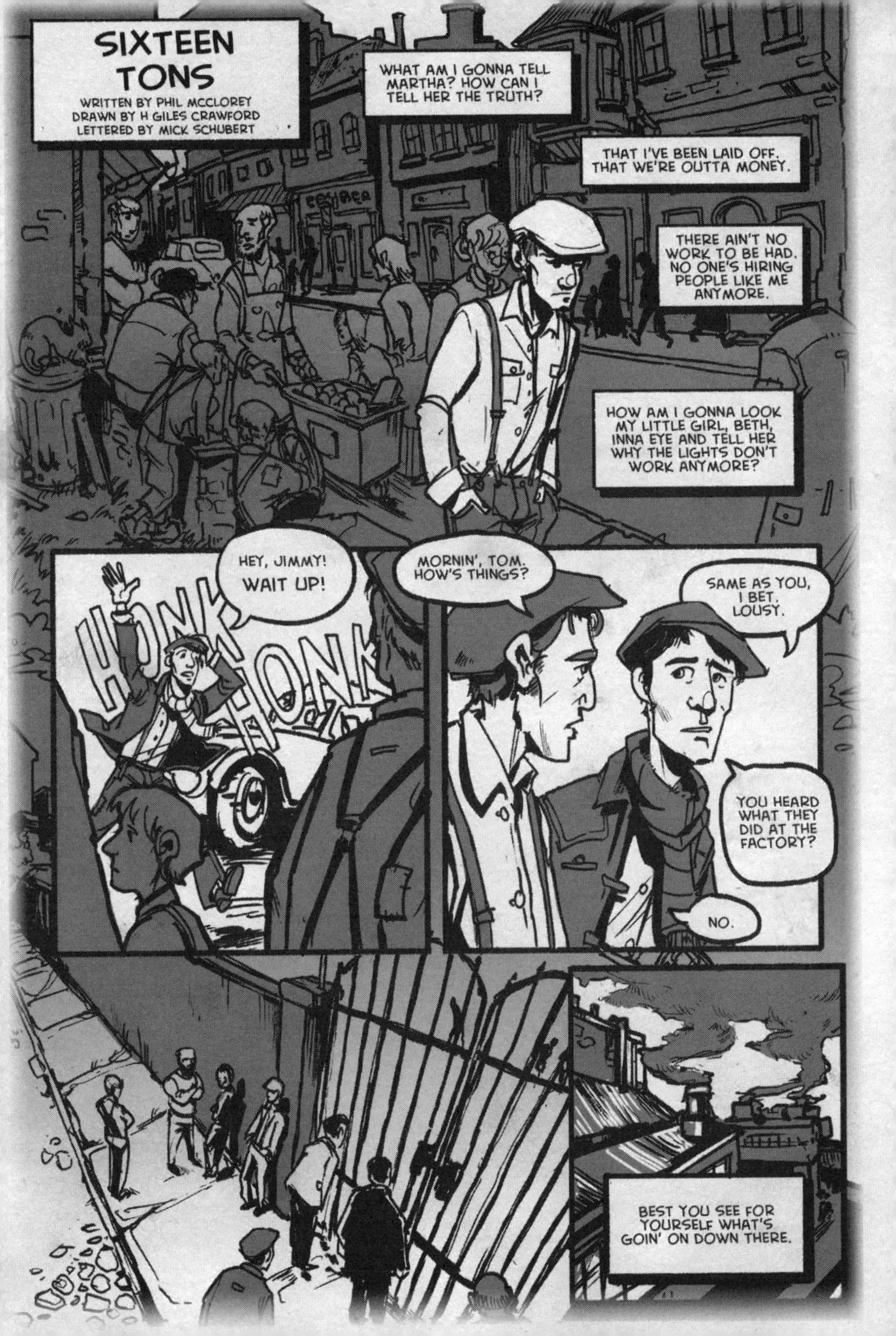
SIXTEEN TONS
WRITTEN BY PHIL MCCLOREY
DRAWN BY H GILES CRAWFORD
LETTERED BY MICK SCHUBERT
WHAT AM I GONNA TELL MARTHA? HOW CAN I TELL HER THE TRUTH?
THAT I'VE BEEN LAID OFF. THAT WE'RE OUTTA MONEY.
THERE AIN'T NO WORK TO BE HAD. NO ONE'S HIRING PEOPLE LIKE ME ANYMORE.
HOW AM I GONNA LOOK MY LITTLE GIRL, BETH, INNA EYE AND TELL HER WHY THE LIGHTS DON'T WORK ANYMORE?
HEY, JIMMY! WAIT UP!
HONK HONK
MORNIN', TOM. HOW'S THINGS?
SAME AS YOU, I BET. LOUSY.
YOU HEARD WHAT THEY DID AT THE FACTORY?
NO.
BEST YOU SEE FOR YOURSELF WHAT'S GOIN' ON DOWN THERE.

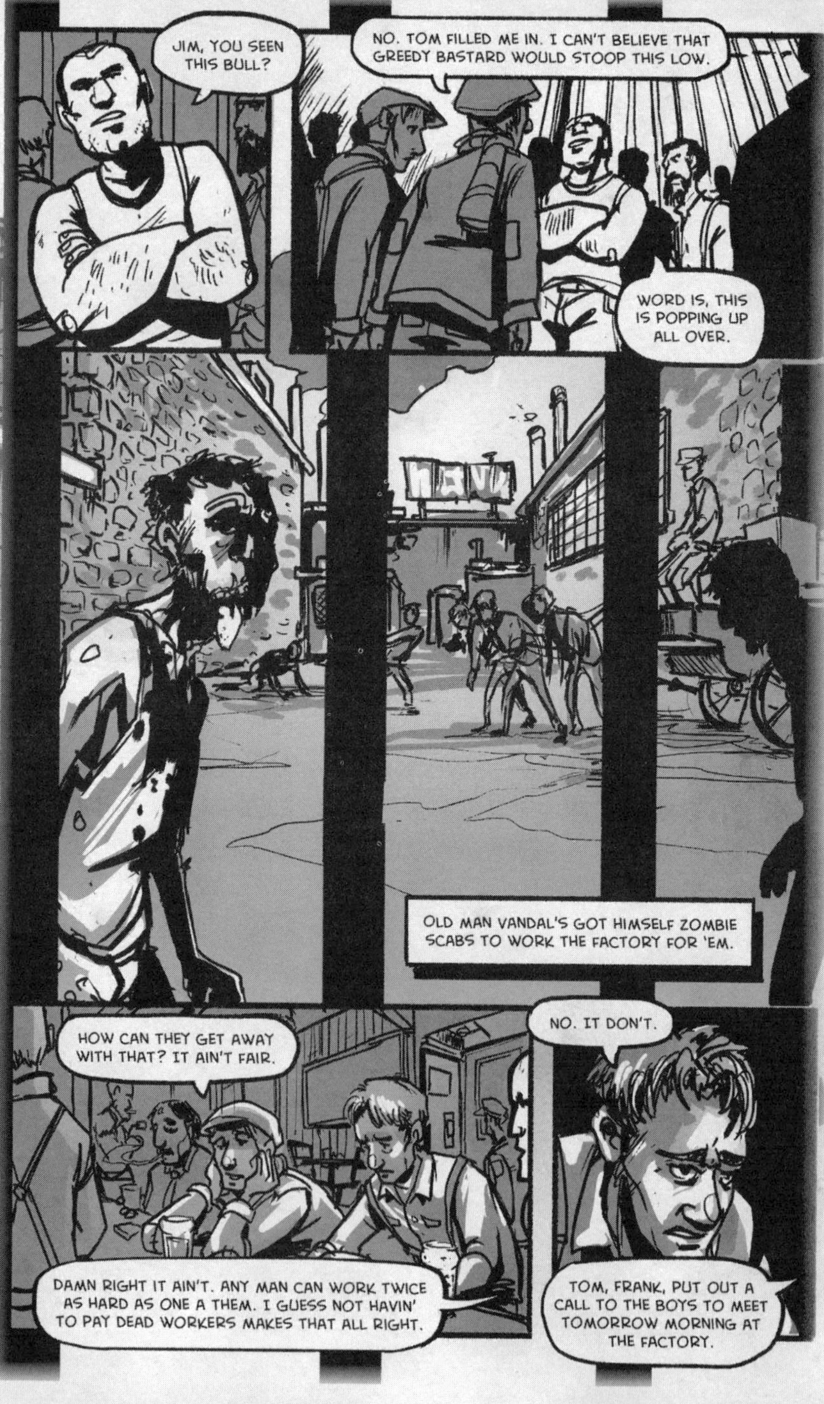
JIM, YOU SEEN THIS BULL?
NO. TOM FILLED ME IN. I CAN'T BELIEVE THAT GREEDY BASTARD WOULD STOOP THIS LOW.
WORD IS, THIS IS POPPING UP ALL OVER.
OLD MAN VANDAL'S GOT HIMSELF ZOMBIE SCABS TO WORK THE FACTORY FOR 'EM.
HOW CAN THEY GET AWAY WITH THAT? IT AIN'T FAIR.
DAMN RIGHT IT AIN'T. ANY MAN CAN WORK TWICE AS HARD AS ONE A THEM. I GUESS NOT HAVIN' TO PAY DEAD WORKERS MAKES THAT ALL RIGHT.
NO. IT DON'T.
TOM, FRANK, PUT OUT A CALL TO THE BOYS TO MEET TOMORROW MORNING AT THE FACTORY.

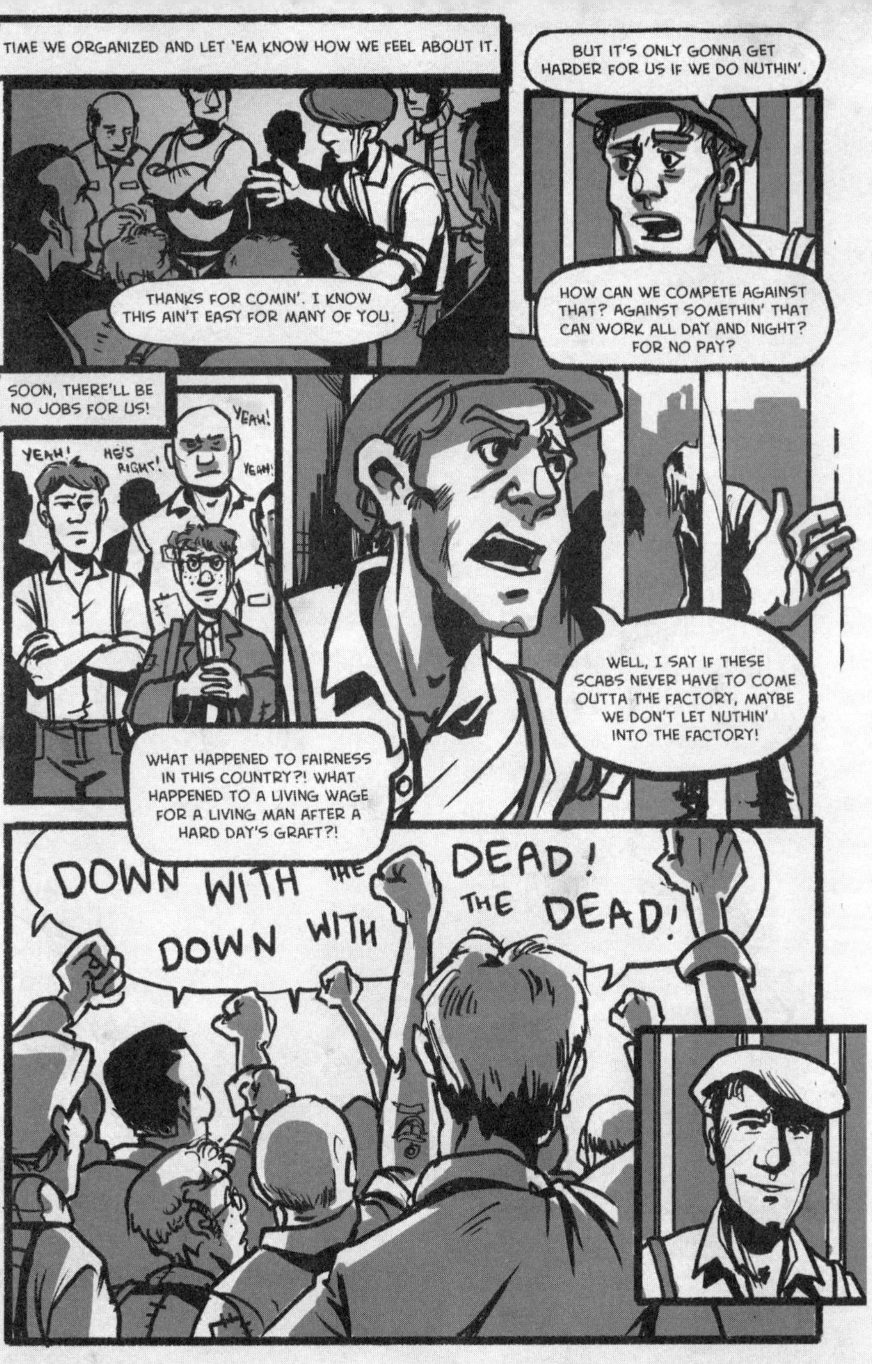

TIME WE ORGANIZED AND LET 'EM KNOW HOW WE FEEL ABOUT IT.
THANKS FOR COMIN'. I KNOW THIS AIN'T EASY FOR MANY OF YOU.
BUT IT'S ONLY GONNA GET HARDER FOR US IF WE DO NUTHIN'.
HOW CAN WE COMPETE AGAINST THAT? AGAINST SOMETHIN' THAT CAN WORK ALL DAY AND NIGHT? FOR NO PAY?
SOON, THERE'LL BE NO JOBS FOR US!
YEAH!
HE'S RIGHT!
YEAH!
YEAH!
WHAT HAPPENED TO FAIRNESS IN THIS COUNTRY?! WHAT HAPPENED TO A LIVING WAGE FOR A LIVING MAN AFTER A HARD DAY'S GRAFT?!
WELL, I SAY IF THESE SCABS NEVER HAVE TO COME OUTTA THE FACTORY, MAYBE WE DON'T LET NUTHIN' INTO THE FACTORY!
DOWN WITH THE DEAD!
DOWN WITH THE DEAD!

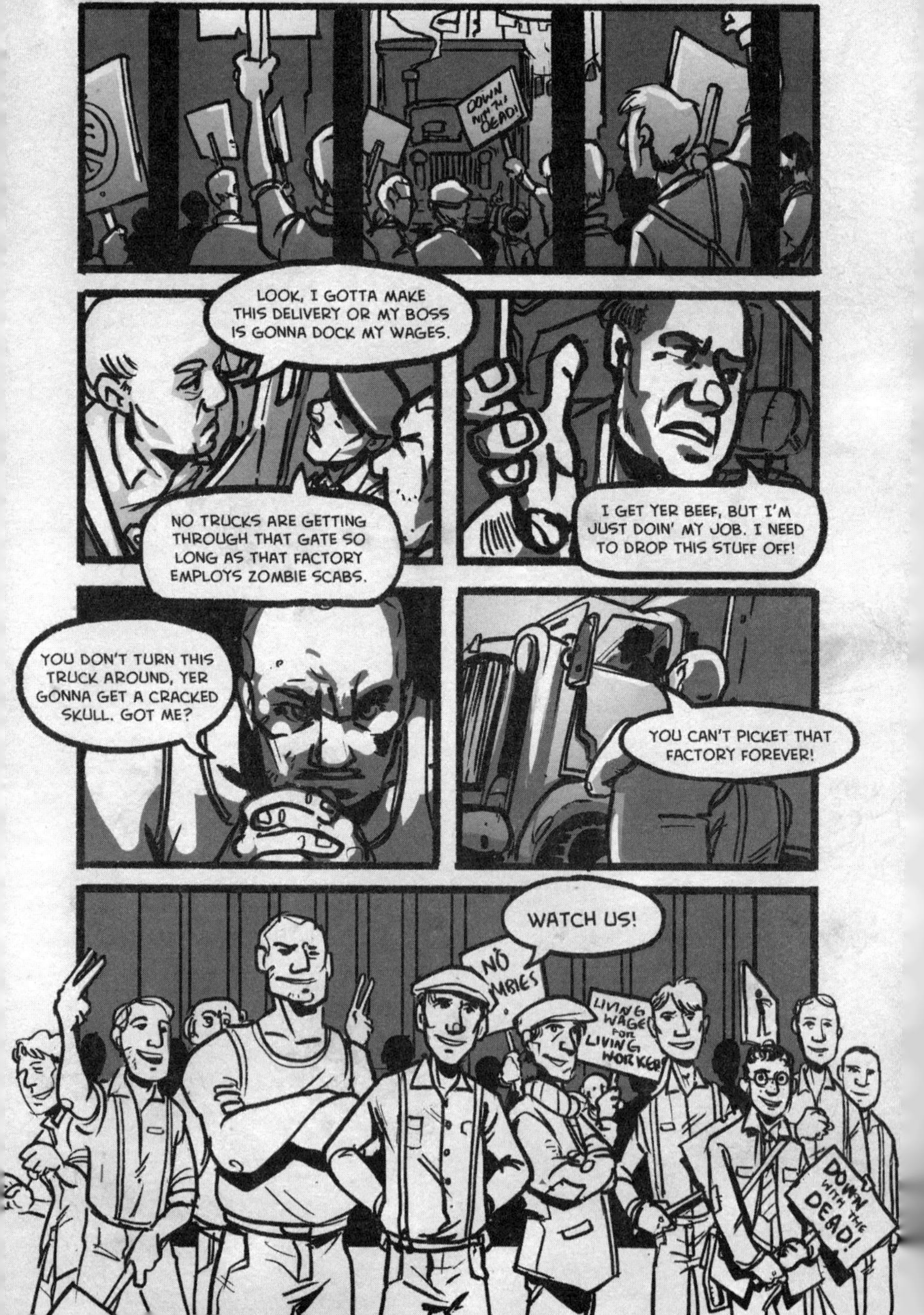
DOWN WITH THE DEAD!
LOOK, I GOTTA MAKE THIS DELIVERY OR MY BOSS IS GONNA DOCK MY WAGES.
NO TRUCKS ARE GETTING THROUGH THAT GATE SO LONG AS THAT FACTORY EMPLOYS ZOMBIE SCABS.
I GET YER BEEF, BUT I'M JUST DOIN' MY JOB. I NEED TO DROP THIS STUFF OFF!
YOU DON'T TURN THIS TRUCK AROUND, YER GONNA GET A CRACKED SKULL. GOT ME?
YOU CAN'T PICKET THAT FACTORY FOREVER!
WATCH US!
NO MBIES
LIVING WAGE FOR LIVING WORKER
DOWN WITH THE DEAD!

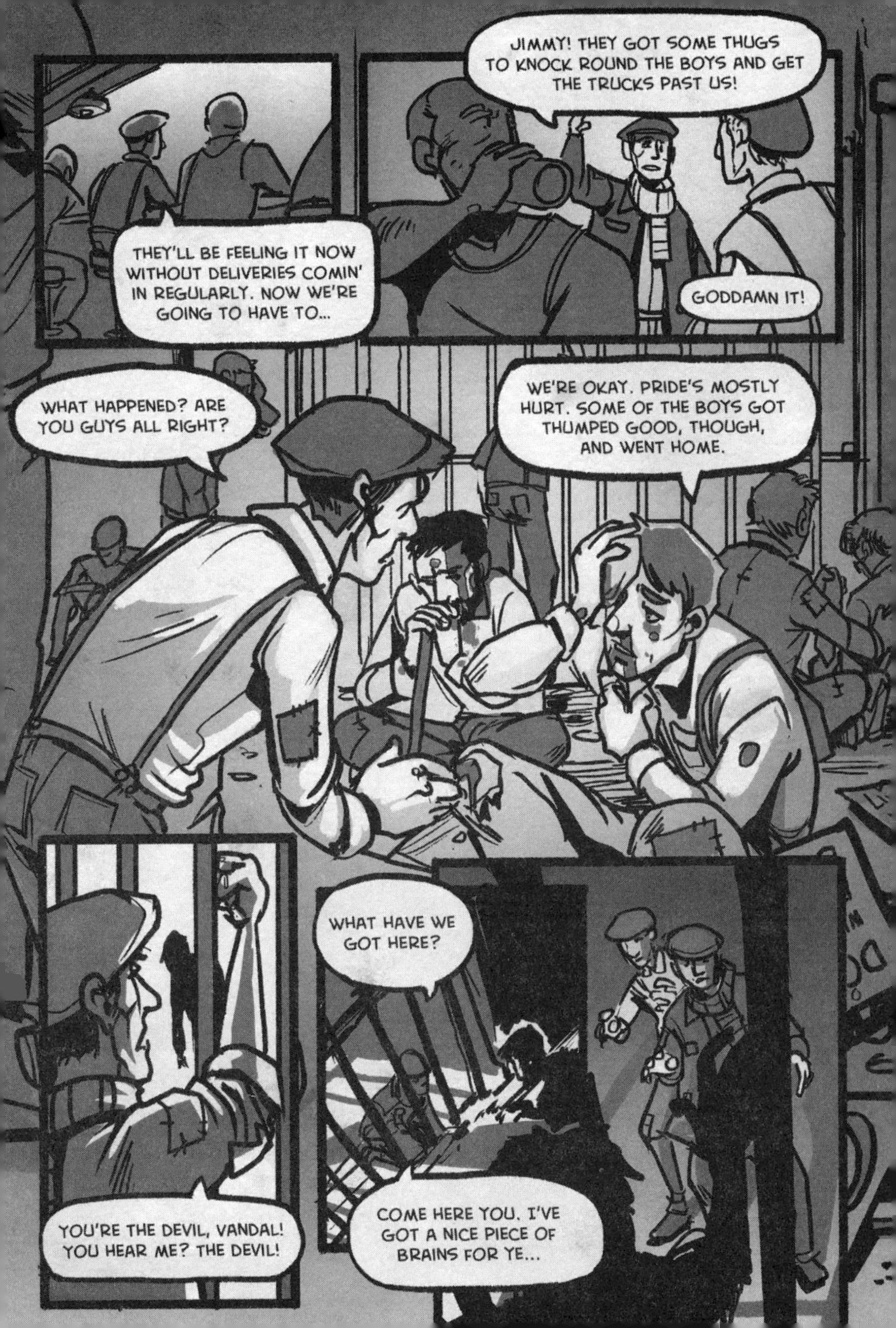
THEY'LL BE FEELING IT NOW WITHOUT DELIVERIES COMIN' IN REGULARLY. NOW WE'RE GOING TO HAVE TO...
JIMMY! THEY GOT SOME THUGS TO KNOCK ROUND THE BOYS AND GET THE TRUCKS PAST US!
GODDAMN IT!
WHAT HAPPENED? ARE YOU GUYS ALL RIGHT?
WE'RE OKAY. PRIDE'S MOSTLY HURT. SOME OF THE BOYS GOT THUMPED GOOD, THOUGH, AND WENT HOME.
YOU'RE THE DEVIL, VANDAL! YOU HEAR ME? THE DEVIL!
WHAT HAVE WE GOT HERE?
COME HERE YOU. I'VE GOT A NICE PIECE OF BRAINS FOR YE...

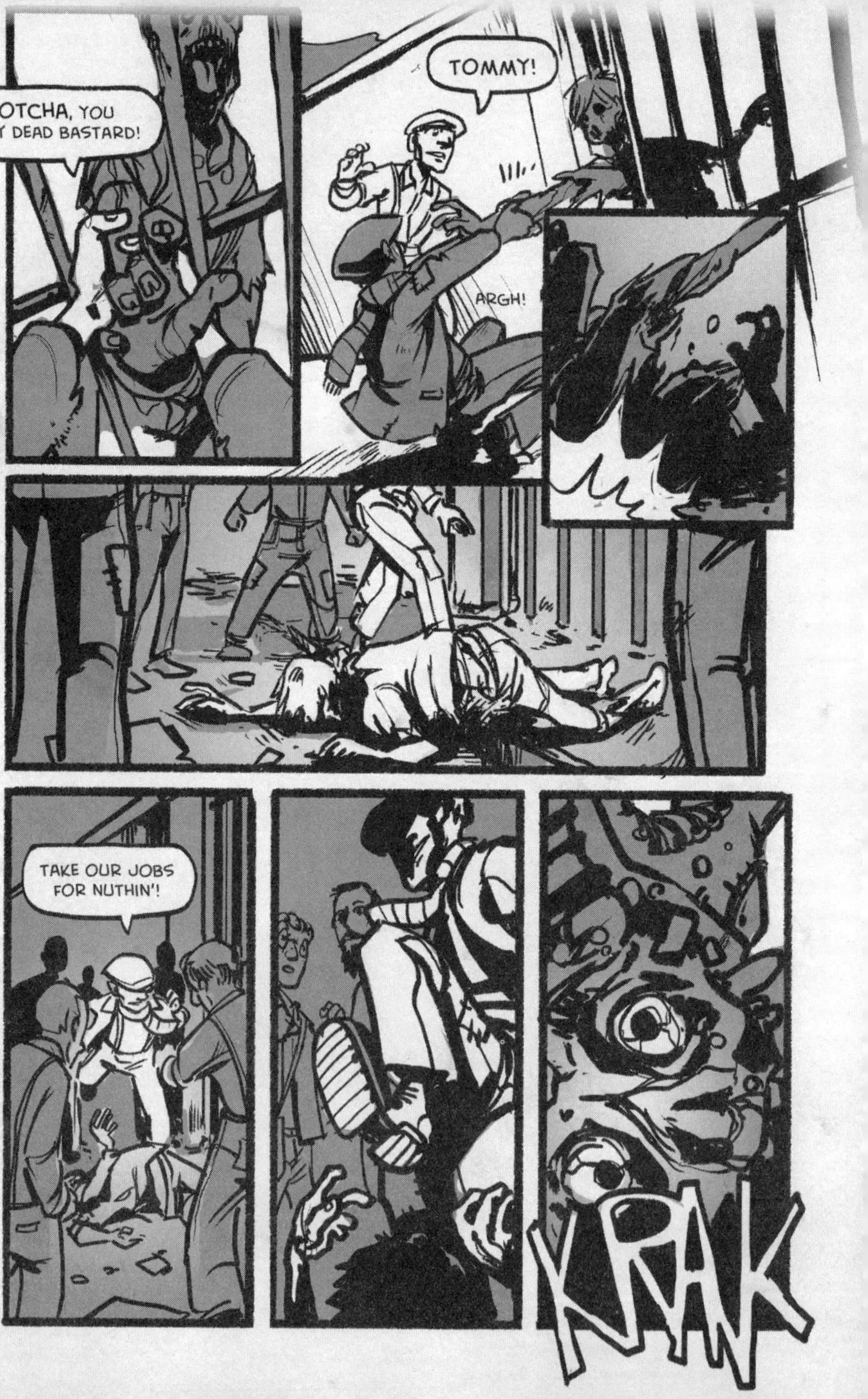
GOTCHA, YOU FILTHY DEAD BASTARD!
TOMMY!
ARGH!
TAKE OUR JOBS FOR NUTHIN'!
KRAK

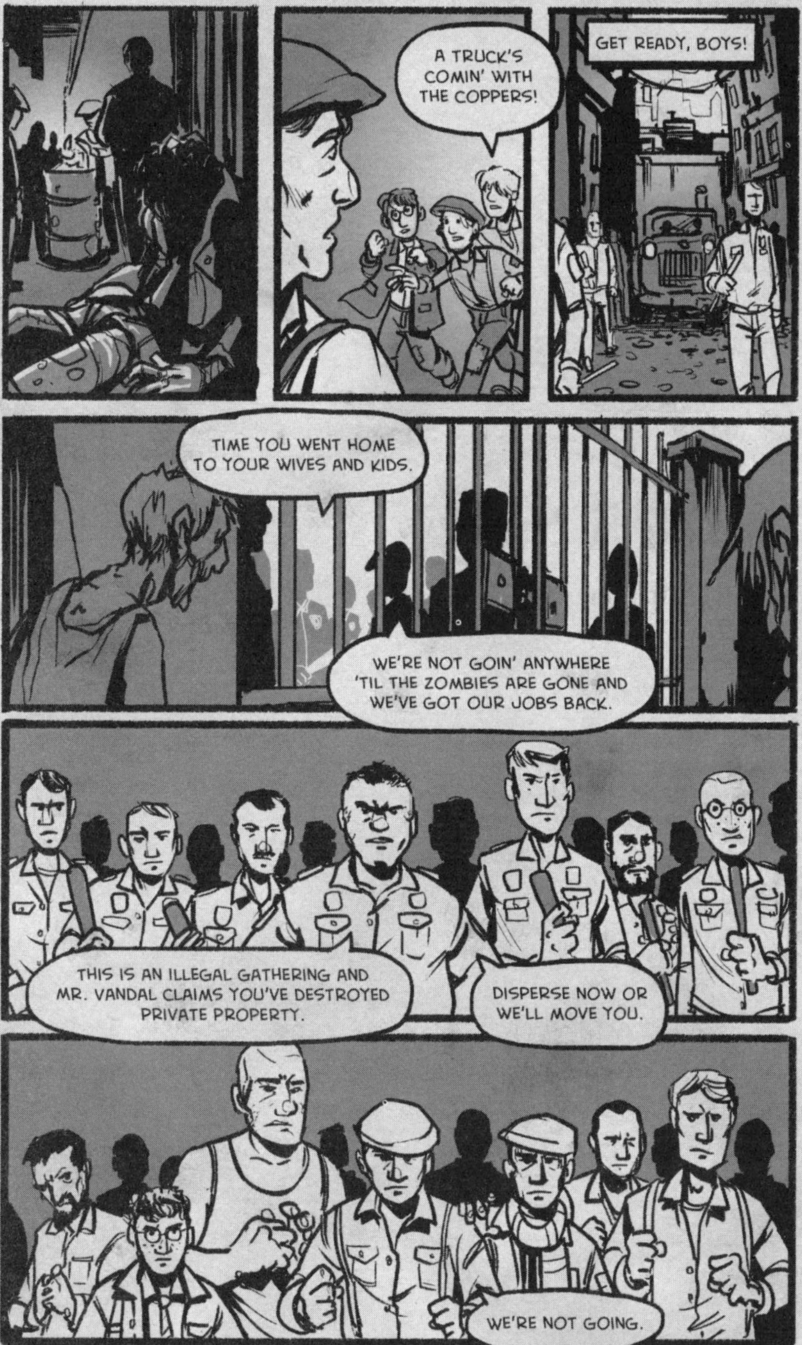
A TRUCK'S COMIN' WITH THE COPPERS!
GET READY, BOYS!
TIME YOU WENT HOME TO YOUR WIVES AND KIDS.
WE'RE NOT GOIN' ANYWHERE 'TIL THE ZOMBIES ARE GONE AND WE'VE GOT OUR JOBS BACK.
THIS IS AN ILLEGAL GATHERING AND MR. VANDAL CLAIMS YOU'VE DESTROYED PRIVATE PROPERTY.
DISPERSE NOW OR WE'LL MOVE YOU.
WE'RE NOT GOING.

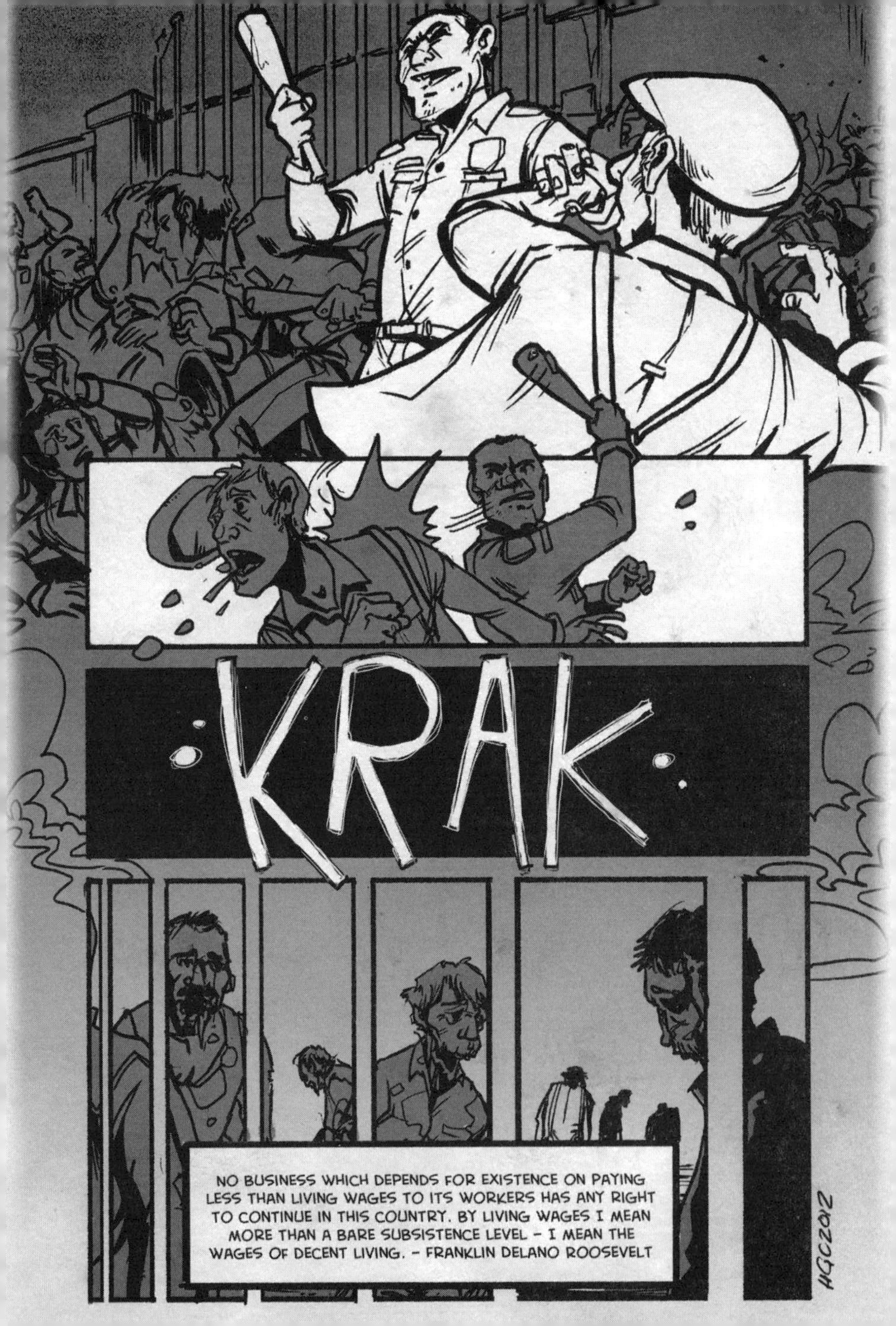
KRAK
NO BUSINESS WHICH DEPENDS FOR EXISTENCE ON PAYING LESS THAN LIVING WAGES TO ITS WORKERS HAS ANY RIGHT TO CONTINUE IN THIS COUNTRY. BY LIVING WAGES I MEAN MORE THAN A BARE SUBSISTENCE LEVEL – I MEAN THE WAGES OF DECENT LIVING. – FRANKLIN DELANO ROOSEVELT
HGC2012

THE Z-MEN

STORY BY:
KYLE KACZMARCZYK

ART BY:
SEAN VON GORMAN

LETTERS BY:
JEFF McCLELLAND

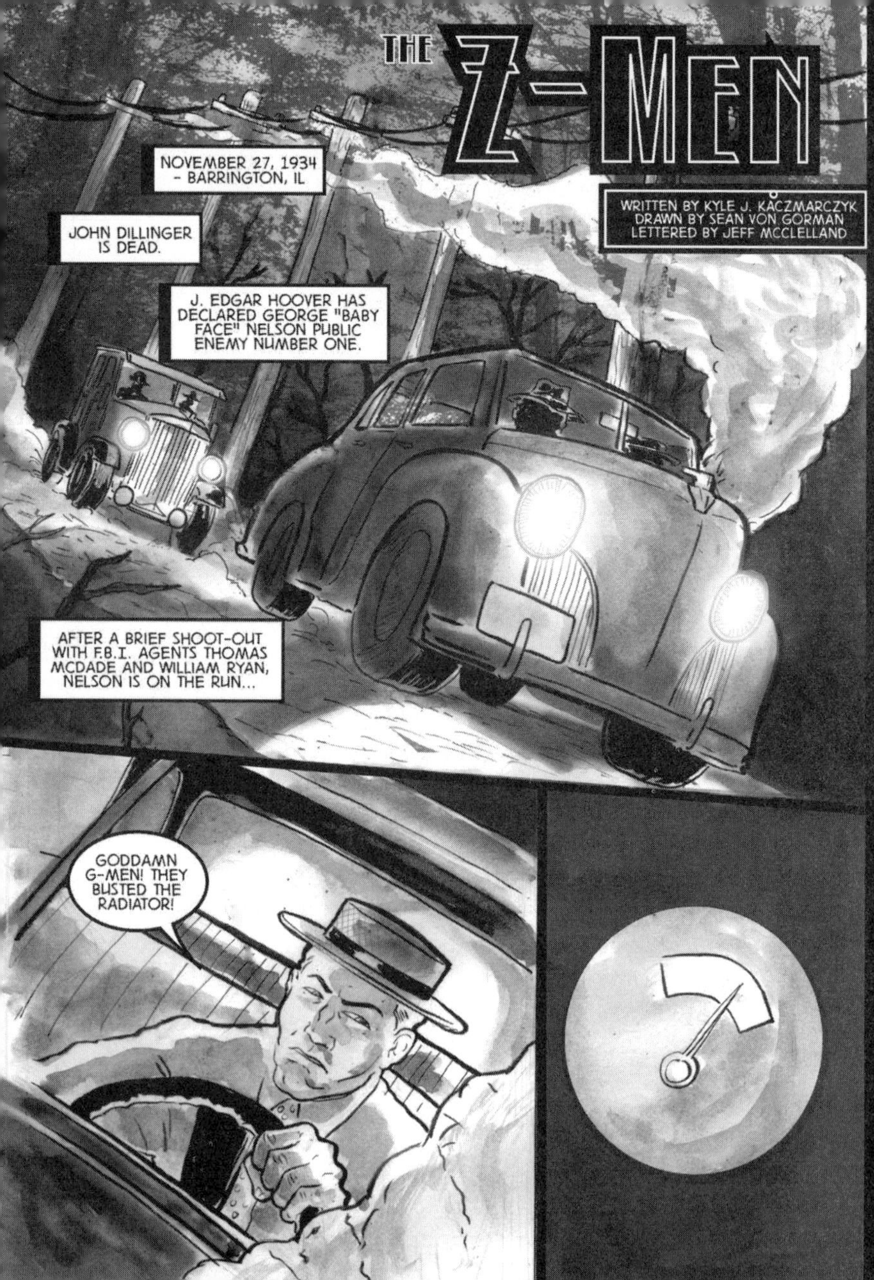

THE Z-MEN
WRITTEN BY KYLE J. KACZMARCZYK
DRAWN BY SEAN VON GORMAN
LETTERED BY JEFF MCCLELLAND
NOVEMBER 27, 1934 - BARRINGTON, IL
JOHN DILLINGER IS DEAD.
J. EDGAR HOOVER HAS DECLARED GEORGE "BABY FACE" NELSON PUBLIC ENEMY NUMBER ONE.
AFTER A BRIEF SHOOT-OUT WITH F.B.I. AGENTS THOMAS MCDADE AND WILLIAM RYAN, NELSON IS ON THE RUN...
GODDAMN G-MEN! THEY BUSTED THE RADIATOR!

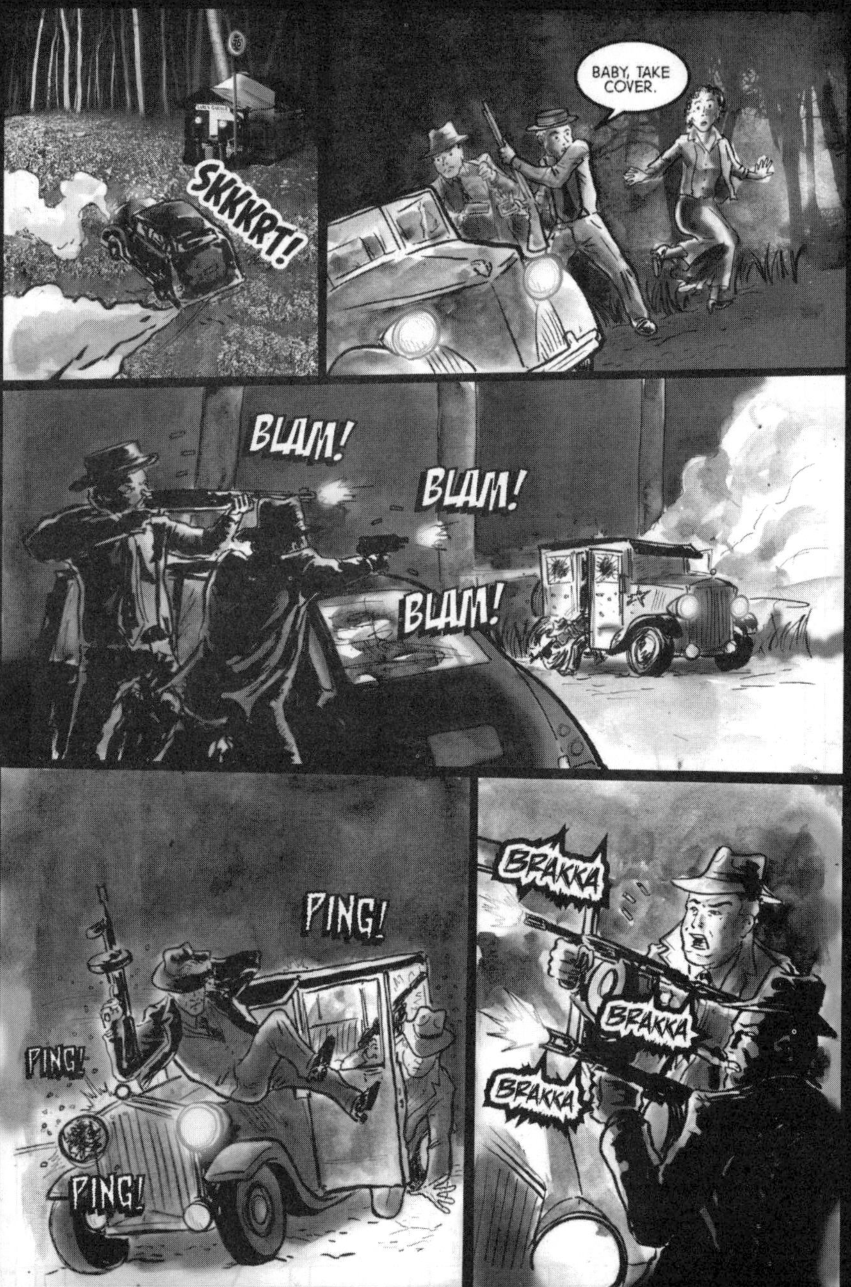
SKKKRT!
BABY, TAKE COVER.
BLAM!
BLAM!
BLAM!
PING!
PING!
PING!
BRAKKA
BRAKKA
BRAKKA

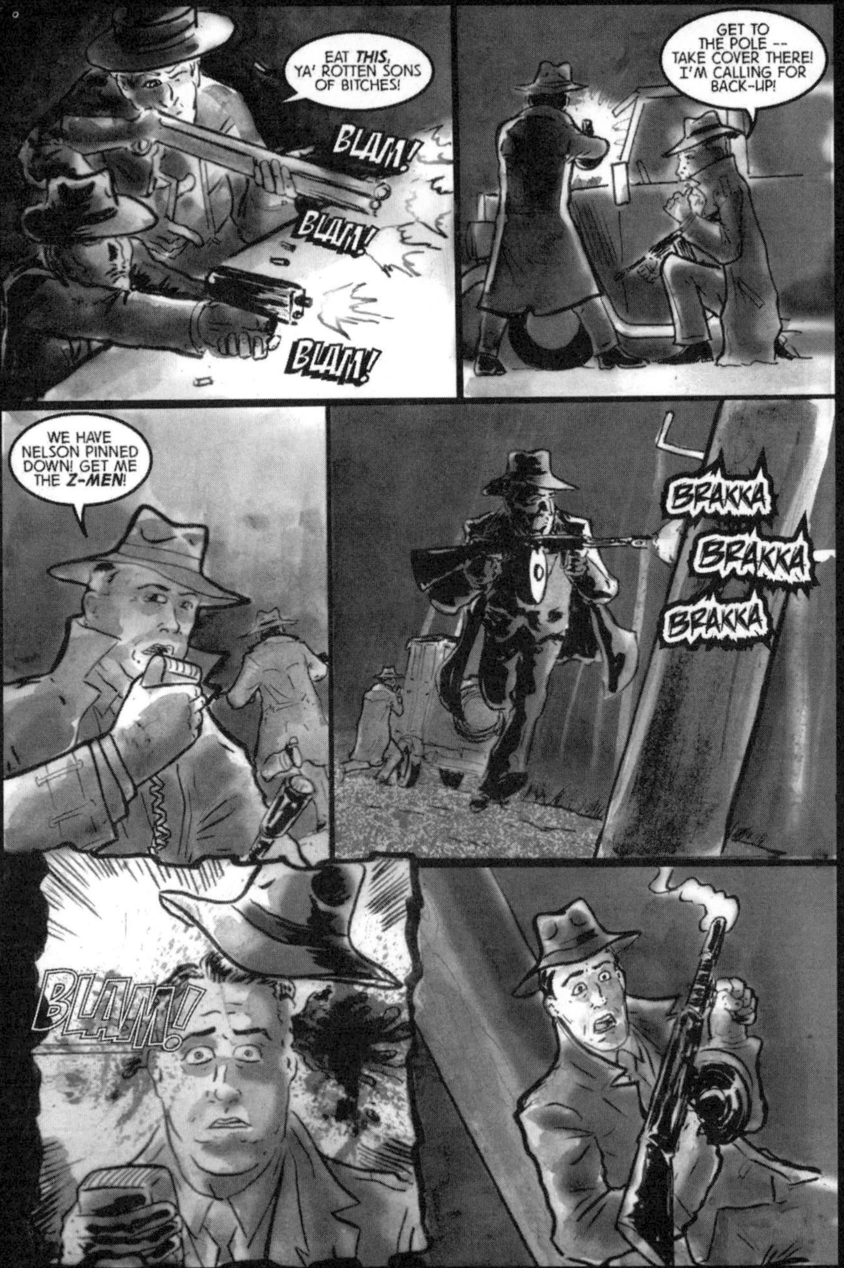
EAT THIS, YA' ROTTEN SONS OF BITCHES!
BLAM!
BLAM!
BLAM!
GET TO THE POLE -- TAKE COVER THERE! I'M CALLING FOR BACK-UP!
WE HAVE NELSON PINNED DOWN! GET ME THE Z-MEN!
BRAKKA
BRAKKA
BRAKKA
BLAM!

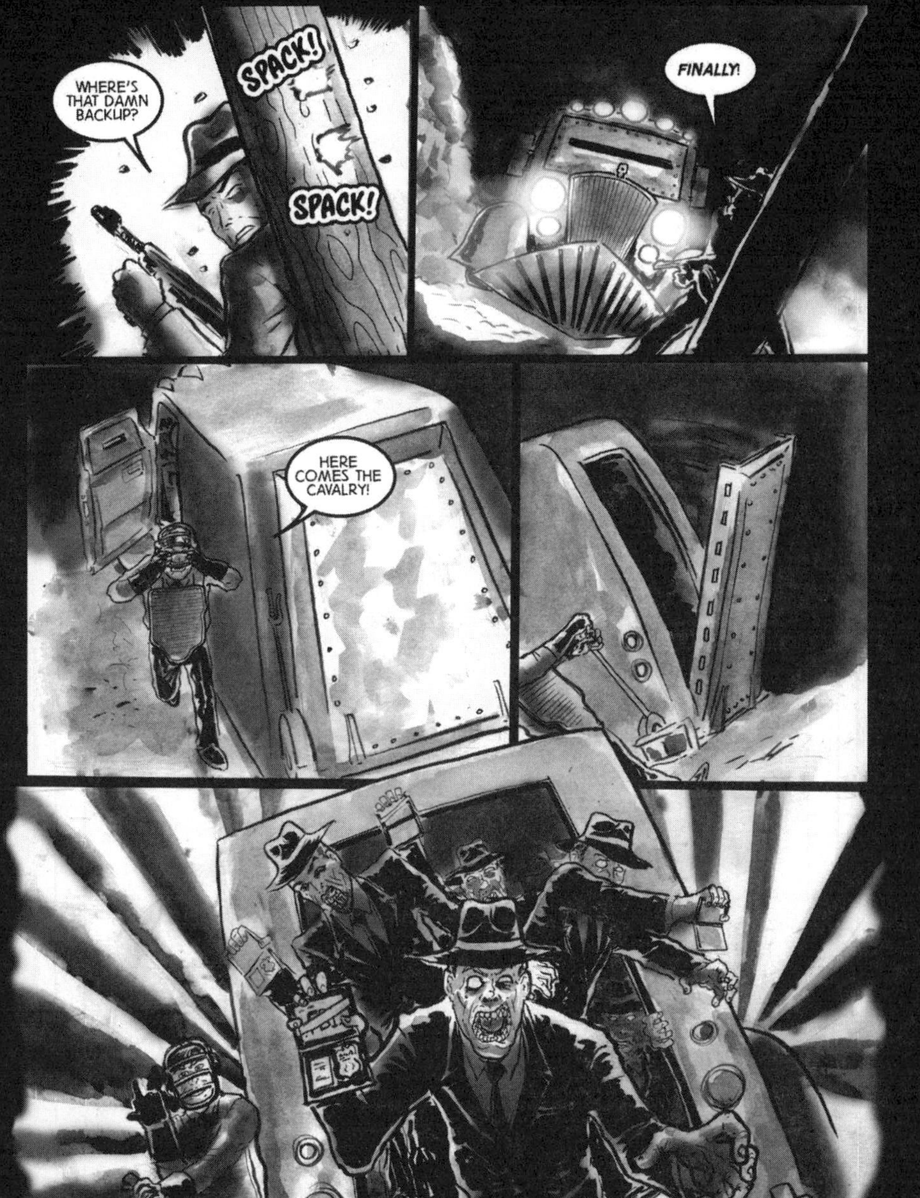
WHERE'S THAT DAMN BACKUP?
SPACK!
SPACK!
FINALLY!
HERE COMES THE CAVALRY!

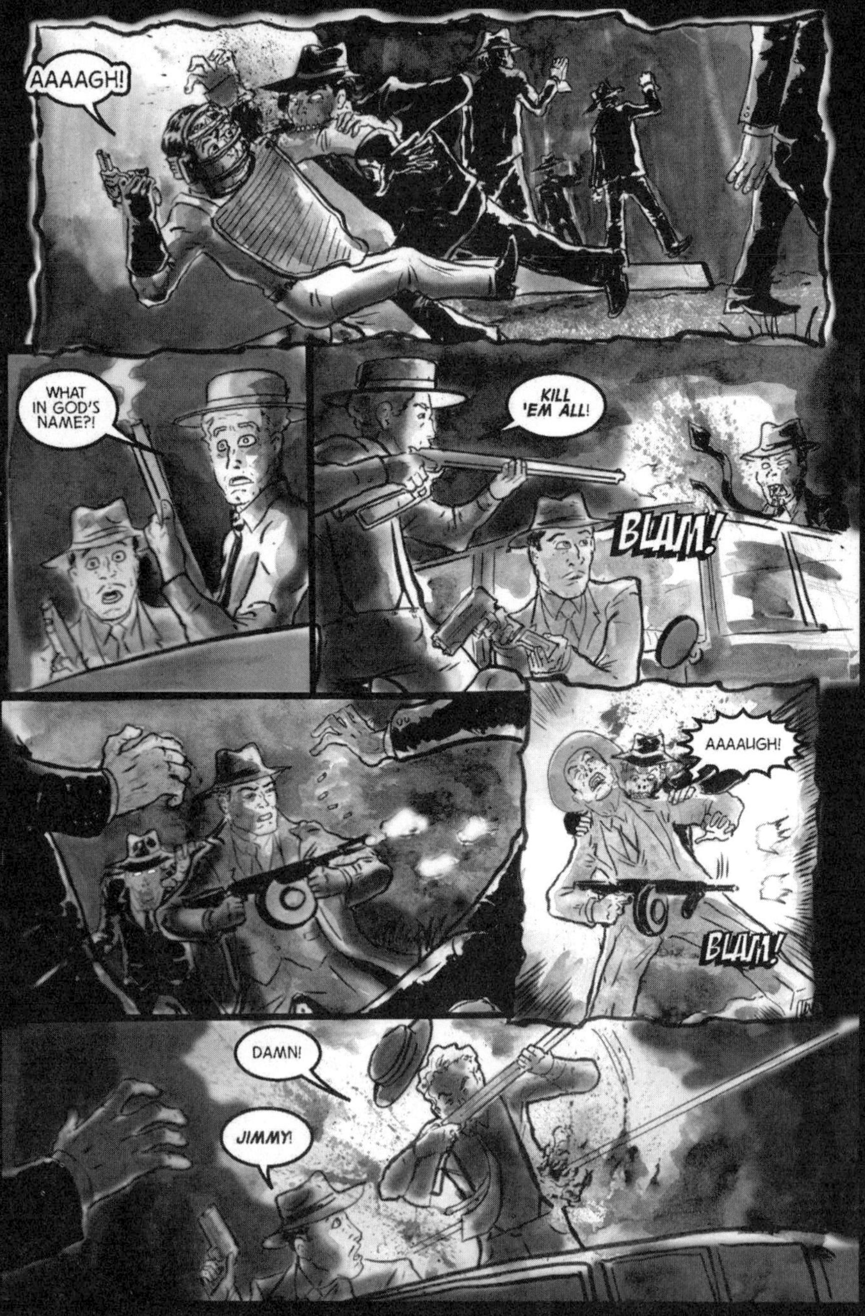
AAAAGH!
WHAT IN GOD'S NAME?!
KILL 'EM ALL!
BLAM!
AAAAUGH!
BLAM!
DAMN!
JIMMY!

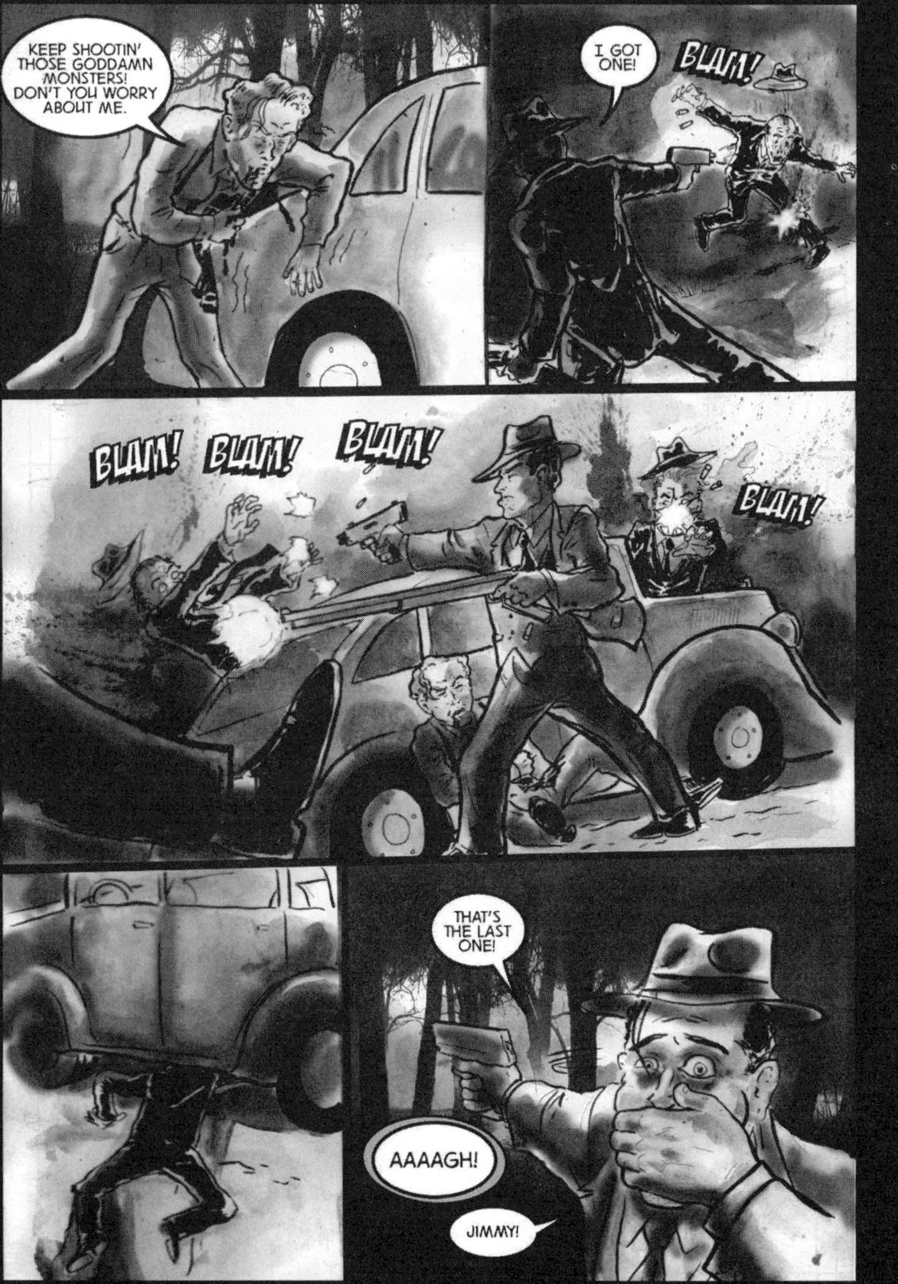
KEEP SHOOTIN' THOSE GODDAMN MONSTERS! DON'T YOU WORRY ABOUT ME.
I GOT ONE!
BLAM!
BLAM! BLAM! BLAM!
BLAM!
THAT'S THE LAST ONE!
AAAAGH!
JIMMY!

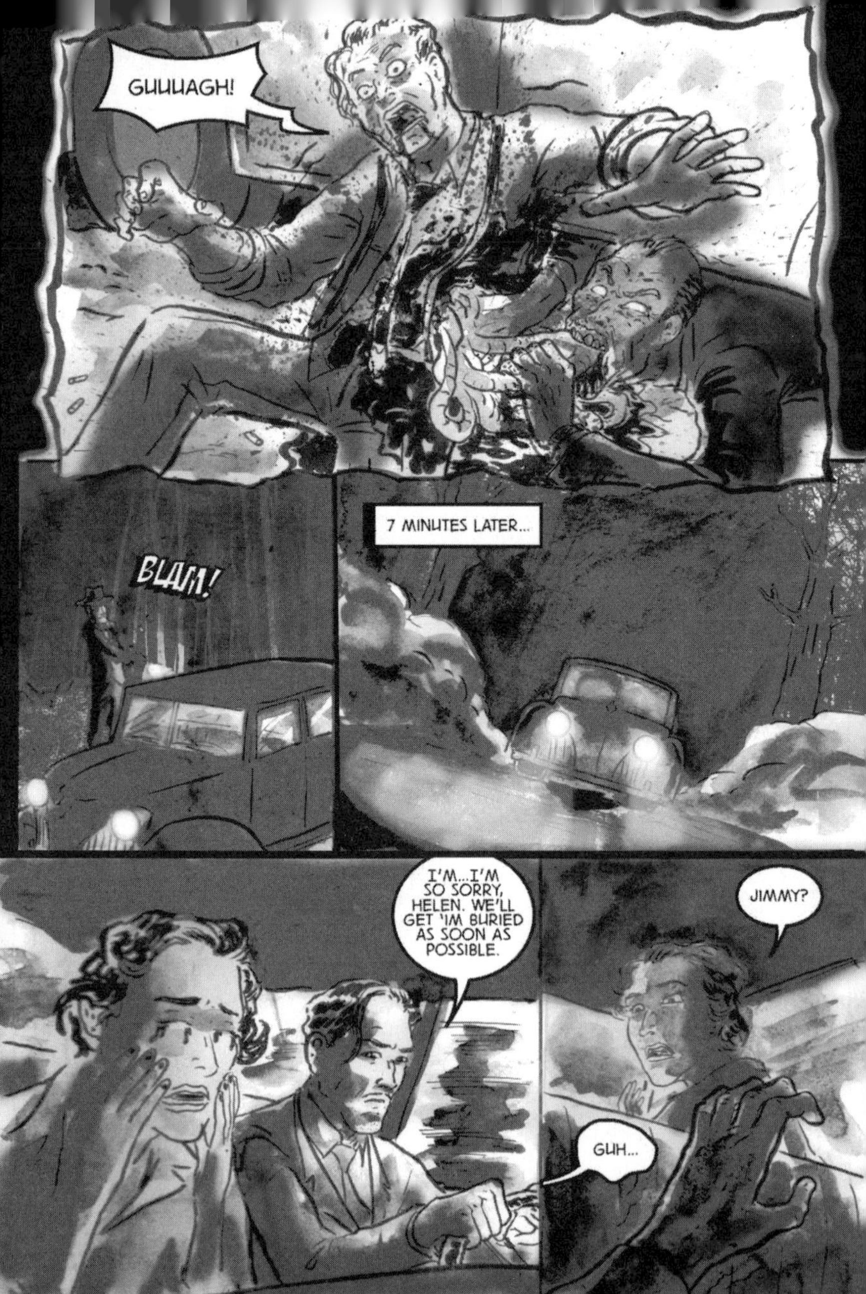
GUUUAGH!
BLAM!
7 MINUTES LATER...
I'M...I'M SO SORRY, HELEN. WE'LL GET 'IM BURIED AS SOON AS POSSIBLE.
JIMMY?
GUH...

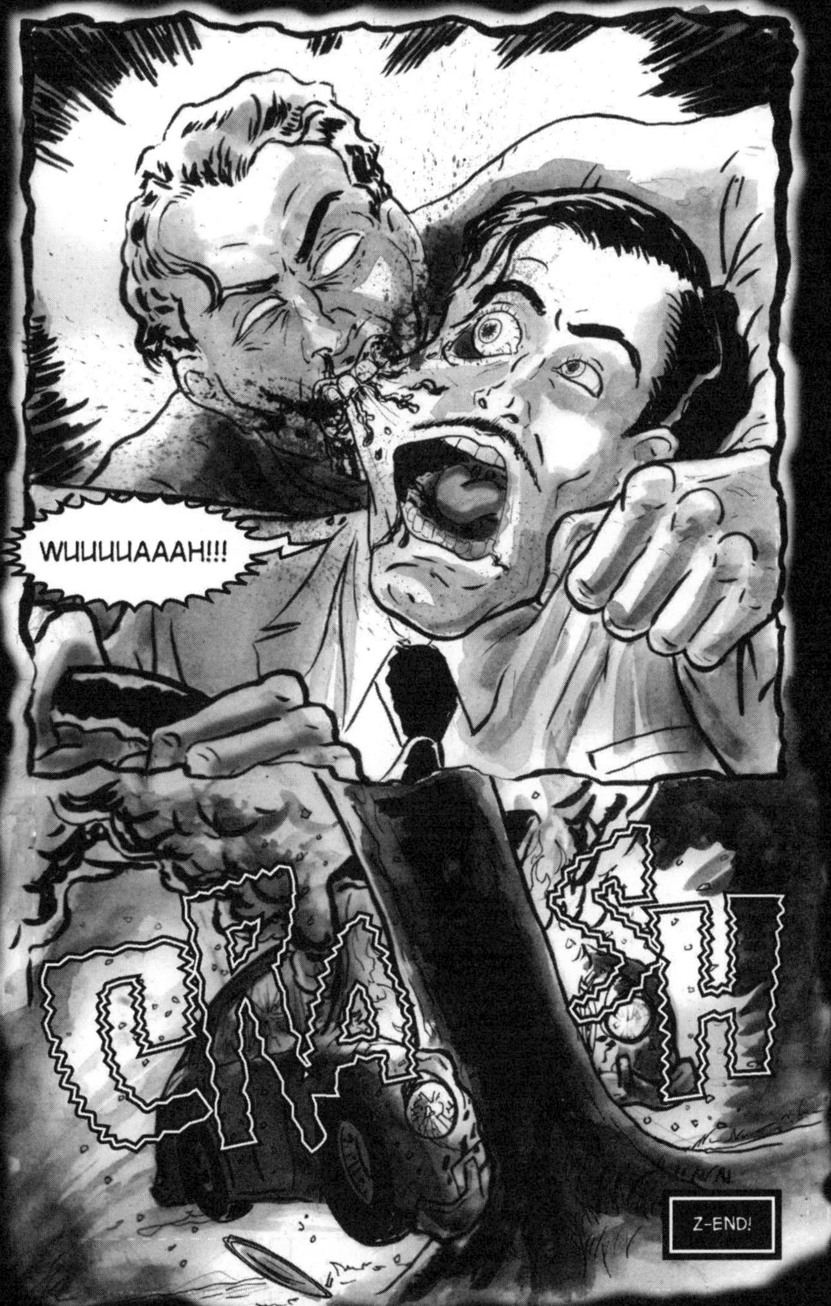
WUUUUAAAH!!!
CRASH!
Z-END!

THE WAR AT HOME

STORY BY:
DANIEL MOSER

ART BY:
MAYSAM BARZA

LETTERS BY:
SHAWN ALDRIDGE

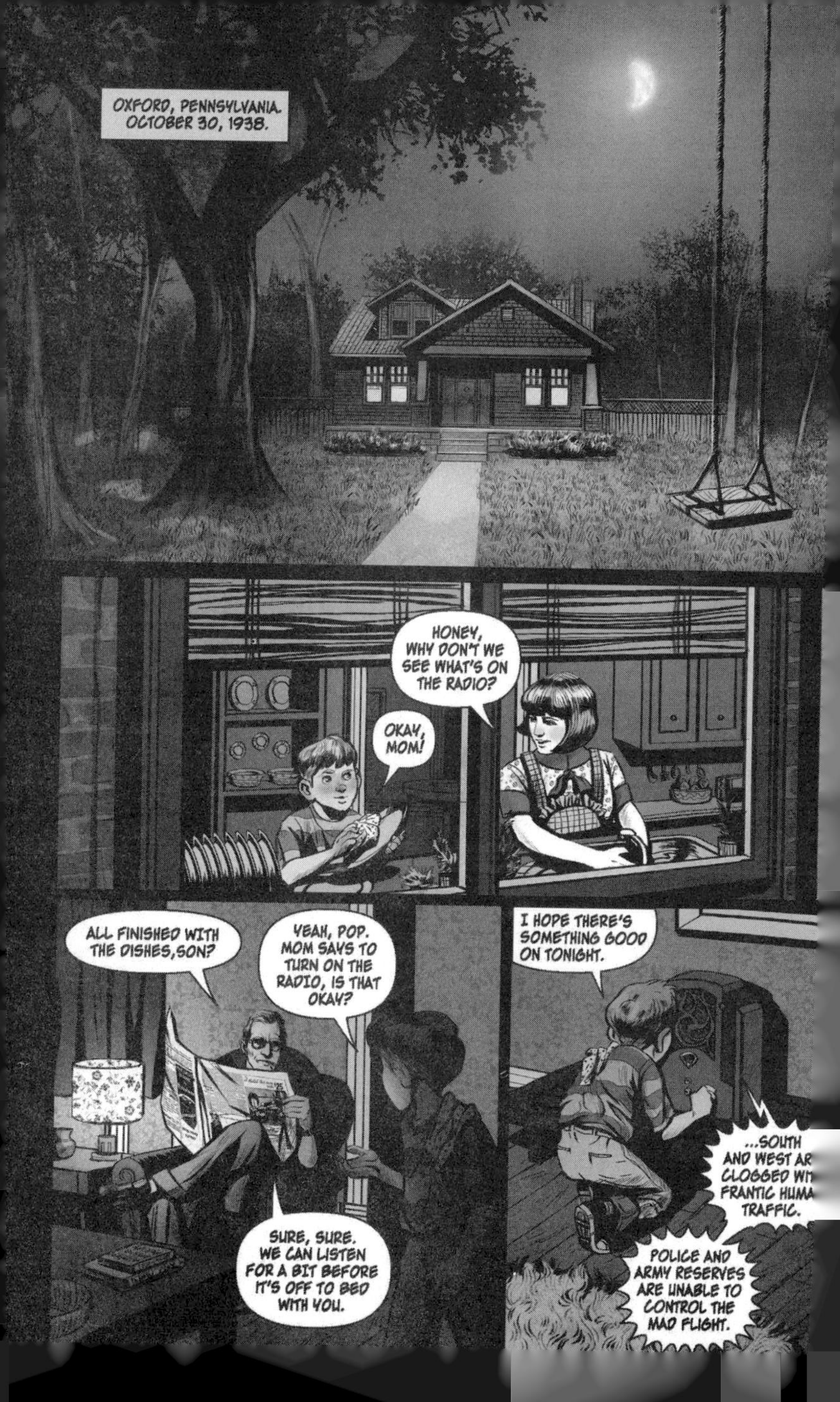
OXFORD, PENNSYLVANIA. OCTOBER 30, 1938.
HONEY, WHY DON'T WE SEE WHAT'S ON THE RADIO?
OKAY, MOM!
ALL FINISHED WITH THE DISHES, SON?
YEAH, POP. MOM SAYS TO TURN ON THE RADIO, IS THAT OKAY?
SURE, SURE. WE CAN LISTEN FOR A BIT BEFORE IT'S OFF TO BED WITH YOU.
I HOPE THERE'S SOMETHING GOOD ON TONIGHT.
...SOUTH AND WEST AR CLOGGED WIT FRANTIC HUMA TRAFFIC.
POLICE AND ARMY RESERVES ARE UNABLE TO CONTROL THE MAD FLIGHT.

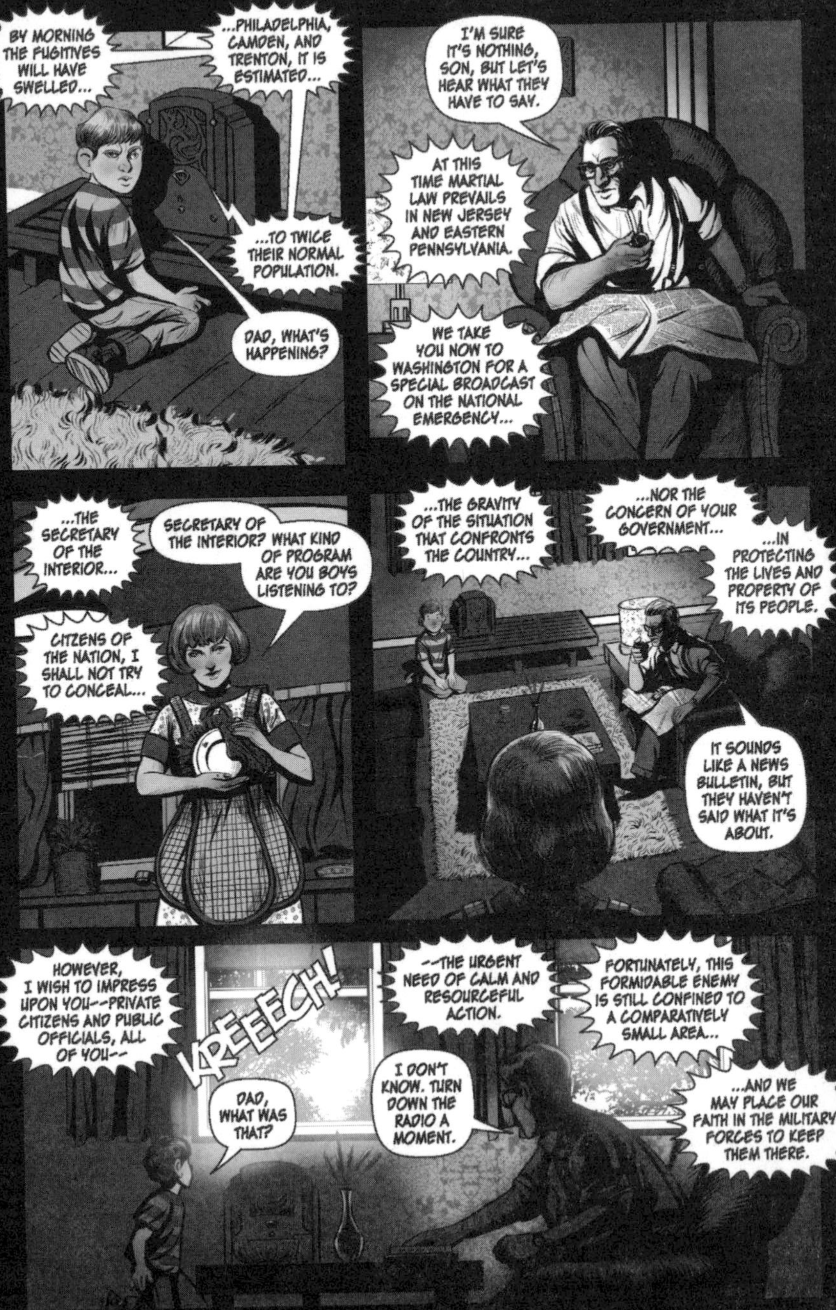
BY MORNING THE FUGITIVES WILL HAVE SWELLED...
...PHILADELPHIA, CAMDEN, AND TRENTON, IT IS ESTIMATED...
...TO TWICE THEIR NORMAL POPULATION.
DAD, WHAT'S HAPPENING?
I'M SURE IT'S NOTHING, SON, BUT LET'S HEAR WHAT THEY HAVE TO SAY.
AT THIS TIME MARTIAL LAW PREVAILS IN NEW JERSEY AND EASTERN PENNSYLVANIA.
WE TAKE YOU NOW TO WASHINGTON FOR A SPECIAL BROADCAST ON THE NATIONAL EMERGENCY...
...THE SECRETARY OF THE INTERIOR...
SECRETARY OF THE INTERIOR? WHAT KIND OF PROGRAM ARE YOU BOYS LISTENING TO?
CITIZENS OF THE NATION, I SHALL NOT TRY TO CONCEAL...
...THE GRAVITY OF THE SITUATION THAT CONFRONTS THE COUNTRY...
...NOR THE CONCERN OF YOUR GOVERNMENT...
...IN PROTECTING THE LIVES AND PROPERTY OF ITS PEOPLE.
IT SOUNDS LIKE A NEWS BULLETIN, BUT THEY HAVEN'T SAID WHAT IT'S ABOUT.
HOWEVER, I WISH TO IMPRESS UPON YOU--PRIVATE CITIZENS AND PUBLIC OFFICIALS, ALL OF YOU--
KREEECH!
--THE URGENT NEED OF CALM AND RESOURCEFUL ACTION.
FORTUNATELY, THIS FORMIDABLE ENEMY IS STILL CONFINED TO A COMPARATIVELY SMALL AREA...
DAD, WHAT WAS THAT?
I DON'T KNOW. TURN DOWN THE RADIO A MOMENT.
...AND WE MAY PLACE OUR FAITH IN THE MILITARY FORCES TO KEEP THEM THERE.

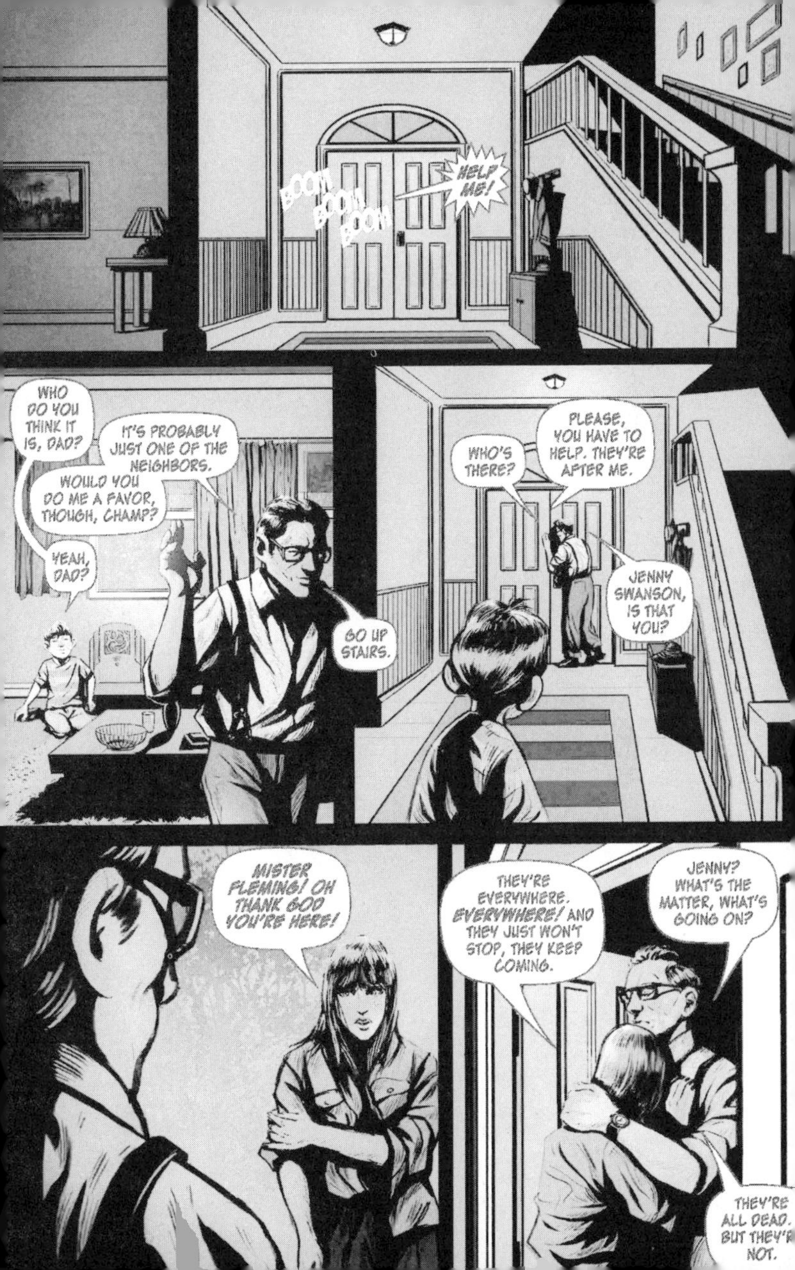
BOOM BOOM BOOM
HELP ME!
WHO DO YOU THINK IT IS, DAD?
IT'S PROBABLY JUST ONE OF THE NEIGHBORS.
WOULD YOU DO ME A FAVOR, THOUGH, CHAMP?
YEAH, DAD?
GO UP STAIRS.
WHO'S THERE?
PLEASE, YOU HAVE TO HELP. THEY'RE AFTER ME.
JENNY SWANSON, IS THAT YOU?
MISTER FLEMING! OH THANK GOD YOU'RE HERE!
THEY'RE EVERYWHERE. EVERYWHERE! AND THEY JUST WON'T STOP, THEY KEEP COMING.
JENNY? WHAT'S THE MATTER, WHAT'S GOING ON?
THEY'RE ALL DEAD. BUT THEY'R NOT.

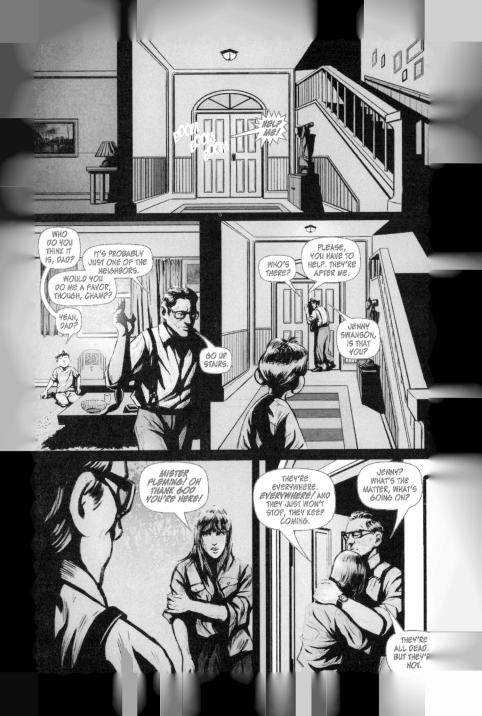

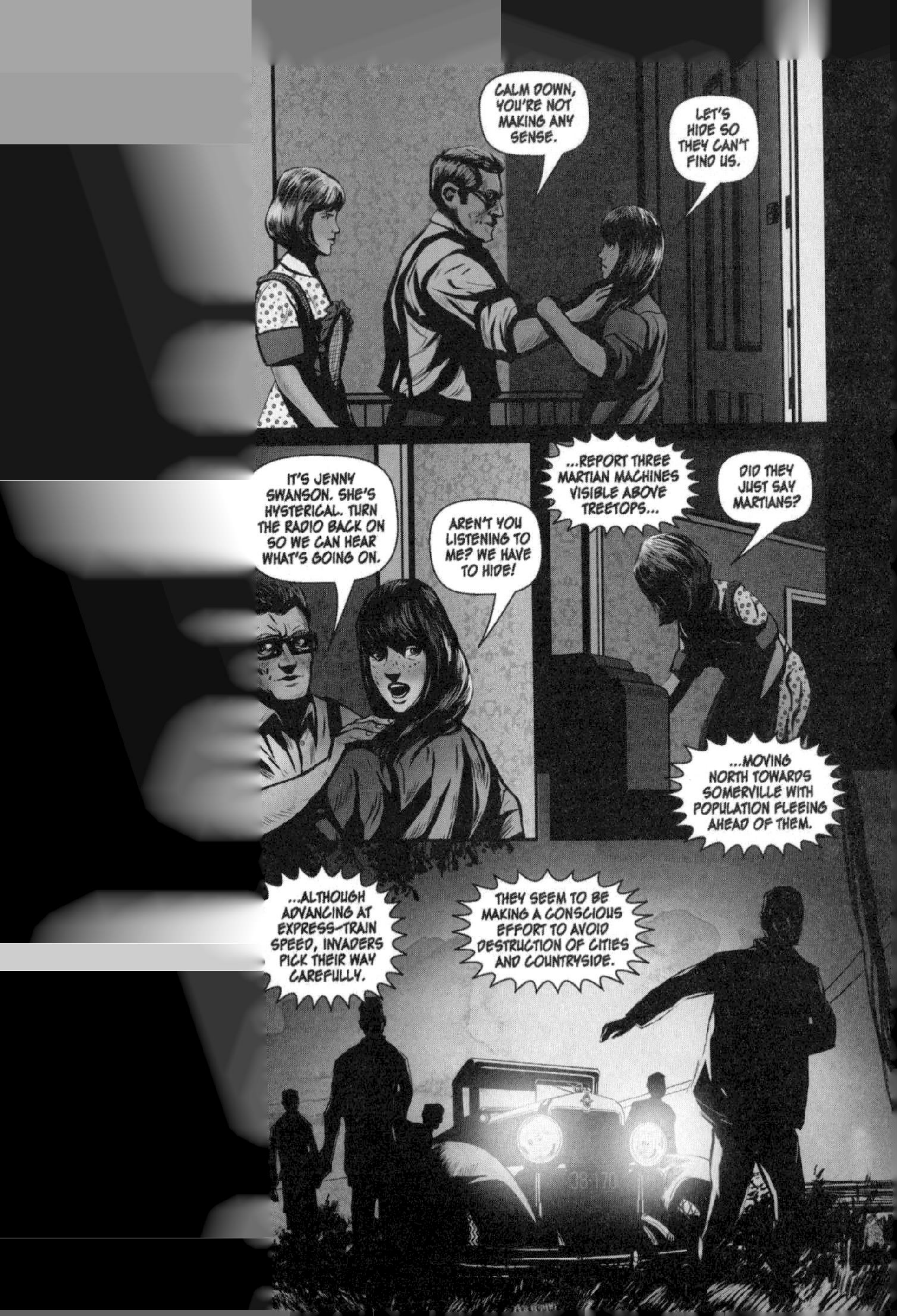

CALM DOWN, YOU'RE NOT MAKING ANY SENSE.
LET'S HIDE SO THEY CAN'T FIND US.
IT'S JENNY SWANSON. SHE'S HYSTERICAL. TURN THE RADIO BACK ON SO WE CAN HEAR WHAT'S GOING ON.
AREN'T YOU LISTENING TO ME? WE HAVE TO HIDE!
...REPORT THREE MARTIAN MACHINES VISIBLE ABOVE TREETOPS...
DID THEY JUST SAY MARTIANS?
...MOVING NORTH TOWARDS SOMERVILLE WITH POPULATION FLEEING AHEAD OF THEM.
...ALTHOUGH ADVANCING AT EXPRESS-TRAIN SPEED, INVADERS PICK THEIR WAY CAREFULLY.
THEY SEEM TO BE MAKING A CONSCIOUS EFFORT TO AVOID DESTRUCTION OF CITIES AND COUNTRYSIDE.

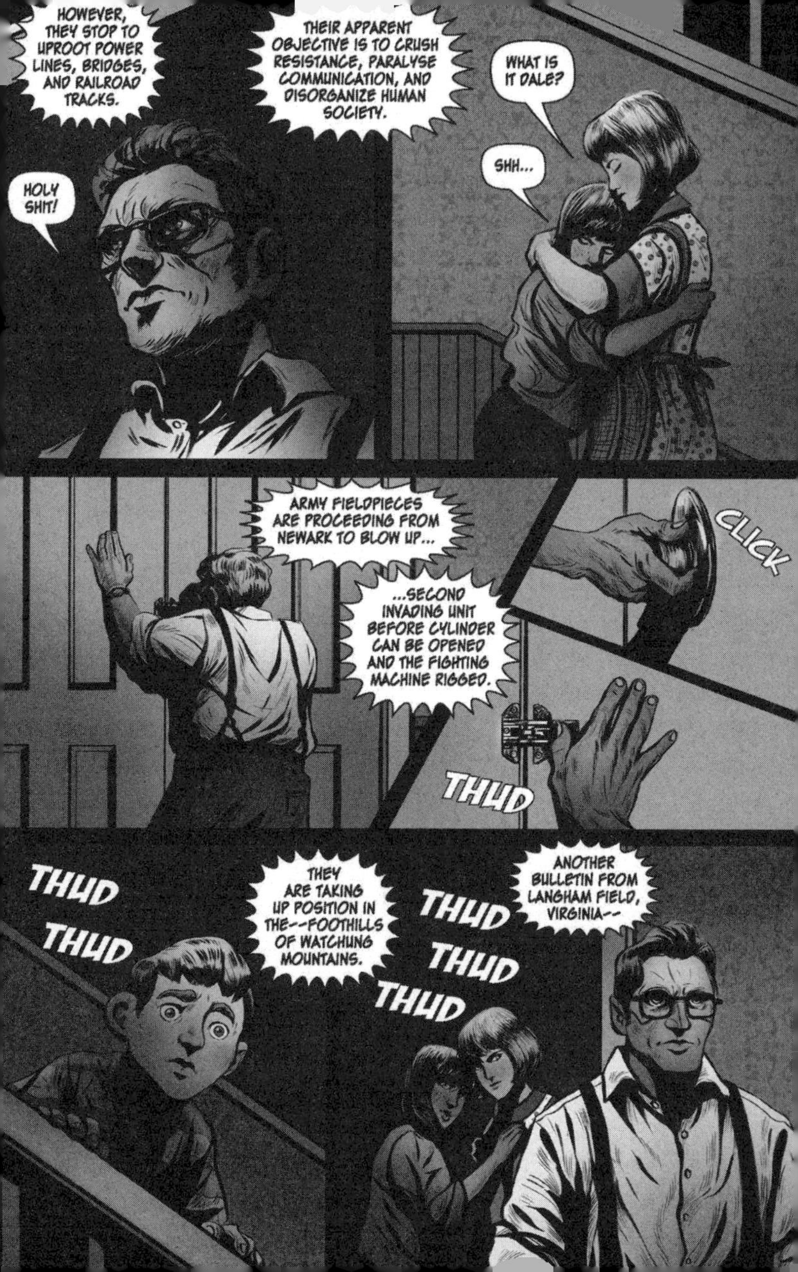
HOWEVER, THEY STOP TO UPROOT POWER LINES, BRIDGES, AND RAILROAD TRACKS.
THEIR APPARENT OBJECTIVE IS TO CRUSH RESISTANCE, PARALYSE COMMUNICATION, AND DISORGANIZE HUMAN SOCIETY.
HOLY SHIT!
WHAT IS IT DALE?
SHH...
ARMY FIELDPIECES ARE PROCEEDING FROM NEWARK TO BLOW UP...
...SECOND INVADING UNIT BEFORE CYLINDER CAN BE OPENED AND THE FIGHTING MACHINE RIGGED.
CLICK
THUD
THUD
THUD
THEY ARE TAKING UP POSITION IN THE--FOOTHILLS OF WATCHUNG MOUNTAINS.
THUD
THUD
THUD
ANOTHER BULLETIN FROM LANGHAM FIELD, VIRGINIA--

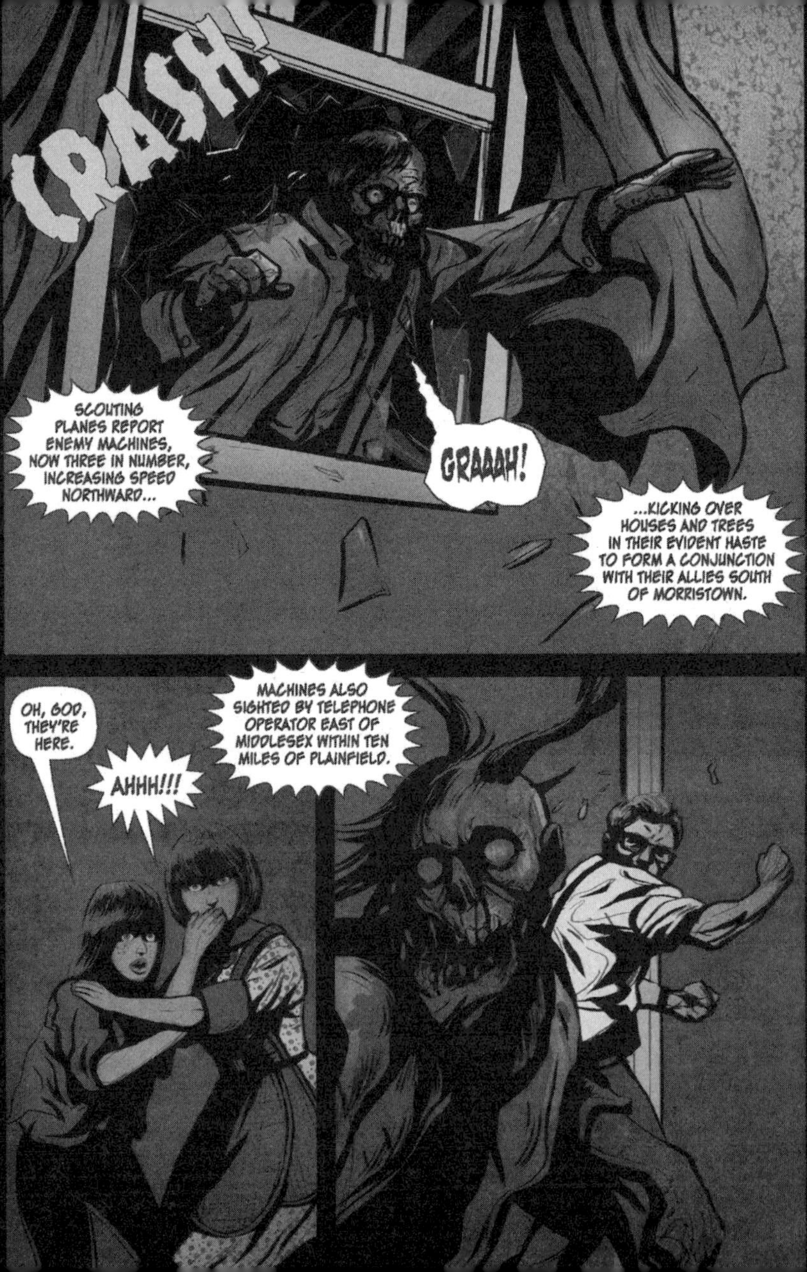
CRASH!
SCOUTING PLANES REPORT ENEMY MACHINES, NOW THREE IN NUMBER, INCREASING SPEED NORTHWARD...
GRAAAH!
...KICKING OVER HOUSES AND TREES IN THEIR EVIDENT HASTE TO FORM A CONJUNCTION WITH THEIR ALLIES SOUTH OF MORRISTOWN.
OH, GOD, THEY'RE HERE.
MACHINES ALSO SIGHTED BY TELEPHONE OPERATOR EAST OF MIDDLESEX WITHIN TEN MILES OF PLAINFIELD.
AHHH!!!

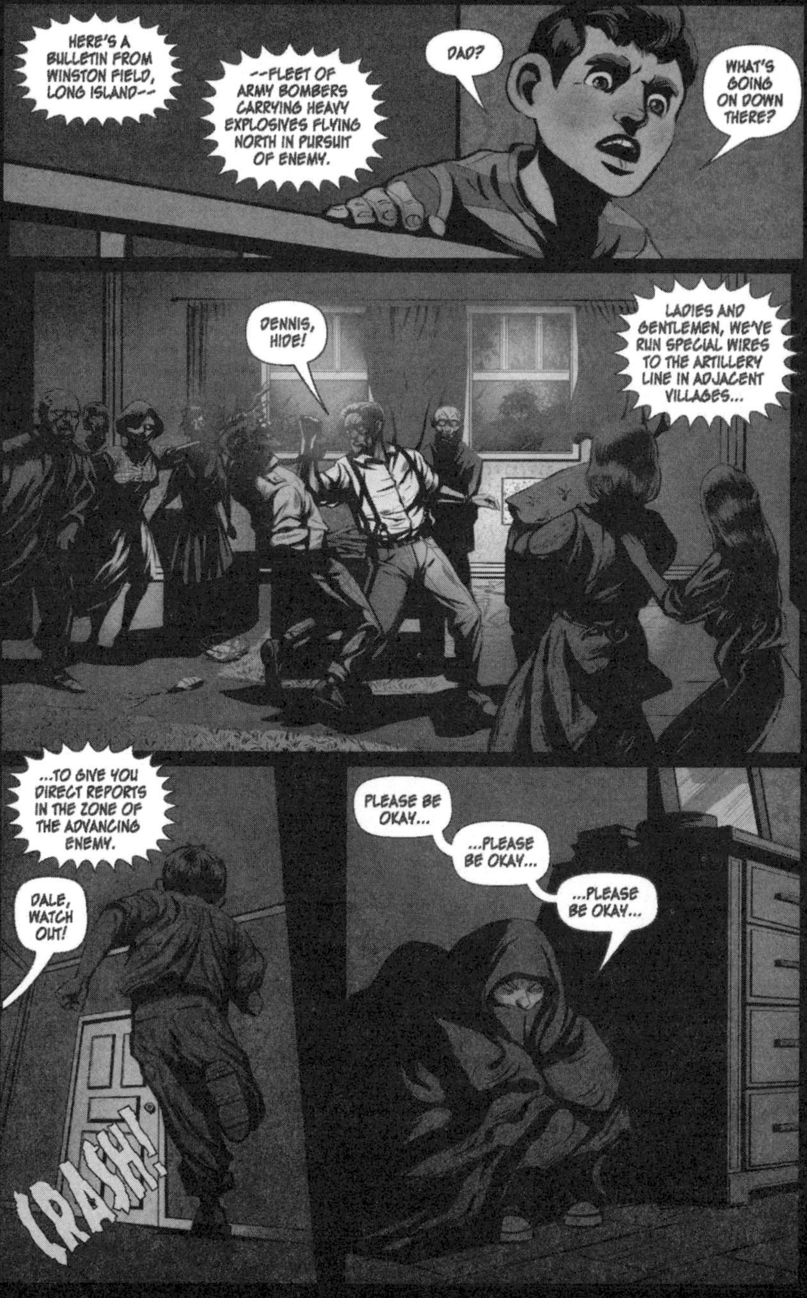
HERE'S A BULLETIN FROM WINSTON FIELD, LONG ISLAND--
--FLEET OF ARMY BOMBERS CARRYING HEAVY EXPLOSIVES FLYING NORTH IN PURSUIT OF ENEMY.
DAD?
WHAT'S GOING ON DOWN THERE?
DENNIS, HIDE!
LADIES AND GENTLEMEN, WE'VE RUN SPECIAL WIRES TO THE ARTILLERY LINE IN ADJACENT VILLAGES...
...TO GIVE YOU DIRECT REPORTS IN THE ZONE OF THE ADVANCING ENEMY.
DALE, WATCH OUT!
CRASH!
PLEASE BE OKAY...
...PLEASE BE OKAY...
...PLEASE BE OKAY...

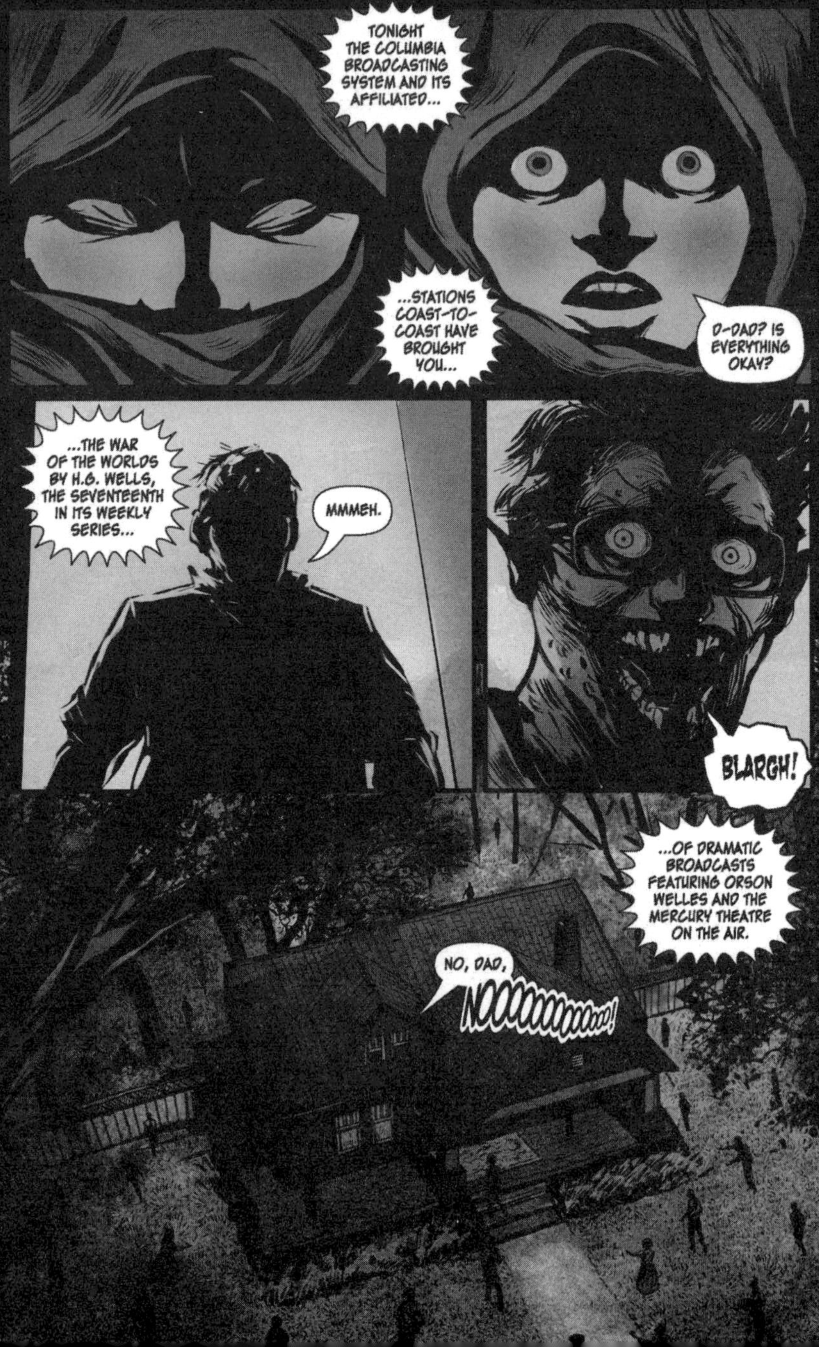
TONIGHT THE COLUMBIA BROADCASTING SYSTEM AND ITS AFFILIATED...
...STATIONS COAST-TO-COAST HAVE BROUGHT YOU...
D-DAD? IS EVERYTHING OKAY?
...THE WAR OF THE WORLDS BY H.G. WELLS, THE SEVENTEENTH IN ITS WEEKLY SERIES...
MMMEH.
BLARGH!
...OF DRAMATIC BROADCASTS FEATURING ORSON WELLES AND THE MERCURY THEATRE ON THE AIR.
NO, DAD, NOOOOOOOOOOooo!

OLD GHOSTS

STORY AND LETTERS BY:
JEFF McCLELLAND

ART BY:
DANIEL THOLLIN

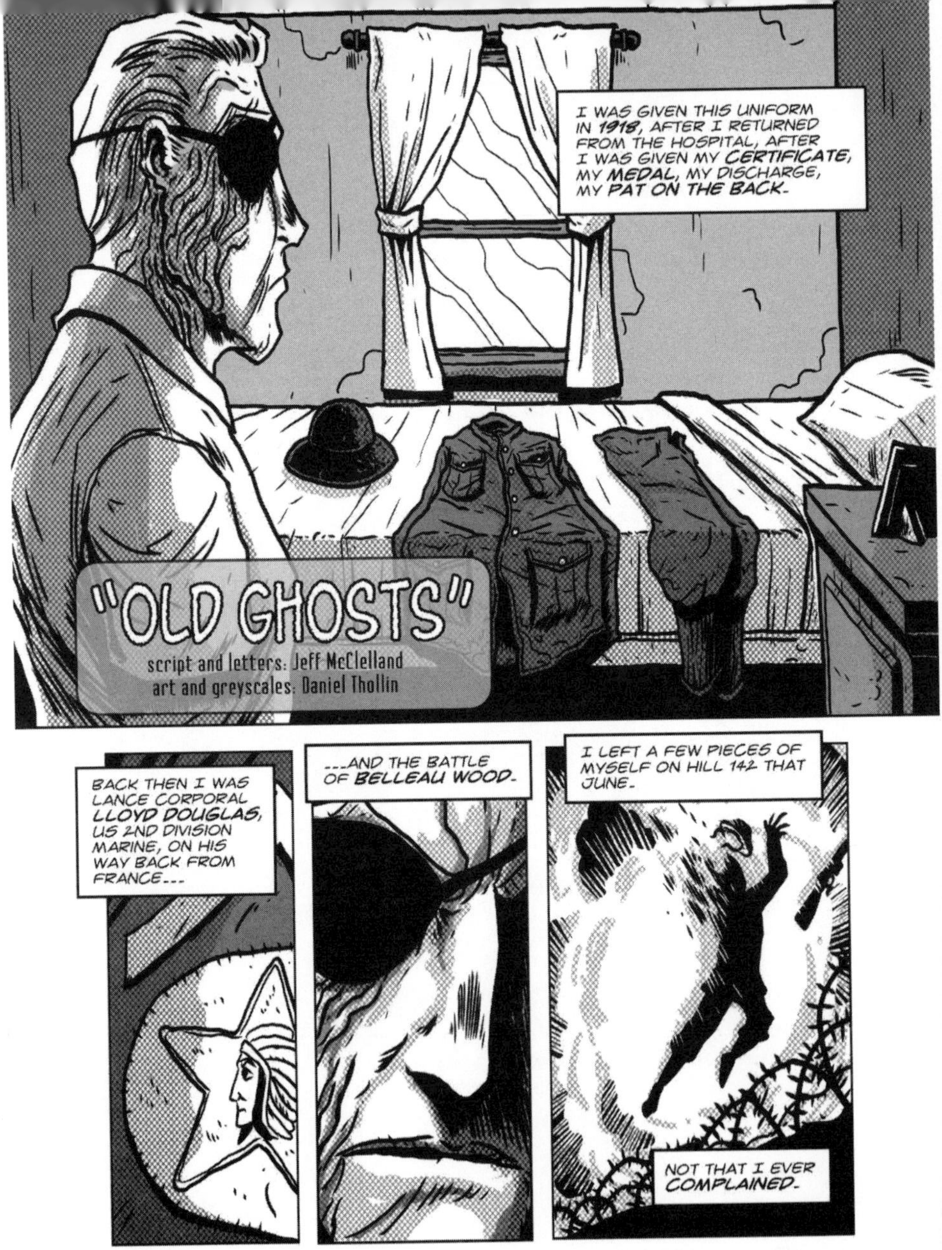
I WAS GIVEN THIS UNIFORM IN 1918, AFTER I RETURNED FROM THE HOSPITAL, AFTER I WAS GIVEN MY CERTIFICATE, MY MEDAL, MY DISCHARGE, MY PAT ON THE BACK.
"OLD GHOSTS"
script and letters: Jeff McClelland
art and greyscales: Daniel Thollin
BACK THEN I WAS LANCE CORPORAL LLOYD DOUGLAS, US 2ND DIVISION MARINE, ON HIS WAY BACK FROM FRANCE...
...AND THE BATTLE OF BELLEAU WOOD.
I LEFT A FEW PIECES OF MYSELF ON HILL 142 THAT JUNE.
NOT THAT I EVER COMPLAINED.

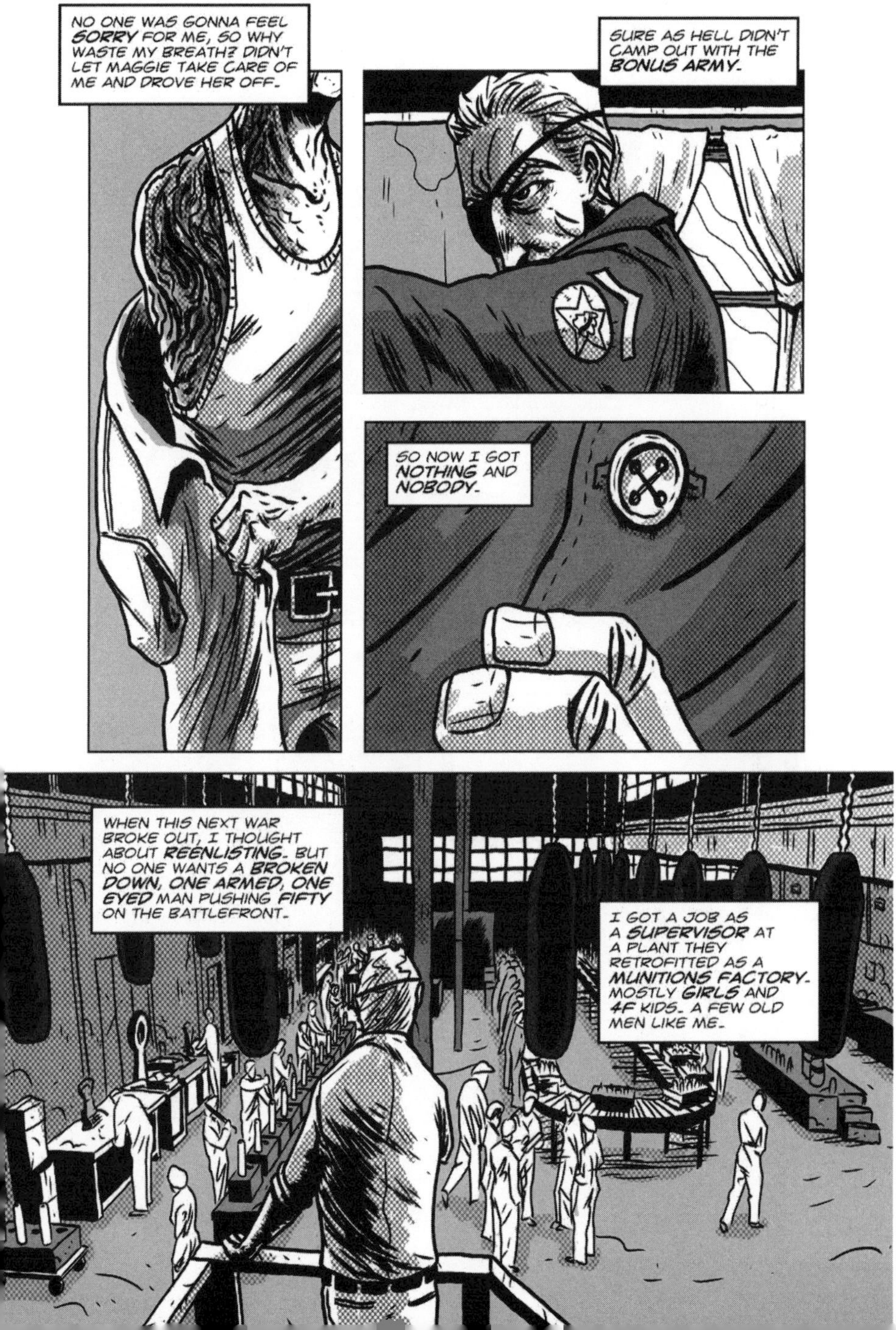
NO ONE WAS GONNA FEEL SORRY FOR ME, SO WHY WASTE MY BREATH? DIDN'T LET MAGGIE TAKE CARE OF ME AND DROVE HER OFF.
SURE AS HELL DIDN'T CAMP OUT WITH THE BONUS ARMY.
SO NOW I GOT NOTHING AND NOBODY.
WHEN THIS NEXT WAR BROKE OUT, I THOUGHT ABOUT REENLISTING. BUT NO ONE WANTS A BROKEN DOWN, ONE ARMED, ONE EYED MAN PUSHING FIFTY ON THE BATTLEFRONT.
I GOT A JOB AS A SUPERVISOR AT A PLANT THEY RETROFITTED AS A MUNITIONS FACTORY. MOSTLY GIRLS AND 4F KIDS. A FEW OLD MEN LIKE ME.

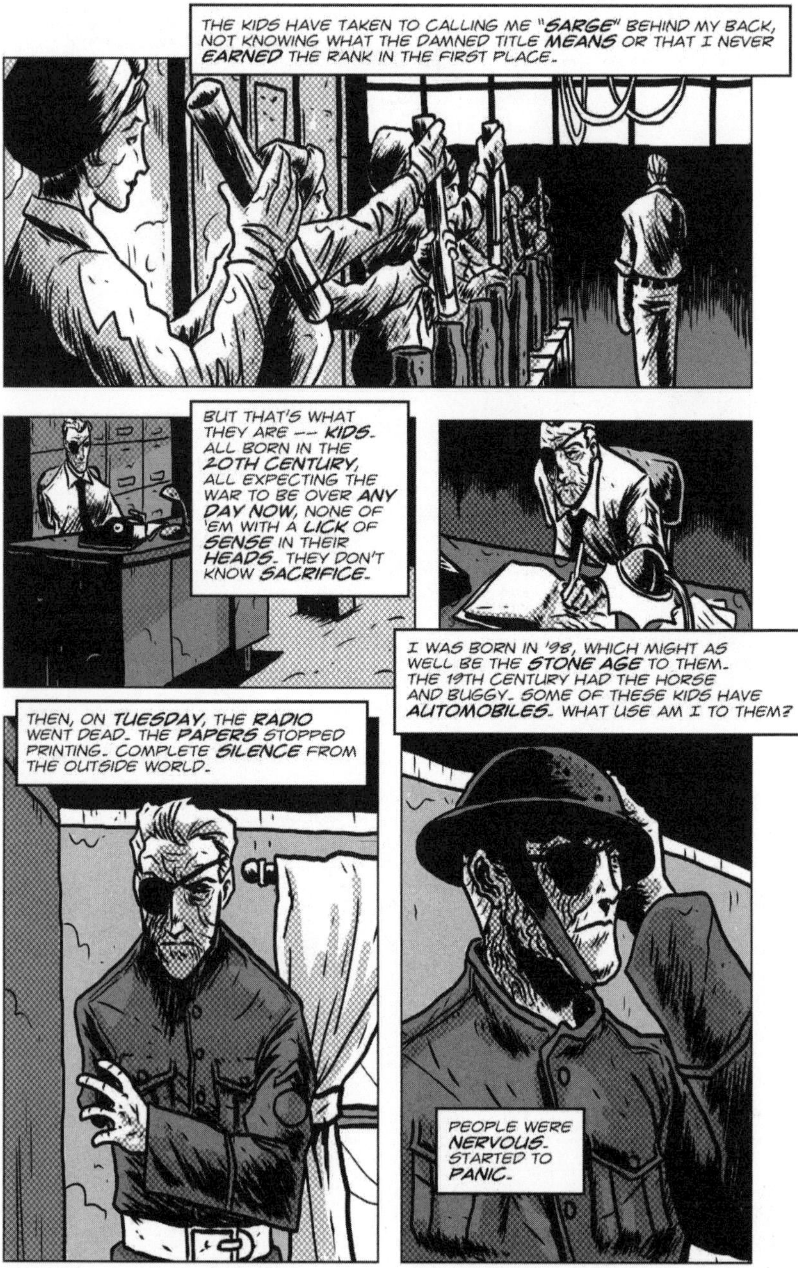
THE KIDS HAVE TAKEN TO CALLING ME "SARGE" BEHIND MY BACK, NOT KNOWING WHAT THE DAMNED TITLE MEANS OR THAT I NEVER EARNED THE RANK IN THE FIRST PLACE.
BUT THAT'S WHAT THEY ARE -- KIDS. ALL BORN IN THE 20TH CENTURY, ALL EXPECTING THE WAR TO BE OVER ANY DAY NOW, NONE OF 'EM WITH A LICK OF SENSE IN THEIR HEADS. THEY DON'T KNOW SACRIFICE.
I WAS BORN IN '98, WHICH MIGHT AS WELL BE THE STONE AGE TO THEM. THE 19TH CENTURY HAD THE HORSE AND BUGGY. SOME OF THESE KIDS HAVE AUTOMOBILES. WHAT USE AM I TO THEM?
THEN, ON TUESDAY, THE RADIO WENT DEAD. THE PAPERS STOPPED PRINTING. COMPLETE SILENCE FROM THE OUTSIDE WORLD.
PEOPLE WERE NERVOUS. STARTED TO PANIC.

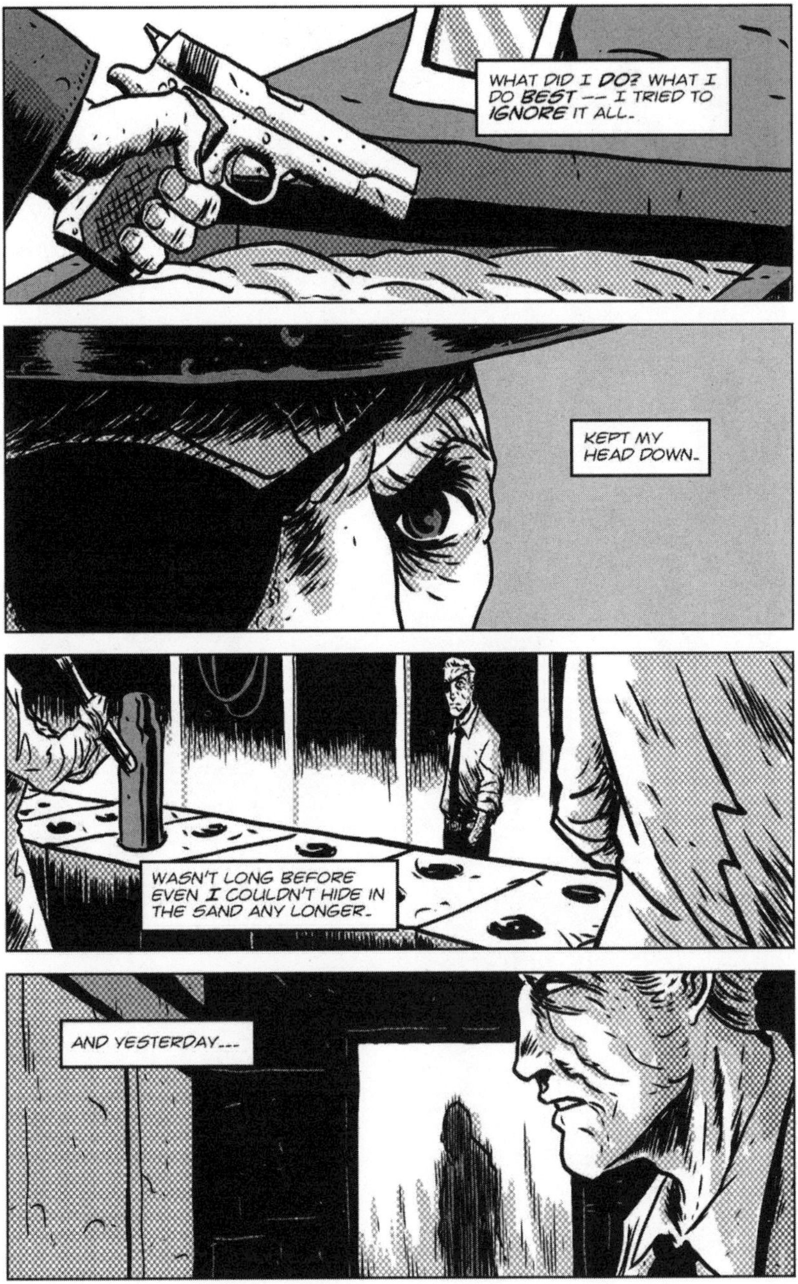
WHAT DID I DO? WHAT I DO BEST -- I TRIED TO IGNORE IT ALL...
KEPT MY HEAD DOWN...
WASN'T LONG BEFORE EVEN I COULDN'T HIDE IN THE SAND ANY LONGER...
AND YESTERDAY...

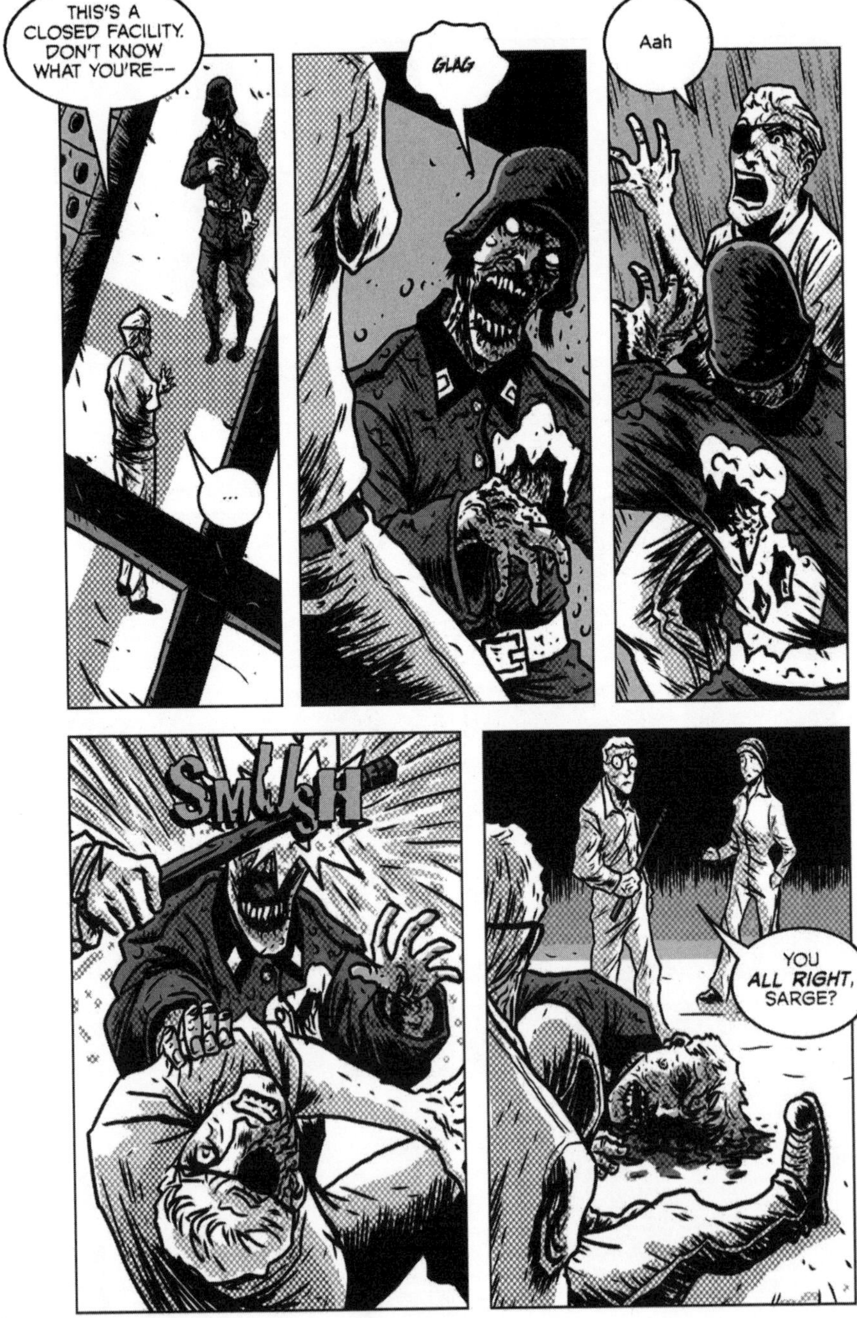
THIS'S A CLOSED FACILITY. DON'T KNOW WHAT YOU'RE--
...
GLAG
Aah
SMUSH
YOU ALL RIGHT, SARGE?

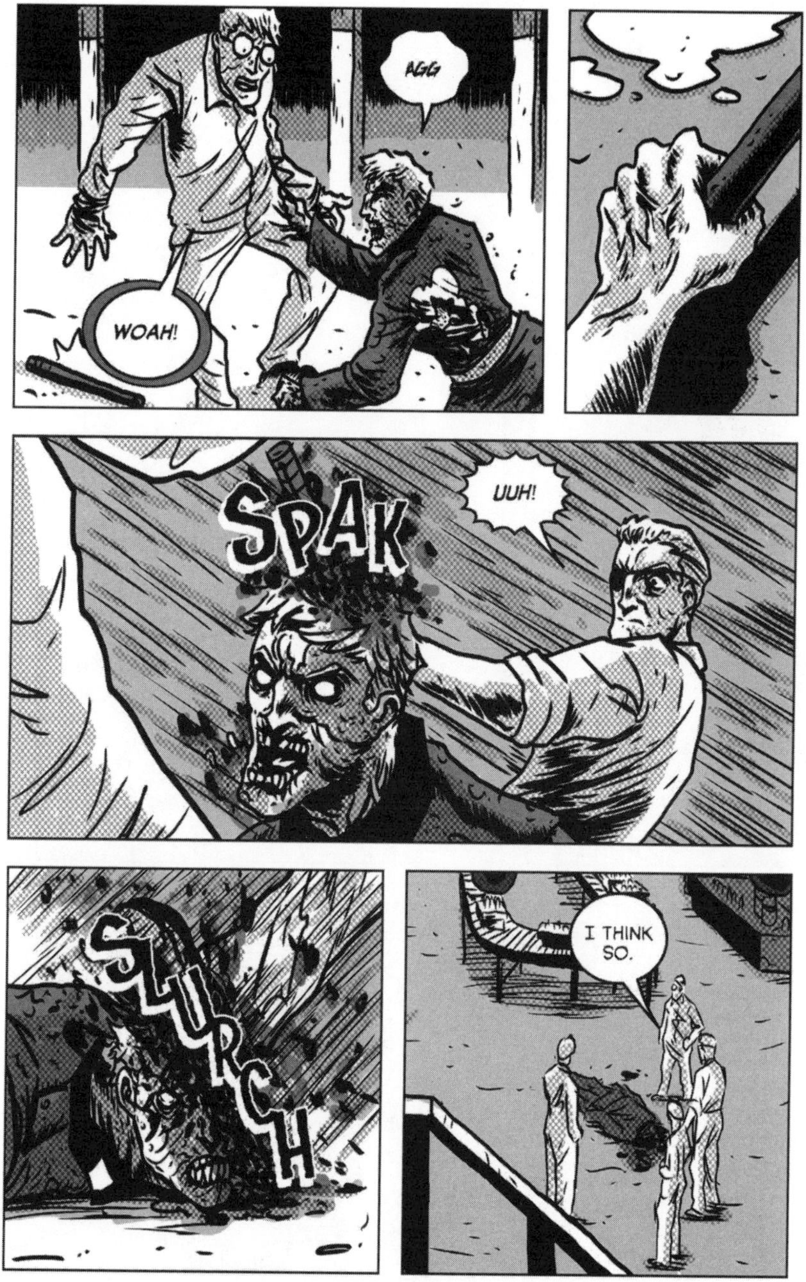
AGG
WOAH!
SPAK
UUH!
SLURCH
I THINK SO.

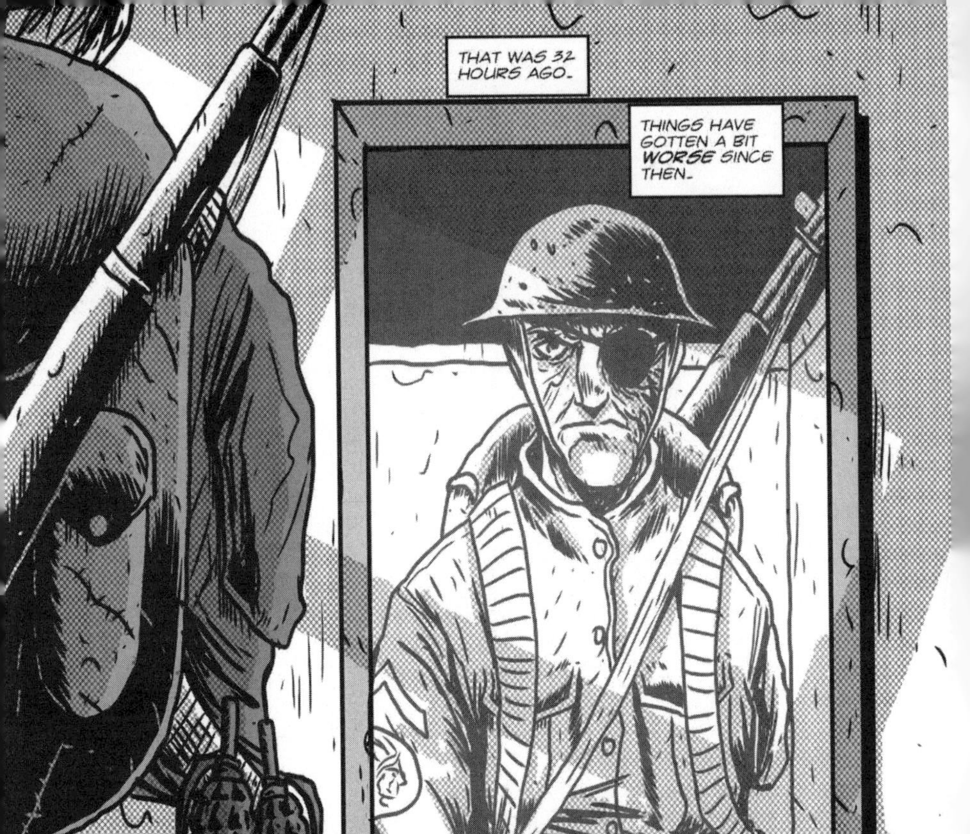
THAT WAS 32 HOURS AGO.
THINGS HAVE GOTTEN A BIT WORSE SINCE THEN.

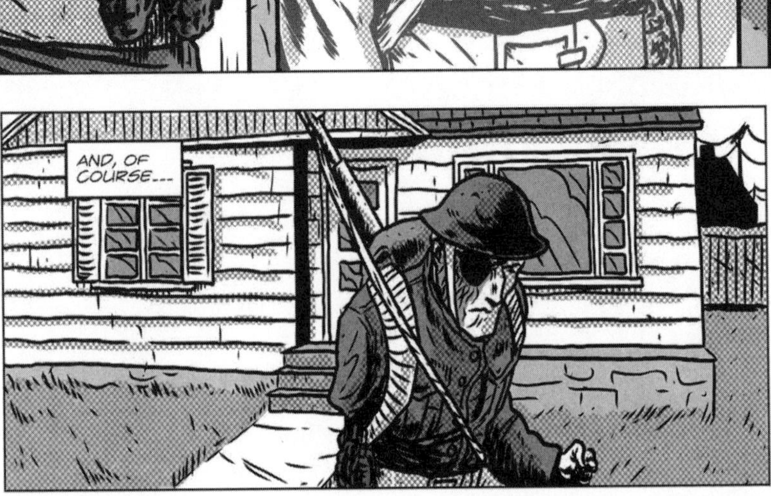
AND, OF COURSE...

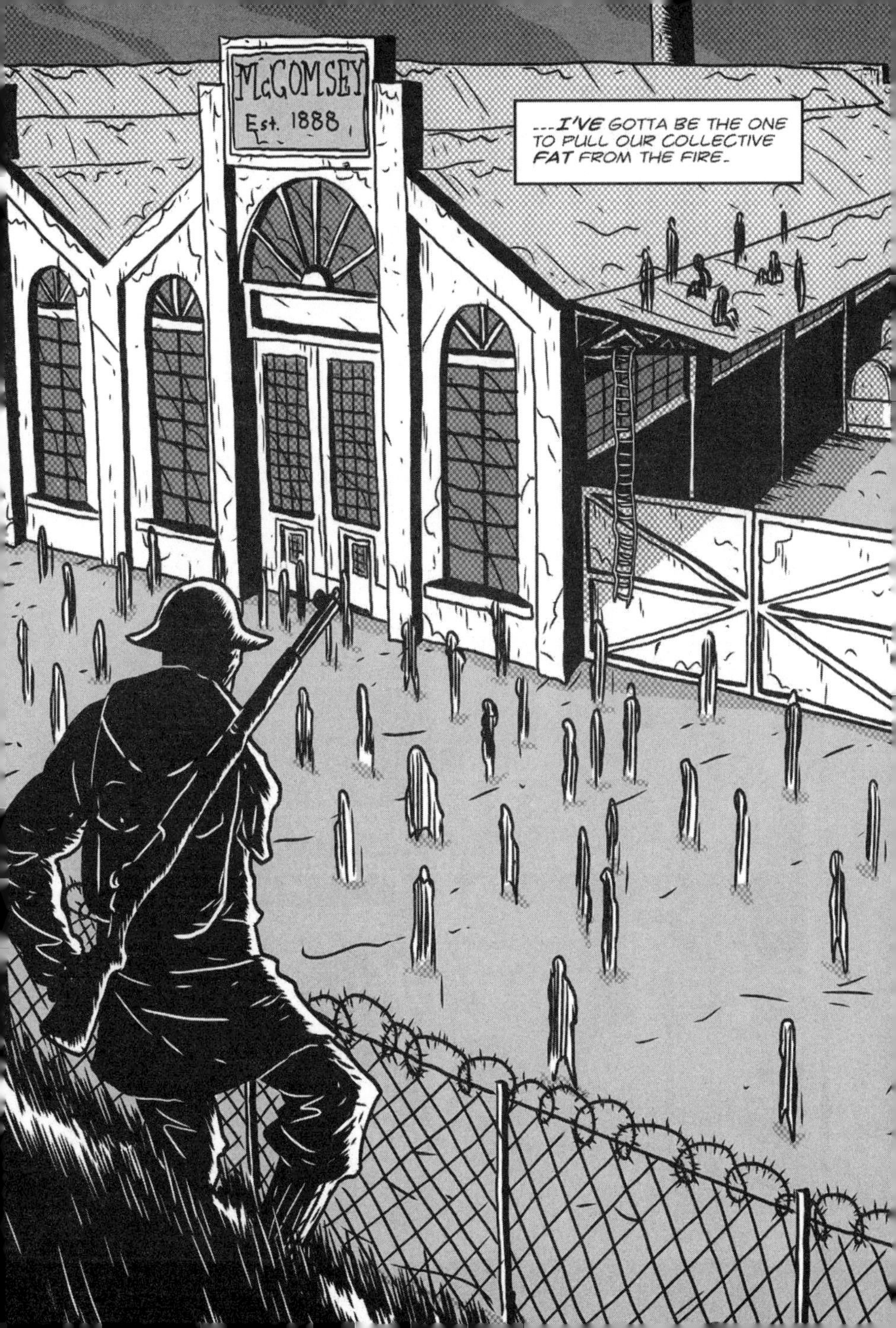
McGOMSEY
Est. 1888
...I'VE GOTTA BE THE ONE TO PULL OUR COLLECTIVE FAT FROM THE FIRE.

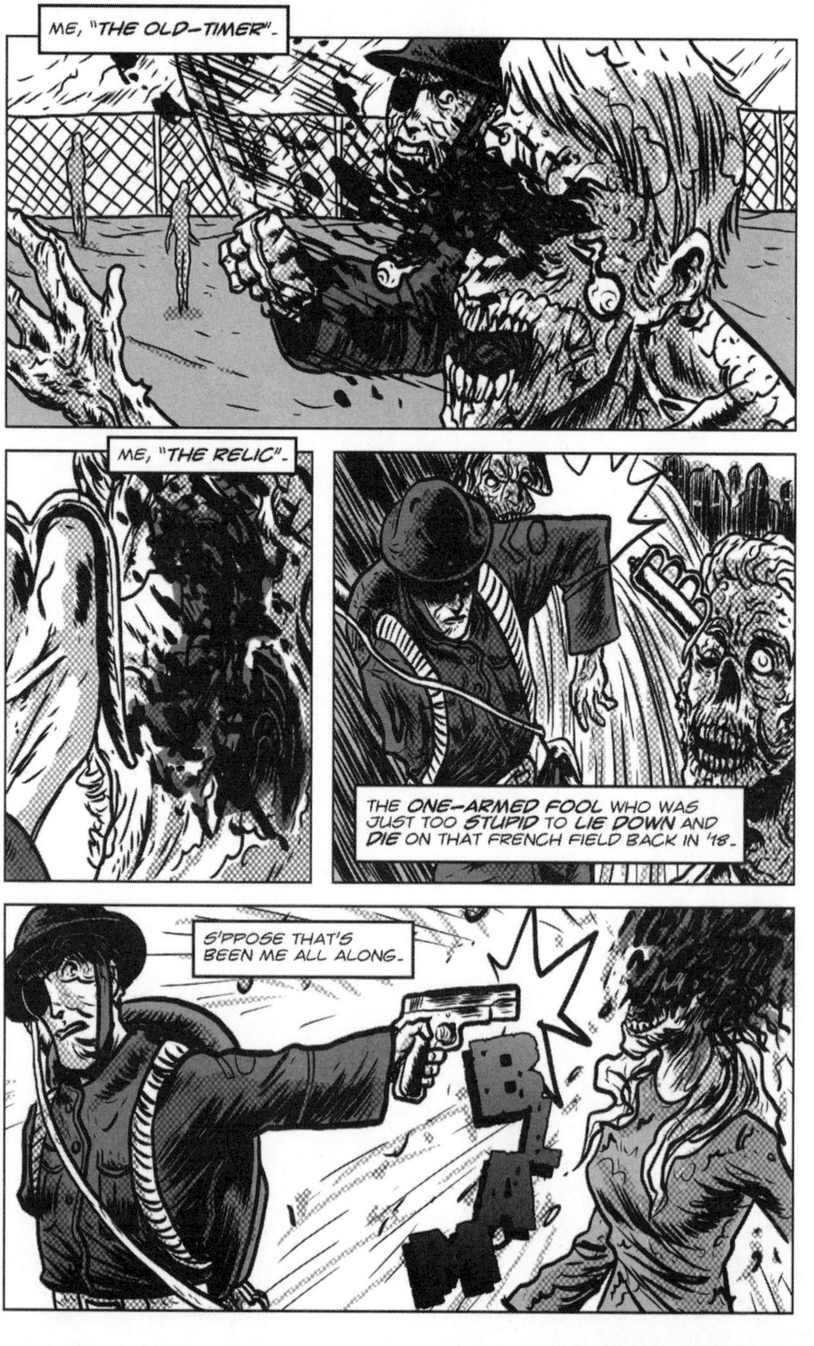
ME, "THE OLD-TIMER"...
ME, "THE RELIC"...
THE ONE-ARMED FOOL WHO WAS JUST TOO STUPID TO LIE DOWN AND DIE ON THAT FRENCH FIELD BACK IN '18...
S'PPOSE THAT'S BEEN ME ALL ALONG...
BLAM

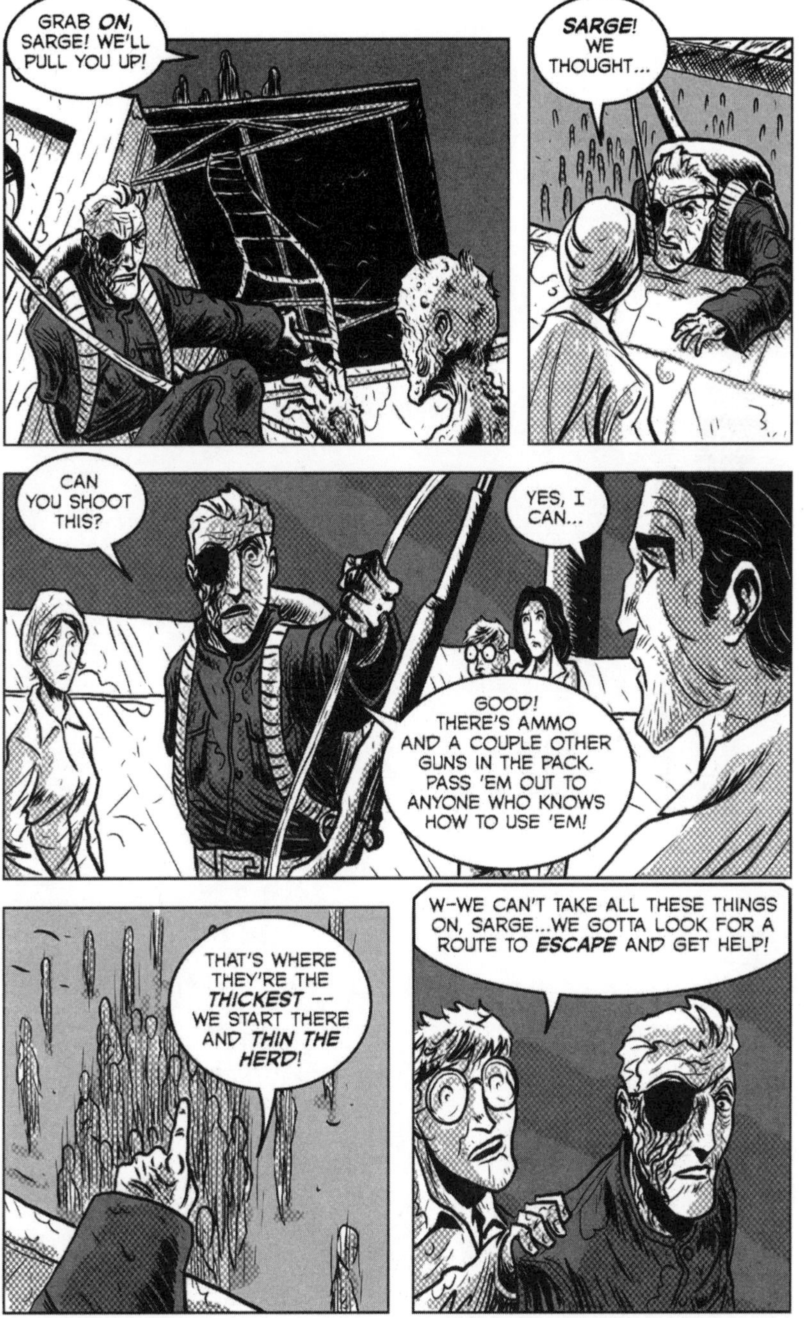
GRAB ON, SARGE! WE'LL PULL YOU UP!
SARGE! WE THOUGHT...
CAN YOU SHOOT THIS?
YES, I CAN...
GOOD! THERE'S AMMO AND A COUPLE OTHER GUNS IN THE PACK. PASS 'EM OUT TO ANYONE WHO KNOWS HOW TO USE 'EM!
THAT'S WHERE THEY'RE THE THICKEST -- WE START THERE AND THIN THE HERD!
W-WE CAN'T TAKE ALL THESE THINGS ON, SARGE...WE GOTTA LOOK FOR A ROUTE TO ESCAPE AND GET HELP!

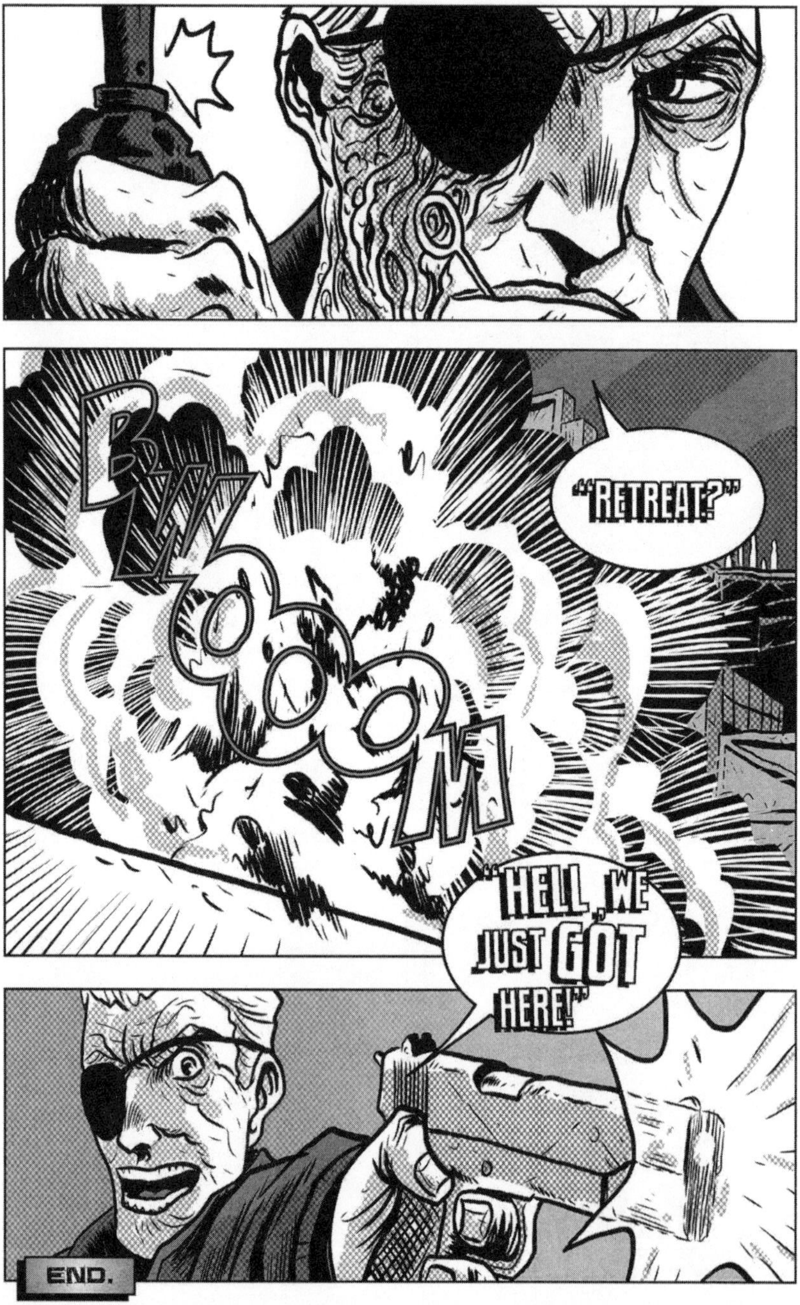

"RETREAT?"
BWOOOOM
"HELL, WE JUST GOT HERE!"
END.

THIS IS LONDON

STORY AND LETTERS BY:
JEFF McCLELLAND

ART BY:
REINE ROSENBERG

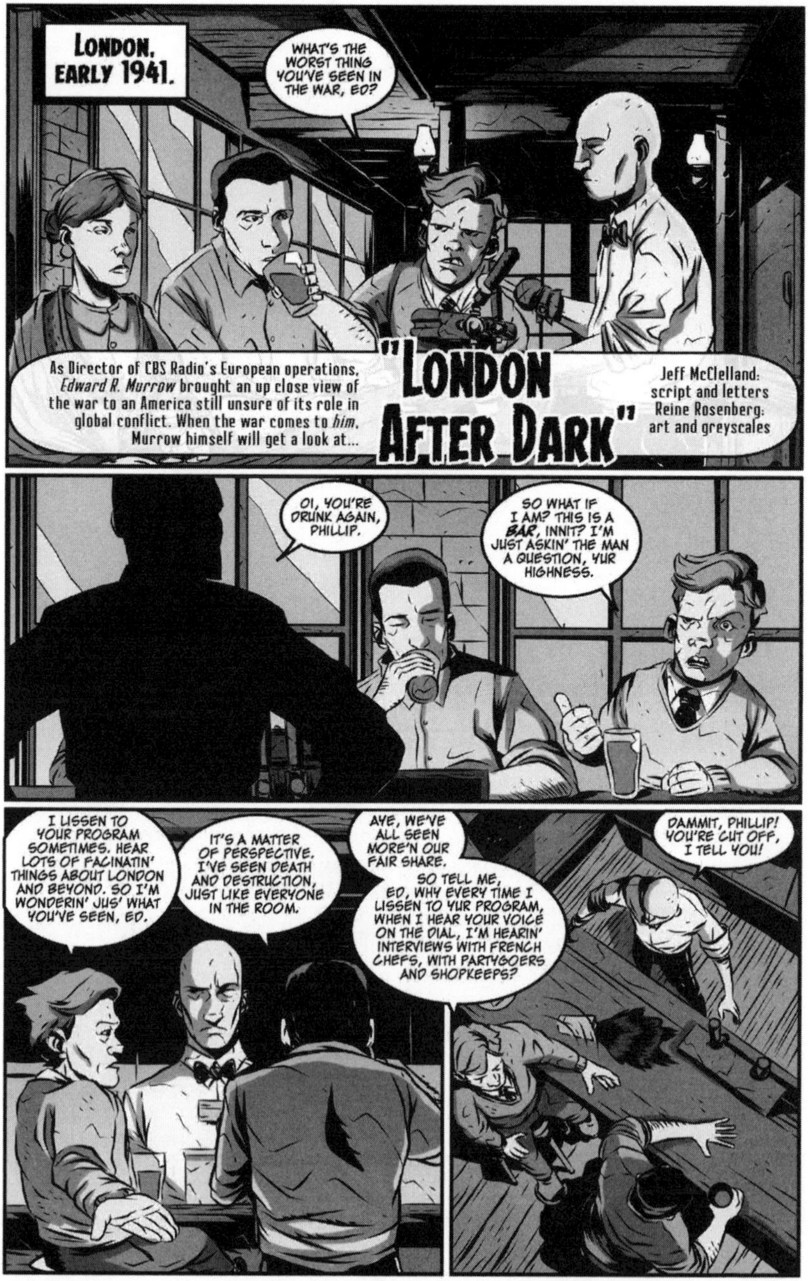
LONDON, EARLY 1941.
WHAT'S THE WORST THING YOU'VE SEEN IN THE WAR, ED?
As Director of CBS Radio's European operations, *Edward R. Murrow* brought an up close view of the war to an America still unsure of its role in global conflict. When the war comes to *him*, Murrow himself will get a look at...
"LONDON AFTER DARK"
Jeff McClelland: script and letters
Reine Rosenberg: art and greyscales
OI, YOU'RE DRUNK AGAIN, PHILLIP.
SO WHAT IF I AM? THIS IS A BAR, INNIT? I'M JUST ASKIN' THE MAN A QUESTION, YUR HIGHNESS.
I LISSEN TO YOUR PROGRAM SOMETIMES. HEAR LOTS OF FACINATIN' THINGS ABOUT LONDON AND BEYOND. SO I'M WONDERIN' JUS' WHAT YOU'VE SEEN, ED.
IT'S A MATTER OF PERSPECTIVE. I'VE SEEN DEATH AND DESTRUCTION, JUST LIKE EVERYONE IN THE ROOM.
AYE, WE'VE ALL SEEN MORE'N OUR FAIR SHARE.
SO TELL ME, ED, WHY EVERY TIME I LISSEN TO YUR PROGRAM, WHEN I HEAR YOUR VOICE ON THE DIAL, I'M HEARIN' INTERVIEWS WITH FRENCH CHEFS, WITH PARTYGOERS AND SHOPKEEPS?
DAMMIT, PHILLIP! YOU'RE CUT OFF, I TELL YOU!

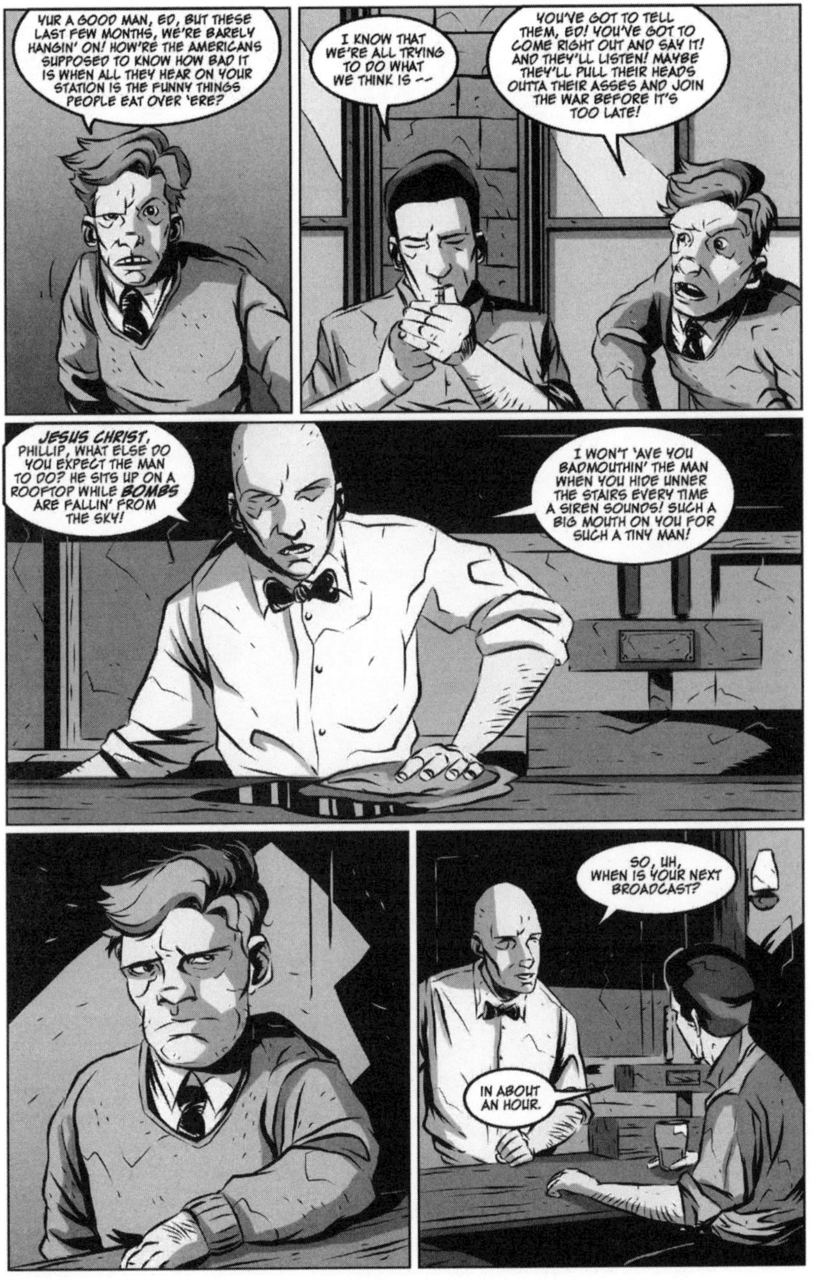
YUR A GOOD MAN, ED, BUT THESE LAST FEW MONTHS, WE'RE BARELY HANGIN' ON! HOW'RE THE AMERICANS SUPPOSED TO KNOW HOW BAD IT IS WHEN ALL THEY HEAR ON YOUR STATION IS THE FUNNY THINGS PEOPLE EAT OVER 'ERE?
I KNOW THAT WE'RE ALL TRYING TO DO WHAT WE THINK IS --
YOU'VE GOT TO TELL THEM, ED! YOU'VE GOT TO COME RIGHT OUT AND SAY IT! AND THEY'LL LISTEN! MAYBE THEY'LL PULL THEIR HEADS OUTTA THEIR ASSES AND JOIN THE WAR BEFORE IT'S TOO LATE!
JESUS CHRIST, PHILLIP, WHAT ELSE DO YOU EXPECT THE MAN TO DO? HE SITS UP ON A ROOFTOP WHILE BOMBS ARE FALLIN' FROM THE SKY!
I WON'T 'AVE YOU BADMOUTHIN' THE MAN WHEN YOU HIDE UNNER THE STAIRS EVERY TIME A SIREN SOUNDS! SUCH A BIG MOUTH ON YOU FOR SUCH A TINY MAN!
SO, UH, WHEN IS YOUR NEXT BROADCAST?
IN ABOUT AN HOUR.

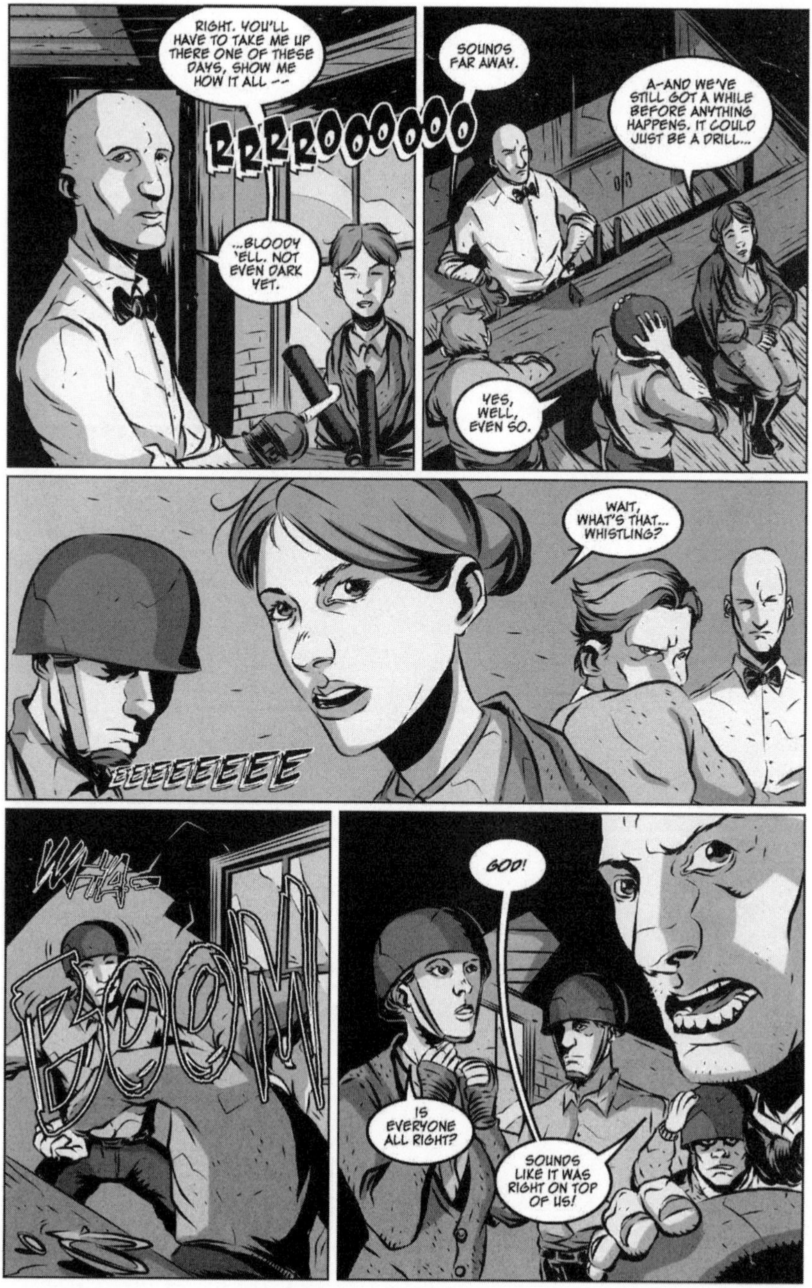
RIGHT. YOU'LL HAVE TO TAKE ME UP THERE ONE OF THESE DAYS, SHOW ME HOW IT ALL --
RRRROOOOOOO
...BLOODY 'ELL. NOT EVEN DARK YET.
SOUNDS FAR AWAY.
A-AND WE'VE STILL GOT A WHILE BEFORE ANYTHING HAPPENS. IT COULD JUST BE A DRILL...
YES, WELL, EVEN SO.
WAIT, WHAT'S THAT... WHISTLING?
EEEEEEEEE
WHA--
BOOOM
GOD!
IS EVERYONE ALL RIGHT?
SOUNDS LIKE IT WAS RIGHT ON TOP OF US!

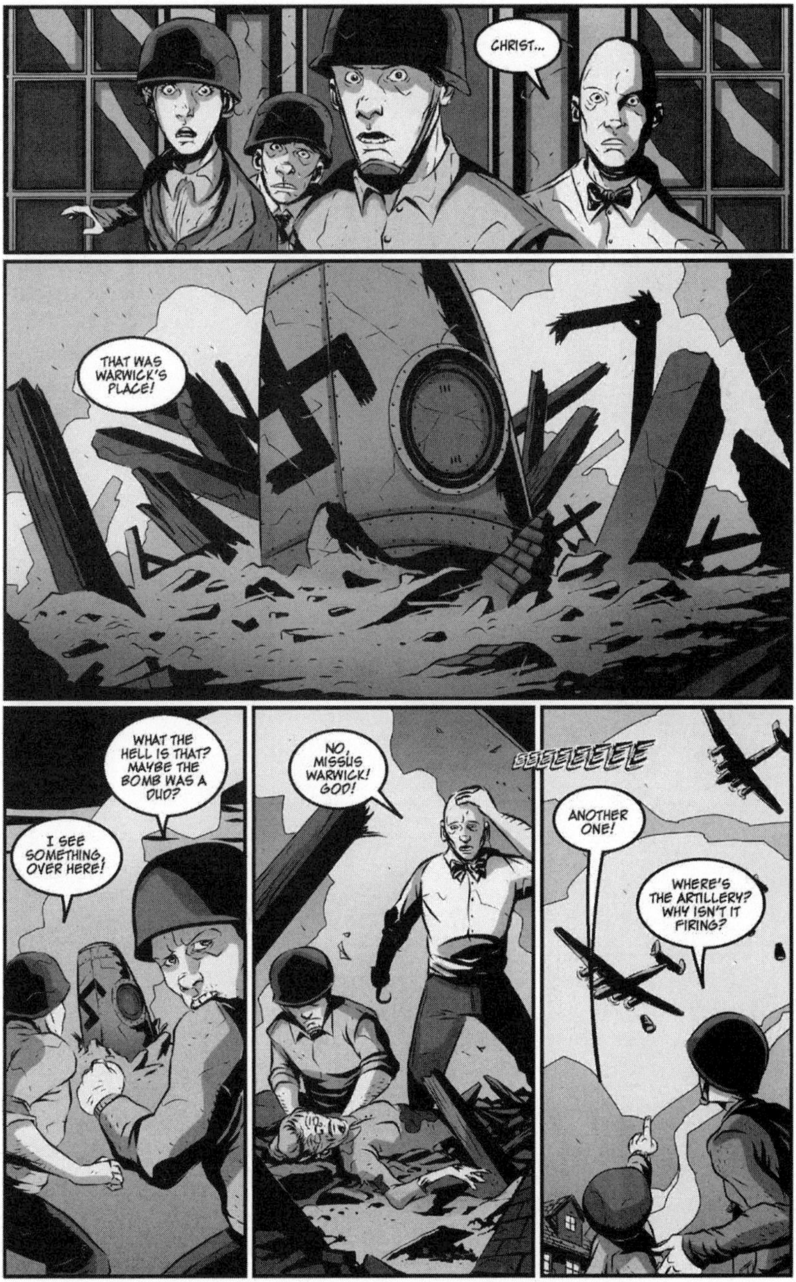
CHRIST...
THAT WAS WARWICK'S PLACE!
WHAT THE HELL IS THAT? MAYBE THE BOMB WAS A DUD?
I SEE SOMETHING, OVER HERE!
NO, MISSUS WARWICK! GOD!
SEEEEEEEE
ANOTHER ONE!
WHERE'S THE ARTILLERY? WHY ISN'T IT FIRING?

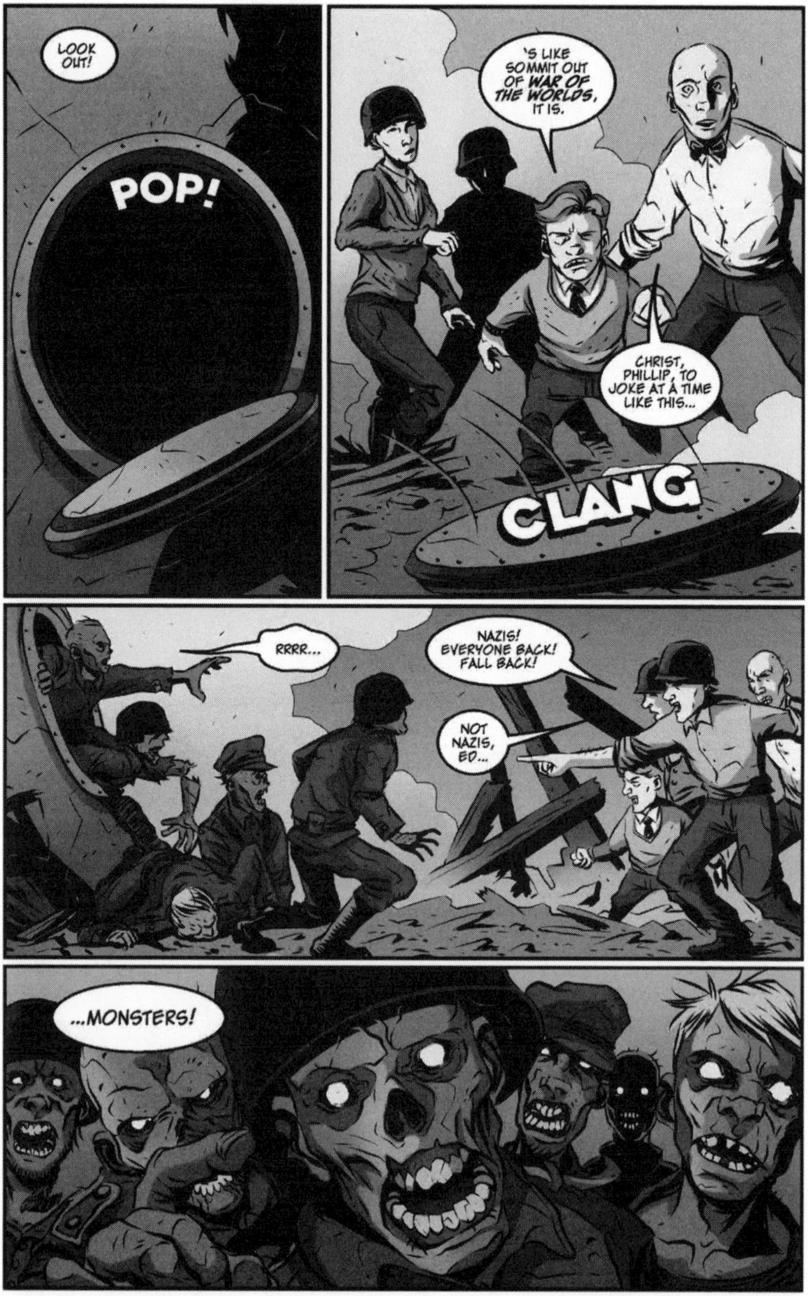
LOOK OUT!
POP!
'S LIKE SOMMIT OUT OF WAR OF THE WORLDS, IT IS.
CHRIST, PHILLIP, TO JOKE AT A TIME LIKE THIS...
CLANG
RRRR...
NAZIS! EVERYONE BACK! FALL BACK!
NOT NAZIS, ED...
...MONSTERS!

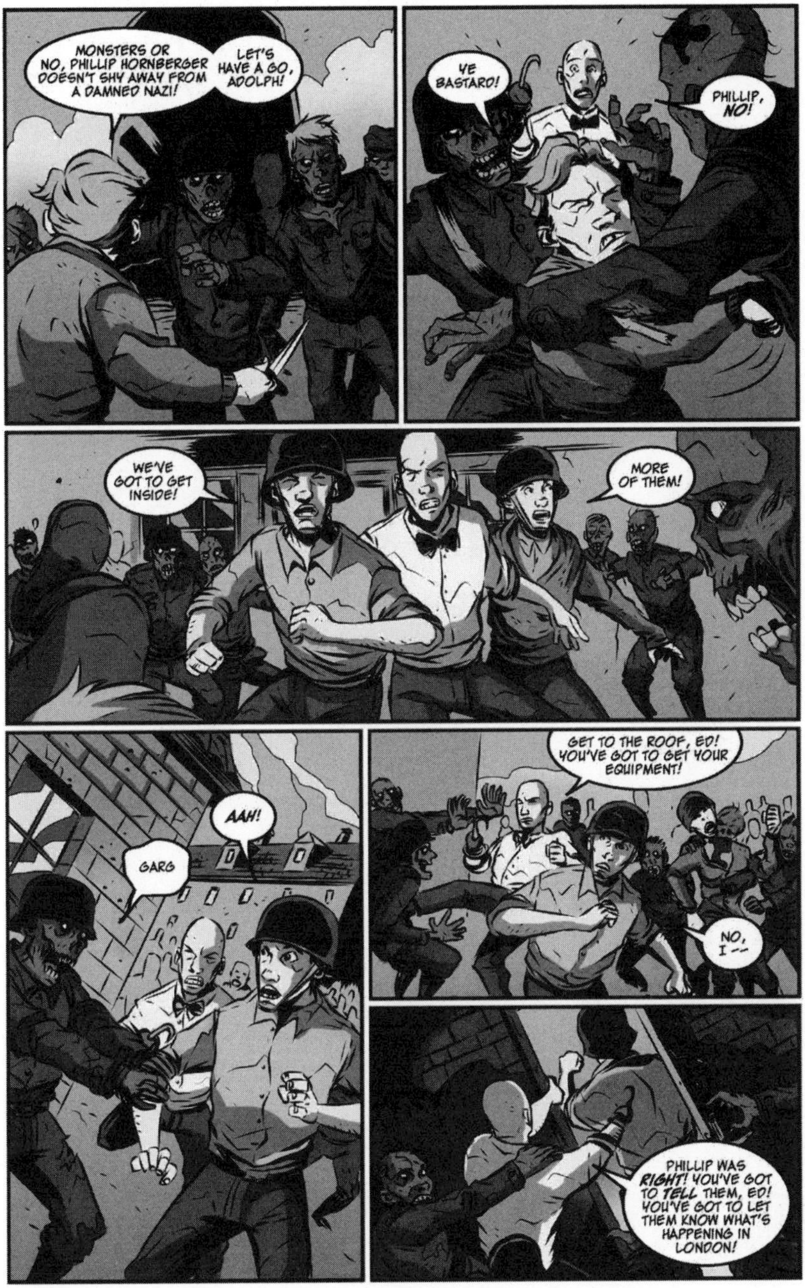
MONSTERS OR NO, PHILLIP HORNBERGER DOESN'T SHY AWAY FROM A DAMNED NAZI!
LET'S HAVE A GO, ADOLPH!
YE BASTARD!
PHILLIP, NO!
WE'VE GOT TO GET INSIDE!
MORE OF THEM!
GARG
AAH!
GET TO THE ROOF, ED! YOU'VE GOT TO GET YOUR EQUIPMENT!
NO, I --
PHILLIP WAS RIGHT! YOU'VE GOT TO TELL THEM, ED! YOU'VE GOT TO LET THEM KNOW WHAT'S HAPPENING IN LONDON!

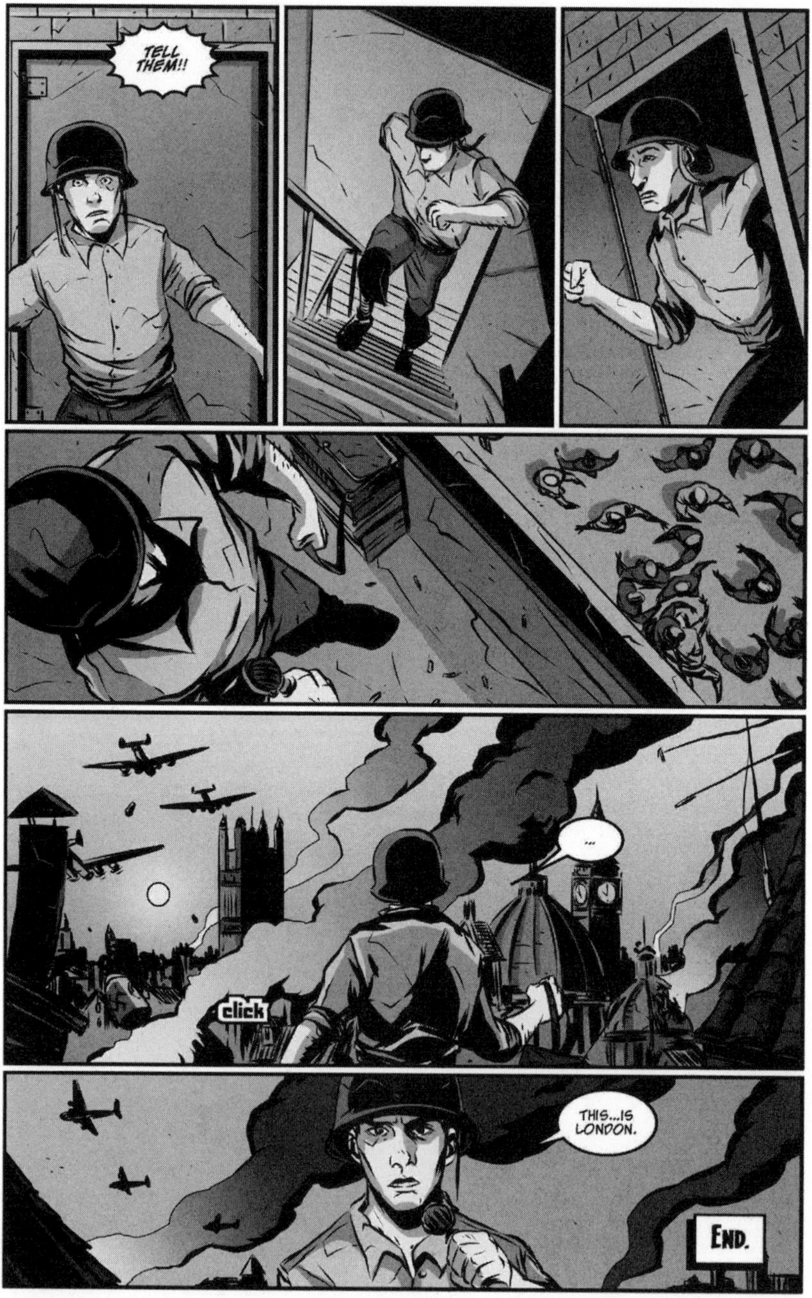
TELL THEM!!
...
click
THIS...IS LONDON.
END.

BOOTS

STORY BY:
CHUCK DIXON

PENCILS, LETTERS AND GRAYSCALES BY:
JEFF McCOMSEY

INKS BY:
STEVE BECKER

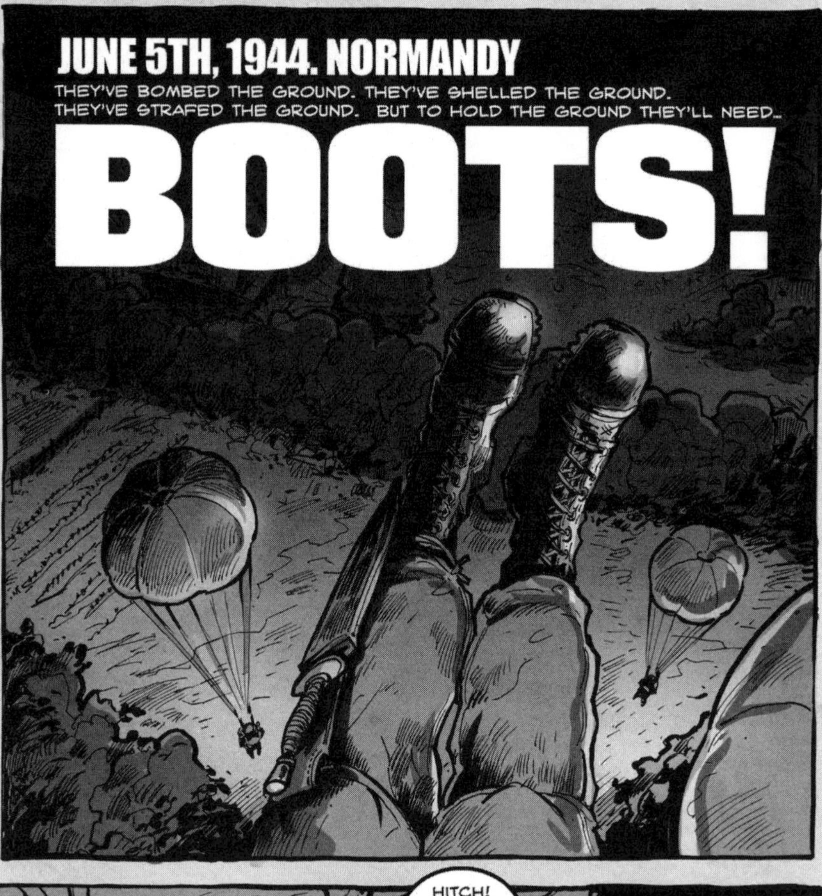
JUNE 5TH, 1944. NORMANDY
THEY'VE BOMBED THE GROUND. THEY'VE SHELLED THE GROUND.
THEY'VE STRAFED THE GROUND. BUT TO HOLD THE GROUND THEY'LL NEED...
BOOTS!

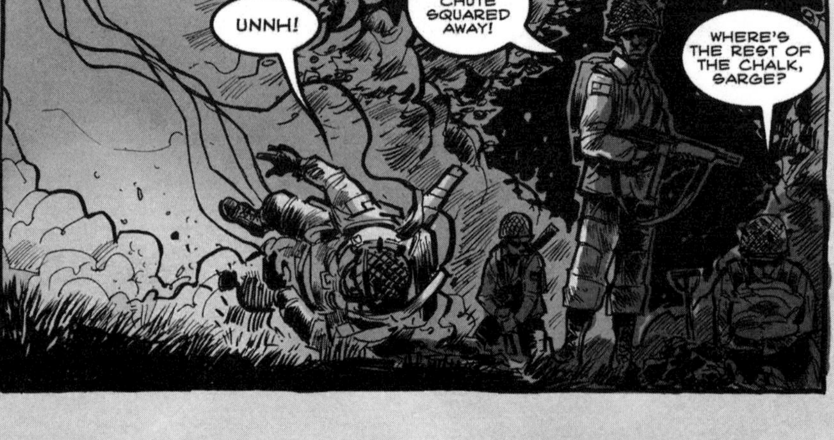
UNNH!
HITCH! GET YOUR CHUTE SQUARED AWAY!
WHERE'S THE REST OF THE CHALK, SARGE?

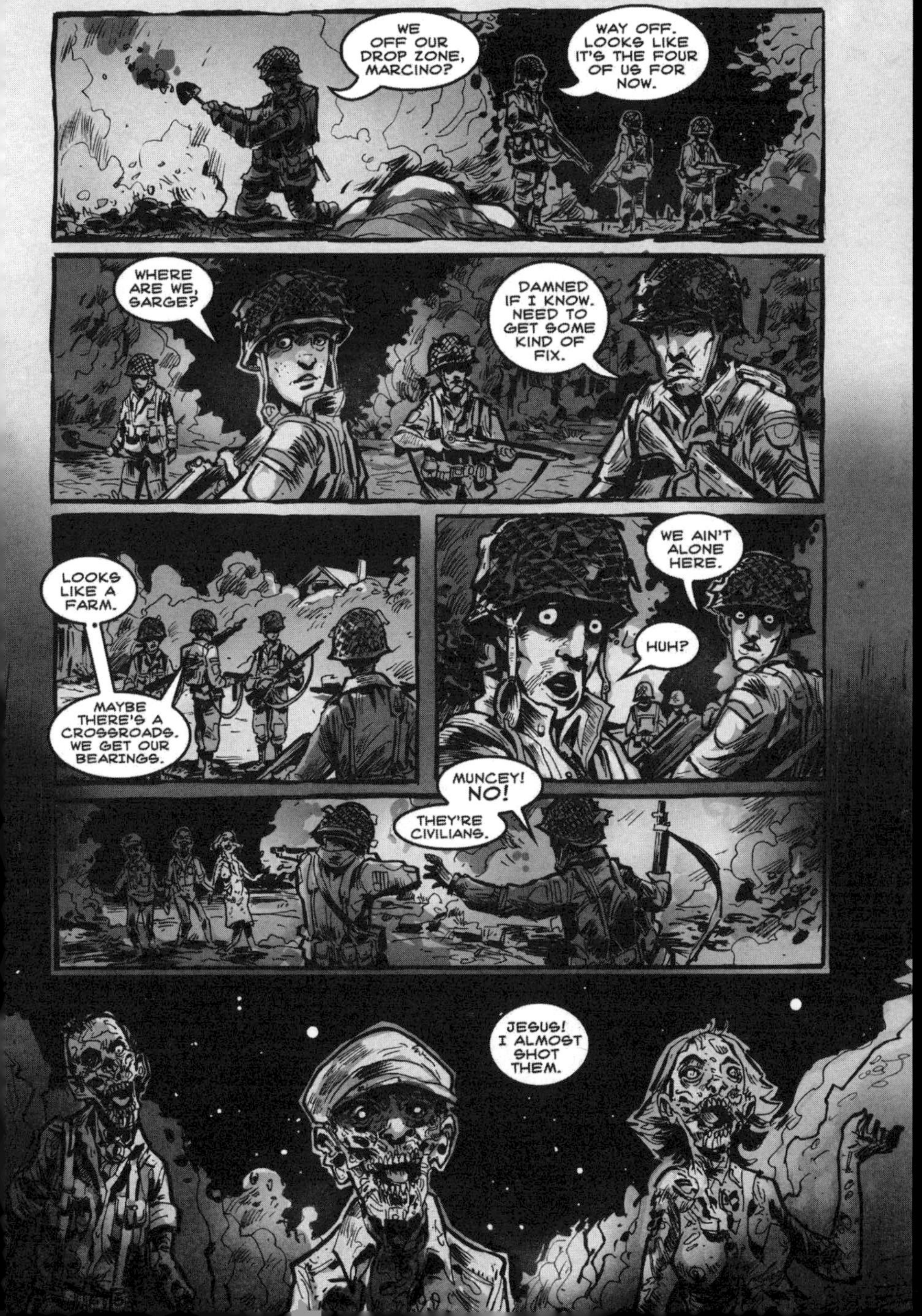
WE OFF OUR DROP ZONE, MARCINO?
WAY OFF. LOOKS LIKE IT'S THE FOUR OF US FOR NOW.
WHERE ARE WE, SARGE?
DAMNED IF I KNOW. NEED TO GET SOME KIND OF FIX.
LOOKS LIKE A FARM.
MAYBE THERE'S A CROSSROADS. WE GET OUR BEARINGS.
WE AIN'T ALONE HERE.
HUH?
MUNCEY! NO!
THEY'RE CIVILIANS.
JESUS! I ALMOST SHOT THEM.

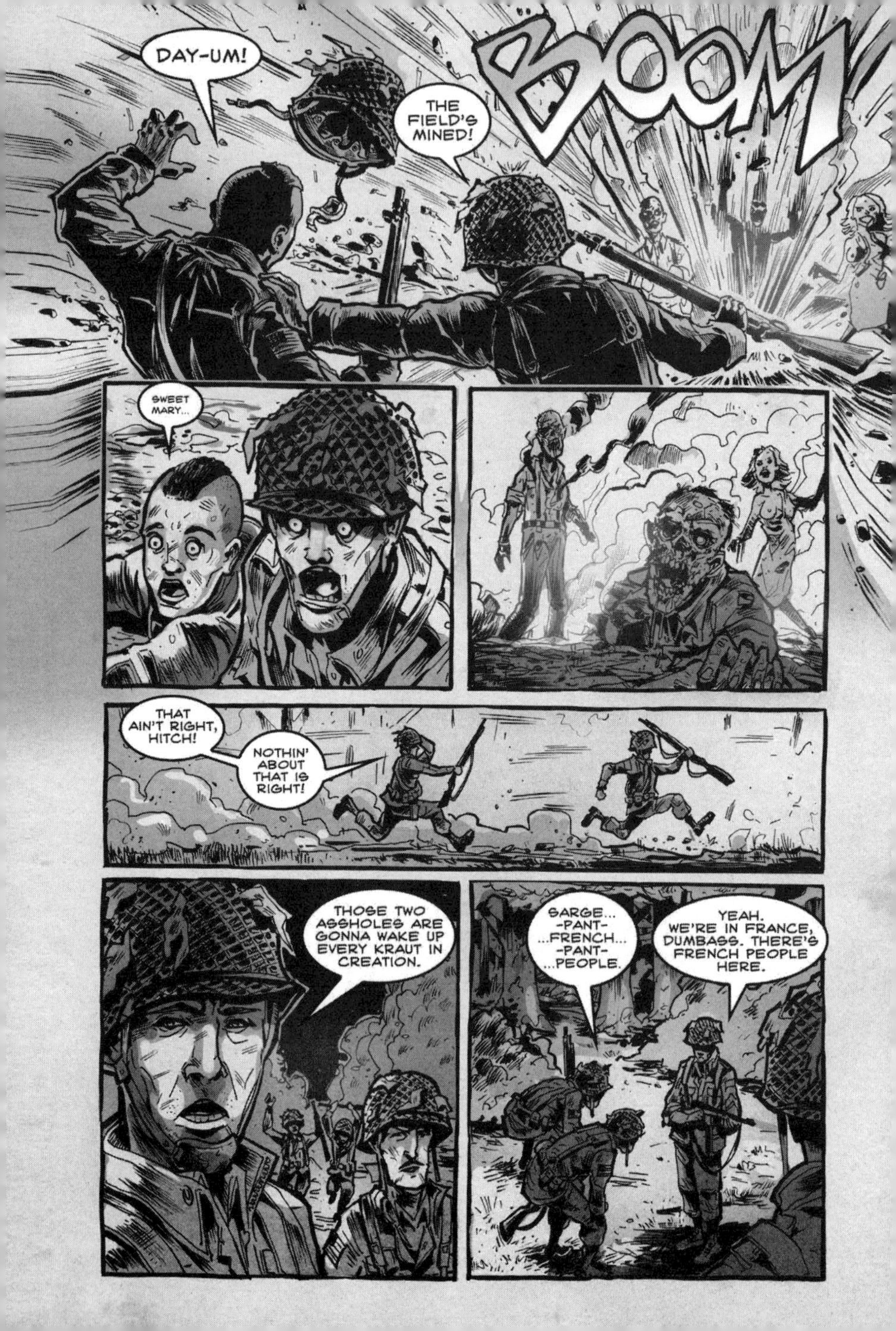
DAY-UM!
THE FIELD'S MINED!
BOOM
SWEET MARY...
THAT AIN'T RIGHT, HITCH!
NOTHIN' ABOUT THAT IS RIGHT!
THOSE TWO ASSHOLES ARE GONNA WAKE UP EVERY KRAUT IN CREATION.
SARGE... -PANT- ...FRENCH... -PANT- ...PEOPLE.
YEAH. WE'RE IN FRANCE, DUMBASS. THERE'S FRENCH PEOPLE HERE.

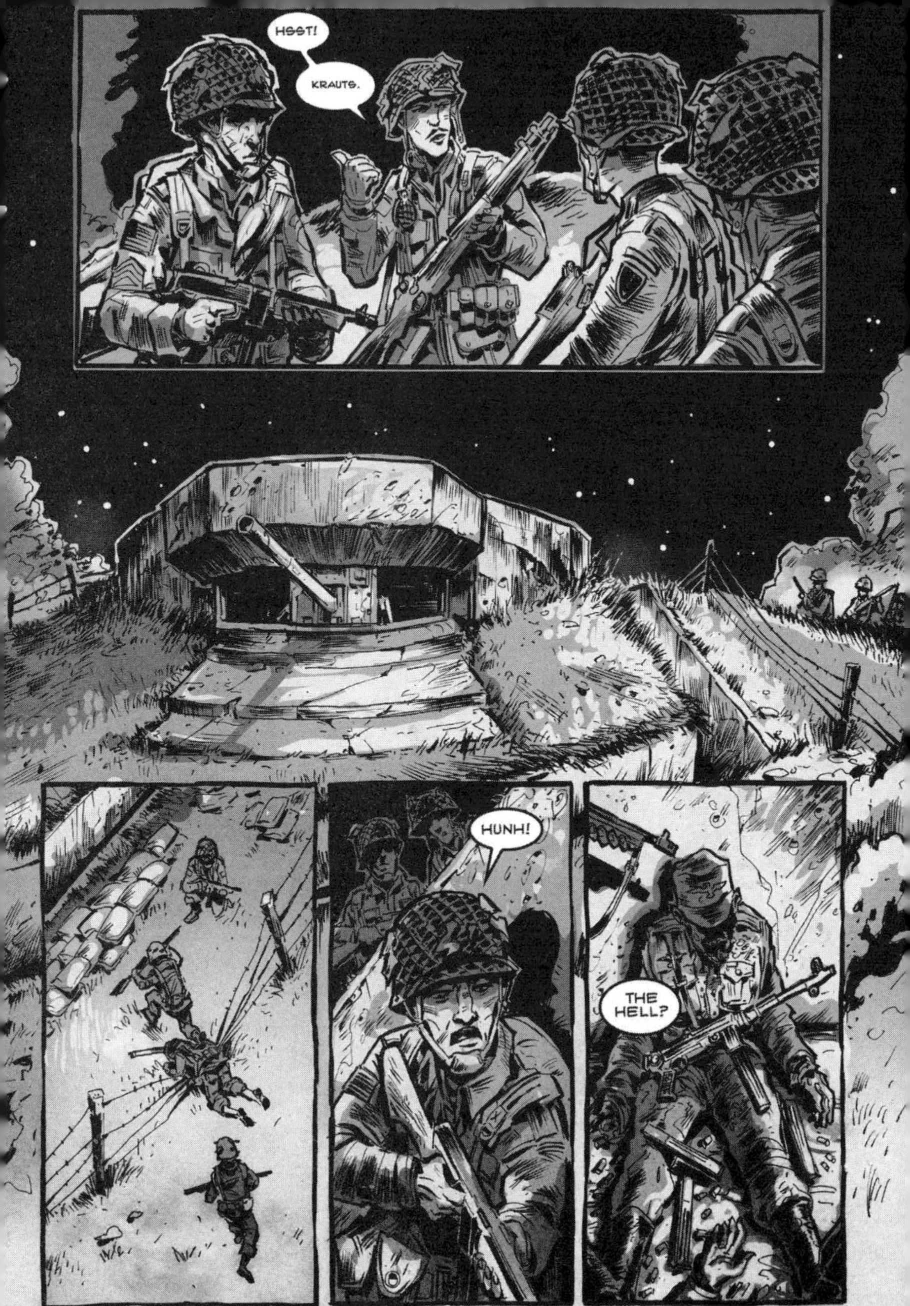
HSST!
KRAUTS.
HUNH!
THE HELL?

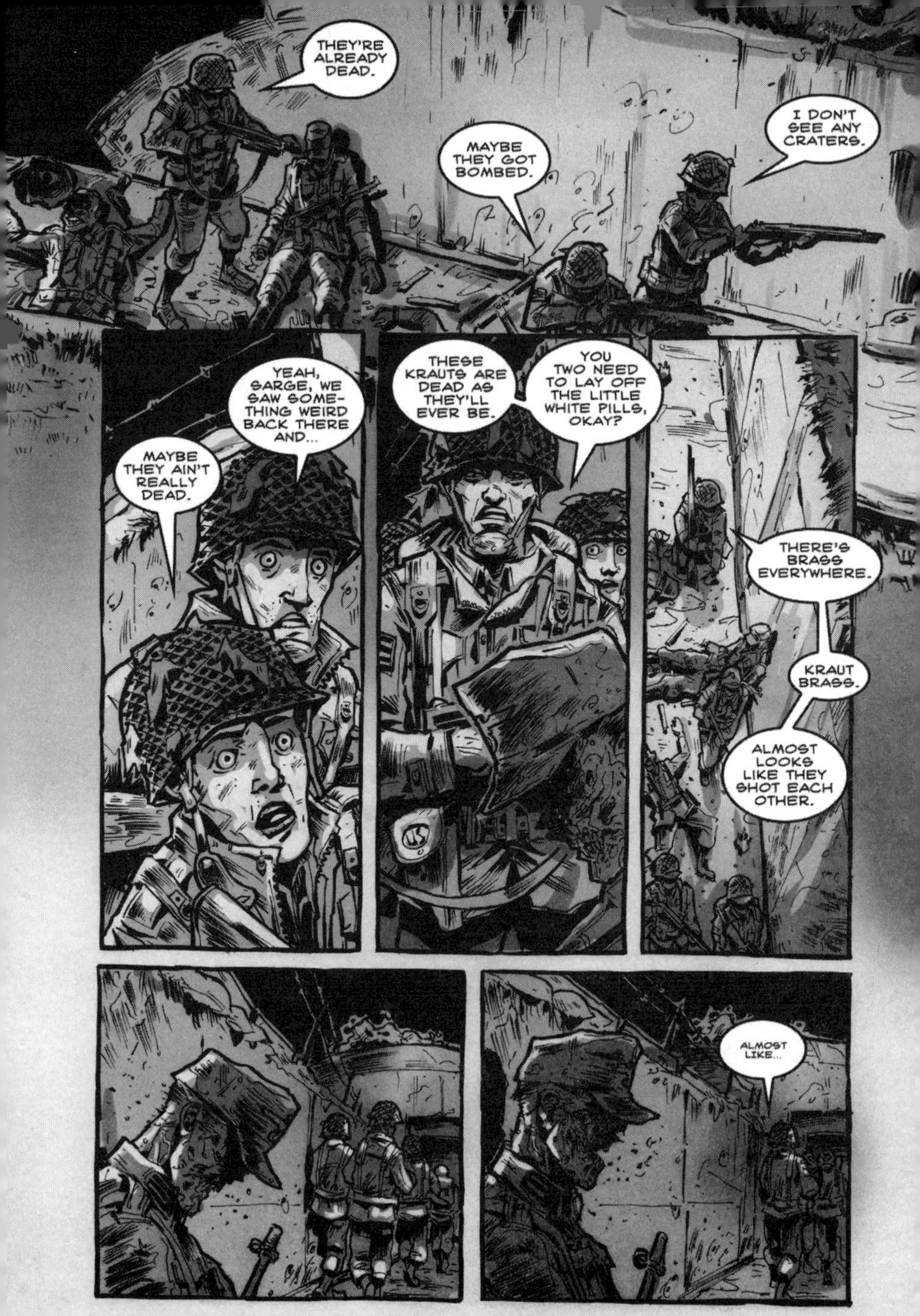
THEY'RE ALREADY DEAD.
MAYBE THEY GOT BOMBED.
I DON'T SEE ANY CRATERS.
YEAH, SARGE, WE SAW SOME-THING WEIRD BACK THERE AND...
MAYBE THEY AIN'T REALLY DEAD.
THESE KRAUTS ARE DEAD AS THEY'LL EVER BE.
YOU TWO NEED TO LAY OFF THE LITTLE WHITE PILLS, OKAY?
THERE'S BRASS EVERYWHERE.
KRAUT BRASS.
ALMOST LOOKS LIKE THEY SHOT EACH OTHER.
ALMOST LIKE...

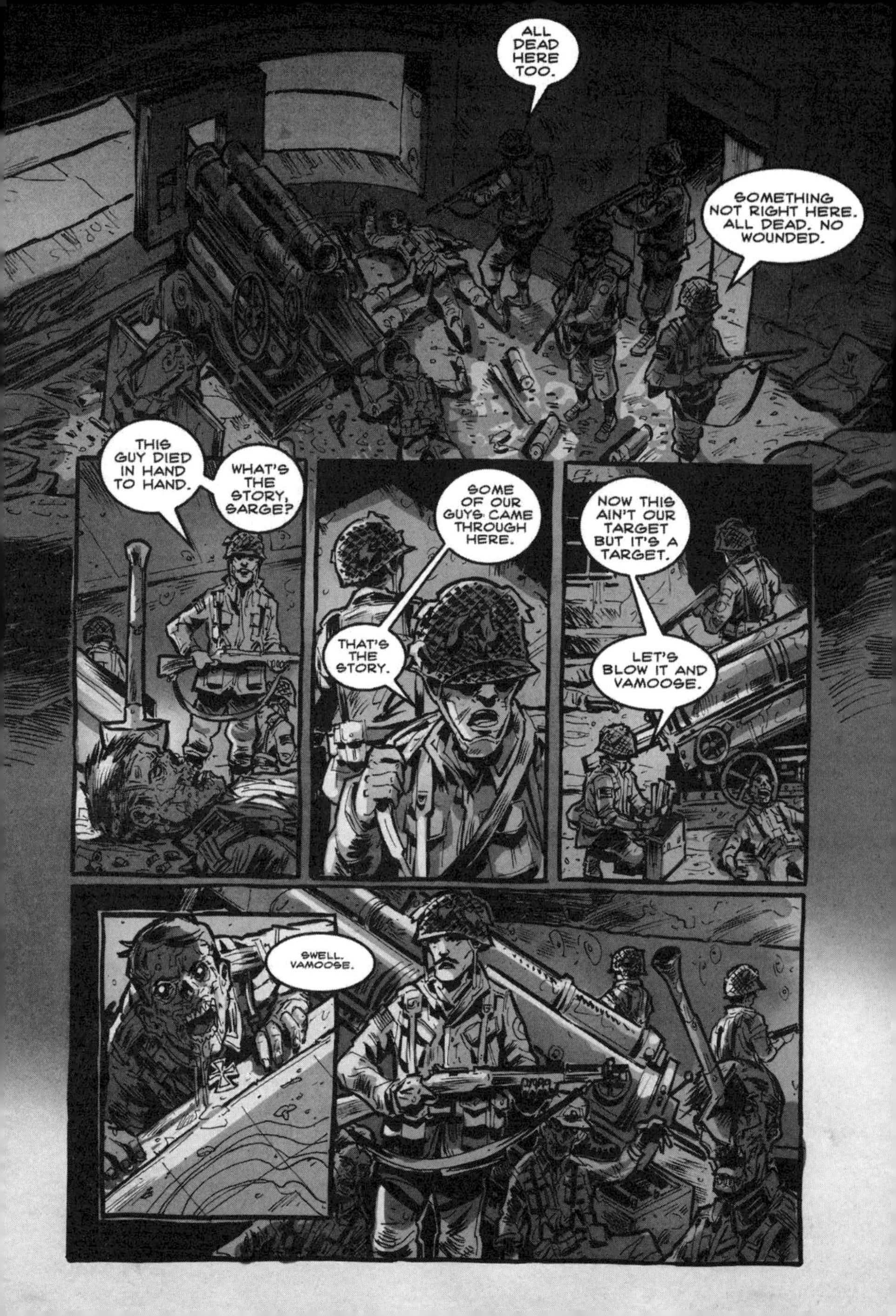
ALL DEAD HERE TOO.
SOMETHING NOT RIGHT HERE. ALL DEAD. NO WOUNDED.
THIS GUY DIED IN HAND TO HAND.
WHAT'S THE STORY, SARGE?
SOME OF OUR GUYS CAME THROUGH HERE.
THAT'S THE STORY.
NOW THIS AIN'T OUR TARGET BUT IT'S A TARGET.
LET'S BLOW IT AND VAMOOSE.
SWELL. VAMOOSE.

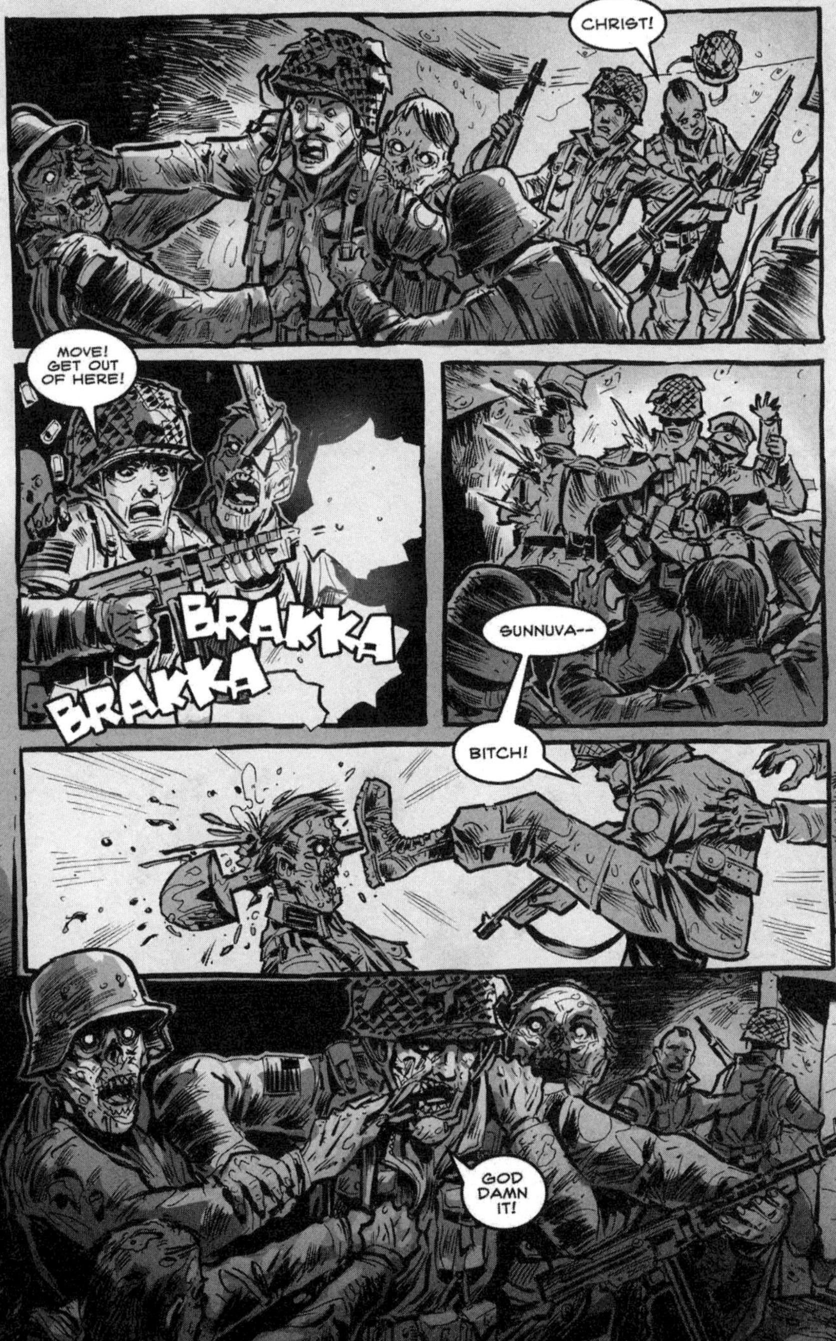
CHRIST!
MOVE! GET OUT OF HERE!
BRAKKA
BRAKKA
SUNNUVA--
BITCH!
GOD DAMN IT!

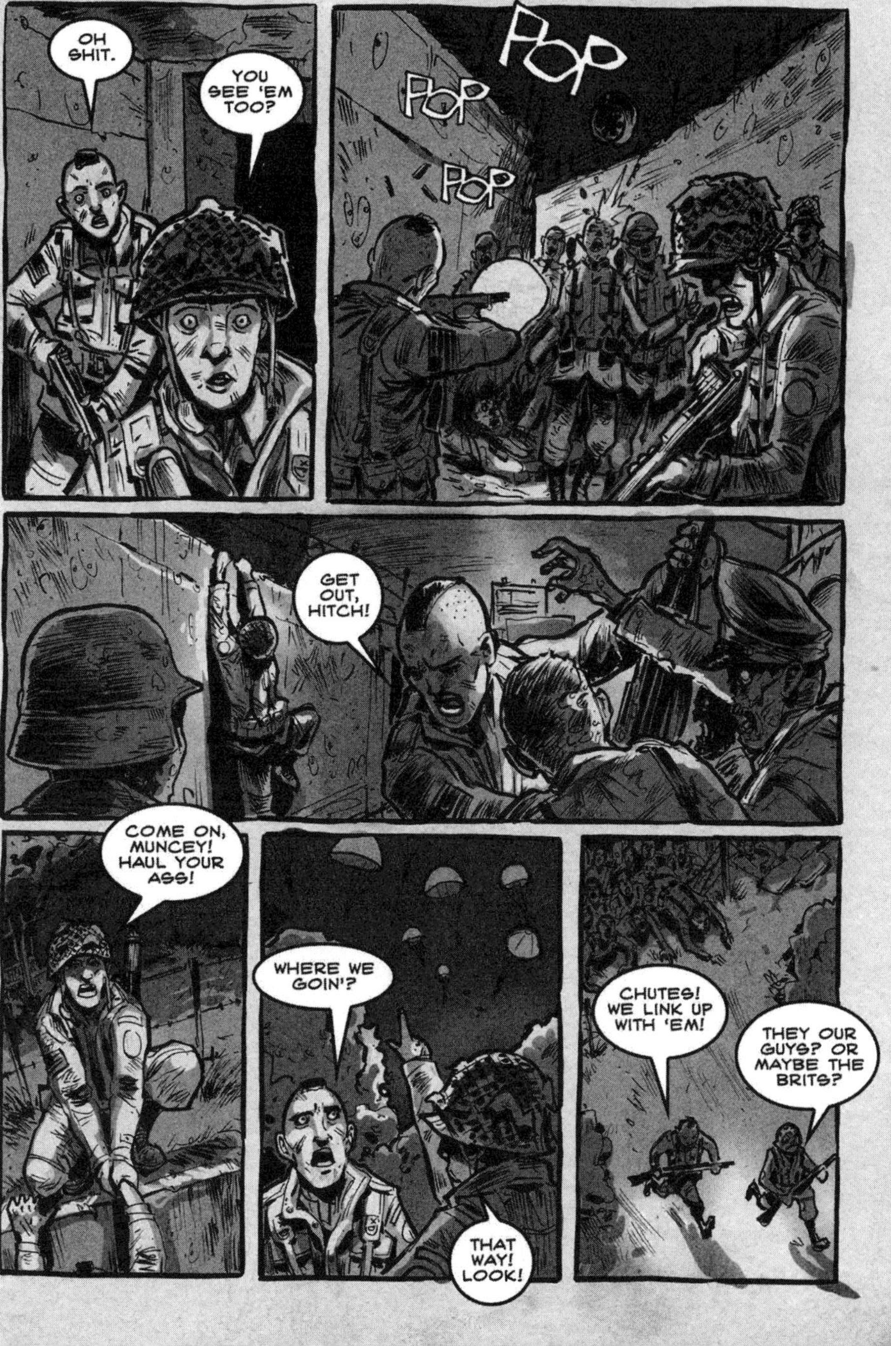

OH SHIT.
YOU SEE 'EM TOO?
POP
POP
POP
GET OUT, HITCH!
COME ON, MUNCEY! HAUL YOUR ASS!
WHERE WE GOIN'?
THAT WAY! LOOK!
CHUTES! WE LINK UP WITH 'EM!
THEY OUR GUYS? OR MAYBE THE BRITS?

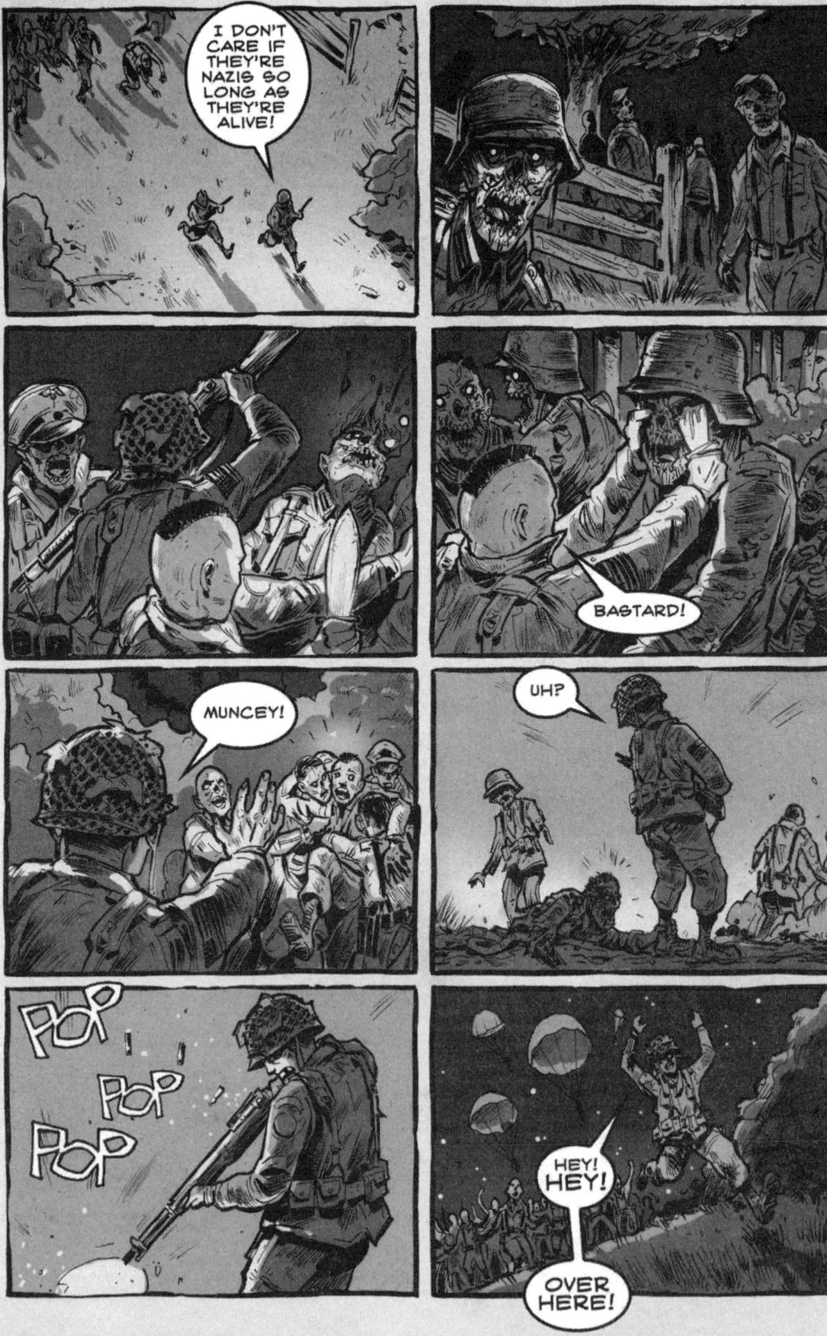
I DON'T CARE IF THEY'RE NAZIS SO LONG AS THEY'RE ALIVE!
BASTARD!
MUNCEY!
UH?
POP
POP
POP
HEY! HEY!
OVER HERE!

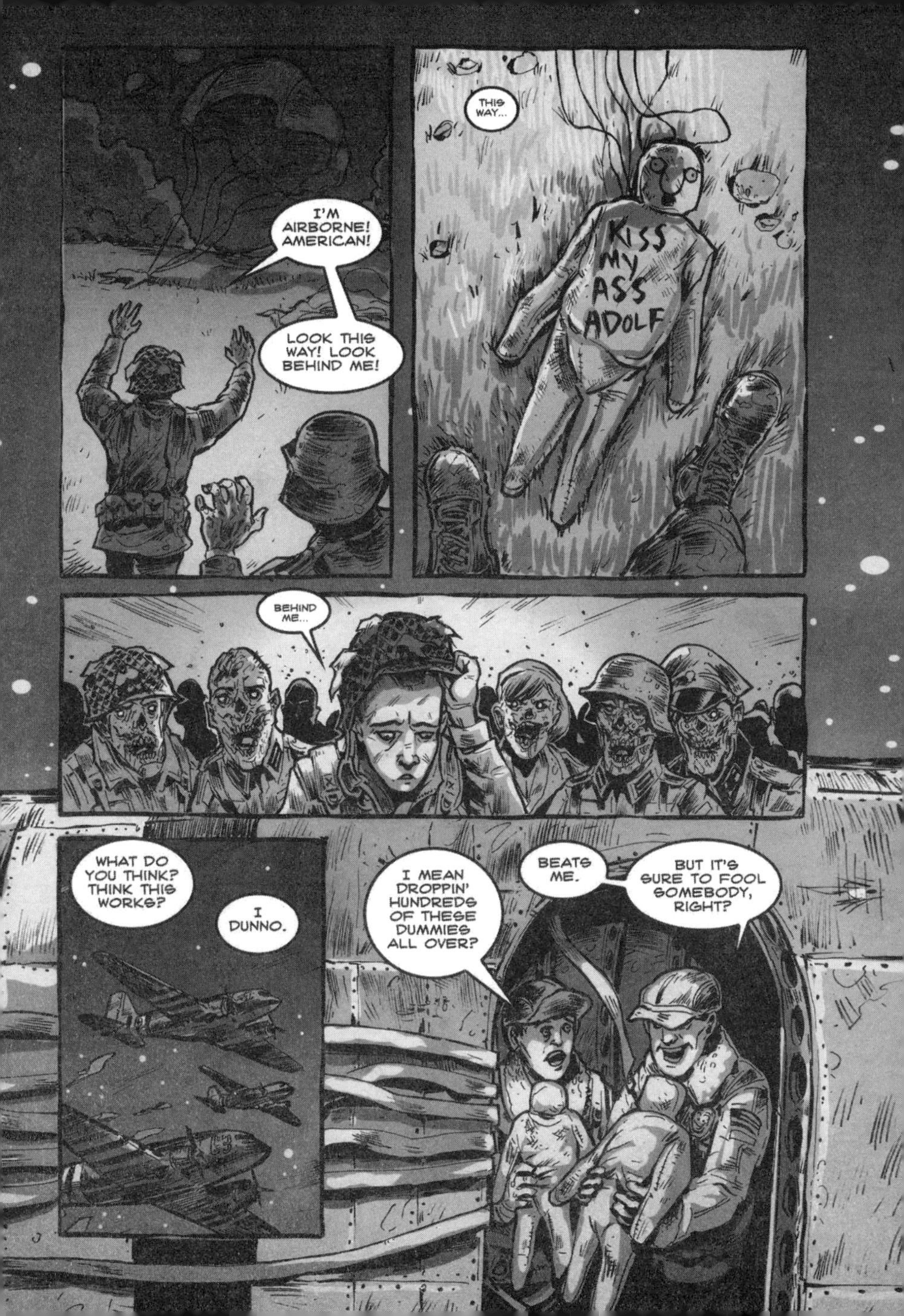
I'M AIRBORNE! AMERICAN!
LOOK THIS WAY! LOOK BEHIND ME!
THIS WAY...
KISS MY ASS ADOLF
BEHIND ME...
WHAT DO YOU THINK? THINK THIS WORKS?
I DUNNO.
I MEAN DROPPIN' HUNDREDS OF THESE DUMMIES ALL OVER?
BEATS ME.
BUT IT'S SURE TO FOOL SOMEBODY, RIGHT?

TO THE LAST MAN

STORY AND LETTERS BY:
JEFF McCLELLAND

ART BY:
LONNY CHANT

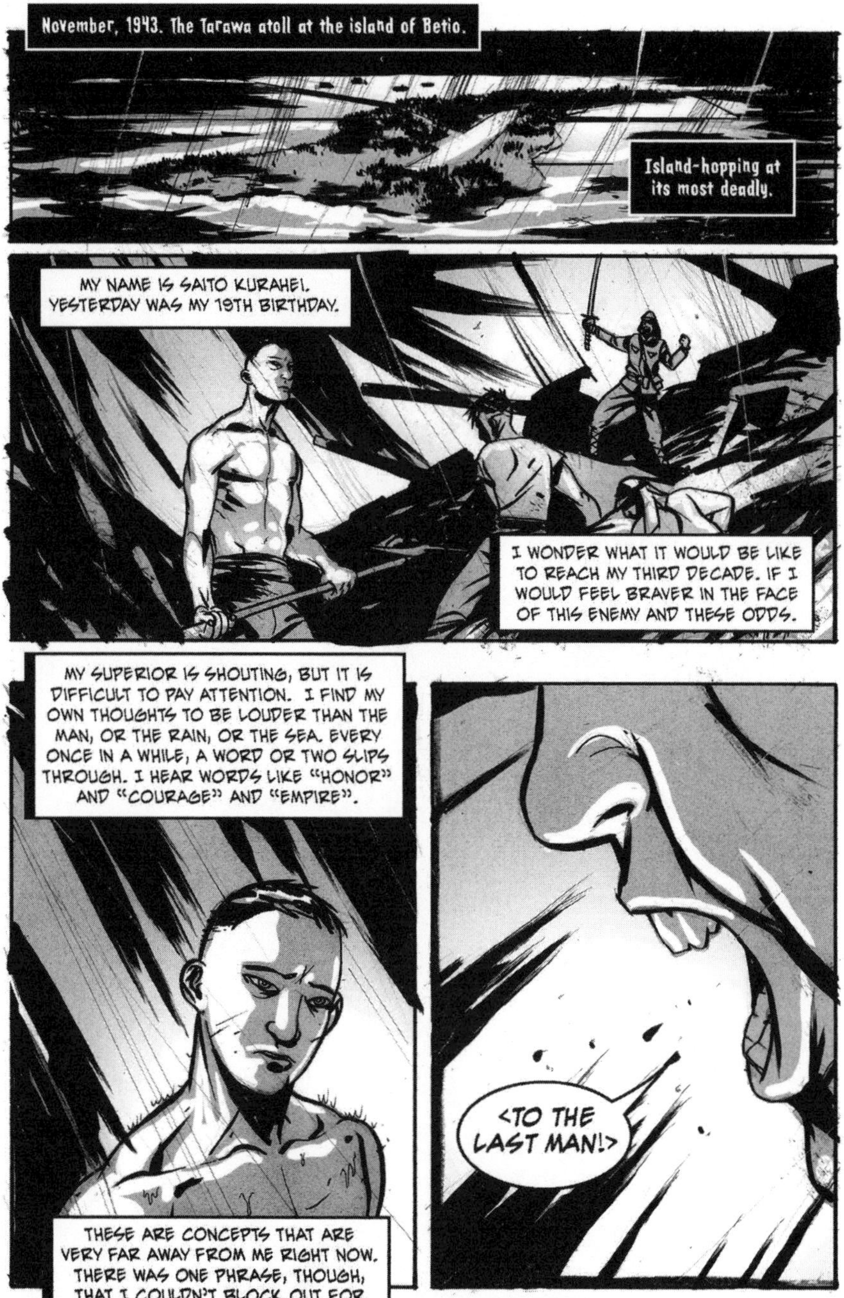
November, 1943. The Tarawa atoll at the island of Betio.
Island-hopping at its most deadly.
MY NAME IS SAITO KURAHEI. YESTERDAY WAS MY 19TH BIRTHDAY.
I WONDER WHAT IT WOULD BE LIKE TO REACH MY THIRD DECADE. IF I WOULD FEEL BRAVER IN THE FACE OF THIS ENEMY AND THESE ODDS.
MY SUPERIOR IS SHOUTING, BUT IT IS DIFFICULT TO PAY ATTENTION. I FIND MY OWN THOUGHTS TO BE LOUDER THAN THE MAN, OR THE RAIN, OR THE SEA. EVERY ONCE IN A WHILE, A WORD OR TWO SLIPS THROUGH. I HEAR WORDS LIKE "HONOR" AND "COURAGE" AND "EMPIRE".
THESE ARE CONCEPTS THAT ARE VERY FAR AWAY FROM ME RIGHT NOW. THERE WAS ONE PHRASE, THOUGH, THAT I COULDN'T BLOCK OUT FOR ITS STUNNING CONSEQUENCE.
<TO THE LAST MAN!>

I FIND MYSELF CONTEMPLATING THOSE WORDS OVER THE NEXT DAYS. WHAT IT WOULD MEAN TO FIGHT "TO THE LAST MAN." IF WHAT WE ARE TOLD IS TRUE, OUR SKILLS AND OUR CAUSE ARE VASTLY SUPERIOR TO THOSE OF THE ENEMY, BUT THE NUMBERS ARE, SIMPLY, NOT ON OUR SIDE.

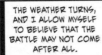

THE WEATHER TURNS, AND I ALLOW MYSELF TO BELIEVE THAT THE BATTLE MAY NOT COME AFTER ALL.

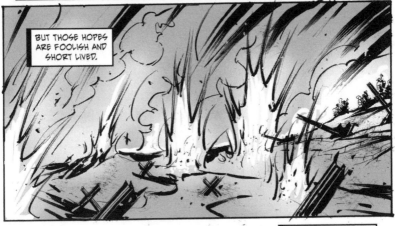

BUT THOSE HOPES ARE FOOLISH AND SHORT LIVED.

AND THE ENEMY IS AS *RELENTLESS* AS IT IS *SUBSTANTIAL*.

I WATCH AS, ONE BY ONE, MY FRIENDS ARE KILLED, THEIR BLOOD COVERING ME AS IF REACHING OUT, DESPERATELY, FOR SAFETY IN ANOTHER.

"TO THE LAST MAN", I THINK.

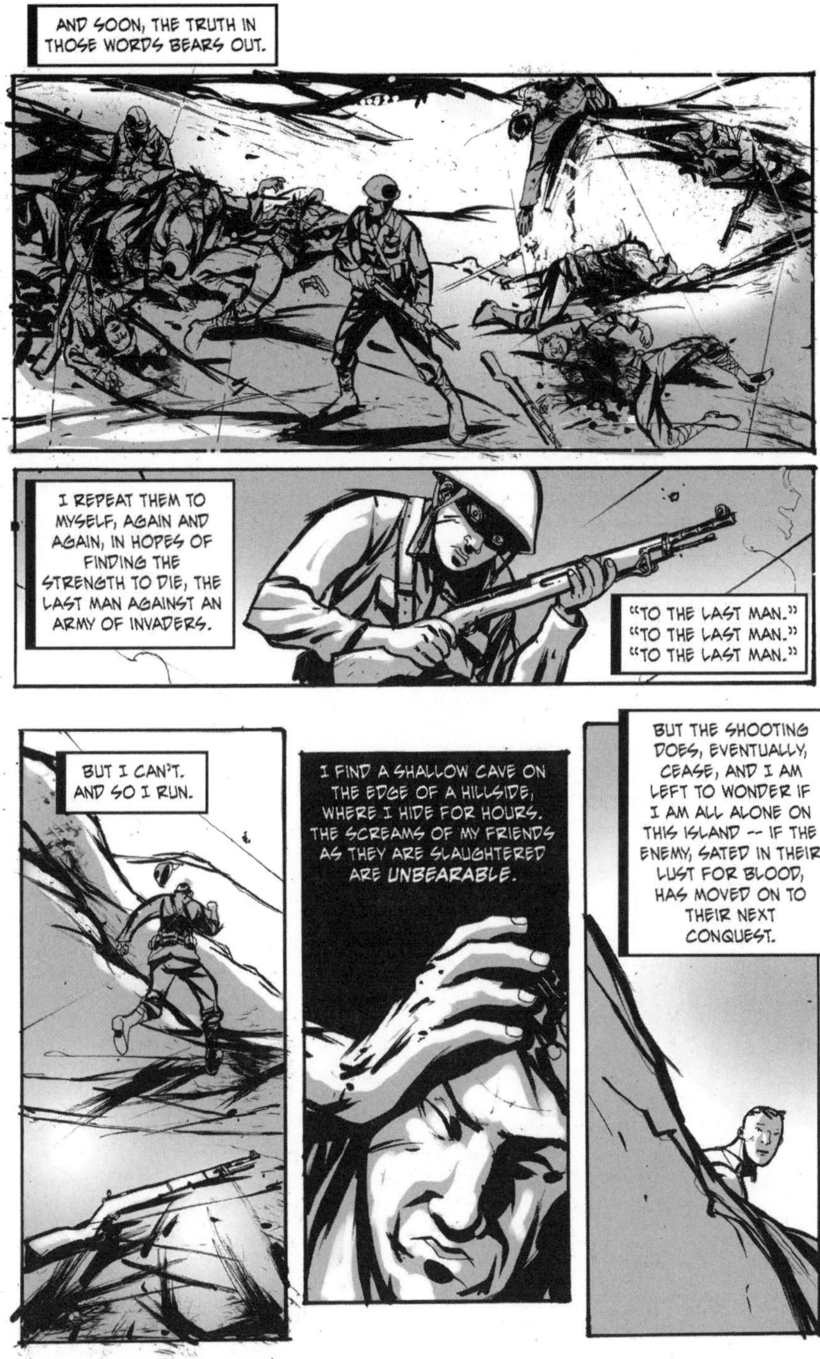
AND SOON, THE TRUTH IN THOSE WORDS BEARS OUT.
I REPEAT THEM TO MYSELF, AGAIN AND AGAIN, IN HOPES OF FINDING THE STRENGTH TO DIE, THE LAST MAN AGAINST AN ARMY OF INVADERS.
"TO THE LAST MAN."
"TO THE LAST MAN."
"TO THE LAST MAN."
BUT I CAN'T. AND SO I RUN.
I FIND A SHALLOW CAVE ON THE EDGE OF A HILLSIDE, WHERE I HIDE FOR HOURS. THE SCREAMS OF MY FRIENDS AS THEY ARE SLAUGHTERED ARE *UNBEARABLE*.
BUT THE SHOOTING DOES, EVENTUALLY, CEASE, AND I AM LEFT TO WONDER IF I AM ALL ALONE ON THIS ISLAND -- IF THE ENEMY, SATED IN THEIR LUST FOR BLOOD, HAS MOVED ON TO THEIR NEXT CONQUEST.

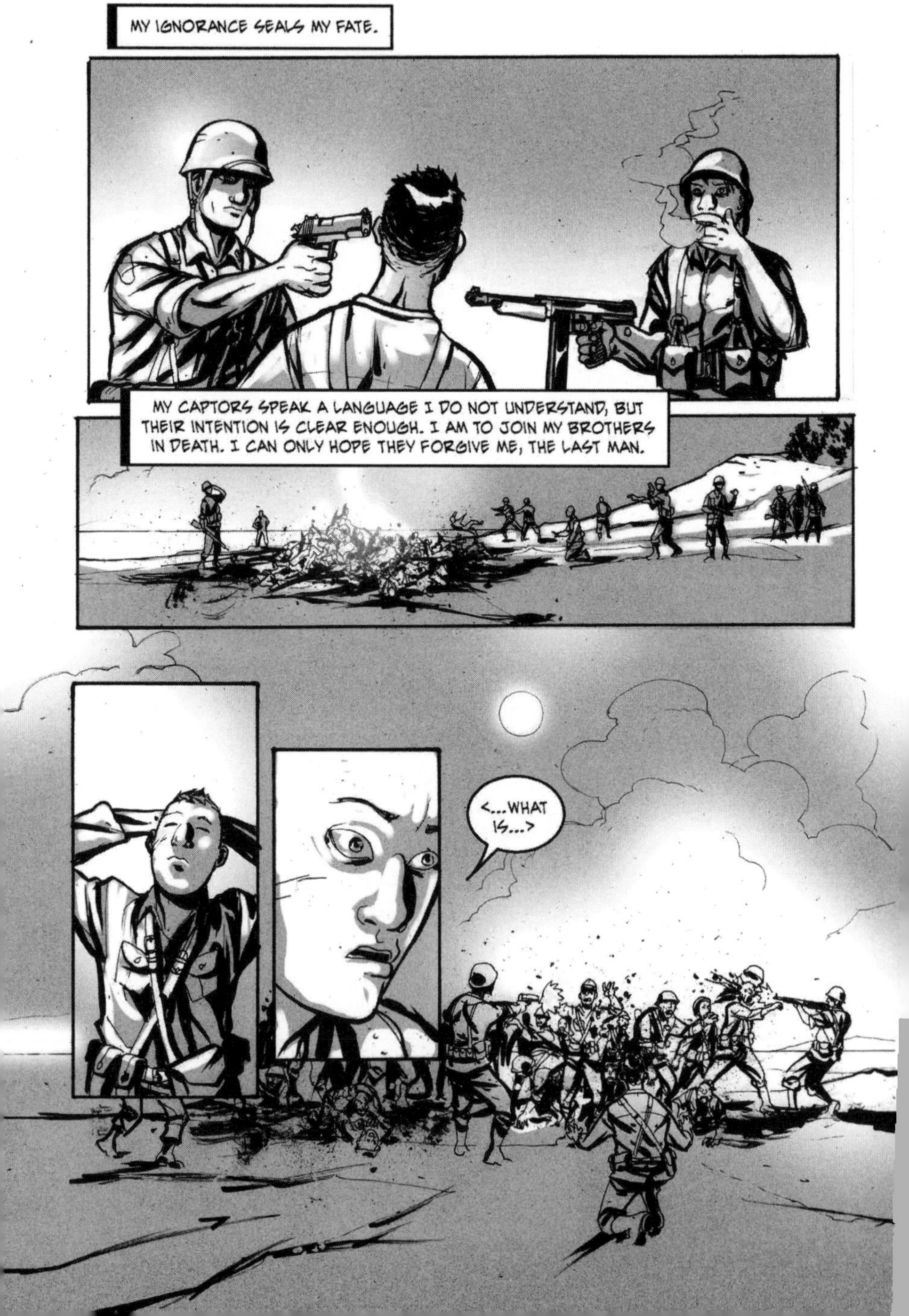
MY IGNORANCE SEALS MY FATE.
MY CAPTORS SPEAK A LANGUAGE I DO NOT UNDERSTAND, BUT THEIR INTENTION IS CLEAR ENOUGH. I AM TO JOIN MY BROTHERS IN DEATH. I CAN ONLY HOPE THEY FORGIVE ME, THE LAST MAN.
<...WHAT IS...>

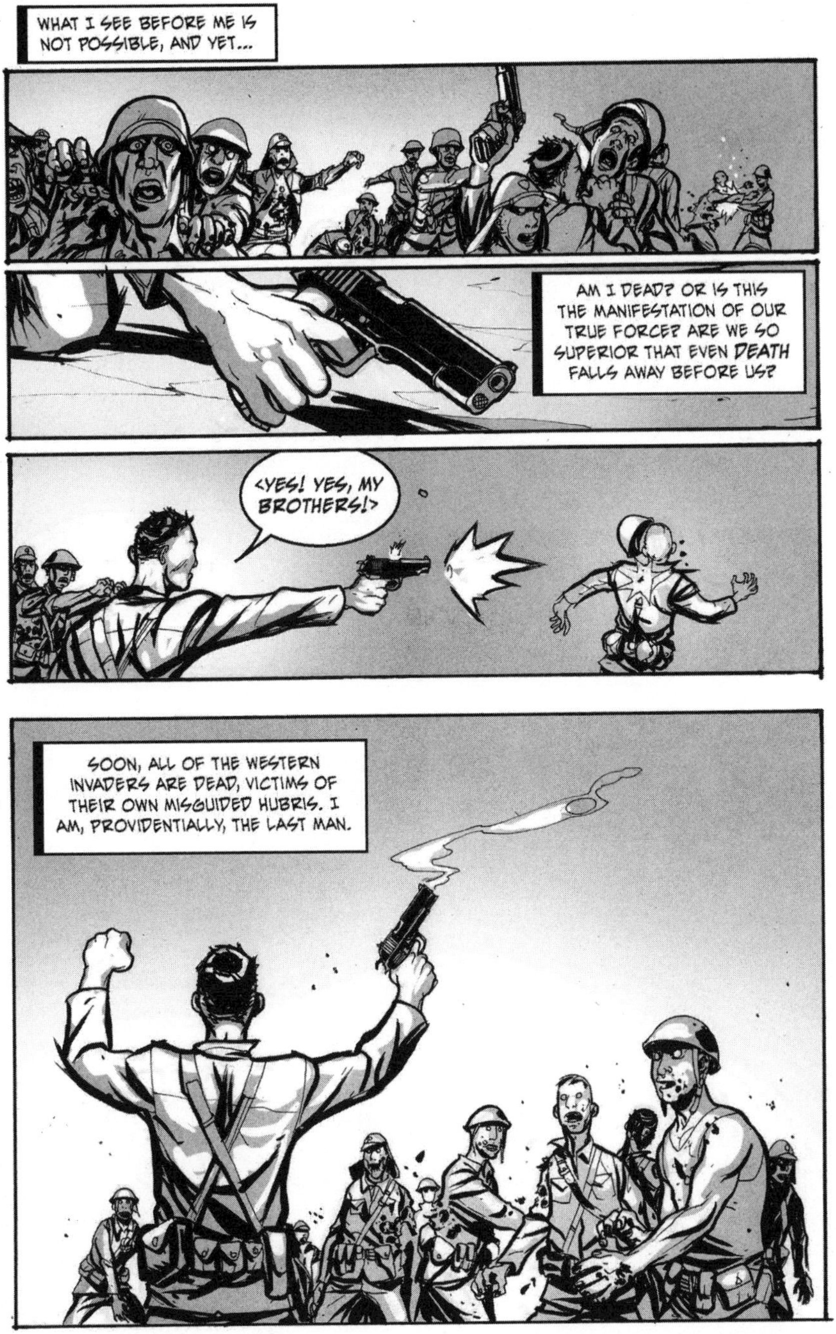
WHAT I SEE BEFORE ME IS NOT POSSIBLE, AND YET...
AM I DEAD? OR IS THIS THE MANIFESTATION OF OUR TRUE FORCE? ARE WE SO SUPERIOR THAT EVEN DEATH FALLS AWAY BEFORE US?
<YES! YES, MY BROTHERS!>
SOON, ALL OF THE WESTERN INVADERS ARE DEAD, VICTIMS OF THEIR OWN MISGUIDED HUBRIS. I AM, PROVIDENTIALLY, THE LAST MAN.

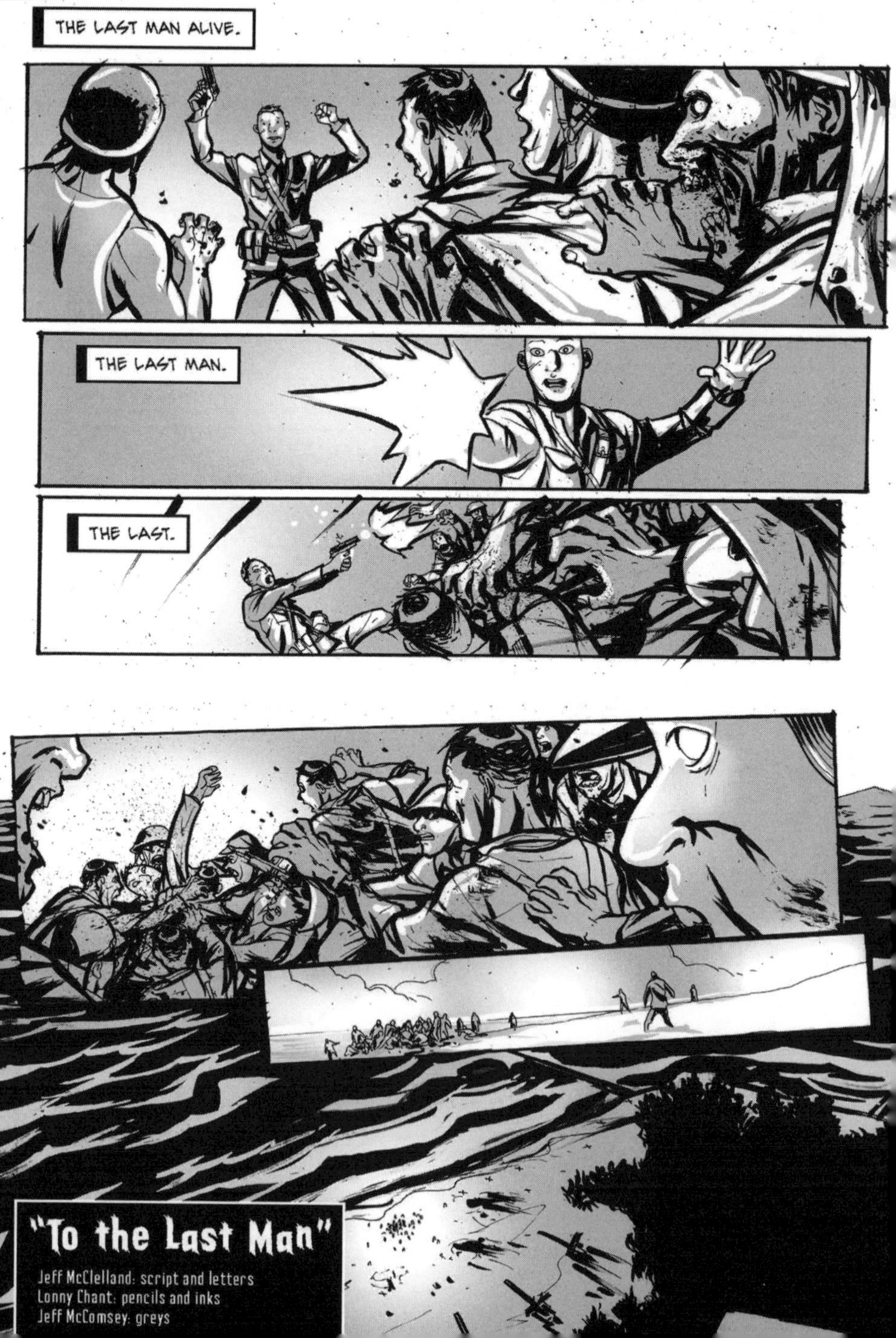

THE LAST MAN ALIVE.
THE LAST MAN.
THE LAST.
"To the Last Man"
Jeff McClelland: script and letters
Lonny Chant: pencils and inks
Jeff McComsey: greys

COLD BLOODED

STORY BY:
JEFF McCOMSEY

ART AND LETTERS BY:
CHARLES FETHEROLF

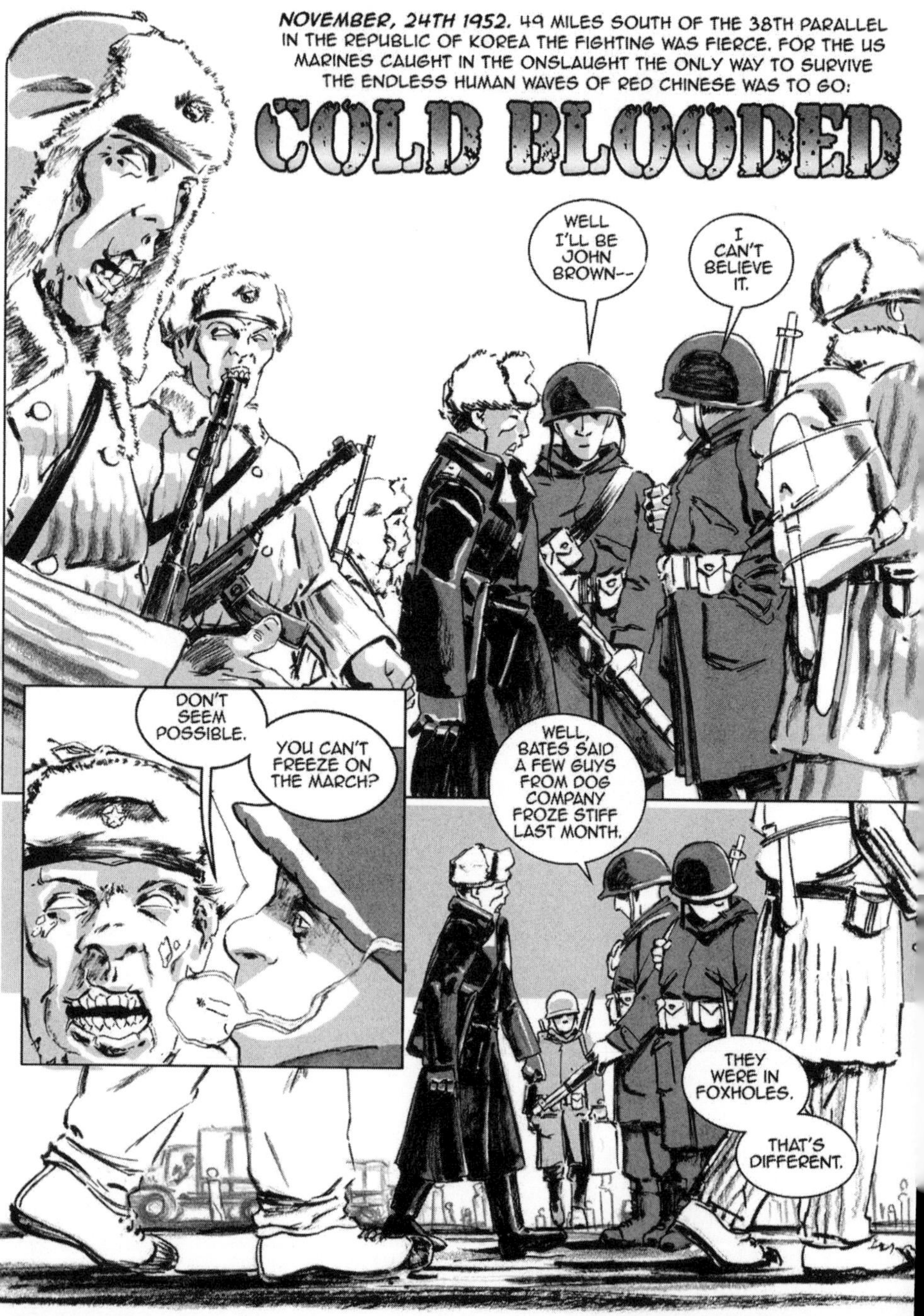
NOVEMBER, 24TH 1952. 49 MILES SOUTH OF THE 38TH PARALLEL IN THE REPUBLIC OF KOREA THE FIGHTING WAS FIERCE. FOR THE US MARINES CAUGHT IN THE ONSLAUGHT THE ONLY WAY TO SURVIVE THE ENDLESS HUMAN WAVES OF RED CHINESE WAS TO GO:
COLD BLOODED
WELL I'LL BE JOHN BROWN--
I CAN'T BELIEVE IT.
DON'T SEEM POSSIBLE.
YOU CAN'T FREEZE ON THE MARCH?
WELL, BATES SAID A FEW GUYS FROM DOG COMPANY FROZE STIFF LAST MONTH.
THEY WERE IN FOXHOLES.
THAT'S DIFFERENT.

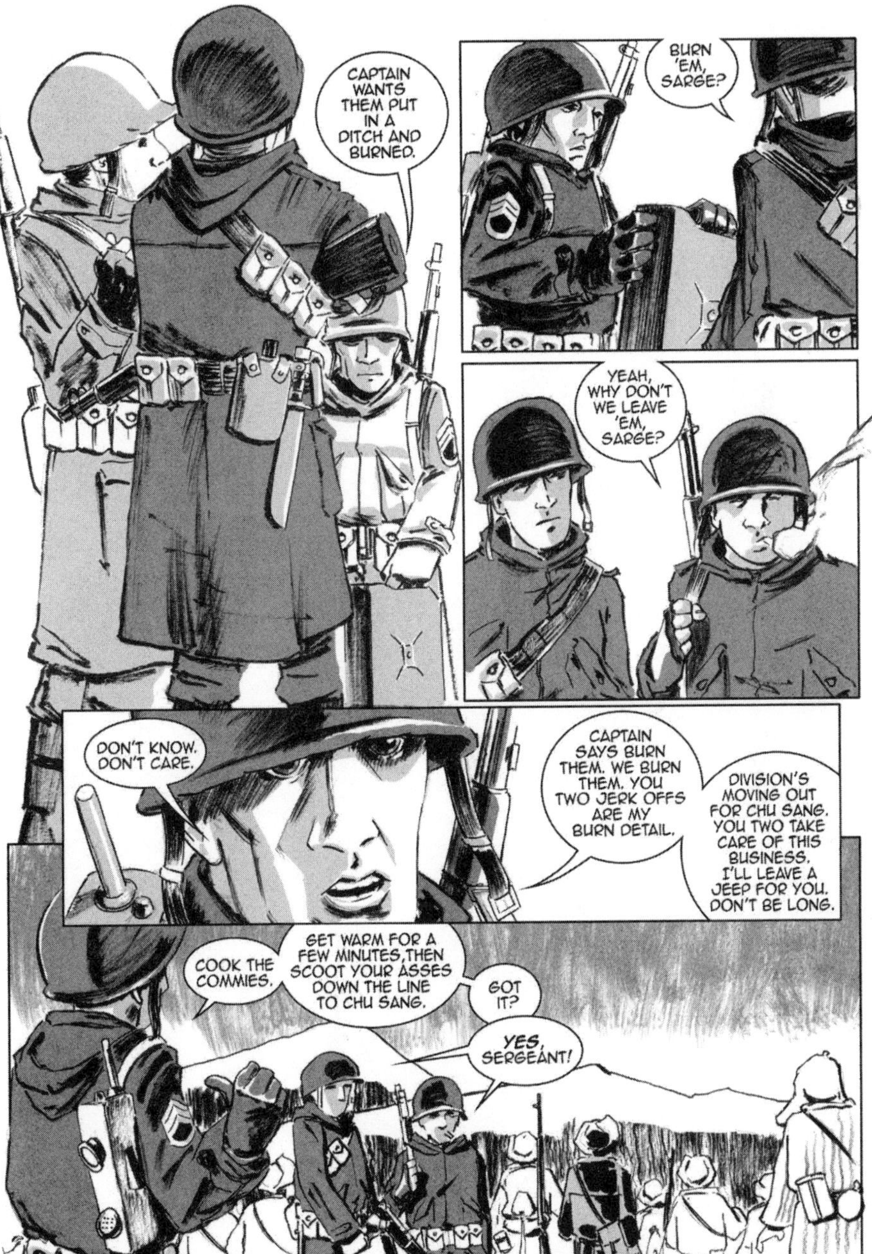
CAPTAIN WANTS THEM PUT IN A DITCH AND BURNED.
BURN 'EM, SARGE?
YEAH, WHY DON'T WE LEAVE 'EM, SARGE?
DON'T KNOW. DON'T CARE.
CAPTAIN SAYS BURN THEM. WE BURN THEM. YOU TWO JERK OFFS ARE MY BURN DETAIL.
DIVISION'S MOVING OUT FOR CHU SANG. YOU TWO TAKE CARE OF THIS BUSINESS. I'LL LEAVE A JEEP FOR YOU. DON'T BE LONG.
COOK THE COMMIES.
GET WARM FOR A FEW MINUTES, THEN SCOOT YOUR ASSES DOWN THE LINE TO CHU SANG.
GOT IT?
YES, SERGEANT!

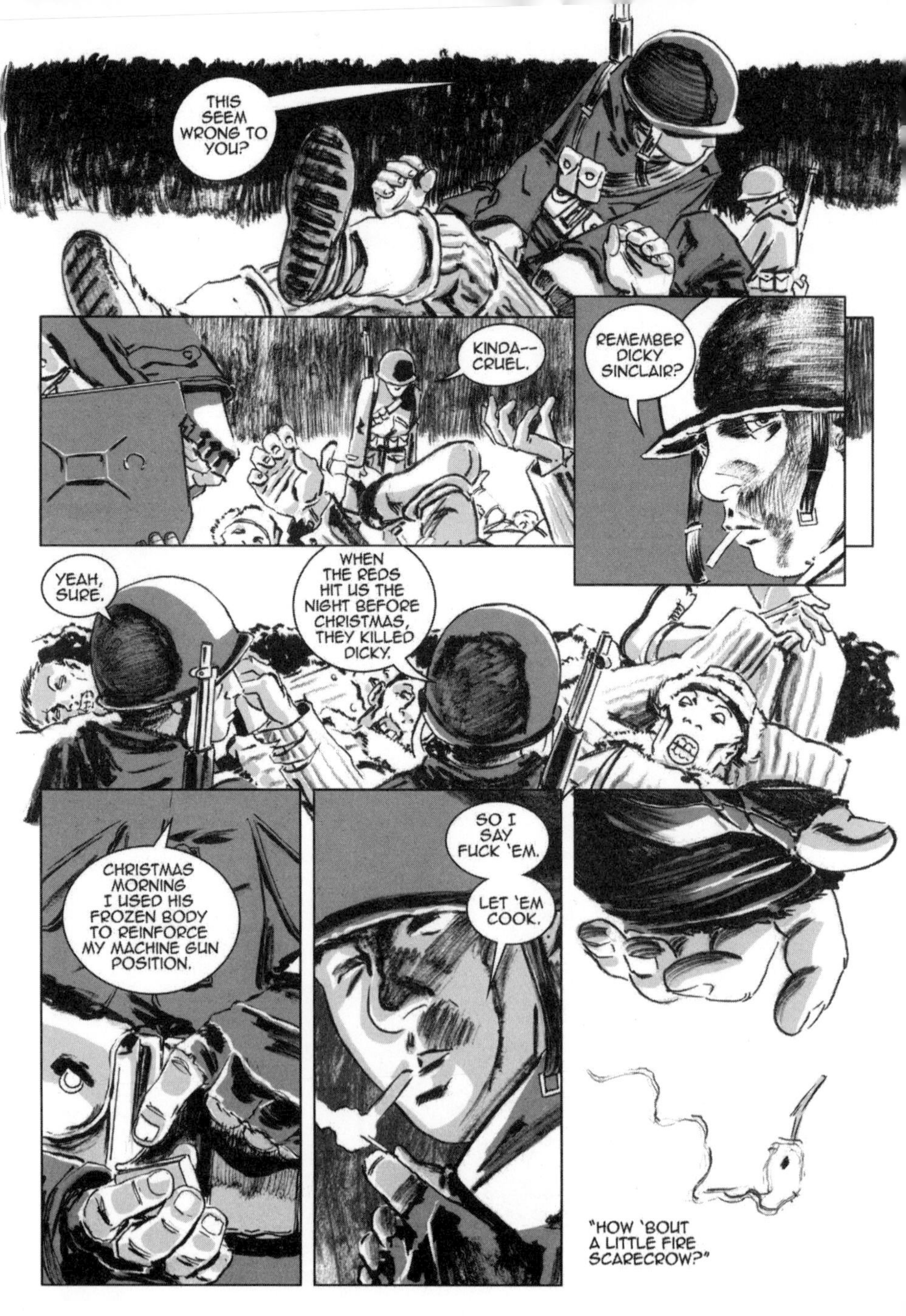
THIS SEEM WRONG TO YOU?
KINDA--CRUEL.
REMEMBER DICKY SINCLAIR?
YEAH, SURE.
WHEN THE REDS HIT US THE NIGHT BEFORE CHRISTMAS, THEY KILLED DICKY.
CHRISTMAS MORNING I USED HIS FROZEN BODY TO REINFORCE MY MACHINE GUN POSITION.
SO I SAY FUCK 'EM.
LET 'EM COOK.
"HOW 'BOUT A LITTLE FIRE SCARECROW?"

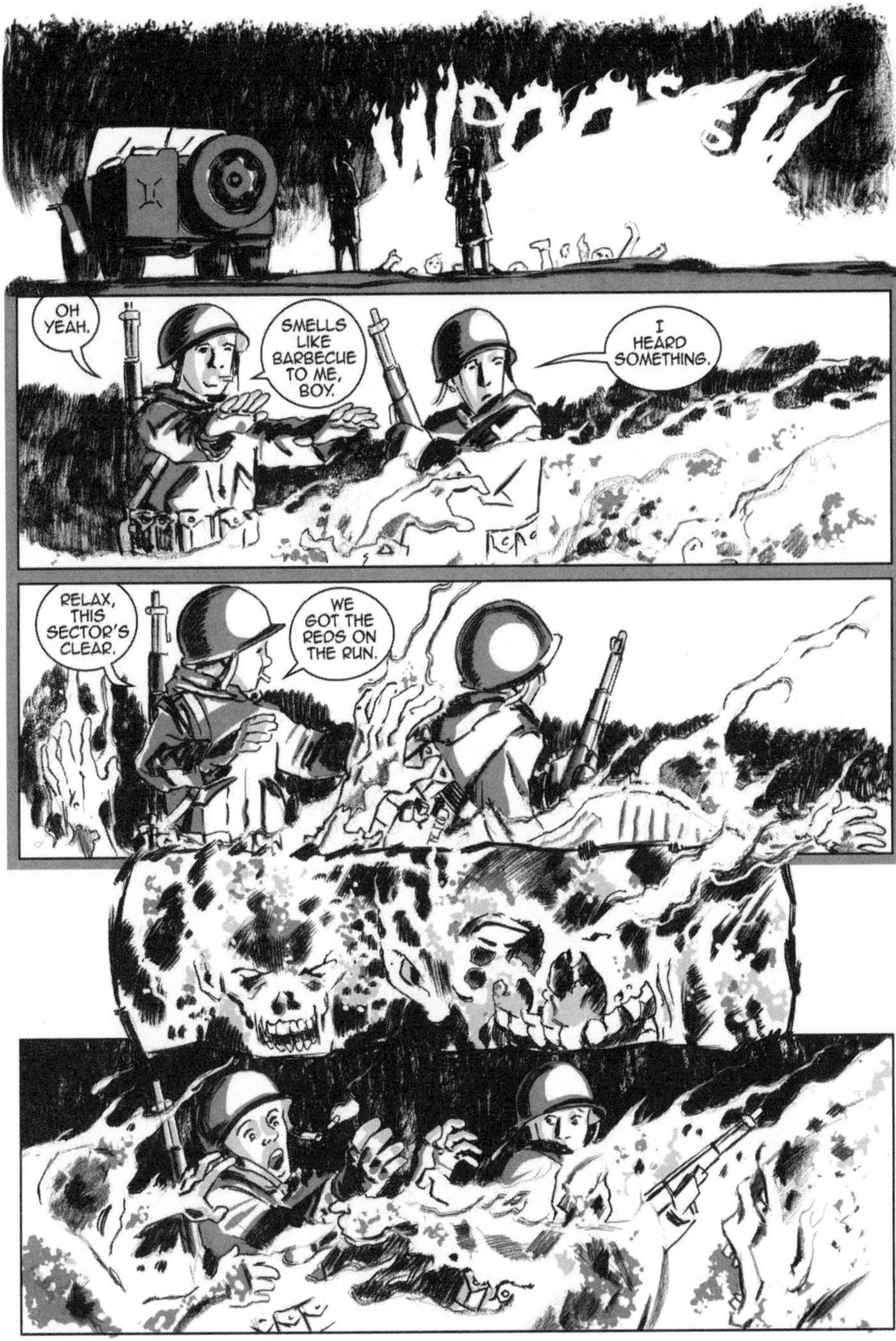
OH YEAH.
SMELLS LIKE BARBECUE TO ME, BOY.
I HEARD SOMETHING.
RELAX, THIS SECTOR'S CLEAR.
WE GOT THE REDS ON THE RUN.

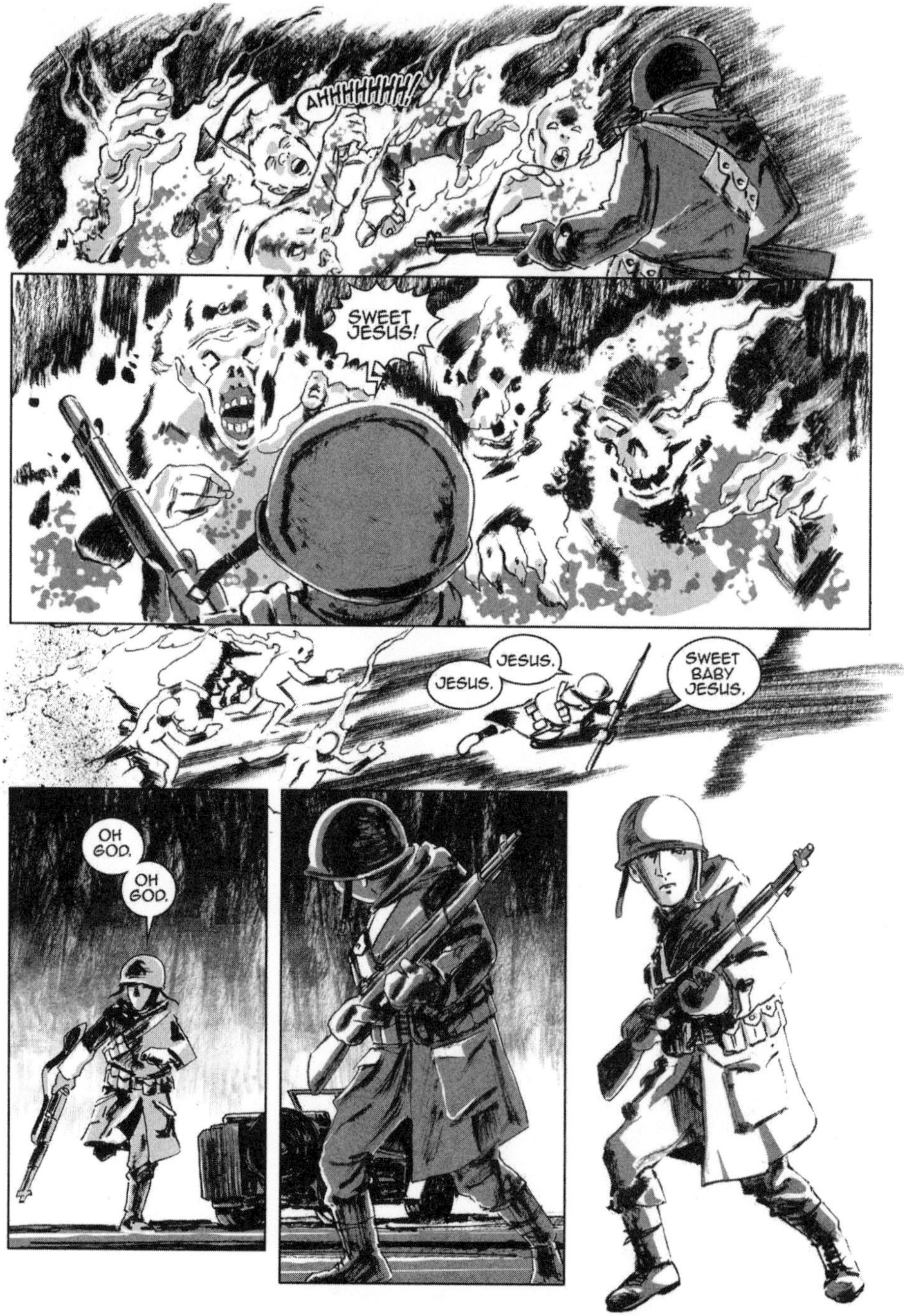
AHHHHHHHH!
SWEET JESUS!
JESUS.
JESUS.
SWEET BABY JESUS.
OH GOD.
OH GOD.

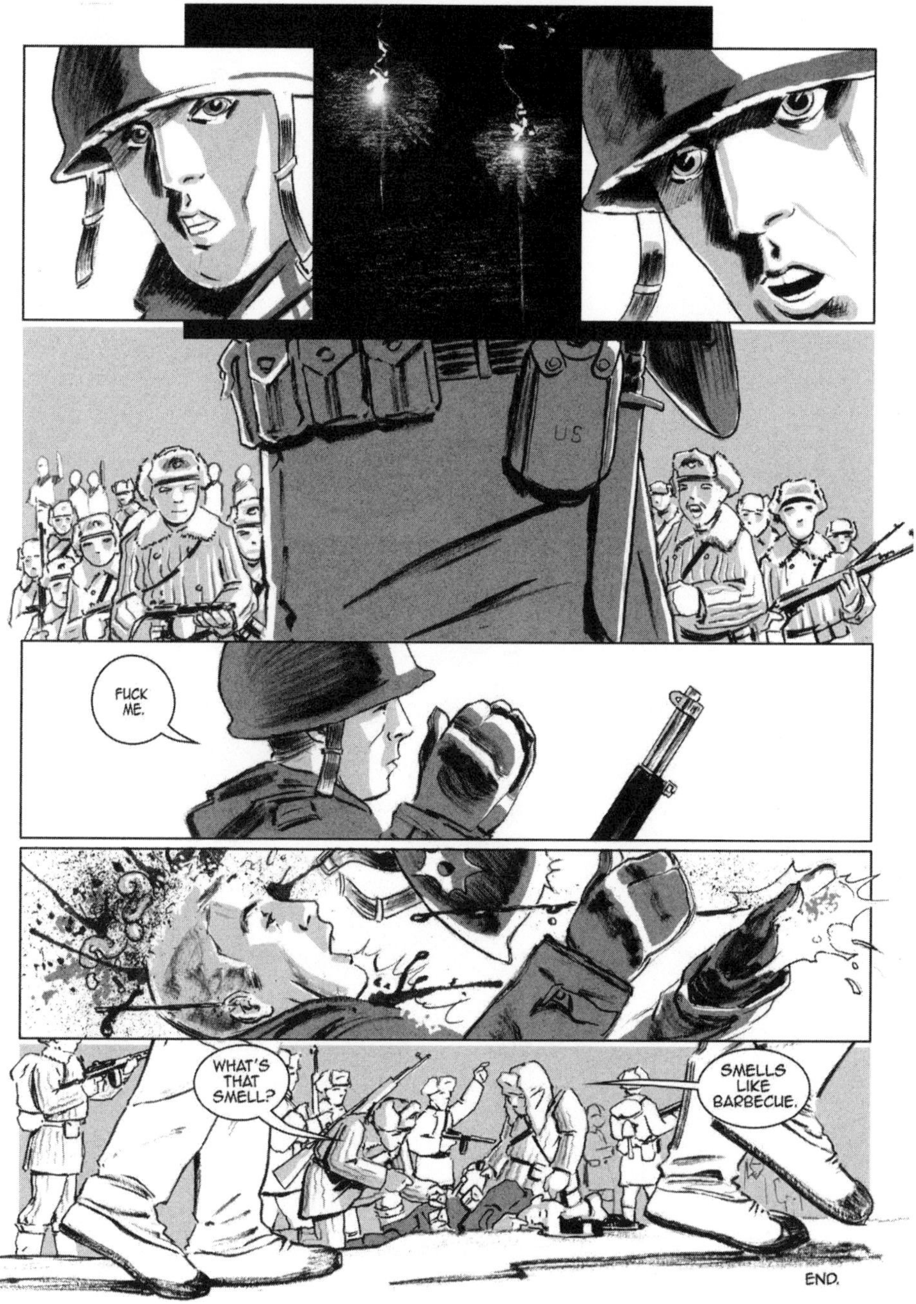
FUCK ME.
WHAT'S THAT SMELL?
SMELLS LIKE BARBECUE.
END.

FOR THE BOYS

STORY BY:
JOEY ESPOSITO

ART BY:
FELIPE CUNHA

LETTERS BY:
JEFF McCOMSEY

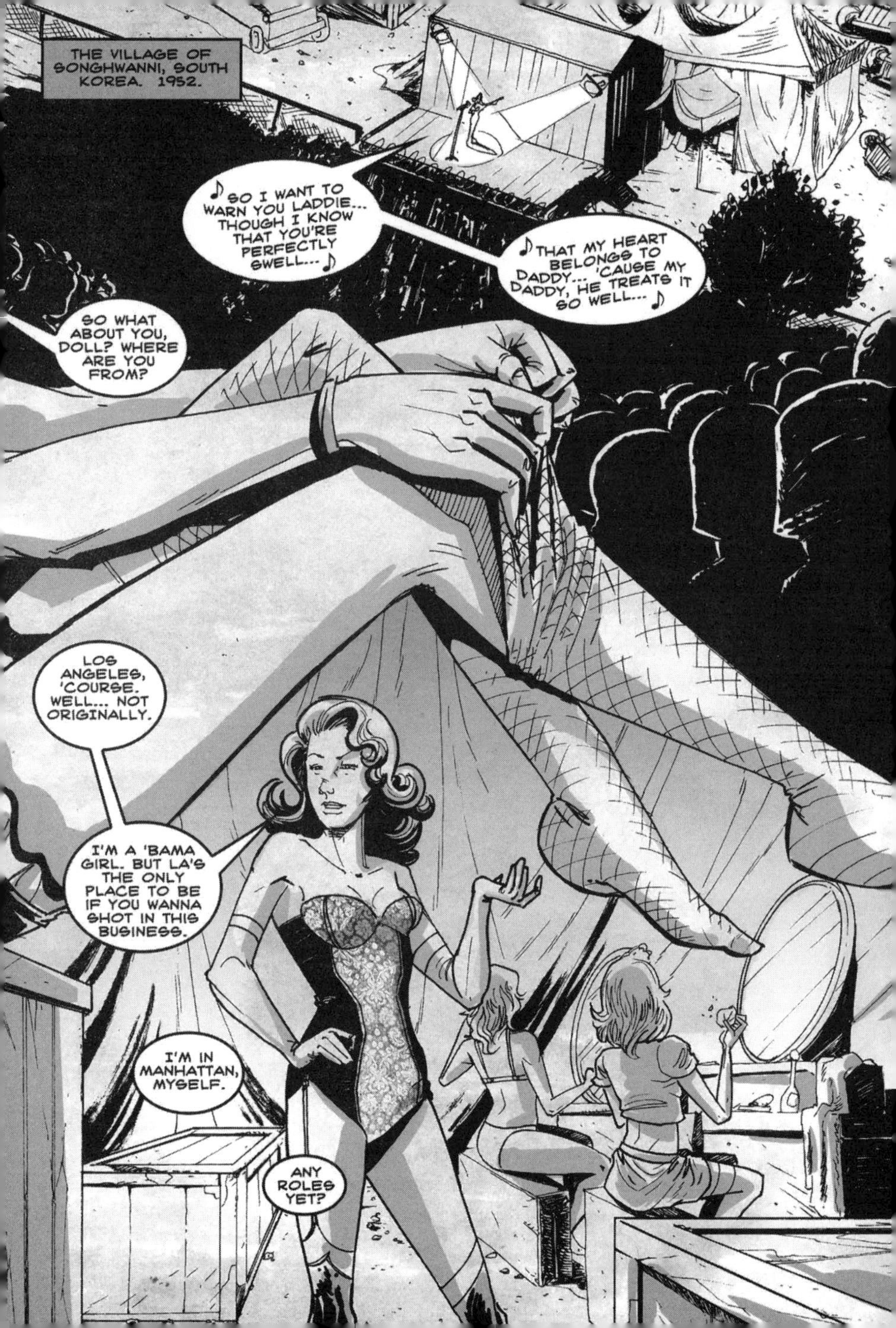
THE VILLAGE OF SONGHWANNI, SOUTH KOREA. 1952.
♪ SO I WANT TO WARN YOU LADDIE... THOUGH I KNOW THAT YOU'RE PERFECTLY SWELL... ♪
♪ THAT MY HEART BELONGS TO DADDY... 'CAUSE MY DADDY, HE TREATS IT SO WELL... ♪
SO WHAT ABOUT YOU, DOLL? WHERE ARE YOU FROM?
LOS ANGELES, 'COURSE. WELL... NOT ORIGINALLY.
I'M A 'BAMA GIRL. BUT LA'S THE ONLY PLACE TO BE IF YOU WANNA SHOT IN THIS BUSINESS.
I'M IN MANHATTAN, MYSELF.
ANY ROLES YET?

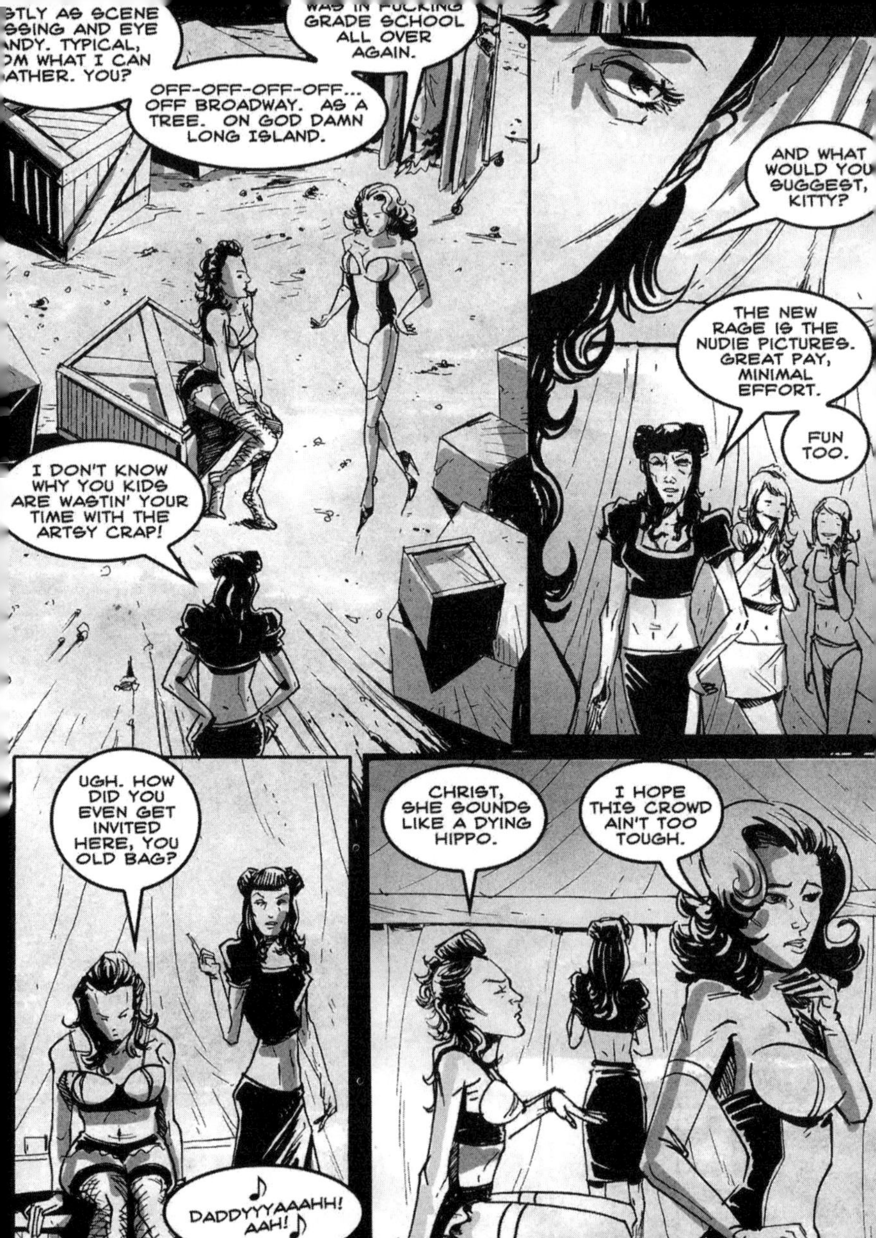
STLY AS SCENE SSING AND EYE ANDY. TYPICAL, OM WHAT I CAN ATHER. YOU?
GRADE SCHOOL ALL OVER AGAIN.
OFF-OFF-OFF-OFF... OFF BROADWAY. AS A TREE. ON GOD DAMN LONG ISLAND.
I DON'T KNOW WHY YOU KIDS ARE WASTIN' YOUR TIME WITH THE ARTSY CRAP!
AND WHAT WOULD YOU SUGGEST, KITTY?
THE NEW RAGE IS THE NUDIE PICTURES. GREAT PAY, MINIMAL EFFORT.
FUN TOO.
UGH. HOW DID YOU EVEN GET INVITED HERE, YOU OLD BAG?
♪ DADDYYYAAAHH! AAH! ♪
CHRIST, SHE SOUNDS LIKE A DYING HIPPO.
I HOPE THIS CROWD AIN'T TOO TOUGH.

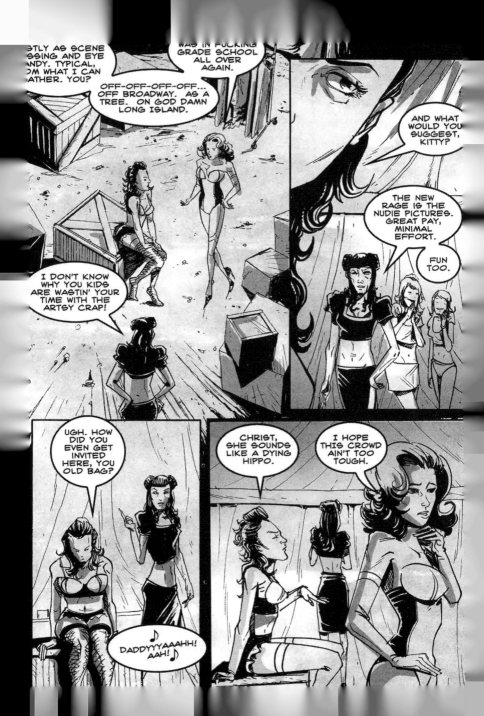

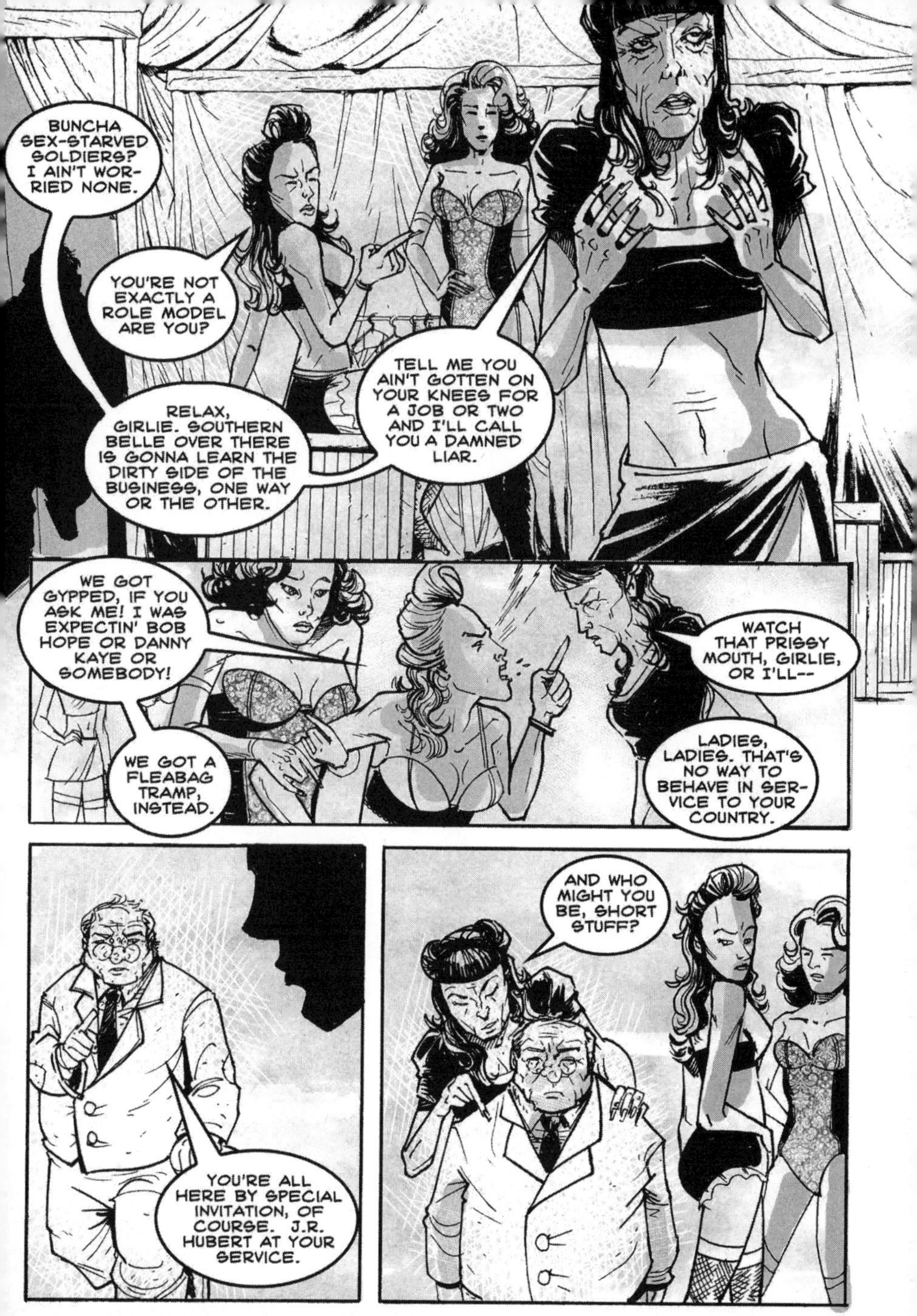
BUNCHA SEX-STARVED SOLDIERS? I AIN'T WOR-RIED NONE.
YOU'RE NOT EXACTLY A ROLE MODEL ARE YOU?
RELAX, GIRLIE. SOUTHERN BELLE OVER THERE IS GONNA LEARN THE DIRTY SIDE OF THE BUSINESS, ONE WAY OR THE OTHER.
TELL ME YOU AIN'T GOTTEN ON YOUR KNEES FOR A JOB OR TWO AND I'LL CALL YOU A DAMNED LIAR.
WE GOT GYPPED, IF YOU ASK ME! I WAS EXPECTIN' BOB HOPE OR DANNY KAYE OR SOMEBODY!
WE GOT A FLEABAG TRAMP, INSTEAD.
WATCH THAT PRISSY MOUTH, GIRLIE, OR I'LL--
LADIES, LADIES. THAT'S NO WAY TO BEHAVE IN SER-VICE TO YOUR COUNTRY.
YOU'RE ALL HERE BY SPECIAL INVITATION, OF COURSE. J.R. HUBERT AT YOUR SERVICE.
AND WHO MIGHT YOU BE, SHORT STUFF?

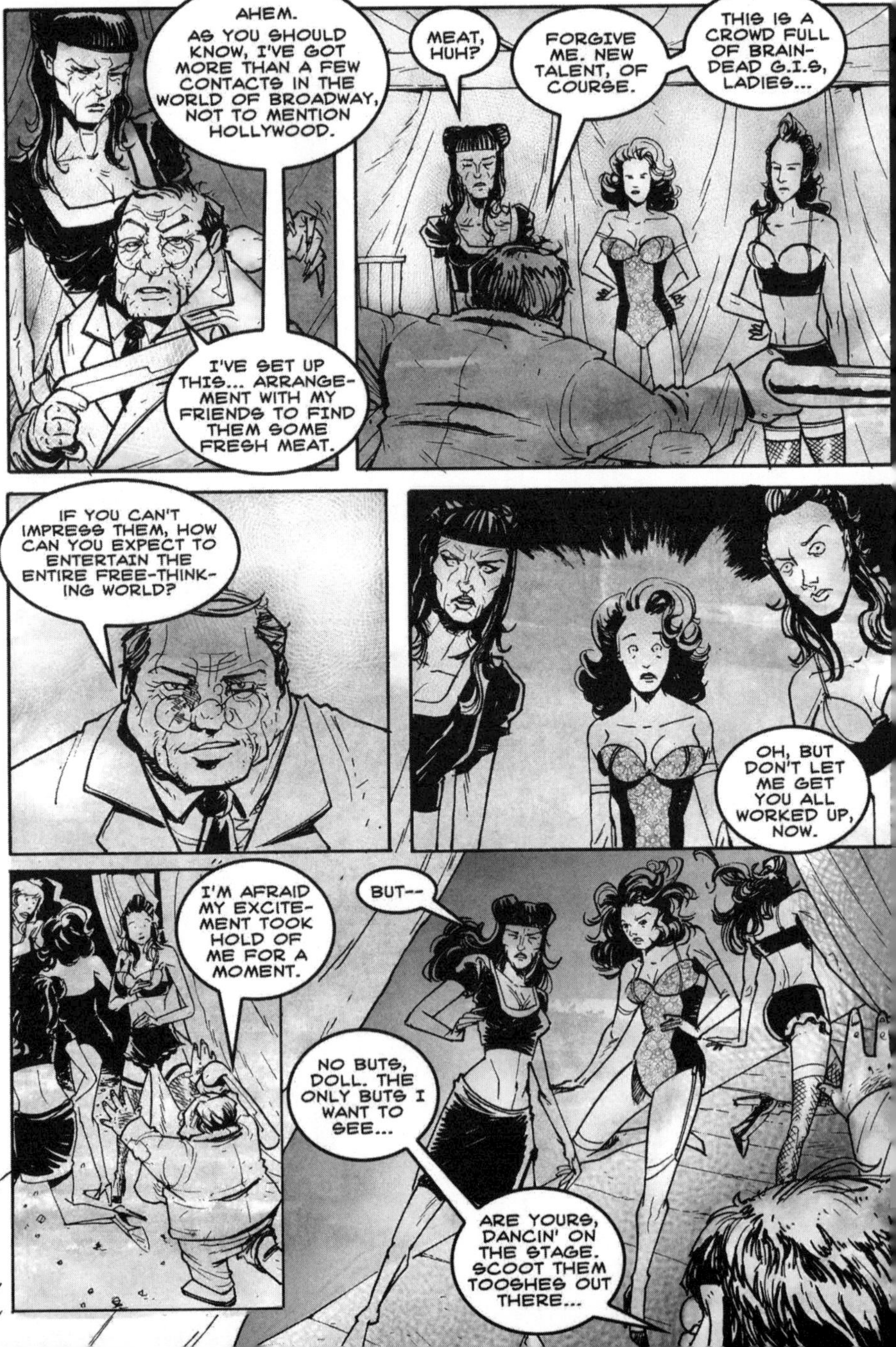
AHEM.
AS YOU SHOULD KNOW, I'VE GOT MORE THAN A FEW CONTACTS IN THE WORLD OF BROADWAY, NOT TO MENTION HOLLYWOOD.
I'VE SET UP THIS... ARRANGE-MENT WITH MY FRIENDS TO FIND THEM SOME FRESH MEAT.
MEAT, HUH?
FORGIVE ME. NEW TALENT, OF COURSE.
THIS IS A CROWD FULL OF BRAIN-DEAD G.I.S, LADIES...
IF YOU CAN'T IMPRESS THEM, HOW CAN YOU EXPECT TO ENTERTAIN THE ENTIRE FREE-THINK-ING WORLD?
OH, BUT DON'T LET ME GET YOU ALL WORKED UP, NOW.
I'M AFRAID MY EXCITE-MENT TOOK HOLD OF ME FOR A MOMENT.
BUT--
NO BUTS, DOLL. THE ONLY BUTS I WANT TO SEE...
ARE YOURS, DANCIN' ON THE STAGE. SCOOT THEM TOOSHES OUT THERE...

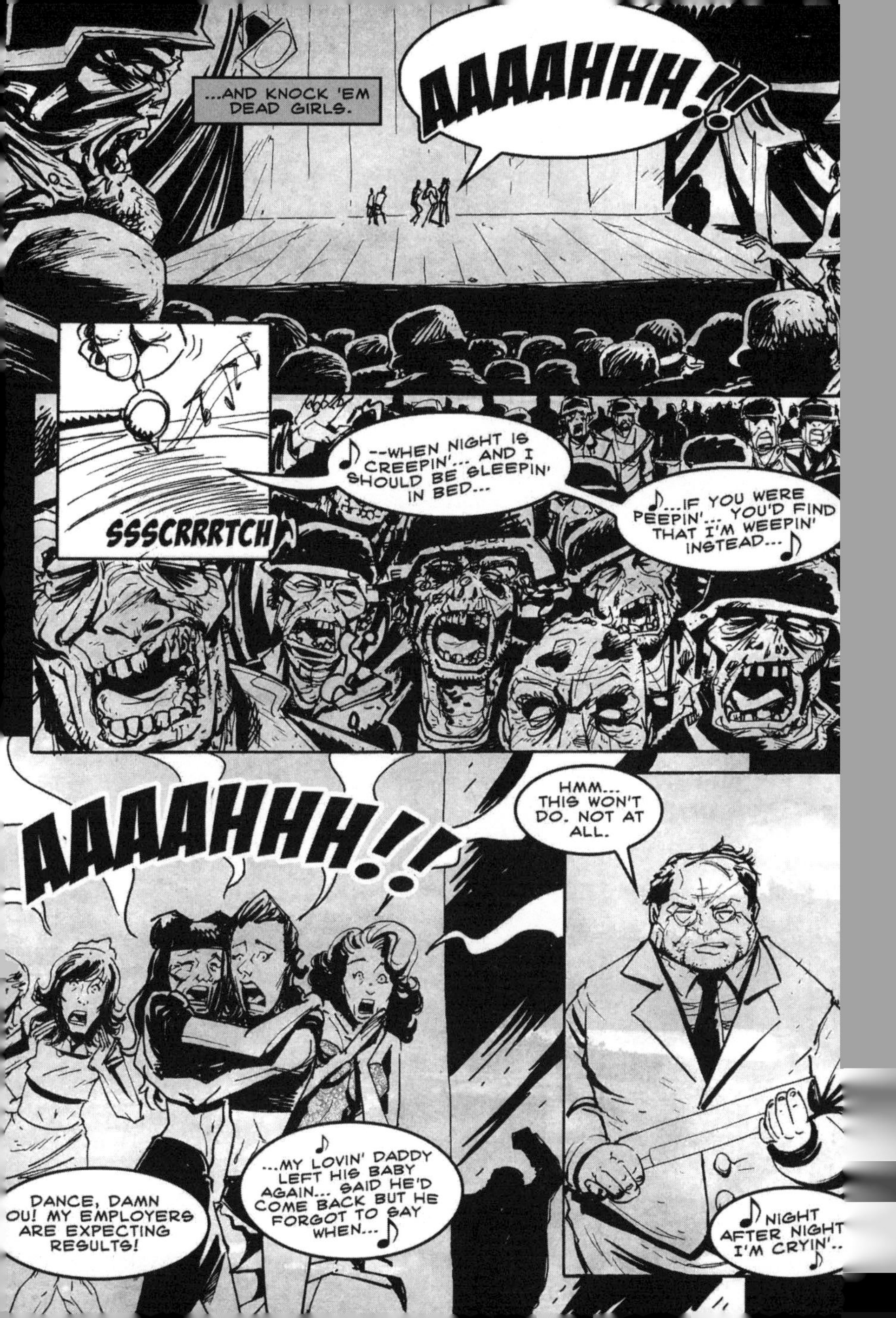
...AND KNOCK 'EM DEAD GIRLS.
AAAAHHH!!
--WHEN NIGHT IS CREEPIN'... AND I SHOULD BE SLEEPIN' IN BED...
SSSCRRRTCH
...IF YOU WERE PEEPIN'... YOU'D FIND THAT I'M WEEPIN' INSTEAD...
AAAAHHH!!
HMM... THIS WON'T DO. NOT AT ALL.
DANCE, DAMN OU! MY EMPLOYERS ARE EXPECTING RESULTS!
...MY LOVIN' DADDY LEFT HIS BABY AGAIN... SAID HE'D COME BACK BUT HE FORGOT TO SAY WHEN...
NIGHT AFTER NIGHT I'M CRYIN'...

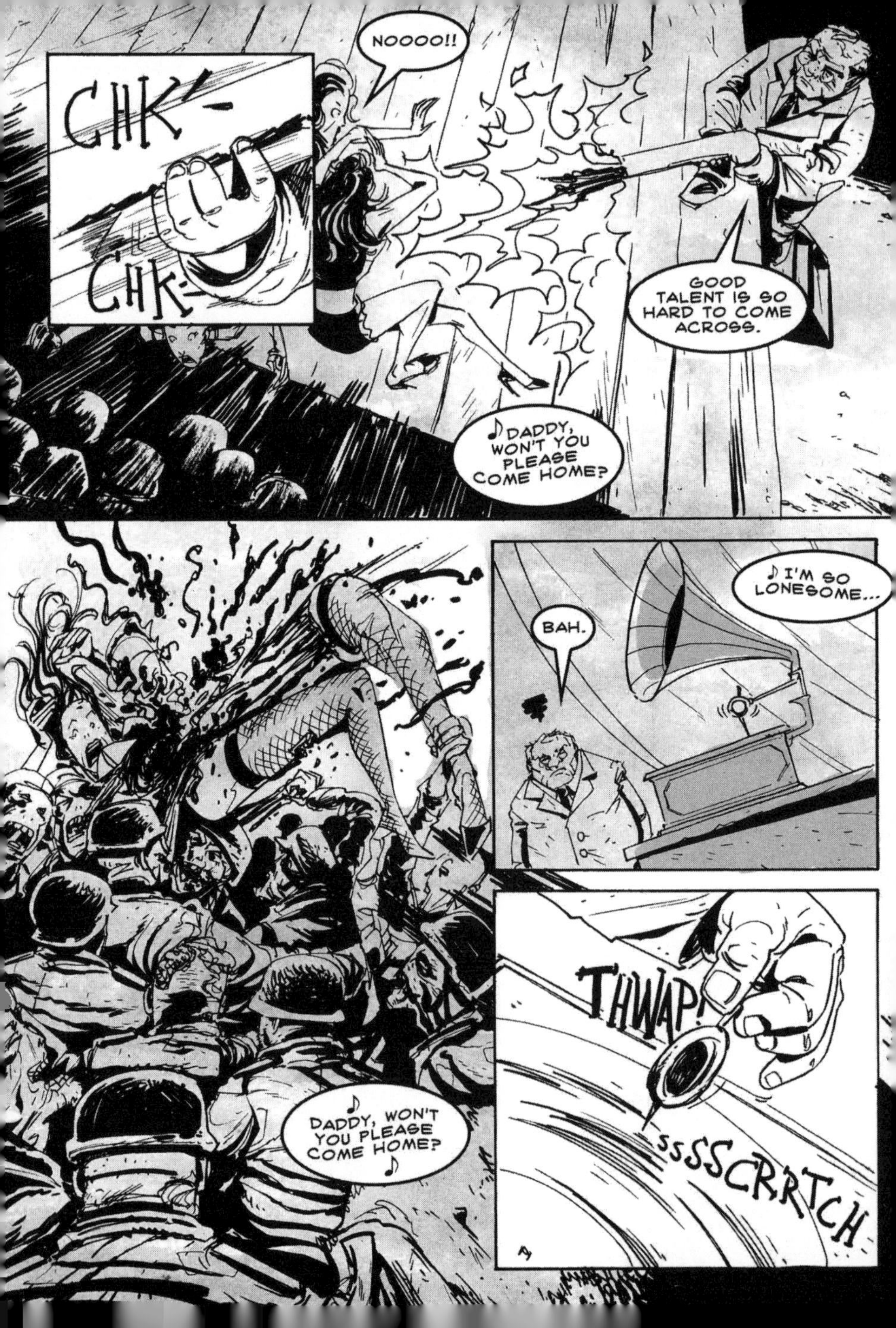

CHK'-
CHK-
NOOOO!!
GOOD TALENT IS SO HARD TO COME ACROSS.
♪ DADDY, WON'T YOU PLEASE COME HOME?
♪ I'M SO LONESOME...
BAH.
DADDY, WON'T YOU PLEASE COME HOME? ♪
THWAP!
SSSSCRRTCH

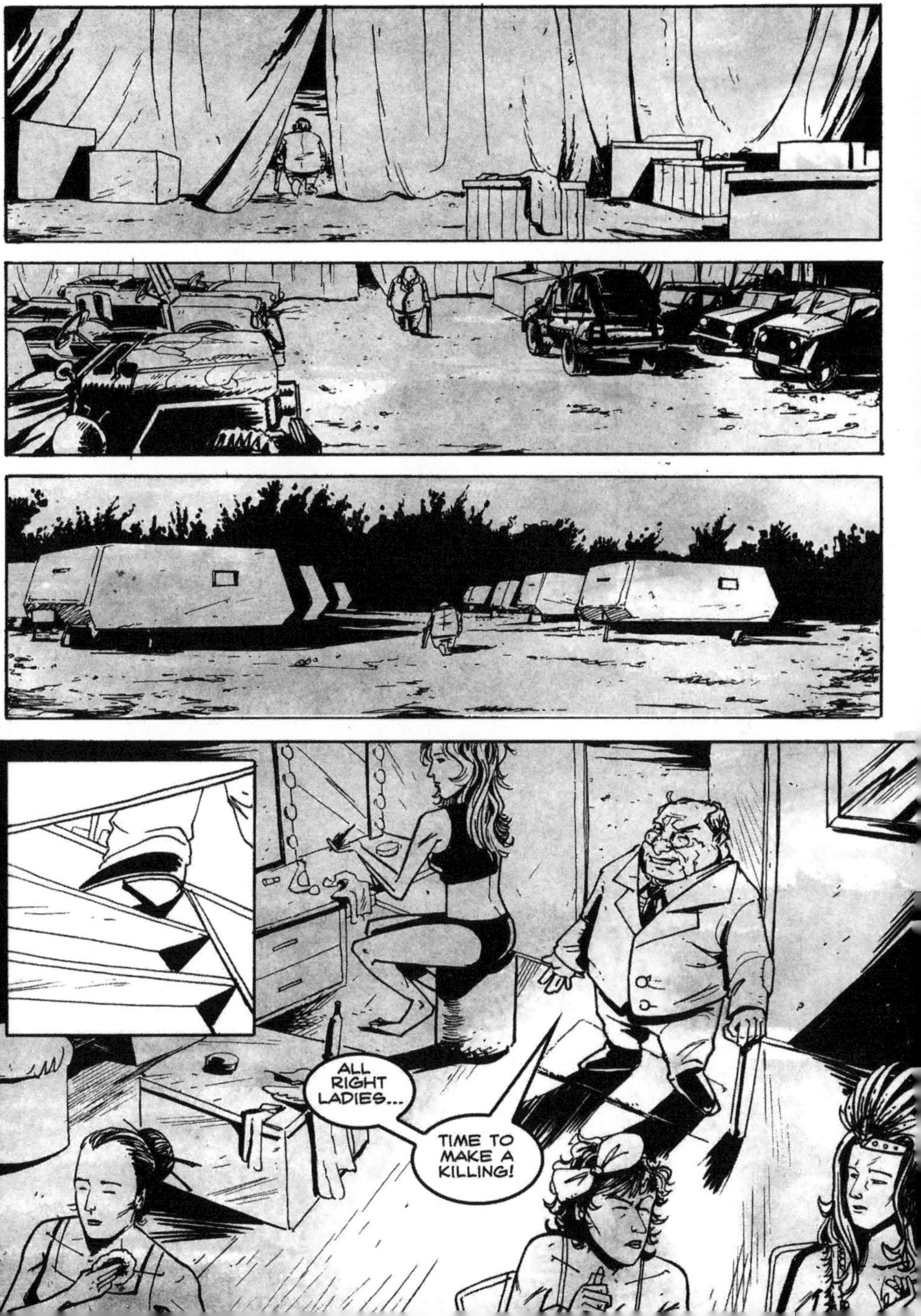
ALL RIGHT LADIES...
TIME TO MAKE A KILLING!

COMPROMISED

STORY BY:
PHIL CHAN

ART AND LETTERS BY:
JOE DUNN

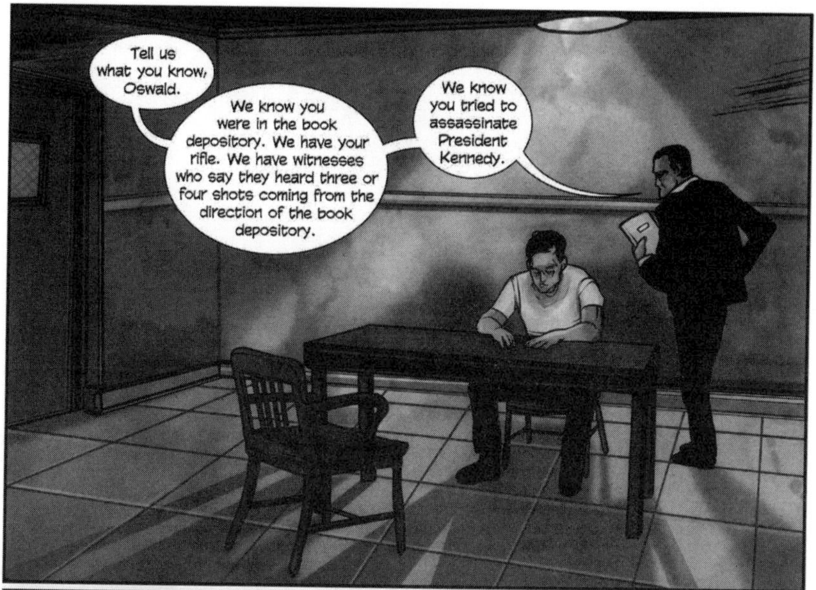
Tell us what you know, Oswald.
We know you were in the book depository. We have your rifle. We have witnesses who say they heard three or four shots coming from the direction of the book depository.
We know you tried to assassinate President Kennedy.

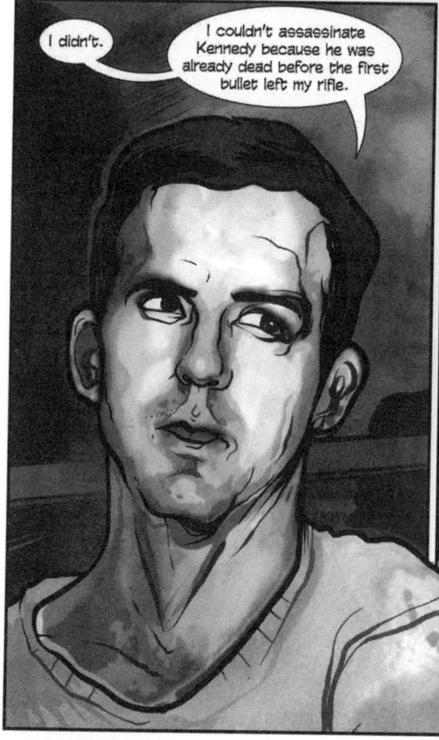
I didn't.
I couldn't assassinate Kennedy because he was already dead before the first bullet left my rifle.

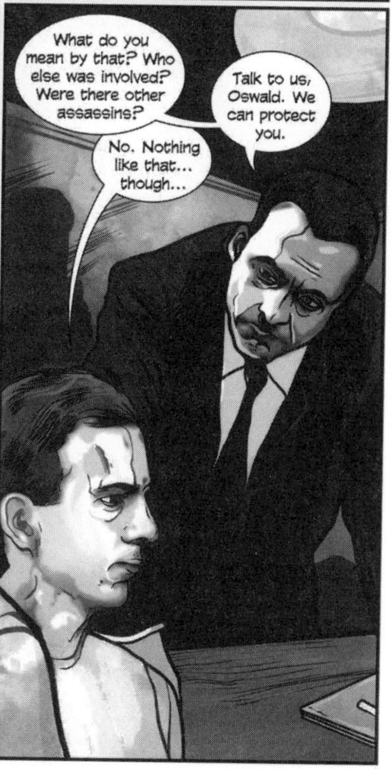
What do you mean by that? Who else was involved? Were there other assassins?
Talk to us, Oswald. We can protect you.
No. Nothing like that... though...

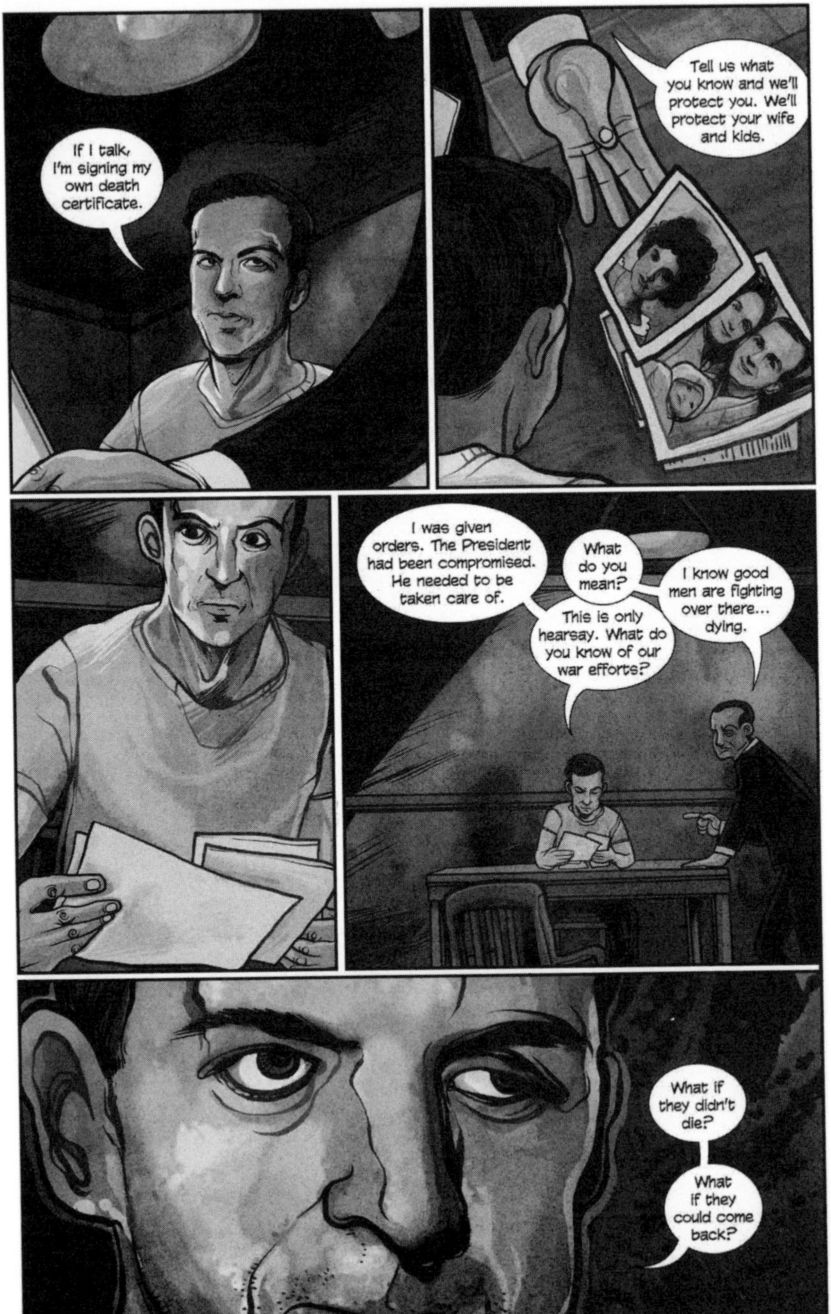
If I talk, I'm signing my own death certificate.
Tell us what you know and we'll protect you. We'll protect your wife and kids.
I was given orders. The President had been compromised. He needed to be taken care of.
What do you mean?
This is only hearsay. What do you know of our war efforts?
I know good men are fighting over there... dying.
What if they didn't die?
What if they could come back?

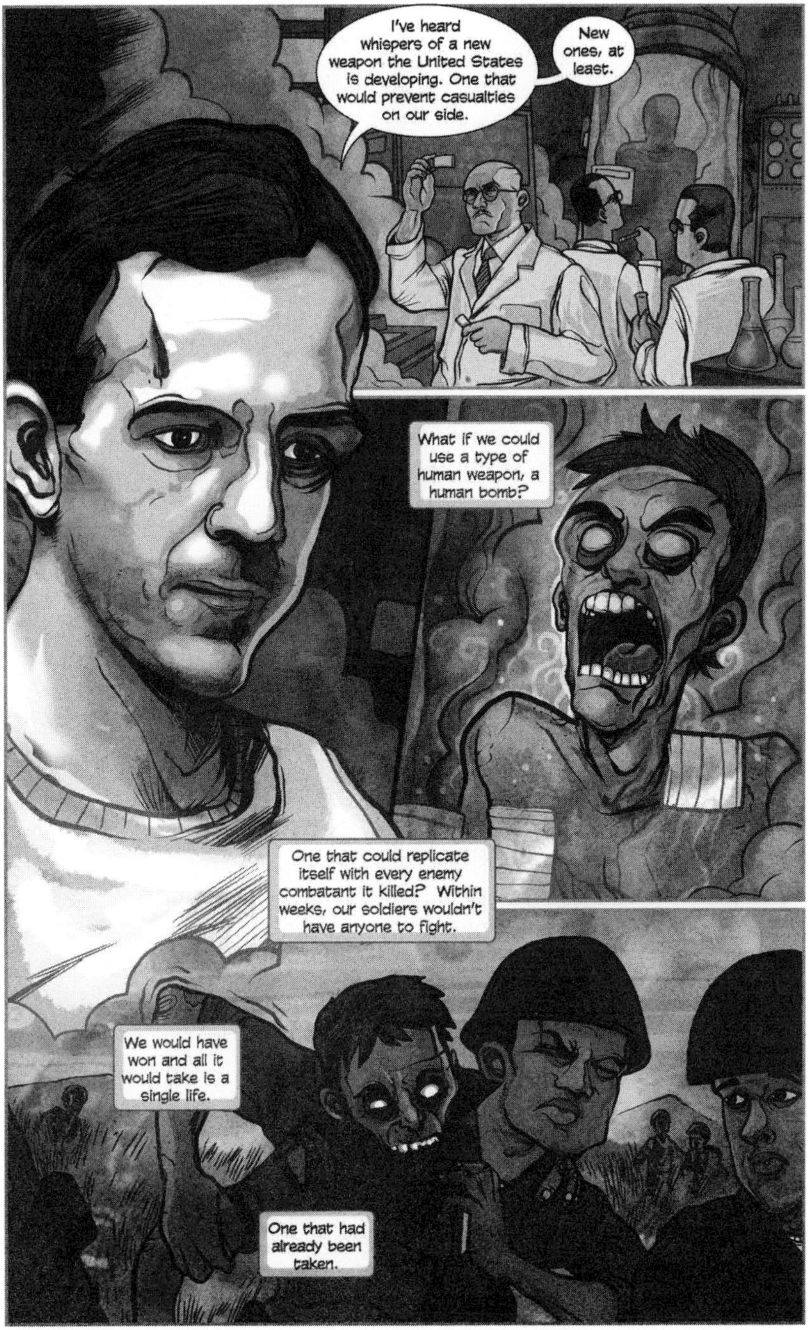
I've heard whispers of a new weapon the United States is developing. One that would prevent casualties on our side.
New ones, at least.
What if we could use a type of human weapon, a human bomb?
One that could replicate itself with every enemy combatant it killed? Within weeks, our soldiers wouldn't have anyone to fight.
We would have won and all it would take is a single life.
One that had already been taken.

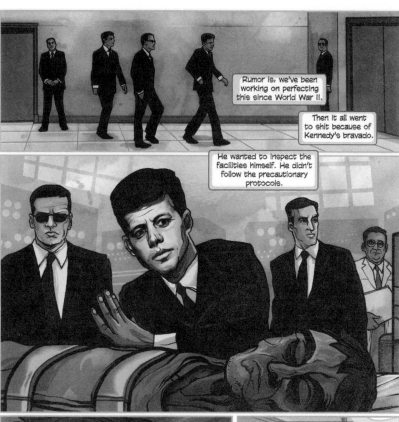

Rumor is, we've been working on perfecting this since World War II.

Then it all went to shit because of Kennedy's bravado.

He wanted to inspect the facilities himself. He didn't follow the precautionary protocols.

He had been compromised.

Of course, the bullheaded man that he is, he dismissed his injury.

But the higher ups knew better. They knew it'd only be a matter of time before he became one of them.

That's when they called me in.

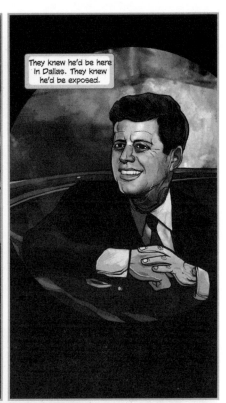

They knew he'd be here in Dallas. They knew he'd be exposed.

Do you really believe all this? That he'd become some sort of undead thing?

What I believe does not matter. I had my orders.

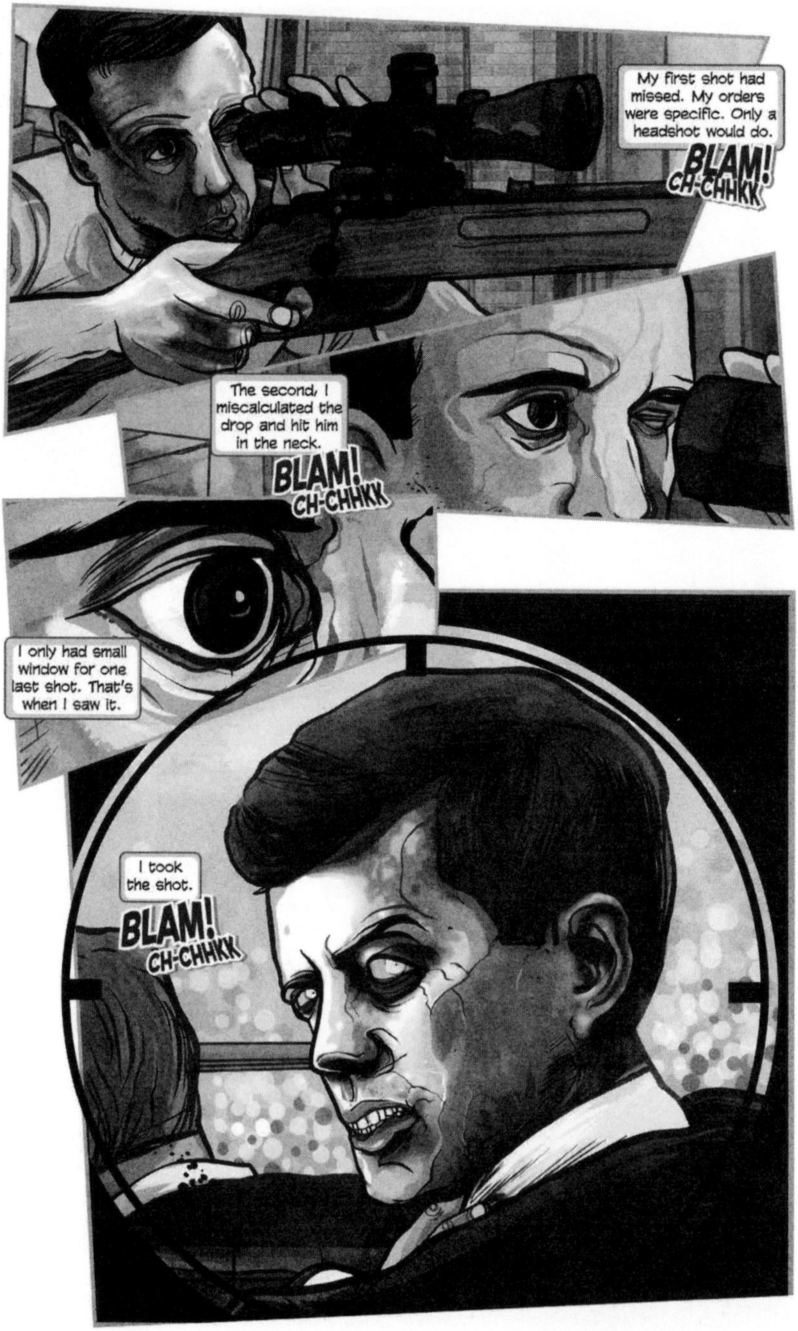

My first shot had missed. My orders were specific. Only a headshot would do.
BLAM! CH-CHHKK
The second, I miscalculated the drop and hit him in the neck.
BLAM! CH-CHHKK
I only had small window for one last shot. That's when I saw it.
I took the shot.
BLAM! CH-CHHKK

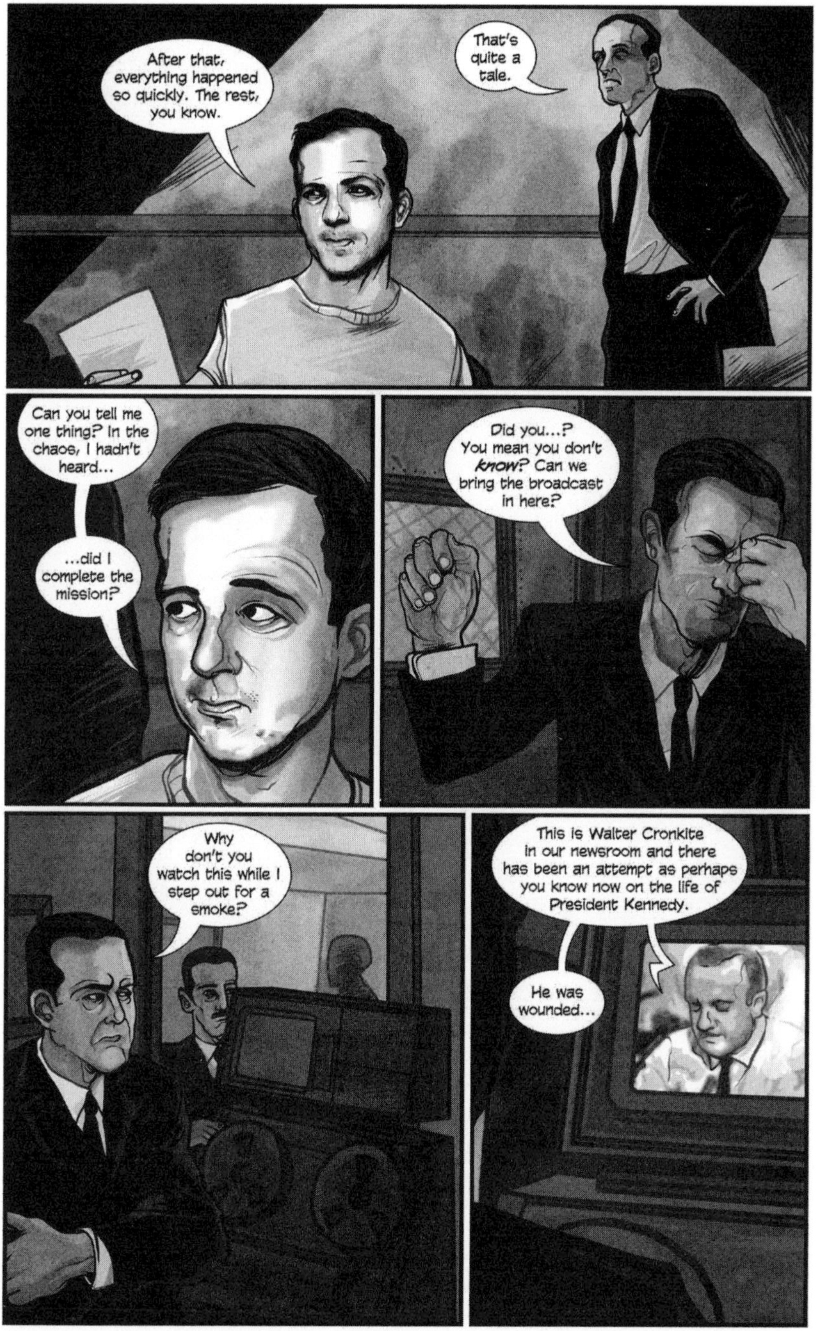
After that, everything happened so quickly. The rest, you know.
That's quite a tale.
Can you tell me one thing? In the chaos, I hadn't heard...
...did I complete the mission?
Did you...? You mean you don't *know*? Can we bring the broadcast in here?
Why don't you watch this while I step out for a smoke?
This is Walter Cronkite in our newsroom and there has been an attempt as perhaps you know now on the life of President Kennedy.
He was wounded...

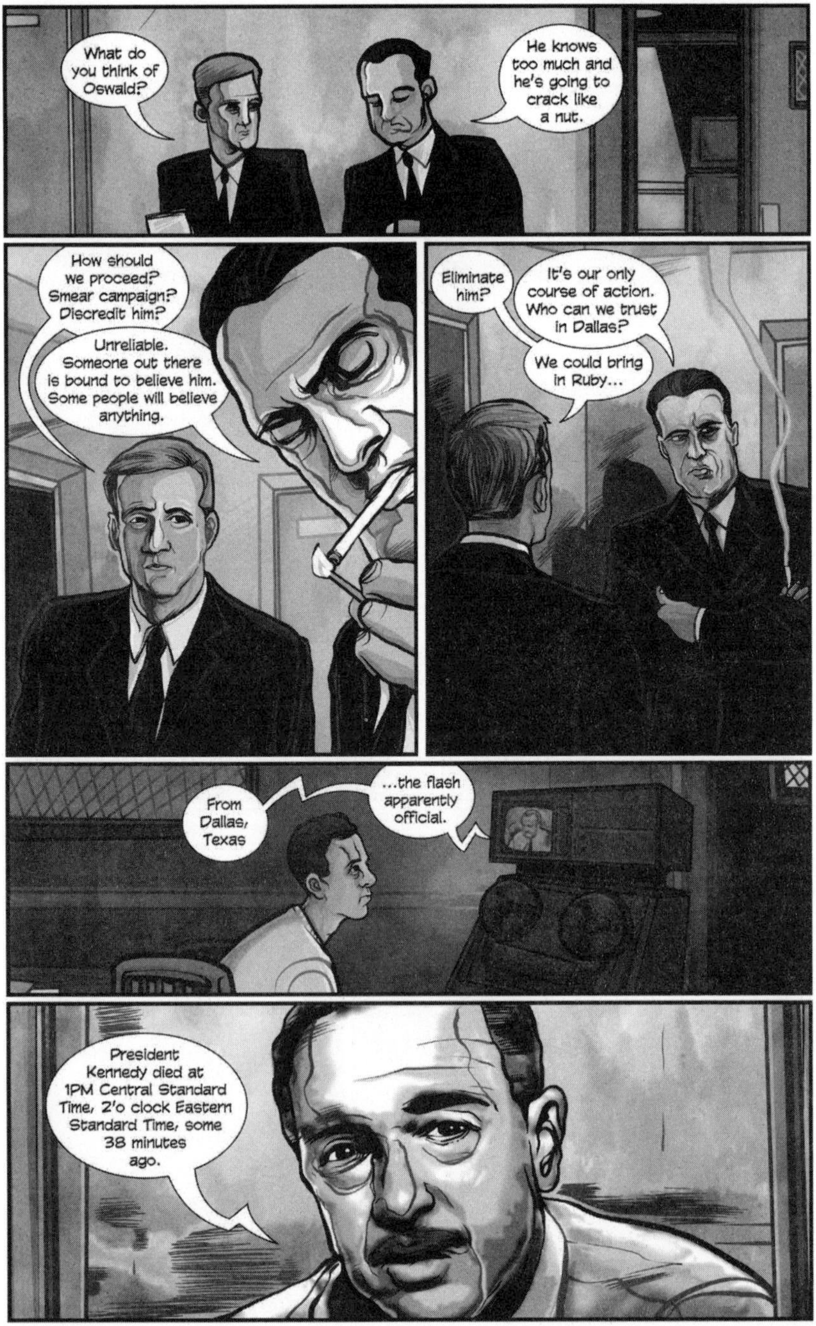
What do you think of Oswald?
He knows too much and he's going to crack like a nut.
How should we proceed? Smear campaign? Discredit him?
Unreliable. Someone out there is bound to believe him. Some people will believe anything.
Eliminate him?
It's our only course of action. Who can we trust in Dallas?
We could bring in Ruby...
From Dallas, Texas
...the flash apparently official.
President Kennedy died at 1PM Central Standard Time, 2'o clock Eastern Standard Time, some 38 minutes ago.

GEMINI 10

STORY BY:
JASON WINN

PENCILS BY:
ALEX DIOTTO

INKS, GREYSCALES AND LETTERS BY:
JEFF McCOMSEY

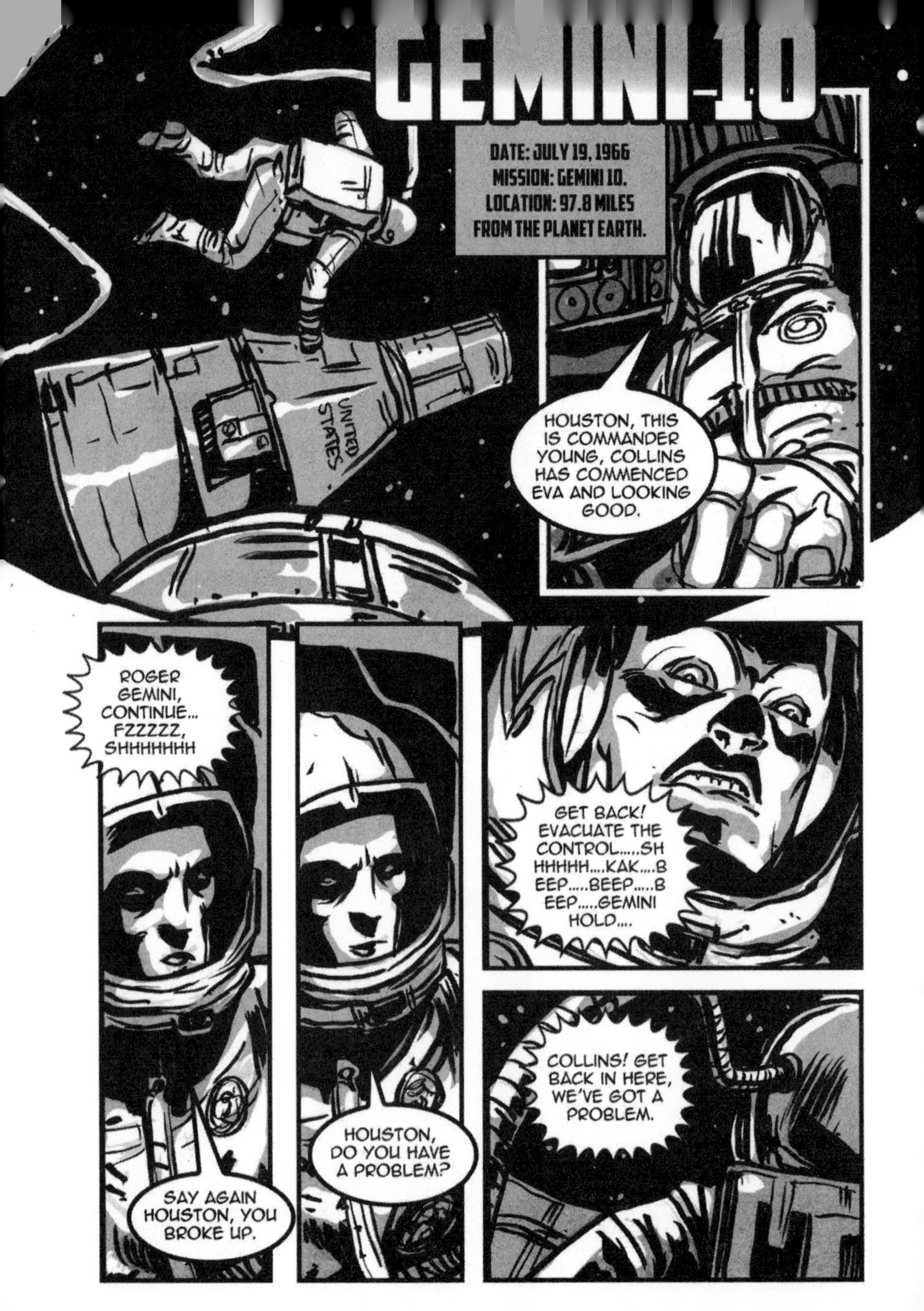
GEMINI 10
DATE: JULY 19, 1966
MISSION: GEMINI 10.
LOCATION: 97.8 MILES
FROM THE PLANET EARTH.
UNITED STATES
HOUSTON, THIS IS COMMANDER YOUNG, COLLINS HAS COMMENCED EVA AND LOOKING GOOD.
ROGER GEMINI, CONTINUE... FZZZZZ, SHHHHHHH
SAY AGAIN HOUSTON, YOU BROKE UP.
HOUSTON, DO YOU HAVE A PROBLEM?
GET BACK! EVACUATE THE CONTROL.....SH HHHHH....KAK....B EEP.....BEEP.....B EEP.....GEMINI HOLD....
COLLINS! GET BACK IN HERE, WE'VE GOT A PROBLEM.

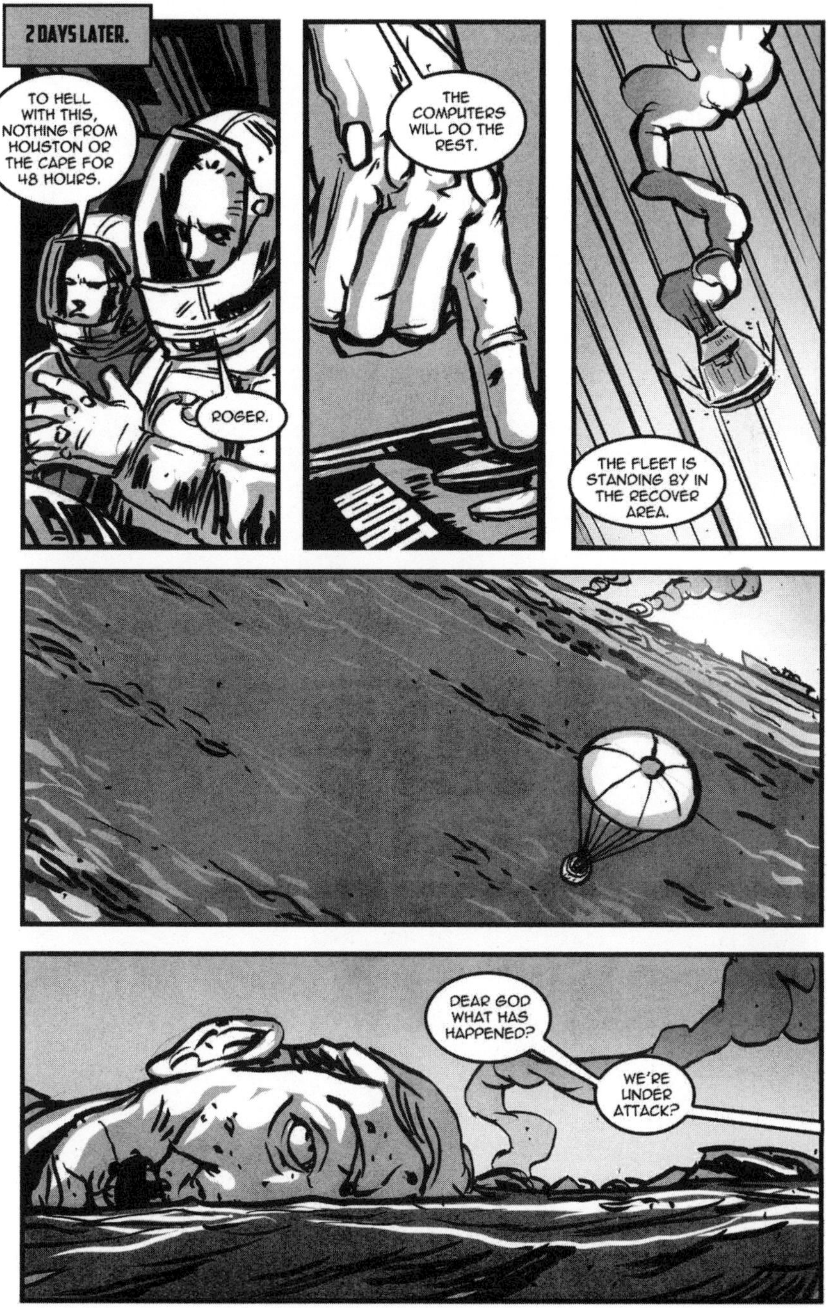
2 DAYS LATER.
TO HELL WITH THIS, NOTHING FROM HOUSTON OR THE CAPE FOR 48 HOURS.
ROGER.
THE COMPUTERS WILL DO THE REST.
ABORT
THE FLEET IS STANDING BY IN THE RECOVER AREA.
DEAR GOD WHAT HAS HAPPENED?
WE'RE UNDER ATTACK?

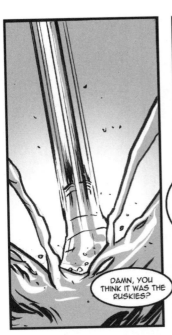

CAN'T THINK OF ANYONE ELSE.

GOD DAMNIT MIKE, WE'RE IN THE MIDDLE OF WORLD WAR 3.

THAT LOOKS LIKE THE WASP OVER THERE. SHE LOOKS TO BE IN BETTER SHAPE THAN THE REST OF THEM.

DAMN, YOU THINK IT WAS THE RUSKIES?

POP!

POP!

LET'S CHECK HER OUT.

POP!

GET BACK GOD DAMN IT, YOU AIN'T BITING ME!

LOWER THAT WEAPON SAILOR! WHAT'S YOUR NAME?

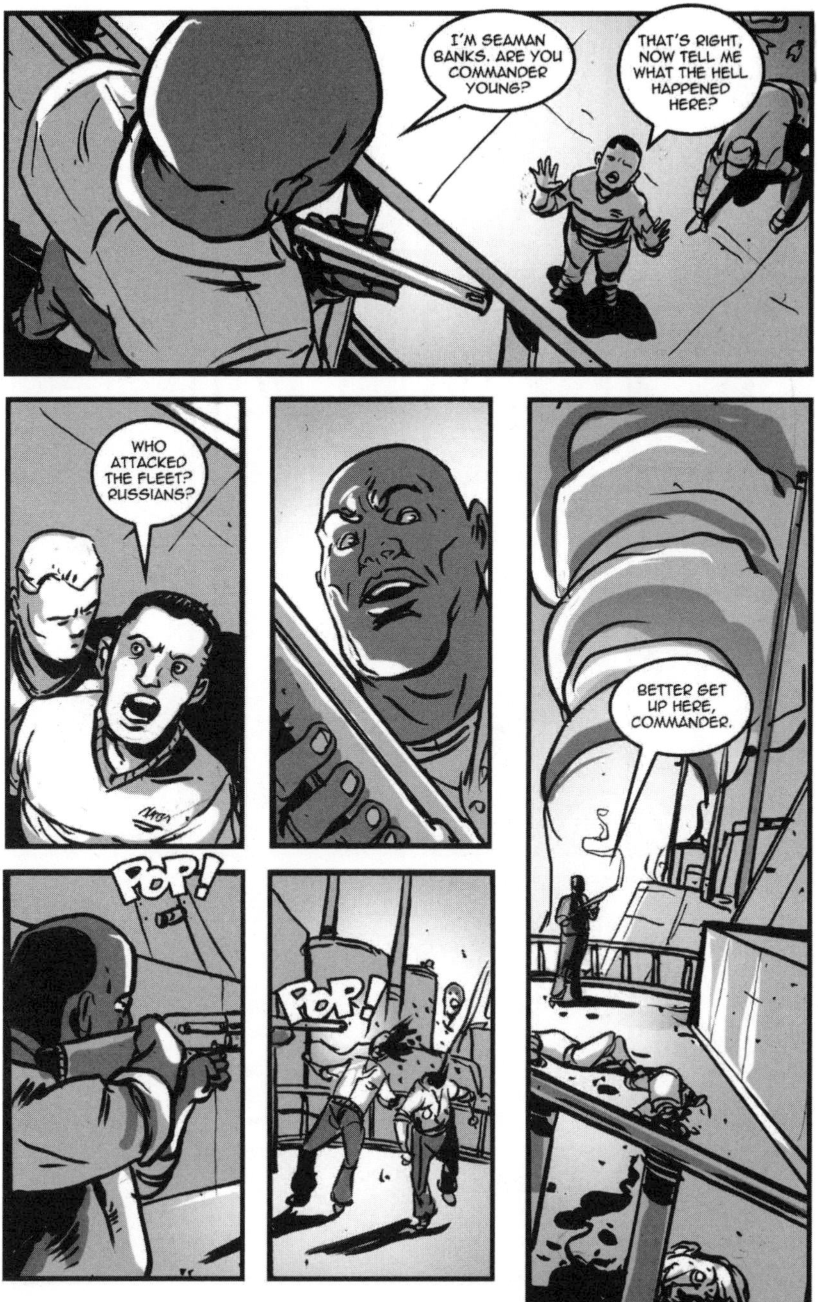
I'M SEAMAN BANKS. ARE YOU COMMANDER YOUNG?
THAT'S RIGHT, NOW TELL ME WHAT THE HELL HAPPENED HERE?
WHO ATTACKED THE FLEET? RUSSIANS?
BETTER GET UP HERE, COMMANDER.
POP!
POP!

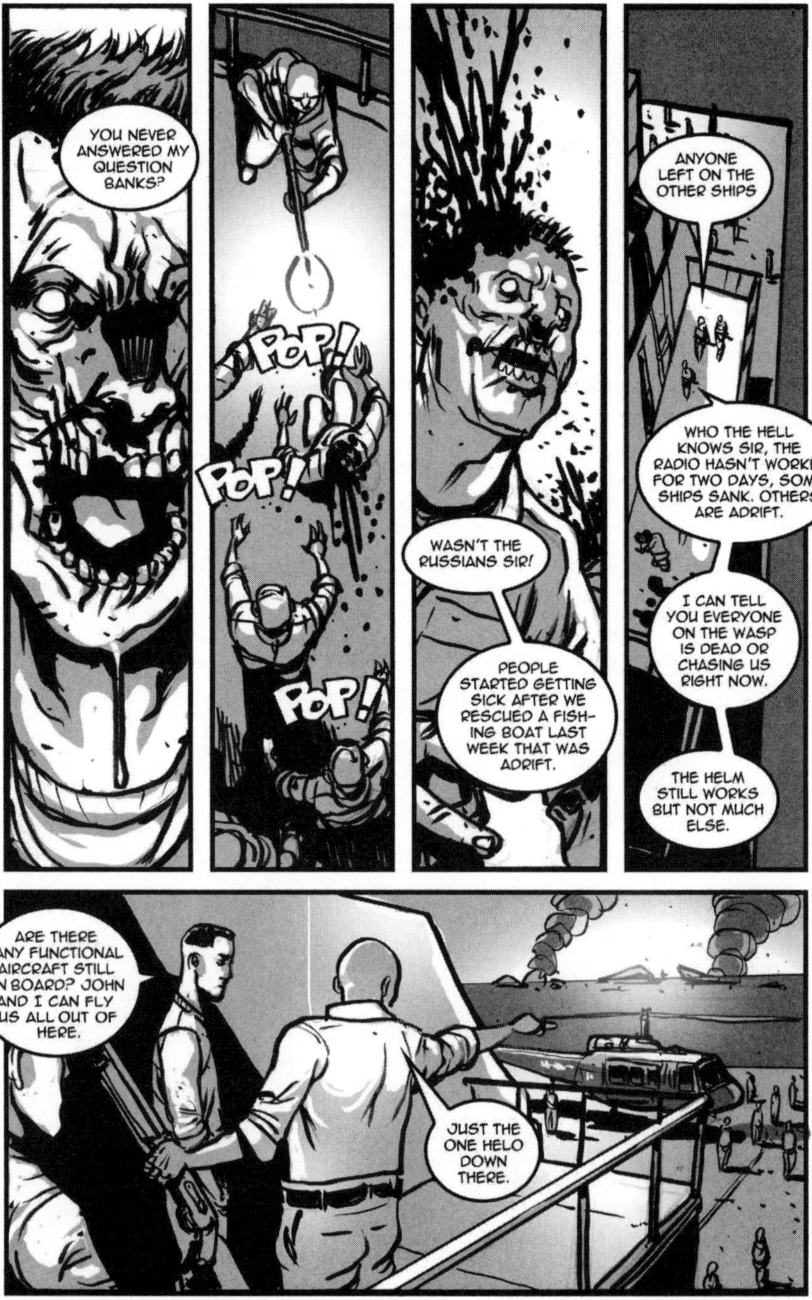
YOU NEVER ANSWERED MY QUESTION BANKS?
POP!
POP!
POP!
WASN'T THE RUSSIANS SIR!
PEOPLE STARTED GETTING SICK AFTER WE RESCUED A FISH-ING BOAT LAST WEEK THAT WAS ADRIFT.
ANYONE LEFT ON THE OTHER SHIPS
WHO THE HELL KNOWS SIR, THE RADIO HASN'T WORKED FOR TWO DAYS, SOME SHIPS SANK. OTHERS ARE ADRIFT.
I CAN TELL YOU EVERYONE ON THE WASP IS DEAD OR CHASING US RIGHT NOW.
THE HELM STILL WORKS BUT NOT MUCH ELSE.
ARE THERE ANY FUNCTIONAL AIRCRAFT STILL ON BOARD? JOHN AND I CAN FLY US ALL OUT OF HERE.
JUST THE ONE HELO DOWN THERE.

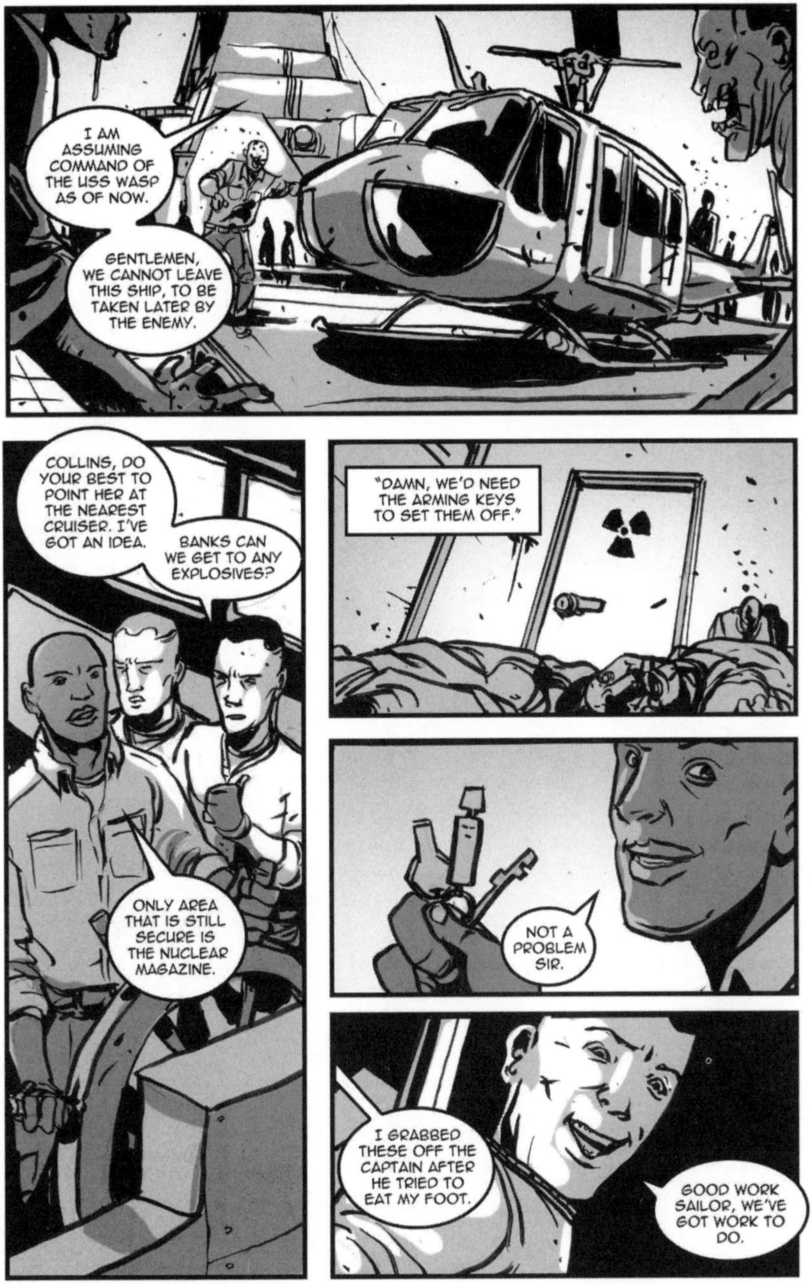
I AM ASSUMING COMMAND OF THE USS WASP AS OF NOW.
GENTLEMEN, WE CANNOT LEAVE THIS SHIP, TO BE TAKEN LATER BY THE ENEMY.
COLLINS, DO YOUR BEST TO POINT HER AT THE NEAREST CRUISER. I'VE GOT AN IDEA.
BANKS CAN WE GET TO ANY EXPLOSIVES?
ONLY AREA THAT IS STILL SECURE IS THE NUCLEAR MAGAZINE.
"DAMN, WE'D NEED THE ARMING KEYS TO SET THEM OFF."
NOT A PROBLEM SIR.
I GRABBED THESE OFF THE CAPTAIN AFTER HE TRIED TO EAT MY FOOT.
GOOD WORK SAILOR, WE'VE GOT WORK TO DO.

BANKS, COLLINS, ARM AS MANY AS YOU CAN.

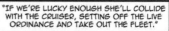

"IF WE'RE LUCKY ENOUGH SHE'LL COLLIDE WITH THE CRUISER, SETTING OFF THE LIVE ORDINANCE AND TAKE OUT THE FLEET."

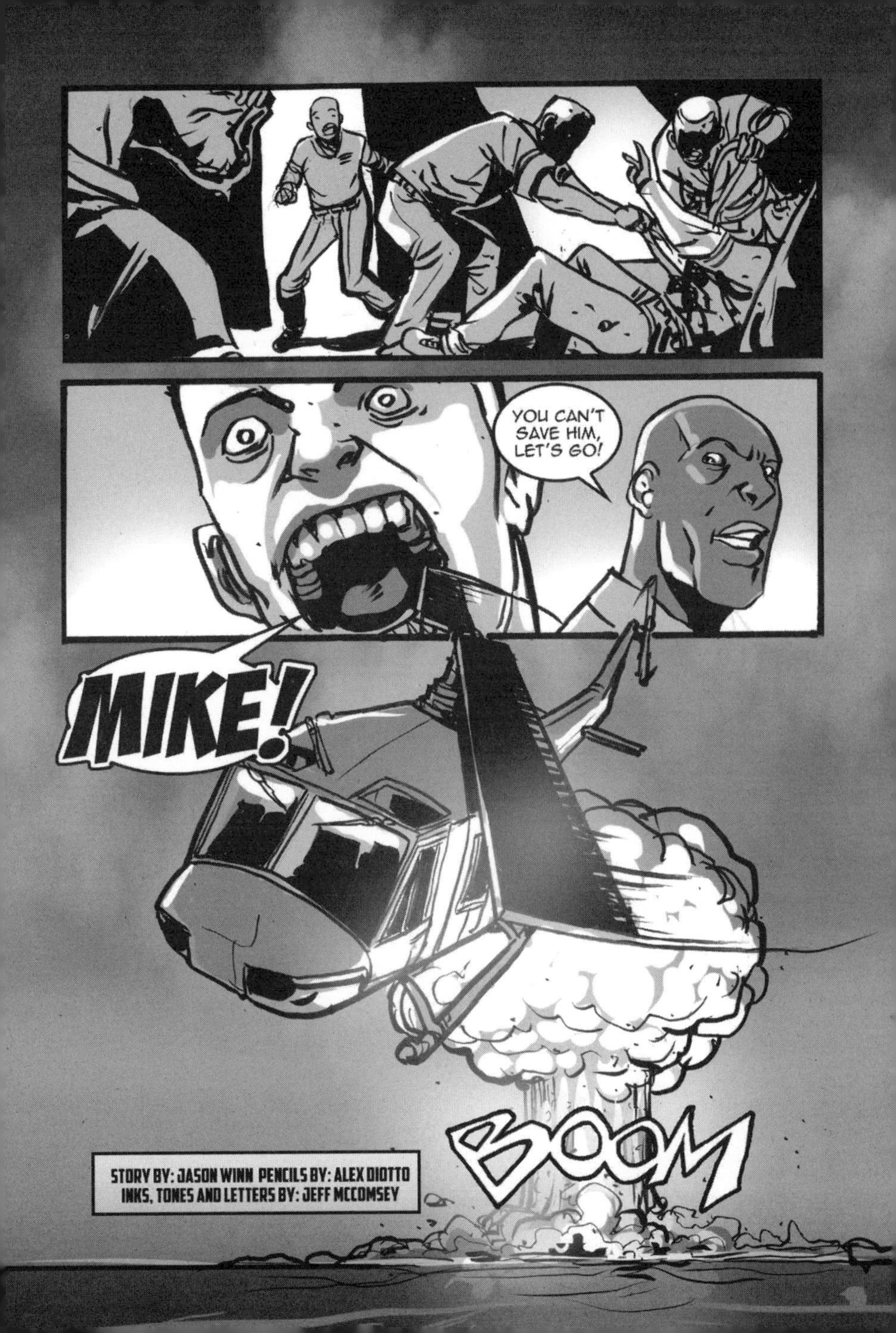
YOU CAN'T SAVE HIM, LET'S GO!
MIKE!
BOOM
STORY BY: JASON WINN PENCILS BY: ALEX DIOTTO
INKS, TONES AND LETTERS BY: JEFF MCCOMSEY

SEA OF TRANQUILITY

STORY BY:
CONOR MAHONEY

ART AND LETTERS BY:
BRANDON CARR

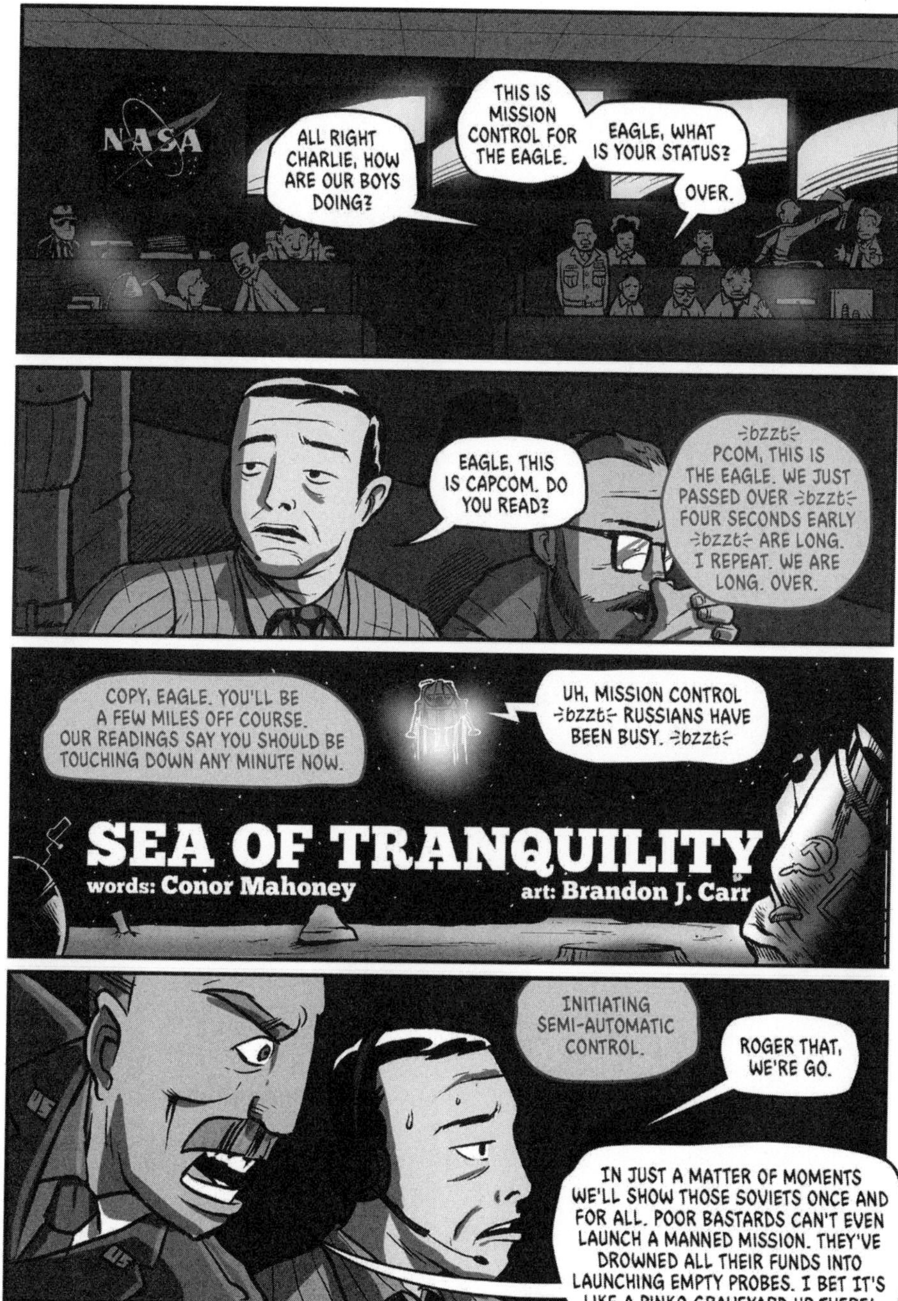

NASA
ALL RIGHT CHARLIE, HOW ARE OUR BOYS DOING?
THIS IS MISSION CONTROL FOR THE EAGLE.
EAGLE, WHAT IS YOUR STATUS?
OVER.
EAGLE, THIS IS CAPCOM. DO YOU READ?
-bzzt- PCOM, THIS IS THE EAGLE. WE JUST PASSED OVER -bzzt- FOUR SECONDS EARLY -bzzt- ARE LONG. I REPEAT. WE ARE LONG. OVER.
COPY, EAGLE. YOU'LL BE A FEW MILES OFF COURSE. OUR READINGS SAY YOU SHOULD BE TOUCHING DOWN ANY MINUTE NOW.
UH, MISSION CONTROL -bzzt- RUSSIANS HAVE BEEN BUSY. -bzzt-
SEA OF TRANQUILITY
words: Conor Mahoney
art: Brandon J. Carr
INITIATING SEMI-AUTOMATIC CONTROL.
ROGER THAT, WE'RE GO.
IN JUST A MATTER OF MOMENTS WE'LL SHOW THOSE SOVIETS ONCE AND FOR ALL. POOR BASTARDS CAN'T EVEN LAUNCH A MANNED MISSION. THEY'VE DROWNED ALL THEIR FUNDS INTO LAUNCHING EMPTY PROBES. I BET IT'S LIKE A PINKO GRAVEYARD UP THERE!

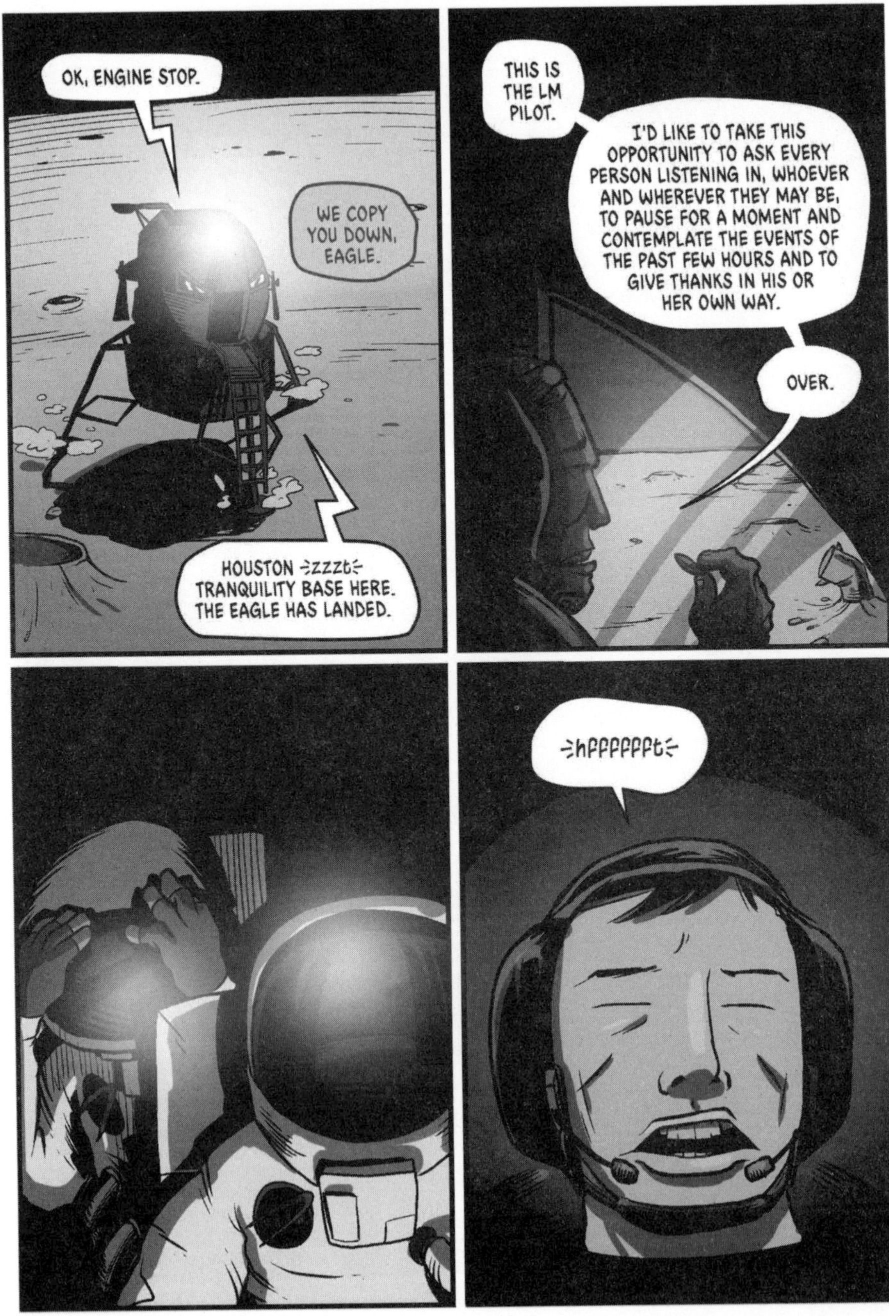
OK, ENGINE STOP.
WE COPY YOU DOWN, EAGLE.
HOUSTON zzzt TRANQUILITY BASE HERE. THE EAGLE HAS LANDED.
THIS IS THE LM PILOT.
I'D LIKE TO TAKE THIS OPPORTUNITY TO ASK EVERY PERSON LISTENING IN, WHOEVER AND WHEREVER THEY MAY BE, TO PAUSE FOR A MOMENT AND CONTEMPLATE THE EVENTS OF THE PAST FEW HOURS AND TO GIVE THANKS IN HIS OR HER OWN WAY.
OVER.
hffffffft

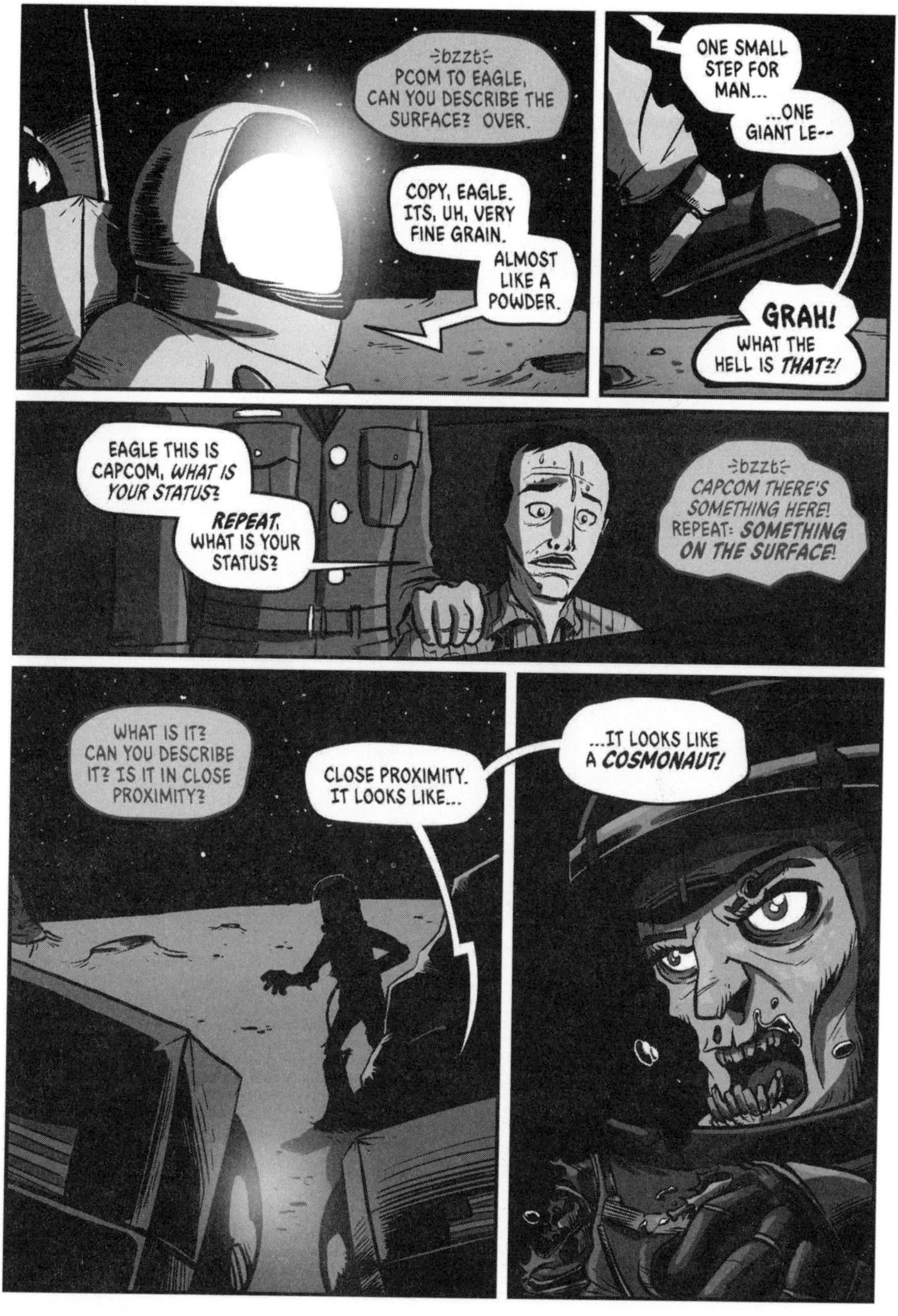

bzzt
PCOM TO EAGLE, CAN YOU DESCRIBE THE SURFACE? OVER.
COPY, EAGLE. ITS, UH, VERY FINE GRAIN.
ALMOST LIKE A POWDER.
ONE SMALL STEP FOR MAN...
...ONE GIANT LE--
GRAH!
WHAT THE HELL IS *THAT?!*
EAGLE THIS IS CAPCOM, *WHAT IS YOUR STATUS?*
REPEAT. WHAT IS YOUR STATUS?
bzzt
CAPCOM THERE'S SOMETHING HERE!
REPEAT: ***SOMETHING ON THE SURFACE!***
WHAT IS IT? CAN YOU DESCRIBE IT? IS IT IN CLOSE PROXIMITY?
CLOSE PROXIMITY. IT LOOKS LIKE...
...IT LOOKS LIKE A ***COSMONAUT!***

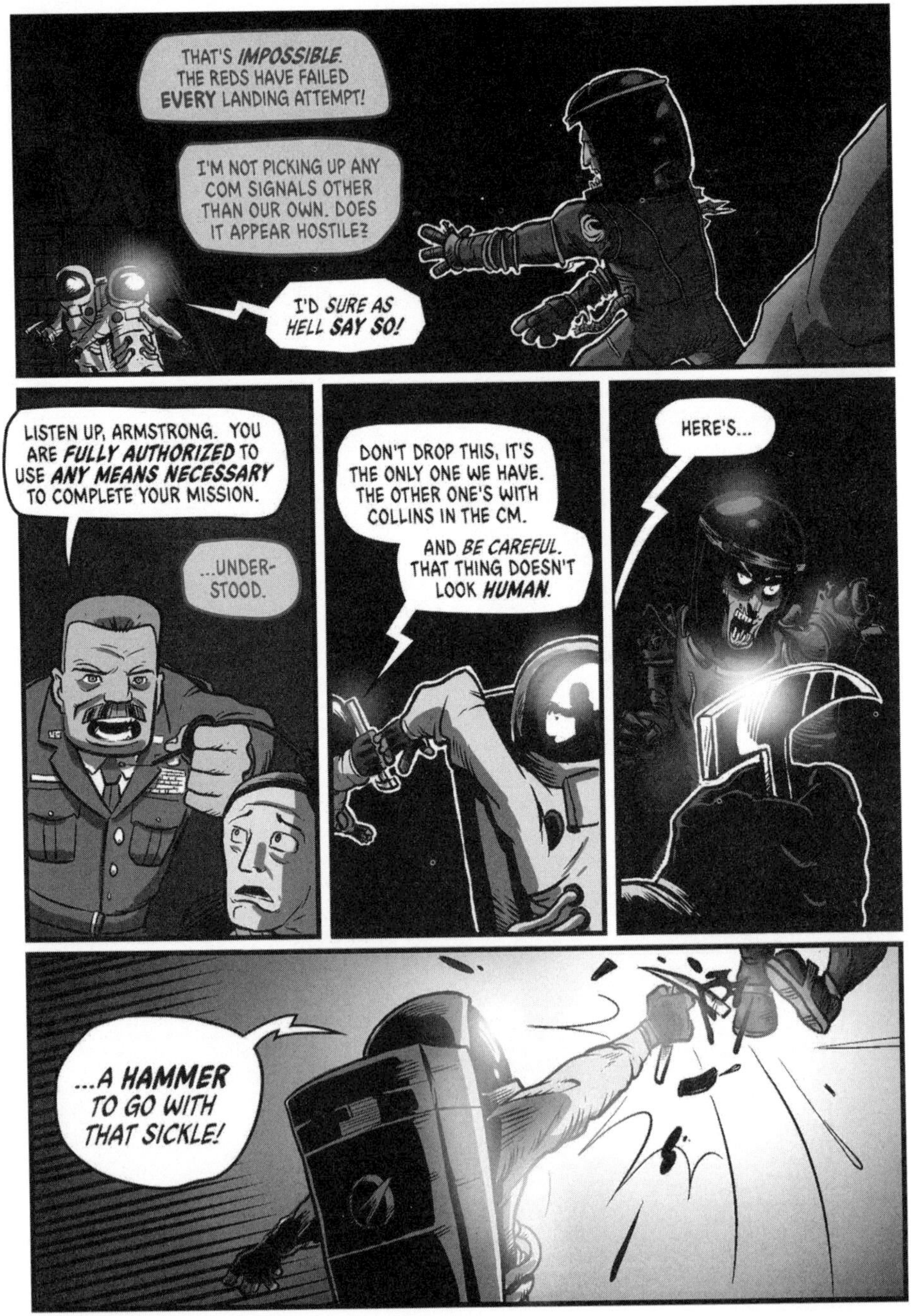
THAT'S *IMPOSSIBLE*. THE REDS HAVE FAILED **EVERY** LANDING ATTEMPT!
I'M NOT PICKING UP ANY COM SIGNALS OTHER THAN OUR OWN. DOES IT APPEAR HOSTILE?
I'D *SURE AS* HELL ***SAY SO!***
LISTEN UP, ARMSTRONG. YOU ARE ***FULLY AUTHORIZED*** TO USE ***ANY MEANS NECESSARY*** TO COMPLETE YOUR MISSION.
...UNDER-STOOD.
DON'T DROP THIS, IT'S THE ONLY ONE WE HAVE. THE OTHER ONE'S WITH COLLINS IN THE CM.
AND *BE CAREFUL*. THAT THING DOESN'T LOOK ***HUMAN***.
HERE'S...
...A ***HAMMER*** *TO GO WITH THAT SICKLE!*

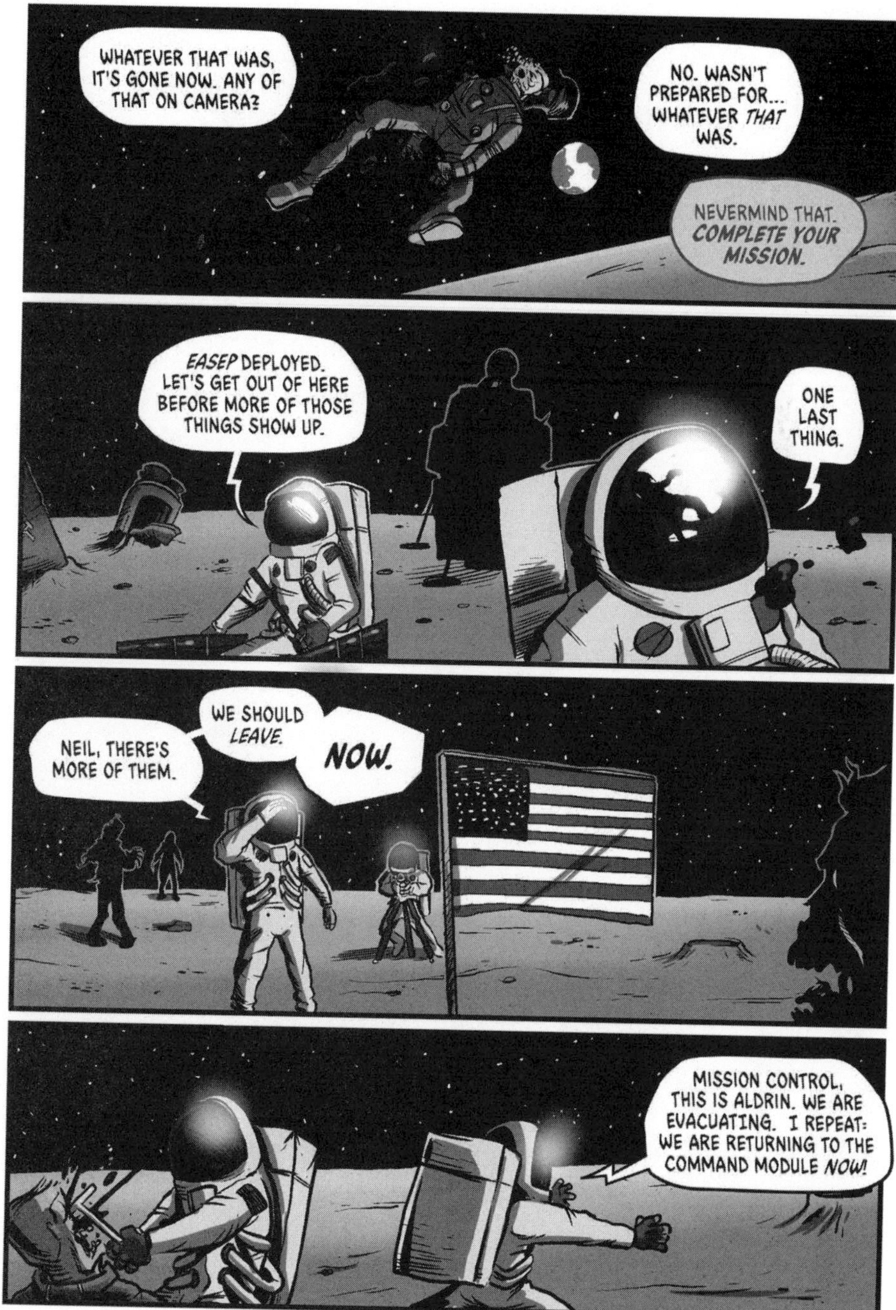
WHATEVER THAT WAS, IT'S GONE NOW. ANY OF THAT ON CAMERA?
NO. WASN'T PREPARED FOR... WHATEVER THAT WAS.
NEVERMIND THAT. COMPLETE YOUR MISSION.
EASEP DEPLOYED. LET'S GET OUT OF HERE BEFORE MORE OF THOSE THINGS SHOW UP.
ONE LAST THING.
NEIL, THERE'S MORE OF THEM.
WE SHOULD LEAVE.
NOW.
MISSION CONTROL, THIS IS ALDRIN. WE ARE EVACUATING. I REPEAT: WE ARE RETURNING TO THE COMMAND MODULE NOW!

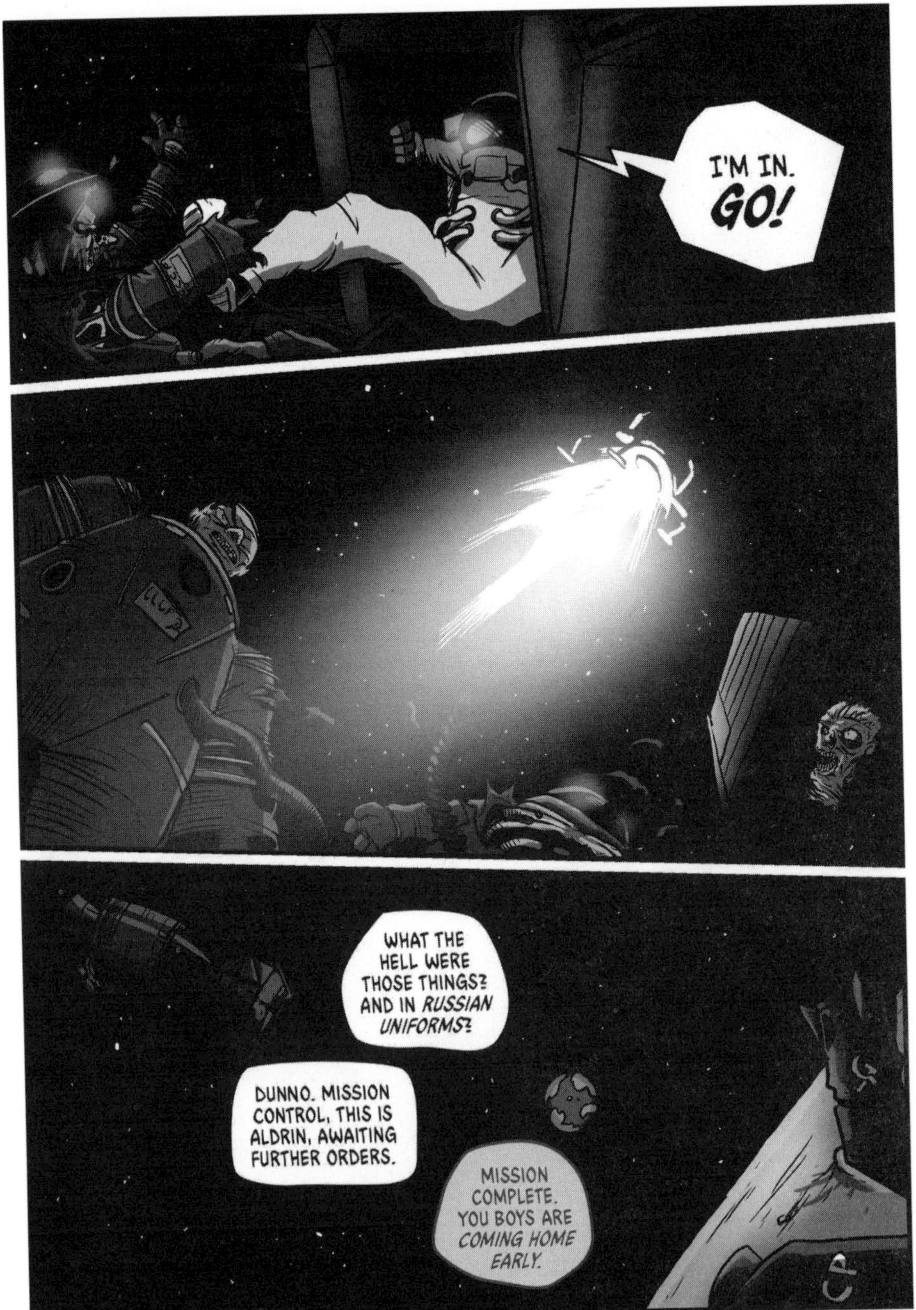
I'M IN. GO!
WHAT THE HELL WERE THOSE THINGS? AND IN *RUSSIAN UNIFORMS*?
DUNNO. MISSION CONTROL, THIS IS ALDRIN, AWAITING FURTHER ORDERS.
MISSION COMPLETE. YOU BOYS ARE *COMING HOME* EARLY.

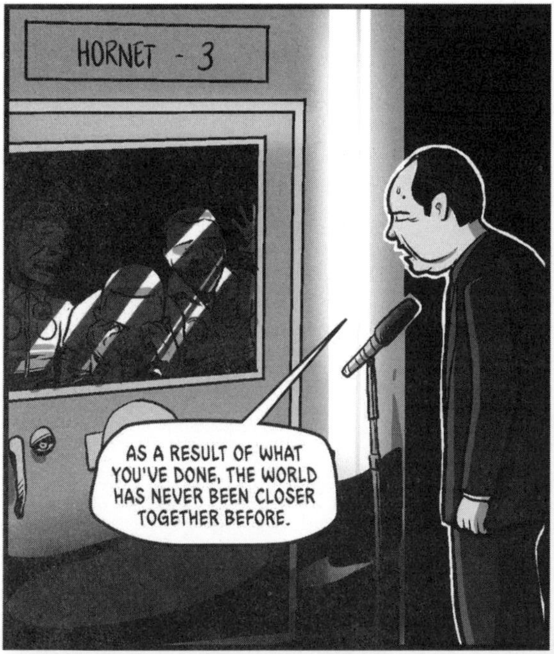
HORNET - 3
AS A RESULT OF WHAT YOU'VE DONE, THE WORLD HAS NEVER BEEN CLOSER TOGETHER BEFORE.

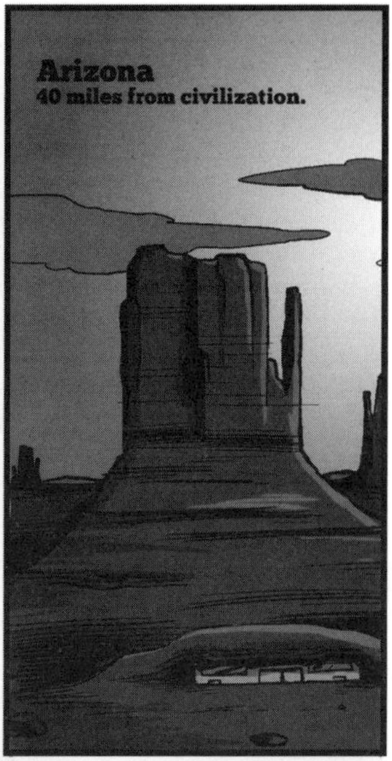
Arizona
40 miles from civilization.

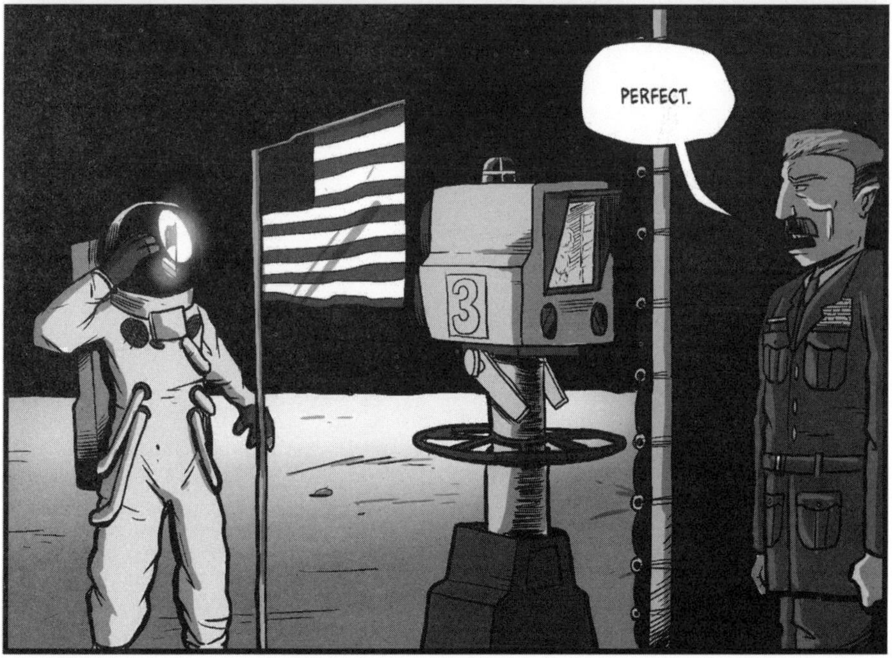
3
PERFECT.

WORLD WAR WOODSTOCK

STORY BY:
MICHAEL MCDERMOTT

ART BY:
ALUISIO CERVELLE SANTOS

LETTERS BY:
JULIE SHELTON

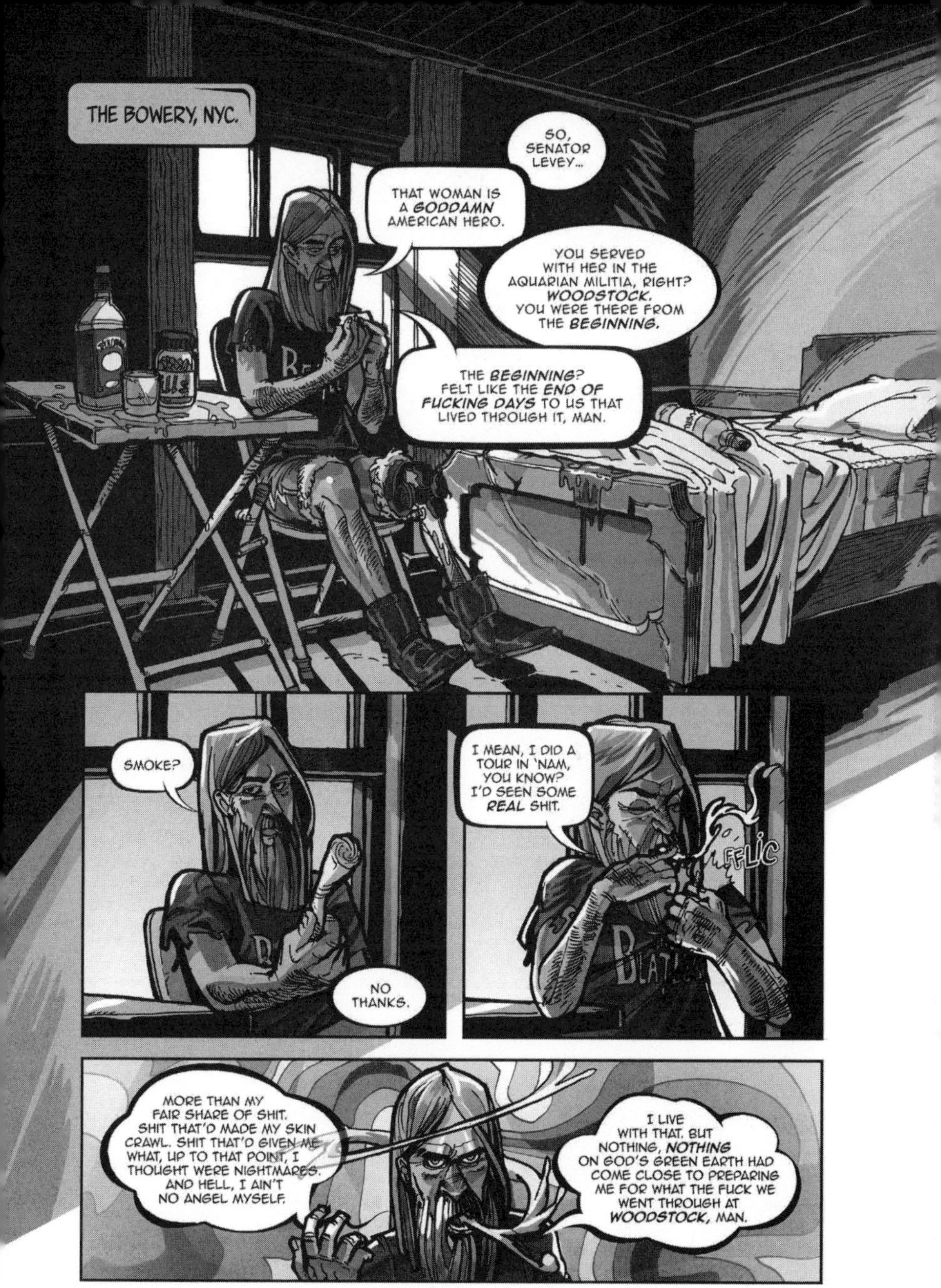
THE BOWERY, NYC.
SO, SENATOR LEVEY...
THAT WOMAN IS A GODDAMN AMERICAN HERO.
YOU SERVED WITH HER IN THE AQUARIAN MILITIA, RIGHT? WOODSTOCK. YOU WERE THERE FROM THE BEGINNING.
THE BEGINNING? FELT LIKE THE END OF FUCKING DAYS TO US THAT LIVED THROUGH IT, MAN.
SMOKE?
NO THANKS.
I MEAN, I DID A TOUR IN 'NAM, YOU KNOW? I'D SEEN SOME REAL SHIT.
FFLIC
MORE THAN MY FAIR SHARE OF SHIT. SHIT THAT'D MADE MY SKIN CRAWL. SHIT THAT'D GIVEN ME WHAT, UP TO THAT POINT, I THOUGHT WERE NIGHTMARES. AND HELL, I AIN'T NO ANGEL MYSELF.
I LIVE WITH THAT. BUT NOTHING, NOTHING ON GOD'S GREEN EARTH HAD COME CLOSE TO PREPARING ME FOR WHAT THE FUCK WE WENT THROUGH AT WOODSTOCK, MAN.

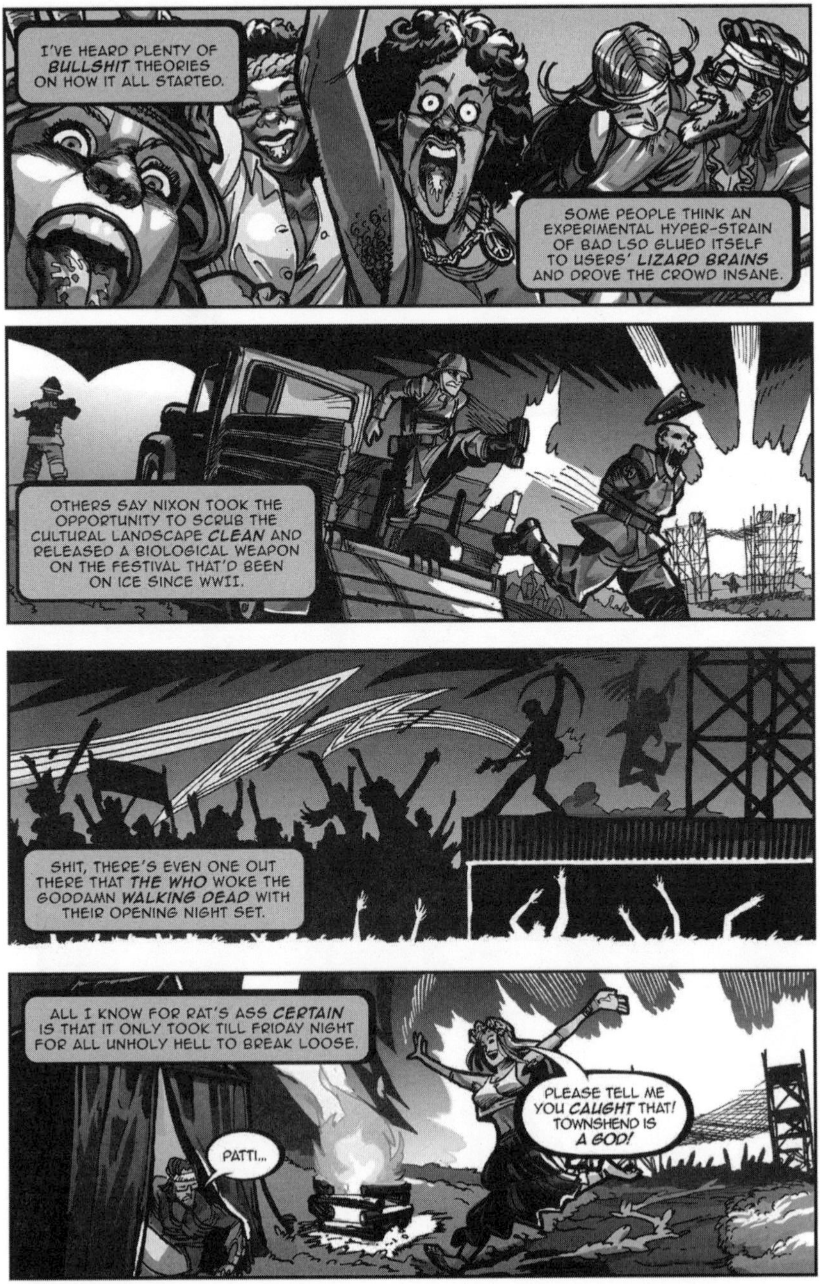
I'VE HEARD PLENTY OF BULLSHIT THEORIES ON HOW IT ALL STARTED.
SOME PEOPLE THINK AN EXPERIMENTAL HYPER-STRAIN OF BAD LSD GLUED ITSELF TO USERS' LIZARD BRAINS AND DROVE THE CROWD INSANE.
OTHERS SAY NIXON TOOK THE OPPORTUNITY TO SCRUB THE CULTURAL LANDSCAPE CLEAN AND RELEASED A BIOLOGICAL WEAPON ON THE FESTIVAL THAT'D BEEN ON ICE SINCE WWII.
SHIT, THERE'S EVEN ONE OUT THERE THAT THE WHO WOKE THE GODDAMN WALKING DEAD WITH THEIR OPENING NIGHT SET.
ALL I KNOW FOR RAT'S ASS CERTAIN IS THAT IT ONLY TOOK TILL FRIDAY NIGHT FOR ALL UNHOLY HELL TO BREAK LOOSE.
PLEASE TELL ME YOU CAUGHT THAT! TOWNSHEND IS A GOD!
PATTI...

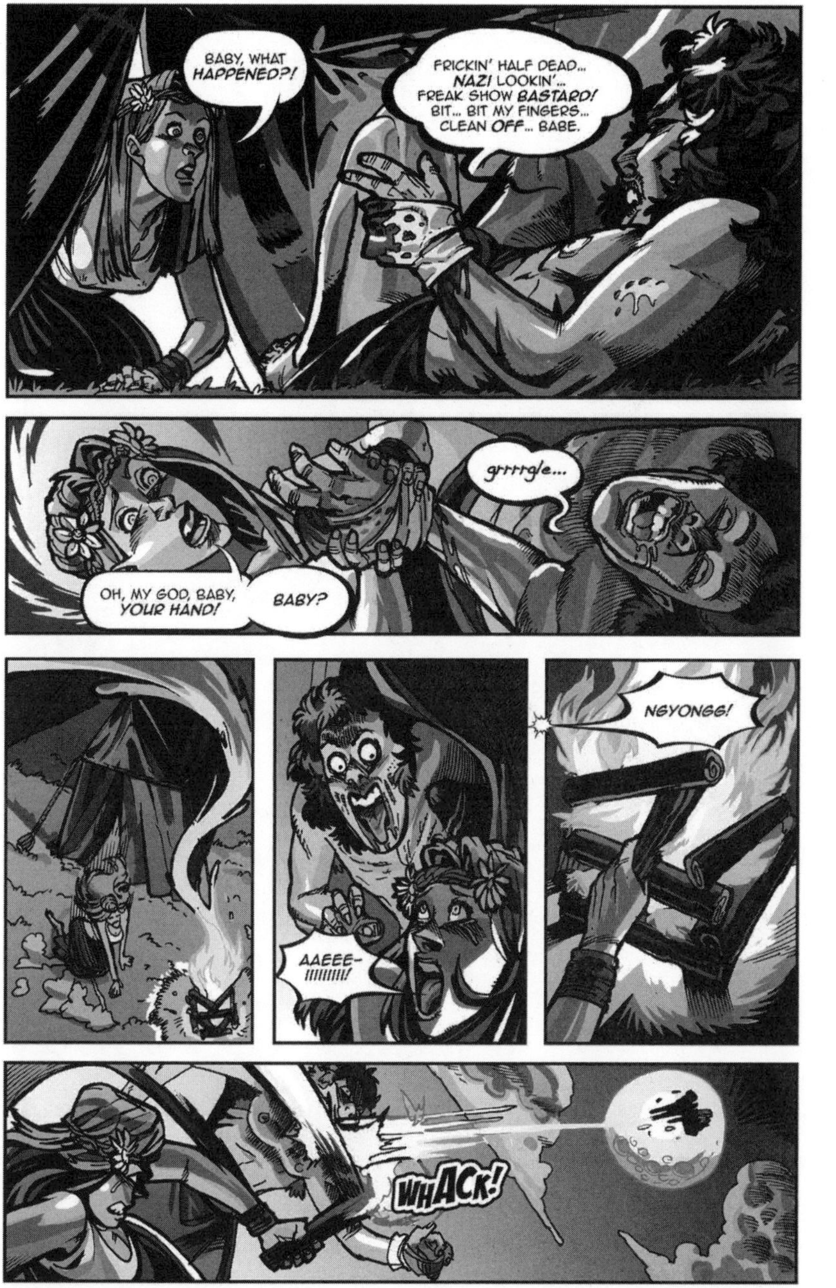
BABY, WHAT HAPPENED?!
FRICKIN' HALF DEAD... NAZI LOOKIN'... FREAK SHOW BASTARD! BIT... BIT MY FINGERS... CLEAN OFF... BABE.
grrrrgle...
OH, MY GOD, BABY, YOUR HAND!
BABY?
AAEEE-IIIIIIIII!
NGYONGG!
WHACK!

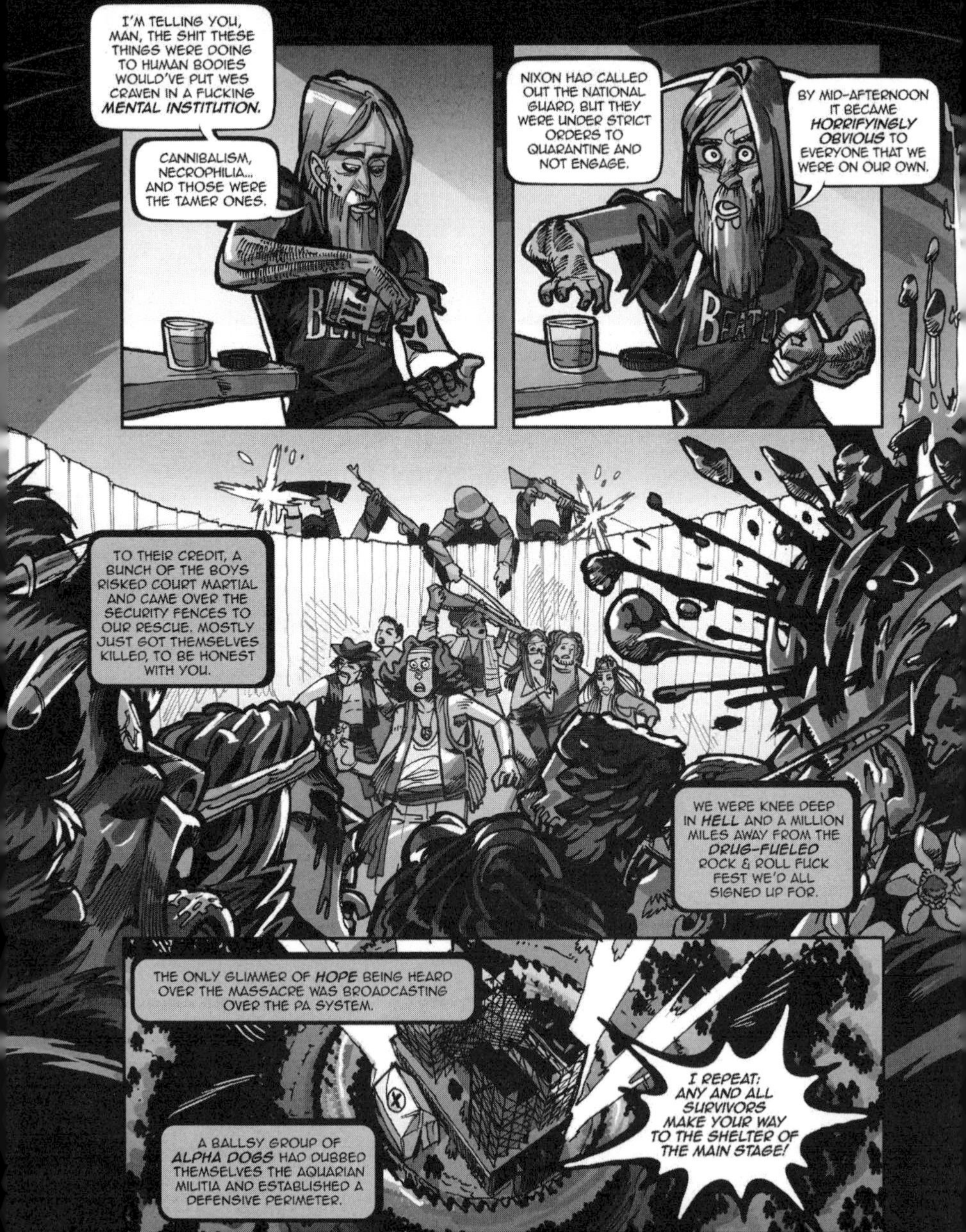
I'M TELLING YOU, MAN, THE SHIT THESE THINGS WERE DOING TO HUMAN BODIES WOULD'VE PUT WES CRAVEN IN A FUCKING MENTAL INSTITUTION.
CANNIBALISM, NECROPHILIA... AND THOSE WERE THE TAMER ONES.
NIXON HAD CALLED OUT THE NATIONAL GUARD, BUT THEY WERE UNDER STRICT ORDERS TO QUARANTINE AND NOT ENGAGE.
BY MID-AFTERNOON IT BECAME HORRIFYINGLY OBVIOUS TO EVERYONE THAT WE WERE ON OUR OWN.
TO THEIR CREDIT, A BUNCH OF THE BOYS RISKED COURT MARTIAL AND CAME OVER THE SECURITY FENCES TO OUR RESCUE. MOSTLY JUST GOT THEMSELVES KILLED, TO BE HONEST WITH YOU.
WE WERE KNEE DEEP IN HELL AND A MILLION MILES AWAY FROM THE DRUG-FUELED ROCK & ROLL FUCK FEST WE'D ALL SIGNED UP FOR.
THE ONLY GLIMMER OF HOPE BEING HEARD OVER THE MASSACRE WAS BROADCASTING OVER THE PA SYSTEM.
A BALLSY GROUP OF ALPHA DOGS HAD DUBBED THEMSELVES THE AQUARIAN MILITIA AND ESTABLISHED A DEFENSIVE PERIMETER.
I REPEAT: ANY AND ALL SURVIVORS MAKE YOUR WAY TO THE SHELTER OF THE MAIN STAGE!

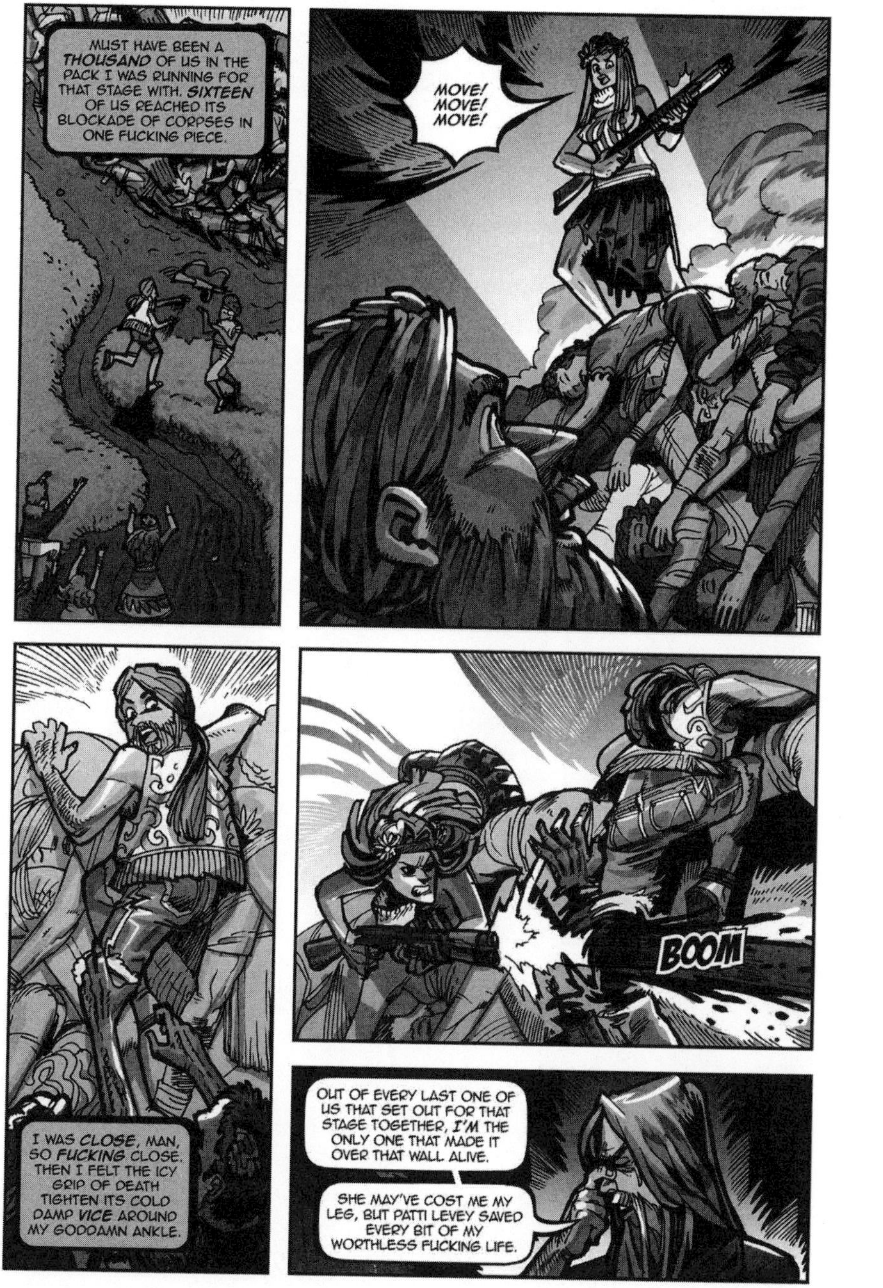
MUST HAVE BEEN A *THOUSAND* OF US IN THE PACK I WAS RUNNING FOR THAT STAGE WITH. *SIXTEEN* OF US REACHED ITS BLOCKADE OF CORPSES IN ONE FUCKING PIECE.
MOVE! MOVE! MOVE!
I WAS *CLOSE*, MAN, SO *FUCKING* CLOSE. THEN I FELT THE ICY GRIP OF DEATH TIGHTEN ITS COLD DAMP *VICE* AROUND MY GODDAMN ANKLE.
BOOM
OUT OF EVERY LAST ONE OF US THAT SET OUT FOR THAT STAGE TOGETHER, *I'M* THE ONLY ONE THAT MADE IT OVER THAT WALL ALIVE.
SHE MAY'VE COST ME MY LEG, BUT PATTI LEVEY SAVED EVERY BIT OF MY WORTHLESS FUCKING LIFE.

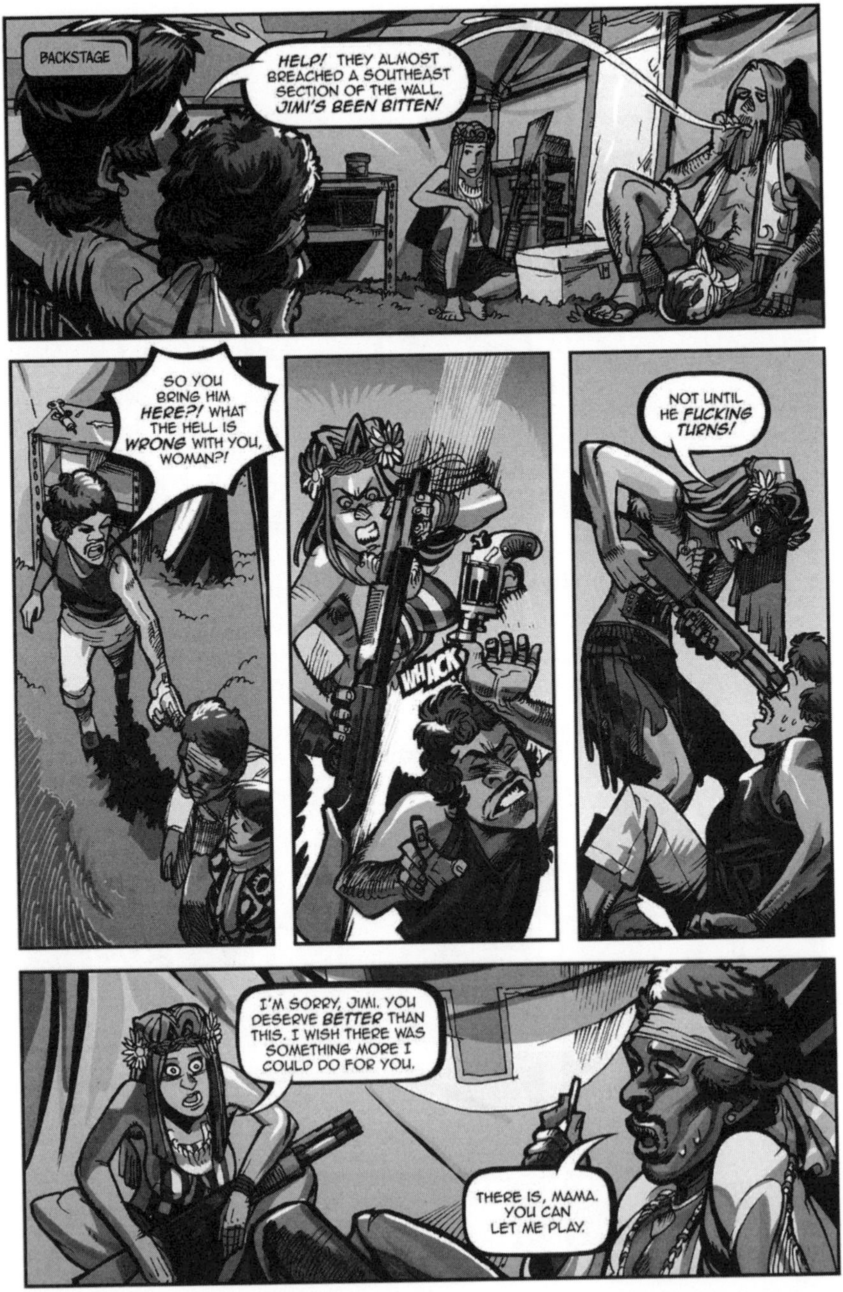
BACKSTAGE
HELP! THEY ALMOST BREACHED A SOUTHEAST SECTION OF THE WALL. JIMI'S BEEN BITTEN!
SO YOU BRING HIM HERE?! WHAT THE HELL IS WRONG WITH YOU, WOMAN?!
WHACK
NOT UNTIL HE FUCKING TURNS!
I'M SORRY, JIMI. YOU DESERVE BETTER THAN THIS. I WISH THERE WAS SOMETHING MORE I COULD DO FOR YOU.
THERE IS, MAMA. YOU CAN LET ME PLAY.

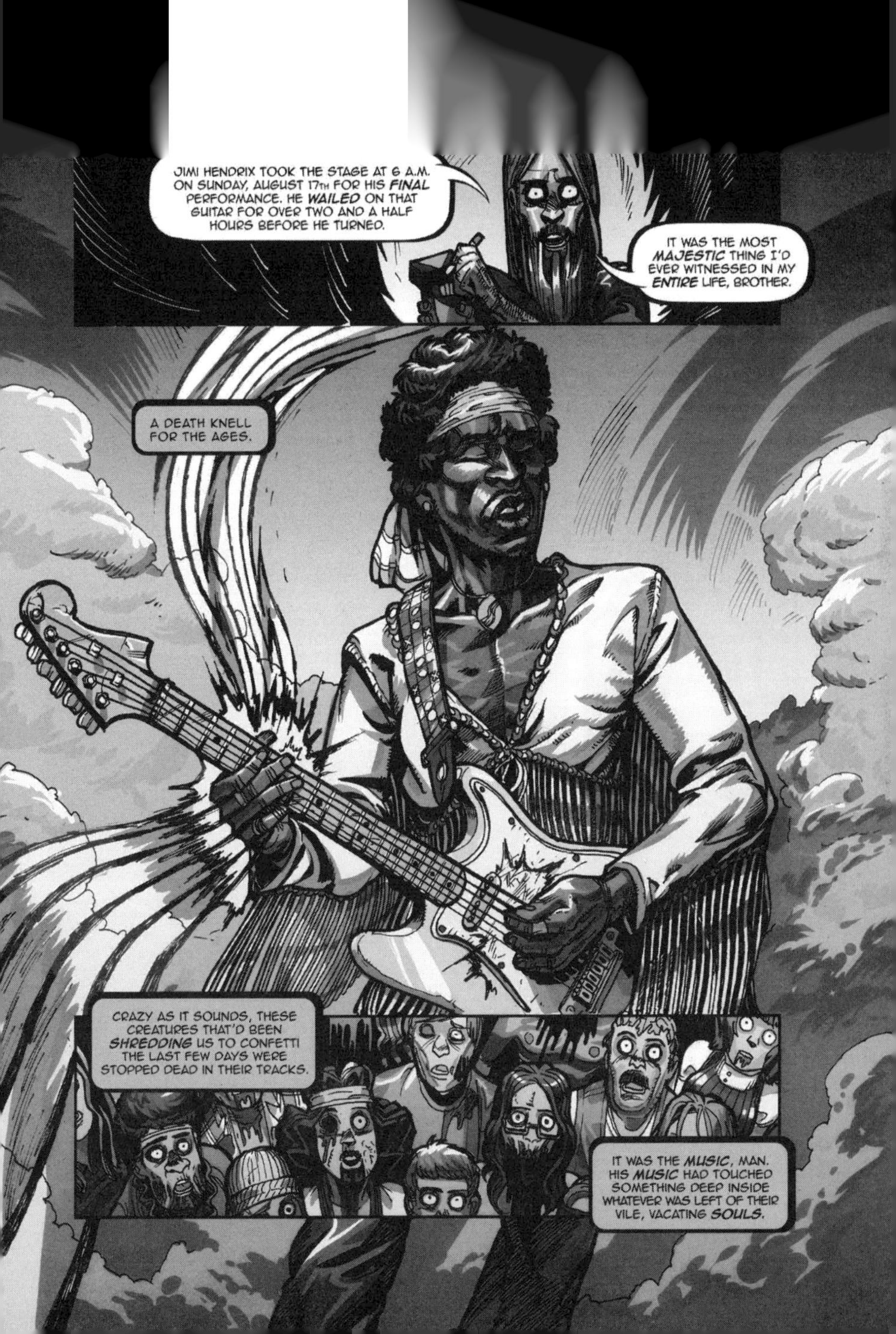
JIMI HENDRIX TOOK THE STAGE AT 6 A.M. ON SUNDAY, AUGUST 17TH FOR HIS FINAL PERFORMANCE. HE WAILED ON THAT GUITAR FOR OVER TWO AND A HALF HOURS BEFORE HE TURNED.
IT WAS THE MOST MAJESTIC THING I'D EVER WITNESSED IN MY ENTIRE LIFE, BROTHER.
A DEATH KNELL FOR THE AGES.
CRAZY AS IT SOUNDS, THESE CREATURES THAT'D BEEN SHREDDING US TO CONFETTI THE LAST FEW DAYS WERE STOPPED DEAD IN THEIR TRACKS.
IT WAS THE MUSIC, MAN. HIS MUSIC HAD TOUCHED SOMETHING DEEP INSIDE WHATEVER WAS LEFT OF THEIR VILE, VACATING SOULS.

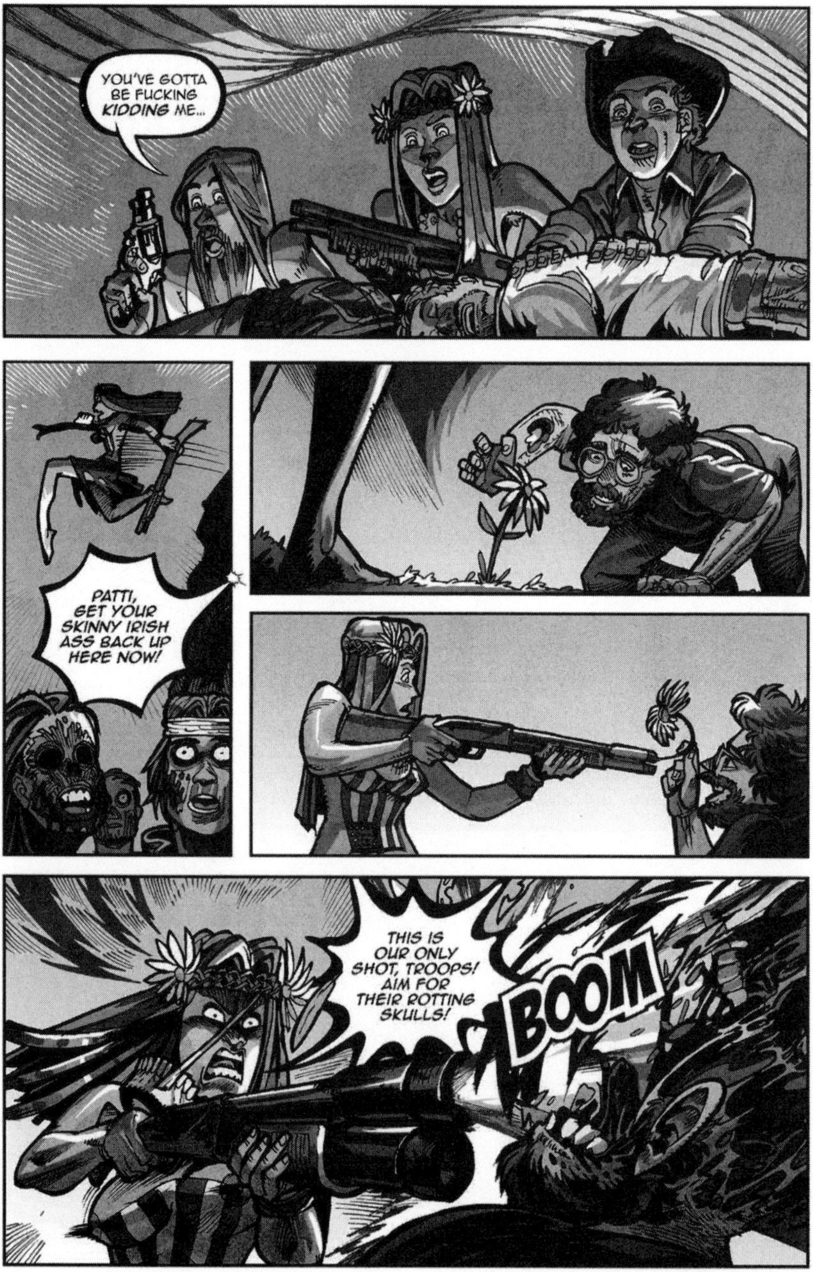
YOU'VE GOTTA BE FUCKING KIDDING ME...
PATTI, GET YOUR SKINNY IRISH ASS BACK UP HERE NOW!
THIS IS OUR ONLY SHOT, TROOPS! AIM FOR THEIR ROTTING SKULLS!
BOOM

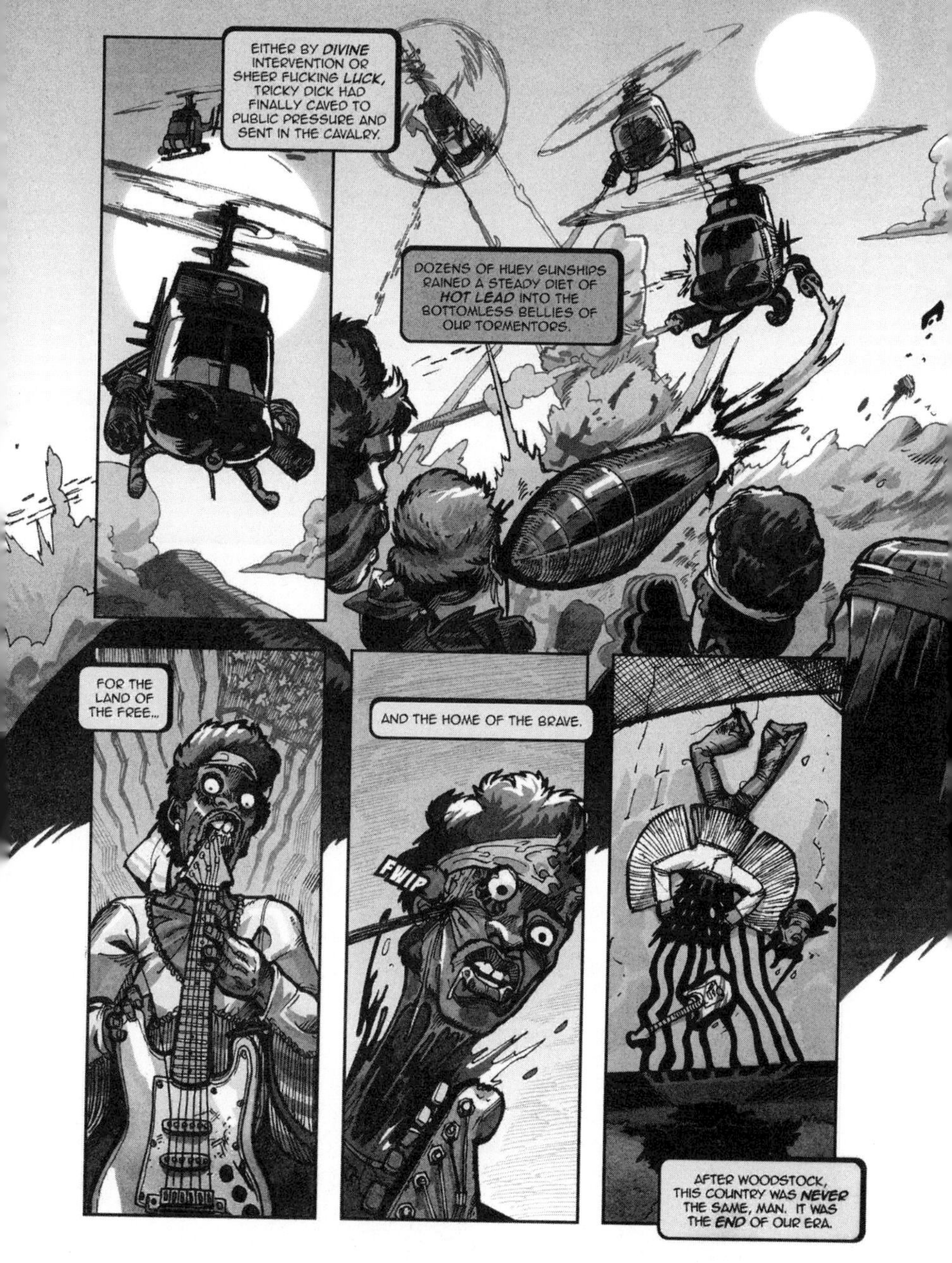
EITHER BY DIVINE INTERVENTION OR SHEER FUCKING LUCK, TRICKY DICK HAD FINALLY CAVED TO PUBLIC PRESSURE AND SENT IN THE CAVALRY.
DOZENS OF HUEY GUNSHIPS RAINED A STEADY DIET OF HOT LEAD INTO THE BOTTOMLESS BELLIES OF OUR TORMENTORS.
FOR THE LAND OF THE FREE...
AND THE HOME OF THE BRAVE.
FWIP
AFTER WOODSTOCK, THIS COUNTRY WAS NEVER THE SAME, MAN. IT WAS THE END OF OUR ERA.

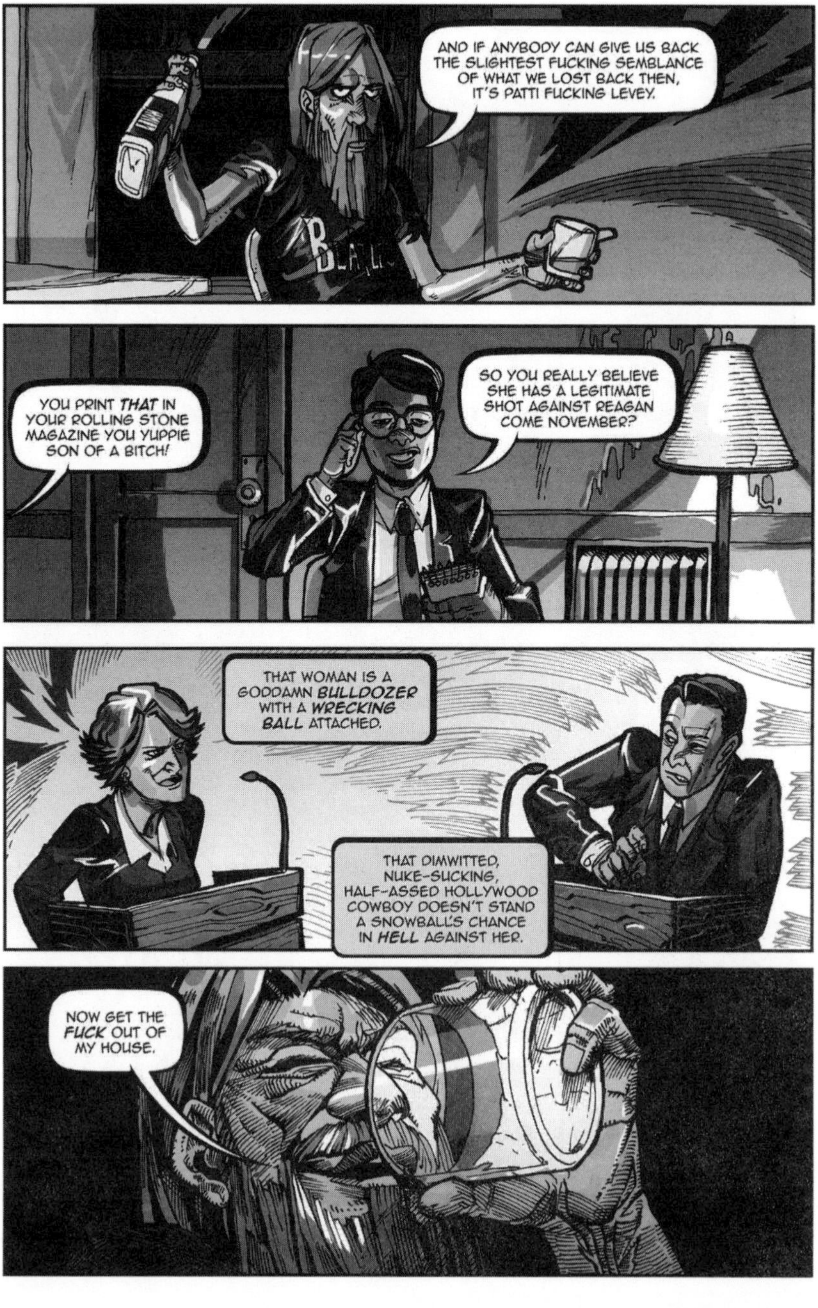
AND IF ANYBODY CAN GIVE US BACK THE SLIGHTEST FUCKING SEMBLANCE OF WHAT WE LOST BACK THEN, IT'S PATTI FUCKING LEVEY.
SO YOU REALLY BELIEVE SHE HAS A LEGITIMATE SHOT AGAINST REAGAN COME NOVEMBER?
YOU PRINT THAT IN YOUR ROLLING STONE MAGAZINE YOU YUPPIE SON OF A BITCH!
THAT WOMAN IS A GODDAMN BULLDOZER WITH A WRECKING BALL ATTACHED.
THAT DIMWITTED, NUKE-SUCKING, HALF-ASSED HOLLYWOOD COWBOY DOESN'T STAND A SNOWBALL'S CHANCE IN HELL AGAINST HER.
NOW GET THE FUCK OUT OF MY HOUSE.

NEW COKE

STORY BY:
MICHAEL ISENBERG
OLIVER MERTZ

ART AND LETTERS BY:
MICHAEL BRACCO

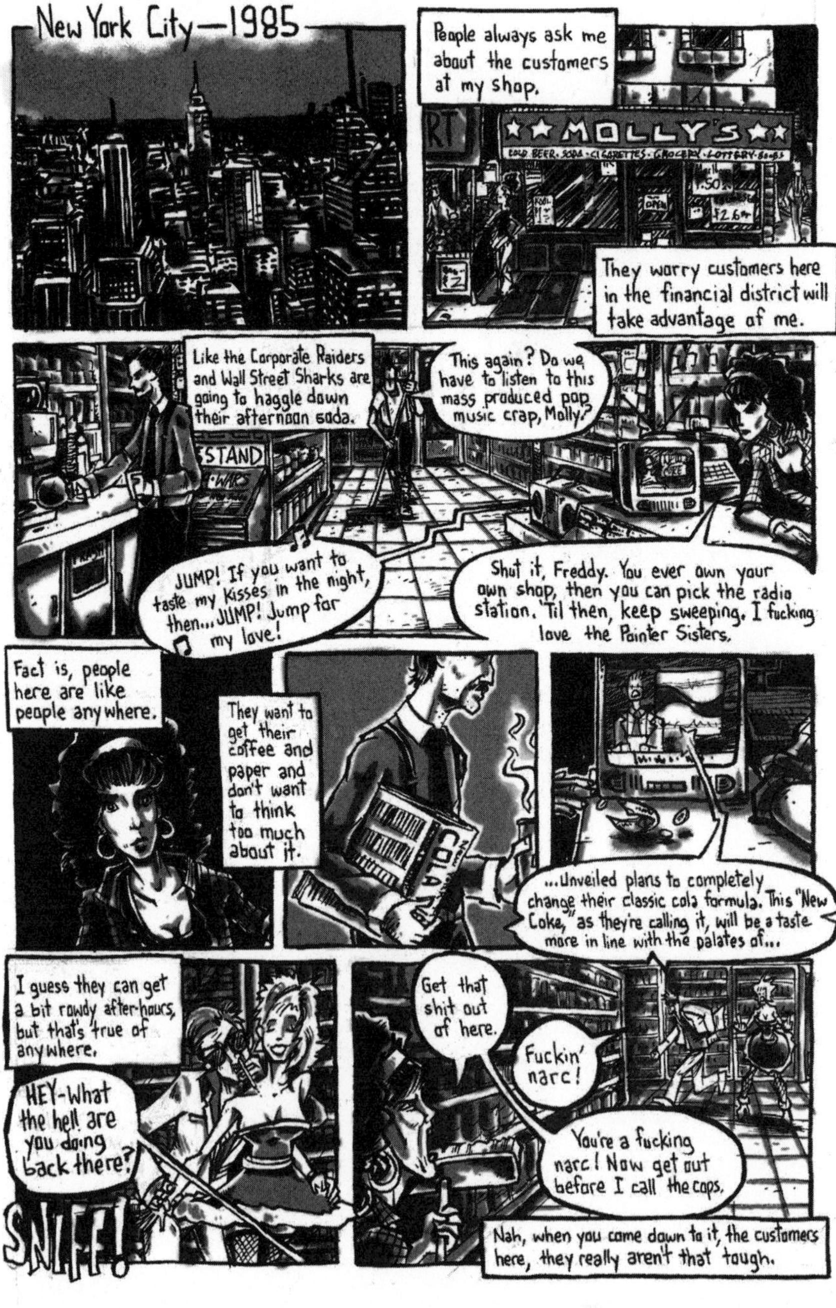

New York City—1985
People always ask me about the customers at my shop.
★★MOLLY'S★★
They worry customers here in the financial district will take advantage of me.
Like the Corporate Raiders and Wall Street Sharks are going to haggle down their afternoon soda.
This again? Do we have to listen to this mass produced pop music crap, Molly?
JUMP! If you want to taste my kisses in the night, then... JUMP! Jump for my love!
Shut it, Freddy. You ever own your own shop, then you can pick the radio station. 'Til then, keep sweeping. I fucking love the Pointer Sisters.
Fact is, people here are like people anywhere.
They want to get their coffee and paper and don't want to think too much about it.
...Unveiled plans to completely change their classic cola formula. This "New Coke," as they're calling it, will be a taste more in line with the palates of...
I guess they can get a bit rowdy after-hours, but that's true of anywhere.
HEY-What the hell are you doing back there?
SNIFF!
Get that shit out of here.
Fuckin' narc!
You're a fucking narc! Now get out before I call the cops.
Nah, when you come down to it, the customers here, they really aren't that tough.

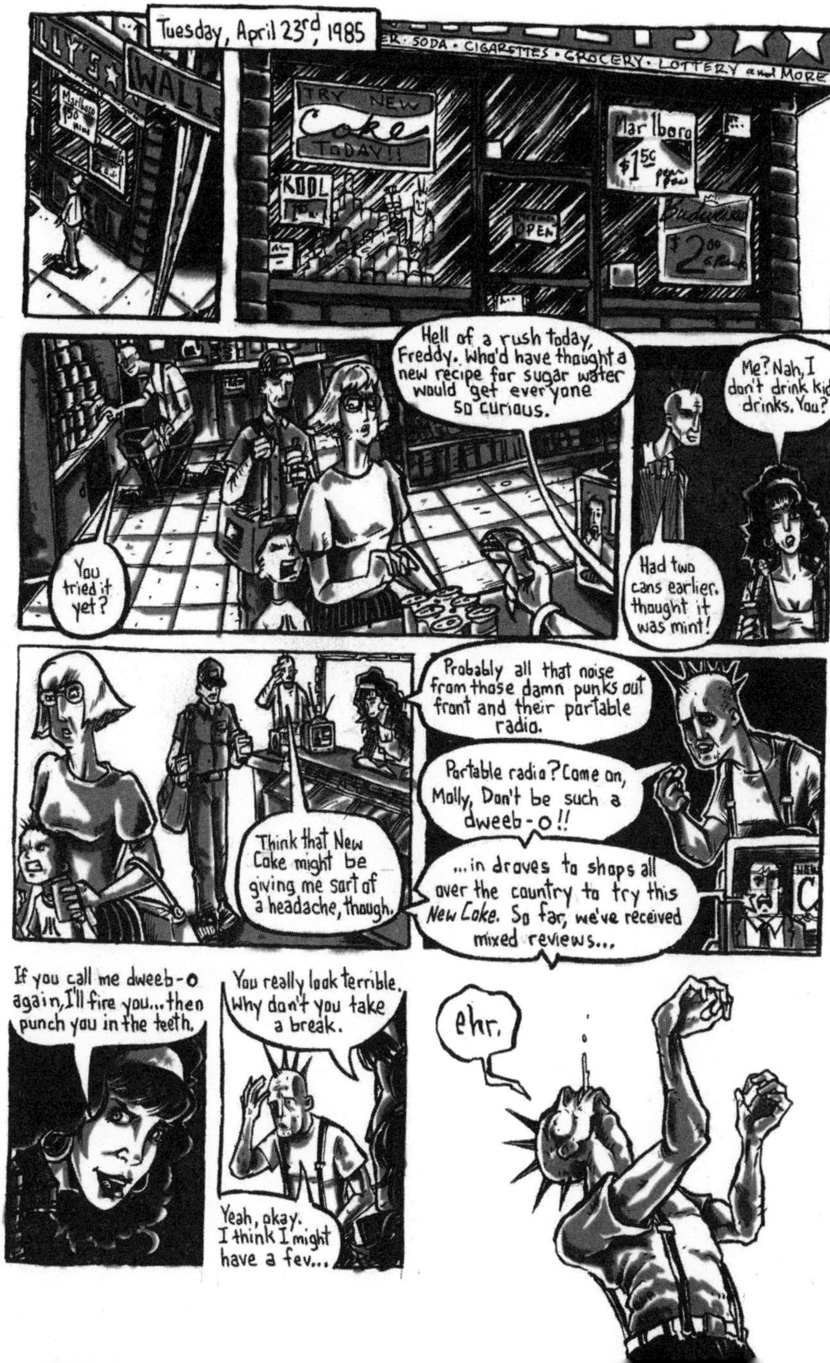
Tuesday, April 23rd, 1985
SODA • CIGARETTES • GROCERY • LOTTERY and MORE
TRY NEW Coke TODAY!!
KOOL
OPEN
Marlboro $1.50
$2.00
Hell of a rush today, Freddy. Who'd have thought a new recipe for sugar water would get everyone so curious.
You tried it yet?
Me? Nah, I don't drink kids' drinks. You?
Had two cans earlier. thought it was mint!
Probably all that noise from those damn punks out front and their portable radio.
Think that New Coke might be giving me sort of a headache, though.
Portable radio? Come on, Molly, Don't be such a dweeb-o!!
...in droves to shops all over the country to try this New Coke. So far, we've received mixed reviews...
If you call me dweeb-o again, I'll fire you...then punch you in the teeth.
You really look terrible. Why don't you take a break.
Yeah, okay. I think I might have a fev...
ehr.

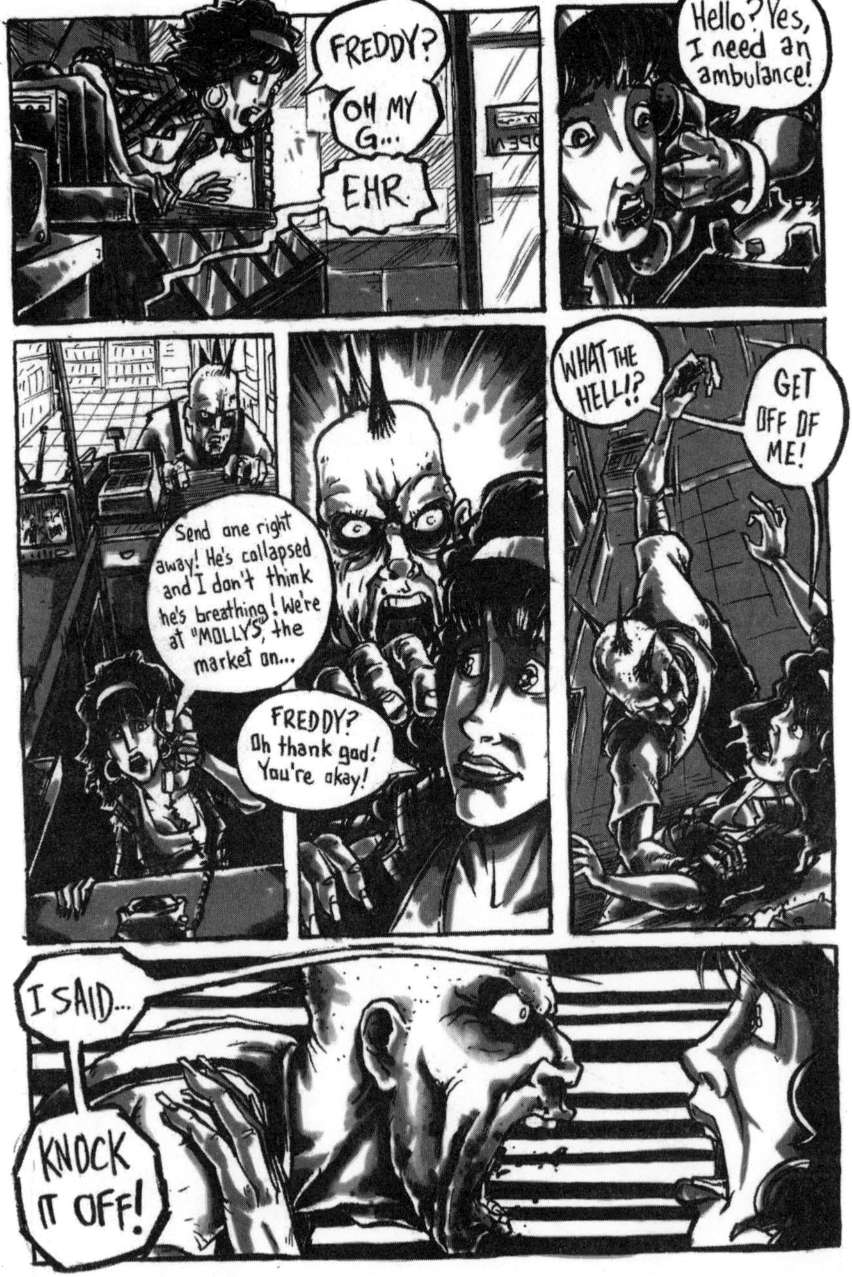
FREDDY?
OH MY G...
EHR.
Hello? Yes, I need an ambulance!
Send one right away! He's collapsed and I don't think he's breathing! We're at "MOLLY'S", the market on...
FREDDY? Oh thank god! You're okay!
WHAT THE HELL!?
GET OFF OF ME!
I SAID...
KNOCK IT OFF!

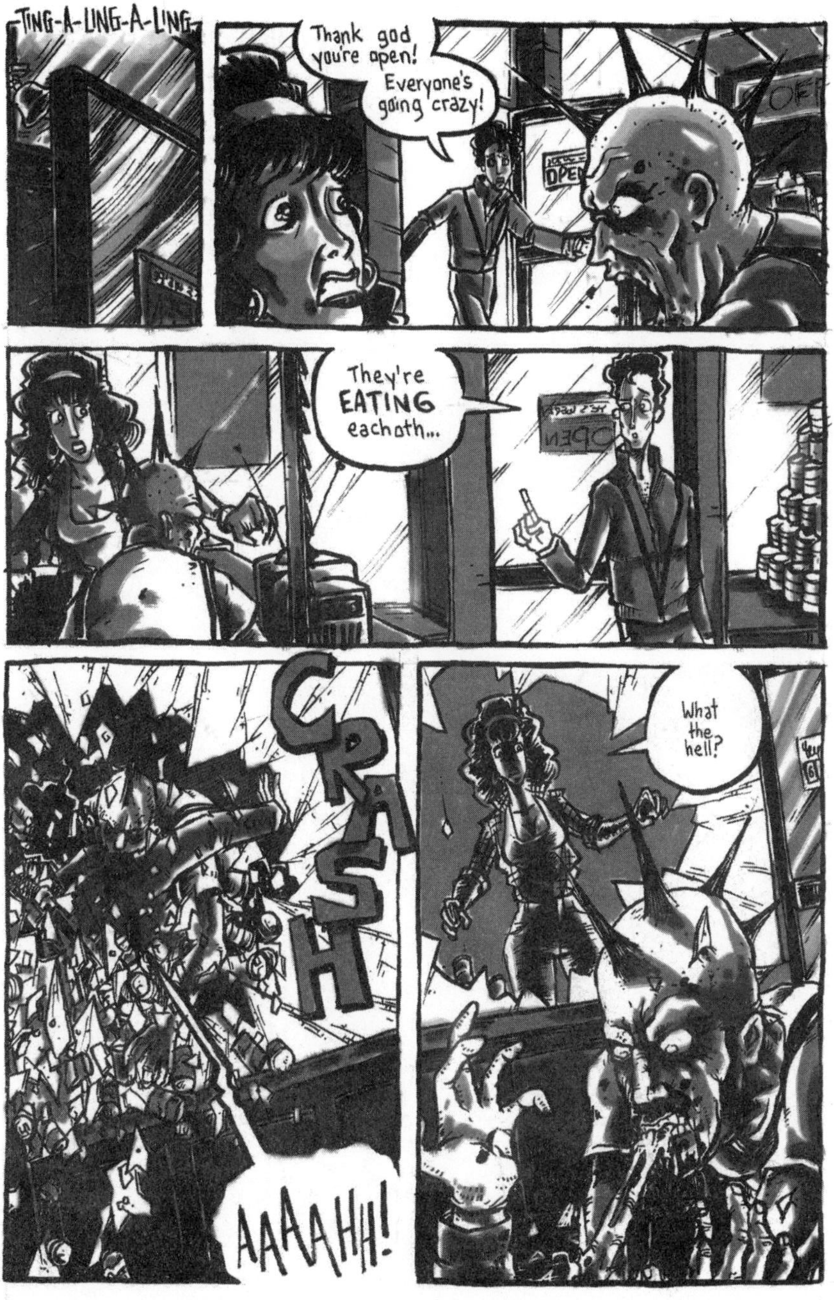
TING-A-LING-A-LING
Thank god you're open!
Everyone's going crazy!
OPEN
They're EATING eachoth...
OPEN
CRASH
AAAAHH!
What the hell?

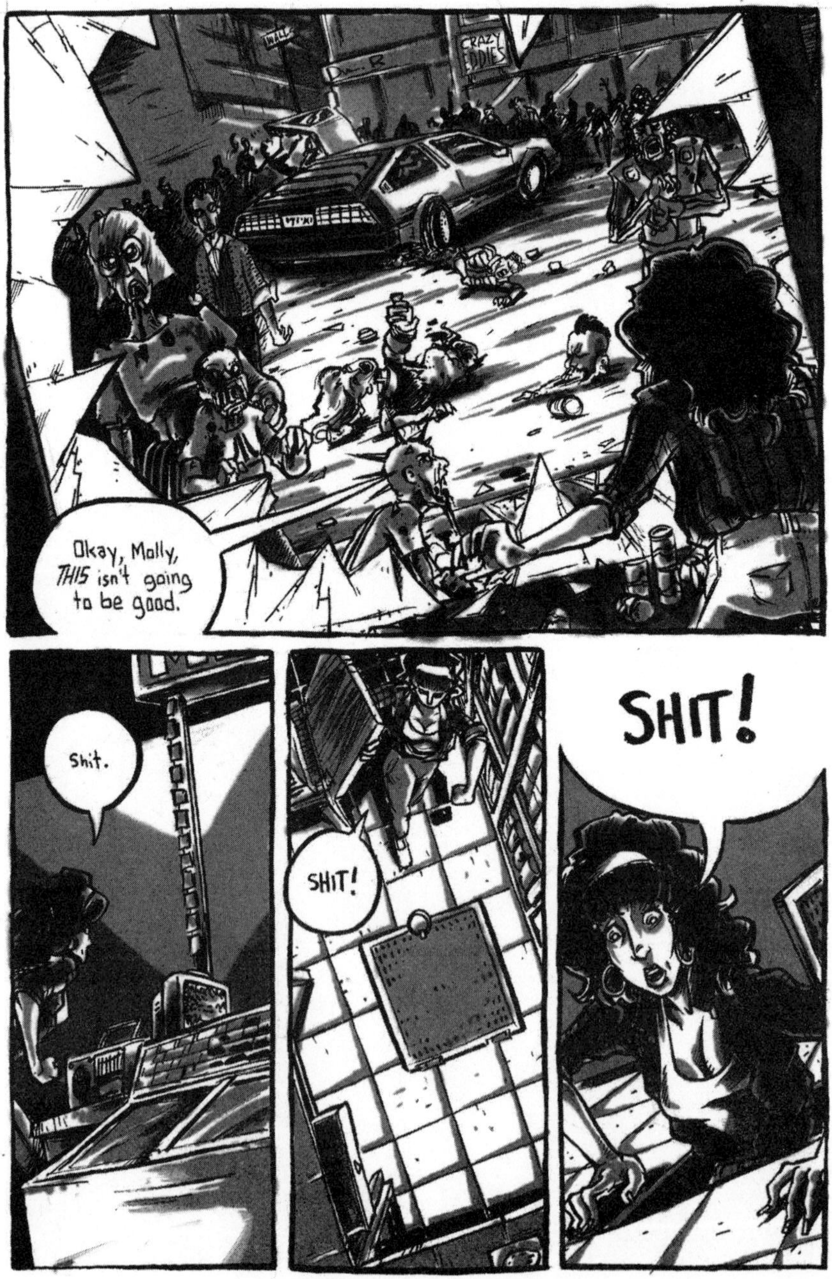

WALL
CRAZY EDDIES
Okay, Molly, THIS isn't going to be good.
Shit.
SHIT!
SHIT!

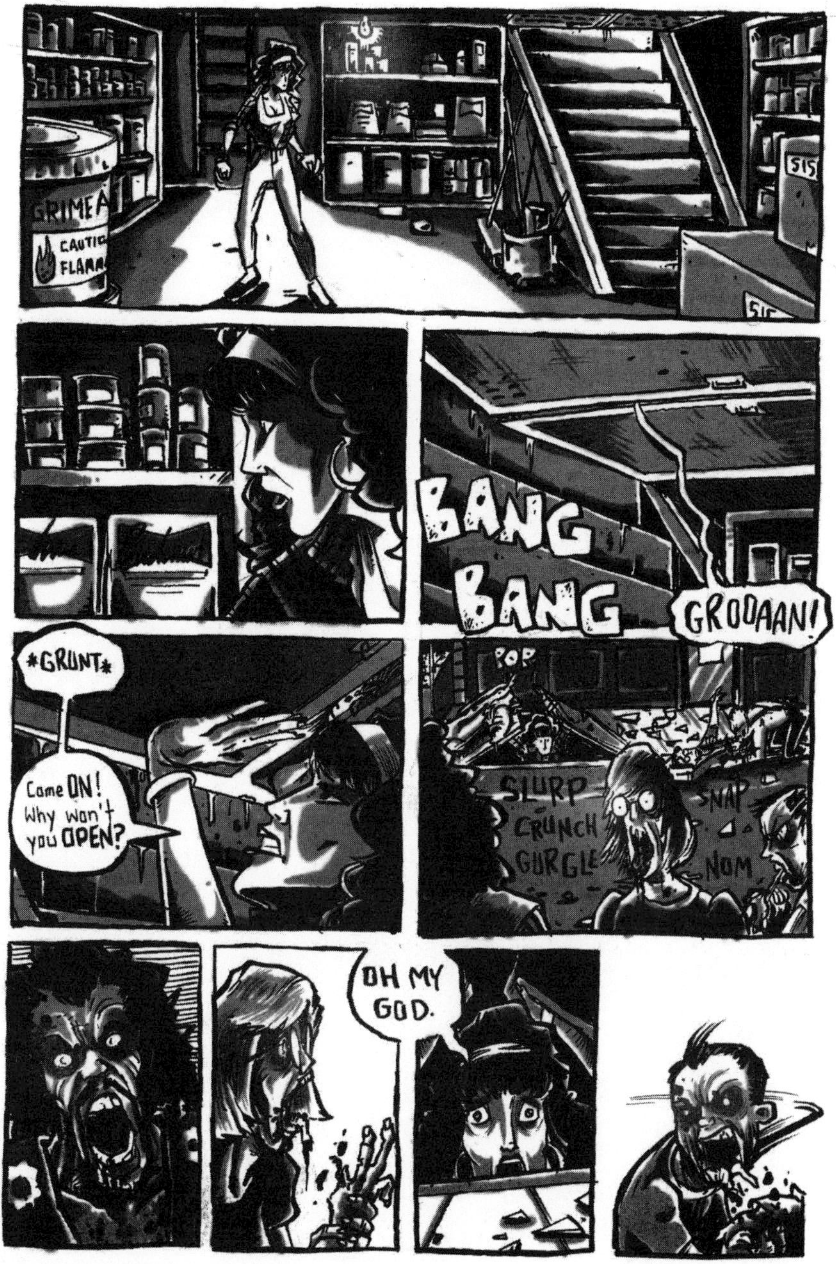
GRIMEA
CAUTIO
FLAMM
BANG
BANG
GROOAAN!
GRUNT
Come ON! Why won't you OPEN?
POP
SLURP
CRUNCH
GURGLE
SNAP
NOM
OH MY GOD.

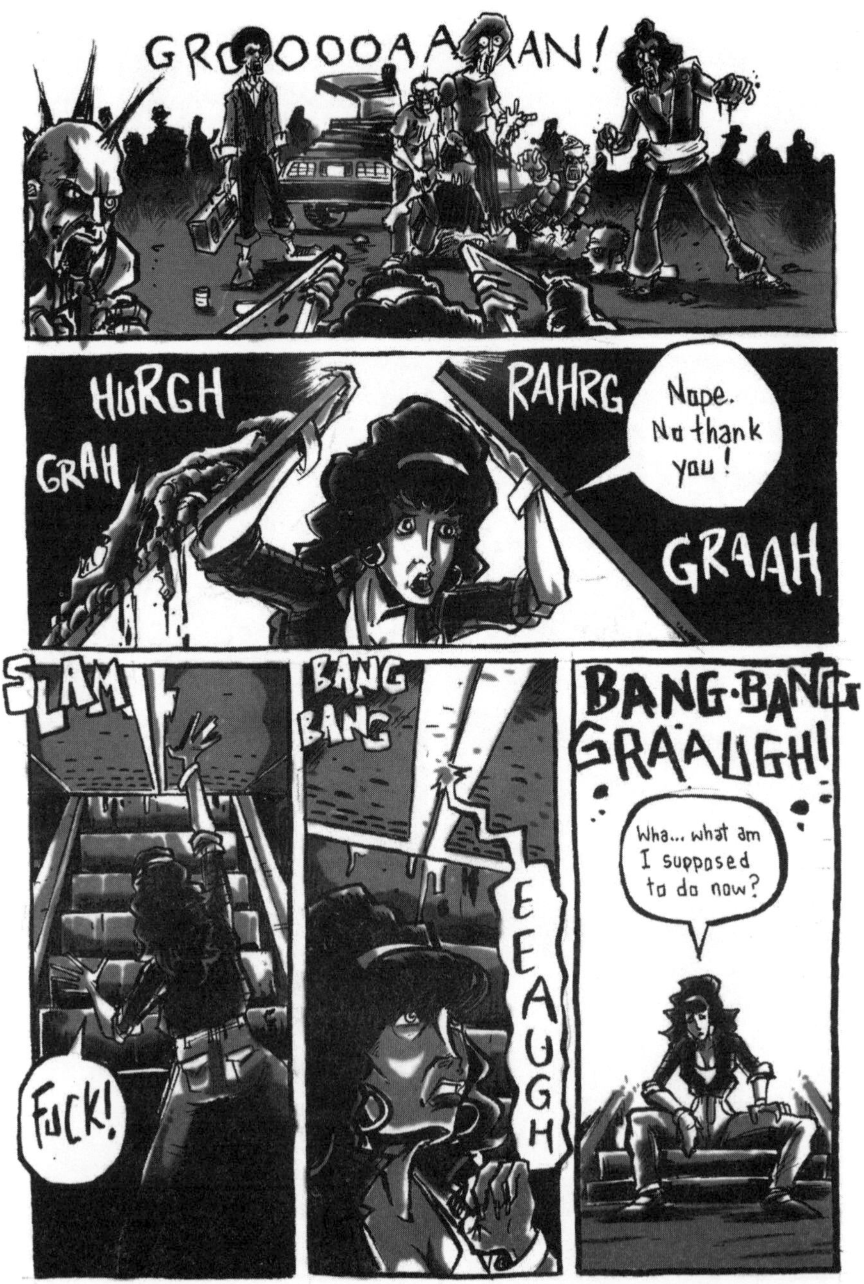
GROOOOOAAAAAN!
HURGH
GRAH
RAHRG
Nope. No thank you!
GRAAH
SLAM
FUCK!
BANG BANG
EEEAUGH
BANG·BANG
GRAAUGH!
Wha... what am I supposed to do now?

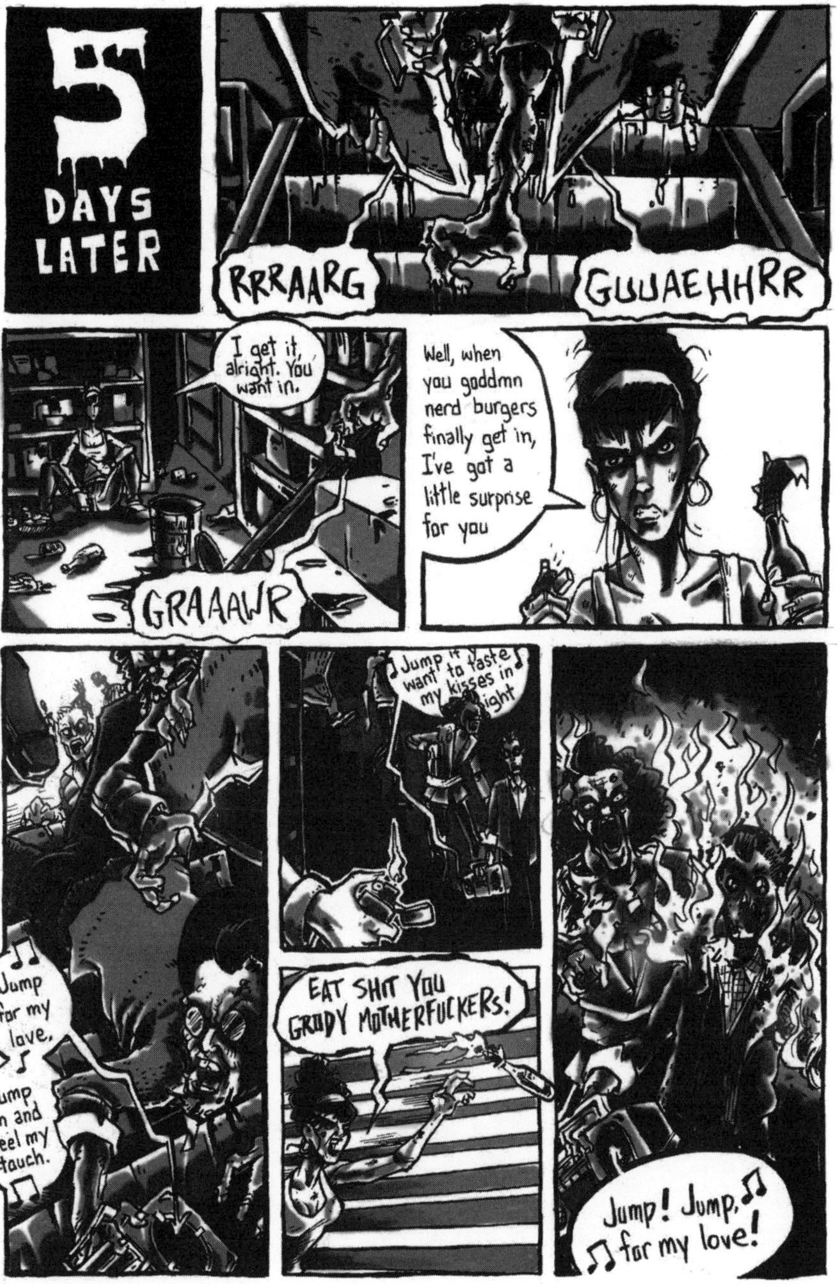
5 DAYS LATER
RRRAARG
GUUAEHHRR
I get it, alright. You want in.
GRAAAWR
Well, when you goddmn nerd burgers finally get in, I've got a little surprise for you
Jump for my love,
Jump in and feel my tauch.
Jump if want to taste my kisses in
EAT SHIT YOU GRODY MOTHERFUCKERS!
Jump! Jump, for my love!

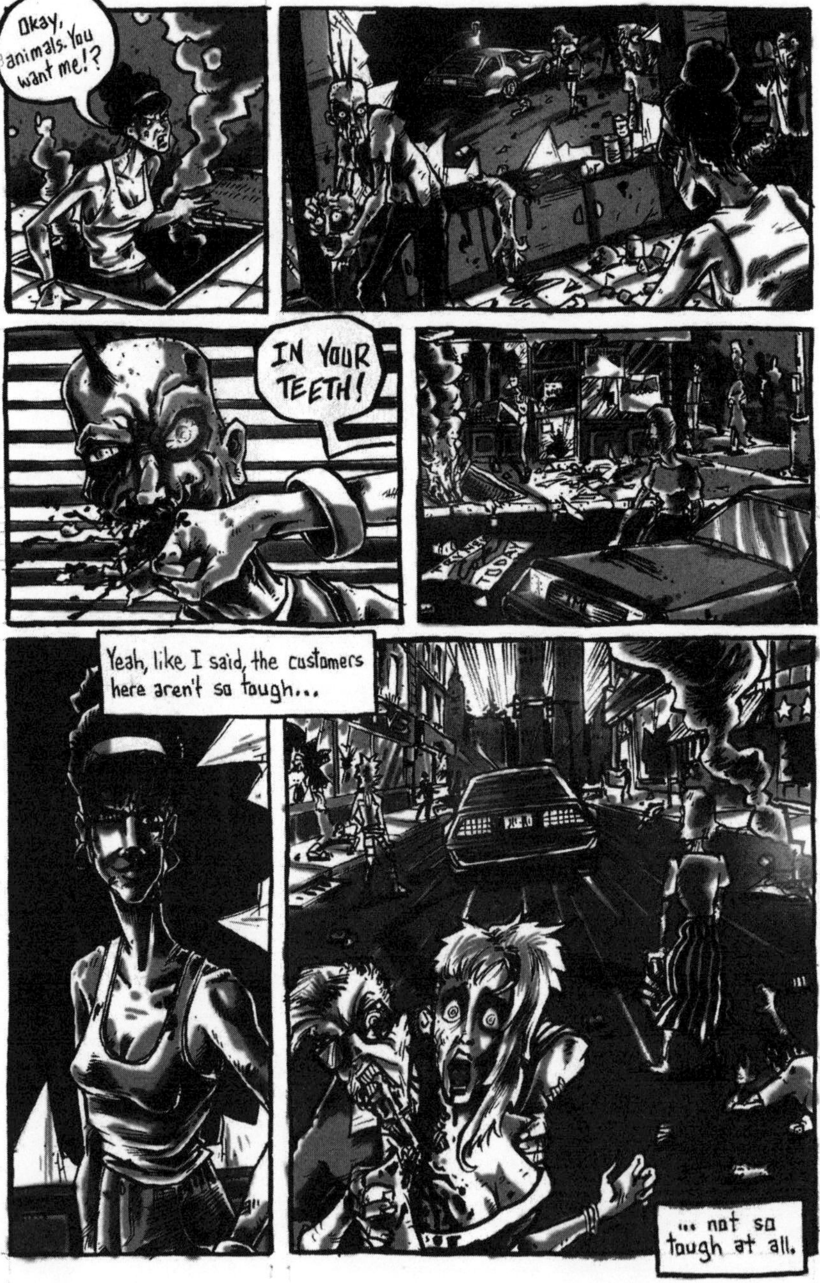
Okay, animals. You want me!?
IN YOUR TEETH!
TODAY
Yeah, like I said, the customers here aren't so tough...
... not so tough at all.

THE BUZZARD

STORY BY:
MICHAEL McDERMOTT

ART BY:
CHRISTINE LARSEN

LETTERS BY:
JEFF MCCOMSEY

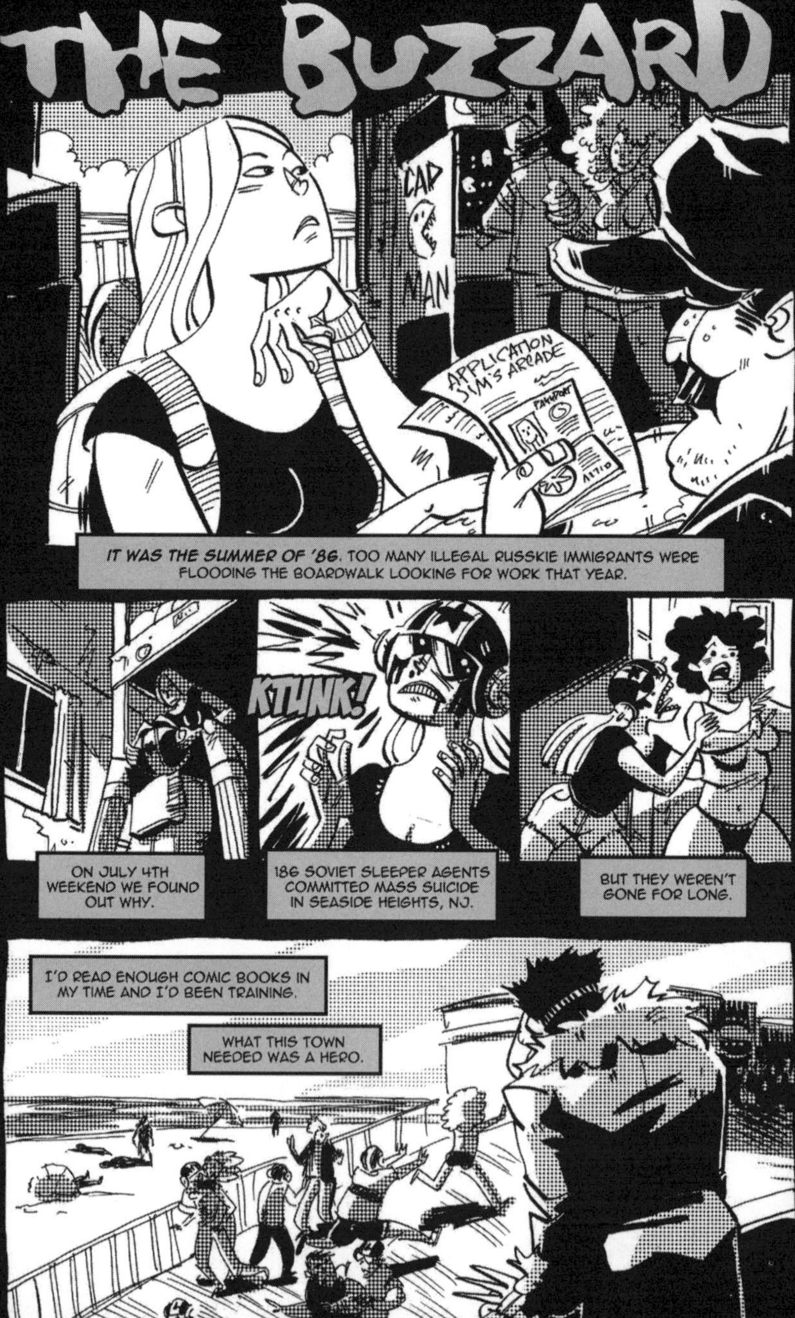
THE BUZZARD
CAP MAN
APPLICATION JIM'S ARCADE
IT WAS THE SUMMER OF '86. TOO MANY ILLEGAL RUSSKIE IMMIGRANTS WERE FLOODING THE BOARDWALK LOOKING FOR WORK THAT YEAR.
ON JULY 4TH WEEKEND WE FOUND OUT WHY.
KTUNK!
186 SOVIET SLEEPER AGENTS COMMITTED MASS SUICIDE IN SEASIDE HEIGHTS, NJ.
BUT THEY WEREN'T GONE FOR LONG.
I'D READ ENOUGH COMIC BOOKS IN MY TIME AND I'D BEEN TRAINING.
WHAT THIS TOWN NEEDED WAS A HERO.

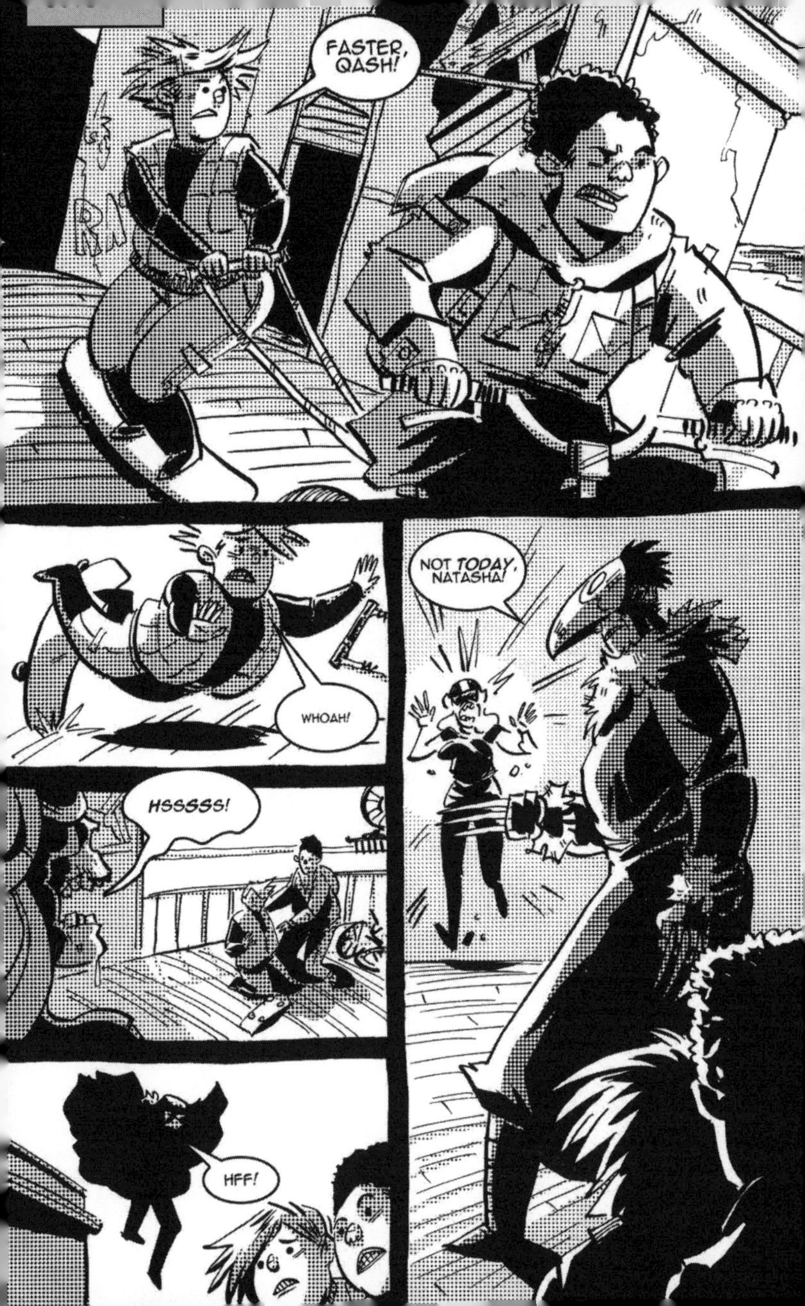
FASTER, QASH!
WHOAH!
NOT TODAY, NATASHA!
HSSSSS!
HFF!

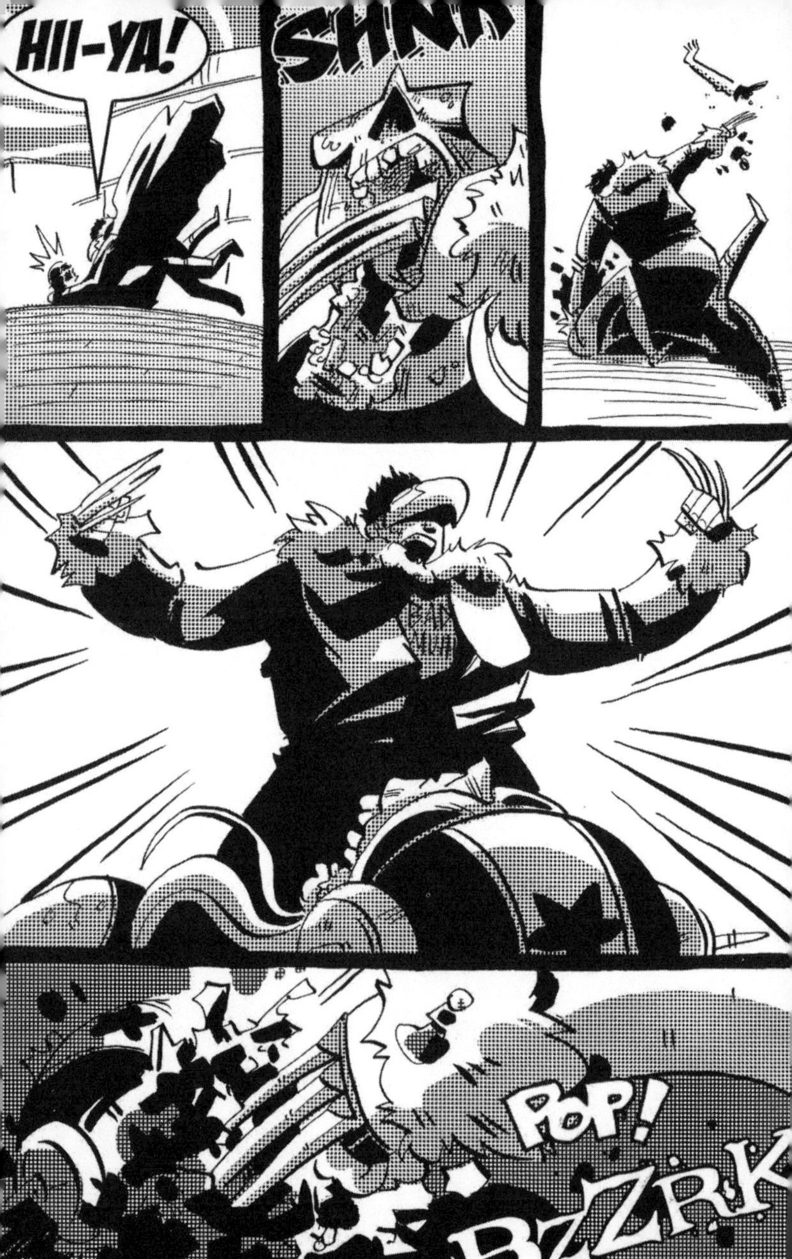
HII-YA!
SHNK
POP!
BZZRK

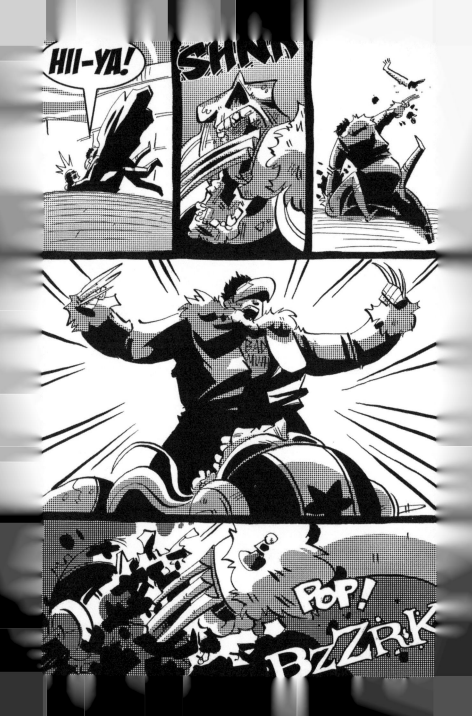

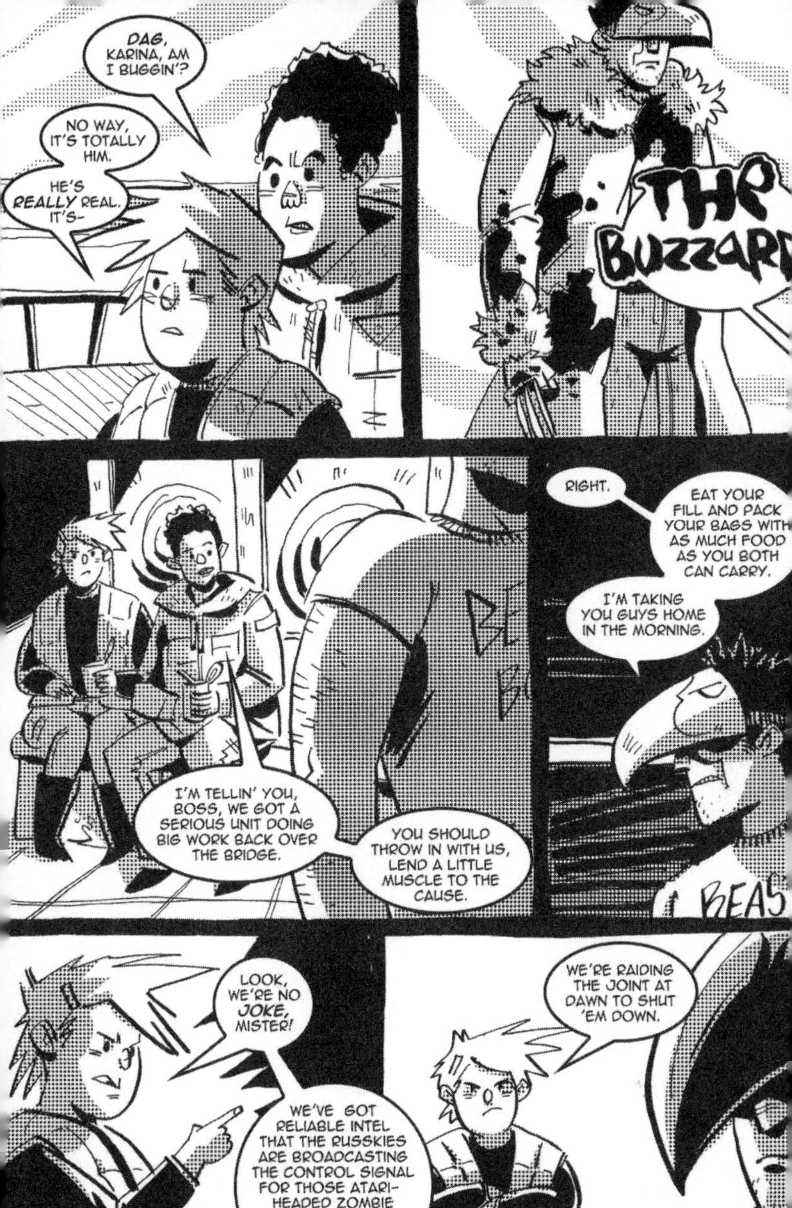

DAG, KARINA, AM I BUGGIN'?
NO WAY, IT'S TOTALLY HIM.
HE'S REALLY REAL. IT'S-
THE BUZZARD
RIGHT.
EAT YOUR FILL AND PACK YOUR BAGS WITH AS MUCH FOOD AS YOU BOTH CAN CARRY.
I'M TAKING YOU GUYS HOME IN THE MORNING.
I'M TELLIN' YOU, BOSS, WE GOT A SERIOUS UNIT DOING BIG WORK BACK OVER THE BRIDGE.
YOU SHOULD THROW IN WITH US, LEND A LITTLE MUSCLE TO THE CAUSE.
LOOK, WE'RE NO JOKE, MISTER!
WE'VE GOT RELIABLE INTEL THAT THE RUSSKIES ARE BROADCASTING THE CONTROL SIGNAL FOR THOSE ATARI-HEADED ZOMBIE FREAK SHOWS OUT OF THE OCCUPIED LAKEHURST NAVAL BASE.
WE'RE RAIDING THE JOINT AT DAWN TO SHUT 'EM DOWN.

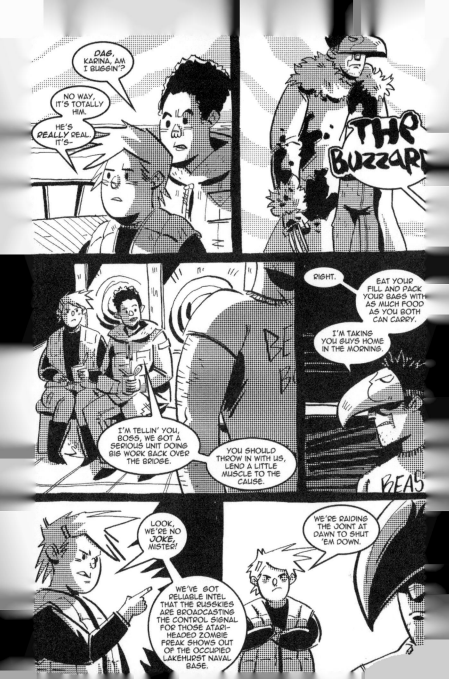

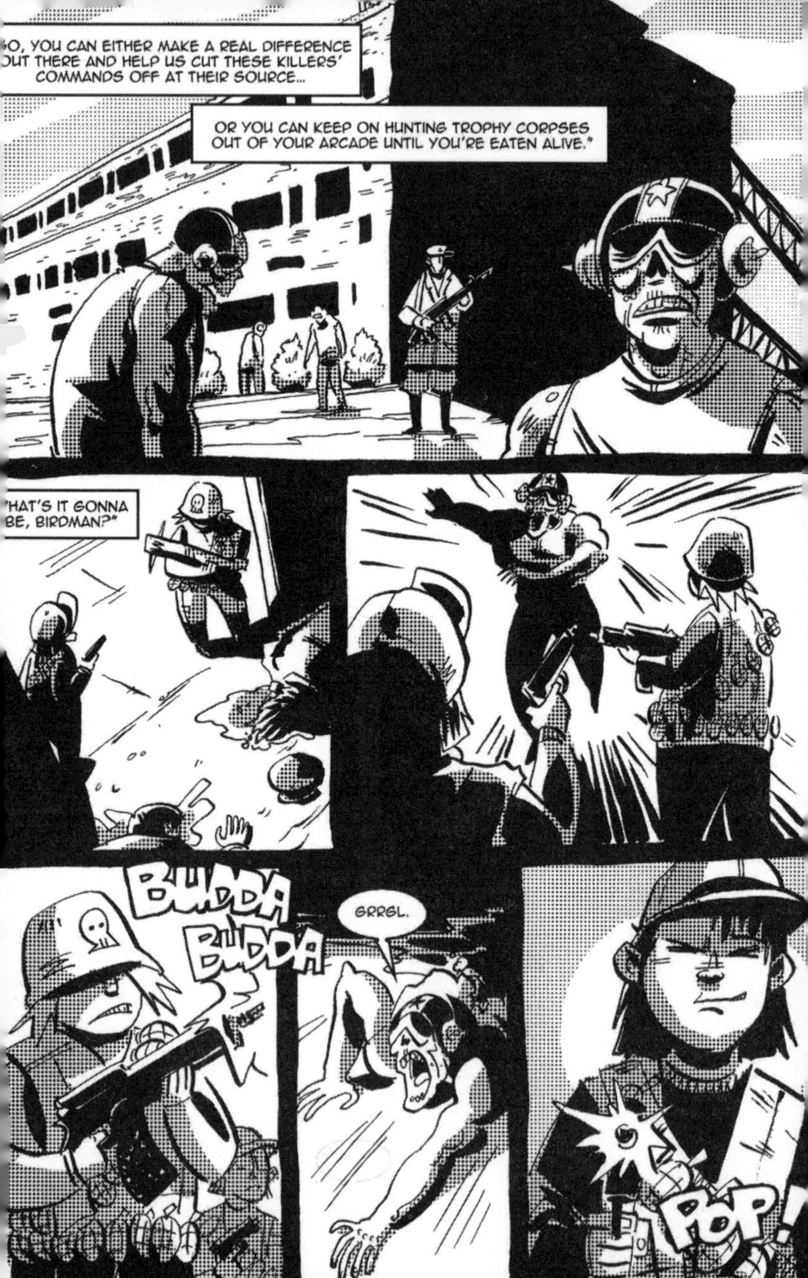

SO, YOU CAN EITHER MAKE A REAL DIFFERENCE OUT THERE AND HELP US CUT THESE KILLERS' COMMANDS OFF AT THEIR SOURCE...
OR YOU CAN KEEP ON HUNTING TROPHY CORPSES OUT OF YOUR ARCADE UNTIL YOU'RE EATEN ALIVE."
WHAT'S IT GONNA BE, BIRDMAN?"
BUDDA
BUDDA
GRRGL.
POP!

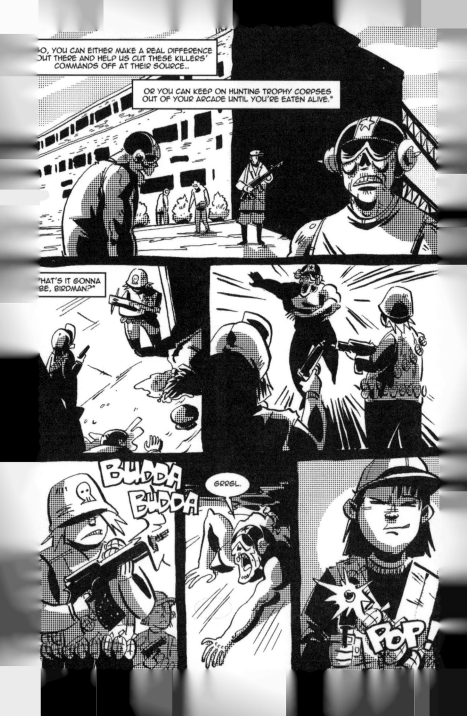

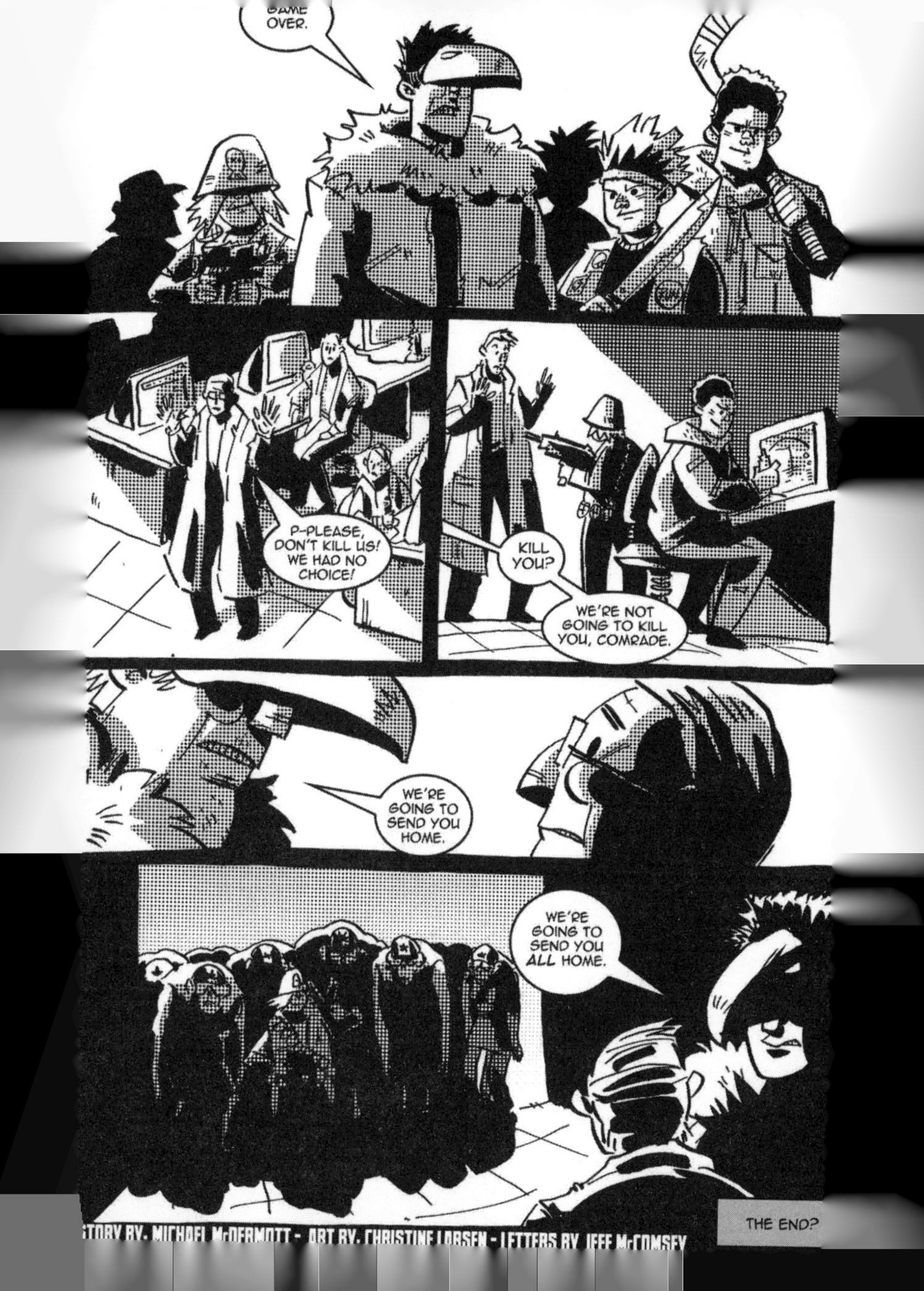
GAME OVER.
P-PLEASE, DON'T KILL US! WE HAD NO CHOICE!
KILL YOU?
WE'RE NOT GOING TO KILL YOU, COMRADE.
WE'RE GOING TO SEND YOU HOME.
WE'RE GOING TO SEND YOU ALL HOME.
THE END?

STORY BY. MICHAEL McDERMOTT - ART BY. CHRISTINE LARSEN - LETTERS BY JEFF McCOMSEY

JACK OF SPADES

STORY AND ART BY:
STEVE BECKER
JEFF MCCOMSEY

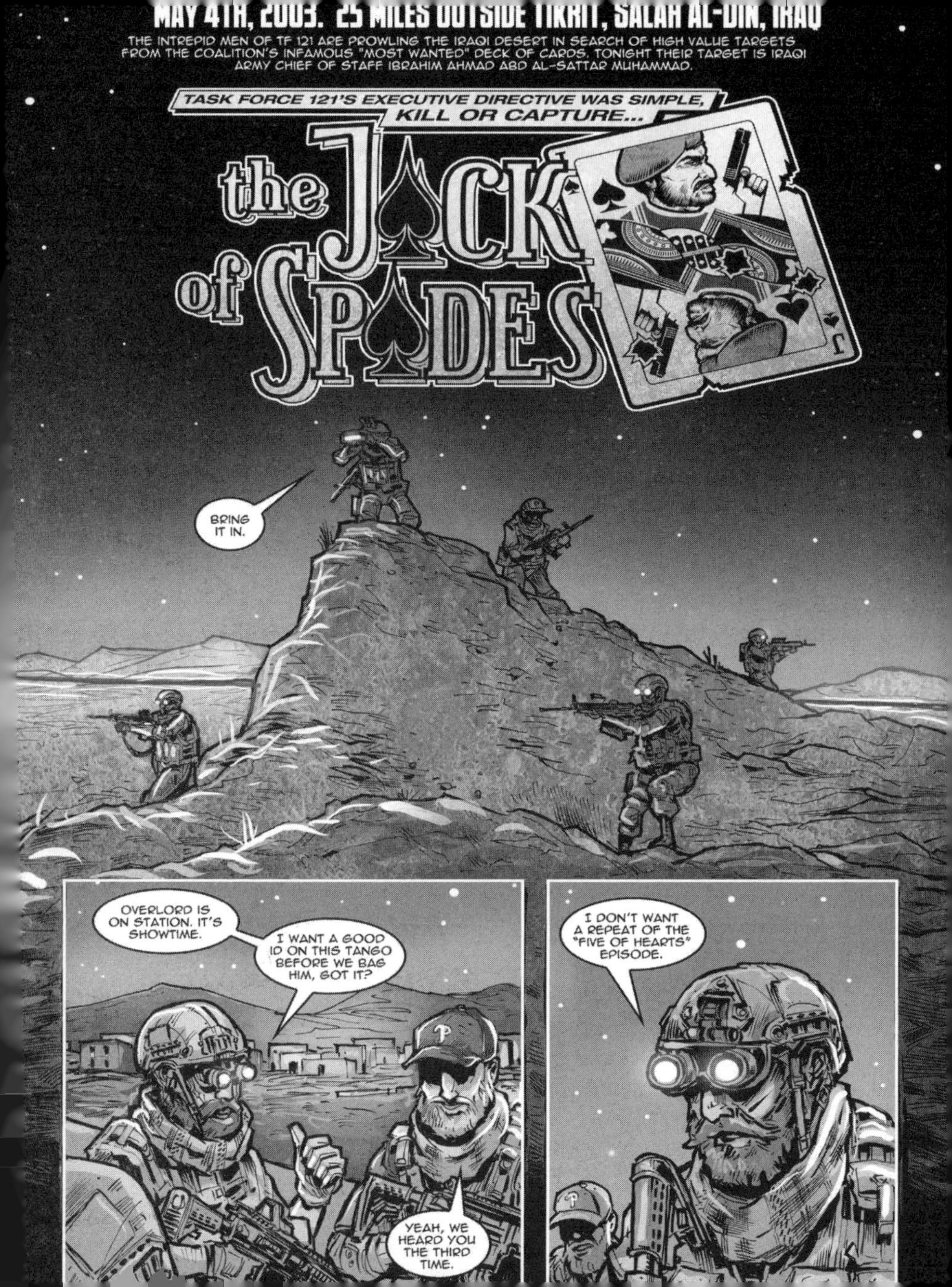
MAY 4TH, 2003. 25 MILES OUTSIDE TIKRIT, SALAH AL-DIN, IRAQ
THE INTREPID MEN OF TF 121 ARE PROWLING THE IRAQI DESERT IN SEARCH OF HIGH VALUE TARGETS FROM THE COALITION'S INFAMOUS "MOST WANTED" DECK OF CARDS. TONIGHT THEIR TARGET IS IRAQI ARMY CHIEF OF STAFF IBRAHIM AHMAD ABD AL-SATTAR MUHAMMAD.
TASK FORCE 121'S EXECUTIVE DIRECTIVE WAS SIMPLE, KILL OR CAPTURE...
the JACK of SPADES
BRING IT IN.
OVERLORD IS ON STATION. IT'S SHOWTIME.
I WANT A GOOD ID ON THIS TANGO BEFORE WE BAG HIM, GOT IT?
YEAH, WE HEARD YOU THE THIRD TIME.
I DON'T WANT A REPEAT OF THE "FIVE OF HEARTS" EPISODE.

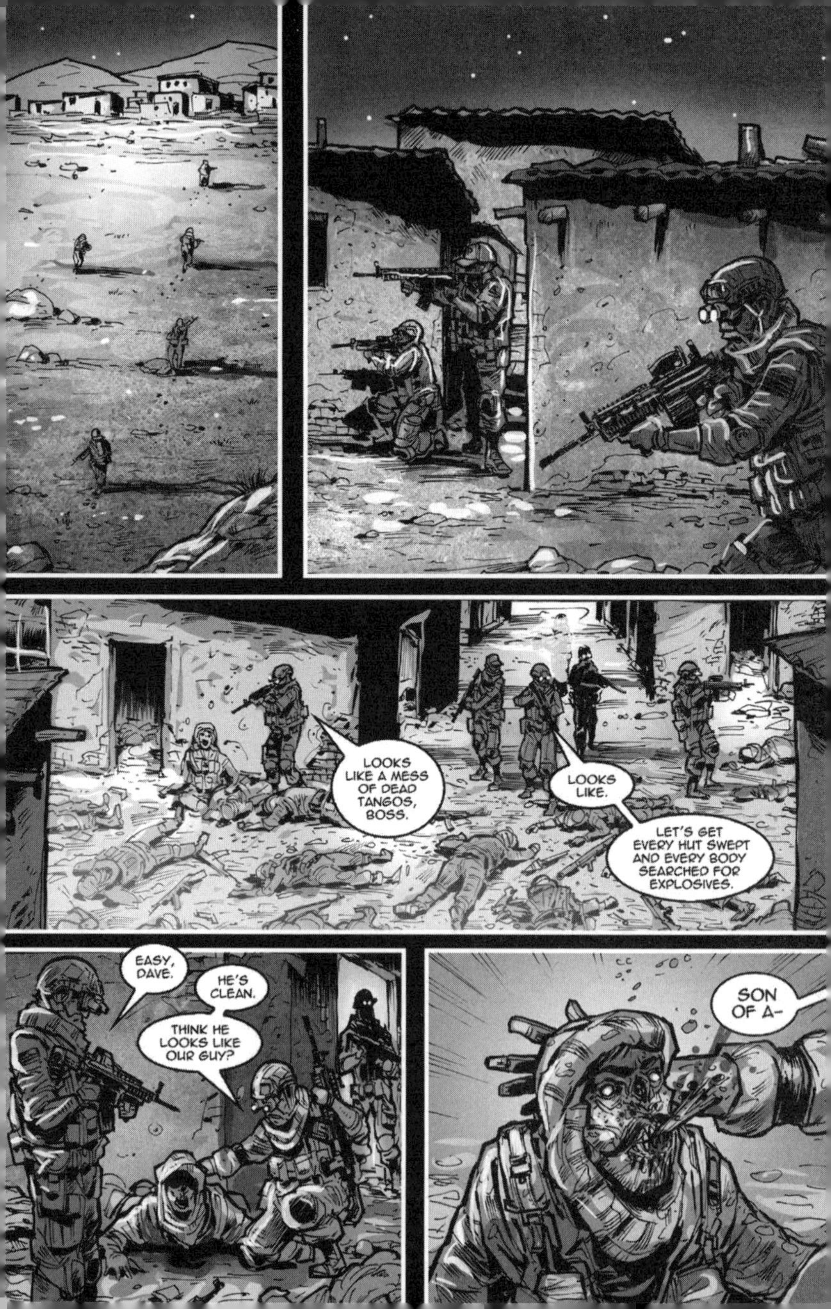
LOOKS LIKE A MESS OF DEAD TANGOS, BOSS.
LOOKS LIKE.
LET'S GET EVERY HUT SWEPT AND EVERY BODY SEARCHED FOR EXPLOSIVES.
EASY, DAVE.
HE'S CLEAN.
THINK HE LOOKS LIKE OUR GUY?
SON OF A-

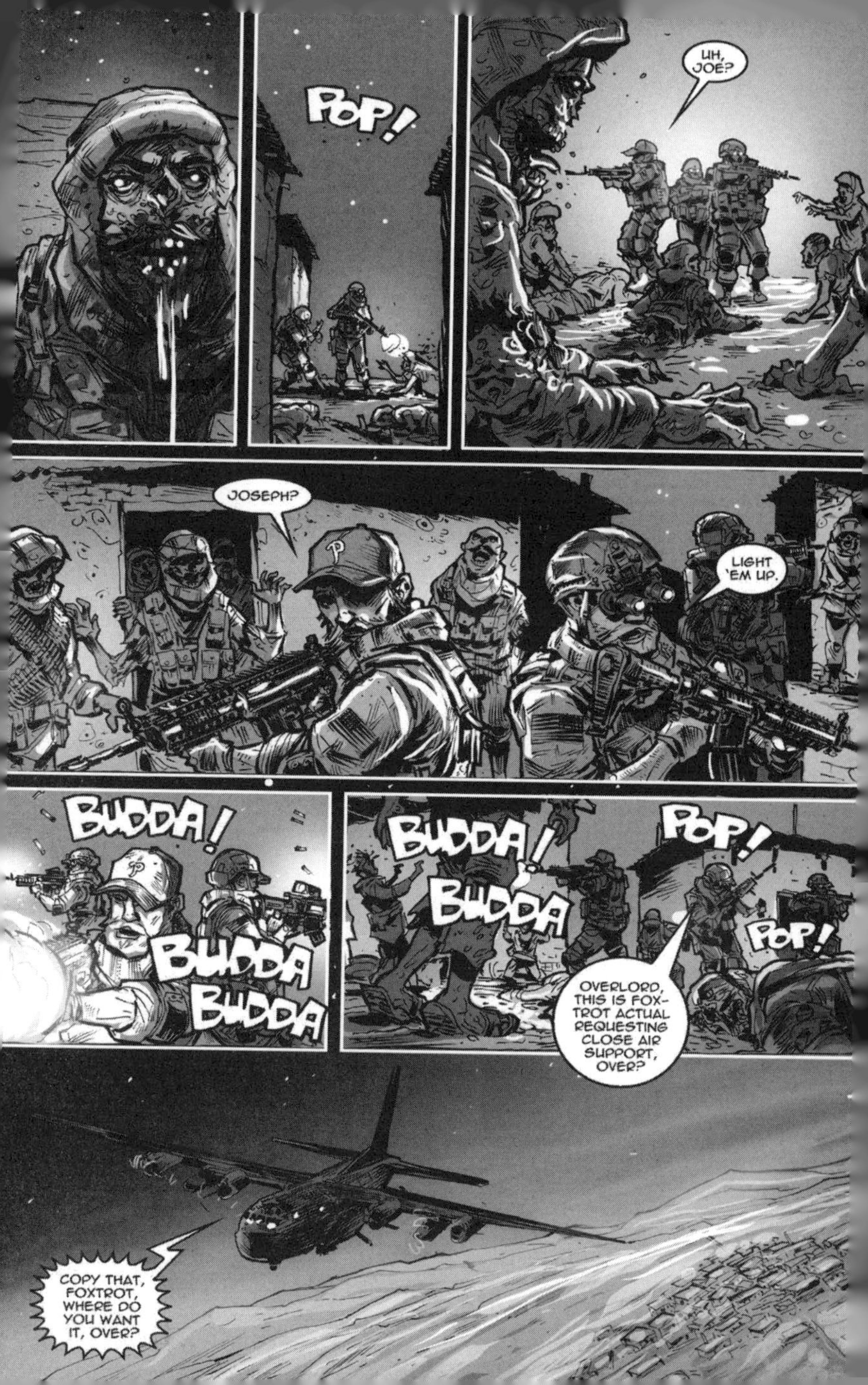
POP!
UH, JOE?
JOSEPH?
LIGHT 'EM UP.
BUDDA!
BUDDA
BUDDA
BUDDA!
BUDDA
POP!
POP!
OVERLORD, THIS IS FOXTROT ACTUAL REQUESTING CLOSE AIR SUPPORT, OVER?
COPY THAT, FOXTROT, WHERE DO YOU WANT IT, OVER?

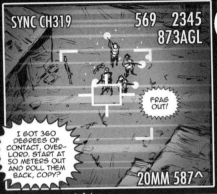

SYNC CH319   569   2345   873AGL

20MM 587^

FRAG OUT!

I GOT 360 DEGREES OF CONTACT, OVERLORD. START AT 50 METERS OUT AND ROLL THEM BACK, COPY?

NEGATIVE FOXTROT. I DON'T HAVE ANY CONTACTS ON THERMAL

UH, WE'VE GOT YOU, FOXTROT BUT I DON'T SEE ANY TARGETS, OVER?

SAY AGAIN, OVERLORD? I GOT TANGOS CRAWLING UP MY NOSE DOWN HERE, OVER?

I GOT BINGO ON THERMAL.

THERMAL?

BUDDA BUDDA

SYNC CH319   569   2345   873AGL

20MM 587^

GO TO INFRARED, OVERLORD!

GOING TO INFRARED. STAND BY, FOXTROT.

SYNC CH319   569   2345   873AGL

20MM 587^

WHOA! I GOT YOUR CONTACTS, FOXTROT!

OK, WE'RE GOING TO GET YOU GUYS SOME TWENTY MIKE MIKE DOWN THERE.

STAND BY, FOXTROT.

WWAAAAAHHHHHHHH

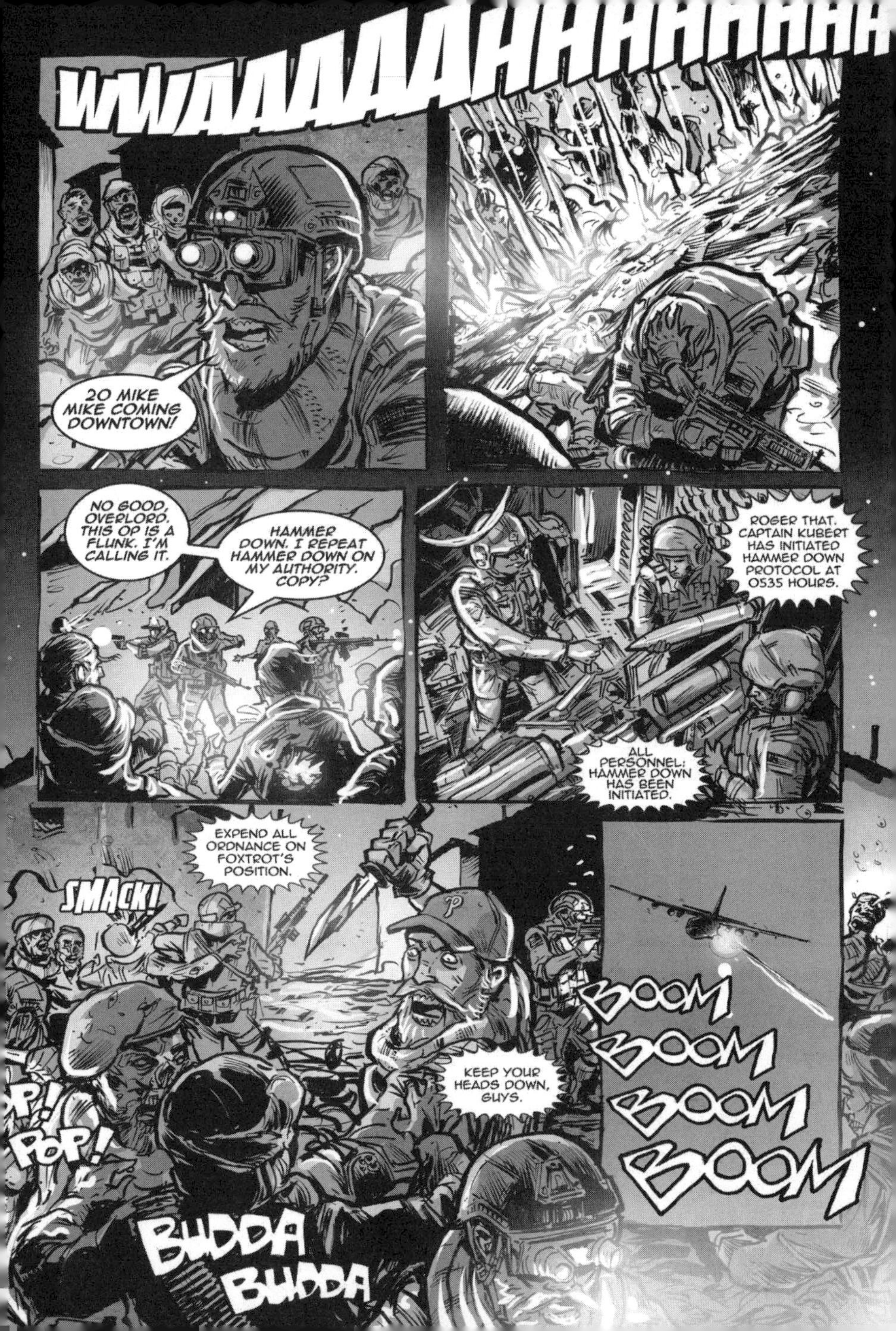
WWAAAAAAHHHHHHHH
20 MIKE MIKE COMING DOWNTOWN!
NO GOOD, OVERLORD. THIS OP IS A FLUNK. I'M CALLING IT.
HAMMER DOWN. I REPEAT HAMMER DOWN ON MY AUTHORITY. COPY?
ROGER THAT. CAPTAIN KUBERT HAS INITIATED HAMMER DOWN PROTOCOL AT 0535 HOURS.
ALL PERSONNEL: HAMMER DOWN HAS BEEN INITIATED.
EXPEND ALL ORDNANCE ON FOXTROT'S POSITION.
SMACK!
KEEP YOUR HEADS DOWN, GUYS.
BOOM
BOOM
BOOM
BOOM
POP!
BUDDA
BUDDA

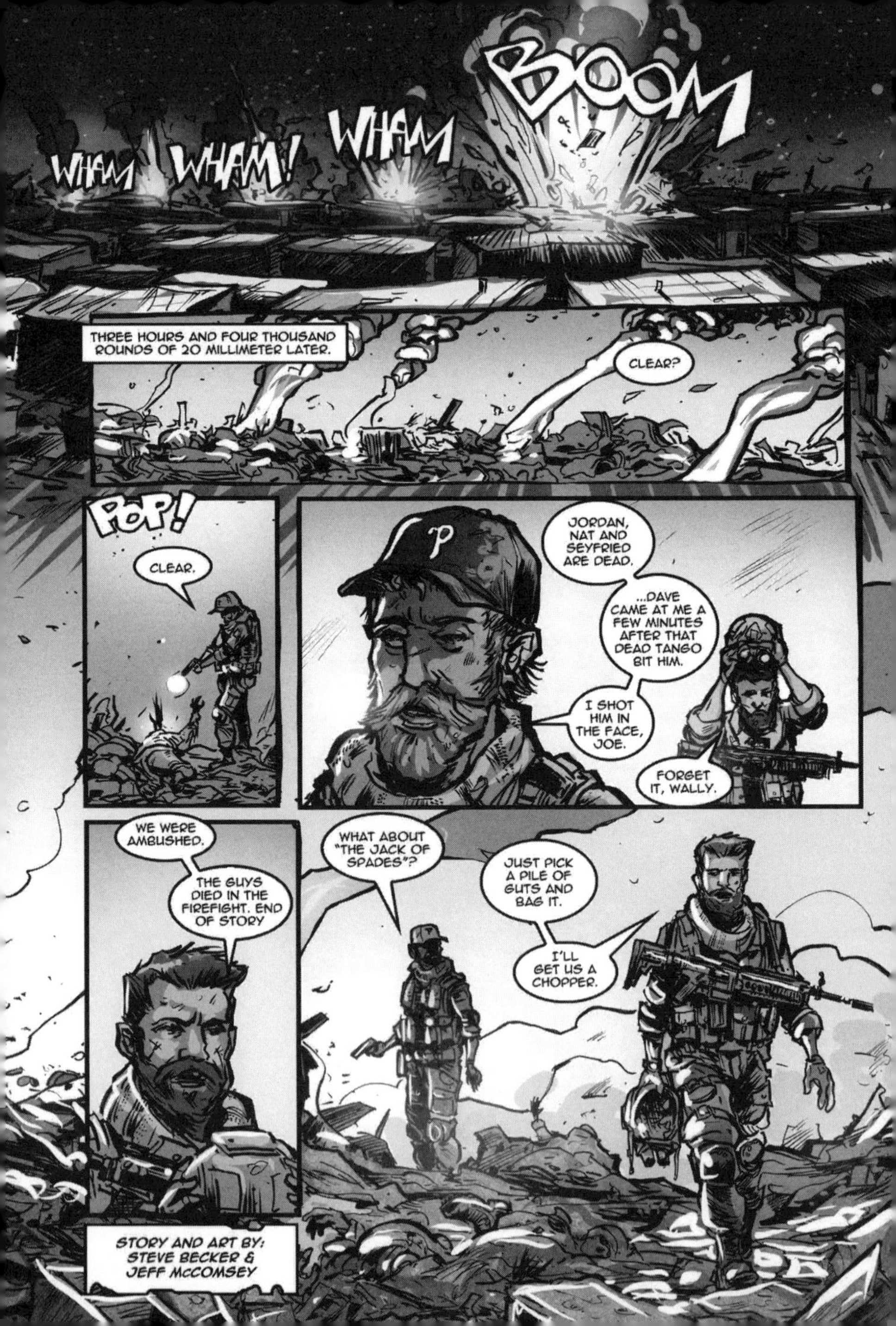
WHAM
WHAM!
WHAM
BOOM
THREE HOURS AND FOUR THOUSAND ROUNDS OF 20 MILLIMETER LATER.
CLEAR?
POP!
CLEAR.
JORDAN, NAT AND SEYFRIED ARE DEAD.
...DAVE CAME AT ME A FEW MINUTES AFTER THAT DEAD TANGO BIT HIM.
I SHOT HIM IN THE FACE, JOE.
FORGET IT, WALLY.
WE WERE AMBUSHED.
THE GUYS DIED IN THE FIREFIGHT. END OF STORY
WHAT ABOUT "THE JACK OF SPADES"?
JUST PICK A PILE OF GUTS AND BAG IT.
I'LL GET US A CHOPPER.
STORY AND ART BY: STEVE BECKER & JEFF McCOMSEY

OUR OWN WARS

STORY BY:
FABIAN RANGEL JR.

ART BY:
JASON COPLAND

LETTERS BY:
PHIL McCLOREY

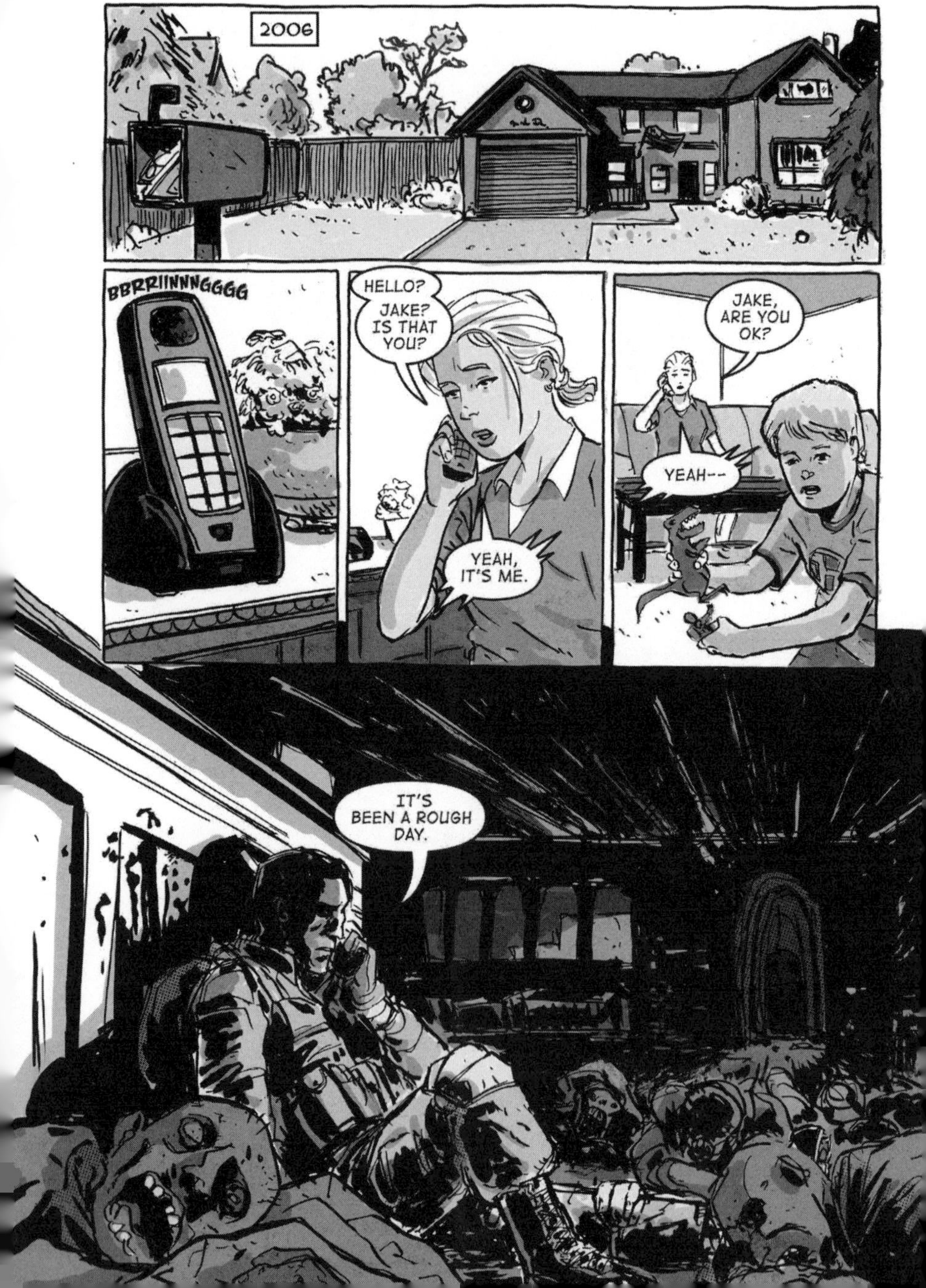
2006
BBRRIINNNGGGG
HELLO?
JAKE? IS THAT YOU?
YEAH, IT'S ME.
JAKE, ARE YOU OK?
YEAH--
IT'S BEEN A ROUGH DAY.

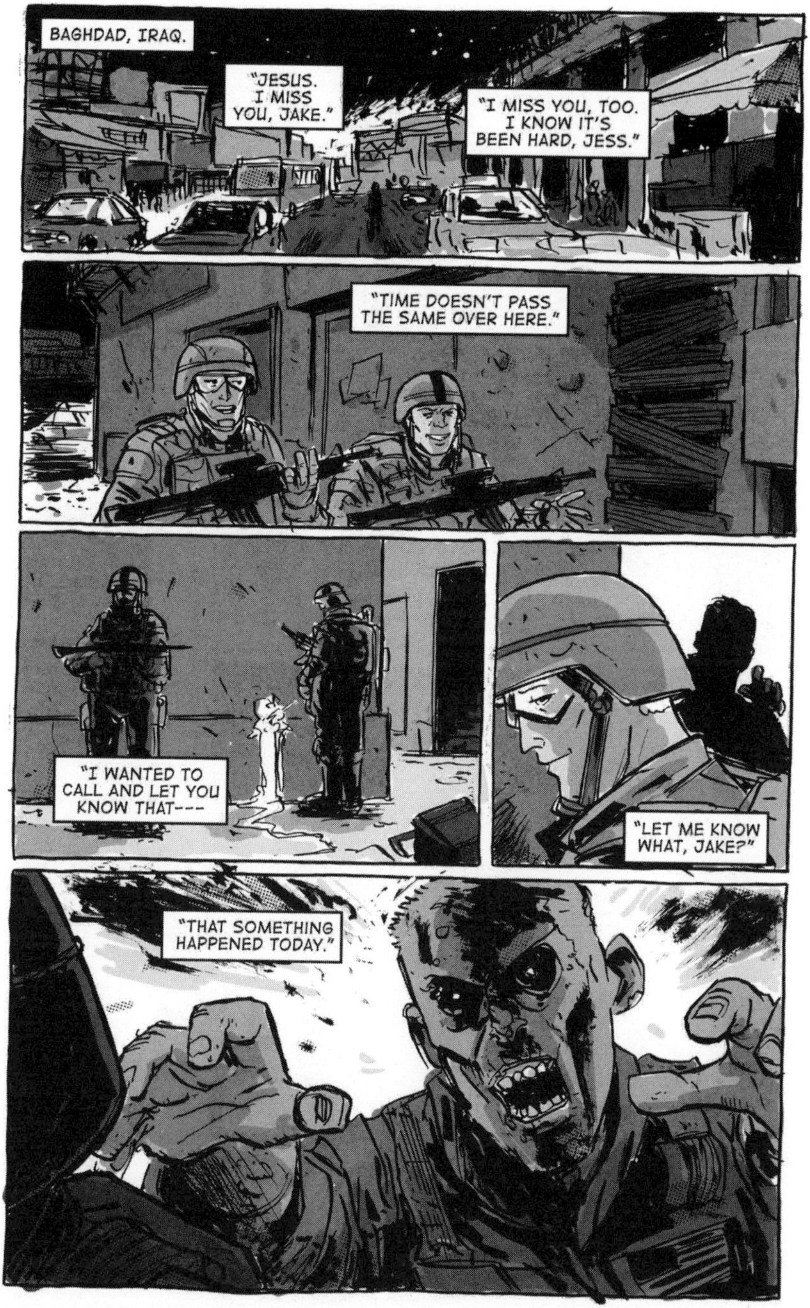
BAGHDAD, IRAQ.
"JESUS. I MISS YOU, JAKE."
"I MISS YOU, TOO. I KNOW IT'S BEEN HARD, JESS."
"TIME DOESN'T PASS THE SAME OVER HERE."
"I WANTED TO CALL AND LET YOU KNOW THAT---
"LET ME KNOW WHAT, JAKE?"
"THAT SOMETHING HAPPENED TODAY."

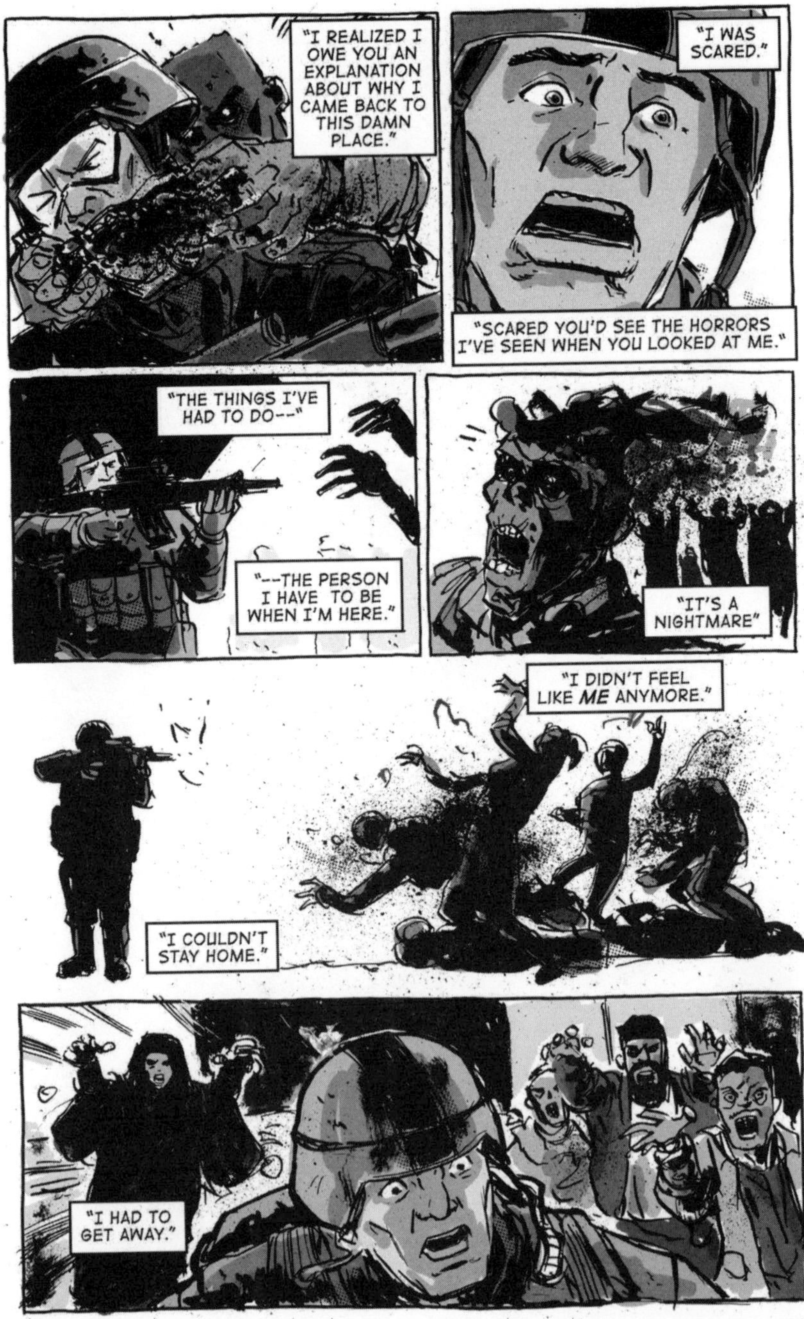
"I REALIZED I OWE YOU AN EXPLANATION ABOUT WHY I CAME BACK TO THIS DAMN PLACE."
"I WAS SCARED."
"SCARED YOU'D SEE THE HORRORS I'VE SEEN WHEN YOU LOOKED AT ME."
"THE THINGS I'VE HAD TO DO--"
"--THE PERSON I HAVE TO BE WHEN I'M HERE."
"IT'S A NIGHTMARE"
"I DIDN'T FEEL LIKE *ME* ANYMORE."
"I COULDN'T STAY HOME."
"I HAD TO GET AWAY."

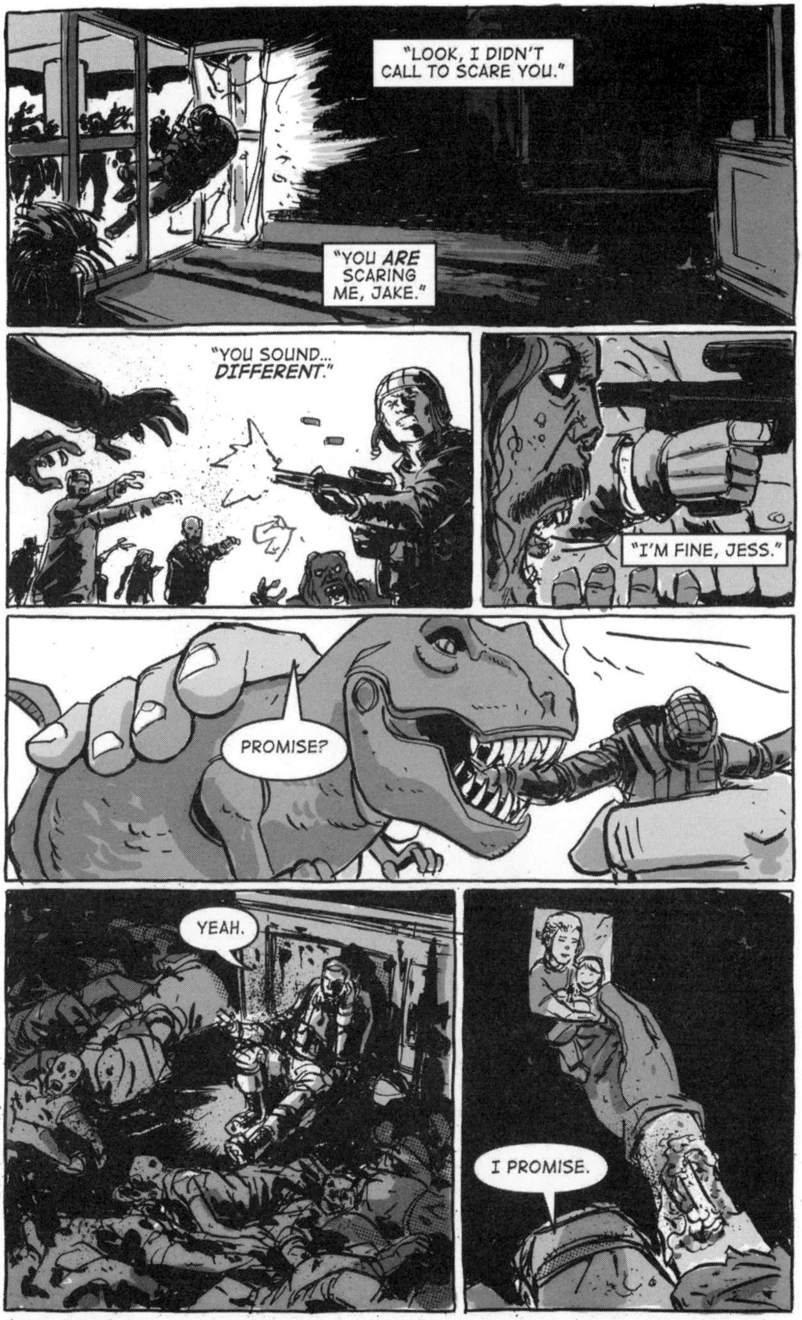
"LOOK, I DIDN'T CALL TO SCARE YOU."
"YOU ARE SCARING ME, JAKE."
"YOU SOUND... DIFFERENT."
"I'M FINE, JESS."
PROMISE?
YEAH.
I PROMISE.

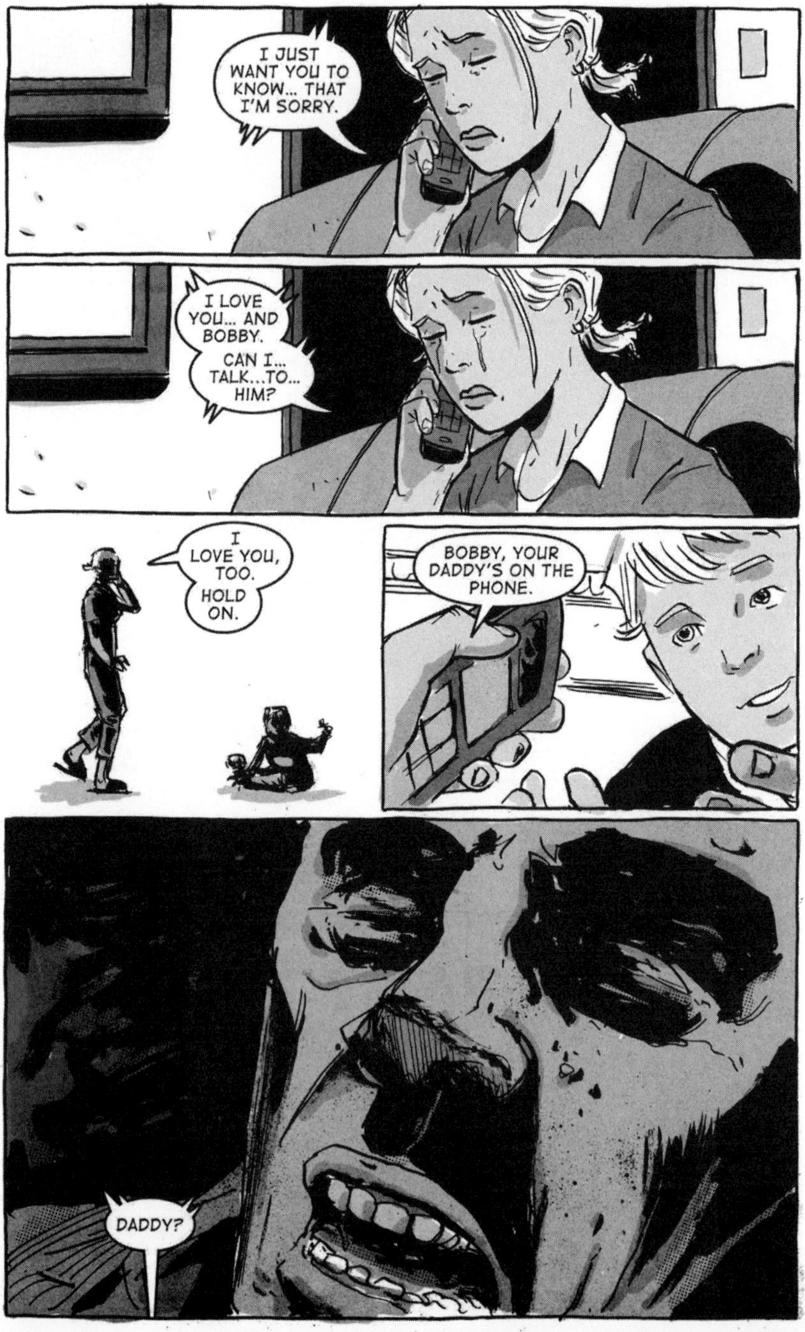
I JUST WANT YOU TO KNOW... THAT I'M SORRY.
I LOVE YOU... AND BOBBY.
CAN I... TALK...TO... HIM?
I LOVE YOU, TOO.
HOLD ON.
BOBBY, YOUR DADDY'S ON THE PHONE.
DADDY?

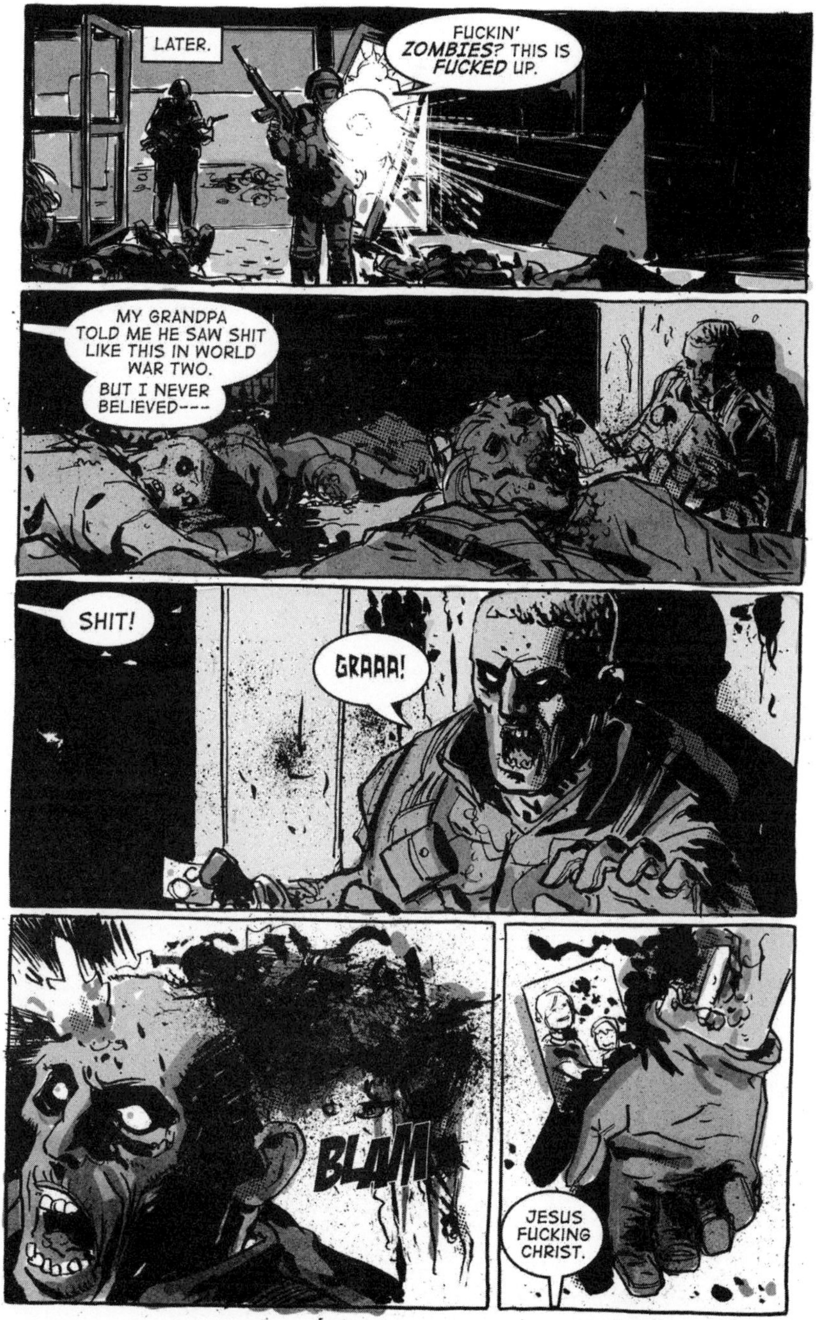
LATER.
FUCKIN' *ZOMBIES*? THIS IS *FUCKED* UP.
MY GRANDPA TOLD ME HE SAW SHIT LIKE THIS IN WORLD WAR TWO.
BUT I NEVER BELIEVED---
SHIT!
GRAAA!
BLAM
JESUS FUCKING CHRIST.

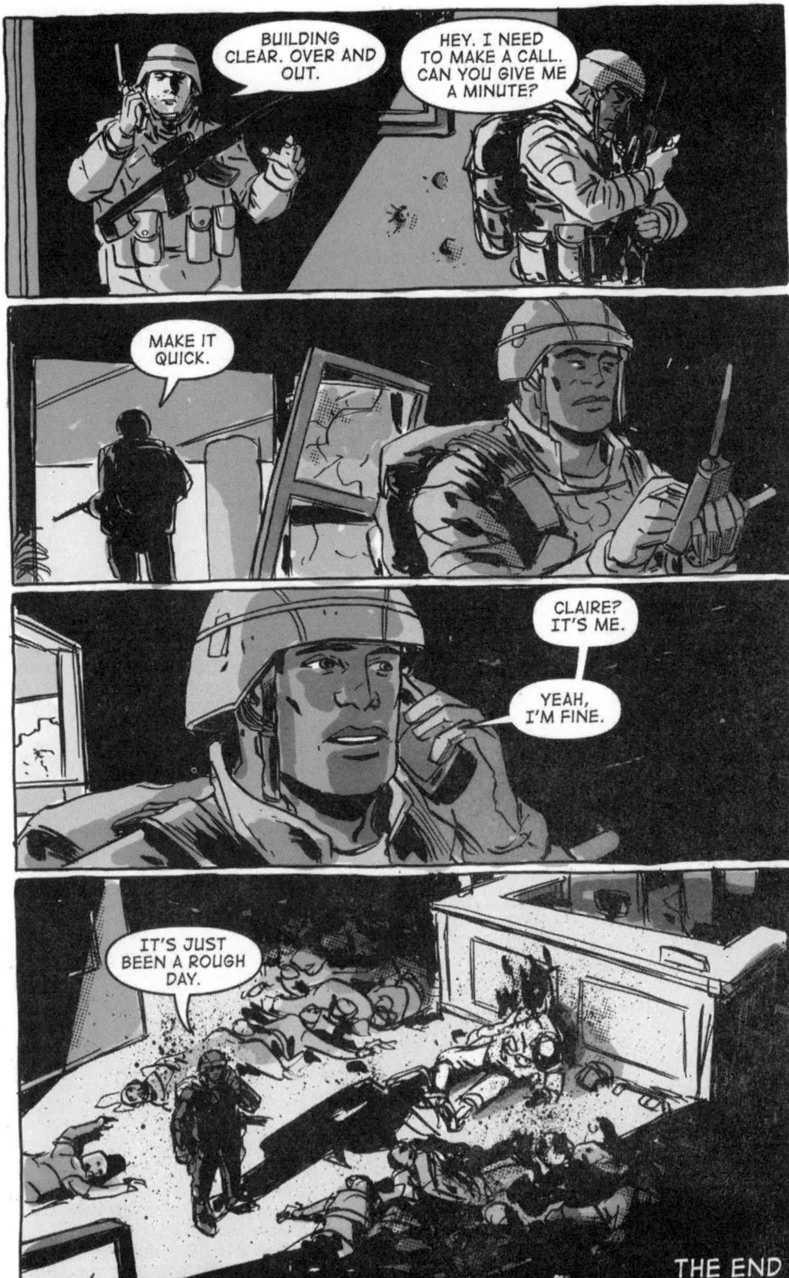
BUILDING CLEAR. OVER AND OUT.
HEY. I NEED TO MAKE A CALL. CAN YOU GIVE ME A MINUTE?
MAKE IT QUICK.
CLAIRE? IT'S ME.
YEAH, I'M FINE.
IT'S JUST BEEN A ROUGH DAY.
THE END

HOPE AND CHANGE
(INTO A ZOMBIE)

STORY AND LETTERS BY:
JEFF McCLELLAND

ART BY:
MIGUEL MORA

GREYSCALES BY:
JEFF McCOMSEY

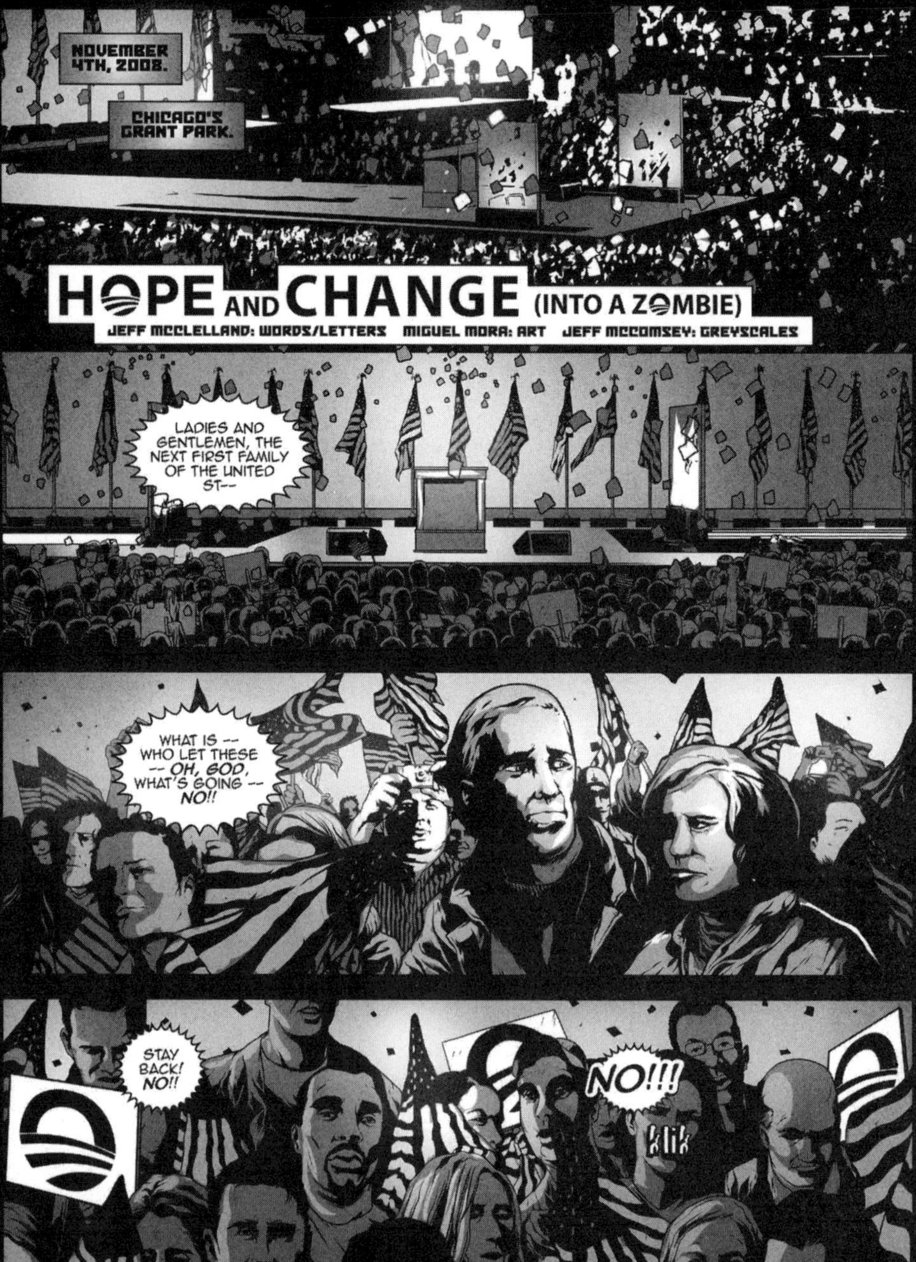
NOVEMBER 4TH, 2008.
CHICAGO'S GRANT PARK.
HOPE AND CHANGE (INTO A ZOMBIE)
JEFF McCLELLAND: WORDS/LETTERS MIGUEL MORA: ART JEFF McCOMSEY: GREYSCALES
LADIES AND GENTLEMEN, THE NEXT FIRST FAMILY OF THE UNITED ST--
WHAT IS -- WHO LET THESE -- OH, GOD, WHAT'S GOING -- NO!!
STAY BACK! NO!!
NO!!!
klik

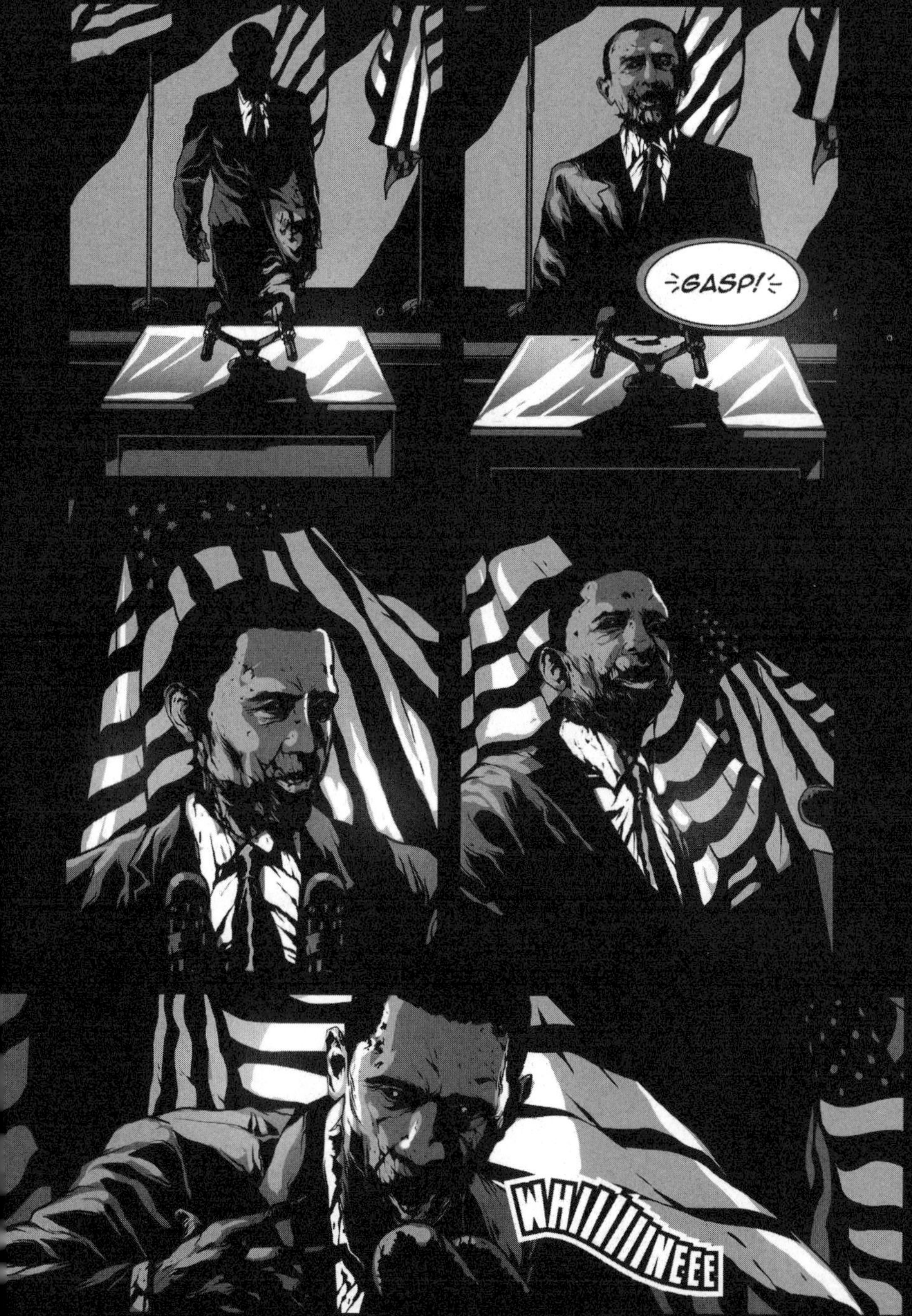
GASP!
WHIIIIIIIINEEE

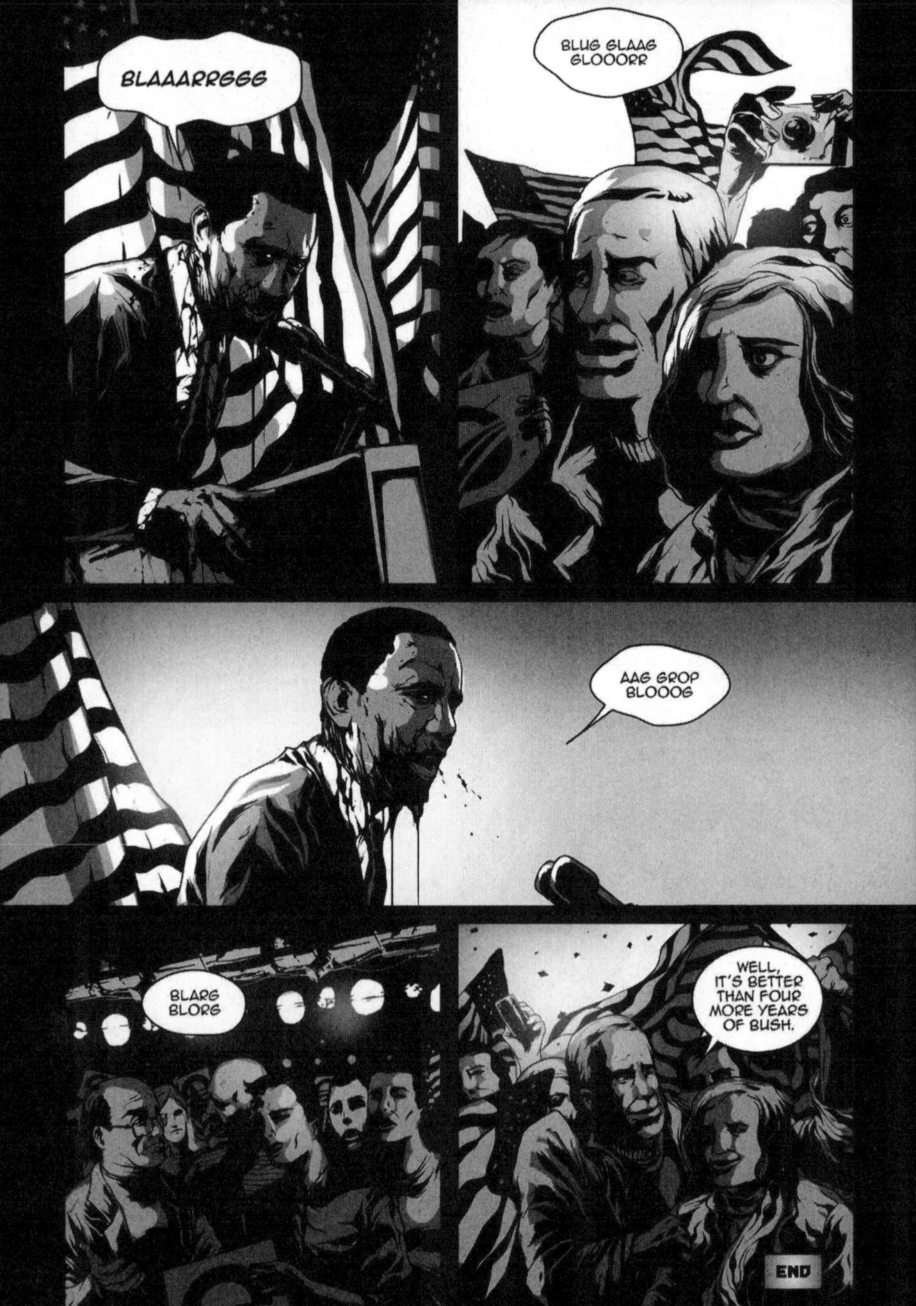
BLAAARRGGG
BLUG GLAAG GLOOORR
AAG GROP BLOOOG
BLARG BLORG
WELL, IT'S BETTER THAN FOUR MORE YEARS OF BUSH.
END

FUBAR

MEDAL OF HONOR GALLERY

ALL GAVE SOME. SOME GAVE MORE.
THESE MEN AND WOMEN DEMONSTRATED CONSPICUOUS
GALLANTRY AND INTREPIDITY AT GREAT RISK TO THIER
SOCIAL LIFE AND FREE TIME ABOVE AND BEYOND
THE CALL OF DUTY.

FUBAR

MEDAL OF HONOR

JEFF "MAD DOG" McCLELLAND

FUBAR

MEDAL OF HONOR

SHAWN "GRIZZLY" ALDRIDGE

FUBAR
MEDAL OF HONOR

DAN "DOWNTOWN" MOSER

FUBAR

MEDAL OF HONOR

MIKE "BLUEBERRY" HAWTHORNE

FUBAR

MEDAL OF HONOR

SOCKO "FACE MAN" JONES

FUBAR
MEDAL OF HONOR

TIGER "HANNIBAL" JONES

FUBAR

MEDAL OF HONOR

CHUCK "D-DAY" DIXON

FUBAR
MEDAL OF HONOR

SAMANTHA "BABYCAKES" HALSEY

FUBAR

MEDAL OF HONOR

APRIL "BABES" MURPHY

FUBAR
MEDAL OF HONOR

JAIME "DR. SEXY" FICKES

FUBAR

MEDAL OF HONOR

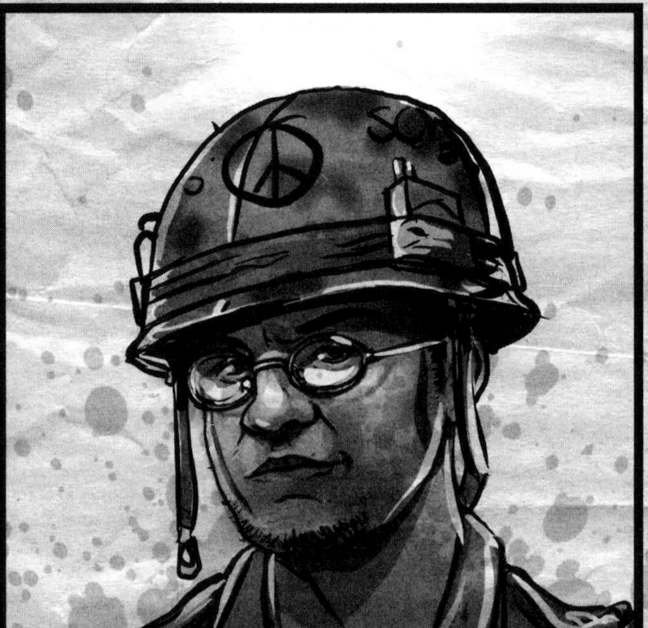
VIVONA

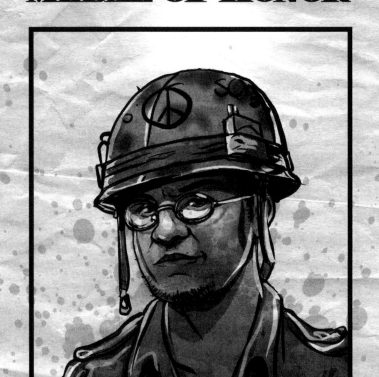

DOMINIC "YEAH BOY" VIVONA

FÜBAR
MEDAL OF HONOR

SHAWN "KWIP" WILLIAMS

FUBAR

MEDAL OF HONOR

PETER "ROCKSTEADY" SIMETI

FUBAR

MEDAL OF HONOR

STEVE "NO BIGS" BECKER

FUBAR
MEDAL OF HONOR

JEFF "NO PROBLEM" McCOMSEY

FUBAR

KICKSTARTER
MEDAL OF HONOR
GALLERY

ALL GAVE SOME. SOME GAVE MORE.
THESE MEN DUG DOWN DEEP AND GAVE MORE THAN WAS
CALLED FOR IN THE NAME OF INDEPENDENT COMICS ABOVE
AND BEYOND THE CALL OF DUTY.

FUBAR

AMERICAN HISTORY Z

DOUG COLLINS

FUBAR

AMERICAN HISTORY Z

DAVE D'ARANJO

FUBAR
AMERICAN HISTORY Z

PHIL KOST

FUBAR

AMERICAN HISTORY Z

JARROD SELSMARK

FUBAR
AMERICAN HISTORY Z

PAWEL GOJ

FUBAR
AMERICAN HISTORY Z

MARCUS TAYLOR

FUBAR

AMERICAN HISTORY Z

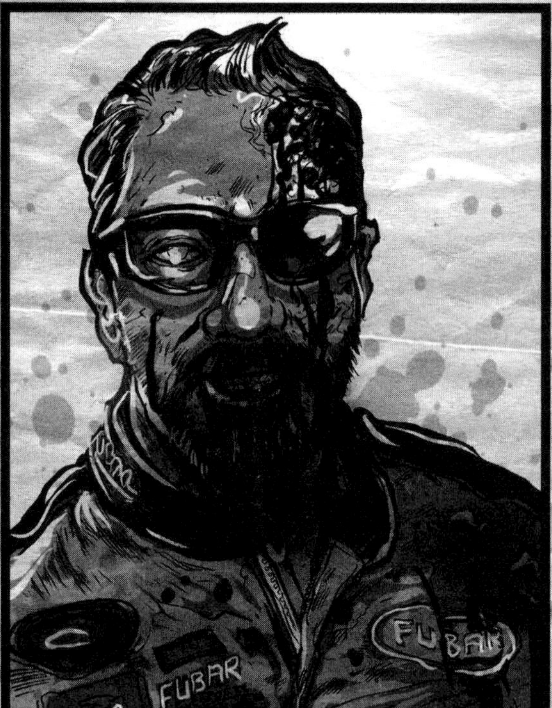
FUBAR
FUBAR
FUBAR
FUBAR

JASON CAREY

FUBAR
AMERICAN HISTORY Z

SEBASTIEN CHAFFAUT

FUBAR
AMERICAN HISTORY Z

BENJAMIN LUNG-TZE LIEW

FUBAR
AMERICAN HISTORY Z

CALLUM BARNARD

FUBAR CENTRAL COMMAND WOULD LIKE
THANK OUR INCREDIBLE KICKSTARTER BACKERS
WHO MADE THIS BOOK POSSIBLE!

Josh Blaylock
Rafer Roberts
Benjamin Fischer
Glenn Møane
Ben Lichius
Steve Willhite
Benjamin Truman
Ken Eppstein
James Kaplan

Kyle J. Kaczmarczyk
Nocturin Lacey-Clarke
Mike Exner III
Lawrence Gill
Damian Eby
Anthony DePietro
Eric Arsenault
Mike Edmonds
Ben Whittenbury
John Wayda
paul glasser
Matt Shaffer
Chris Keane
Michael J Farineau
Michael
Peter Thomas
Shawn Aldridge
Luke Kwek
Joe Fello
Alexander P Bannon

JUAN CALLE
Doug Shank
Preston Cockey
Jason Rapp
Dr. Stephen Derose
Jim Runyan
Brad Roberts
Benjamin Dow
Patrick Reidy
Richard Mays
Joel Kovach
Michael Skovgaard Rosenberg
George Smolar
James Welch
Andrew Radespiel
Ryan French
Kyle Morgan
Chase Acker
Matt Carr
Conor Toleson
Kevin Kappel
Victor Pisconte
Kevin Donovan
Caleb Michael Smith

Michael Blair
Keith Shafer
Steve Petusky
Mark Pengryn
Ethan Soskel
Rob Vaughn
Benjamin Meadows
Ryan Adcock
Justin Brewer
Delbert Hewitt Jr
Arik Nachmias
John D'Aprix IV
Heather Yanoska
Eric Spohn
David Verbsky
John MacLeod
Brian Iglesias
Michael Perkins
Louis Decenzi
Aaron Lucchesi
Christine Lawrence
Jason Winn
Heikki Penttilä
Bill Dowis
Tor Karlsson
Scott Dancer
Mike Thomas
Armando Chavez
Eric Ramos
Jason Copland
Parker Lindstom
Steve Tracy
Jennie Wood
Tracy Cox c/o NSVRC
Gregory Kane
Stephen Huber
Adam J. Monetta
Cory Lievers
Oliver Mertz
Lucas Duffy
Rob Croonenborghs
Basil Yong Wei Hee
Joshua R Andress
Christopher W Broden
Jeff Schultz
Ryan Murray
INDIO
Michael Torem
Jeffrey Maslany
Paul Nordland
Desmond Walsh
nicholas compton
Zach Quayle
Hart Rossman
Rhonda Chase
rory sampson

Matthew Midgette
Ezra Atikune
Brad dancer
Adam Whitcomb
Geoff Skinner
Rich Laux
Peter Harper
Dain Eaton
Robert Untucht
Jeff Stein
Sean Frost
Brian Bobb
Marco Piva
Adrian Sun
Anthony Eager
Joseph Fernandes
Christopher Hughes
Neil Sakamoto
Stuart McIntosh
Ruediger Fleck
Ivan Ross
Luca T Romano
Thayne Clark
Ryan Thompson
James Burzelic
Chris Call
Daniel Laloggia
Max Blanchard
Justine Campbell
kevin Appleby
Abilash Pulicken
KLINGER Axel
Nick Buchan
Leonard Chew
Niall Lindsay
aaron jurkis
Hugh Hamilton
Sarah Braly
Lee Cherry
Cary Renquist
Jay Chang
Brandon Spickard
Ryan fitzgibbon
Lars Ivar Igesund
Pieter Goris
Jef Mertens
Anthony Gunther
Jack Taylor
David Sander
Gregory Dalesandre
Chris CarleyJoseph
Mattera
Dan Haskins
James Greene
Christopher Buehl

FUBAR CENTRAL COMMAND WOULD LIKE THANK OUR INCREDIBLE KICKSTARTER BACKERS WHO MADE THIS BOOK POSSIBLE!

Roderick Taylor
Ken Holt
Steffen Beth
Santiago Anglés
Janne Ketola
Christoph Haar
Jeroen Claes
Simon Varley
Milan Janosik
Kevin Kortekaas
Kevin Schantz
Brad Brown
Brian Federici
Benjamin Mialot
Robert W. Triplett
Nicolas Al-Ama
Magnus Jacobsson
Luke Wild
Jim Norton
Tom James Allen Jr.
Gregory Morris
Sean Lambert
Joshua Turner
Aaron Edwards
Thomas Hill
Andy Bates
Wei Jen Seah
Ryan Wolfe
Cameron Fong
Tourino Pablo
Andrew Gillespie
Andrey Dolganov
Brandon Eaker
Raymond Zhao
Tony R Nunes
Red Sky Comics
Bryan Barnes
Daniel M Andersen
Ken Nagasako
Brent Kevinsen
Jean-François Lebret
Markus Liukka
Frank Castro
Andrew Parr
Christian Guy
Chris Peterson
Martha Fischer
Joe D. Espinosa
Evan Rattner
Eric E. Johnson
John Robson
Denis Chistyakov
David Ludowici
Daniel Sandoval
Niels Christian Selchau-Mark
Kirk Spencer
Joona Ruuhiala

EXTRA SPECIAL THANKS TO OUR MEDAL OF HONOR BACKERS!

Benjamin Lung-Tze Liew
Phil Kost
Shawn Williams
Jarrod Selsmark
Pawel Goj
Doug Collins
Sebastien CHAFFAUT
Marcus Taylor
Dave D'aranjo
Jason Carey
Jeff McClelland

A DISTINGUISHED EXTRA SPECIAL THANKS TO OUR FUBAR FOR LIFE BACKER!

Callum Barnard

PIN UPS BY:

DANIEL THOLLIN
JOE PALUMBO
ERIK REGESTER

FUBAR
AMERICAN HISTORY Z

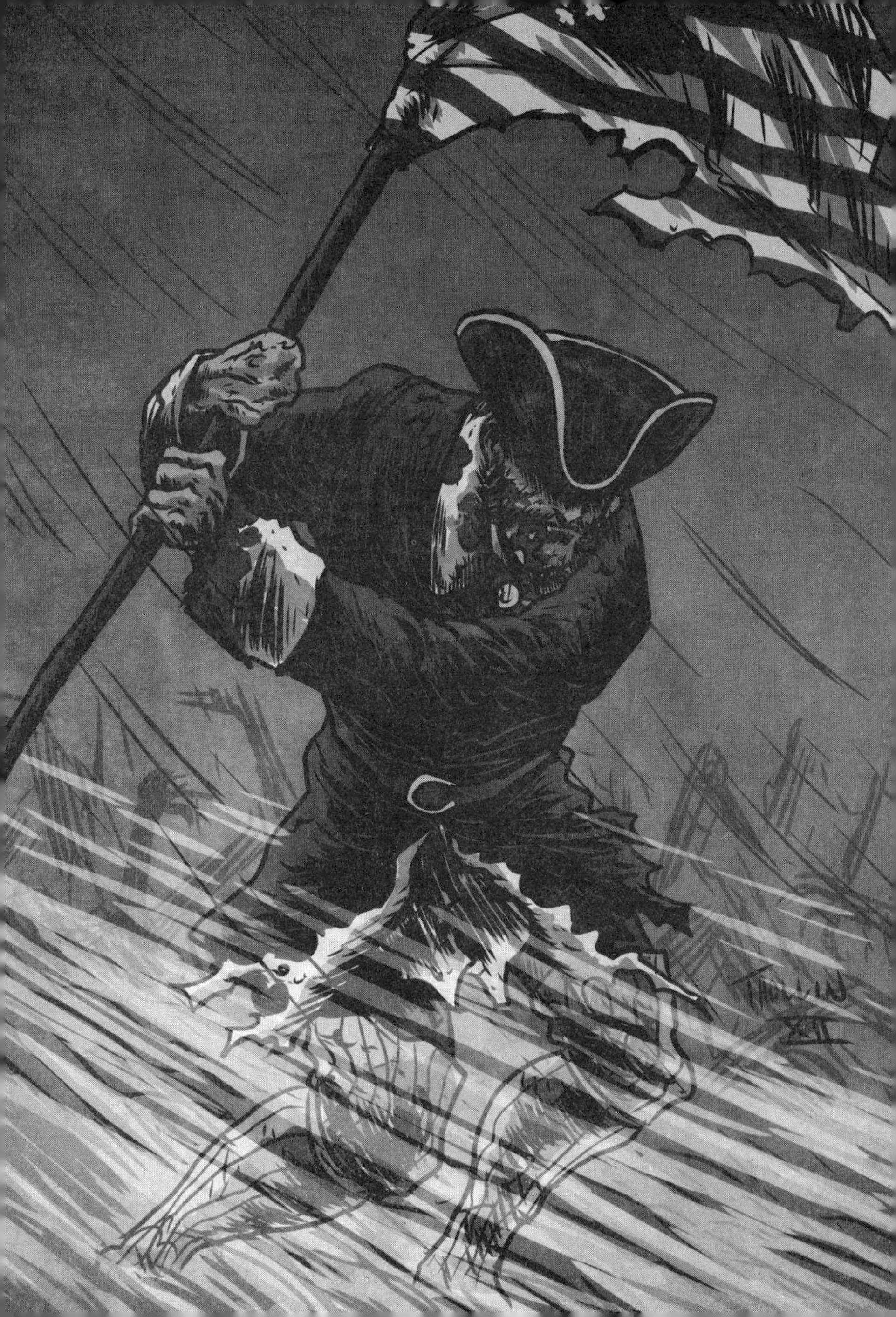

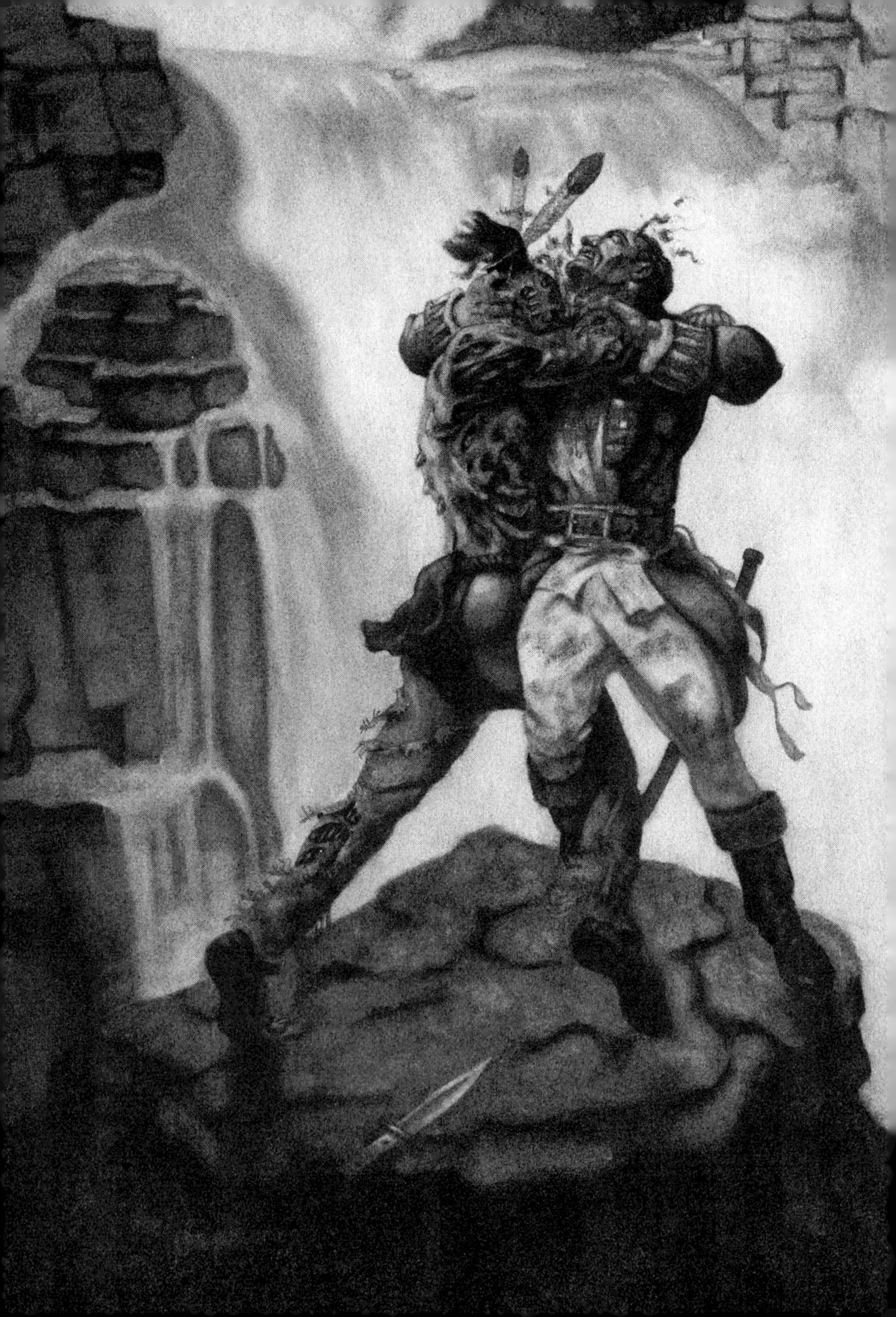

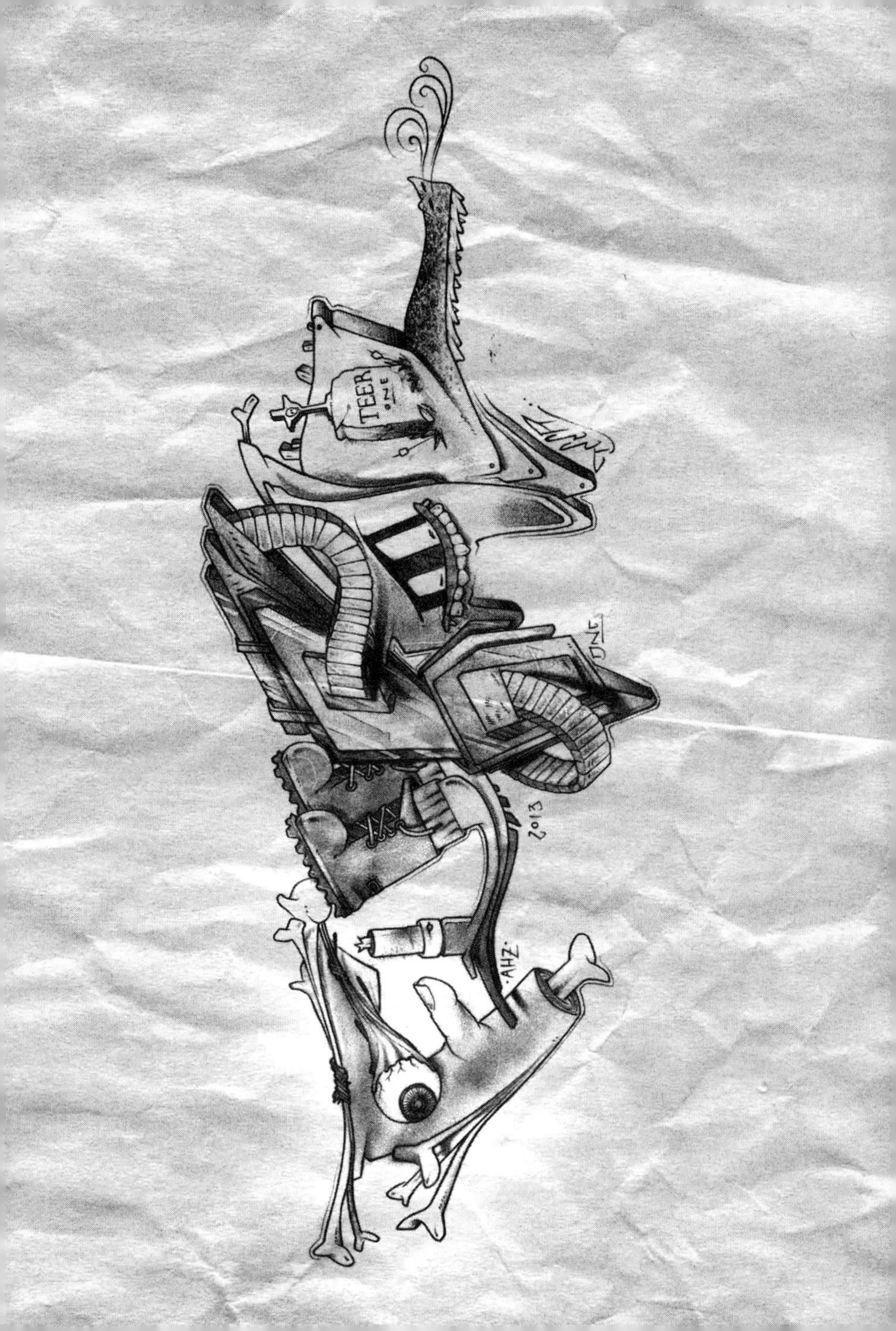
TEER
ONE
2013
AHZ

SKETCHES

JOE DUNN

STEVE BECKER

DANIEL THOLLIN

ROB CROONENBORGHS

JASON COPLAND

STEVE WILLHITE

SKETCHES

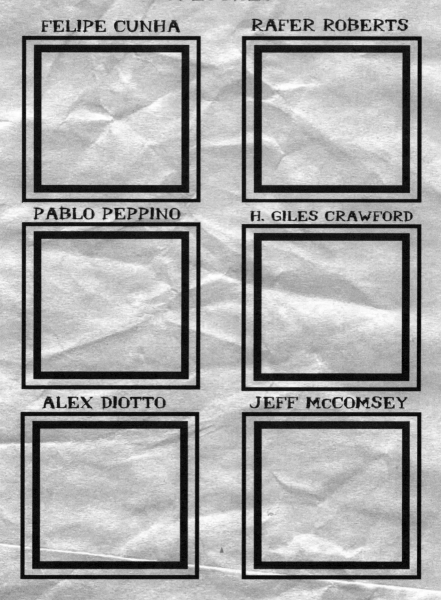

FELIPE CUNHA

RAFER ROBERTS

PABLO PEPPINO

H. GILES CRAWFORD

ALEX DIOTTO

JEFF McCOMSEY

SKETCHES

JOHN BROGLIA

ANDRES ESPARZA

GLEN OSTRANDER

ALUISIO CERVELLE SANTOS

JACOB WARRENFELTZ

PEEBO MONDIA

SKETCHES

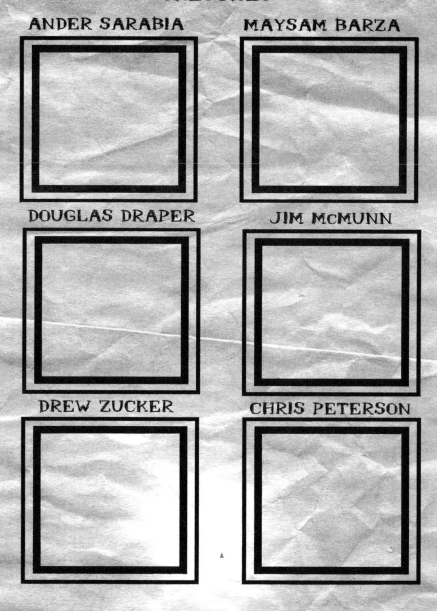

ANDER SARABIA

MAYSAM BARZA

DOUGLAS DRAPER

JIM McMUNN

DREW ZUCKER

CHRIS PETERSON

SKETCHES

WILL PERKINS

JOHN SHINE

DOMINIC VIVONA

ERIC SPOHN

SEAN VON GORMAN

REINE ROSENBERG

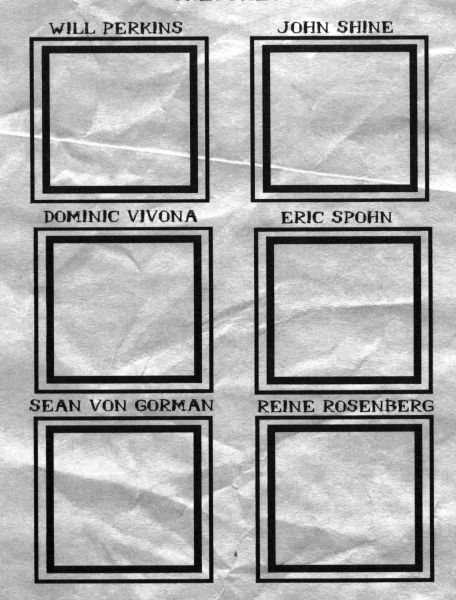

SKETCHES

CHARLES FETHEROLF

BRANDON CARR

MICHAEL BRACCO

CHRISTINE LARSEN

MIGUEL MORA

DAVID STOLL

AMERICAN HISTORY EDITION!

WHO WAS THE MOST DECORATED (POSTHUMOUS) VETERAN OF WORLD WAR 1 WITH 679 CONFIRMED ZOMBIE KILLS?

A. PFC. JAMES DARMODY
B. SGT. ALVIN YORK
C. CPL. RICHARD HARROW

WHAT REVOLUTIONARY WAR FIGURE WAS QUOTED AS SAYING, "I REGRET THAT I HAVE BUT ONE BARREL TO GIVE YOU ROTTING ZOMBIE REDCOATS!" BEFORE BEING EATEN ALIVE?

A. BENENDICT ARNOLD
B. GEORGE WASHINGTON
C. NATHAN HALE

WHAT BRITISH COMMANDO WEAPON WAS ADOPTED BY US SPECIAL FORCES IN VIETNAM TO ELIMINATE ZOMBIES QUIETLY?

A. THE WOBBLY STABBER
B. THE PRANGER KNIFE
C. THE FAIRBAIRNE SYKES DAGGER

WHAT PIECE OF ORDINANCE WAS SUCCESS-FULLY DEPLOYED IN THE KOREAN CONFLICT TO STOP THE "HUMAN WAVES" OF ZOMBIE CHINESE INFANTRY?

A. M28 DAVY CROCKET
B. M6M-5 CORPORAL
C. M65 ATOMIC CANNON

AMERICAN HISTORY EDITION!

WHICH US PRESIDENT WOULD ENGAGE IN
FISTICUFFS WITH ZOMBIE ROBBER
BARONS FOR HIS MORNING EXCERCISE?

A. TEDDY ROOSEVELT
B. WILLIAM HOWARD TAFT
C. CALVIN COOLIDGE

WHAT IS THE NAME OF THE ACTOR WHO
SAVED MARY TODD LINCOLN FROM BEING
EATEN ALIVE AT FORD'S THEATER?

A. BUSTER KEATON
B. JOHN WILKES BOOTH
C. GARY COOPER

350 PAGES CHOCKED FULL OF FACE BITING HISTORICAL ZOMBIE MADNESS!

38 STORIES BROUGHT TO YOU BY A LARGE ARMY OF SMALL PRESS COMMANDOS!!

NOW THAT YOU'VE TAKEN THE QUIZ YOU'RE
READY TO PICK UP THE MASSIVE EPIC:
FUBAR AMERICAN HISTORY Z
AVAILABLE IN APRIL AT YOUR LOCAL COMIC
SHOP!

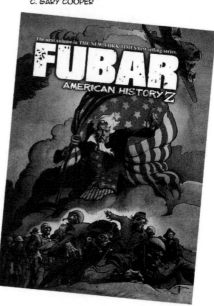

ANSWERS: 1.B 2.C 3.C 4.C 5.A 6.B

FUBAR

WWW.FUBARPRESS.COM

SCORE AREA K5 ONLY

To score multiple target combat course add the total of K5's on all targets

Scoring for alternate qualification	SUB. TOTAL
X, 9, 8 rings........................ = 5	
7 ring........................ = 2	
All other hits on silhouette........................ = 0	
TOTAL	

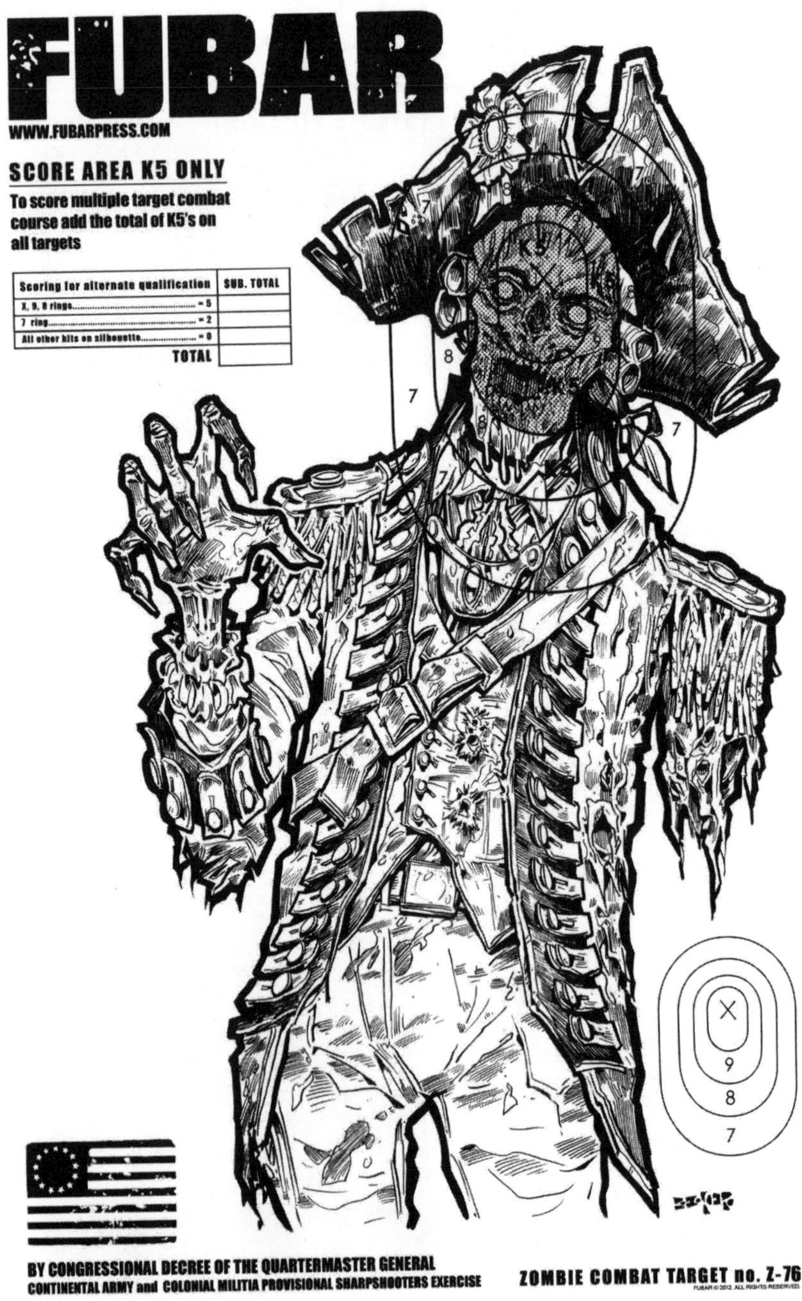
K5
8
7
X
9
8
7

BY CONGRESSIONAL DECREE OF THE QUARTERMASTER GENERAL
CONTINENTAL ARMY and COLONIAL MILITIA PROVISIONAL SHARPSHOOTERS EXERCISE

ZOMBIE COMBAT TARGET no. Z-76

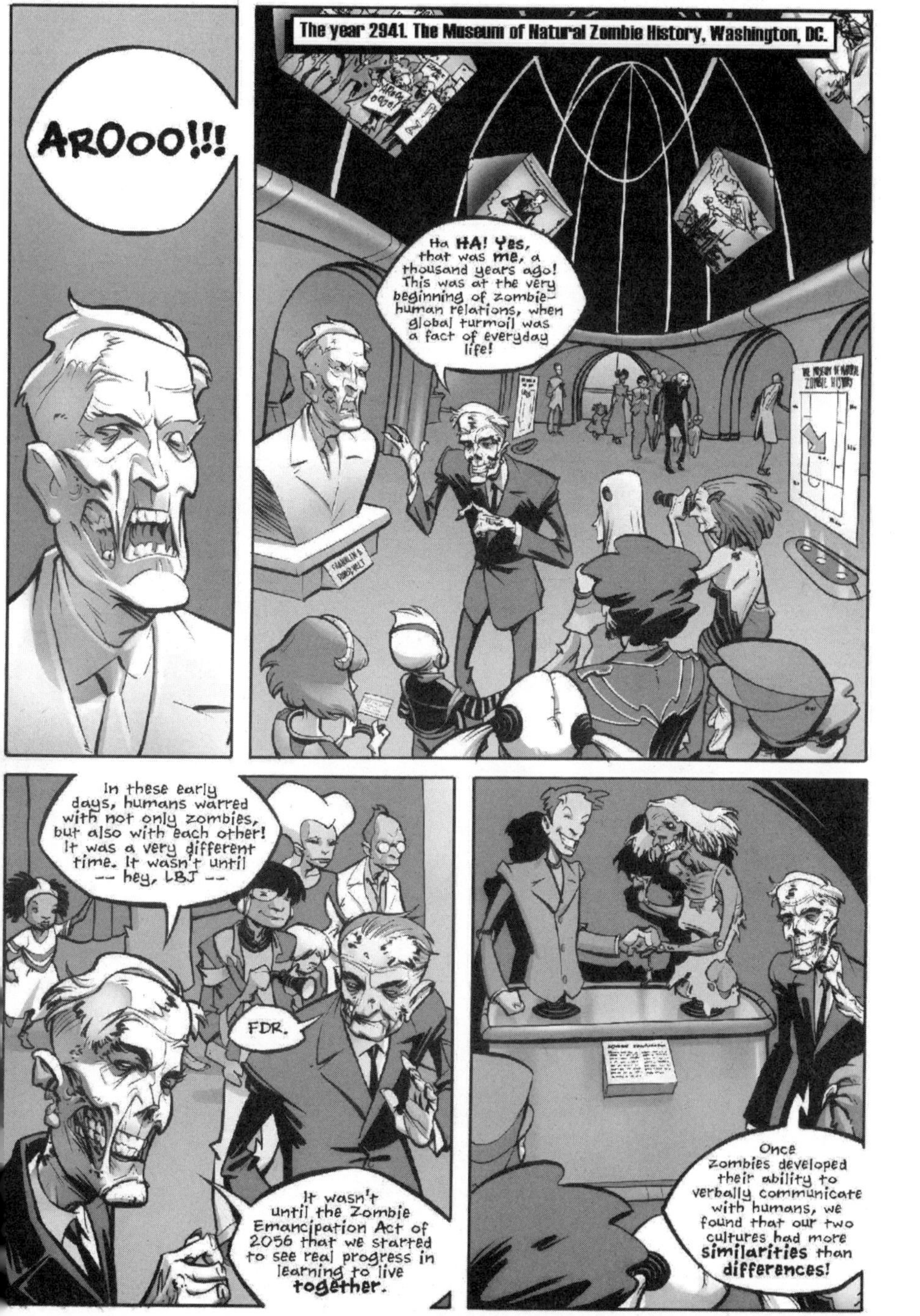
AROOO!!!
The year 2941. The Museum of Natural Zombie History, Washington, DC.
Ha HA! Yes, that was me, a thousand years ago! This was at the very beginning of zombie-human relations, when global turmoil was a fact of everyday life!
In these early days, humans warred with not only zombies, but also with each other! It was a very different time. It wasn't until -- hey, LBJ --
FDR.
It wasn't until the Zombie Emancipation Act of 2056 that we started to see real progress in learning to live together.
Once zombies developed their ability to verbally communicate with humans, we found that our two cultures had more similarities than differences!

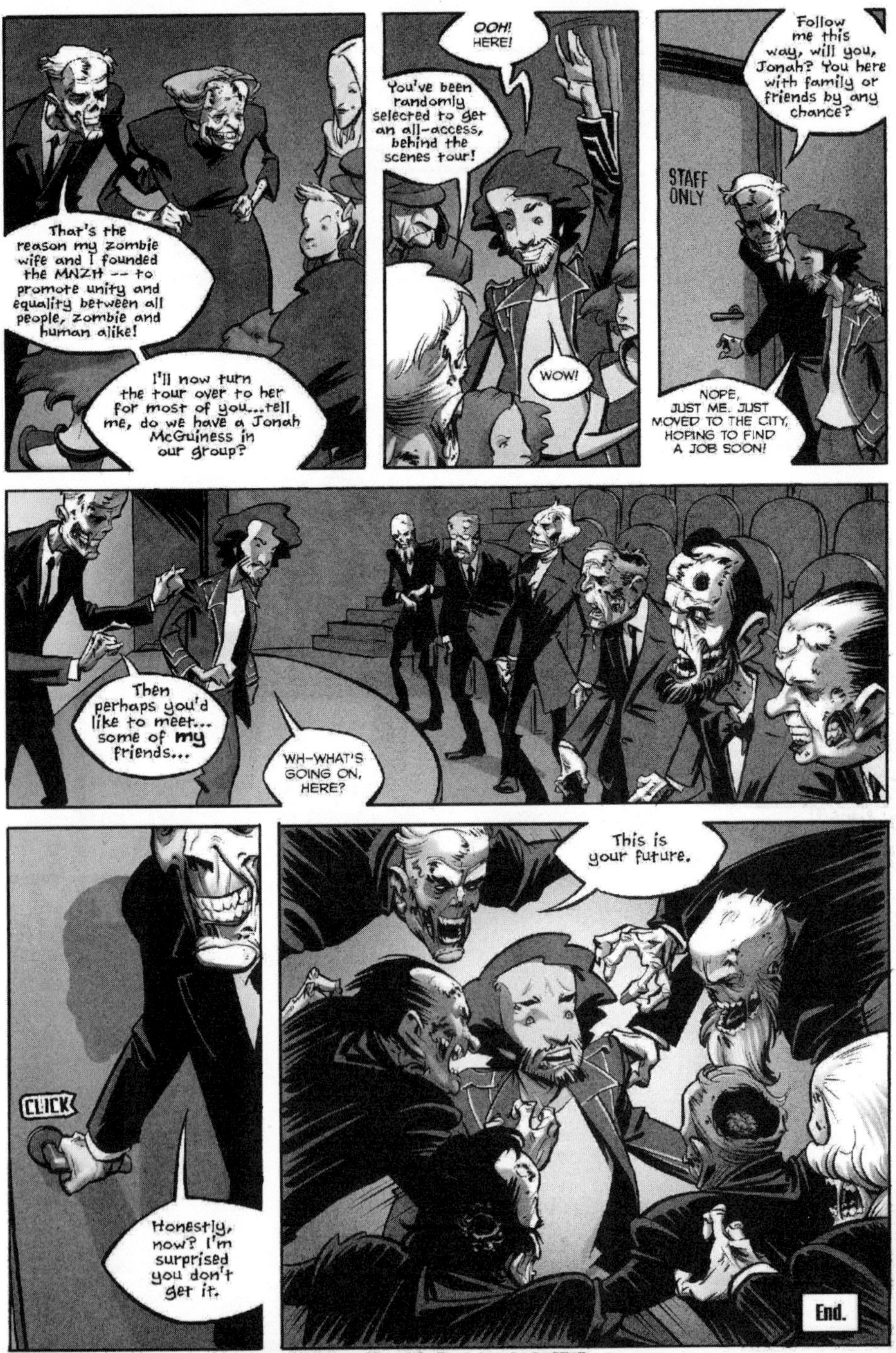
That's the reason my zombie wife and I founded the MNZH -- to promote unity and equality between all people, zombie and human alike!
I'll now turn the tour over to her for most of you...tell me, do we have a Jonah McGuiness in our group?
OOH! HERE!
You've been randomly selected to get an all-access, behind the scenes tour!
WOW!
Follow me this way, will you, Jonah? You here with family or friends by any chance?
STAFF ONLY
NOPE, JUST ME. JUST MOVED TO THE CITY, HOPING TO FIND A JOB SOON!
Then perhaps you'd like to meet... some of **my** friends...
WH-WHAT'S GOING ON, HERE?
CLICK
Honestly, now? I'm surprised you don't get it.
This is your future.
End.

Jeff McClelland and Leonardo Pietro present "F.D.Arrrgh" part 3: "The Future Looks Bite"